A History of

the United States

(Volume V)

The Period of Transition 1815-1848

Edward Channing

Alpha Editions

This edition published in 2019

ISBN : 9789353805555

Design and Setting By
Alpha Editions
email - alphaedis@gmail.com

A HISTORY

OF

THE UNITED STATES

BY

EDWARD CHANNING

VOLUME V

THE PERIOD OF TRANSITION

1815–1848

New York

THE MACMILLAN COMPANY

1927

Norwood Press
J. S. Cushing Co. — Berwick & Smith Co.
Norwood, Mass., U.S.A.

CONTENTS

MAPS

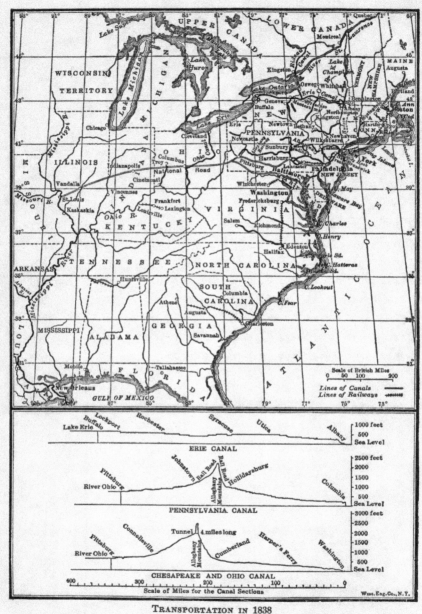

TRANSPORTATION IN 1838

(From Stevenson's *Civil Engineering of North America*. The profiles are from
Trotter's *Observations*, 1839)

A HISTORY OF THE UNITED STATES

CHAPTER I

THE WONDERFUL CENTURY

THE Roman Emperor Tiberius travelled two hundred miles in northern Italy in twenty-four hours; in 1800 President John Adams, journeying from Washington to his home in Quincy, Massachusetts, was fortunate if he could cover fifty miles in one day.[1] By the middle of the nineteenth century fifty miles an hour was no uncommon speed on an American railroad. In the last seventy years the application of steam and electricity to the movement of machinery and the invention of the internal explosion engine have again accelerated the rate of human travel, have made all parts of the earth accessible to man, and have provided for the navigation of the air above and the waters underneath and for the transmission of intelligence and administrative orders from one part of the world to another without other medium than the atmosphere. Why all this should have happened in the Wonderful Century from 1815 to 1914 — in the hundred years between the world-wide wars — is hard to ascertain. Coal, iron, steam, electricity, have all been present in the earth and in its atmosphere from the

[1] See the present work, vol. iv, 2–8, 75, and Caroline A. J. Skeel's *Travel in the First Century after Christ*, 69. Tiberius was hastening to his dying brother, but "the Dictator Julius" rode one hundred miles a day in a hired coach. Fifty or forty miles was the usual speed for ordinary travellers. I am indebted to Professor Clifford H. Moore of Harvard University for this reference.

carboniferous age and yet they have not been used as they now are until the era of machinery. Why was it left for Watt to utilize steam, for Fulton to apply steam to the propulsion of boats, for Stephenson to make the first practicable locomotive, and for Morse to use electricity for the transmission of thought? These are questions at present insoluble. Certain it is that the American mind, which had concerned itself only with political organization, suddenly turned to other problems of human existence and became renowned for fertility of invention, for greatness in the art of literary expression, and for the keenest desire for the amelioration of the lot of humanity.[1]

For forty years before 1815 the world had been at war and the French Revolution was the greatest wrecker of complacency that had occurred in modern times, — before 1914. In itself, war is a frightful scourge; but in its effects it oftentimes has produced most beneficent results. Wars and revolutions lead to readjustments in social relations, in political affairs, and in the mental outlook of nations and of races. Ordinarily, our rules and regulations, our ordinances, and our laws are directed to the preservation of human life, to the protection of individual liberties, and to the conservation of property. In war, on the other hand, our design is to kill, to destroy, and to make existence painful to men and women on the other side of the boundary line. In such times, the mind breaks adrift from its everyday moorings and turns to thoughts and theories that in peaceful hours seemed fantastic and incapable of attainment. War leads to a loosening of the mind, to a breaking

[1] McMaster treated the social condition of the American people in 1784 in the first volume of his *History*. Henry Adams devoted six chapters of the first volume of his *United States* to a description of the social and intellectual conditions of the American people in 1800, — the last four of these chapters presenting a remarkable analysis of the American mind in the early years of the nineteenth century.

of associations, to new thoughts and groupings; and humanity leaps from one stage of civilization to another. In the thirty-five years after 1815, men and women threw off the shackles of the past : they exalted the position of the individual in society, burst the bonds of education and religion, experimented with schemes to better human life, sought the abolition of slavery, and the reformation of drunkards and criminals. All this led to the giving the masses of the people more direct participation in the government of town, city, county, State, and Nation. Unfortunately with the good there was also the bad, for war leads to a slackening of the moral sense, and to an increase in the desire for rapid gain. In such times, men forget their obligations to their fellow men and embark on speculative ventures without other thought than self-enrichment. This was particularly true after the fall of the Napoleonic Empire, for great discoveries in mechanics, in chemistry, in physics, in biology, and in the medical sciences gave opportunities of pecuniary profit that the world had never dreamed of before in historic times. For America, the most important of them all was the application of the new inventions to the transportation of persons and of goods and to the transmission of intelligence and of administrative orders from one part of the country to another. Modern life in all its branches from day to day, in peace and in war, depends upon the mobility of men and of things, for it is this that makes possible the association of human beings for the prosecution of sociological, political, and economic objects.[1] It enables them to work in larger units and results in the enormous and rapid accumulation of wealth. After

[1] The beginnings of the machine-made world can be visualized by a study of *The Emporium of Arts & Sciences* that was edited by John R. Coxe and Thomas Cooper and published at Philadelphia in the years 1812–1814.

For a radically different view of the

pondering these things and viewing the tremendous development of production and the enormous accumulation of wealth which has gone on with constantly accelerated speed from one decade to another, one turns to Webster's exhortation that in the "days of disaster, which, as they come upon all nations, must be expected to come upon us also," we may turn our eyes to the standards of the Fathers of the Republic and be assured that "the foundations of our national power are still strong."

In 1815, the horse-drawn stage, the ox-drawn wagon, and the wind-propelled sloop or schooner formed the main reliance of traveller and forwarder. The roads were, for the most part, of the colonial dirt type. Already, a glimpse of the future might be discerned in a few stone roads leading out from the largest towns, a few miles of canals connecting important water courses, and a few steamboats plying along the coast and on the Ohio and Mississippi rivers; but the lack of capital and the want of technical skill stood in the way of rapid development. The country was new, the demands for capital and labor were great, banking facilities few, and credit was in its infancy. Moreover, knowledge of modern business methods was lacking, except in a few isolated spots. There was not a technical school in the country and, except for a score of men — all of them born on the other side of the ocean — there was no mechanical skill anywhere to be found and there were no machine-shops where actual mechanical work could be done.

The first advance toward the betterment of transportation facilities was the construction of stone roads after the mode

---

main springs of our national development from that given in the text, see Frederick J. Turner's "Contributions of the West to American Democracy" in the *Atlantic Monthly* for January, 1906; his *Rise of the New West* in Albert Bushnell Hart's *American Nation* series; and his *The Frontier in American History* (New York, 1920).

proposed by John Loudon McAdam. This extraordinary man was born in Scotland, came to America with an uncle, and went back to Britain with the Pennsylvania Loyalists in the year 1783. By analysis and experiment, helped by observation, McAdam found that by the use of small angular stone fragments — none of them exceeding an inch in any one dimension — spread ten inches deep, a roadway could be constructed that would grow stronger with time and use. Moreover, it could be made nearly flat and laid over soft ground as well as on rock foundation. The expense of such a road was small in comparison with any kind of block pavement and could be kept in repair at small annual cost.[1] The establishment of the new government under the Constitution greatly stimulated the demand for better facilities for transportation in America and this demand grew more and more insistent in the years of embargo and war.[2] As no State or community, in the crude methods of taxation then prevailing, could provide the means for the construction of any extensive system of roadway private enterprise came in. Corporations were formed often with financial aid from the State; they procured the rest of their capital by lotteries and they charged tolls for the use of their highways. These were called turnpikes and that word, of somewhat obscure origin, was generally used as synonymous with an artificial stone road. In the first twenty-one years of the century, from 1800 to 1821, twelve hundred miles of road, nearly all of it of approved construction, were built. Soon after that time canals and railroads attracted public attention, and the turnpikes failed to

[1] See John L. McAdam's *Remarks on the Present System of Road Making* (London, 1824), 34, 35. There is no adequate account of McAdam's life and work. His evidence before a committee of the House of Commons, on pp. 199–236 of this book, gives the best idea of his career and invention.

[2] See ch. x for a treatment of the political and constitutional aspects of internal improvements.

pay expenses and had to be taken over by the public. In these years, the State of Pennsylvania had subscribed nearly two million dollars to the capital stock of the road companies within her limits, besides contributions that had been made by counties and towns. The construction of bridges on these roads was usually undertaken by other companies which were also often aided by public authorities.[1] Most of these bridges were of timber, with stone abutments in some cases, and they were constantly being destroyed by ice, flood, or fire.

Albert Gallatin made the first suggestion as to giving federal aid to the building of roads. On February 13, 1802, he wrote to William B. Giles of Virginia, who was then chairman of the committee to consider the admission of Ohio into the Union. Gallatin proposed that one-tenth part of the net proceeds of the land that was hereafter sold by the national government within the boundaries of the new State should be applied towards making roads from the Atlantic seaboard to the Ohio Valley, and, later, to the Mississippi. Giles followed Gallatin's recommendation and Ohio was admitted to the Union with such a condition in the act of Congress.[2] In 1806, Congress authorized the President to appoint three commissioners to survey a road from Cumberland, Maryland, to the Ohio and appropriated thirty thousand dollars to defray the expense of laying out and making the road,[3] — and Thomas Jefferson, as Presi-

[1] See the section on "Turnpike, or Artificial Roads" in Gallatin's *Report . . . on . . . Public Roads and Canals*. The writings of early travellers are filled with the discomforts and delays of stage-coach travel over these roads. Zadok Cramer states that in the year 1813 no less than 4055 wagons passed along "the great road" from Philadelphia to Pittsburg (*Navigator*, 9th ed., p. 63 note).

[2] Adams's *Writings of Gallatin*, i, 76; *Annals of Congress*, 7th Cong., 1st Sess., 1100. The debate follows on succeeding pages, but relates almost entirely to the constitutional questions involved. The act is in the same volume, 1349.

[3] See *Annals of Congress*, 9th Cong., 1st Sess., 1237. For a report of the commissioners, see "Message from the President of the United States, trans-

dent, by his signature approved the act. In this case the consent of the States through which the road should run was to be obtained before beginning the actual work of construction. Within the next dozen years or so, this road was constructed from Cumberland on the Potomac in Maryland, to Wheeling on the Ohio in the western part of Virginia.[1] The eastern portion of the Cumberland Road — or National Road — followed generally the lines of the old Braddock Road, which had itself pursued roughly the course of an Indian path. In later years the National Road was continued westwardly through Ohio and Indiana to central Illinois, and it was proposed to build a connecting line southward from Zanesville in central Ohio, to Maysville in Kentucky on the Ohio River and thence to Lexington and southwestwardly, even to the lower Mississippi. From 1816 for ten or fifteen years, the eastern and middle portions of the Cumberland Road were literally crowded with emigrants, their families, and wagons laden with household goods and chattels, pursuing their westward way.[2] In later years it was equally crowded with wagons bringing the products of western farms to the markets of the East. Farther south, through Cumberland Gap and along the Wilderness Road, a smaller tide of emigration sought Kentucky and the country south of the Ohio River, and, at a later time, many of these migrants or their children crossed that stream into the States of the Old Northwest.

mitting a Report of the Commissioners appointed under . . . 'An act to regulate the laying out and making a road from Cumberland,'" etc., dated January 31, 1807.

[1] For an enumeration of the acts, see *Statutes at Large*, ii, 357 and note.

[2] For an account of this road, see Jeremiah S. Young's *Political and Constitutional Study of the Cumberland Road*, Archer B. Hulbert's *Cum-*

berland Road, and Thomas B. Searight's *The Old Pike. A History of the National Road*, but none of these books is satisfying.

Mahlon Dickerson of New Jersey stated in the House of Representatives (February 1, 1827) that the Cumberland Road had cost fourteen thousand dollars a mile up to 1823, or about one and a quarter million dollars for a road 130 miles long.

The opening of the canal between Liverpool and Manchester, England, in 1772, gave a great impulse to the providing of internal water communications everywhere. The Revolution postponed all such attempts in America, but in 1783 Washington noted that the Mohawk River with Wood Creek and Lake Oneida offered what seemed to be a practical route to the western country.[1] As a Virginian, however, his interests and sentiments pointed to the improvement of the James and Potomac rivers by clearing their beds, accelerating the current in places by constructing wing dams, digging canals around the falls and impassable rapids, and connecting the highest point of river navigation by roadways with the Mississippi system. Companies were formed, individuals subscribed for stock, and States also were induced to face the tax payers by voting money for the schemes;[2] but nothing of any importance was ever accomplished and the canal and canal rights of the Potomac Company and its successor, the Chesapeake and Ohio Canal Company, proved only hindrances in the way of the construction of the National Road and later of the Baltimore and Ohio Railroad. Early in the new century, a water route from the Mohawk to Lake Ontario was opened. It accommodated ten-ton boats at ordinary stages of the river, but, owing to its dependence upon variable water supplies, it was never satisfactory.

[1] Washington's *Writings* (Ford), x, 325.

[2] See John E. Semmes's *John H. B. Latrobe and his Times, 1803–1891*, pp. 336–352; Corra Bacon-Foster's *Early Chapters in the Development of the Potomac Route to the West* (reprinted from the *Records* of the Columbia Historical Society, vol. 15); G. W. Ward's "Early Development of the Chesapeake and Ohio Canal Project" in *Johns Hopkins Studies*, xvii; and John Pickell's *A New Chapter in the Early Life of Washington, in connection with Narrative History of the Potomac Company* (New York, 1856). The "Report" of a committee of the House of Representatives (May 22, 1826, 19th Cong., 1st Sess., No. 228) is a convenient account of the connection between the Potomac and the Chesapeake and Ohio projects. See also *Journal of the Internal Improvement Convention . . . 8th Day of December, 1834,* which is preceded by an interesting map.

Many short canals were dug to overcome obstructions in otherwise navigable streams and attempts were made to connect the bays and sounds of the coast, to provide a line of communication from Boston to Charleston that would be sheltered alike from storm and foe. When Secretary of War Henry Knox had a route surveyed across Cape Cod on the line of the present canal, he estimated the expense of constructing the canal at half a million dollars![1] Robert Morris advocated connecting the Delaware and Ohio by canals wherever possible, with roads between.[2] John Nicholson, writing to Jefferson[3] from Herkimer, New York, in 1806, proposed that the national government should open communications for vessels of eighty tons between the Hudson and Lake Ontario and thence to the Ohio and the Mississippi, using canals wherever necessary. Nothing came of any of these schemes at the time; but in 1803, the Middlesex Canal[4] connecting the Merrimac with Boston Harbor was opened.

The discussions over the Cumberland Road project and the growing interest in canals culminated in a resolution of the Senate requesting Gallatin to prepare and report a plan for "the application of such means as are within the power of Congress, to the purposes of opening roads, and making canals." The Secretary of the Treasury replied on April 4, 1808, with one of the most remarkable documents

[1] The locks were to be 120 feet long. The labor was estimated to cost about $250,000, the mechanical utensils to be used were estimated at $3600 and $1800 was allowed for contingencies. "Knox Papers" and The Medley or Newbedford Marine Journal for February 3, 1797.

[2] Hazard's Register, ii, 119–122. A convenient statement of the knowledge of the time in regard to canals may be found in A Treatise on Internal Navigation (Ballston Spa, 1817).

[3] Thomas Jefferson Correspondence (Boston, 1916), p. 136.

[4] See "The Middlesex Canal" in Lowell Historical Association's Contributions, iii, 273–308; and G. Armroyd's Internal Navigation of the United States, 32. Writing to Knox in 1793, James Sullivan and Ishem Russell declared that they needed a man "skilled in canal business" to survey the proposed Middlesex Canal. They had heard that "such an Artist" was at Philadelphia. See "Knox Papers" under date.

that ever came from his pen.[1] In it he proposed constructing a line of canals along the Atlantic coast and other systems connecting the seaboard with the Mississippi Valley and the St. Lawrence. This plan, if carried out, together with turnpikes and connecting roads, he thought would cost twenty million dollars. The cost of the canals would be more than sixteen million dollars and the connecting roads or canals about three or four millions more. Two Appendixes to the "Report," written by B. H. Latrobe and Robert Fulton, were printed at the time. In a postscript to the former, Latrobe describes "rail roads." These, he wrote, were constructed of iron or of timber covered with rails of cast iron forming in section the letter "L" on its back; the gauge of these railroads was from three and a half to five feet and the total cost of such a road with "a set of returning ways" would be about ten thousand dollars a mile. The carriages to run on these roads might be of various dimensions, but they were to have low cast iron wheels fastened to the axle. Astonishing loads, Latrobe wrote, could be drawn on these railroads with one horse. The objection to them was that ordinary carriages could not travel upon them, but even with this disadvantage, they might supplement internal navigation.[2] Fulton argued most strongly

---

[1] *Report of the Secretary of the Treasury, on the Subject of Public Roads and Canals; made in pursuance of a Resolution of Senate, of March 2, 1807, April 12, 1808, Printed by Order of the Senate* (Washington, 1808) and *American State Papers, Miscellaneous,* i, No. 250 (pp. 724–921). The separate issue does not contain Appendixes A–D; these are printed in the *State Papers* and contain much information on contemplated internal improvements. Interesting items concerning the Cumberland Road are in Henry Adams's *Writings of Gallatin,* i, 78, 79, 304, 305, 309, 395. Gallatin's *Report . . . of Public Roads and Canals,* with Ap-

pendixes E and F, is appended to *A Treatise on Internal Navigation* (Ballston Spa, 1817).

[2] John Stevens of Hoboken, New Jersey, whose steam propelled *Phœnix* almost anticipated Fulton's sidewheeled *Clermont* published in 1812 a pamphlet entitled *Documents tending to prove the Superior Advantages of Rail-Ways and Steam-Carriages over Canal Navigation* (reprinted in Abbatt's *Magazine of History,* Extra Number — No. 54). In this Stevens argued that railroads on which wagons could be hauled by horse or steam power would be much cheaper and better than canals.

for the construction of canals, which were vastly superior to any form of turnpike. He calculated that the saving on the transportation of one barrel of flour for one hundred and fifty miles, if carried by canal instead of by road, would be one hundred and fifty cents, which was equal to the existing import duty on thirty pounds of coffee or thirty gallons of molasses, and the saving on the bringing of fifty thousand cords of wood to a city of fifty thousand inhabitants in one year would pay all the duties levied by the government on those people during that time and leave a surplus.[1] It followed, therefore, that canals could be dug and operated at public expense with a great saving of money and of effort, even though they were operated free of toll.

The Erie Canal [2] stands out from all others of that period in its influence on building up the industries of the East, peopling the farms of the West, and providing the laboring masses of large portions of Europe with food. It has been so successful that its origin has been clouded by the claims of many persons and their descendants. It makes little difference to whom the idea first occurred, for the canal would not have been dug when it was had it not been for the powerful, continuing support given to the project by De Witt Clinton [3] and to him, therefore, must fairly be given the credit for its construction. The Western Inland Lock Navigation Company had provided a somewhat uncertain

[1] This matter is summarized from Fulton's *Treatise on the Improvement of Canal Navigation* (London, 1796).

[2] On the New York canals, see Noble E. Whitford's *History of the Canal System of . . . New York* (2 vols., Albany, 1906, — forming the *Supplement* to the *Annual Report* of the State Engineer for 1905, and issued separately with the above title) and Meyer and MacGill's *History of Transportation*, 180–195, etc. Whitford has a long bibliography and biographical sketches of the canal engineers in his second volume.

[3] Clinton published essays under the names of "Atticus," "Hibernicus," and "Tacitus" and he was president of the New York Association for the Promotion of Internal Improvements which published *Considerations on the Great Western Canal from the Hudson to Lake Erie* in 1818. Of these papers his *Canal Policy*, printed in 1821, had the greatest influence.

navigation between the Mohawk and Lake Ontario using existing water courses wherever possible.[1] The Erie Canal, on the other hand, was constructed independently of any parallel river or lake navigation[2] and connected the Mohawk with the Great Lake system above Niagara Falls; it ran by the side of the Mohawk and even crossed it, but never utilized its bed. The canal was close to Lake Ontario, but soon changed its course for Lake Erie. Its only dependence upon lakes and rivers was for the necessary water to operate the locks. In this way it avoided all the dangers and difficulties besetting river navigation: high water, low water, rapids, rocks, and tumultuous current — and connected the Hudson with the navigation of the continental interior and not with that of the St. Lawrence Valley.[3] The digging of the Erie Canal was authorized by the New York legislature in 1817 at the expense of the State, application having been made in vain for national assistance.[4] There proved to be many critical engineering problems to be solved and no trained engineers to face them. The difficulties of the enterprise may almost be said to have laid the foundation of American constructive engineering, for they were studied and overcome in a manner that aroused the admiration of English experts who visited the canal. As at first con-

---

[1] For the doings of this company, see the *Report of the Directors of the Western Inland Lock-Navigation Company . . . 16th February, 1798;* Buffalo Historical Society's *Publications,* ii, 157; and Elkanah Watson's *History of the Rise . . . of the Western Canals,* 92, 93.

[2] The bed of Tonawanda Creek for ten or twelve miles was used for the canal; otherwise it followed an artificial channel.

[3] The Champlain Canal connecting the Hudson and St. Lawrence systems was opened in 1822; in twelve months, from October 1, 1825, it brought in seventy-three thousand dollars in tolls. See Whitford's *Canal System,* i, 113, 416–418, 979–987, ii, 1064.

[4] For maps and profiles of New York canals, see *Engravings . . . accompanying the Annual Report . . . on the Canals for 1859.* There is an excellent short "Account of the Grand Canals" in *A Brief Topographical and Statistical Manual of the State of New York* for 1822. A reduced profile of the Erie Canal and some interesting details are to be found in the *Biography of William C. Young,* — one of the early surveyors.

structed, it was 363 miles long and the highest point was at Lake Erie, 568 feet above the Hudson at Albany. Owing to the fact that the canal ascended and descended to avoid expensive cuttings or embankments, the total lockage was increased to about 700 feet.

The effect produced by the opening of the Erie Canal was immediate and great.[1] It provided a comparatively easy and uninterrupted mode of transportation from the Hudson to Lake Erie. It facilitated the movements of western emigrants and provided a commercial outlet for the surplus products of their farms. At once the increase in the demand for food by the western emigrants raised the price of grains along the western portions of the canal, but this was temporary. Salt making at Salina, or Syracuse, and the manufacturing of many kinds of household goods developed at several points along the canal; but its greatest effect was to stimulate the growth of New York City. The older Western Inland Lock Navigation Company's canal and slack-water system had lowered the cost of transportation between the Hudson River and Lake Ontario, but it was unsuitable for the conveyance of bulky and heavy goods, because everything had to be shifted from boat to wagon and back again several times to pass the falls and rapids of the Mohawk. Sections of the Erie Canal were open for traffic as soon as completed. By 1825, when it was opened for its full length, the cost of transportation of one ton of merchandise from Buffalo to New York City was reduced from one hundred dollars to less than eight dollars.[2]

[1] For some illustrative figures, see Note III at end of chapter.

[2] Meyer and MacGill's *History of Transportation*, 168 note. In 1882, the State auditor reported that the gross revenue of the Erie Canal to date was $121,461,871.09, the gross expenditure, exclusive of interest on the debt, $78,862,153.84, leaving a balance of $42,599,717.25. After this there were no more tolls to be collected, as the canals of the State were made free. Whitford's *History of the Canal System . . . of New York*, i, 317.

In other words the conveyance of merchandise between the Great Lakes and the seaboard was now a commercial possibility. The outstanding and continuing result was the decline in prosperity of all the seaports on the Atlantic coast, north and south of New York, in comparison with the wonderful growth of that commercial metropolis.[1]   As early as 1827 Governor Troup of Georgia wrote that the wheat of western New York was already supplanting that of Georgia in the Savannah markets, for no fertility of soil or geniality of climate can overcome "a difference of freight of five to one."   Since 1825 the Erie Canal has been reconstructed again and again, and, practically following its course, run the railroads, from Lake Erie to the Hudson.   The ultimate influence of the break in the Appalachian system through which these lines of transportation run may be seen in the fact that in 1910 nearly three-quarters of the inhabitants of the State of New York lived within five miles of the line of water communication between New York Harbor and the eastern end of Lake Erie.   Had there been no Erie Canal the development of that region would have been delayed for twenty or thirty years until the railroads reduced transportation costs, but it would have come then.   The settlement of the Old Northwest, north of the line of the National Road, would also have been greatly retarded, so greatly retarded, indeed, that the War for Southern Independence might have terminated otherwise than it did. Finally, the part played by lessening costs of transportation on social evolution may be seen in the fact that of the four

---

[1] In 1829 a paragraph in Hazard's *Annals of Pennsylvania* (iii, 320) stated that one hundred weight of goods could be transported from New York City to Middleburg in central Ohio, a distance of 750 miles, all the way by water by the Hudson River and Lake Erie and by the Erie and Ohio canals, for $1.37½; on the other hand, it cost $1.50 to transport the same weight of goods by wagon from Philadelphia, 140 miles, to Milton in central Pennsylvania.

hundred and sixty men of highest literary attainment who were born and nurtured in the United States between 1815 and 1850, three hundred and fifty-eight first saw the light of day in the section north of the Potomac and east of the Ohio.

The Pennsylvanians earlier had enjoyed an almost complete monopoly of western traffic between the Atlantic and the Mississippi Valley and north of the Potomac. Conestoga wagons lined the roads leading westwardly through Pennsylvania. This traffic had centred at Pittsburg for so long a time that at first the Pennsylvanians were disposed to minimize the dangers of impending competition through the Mohawk Valley. They may also have been deterred from taking up any canal projects through their own State by the great difficulty of overcoming the mountains that nature had flung from north to south across its limits.[1] With the actual opening of the Erie Canal, more attention was paid to westward transportation and, in 1834, an independent route by canal and railroad was opened from Philadelphia to Pittsburg. This system was often referred to as the Portage Railway from the name of the project

[1] The following facts are taken from a "Comparison of the Great Routes proposed to unite the Atlantic with the Great Lakes" in the "Biddle Manuscripts" in the Library of Congress under date of February 12, 1825.

No. I.	New York, by her Grand Canal	Lockage	655 ft.	Distance	506 miles
No. II.	The National Route by Harrisburg, Wilkesbarre; Seneca Lake to Lake Erie	"	1593 "	"	511 "
No. III.	Philadelphia by Schuylkill, Harrisburg to Lake Erie . .	"	2033 "	"	559 "
No. IV.	Trenton by Easton, Lehigh, Wilkesbarre to Lake Erie, by upper tunnel	"	3266 " }	"	436 "
	By lower do.	"	2700 "		
No. V.	From Washington City, by Potomac River and Cumberland, to Lake Erie	"	4833 "	"	559 "
No. VI.	From Philadelphia by Union Canal, Juniata to Alleghany and thence to Lake Erie . .	"	4410 "	"	650 "

by which the mountainous mass was overcome. The total distance from Philadelphia to Pittsburg by this route was 395 miles. David Stevenson, a British engineer, made the journey over this line in 1837. He covered the whole distance in 91 hours' travelling time. He went by railroad from Philadelphia to Columbia on the Susquehanna and then by canal and slack-water navigation to the eastern end of the Portage Railway. The highest point of the portage was 2326 feet above the mean level of the Atlantic Ocean.[1] This was overcome by ten inclined planes with stretches of level railroad in between. The planes were from 1480 feet in length to over 3000 feet, the height varied from 150 feet to 307 feet. Up these planes, railroad cars and canal boats were hauled by an endless rope, actuated by stationary engines, of which there were two at the head of each plane. Bits of railroad from one-sixth of a mile to thirteen miles in length connected the planes. Stevenson took seven hours to pass over the Portage Railway. In the first seven months that it was open nineteen thousand passengers and thirty-seven thousand tons of merchandise were conveyed over it, — a most convincing proof of the necessity of this particular internal improvement, whether it could or could not compete with the New York route or whether it ever repaid the cost of construction or, indeed, of operation.

The temporary success of the early trunk line canals incited the people of other parts of Pennsylvania to demand the construction of canals,[2] either connecting their towns with

[1] See David Stevenson's *Sketch of the Civil Engineering of North America*, 262–274. A most interesting and ample account, giving helpful illustrations, including one of an inclined plane, is "The Evolution, Decadence and Abandonment of the Allegheny Portage Railroad," by W. B. Wilson, in the *Annual Report* of the Secretary of Internal Affairs of Pennsyl- vania for 1898–99, Pt. iv, No. 8, xli– xcvi. There is a brief and clear ac- count of the Portage Railway and of the connecting systems in C. B. Trego's *Geography of Pennsylvania* (1843), 147–156.

[2] The canal commissioner's report forms "Appendix" to vol. ii of *The Journal of the Senate* of Pennsylvania of 1833–34.

the main system or, in some cases, merely for transportation
of goods from one town or county to another. The legislators could not resist these appeals and multitudinous
canals were dug. Many of them had no economic justification whatever and few of them provided enough business
to repay the cost of operation. Moreover, there was great
inefficiency in the construction and carrying on of these
public utilities and there was also corruption and extrava-
gance. The State, too, had gone into the venture of public
ownership and operation without making any adequate
financial provisions. In the end the people of Pennsylvania
found themselves burdened with canals, most of them not
paying expenses and unable to compete with the railroad
systems when they came to be built.[1]

West of the Alleghanies, the canal fever raged with nearly
as great severity as it did on the Atlantic seaboard. In 1822,
the Ohio legislature authorized a survey to be made to
determine the practicability of connecting Lake Erie with
the Ohio River by a canal. The committee reported in
1823, and ten years later the canal was opened for business
from the "southwesterly corner of the Village of Cleveland"
to Portsmouth on the Ohio. It was 308 miles in length
and its summit was 395 feet above Lake Erie and 491 feet
above its entrance into the Ohio. On portions of the route,
there were serious engineering difficulties and the sudden
risings of rivers more than once seriously interfered with the
maintenance of the canal after it was opened and occasioned
large and recurring expenditures. In the early years the

---

[1] See Thomas K. Worthington's
"Historical Sketch of the Finances
of Pennsylvania" in the *Publications*
of the American Economic Association, vol. ii. There is a good deal of
interesting matter relating mainly
to the Chesapeake and Ohio Canal
scheme, but useful also, as showing
the best thought of the time on transportation, in the *Journal of the Internal Improvement Convention* that was
held at Baltimore in 1834 and in the
"Report" that accompanies it.

traffic on this canal was heavy, — the tolls, fines, and water rents in 1837 amounted to nearly three hundred thousand dollars.[1] Its early success led to visions of vast interior navigations. Some of these were abundantly realized, but for the most part there was disappointment. There were many other western canals, the most important, perhaps, being the Illinois and Michigan Canal which was designed to connect Chicago with the Mississippi system.[2] Work was begun on it in 1836 and continued off and on for a dozen years greatly to the relief of many groups of settlers in northern Illinois, who otherwise would have found difficulty in securing the necessities of existence.

The Southerners also projected extensive systems of canals; one from the Tennessee River to the Atlantic Ocean and another from the Flint to the Savannah,[3] but the only southern canal of any length to be constructed in this period was that connecting the Santee and Cooper rivers in South Carolina. It was very expensively con-

[1] See "Annual Reports" of the Ohio Canal Commissioners; W. F. Gephart's Transportation . . . in the Middle West, 107–128; Dr. R. B. Way's article on the "Mississippi Valley and Internal Improvements, 1825–1840" in Mississippi Valley Historical Association's Proceedings, iv, 153–180; James L. Bates's Alfred Kelley, 69–93; and the History of the Ohio Canals published by the Ohio State Archaeological and Historical Society in 1905. An earlier and shorter account is Charles M. Morris's essay in American Historical Association's Papers, iii, 107–136. There is a valuable "List of Works relating to Ohio Canals" in C. B. Galbreath's Ohio Canals, 8–17, published by the Ohio State Library in 1910.

On Indiana, Logan Esarey's article in the Indiana Historical Society's Publications, v, No. 2, is detailed and careful; and much out-of-the-way material can be gleaned from The State of Indiana Delineated that was published at New York in 1838.

[2] See James W. Putnam's "Illinois and Michigan Canal" forming vol. x of Chicago Historical Society's Collections, and see also the Illinois State Historical Library's Collections, vii, pp. lxii-lxxvii.

[3] E. J. Harden's Life of George M. Troup, 174, 180. In 1824 Governor Troup advocated undertaking a system of internal improvements by the State of Georgia. If this were done, instead of "decaying cities and a vacillating trade . . . seeking an emporium elsewhere than within her own limits, she will witness the proud and animating spectacle of maritime towns restored and flourishing, new ones rising up — her trade steady and increasing — . . . and she may witness . . . the Western waters mingling with her own, and the trade of Missouri and Mississippi floated through her own territory to her own

structed and without adequate engineering oversight.[1] It
was of small utility, was dug and operated by a private
corporation, and is interesting mainly as an example of
Southern desire for better transportation facilities.[2] In the
country as a whole, in 1830, there were 3908 miles of canal
either finished or well advanced toward completion and
6833 miles more either under construction or actively contemplated.[3] These canals were constructed at vast out-
lays for those days. States and municipalities issued bonds
to provide the necessary funds out of all proportion to their
ordinary taxable receipts.[4] With the coming of the steamboat and the railroad, most of the canals went out of use
and, finally, in many instances they proved to be menaces
to the public health. The great changes that the application of steam to transportation on coastal and inland
waters and on the land itself were to make within a score of
years could not have been foreseen by the statesmen,
financiers, and promoters of that time, and they should not
be held blameworthy for these miscalculations. Of all
the canals, the Erie alone retained its vitality. Even as
late as 1860, it had a grain tonnage equal to that of the
railroads paralleling its course, partly because the roads
paid heavy taxes from which the canal was exempt.

It is an interesting thought how one invention supplants
another. For a time, the cry was for roads and more roads;
the Nation, the States, and private companies undertook
their construction and operation usually in return for tolls

seaports, and all this within the compass of her own resources."
  [1] U. B. Phillips's *Transportation in
the Eastern Cotton Belt*, 34-43.
  [2] Alexander Trotter's *Observations
on the . . . Credit of such of the States
. . . as have contracted Public Debts*
(London, 1839), chs. v-viii. J. A.
Morgan's "State Aid to Transportation in North Carolina" in the *North*

Carolina Booklet, x, 122, and the "Mur-
phey Papers" in the North Carolina
Historical Commission's *Publications*,
ii, 103-151.
  [3] George Armroyd's *Internal Navigation*, 447-482.
  [4] See B. R. Curtis's "Debts of the
States" in *The North American Review* for January, 1844.

that were levied on all traffic passing over them. Then came the canals which rendered partially useless the stage-coach and the wagon, and also the stone road except for merely local purposes. In their turn the canals were hardly completed as a system when the steamboat and the railway took business away from them. Is it not possible that the automobile and motor-truck with the airplane and the electrically propelled car will one day, and perhaps a not far distant one, likewise deprive the railroad of its place in the transportation system of this country?

The *Clermont* and the *Phœnix* made their trial trips in 1807; but the application of steam to movement by water did not become effective on the seaboard until after the close of the War of 1812 [1] or on the Mississippi until about 1819, and even later on the Great Lakes. The speed of the first boats was very slow, from four to six miles an hour, — a rate of progression that was ineffective against the current of a rapidly running river. The early Hudson River steamboats took thirty-six hours to make the run between Albany and New York City which is now covered in a quarter of that time.[2] By 1820, however, they were carrying sixteen

---

[1] For the history of the steamboat in America, see Stevenson's *Sketch of the Civil Engineering of North America*, 116–169. The successive editions of Samuel Cumings's *Western Pilot* from 1825 to 1841 give an account of the Ohio River and the Mississippi River below the Missouri and of the towns and settlements along the banks of those streams.

[2] *The Republican Crisis*, July 22, 1808. The "Telegraph Coach" with seats for eight passengers only was advertised to make the run from Albany to Buffalo in fifty-six hours, or ninety-two hours in all by steamboat and coach from New York City to Buffalo, — four days for the run that is now made in half a day or less. See *The Stage, Canal, and Steamboat Reg-*

ister for 1831 (Utica, N. Y., p. 5). My attention was called to this book by Mr. F. S. Owen. The time by the mail-coach from Boston to New York, 210 miles, was forty-one hours and the fare $11.00; but by going somewhat slower by stage and steamboat from New London, Providence, or Norwich, the fare was $7.25 (*The New England Almanac and Masonic Calendar* for 1828, stage-list at end).

The rates of postage had increased since 1800, being 15 cents in 1816 for ninety miles for a single letter as against 10 cents in 1800 and 12½ in 1832. The rate on the shortest distance, under 30 miles, was reduced in this later year from .12 to .06. See the present work, vol. iv, 6, and almanacs of the period.

thousand passengers a year between the two cities at a fare
of six dollars for each person. By that time, traffic through
Long Island Sound was also active, steamers running to
Norwalk, Hartford, New London, and even to Providence
in Rhode Island. The use of steamboats from New York
southward grew more slowly, but after 1820 there were
many of them plying along the seaboard. In 1825, Nicholas
Biddle wrote to William H. Crawford, who was then at
Washington slowly recovering from an illness. He invited
him to come to Philadelphia and wrote that the "steamboats will render the travelling very easy — and in less than
four and twenty hours you can be in Philadelphia," — a
distance that is now covered by train in one-eighth of that
time.[1] The route followed in 1825 was from Washington
to Annapolis by coach, across Chesapeake Bay by steamer,
thence to Newcastle, Delaware, by coach, and up the bay
and river by steamer to Philadelphia. This does not sound
very inviting at the present time, but the people of those
days were accustomed to great hardships in travelling.

The first steamer to be launched in the Mississippi
Valley was the *New Orleans*, which was built at Pittsburg
in 1811. She was constructed for Livingston, Fulton, and
Nicholas Roosevelt, and was built under the superintendence
of the last named. In September, 1811, she started down
stream with Mr. and Mrs. Roosevelt as passengers. After
some delays, while awaiting high water at the falls of the
Ohio at Louisville, she passed them safely and in due course
reached New Orleans.[2] For two years she plied between
that city and Natchez, but in 1814 was destroyed by accident. In 1815, the *Enterprise* that had been built at Browns-

[1] "Biddle Manuscripts" in Library
of Congress, under date of February
15, 1825.

[2] See J. H. B. Latrobe's "First
Steamboat Voyage on the Western
Waters" in Maryland Historical So-
ciety's *Fund-Publication*, No. 6.

ville, in Pennsylvania, not only went down the river, but ascended against the current to Louisville and thence to Pittsburg, thereby demonstrating the possibility of river steamboat navigation.[1] The building of steamboats now proceeded with rapidity and before the end of 1819, no less than sixty of them had been launched on the waters of the Mississippi or its affluents. It seems to be impossible to estimate the number of steamboats plying on the Mississippi and its branches at any one time, for the life of a river steamer was brief. The boats were flimsily constructed, the engines were weak and clumsy, and the boilers were poorly put together. The sudden and frequent changes from motion to rest at the various landings made it very difficult to control the making of steam. The pressure was very uneven and resulted in blowing out of cylinder heads and bursting of boilers, — the burning of the boat being an almost inevitable result. The navigation of the rivers was also peculiarly perilous. In addition to shoals and swiftly running currents, they were infested with drifted trees that had become anchored by their branches to the river bottoms with the trunks swinging down the stream at an angle of from thirty to fifty degrees. These were the snags, planters, and sawyers that brought many a steamboat to an early end.[2] For these reasons, the life of an early Mississippi steamboat was about four years, which was

[1] Ben Casseday's *History of Louisville*, 129.

[2] J. T. Scharf's *History of Saint Louis*, ii, 1094–1123, which is repeated in E. W. Gould's *Fifty Years on the Mississippi*, ch. xxiv; De Bow's *Commercial Review* for 1849, pp. 279–288. Chapter xii of James Hall's *Statistics of the West* (Cincinnati, 1836) is an interesting early account. A table on pp. 252–263 gives the names, tonnage, and dates of building and loss of all western river steamboats to

1836. Donald McLeod (*History of Wiskonsan*, Buffalo, 1846) estimated that in 1842 there were 450 steamers on the Mississippi River and its affluents with an aggregate tonnage of 90,000 and valued at more than seven million dollars.

The spirit of western steamboat navigation of this early time is set down in John Hay's "Jim Bludso" with a vigor and truthfulness that one seldom finds in this world.

later increased to six. In 1836 there were only eighty-seven
steamboats on the river that had been launched before
1830. In 1835 the fare for cabin passage including board
from Wheeling to New Orleans, a distance of 1908 miles,
was thirty-five dollars and deck passage one-quarter as
much, the passenger "finding himself." [1] The ten years
between 1840 and 1850 saw river navigation at its height;
then the railroads grew quickly west of the mountains and
set a limit to the commerce of the northern Mississippi
Valley by way of New Orleans.

Steamboats made their appearance on the Great Lakes
at a later day than they did in the Mississippi region. The
Walk-in-the-Water made her first trip in 1818 on Lake Erie.
With the opening of the Erie Canal the demand for steam
navigation grew and it was supplied. In 1834, it was arranged to run a weekly steamboat from Buffalo to Chicago
during the summer. In 1837, there were said to be forty-two
steamboats in active employment on Lake Erie and six
more on the stocks.[2] By 1840, they had established regular
business with the harbors on Lake Michigan. From that
time on, steamer traffic on the Lakes exercised an extremely
important influence on the settlement of the northern part of
the Old Northwest. By 1848, the time from New York to St.
Louis by rail and steamer had been cut down to eight days and
could be made with a fair amount of comfort and certainty.

The application of steam to transportation on land was
demonstrated to be commercially possible by George
Stephenson, an Englishman. There were locomotive engines
as good as Stephenson's from the theoretical point of view,

[1] Hall's *Statistics of the West*, 249.
Many interesting details are given in
Monette's "Progress of Navigation
. . . of the Mississippi" in the Mississippi Historical Society's *Publications*, vii, and L. S. Henshaw's "Early

Steamboat Travel on the Ohio River"
in *Ohio Archæological and Historical
Quarterly*, xx, 358.
[2] J. N. Larned's *History of Buffalo*,
i, 33, 45.

but he managed to combine correct mechanical appliances with a commercially profitable line of railroad.[1] He constructed the Liverpool and Manchester railway in the face of doubt and legislative refusal of aid. It was open for traffic in September, 1830, and its success spurred on the building of railroads in Europe and more extensively in America. The earliest or one of the earliest railroads to be built was the five miles of "way leaves" that connected near-by collieries with Sunderland, England, and was in working order in 1723.[2] These early railroads were used to haul the coal from the pit to the shipping point. Almost one hundred years later, Stephenson equipped the railroad leading from a colliery to Durham with a steam locomotive that drew seventeen loaded wagons at four miles an hour.[3] The first railroads to be built in America were one on Beacon Hill, Boston, and another in Delaware County, Pennsylvania, in the first decade of the nineteenth century, but the details are indefinite. The third railroad or tramroad or possibly the fourth was built at Falling Creek, Virginia, in 1810. It was about a mile long and at one point ran across a trestle some seventy-five feet high. One of the rails was grooved and the other tongued to fit corresponding wheels on either side of the wagon. The sixth road was

[1] As was the case with Fulton, Stephenson combined the devices and experiences of his predecessors in the production of a machine that would go commercially and keep on going profitably: these were the smooth wheel in place of the cog wheel of earlier types, the exhausting the steam from the cylinders directly into the chimney, thus creating a strong draft without the use of bellows, and the making of a tubular boiler in which twenty-five three-inch copper tubes conducted the heated gases from the furnace to the chimney. It was not until the making of the "Rocket" in 1829 that these inventions were combined to produce a practicable locomotive. See Samuel Smiles's *George Stephenson* and William H. Brown's *History of the First Locomotives in America.*

[2] Royal Historical Manuscript Commission's *Report on Welbeck Abbey Manuscripts,* vi, 104.

[3] William H. Brown's *First Locomotives in America* (ed. 1871), 55. Lewis H. Haney's "Congressional History of Railways in the United States to 1850," forming *Bulletin* No. 211 of the University of Wisconsin, contains much useful information in a brief compass.

built at Quincy, Massachusetts, in 1826. This road had wooden rails laid on stone sleepers and covered with iron plates, the wheels of the wagons being flanged.[1] These railroads were all for the transportation of heavy material for short distances. They were either gravity roads or the propelling power was provided by horses, or, on one of the later roads, by men.[2] Some of the early roads, especially in Pennsylvania, were constructed at public expense. These were open to any one who had the necessary locomotive or horse equipment and on one of them the regulations provided that the slower conveyance, whether steam or horse drawn, when overtaken by a speedier must make for the first siding and allow the swifter to pass.[3] The first steam locomotive to be used in America was the "Stourbridge Lion" which was imported from the Stephenson engine works in 1829.[4] For some time it was blocked up in the yard of a machine shop and operated with steam from a stationary boiler to run the machinery of the shop. At a later time it was used on the Delaware and Hudson railroad, but was too heavy for the rails and disappeared. The natural prejudice against the employment of steam locomotives comes out in a conversation with Governor Troup

[1] See article by James L. Cowles in *Boston Evening Transcript* for May 12, 1900; W. Hasell Wilson's *Brief Review of Railroad History*, 20; and George Smith's *History of Delaware County*, 389. The best brief account of land transportation with helpful illustrations is George G. Crocker's *From the Stage Coach to . . . the Street Car*.

[2] The advantages of railways are set forth in the *Report* as to the practicability and expediency of constructing a railway from Boston to the Hudson River that was presented to the Massachusetts House of Representatives in January, 1827.

[3] As the early Pennsylvania railroads were built at public expense, they were open for use by any one who had the proper equipment upon payment of a toll. The rules provided that no car should carry more than three and a half tons and no "burden car" should travel faster than five miles an hour. The occasional shipper found it too expensive to provide the vehicles with flanged wheels to run on the rails, and the business drifted into the hands of individuals or companies. See abstract of Antes Snyder's article in *Scientific American Supplement*, November 28, 1903.

[4] W. H. Brown's *First Locomotives in America*, 74–92.

of Georgia in which he assented to the advisability of railroads, but as for the employment of steam locomotives exclaimed, "Good God, I cannot stand that; I will go to the extent of horse power."

The "historic moment" in the railroad history of America was on July 4, 1828, when Charles Carroll of Carrollton, the sole surviving Signer of the Declaration of Independence, laid the "corner stone" on the line of the contemplated Baltimore and Ohio Railroad.[1] The first steam railroad to be operated in the United States was the Charleston and Hamburg Railway connecting South Carolina's great seaport with the Savannah River, opposite Augusta, in the State of Georgia. It was constructed partly at the cost of South Carolina to divert the commerce of the upper Savannah River to Charleston, which had been the point of transshipment for the interior trade in colonial days. It was an attempt to revive the waning fortunes of Charleston, which were already beginning to feel the effects of competition with the cotton lands of Alabama and Mississippi and the diversion of trans-Atlantic traffic to New York, and other northern seaports. The new railway was lightly built, running for miles over low trestles, and the final approach to the Savannah River was made by an inclined plane. The stage-coaches had carried twelve passengers or so a week between Charleston and Augusta; after the opening of the railroad in October, 1833, the number of passengers increased to fifty a day. The South Carolinians deserve great credit for the energy and public spirit that they displayed in carrying through this enterprise. As an instrument of transportation, however, the road was not a success because the Georgians forbade its extension across

[1] Lewis A. Leonard's *Life of Charles Carroll of Carrollton*, 229–231 and   Brown's *First Locomotives in America*, 93.

the river and constructed a railroad of their own to tap the resources of the State above Augusta and to concentrate commerce at Savannah.[1]

The first engines used on the early railroads were very light and of small power, and the earliest lines were built with sharp curves and steep pitches. These could be overcome in dry weather, but a very small amount of moisture on the rails stalled the locomotives. An example occurs in the early history of the Philadelphia and Germantown Railway, which was very steep in places. It advertised that a locomotive engine will depart daily with a train of passenger cars "when the weather is fair"; when not fair, cars drawn by horses will be used.[2] So uncertain was early steam locomotion in New England that trains were sometimes lost in rain or snow and it was thought expedient to provide relays of horses at convenient spots to rescue any locomotive that might be unable to proceed. It was also thought dangerous to run in the darkness and therefore all motion on these roads came to an end at sundown.

The electric telegraph came into existence most opportunely to make possible the running of trains on the railroads with the minimum of danger and the maximum of speed and certainty of operation. As was the case with Fulton, so Samuel Finley Breese Morse[3] was a portrait painter by profession. He was the son of Jedidiah Morse, the geographer and a Calvinistic minister. Permitting the son to study art must have seemed a good deal like consigning

[1] U. B. Phillips's *History of Transportation in the Eastern Cotton Belt*, ch. iii; T. D. Jervey's *Robert Y. Hayne and his Times*, using index; H. Hammond's *South Carolina*, 629–633; *Handbook of South Carolina* (2nd ed., 1908), pp. 505–508; and Meyer and MacGill's *History of Transportation in the United States*, 422–427.

[2] *History of the Baldwin Locomotive Works, 1831 to 1907*. A facsimile of the above advertisement is on p. 13.
[3] See E. L. Morse's *Samuel F. B. Morse: His Letters and Journals* (2 vols., Boston, 1914), and Samuel I. Prime's *Life of Samuel F. B. Morse, LL.D.* (New York, 1875).

him to perdition; but his parents consented and the profits of the "Geographies" provided the necessary funds. While returning home from one of his European trips, a fellow passenger — Dr. Charles T. Jackson of Boston — asserted that the electric current went instantly from one end of a line of wire to the other. At once Morse declared that if that were so there was no reason why "intelligence may not be transmitted instantaneously by electricity." From that moment telegraphy occupied Morse's mind to the exclusion of everything else except that he was obliged to exercise his profession to procure bread. In devising the telegraph, he freely used information that he obtained from Joseph Henry, Alfred Vail, Ezra Cornell, and others; but the successful assembling of their ideas and combining them with his own to produce a workable electric telegraph has given him deserved immortality.[1] The first line was opened in 1844. It immediately attracted attention and the telegraph came into common use within a few years; but Morse's later life was very largely occupied with defending his invention against the infringements of others.

The first improvement in the railroad was the substitution of the solid U-shaped iron rail for a combination of strap-iron and wood. The next was to substitute wooden trans-

[1] An account of the origin and development of Morse's invention by William B. Taylor was printed in the *Annual Report* of the Smithsonian Institution for 1878, pp. 262–360, under the title of "Henry and the Telegraph." See also Alfred Vail's *Description of the American Electro Magnetic Telegraph: now in operation between the Cities of Washington and Baltimore* (Washington, 1845) and J. C. Vail's *Early History of the Electro-Magnetic Telegraph. From Letters and Journals of Alfred Vail* (New York, 1914). Morse, himself, prepared an account in 1867 entitled *Modern Telegraphy*, which has, as an appendix,

depositions from various persons exposing errors of dates and statements of his opponents. The telegraph companies and the miles of wire in operation in 1850 are given in *Report of the Superintendent of the Census for 1852*, p. 112.

As a scientific man Joseph Henry probably deserves in our history the place next to Franklin; but he was an experimenter rather than an exploiter and the oblivion that attends the man in the laboratory seems to have surrounded him. See *A Memorial of Joseph Henry. Published by Order of Congress* (Washington, 1880).

verse sleepers laid on the surface of the road bed instead of on the stone posts or walls that were used at first and found to be inelastic and disturbed by the frosts of northern winters. As it was financially impossible to build reasonably straight and level road beds in a new country and over the mountainous approaches of the Appalachians, it proved to be feasible to change the form of the locomotive by providing it with four front wheels on a truck to which the engine was attached on a pivot. A locomotive mounted in this way could go around a sharp curve, and then the same principle was applied to the coaches or cars in which the passengers rode or freight was carried. This again led at once to the substitution of a long boxlike car for a replica of the old stage-coach, which had been the form of the first railroad passenger conveyances. Then a doorway was cut in the end, the passengers were seated on either side of an aisle, and thus the American locomotive and coach were evolved.

With each improvement of the steamboat and the railroad, speed was increased and the conditions of travelling were improved. In 1817, the time from Boston to New York had been cut down from eighty hours to forty or so. Passengers left New York by boat on Monday, Wednesday, or Friday morning for New Haven, where they transshipped to another boat for New London and from there proceeded by stage-coach to Providence and Boston. In 1826, the time was further reduced to twenty-four hours.[1] From New York southward, one went by railroad through New Jersey. In 1833, Adams travelled over this line. He timed the rate of speed at sixteen miles in fifty minutes; "We had flakes of fire floating about us in the cars the whole time," he wrote. Between Amboy and Bordentown a wheel on one of the coaches burst into flame and slipped

[1] J. Q. Adams's *Memoirs*, iv, 4; vii, 315; viii, 541; ix, 30; xii, 70.

off the rail. One of the cars was overset and the side crushed in. Two persons were killed and one only in that car escaped unhurt. In the same year Audubon, journeying southward,[1] from Petersburg, Virginia, was dragged in a "car drawn by a locomotive" at the rate of twelve miles an hour and "sparks of fire" came into the car in such quantities that the passengers were kept constantly busy extinguishing them on their clothes. In 1844, Adams left Baltimore at nine o'clock in the morning and reached the Astor House in New York before midnight of the same day.

These improvements in transportation were greatly for the public benefit. They were essential to the peopling of the West and to the building up of the industries of the East.[2] Capital was in scant supply and the citizens naturally turned to the public authorities for aid. The federal Congress, State legislatures, and the cities and towns answered the demand. The Erie Canal was constructed by the State of New York; States and cities subscribed to the stock of road companies, and legislatures gave promoters the right to hold lotteries. When the railroads came, therefore, the people were accustomed to public contribution. In the western country especially, public aid was very necessary because roads, canals, and railroads could not possibly earn any return on the money invested in them, until the country served by them had been cleared and was producing a surplus for transportation. The result was a mass of public debt which was, for the most part, entirely justifiable from economic and political standpoints, but was none the less burdensome. It was under these circumstances that many of these States went into the banking business with the

---

[1] F. H. Herrick's *Audubon*, ii, 53.
[2] G. S. Callender's "Early Transportation and Banking Enterprises of the States" in *Quarterly Journal of* *Economics*, xvii; D. R. Dewey's "State Banking Before the Civil War" (*Senate Documents*, 61st Cong., 2nd Sess., vol. 34).

expectation, apparently, that they could secure enough
profits from banking to relieve themselves of a part, at
least, of the burdens of railroad building. In many cases
these hopes proved to be elusive, but in some States, notably
in Virginia[1] and South Carolina, the State banks were well
managed and profitable. The Bank of South Carolina was
founded in 1812. The act for its establishment provided
that all the assets of the State should form its capital and
that all the taxes collected by the State should be deposited
in it. The bank might receive private deposits, discount
bills of exchange, loan money even on mortgages, and issue
paper currency; but the amount loaned on real property
was to be apportioned among the election districts, according
to the number of representatives in the Assembly.[2] The
income of this bank was regarded as a part of the revenue
of the State. This act was amended from time to time
and the operations of the bank aroused jealousies and envy
on the part of legislators and of financial institutions. It
lived down all these troubles and in 1847 had received and
paid out over twenty-eight million dollars.

Three journeys made in 1796, 1836, and 1845 reflect the
changing conditions of travel. The first was made by Moses
Austin,[3] who left Virginia on December 8, 1796. He and
his comrades rode on horseback about thirty miles a day
to Harrodsburg, Kentucky, which they reached on the 23rd
of that month. On the 29th they crossed the Ohio by ice
and by boat and on the 9th of January reached Kaskaskia
on the Mississippi, having been almost exactly a month on

[1] Richard L. Morton's "Virginia
State Debt and Internal Improvements, 1820–38" in *Journal of Political Economy*, xxv, No. 4, April,
1917; and William L. Royall's *History of Virginia Banks . . . Prior to
the Civil War*.

[2] See *A Compilation of All the Acts
. . . in Relation to the Bank of the State
of South Carolina* (Columbia, S. C.,
1848).

[3] *American Historical Review*, v,
523.

the way. The second journey was made by Lucian Minor.[1]
He left Baltimore by stage on November 29, 1836, over the
National Road, which he described as a "fine McAdamized
turnpike."   On December 6 he left Wheeling by steamboat for Cincinnati. The ice was running in the river and
the voyage proved to be full of peril. But he reached Louisville on the 16th. There he passed through a canal with
two locks which had cost nearly a million dollars, five-
sevenths being paid by the United States. At Louisville
he stayed at the Galt House, which he described as "a new
and elegant hotel, almost vieing with the Tremont of
Boston"; he had a warm room on the fourth story and clean
towels. On December 21 he reached Shawneetown in
Illinois. Nine years later, in May, 1845, W. W. Greenough [2]
travelled by steamer and railroad from Detroit to Boston
in less than three days and a half.

By 1840 there were nearly three thousand miles of steam
railroad in operation in the United States. About one-half
of this mileage was in the Middle States, — Pennsylvania
with seven hundred and fifty miles having the greatest
extent of railroad of any State in the country. Indeed,
there were more miles of railroad in Pennsylvania than in
all the Southern States put together. In the next ten years
the railroad mileage tripled to about nine thousand miles in
all. By this time, New York had outstripped Pennsylvania
and Massachusetts was pressing hard upon the Keystone
State. In 1850, something less than one-quarter of the
total mileage was in the States south of the Potomac and the
Ohio. The seasonal variation of cotton and tobacco carriage
in that region and the multiplicity of navigable waters made
against railroad building. In Kentucky there were only

[1] Massachusetts Historical Society's
Proceedings, 2nd Ser., vii, 264.

[2] Massachusetts Historical Society's
Proceedings, vol. 44, p. 339.

seventy-eight miles of completed railroad, and in Virginia there were less than four hundred miles in comparison with thirteen hundred in New York. Georgia, indeed, in 1850, was the only Southern State that had a railroad system in actual operation that was at all comparable to those of the States of the Northeast.[1]

Important as transportation has been in determining the growth of cities and towns and the settlement of farming areas — in the development of the material side of life — the effect of these new forces on the relation of man to man has been even greater. By making practicable the working together of human beings in larger units it has conduced to the development of democracy and direct government; democracy has outgrown the town and State until now, from the Atlantic to the Pacific, from Canada to Mexico, the whole force of the community in a brief space of time can be thrown in any one desired direction. Peering into the future and embarking on the dangerous path of prophecy, it is not at all out of the realm of possibility that the same forces that have broken down sectional barriers within national borders will shatter national barriers themselves and racial lines, too, and lead to international action on a scale and in directions hitherto undreamed of. So, too, in a similar way and for similar reasons the old associations of man to man, of the employer and employed working together, side by side, have disappeared. The man of executive mind and of power can now direct far more than the gang of working men laboring by his side or within easy reach by eye or horse; he now can administer a factory or a group of them, or even groups of groups scattered widely over the

[1] These figures are taken from the table in Poor's *Manual of the Railroads of the United States, for 1868-69,* p. 20. For somewhat different fig-ures, see Dudley Leavitt's *New-England Almanack . . . for the Year 1841,* pp. 41, 42.

country or the world. Entrepreneurs combining together
can conduct operations limited only by the demand for
their goods, without much regard to distance, country, or
clime. So, also, labor has been forced to act in larger and
larger units, to disregard political barriers, and even to leap
over the bounds of race and religion : the town guild has
become the labor union by federation extended to many
trades and employments and tending to disregard the lines
of political and physical geography. Under these circumstances, schemes of living and working that have
hitherto been impracticable are every day coming to be
more and more the usual mode of action.

NOTES

I. General Bibliography. — Hildreth's annalistic work stops with the year 1820 and Henry Adams's survey of the administrations of Jefferson and Madison closes with the accession of Monroe in 1817. James Schouler's *History of the United States* (vols. iii-iv) is the only work of the formal historical type that covers the period from 1815 to 1850 in detail. It is especially worthy of note for this time because the author takes a sympathetic view of Jacksonianism. McMaster's *History of the People of the United States* (vols. iv-vii) covers the period in a most comprehensive manner. The author has discarded the sprightly style of the opening part of his work and the volumes are unusually hard reading; but owing to the mass of detail in them and to the abundance of quotation and citation, they are extremely useful. Possibly most readers will find Schurz's *Clay,* Lodge's *Webster,* and Shepard's *Van Buren,* in the " American Statesmen" series, more useful than either Schouler or McMaster. Books dealing with the more important topics of this era will be cited in later notes.[1]

II. Transportation. — The best general work is Meyer and Mac-Gill's *History of Transportation . . . before 1860* (Washington, 1917). A much shorter, but useful essay is Henry V. Poor's *Sketch of the Rise and Progress of the Internal Improvements . . . of the United States;* this was first printed as an introduction to his *Manual of the Railroads* for 1881 and was published separately with the same title, but with a slightly different pagination. An earlier comprehensive sketch is contained in the *Report of the Superintendent of the Census for December 1, 1852.* David Stevenson's *Sketch of the Civil Engineering of North America* (London, 1838) and George Armroyd's *Connected View of the Whole Internal Navigation of the United States* (Philadelphia, 1830) have already been mentioned several times, — a list of canals completed and projected is on pp. 454–489 of the latter. Part iv of the second volume of Noble E. Whitford's *History of the Canal System of the State of New York* is a comprehensive view of the " Canals of the United States and Canada."[2] G. G. Huebner's and

[1] The student of inquiring mind can find information arranged in usable form in the State Gazetteers, of this period, especially T. F. Gordon's *Gazetteer of the State of New York* that was published at Philadelphia in 1836, but really has a much wider significance than its title implies.

[2] A vast amount of useful information on these topics and on social and political matters, also, may be easily gathered from the successive volumes

T. W. Van Metre's articles on " The Foreign Trade of the United States since 1789," " Internal Commerce," and " The Coastwise Trade" in E. R. Johnson and associates' *History of Domestic and Foreign Commerce of the United States* give a convenient conspectus of the subjects studied.

III. The Effect of the Erie Canal. — It appears from Delaval Carpenter's *Address to the People of the United Kingdom, on the Corn Laws* (London, 1840) that the price of wheat in England by the quarter of eight bushels was 65 shillings in 1820, 43 in 1822, 66 in 1825, and thereafter varied from fifty-six to sixty-six until 1833, when it went to fifty-two; in 1835 it went to the lowest point, 40 shillings a quarter; but in 1838 it was up again to sixty-three shillings. The price of wheat in America had similar inexplicable variations. In 1820, flour by the barrel was $6.00 at New York; in 1829 it was $8.50, in 1831 was $6.12, in 1835 just under $5.00, and in 1837, $11.00 a barrel.[1] It would seem from this that other factors than cheapness of transportation between the Great Lakes and the seaboard governed the price of food.[2] The figures and titles in this Note were given to me by Mr. F. E. Milligan of Pittsburg, Pennsylvania.

of Hezekiah Niles's *Weekly Register*, published at Baltimore from 1811 onward; and Samuel Hazard's *Register of Pennsylvania*, the first volume of which was published at Philadelphia in 1828 and the six volumes of his *United States Commercial and Statistical Register*, which was published at the same place beginning with 1839.

[1] According to the *Parliamentary Papers* (Accounts and Papers, 1843, liii, No. 177, p. 18) the "Annual Average Prices" of wheat in England and Wales per "Imperial Quarter" were:

> 67s, 10d, in 1820
> 44s, 7d, in 1822
> 68s, 6d, in 1825
> 52s, 11d, in 1833

> 39s, 4d, in 1835
> 64s, 7d, in 1838

[2] See also tables of the exports of wheat, flour, and manufactures in Thomas G. Cary's *Use of the Credit of the State for the Hoosac Tunnel* (Boston, 1853), pp. 22, 23.

De Bow's *Review* for July, 1849, p. 82, gives a table of the aggregate value of breadstuffs and provisions exported by five-year periods:

> 1821–1825 = $66,690,537
> 1826–1830 = $59,657,484
> 1831–1835 = $67,705,481
> 1836–1840 = $63,054,453
> 1841–1845 = $80,016,657

The smallest amount exported in a single year was $9,588,359 in 1837; and the largest amount was $68,701,921 in 1848.

CHAPTER II

THE WESTWARD MARCH

THE migration from the "Old Thirteen States" on the Atlantic seaboard and from European countries to the Mississippi Valley is one of the marvellous phenomena of history.[1] The coming of the Germanic hordes to western Europe in the days of Alaric, the West Goth, and Attila, the Hun, and their overthrow of the Roman Empire is comparable to it by reason of far-reaching success; it has no relation to the occupation of the trans-Appalachian region in point of size. Moreover, the Germanic invasions destroyed, or greatly modified, the most highly developed institutions of that time; the migration across the Alleghanies and the occupation of the Mississippi Valley substituted civilization for savagery at the cost of the extinction of the original occupiers of the land, to the accompaniment of warfare, treaties, and the inevitable effects of the contact of savagedom with the vices and diseases of civilization.

Transappalachia includes the greatest portion of the United States. Measuring across the continent from Cape Henlopen on the Atlantic to Cape Mendocino on the Pacific, seven-eighths of this territory is to the west of the Appalachian Mountains. In 1815 the United States was limited on the west and on the south, but by the Florida Treaty of 1819, the Oregon Treaty of 1846, and the treaties following

---

[1] For the earlier time, see the present work, vol. ii, 550 and fol.; iii, 15–24; vol. iv, ch. ix.

on the close of the Mexican War the boundaries of the
homelands of the United States were established as they
are today. Transappalachia may be roughly divided into
the Mississippi Valley with the accompanying alluvial-
coastal plains, the Rocky Mountain region, and the Pacific
Coast. For practical historical purposes the country west
of the Appalachians may be regarded as divided by the one
hundred and fourth meridian which forms the eastern
boundary of the present States of Montana and Wyoming.
It is with the eastern section that the present chapter is
concerned. Journeying westwardly from the Alleghany
Mountains, one came, in the old days, to a densely forested
country extending almost from the Lakes to the Gulf.
The hardwood trees were of no structural value at that
time, but they offered a great impediment to the pioneer
as they must be cut down before corn could be grown for
the sustenance of himself and his family. Nevertheless,
for years the pioneers hesitated to go out from the
protection of the trees to the naked prairies beyond, for
there, there was no shelter from the summer's sun or the
winter's storms. Moreover, surface water was scarce,
although, as the pioneers did not know, by sinking wells it
might be obtained almost anywhere. The prairies stretch
westwardly to about the ninety-seventh meridian, where
they are succeeded by higher and drier level tracts known as
the "high plains." It is not known why there are no trees
on the prairies and the plains. The best explanation
perhaps is that forests to live require a certain amount of
moisture.[1] When the rainfall is below that point, minor

[1] See papers by J. D. Dana, A.
Winchell, and Leo Lesquereux in
Silliman's *American Journal of Science
and Arts*, vols. xxxviii, xxxix, and xl;
and John D. Caton's comments on
Lesquereux's theories in his *Miscel-*
lanies, ch. ix. See also Bowman's
Forest Physiography, 427; Daniel E.
Willard's *Story of the Prairies;* and W.
V. Pooley's *Settlement of Illinois*. An
interesting old-time view is in James
Hall's *Statistics of the West*, ch. vi.

factors, that ordinarily would have little influence, become decisive. Thus in a region of abundant rainfall, a fire started by lightning would have slight effect, but in a drier country it might prove fatal to tree life. So, too, the pulverization of the surface soil by drought keeps the scanty supply of water near the surface and thereby prevents the reforestation of burned-over areas. With artificial encouragement, trees can be grown as far west as the one hundred and fourth meridian, except in limited areas where special considerations apply.

South of the Ohio River and between the mountains and the Mississippi, the country is suited to the production of corn, tobacco, and cotton. The Black Belt, extending from western Georgia to the Mississippi River, possesses a dark soil which in its pristine condition is exactly suited to the needs of the cotton plant, and the rainfall and temperature of this belt of land are also exactly what the growing cotton demands.[1] Northward of the Ohio River, corn and wheat grow luxuriantly. Indeed, nowhere else on the earth's surface is there a block of half a million square miles of land so thoroughly suited to the needs of agricultural man as eastern Transappalachia and impinging upon it are areas of iron and coal and copper, in richness beyond the dreams of the most ambitious manufacturer.

The obstacles to the occupation of this country had been the difficulty of reaching it from the Atlantic seaboard and the lack of surplus population in that section to take advantage of such means of transportation as then existed. In 1800 there were not enough people living in the original States

[1] See J. W. Mallet's *Cotton . . . the Actual Conditions and Practice of Culture in the Southern or Cotton States of North America* (London, 1862). Professor Mallet was analytic chemist of the Alabama State Geological Survey and a Ph.D. of Göttingen. A modern book on the same subject is C. P. Brooks's *Cotton: its Uses, Varieties, Fiber Structure, Cultivation, and Preparation for the Market and as an Article of Commerce* (New York, 1898).

to more than scratch the surface of opportunity. Those who sought the lands over the mountains in the earlier time were actuated mainly by the love of adventure, by the lure of the wilderness; stern economic necessity had not as yet touched the people of the older settled area. From 1800 to 1820, the embargo, the war, and the hard times spurred on migration; but it was not until the financial revulsion of 1837 and the critical years thereafter that eastern people sought the western wilds in great numbers. This gradual strengthening of the tide of emigration from east to west synchronized with the development of the new modes of transportation.[1] Until the opening of the National Road, travel toward the Mississippi Valley was arduous, dangerous, and prolonged, — and that highway served mainly the needs of Pennsylvania and the States to the southward. It was not until the Erie Canal and connecting links of transportation became available about 1830 that emigrants from New York and New England could gain the western country with any fair degree of safety, speed, and comfort.[2] By 1840 the railroad began to influence migration, but only to small distances from tidewater. It was not until after 1850 that this mode of transportation became an important element in the settlement of the Northwest.

A contributory cause to the growing march of westward migration was the development of the national land system. Land acts were passed in 1800, 1820, and 1841, and the movement increased in volume after each one of those years, but whether there was any direct relation between these two facts cannot be stated. It is certain that the land legis-

[1] Professor Albert P. Brigham has a readable article on "The Great Roads across the Appalachians" in the *Bulletin* of the American Geographical Society for June, 1905. Moses Guest gives an interesting account of the Pennsylvania route before the days of the Portage Railway in his *Journal* (ed. 1824, p. 147).

[2] See Michigan Political Science Association's *Publications*, iv, 13.

lation explains some of the peculiarities of western settlement and, therefore, would better be briefly examined. In 1785, when the land ordinance was passed, western public lands were looked upon as prospective producers of wealth for the States of the Confederation and the idea that the lands were a valuable financial asset to the older settled part of the country remained into the constitutional period as can be seen in the land act of 1796.[1] In 1800, while the Federalists were still in control of the government, a land law was passed that marked the beginning of a different policy.[2] In the future, the national domain should be used for the benefit of the country as a whole by encouraging the settlement of unoccupied lands. In the future, land would be sold in good sized lots to settlers at a minimum price of two dollars an acre, a portion being paid down at once and the remainder in instalments at interest, — the government, on the other hand, allowing a discount for cash on the payments that might be deferred. The mode of surveying that had already been adopted was continued with some alterations. Under this system, settlers often outran the surveyors and demanded recognition of their preëmption rights. It is easy to see how many complications might arise. Men were often tempted to buy as much land as they had money in hand to pay the first instalment; and,

---

[1] For this and later land laws see *Annals of Congress* and *Statutes at Large* under date; these laws and illustrative matter have been collected in four volumes as *House Miscellaneous Documents*, 47th Cong., 2nd Sess., No. 45 (Washington, 1884). For a scholarly résumé of the earlier history of the land system, see Payson J. Treat's *National Land System, 1785–1820*.

[2] See however, Robert E. Chaddock's *Ohio before 1850*, p. 54. He writes "In 1800, when the party of Jefferson came into power, and W. H. Harrison, himself a Virginian, was Ohio's delegate in Congress, a new act was secured, largely through his influence, which permitted tracts of 320 acres to be purchased by individuals." It is perhaps needless to point out that in 1800, the Federalists were still in power and this act was approved by President John Adams. Harrison did favor it, but one of the strongest opponents of it was Henry Lee, likewise a Virginian, and father of Robert E. Lee.

with the frontiersman's speculative hopes, relied on the future to provide the funds necessary for the deferred payments. As long as everything went well — as long as the Indians kept quiet, new settlers came pressing in from the East, and frost and malarial sicknesses held off — the lands would constantly increase in value and a man by selling off part of his holdings could raise the money to pay the instalments as they came due. After 1810 for a dozen years or so, there were Indian troubles, sicknesses, and droughts which culminated in financial distress. On September 30, 1819, it appeared that settlers owed to the United States government more than twenty-four million dollars of unpaid instalments. The condition called for a remedy and had been calling for a remedy ever since the passage of the act. So, too, had the case of the unauthorized dwellers on the government land, the squatters as they were later called. If the object was to increase the power and strength of the United States by the rapid occupation of lands and the building of homes, why should men wait for surveyors to run their chains over bog and mountain? Why not take a bit of good land and pay for it when the surveyor did come? But this of course created trouble. Not infrequently it happened that when a man had regularly purchased land, he would find one of these preëmptioners already living upon it. Sometimes the matter might be amicably settled by payment for improvements, but often there was friction.[1] Settlers were constantly appealing to Congress for extensions of time in which to make their payments or to have their squatter rights legalized. Congress might have insisted upon the law being rigidly enforced or it might have provided some entirely new system. It did neither, but granted extension

[1] For a description of the mode by which the settlers overrode the law, see Alfred Brunson's "Circuit Rider's Horseback Tour" in *Wisconsin Historical Collections*, xv, 277.

of credit no less than thirteen times and passed no less than thirteen preëmption acts that were limited in their application. At length in 1820, Congress put an end to the credit system and provided that lands should be sold in eighty acre lots at a minimum price of one dollar and a quarter an acre. Twenty-one years later, in 1841, it passed a general preëmption law, and twenty-one years after that President Lincoln put his name to the Homestead Act by which it was hoped that actual settlers would acquire farms practically without money payment.[1] In all these earlier years, Congresses and Presidents, generally, stood firmly against making special grants or special exceptions, but there were some instances and some of them were entirely commendable as the presents in 1803 and 1825 of thousands of acres of the public lands to General Lafayette.

The first settlers were backwoodsmen, or frontiersmen, or pioneers, or pathbreakers, — they cannot be called farmers or planters because as soon as they had brought a little patch of ground into farming condition, they sold out to the next comer and moved away into the wilderness. They were temporary reversions to the hunter type; they did not belong to the agricultural stage. They loved solitariness and the smell of the smoke of a neighbor's chimney was in itself enough to drive them back to the wilderness road. The mother and children had as great a fondness for the life of the fringe of civilization as the father and moved willingly on and on with him. Daniel Boone is the stock representative of this type and he is a very good one, because not until age stiffened his limbs could he be brought to quiescent living. Next came the farming and planting pioneers

[1] Emerick's "The Credit System and the Public Domain" in the *Publications* of the Vanderbilt Southern History Society (No. 3) and San-born's "Some Political Aspects of Homestead Legislation" in *American Historical Review*, vi, 19.

following hard on the first rank of wilderness invaders. They exhibited some symptoms of settled existence, building better cabins than the half-faced camps. They cultivated the fields for several years until the ground was free from stumps, the soil pulverized, and neighbors appeared. Then the "Western Fever" seized upon them and drove them once more to the wilderness: — to the Connecticut River, to New York State, to the Western Reserve, to Illinois, to Minnesota and beyond.[1] An interesting example of this restless type was Hezekiah Lincecum and his son, Gideon. The latter was born in Georgia in 1793. In the course of the next ten years or so, the family lived in eight or nine different places in Georgia and South Carolina. The Lincecums [2] then settled for a time near Tuscaloosa, in Alabama, and finally on the Tombigbee River near Columbus, Mississippi. There Gideon struck out for himself. He became a self-taught doctor and collector of insects and lived his last years in Texas and in Mexico. Although belonging to a later generation Hamlin Garland's family well represents the farming wanderer. The grandparents left Maine before the Civil War and moved by canal and steamer to Wisconsin. Hamlin's father was a soldier in the Union army. Returning to his Wisconsin home, he lived there for a time; then "Fair freedom's star" pointed to the sunset

[1] "At first the west was the Connecticut river; then the hill country of Western Massachusetts . . . and finally the regions beyond." Aaron W. Field's "Sandisfield: Its Past and Present" in Berkshire Historical and Scientific Society's *Collections* for 1894, p. 81. In point of fact, the Atlantic beach was really the first frontier, because the three thousand mile voyage across the ocean brought to many a man and woman entirely new ideas of the responsibilities and possibilities of life. Owing to the shifting geographical position of "the West," it has been found advisable to use a definite geographical term — Transappalachia — to describe the country beyond the Old Thirteen. At the present time (1920) there seems to be a reaction against the term "the West" as used by Mr. Field, for W. P. Shortridge in *Minnesota Historical Bulletin*, iii, 116, speaks of the region beyond the Alleghanies as "the first real American West."

[2] Mississippi Historical Society's *Publications*, viii, 443–519. See also Southern History Association's *Publications*, i, 89–97.

regions and away he and his wife and children went to
Minnesota, to Iowa, to southern Dakota.[1]　In reading this
family life story, one is impressed, as he is with the life
stories of other migrant farming families, with the absence
of home ties. They had no feelings of affection for the houses
and lands that they left behind ; they only looked to the
future and over the mountains and rivers to the westward.
As years went by and the fringe of settlement moved out
from the wooded country to the prairies, the hunting pioneers
disappeared.　Now, when the railroad brings immigrants
from the Atlantic coast in one journey to the railhead on
the prairie, the first comer is no longer a farming migrant,
but himself belongs to the group of home making farmers
or homesteaders, as they might well be called.

The magnitude of the westward movement and its meaning can best be expressed, perhaps, by a study of population
statistics of different parts of the country in years that are a
generation apart.　In 1790, ninety-four per cent of the
total population of the country of about four million human
beings lived in the Old Thirteen States, the takers of that
census reporting under one-quarter of a million people in
the western settlements.　By 1820 practically one-quarter
of the whole population of nine and a half million people

---

[1] Hamlin Garland's *A Son of the
Middle Border*. The author himself
came to Boston for training in literature and then removed to New York,
and in 1893 brought back his parents
from their Dakota farm to Wisconsin.

The family history of my colleague,
Professor Frederick Jackson Turner,
furnishes an admirable example of a
migrant and re-migrant family. The
first immigrants from England settled
in eastern Massachusetts. Thence,
after a good interval, the Turners
took up the westward march, going
first to Connecticut, and then northwestwardly through Massachusetts to
the Vermont and New York shores of
Lake Champlain. After tarrying there,
representatives of the family moved to
Michigan and Wisconsin and Nebraska; some of them, revivified by
contact with the western wilderness,
returning to their first landing place
in the New World.

A good illustration of re-migration
is the Ohio Society of New York.
In 1889 a list of its 303 members,
giving the places in Ohio whence
they had come to New York, was
printed in Henry Howe's *Historical
Collections of Ohio*, i, 177–183.

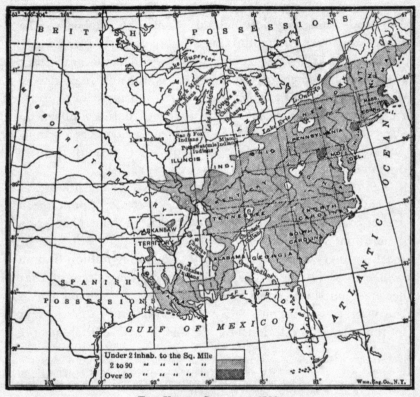

THE UNITED STATES IN 1820
(From *The Statistical Atlas* of the Twelfth Census.)

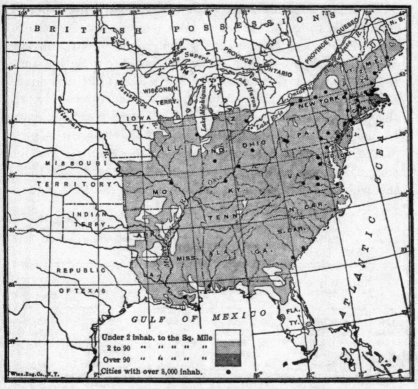

THE UNITED STATES IN 1840
(From *The Statistical Atlas* of the Twelfth Census.)

lived beyond the western limits of the Atlantic seaboard States, and in 1850, forty-five per cent of the twenty-three million inhabitants of the United States lived there. Since that time, the proportion has slowly increased, until in 1910, nearly fifty-nine per cent of the dwellers in the homelands lived to the westward of Pennsylvania and New York and the other original thirteen States.[1] So great, on the other hand, has been the growth of urban population that in 1910 as many people lived within a radius of thirty miles of the New York custom house as inhabited the country to the westward of the one hundred and fourth meridian, even to the shores of the Pacific Ocean. By far the greatest part of the increase in the newer part of the country was by emigration from the older States on the seaboard. In 1820, the western population, instead of being less than half a

[1] The following table is compiled from the *Compendium of the Seventh Census* (1850), pp. 40, 41; *Census* of 1870, vol. i, p. 4; and *Census* of 1910, vol. i, p. 146 and fol. It illustrates the points noted in the text and gives comparisons of a later date:

	TOTAL POPULATION IN UNITED STATES	POPULATION OF ATLANTIC SLOPE	% OF POP. ON ATLANTIC SLOPE	POPULATION OF TRANSAPPALACHIA	% OF POP. IN TRANS-APPALACHIA
1790	3,929,827	3,708,116	$94\frac{7}{10}$	221,711	$5\frac{3}{10}$
1820	9,638,131	7,013,154	$72\frac{7}{10}$	2,624,977	$27\frac{3}{10}$
1850	23,191,876	12,729,859	$54\frac{9}{10}$	10,462,017	$45\frac{1}{10}$
1870	33,589,377	15,752,507	$46\frac{9}{10}$	17,836,870	$53\frac{1}{10}$
1900	75,994,575	31,490,175	$41\frac{9}{10}$	44,504,400	$58\frac{1}{10}$
1910	91,972,266	38,063,468	$41\frac{7}{10}$	53,908,798	$58\frac{3}{10}$
1920	105,708,771	43,651,927	$41\frac{3}{10}$	62,056,844	$58\frac{7}{10}$

In 1800 the total urban population of the United States as a whole was less than one-quarter of a million; in 1850 it was over two millions, and in 1920 it was approximately fifty-four millions as against fifty millions as the total rural population of the country. In 1910 the total population of the States west of the 104th meridian, which is the western boundary of the Dakotas and Nebraska, was 6,825,821 and at the same time there were more than 7,225,416 human beings living within a radius of thirty miles of the New York custom house. In fact, in 1910 more people lived on Staten Island in New York Harbor than in the whole State of Nevada. The people of Nevada were represented by two Senators in Congress, while the people of Staten Island were represented by $\frac{1}{108}$ part of two Senators.

million as it would have been by the usual excess of births
over deaths, was over two and a half millions;[1] at
least one million and a half of this increase represented immigrants from the older States. In the second thirty years
from 1820 to 1850, the inhabitants of Transappalachia more
than doubled by some five millions; the seaboard section,
notwithstanding the great immigration from Europe in the
last ten years of that time failing to double by at least two
millions. It would seem probable, therefore, that in those
two decades, the West took at least four million people out
of the East. When we consider also that the migration
from the farms to the manufacturing towns and commercial
cities was very large in these sixty years, especially in the
last thirty of them, we can realize what a strain was placed
upon the old rural population.

Looking over the figures given in the "Census of 1850,"
one is impressed with the large proportion of the migration
from the four South Atlantic States. Two-fifths of the free-
born South Carolinians — whites and blacks — were then
living outside of the State of their birth. This was a larger
proportion of emigrants than from any other State in the
Union, but nearly one-third of the Virginians and North
Carolinians and nearly one-quarter of the Georgians had

---

[1] The figures given in the text are
based upon somewhat intricate calculations about which there may be a
good deal of doubt. In a new country population is supposed to double
by natural reproduction about every
thirty years, but the rate declines
rapidly as a country emerges from the
pioneer stage. Some of the accretion
of the population of Transappalachia
was due to the acquisition of Louisiana
which brought two hundred thousand
people into the United States at one
time. On the other hand, the influence of the War of 1812 may be
eliminated, if we accept William Jay's

estimate of the total loss of the American army in the whole war, including
those killed in action and those dying
of disease and wounds, as less than
twenty-five thousand. See the present work, vol. ii, 492 note and William Jay's "Table of the Killed and
Wounded in the War of 1812" in New
York Historical Society's *Collections*,
Second Series, ii, 447–466.

For other calculations limited to
New Englanders, see Professor Turner's "Greater New England in the
Middle of the Nineteenth Century"
in American Antiquarian Society's *Proceedings*, October, 1919.

likewise sought the newer lands. The inhabitants of the
Southwest from Alabama to Arkansas and Texas were
almost entirely from the Old South ; there were some foreign
born immigrants and rather more from the Northern States,
especially in Texas, but most of the settlers were Southerners
born and bred. Moreover, Southerners crossed the Ohio
River from western Virginia and from Kentucky and formed
the predominant element in the Old Northwest, south of
the line of the National Road. Indeed, the New Englanders
at Marietta and vicinity were almost the only Northerners
in this region. The causes of this Southern migration are
easily found in the crude methods of agriculture of that
region and in the tremendous demand for cotton that developed almost beyond belief in each decade from 1800. The
area of cotton culture rapidly grew and the cultivation of the
plant became more intense, more a matter of business, of the
application of capital to labor. The units of cultivation grew
larger and the small farmer could no longer compete with
the man of capital. By 1830 cotton growing had spread
from western Georgia to the Mississippi River. The
planters in the older States could not compete with the
cotton growers of the "black belts."[1] The only thing for
the less advantageously situated planters and farmers to
do was to go to the newer cotton lands and westward they
went. George Tucker, a Virginian, writing in 1824,[2] declared that "the west" was "the *el Dorado* of all bad managers"; but he was unjust to his neighbors, for it was the

---

[1] See Phillips's "Origin and Growth
of the Southern Black Belts" in
American Historical Review, xi, 798-
816. Some conditions of life in the
South and circumstances of migration are vividly set forth in Edwin J.
Scott's *Random Recollections* (Columbia, S. C., 1884).

[2] See his *Valley of Shenandoah;*

or Memoirs of the Graysons, i, 169.
This work of fiction, which was printed
in two volumes at New York in 1824,
gives an intimate view of the life of the
planters of Virginia by one of themselves; Paulding's *The Banks of the
Ohio; or Westward Ho!* (3 vols.,
London, 1833) is a remarkable picture
in prose of the Virginia migration.

general economic condition of Virginia planting life and not especially bad management that made migration inevitable. The tobacco plant was a destroyer of the soil and Virginia methods were undoubtedly extravagantly wasteful. Washington and Jefferson were both of them disturbed at the outlook. They studied books and corresponded with eminent agriculturists in other parts of the United States and in Europe, but both of them seem to have been helpless in introducing thorough-going reforms even on their own estates. Then, as the century advanced, Kentucky-grown tobacco appeared in the markets and added to the distress of the Virginians. The years after 1815, instead of bringing relief from the conditions of embargo and war, only increased the troubles of the tobacco men. Droughts and insect-pests were added to the pressure of old debts, and the hard times in the cotton region greatly lessened the demand for Virginia slaves, which were offered for sale by the thousands.[1] Jefferson's experience is interesting. It would seem that an estate of over five thousand acres with one hundred and thirty-two slaves might have been made to pay, but it is very doubtful if Jefferson ever secured any net return from his property.[2] In fact, as the tobacco acreage on Virginia's exhausted fields diminished, the amount of labor, as measured by the number of slaves, increased so that the plantation slowly ate itself up. Virginia planters, following the example of the South Carolinians, migrated to the westward, taking their slaves with them,

[1] *Speech of Thomas J. Randolph . . . on the Abolition of Slavery . . . Jan. 21, 1832*, p. 11. Ambler, citing Thomas Marshall, states that the agricultural products of Virginia in 1831-32 were "worth no more than they had been eighty years prior when the population was only one-sixth as large." *Sectionalism in Virginia*, p. 111. Pages 110–117 of this book give an inter-esting picture of the condition of Eastern Virginia at the time of the westward migration.

[2] See the "Jefferson Papers" in the cabinet of the Massachusetts Historical Society under date of August 11 and 27, 1819, and his Account Book for 1823. "A List" of Jefferson's property is in the same collection under date of May 14, 1815.

or one or two members of the family with some of the slaves established new homes in Transappalachia. In these years, the population of eastern Virginia including the Valley of the Shenandoah was actually declining, — in 1840 there were 26,000 fewer inhabitants living there than in 1830.[1]

It will be interesting to study the migration from a more personal point of view. There were the Cabells of Virginia who were connected by marriage with the Brecken-ridges of Kentucky and Missouri and with the Shelbys of Alabama; and there are few States of the Union that have not representatives of the Cabells and their kin. The best known Southern-Western migrating family was that of Jefferson Davis. His grandfather came to Pennsylvania from Wales and moved to Georgia. His father went next to western Kentucky, where the future President of the Confederacy was born in the year 1808. In infancy he was taken by his father to Louisiana and then to Mississippi. Also in western Kentucky, and one year later in point of time, Abraham Lincoln first saw the light of day. His ancestors had come to Massachusetts in 1637 and the family had moved slowly through New Jersey, Pennsylvania, and Virginia to Kentucky, leaving members behind at various points of the route.[2] Abraham Lincoln with his father and mother crossed the Ohio River to Indiana and later he removed to central Illinois. Of the other two great characters in the secession struggle, General Grant belonged to a Massachusetts family[3] that migrated to Ohio by way of

[1] These figures were compiled for me by Mr. R. L. Morton. From them it appears that the white population of the Piedmont district actually decreased over 4% in the decade. J. B. Harrison in his *Review of the Slave Question . . . By a Virginian* (Richmond, 1833), p. 19, gives figures that show that the white population of nine Virginia counties below the head of tide-water had decreased by 3274 between 1820 and 1830; and five Piedmont counties had likewise suffered a loss of 1522 white inhabitants in those years.

[2] For a complete and careful account of the Lincoln family, see Lea and Hutchinson's *Ancestry of Abraham Lincoln* (Boston, 1909).

[3] Arthur H. Grant's *The Grant Family . . . Descendants of Matthew Grant*.

Pennsylvania; the immediate family of his great opponent, Robert E. Lee, remained persistently in Virginia, being the only one of the four to have no Western associations.

Viewing the course of the movement from a more general standpoint, one is impressed by the part played by Vermont and central and western New York and western Pennsylvania as temporary abiding places for these western going families. An almost endless procession begins in Massachusetts and moves through Connecticut or western Massachusetts, to Vermont or to the New York shore of Lake Champlain. There a family remained for a generation or two and then in the 1820's moved to the "Genesee country"[1] in western New York, and then another generation went farther west. If the migrant family found itself in western Connecticut, the line of march was often farther south through New Jersey and Pennsylvania to Ohio, or sometimes even farther south to Kentucky by way of Virginia. The liberal institutions of Vermont coupled with an abundance of vacant land drew people to that northern country; but the life there was very hard, the labor severe, and the reward small. Western New York attracted families of passage by its greater economic opportunity, and also because in a larger and rapidly growing State the chance for service and personal advancement was much greater there than in a smaller and longer settled community. Frequently ill health necessitated a freer open-air life and drove many a promising, but physically weak, lad from eastern town or farm to the western wilderness,[2] as was the case with Luther Burbank.

The great migration from central and western New York

[1] A good example is to be found in the family of William L. Sill of Wyoming. He was born in Wisconsin, his father was a native of New York; his mother was from Vermont and his paternal grandfather from Connecticut.

[2] W. S. Harwood's *New Creations in Plant Life.*

between 1830 and 1840 is not easily accounted for. At first sight it would seem that the opening of the Erie Canal, by subjecting the farmers of that region to the competition of the workers of the fertile lands tributary to the Great Lakes, would so have reduced the price of flour and other agricultural products that the New Yorker would abandon his farm and proceed to a new country. It does not appear, however, that the price of flour at New York City and at Philadelphia was materially affected by the radical reduction in the cost of transportation from Buffalo to tide-water. Moreover, the marvellous increase in the manufacturing population of the Northeast created a new demand for agricultural products, for these workers abandoned the production of food for the making of shoes, cloth, and other commodities. It is probable that, contemporaneously with the drifting into towns, there was a change in the taste in food from bread made of corn and the dark grains to bread made from wheaten flour. Owing to the shifts in the methods of census taking, it is impossible to state the growth of the urban population as distinguished from the rural at different periods. All that can be said is that in the first half of the nineteenth century the urban and suburban population had grown from something like a quarter of a million in 1800 to about ten times that amount, or two and a half millions in 1850; none of these town dwellers produced much, if any, food, and every one of them had to be fed by the labor of others. The Northeastern farmer of the olden type was of about the best human material that America has ever seen. He lived an almost ideal political and social democratic existence. With a change in agricultural conditions that the use of machinery brought in, with the establishment of manufacturing, and the coming of immigrants of other stocks, an abandonment of the old life was

necessary, for a part of the family, at any rate.[1] Some of
the children became prosperous farmers in Illinois or other
Western States, others of them entered business or manufacturing life in the towns of the Eastern States, and after a
generation or two became prosperous manufacturers or
commercial men or bank presidents or entered one or another
of the learned professions. Some of the western wanderers
were attracted to Transappalachia by ideals of freedom or the
probability of economic independence offered by a farm in
the new country. But many men sought speculative
opportunities there; not a few, who had read law, per-
ceived a chance to acquire wealth in the endless litigation
that was sure to arise over western lands; and others sought
political preferment in new communities where positions were
not already held by well known men. In the earlier years,
the emigrant moved by short stages from one State to
another; but after 1840 steamboat navigation on the Lakes
made it almost as easy to go from Buffalo or Cleveland to
Milwaukee or Chicago as it was to go to Toledo or Detroit.

The story of a few families will illustrate the points made
in the preceding paragraph. Of New Englanders, perhaps,
the Fairbanks family is the most interesting: the immigrant
Jonathan Fairebanke came from England to Massachusetts
in the 1630's and at Dedham built a house which is still
standing and was occupied by members of the family for
eight generations. Descendants of the original settler to
the number of a thousand or more have lived in thirty-four
States of the Union: at Monroe and at Leon in New York;
at Madelia in Minnesota; at Waupun. in Wisconsin, at
Berkeley, California, and elsewhere. The first Fairbanks

[1] See Charles F. Emerick's "Analysis of Agricultural Discontent in the
United States" in *Political Science
Quarterly*, xi, 436, 437; the early history of Daniel Webster admirably illustrates the motive of migration from
the "old farm" to city or prairie.

were farmers, but the later ones, or some of them, have entered many occupations. Among them were Thaddeus Fairbanks of St. Johnsbury, Vermont, who invented the standard scales that bear his name; Nathaniel Kellogg Fairbank, who began as an apprentice to a bricklayer in Sodus, Wayne County, New York, and ended his life in Chicago as a princely manufacturer; and Charles Warren Fairbanks of Indianapolis, who was Vice-President of the United States.[1] There are many other families with similar histories, as that of Henry Kingsbury who came to Massachusetts from England in the *Talbot* in 1630. Since then nearly two thousand of his descendants have lived in thirty States or territories of the Union.[2] One might go on for page after page giving repeated references and mentioning family after family, but it would be a mere fortifying of a story that is beyond dispute. Indeed, of the seven Presbyterian ministers commemorated in Hotchkin's "Western New York," five came from Connecticut and of the three hundred and sixty-eight original settlers of Chautauqua County, nearly one-half were New Englanders.[3] New York stood in the relation of foster parent to thousands of families who paused there a generation or two on the way from New England to Ohio and the States farther west, even to the shores of the Pacific Ocean. On the other hand, it is notice-

[1] See Lorenzo S. Fairbanks's *Genealogy of the Fairbanks Family in America, 1633–1897.*

[2] F. J. Kingsbury and M. K. Talcott's *Genealogy of the Descendants of Henry Kingsbury of Ipswich and Haverhill, Mass.* Of the nine uncles of a lady from Maine of my acquaintance six went to California, made some money, and then abandoned the Golden West. Four of them returned to New England; the other two settled in Georgia and Kentucky.

[3] Besides Hotchkin, see Lockwood L. Doty's *Livingston County, New York* (Geneseo, 1876); Andrew W. Young's *Chautauqua County, New York* (New York, 1848); O. Turner's *Pioneer Settlement of Phelps and Gorham's Purchase* (Rochester, 1870); and an almost endless number of biographies, local histories, and publications of historical societies. A tabulation of five volumes of *The Mayflower Descendant* shows that descendants of the Pilgrims have lived or are living in almost every part of the United States and outlying possessions.

able that the families of the original Dutch settlers of New Netherland, to an even greater extent than the Pennsylvania Germans, stayed in their first homes.

Thousands of family stories present certain elements of similarity. There is the closing of the old home, the packing of household goods and children, sometimes the mother and grandmother, into a wagon drawn by two, four, or six horses or oxen and sometimes by a mixed team. Often the elder children and the mother walked with the father, an uncle or two, and possibly a hired man. There were always troubles with the road whether one went south or north or through the Middle States. There were rivers to be forded, mountains to be crossed, and swamps to be passed. Following the southern and middle routes, one went directly from one's former home to the newer place of living. In the North, the first part of the journey was sometimes made wholly or partly by canal boat, from the Hudson westward to Buffalo. There the travelling family with its paraphernalia and animals embarked on a steamboat to go by water to a port in Michigan, or Wisconsin, or Illinois and then to take up the landward march. These journeys were not mere matters of days or weeks, but often consumed a month or more. The desires of the emigrant were often aroused to join the westward movement by letters received from a brother who had gone before [1] or by alluring circulars from land speculators who were able to acquire large tracts on credit under the act of 1800. Later the transportation companies became active and touted for business.[2]

[1] Dr. Solon J. Buck in the "Introduction" to the "Letters of Gershom Flagg" states that five of Flagg's brothers and sisters followed him to Illinois.

For roads, distances, steamboats, and canal routes, see the map accompanying S. A. Mitchell's *Traveller's* *Guide through the United States* (1838). Insets give detailed information as to roads, etc., in the vicinity of the leading cities.

[2] John T. Blois in his *Gazetteer of the State of Michigan* (Detroit, 1838, p. 160) says that in Michigan in 1837 a farm of 80 acres of government land

Arrived at the new home or the place that was to be a new home for five or ten years, the family either moved into a frontier hut that had been erected on a half cleared farm, or, if the emigrant took up land that had not been touched it would be necessary to build a shelter and then construct a log house. Everything was of the rudest type, necessarily so in the existing conditions of transportation. Then followed the work of clearing the land or of continuing the clearing operations of an earlier occupier. Throughout large portions of the western country fevers and agues and stomachic troubles beset the settlers. They generally attributed these disorders to the turning up of large areas of sod or decaying humus in the forested tracts. Probably they were malarial infections and were unavoidable in the existing condition of hygienic science. They certainly were not diminished by the sudden change in the condition of the soil covering. As to remedies, the pioneers had vigorous constitutions, otherwise they could hardly have survived the combination of disease and "cure"; and under the circumstances there was likely to be resort to alcohol either in the form of a beverage or in the more insidious guise of a medicine. When one had cleared his land and got his fields in fair producing order, there was usually no market for whatever surplus grain or live-stock the farm might produce and, therefore, there was no money with which manufactured commodities could be purchased. The early farms were perforce self-sustaining in that the women made the clothes from the wool, the flax, or the skin, the men of the family helping in the heavier work, as boot-making. One of the most interesting accounts of early western life

cost $100.00, or a farm of 640 acres cost $800.00; therefore a "father may sell his small farm in the East for a sum that will purchase a dozen large ones in the West, of the best quality of land." By migration, he would better his own condition and that of each member of his family, who would soon become independent.

was written by Gershom Flagg, an early New England
settler in southern Illinois. He raised corn and wheat by
the hundred bushels and could do nothing with it. In
1820 corn was selling at from twelve and one-half cents to
twenty cents a bushel at Edwardsville in Illinois.[1] A
settler in the earlier days was almost immobile. Public
conveyances ran infrequently, if they ran at all, the fares
were very high and the distances to be travelled long.
About the only way, therefore, to get a change of scene was
to migrate to some other part of the country. If one
lived within a day's journey of a navigable river, the case
was perhaps a little better, but even the teaming of farm
produce to a steamboat landing for twenty or thirty miles
was extremely difficult and expensive. It was under these
circumstances that the farming population of the newer
country, territory, or State, welcomed any kind of suggested
improvement in transportation, whether road, canal, or steam
railroad, and cheerfully consented to the incorporation of
banks and to the incurring of debt on the part of the State
or town for the purpose of encouraging the opening of lines
of transportation.

Religion, idealism, or economic causes often led the migration to assume a group form. There are examples of
concerted movement from the old Puritan settlements, of the
transplanting of Southern Quaker "Meetings," and of the
removal from Europe to America of particularistic groups
whose religious views or social doctrines were displeasing to
some European ruler. The migration from Granville,
Massachusetts, to Granville, Ohio, in 1805, is probably the

[1] Gershom Flagg's "Letters" in
Illinois State Historical Society's *Transactions* for 1910, p. 167. Corn had
been selling at 33 to 50 cents in 1819;
in 1818 and again in 1825 it was as
high as 75 cents a bushel. These
prices are for St. Louis and Edwardsville, Illinois, which was within easy
teaming distance of the Mississippi.
Farther inland the prices of farm
produce must have been very much
less.

most perfect example of the continuance of the old Puritan system of group migration.[1] In this case, a "church" of the old New England type had previously been organized and a constitutional agreement drawn up and signed in the old Granville and land acquired in the new. In the first migration one hundred and seventy-six persons participated, fifty-two of them being heads of families; in most cases the weaker members were left behind to follow on later. They laid out their town on the New England model, with a public square in the centre where they erected a log house that in the earlier years served for religion, business, and education. In 1831, the people of Bergen in New York, incited by religious zeal, determined to become a church in the wilderness as the Pilgrims had before them. Five years later, just before starting on their westward way, they covenanted "with God and with one another" to found such a church. In 1836 and in 1837, about fifty persons, included in seven or eight families, left Bergen and journeyed to Illinois, across Canada, southern Michigan, and northern Indiana. They occupied nine weeks on the journey and founded the settlement of Geneseo[2] near a similar colony called Princeton,

---

[1] See Henry Bushnell's *History of Granville, Licking County, Ohio* (Columbus, Ohio, 1889) and *The Granville Jubilee, celebrated at Granville, Mass., August 27 and 28, 1845* (Springfield, 1845).

Ordinarily, little reliance can be placed on names of towns and townships in deducing institutional relationships. In 1816 Gershom Flagg states that there were then in Ohio 3 Concords, 6 Fairfields, 11 Madisons, 7 Salems, and 8 Springfields. See Flagg's "Letters," p. 143, and note and Mrs. Martin's "Origin of Ohio Place Names" in *Ohio Archæological and Historical Publications*, xiv, 272. It is interesting to note that Hubert Howe Bancroft, the maker of the *History of the*

Pacific States and long resident in San Francisco, was born in Granville, Ohio; his ancestors having lived in Granville and West Springfield, Massachusetts, the first of them landing at Lynn in 1632.

[2] *Memorial Address . . . of the Settlement of Geneseo, Illinois.* Other instances of group migration from New England are those from Vermont to Vermontville in Michigan (Michigan Pioneer and Historical Society's *Collections*, xxviii, pp. 197–265) and from Durham in Connecticut to Durham in New York (William C. Fowler's *History of Durham*, 209, 214, and Lois K. Mathews' *Expansion of New England*, 228–230).

which had been established in 1831 by people of Northampton, Massachusetts.

Most of the early settlers of Ohio and Indiana and southern Illinois were from the Southern States and Pennsylvania, sometimes directly and sometimes by way of Kentucky. Many of them were attracted to Ohio by the cheapness of the land as well as by the fertility of the soil. Large tracts had been assigned to Virginia at the time of the cession and a great deal of this land had been turned over to Virginia's Revolutionary soldiers to satisfy their claims under the bounty laws of that State,[1] and, besides, Virginia had made many private grants in the Ohio region before the cession. Many of the soldiers and other grantees sold their warrants for what they would bring to speculators, who in turn sold them below the government rate to actual settlers. It has often been asserted that many of the early Ohio colonists left their Southern homes because they disliked the slave system and that others had been driven out of the South by the increasing competition of slave labor. This was true in some cases, but probably the aversion to slavery on the part of the Southern settlers in Ohio has been overemphasized. It certainly strongly influenced the migration of Quakers from Virginia, the Carolinas, and Georgia to the free country north of the Ohio River. This movement continued throughout the first thirty years of the century. In some cases the clearance of the Quakers from their old homes to the interior resulted in the transference of their meetings as a whole. In other cases, some members remained behind, but most of these or their children probably joined the earlier emigrants in the years of deepening slavery and secession feeling in the Southern States. An idea of the

[1] Payson J. Treat's *National Land System, 1785-1820*, p. 329. Virginia laws promised 15,000 acres to a major general and from 100 to 300 acres to a private, according to the length of service.

size of this Quaker migration may be gathered from the fact that letters transferring the membership of nearly two thousand persons from meetings in the Southern States to the Miami Meeting were received in the four years from 1803 to 1807 ; and the minute books of Cedar Creek Meeting and South River Meeting in Virginia contained more than one hundred letters of dismissal to Ohio, — which probably meant the migration of four times as many persons. The Friends went to Cincinnati, to Miami County, to Fairfield, to Plainfield, and to other places in Ohio.[1] Their aversion to slavery grew rather than weakened as the years went by and this, combined with their industrious and law-abiding habits, made them an exceedingly important element in the State.

Whatever may have been the case with the Southern settlers of Ohio, the Southern colonists of Indiana and Illinois were not impelled by any religious or idealistic motives, but crossed the Ohio River, either because of the love of adventure or because on the northern side they hoped to make a living more easily than they could in western Virginia or Kentucky. Until 1840, Indiana and southern Illinois were distinctively Southern in thought and institutions. The Black Swamp protected Indiana from invasion from the north and the distance of the inhabited parts of Illinois from the southern end of Lake Michigan made against migration by way of the Great Lakes.[2] The

[1] Harlow Lindley's "The Quakers in the Old Northwest" in *Proceedings of the Mississippi Valley Historical Association*, v, 60–72; Stephen B. Weeks's "Southern Quakers and Slavery" in *Johns Hopkins University Studies*, extra volume xv, ch. x; the *Annals of Newberry* by J. B. O'Neall and J. A. Chapman (Newberry, S. C., 1892) specially Part ii, § i; and *Our Quaker Friends of Ye Olden Time* (Lynchburg, Va., 1905).

[2] S. J. Buck's "The New England Element in Illinois Politics before 1833" (Mississippi Valley Historical Association's *Proceedings*, vi, 49) brings together with abundant citations many interesting and not easily get-at-able facts as to early Illinois population; and the map accompanying S. A. Mitchell's *Illinois in 1837* provides tangible information as to county lines, canals, towns, etc.

settlers of southern Indiana and Illinois had none of the anti-slavery sentiments of the Southern settlers of Ohio. Indeed, they would gladly have introduced slavery into their new homes and came very near doing so.[1]

Apart from the Northern and Southern groups that have just been mentioned, one of the first religious communities to appear in the Western country after 1800[2] was led by George Rapp, a Würtemberger, who had lost faith in Lutheranism, had denounced its vices and corruptions, and had found it desirable to abandon the land of his birth. With his followers he migrated to Pennsylvania and later sought the Wabash Valley in Indiana. There they established a home in the wilderness which they named Harmony; but the spot was unhealthy. In 1825 they sold out their farms and village to Robert Owen and, returning to Pennsylvania, established the town of Economy on the Ohio River about eighteen miles from Pittsburg. The Rappists were celibates and communists and believed that the second coming of Christ and the end of the world were so near that they themselves would see them. Another German religious body to come to Pennsylvania was that composed of the followers of Joseph Bimeler or Bäumeler. He also was a Würtemberger and either he or one of his comrades had warned Napoleon of his danger, owing to the multitude of souls he was hurrying into eternity. Bimeler and his

---

[1] See T. C. Pease's *The Frontier State* (*Centennial History of Illinois*, ii) ch. iv; N. D. Harris's *History of Negro Servitude in Illinois*, chs. iii and iv; E. B. Washburne's *Sketch of Edward Coles*, 61–198; and William H. Brown's "Historical Sketch of the Early Movement in Illinois for the Legalization of Slavery" (*Fergus Historical Series*, No. 4).

[2] For the earlier German communities in Pennsylvania, see the present work, vol. ii, 411, and the books there cited; and also J. I. Mombert's *Lancaster County*, 354–362; and Hinds's *American Communities* (2nd ed.), 16–26. For the Rappists, see *ibid.*, 69–98, and the books cited on the latter page; and especially J. H. Bausman's *Beaver County, Pennsylvania*, ii, 1004–1030; and also G. B. Lockwood's *The New Harmony Movement*, 7–42.

A list of books on American communities is in note to ch. xv, below.

people landed at Philadelphia in 1817. They soon moved to Ohio, calling the place of their settlement Zoar. As was the case with the Rappists, communism had been no part of the original scheme of Joseph Bimeler; but the struggle with the wilderness convinced the Zoarites that in no other way could they succeed in keeping body and soul together. For a time, too, celibacy was the rule, but later on marriage was permitted.

Another communal experiment of this early time is that which is associated with the name of Robert Owen. He was a native of Wales who had some very pronounced theories as to property and modes of living.[1] He had been a mill manager in Scotland and had greatly contributed to the success of the establishment in his charge by reducing the hours of labor, increasing the wages of the operatives, and providing for the happiness of the working people. At one time he had hit upon the belief that the way to cure most of the evils of society was for men to associate together, to eliminate the distributing middleman, but otherwise to be free to work out their own salvations. In 1820, the idea came to him that reason indicated the grouping of human beings into villages of about a thousand souls apiece. Each person in one of these settlements should be allotted an acre of land or possibly two; families should live separately in contiguous houses, the members taking their meals in a common dining-room.[2] Individualism would disappear and each and every one would work for the benefit of all. Owen thought that his plan to be successful should be tried on a

[1] Duke Bernard of Saxe Weimar, on the occasion of Owen's death, wrote that his wish had been "to renovate the world, to extirpate all evil, to banish all punishments, to create like views and like wants, and to guard against all conflicts and hostilities"; G. J. Holyoake's *Life and Last Days*

of Robert Owen (London, 1871), p. 4. *R. Owen at New Lanark; . . . By One formerly a Teacher at New Lanark* contains many illustrative anecdotes of Owen's early life.

[2] Owen's *Report to the County of Lanark* (ed. 1821), pp. 24–26.

great scale, but not raising the necessary funds, he decided to try it on a small scale. He bought out the Rappist improvements in Indiana, and in 1825 he led his colonists thither, and renamed the settlement New Harmony. The course of life there ran anything but smoothly after the first few months. There was incessant debating and constitution making, but very little labor. In 1827, the experiment as a community came to an end, but most of the Owenites remained in Indiana, although Robert Owen, himself, eventually returned to England.[1]

The story of the founding and early days of any one of the newer States is merely a replica of that of western New York, western Pennsylvania, Kentucky, or Tennessee. When New Englanders and New Yorkers moved to the newer country, they carried with them their churches, their schools, and their ideas of corporate responsibility.[2] The Southerners in their migration likewise carried to their new homes their strong individualism and their peculiar labor institutions. In Ohio, Indiana, and Illinois, the two sets of ideas began to jostle one another as these States received more Northern immigrants. For a time, there was a good deal of friction, but finally a conglomerate institutional fabric was worked out under which Southerner, Pennsylvanian, and Northerner lived together side by side in reasonable harmony. After 1850, when the rapidly growing network of railroads opened the "Middle West" to Northern influences and Northern markets, the old North-

[1] For Robert Owen and his experiments, see his *Life* (1 vol., London, 1857) by himself and a *Supplementary Appendix* (London, 1858); W. L. Sargent's *Robert Owen* (London, 1860); *New Views of Mr. Owen of Lanark* (London, 1819); Owen's *New View of Society* (3rd ed., London, 1817); and George B. Lockwood's *New Harmony Communities* and *New Harmony Move-*

[2] John T. Blois (*Gazetteer of the State of Michigan*, 157, 158) says that of the white population in Michigan in 1837, the greater portion, estimated at nearly two-thirds, is from New England or western New York, or is composed of "New Englanders or their descendants, and mostly of the latter."

ment and the books mentioned on p. 381.

west rapidly changed its political and social alignment. Michigan and Wisconsin had no Southern elements in their populations, but both of them in the 40's and 50's were to be powerfully influenced by bands of immigrants from Germany and Scandinavia.

The perusal of diaries, journals, and letters written by these early settlers of Transappalachia convinces one of the attachment of these pioneers to the homes of their youth, and to the ideals of the communities whence they came. The direct contact with nature and the hardness of frontier life brought back to the race those qualities that easier existence seemed to have softened. As the Reverend J. D. Butler of Madison, Wisconsin, phrased it in 1870 : "Through a change of base men secure a vantage-ground for a new start after failure, they gain a fair field for new experiments, they plunge into that necessity which is the mother of invention, — they cast off in their long march valueless heirlooms, mental no less than material, — they are roused to the utmost endeavors by new hopes, new havings, new potentialities of progress." [1]

[1] C. K. Williams's *Centennial Celebration of the Settlement of Rutland, Vt.*, 51. It is remarkable how evanescent has been the influence of these new conditions, for the American people is now and has been for some years among the most conservative of the nations of the earth.

NOTES

I. Bibliography. — Professor Frederick Jackson Turner's *The Frontier in American History* (New York, 1920) is by far the best book on the subject and, besides, itself is an embodiment of the pioneer spirit. Detailed citations are given in the footnotes of this book and also in Turner's *List of References on the History of the West*, published by the Harvard University Press, and in the later sections of Channing, Hart, and Turner's *Guide to the Study and Reading of American History*. When he was at the University of Wisconsin, Professor Turner broke away from the ordinary path of American historical endeavor and with his students organized the study of "the West" on a new basis. In a series of articles in the *Atlantic Monthly* and in other publications,[1] he set forth his ideas. His students, in the volume of "Turner Essays"[2] and in separate contributions, have reinforced their master's theories. J. W. Monette's *History of the Discovery and Settlement of the Valley of the Mississippi* was published in 1846;[3] it contains a mass of information and reflects the thoughts of an early inhabitant of that part of the country. James Hall's four books[4] well set forth the condition of the West at about the same date. Lois K. Mathews's *Expansion of New England* treats the Northern stream of migration and Ulrich B. Phillips in his "Origin and Growth of the Southern Black Belts" in *American Historical Review*, xi, 798, in his chapters in *The South in the Building of the Nation*, and in his *History of Transportation in the Eastern Cotton Belt* has done excellent work for the Southern

---

[1] Among them may be mentioned "The Significance of the Frontier" in American Historical Association's *Report* for 1893 (reprinted with some changes in Wisconsin Historical Society's *Proceedings* for December, 1893; and also as chapter ii of C. J. Bullock's *Selected Readings in Economics*); "The Significance of the Mississippi Valley in American History" (Mississippi Valley Historical Association's *Proceedings* for 1909); "The Middle West" (*International Monthly*, iv); and "The Colonization of the West, 1820–1830" (*American Historical Review*, xi, 303–327) and with some changes as chapter v of his *Rise of the New West*.

[2] *Essays in American History dedicated to Frederick Jackson Turner* (New York, 1910).

[3] Two articles by Monette, one on "The Progress of Navigation and Commerce on the . . . Mississippi River and the Great Lakes," the other on "The Mississippi Floods," are printed in the *Publications* of the Mississippi Historical Society, vol. vii.

[4] *Sketches of History, Life, and Manners, in the West* (2 vols., Philadelphia, 1835); *Statistics of the West* (Cincinnati, 1836); *Notes on the Western States* (Philadelphia, 1838); and *The West: its Commerce and Navigation* (Cincinnati, 1848).

part of the movement. Possibly McMaster's chapters in the fourth, fifth, and sixth volumes of his *History of the People of the United States* taken together form the best bit of writing on the subject that has been done. Among the isolated monographic works the best are Solon J. Buck's *Illinois in 1818* (Springfield, Ill., 1917); George N. Fuller's *Economic and Social Beginnings of Michigan* (Michigan Historical *Publications*, University Series, vol. i); Frederick Merk's *Economic History of Wisconsin during the Civil War Decade* (Wisconsin Historical Society's *Publications*, " Studies," vol. i) and the second part of Reuben Gold Thwaites' *Wisconsin* in the " American Commonwealth " series.[1] Almost innumerable works of travel, exploration, and trade were printed or, at all events, written about the country between the Mississippi and the Rockies before 1846. A mass of these narratives has been gathered by Thwaites in his *Early Western Travels* (32 vols.) and by H. M. Chittenden in *The American Fur Trade of the Far West* (3 vols.).[2] Besides, there are books without number: county histories, family histories, town histories, reminiscences, and diaries.[3] Each state has its historical society and the Mississippi Valley Historical Association has gathered into its *Proceedings* and into the *Review*, that is published under its auspices, material that is necessary for the student of this portion of American history.

II. **Indian Treaties**. — The treaties made with the Indians relating to cessions and compensations were numbered by the hundreds, most of them since 1850. They are calendared and the geographical extent of the cessions noted in the 18th *Report of the Bureau of American Ethnology*, Pt. ii. The treaties themselves were printed in 1826 in a volume entitled *Indian Treaties, and Laws and Regulations relating to Indian Affairs*, again in 1837 in *Treaties between the United States of America and the several Indian Tribes, from 1778 to 1837*, a third

[1] W. V. Pooley's "Settlement of Illinois from 1830 to 1850" (*Bulletin of the University of Wisconsin*, No. 220) and B. H. Hibbard's "History of Agriculture in Dane County" in *ibid.*, Economic Series, i, are of greater value and wider application than their titles indicate.

[2] Solon J. Buck's bibliography of *Travel and Description, 1765–1865*, forming vol. ix of the *Collections* of the Illinois State Historical Library, is excellent within the years treated.

[3] One of the best contemporary descriptions of Western life is Baynard R. Hall's *The New Purchase: or, Seven and a Half Years in the Far West. By Robert Carlton, Esq.* (2 vols., New York, 1843). Substantially the same material was published in one volume at New Albany, Indiana, in 1855. In 1916, an "Indiana Centennial Edition" edited by J. A. Woodburn was published at Princeton, N. J.

time in volume vii of the *Public Statutes at Large of the United States* and in 1904, in *Indian Affairs. Laws and Treaties*, edited by Charles J. Kappler, vol. ii (Senate Document, No. 319, 58th Cong., 2nd Sess.). There are differences in the text of the treaties as printed in these several publications, and some treaties are in one and not in any of the others. The whole subject of Indian relations and of the United States Indian factory system needs careful and extended treatment. Up to the present time, Cyrus Thomas's " Introduction " to the Bureau of Ethnology's volume above cited, and the " Table of Contents " to the volume of 1837 of Indian treaties already mentioned are the best official statements of the Indian relations, but chapters xiii and xv in M. M. Quaife's *Chicago and the Old Northwest* gives one, perhaps, the best insight into the matter that can be had. The official story down to 1826 as told in documents is in the two volumes of *American State Papers, Indian Affairs.*

CHAPTER III

THE URBAN MIGRATION

THE westward movement forms a distinct picture in our annals. No less distinct, but much less known, is the rise of manufacturing and commercial cities and towns, principally in the Northeast, and the development therein of classes and of an industrial social system. The more venturesome of the sons and daughters of the settled population of the seaboard sought the fertile farming lands of the West; others, of a mechanical turn of mind, or ambitious of gain, or addicted to books, found employment in the factories, countinghouses, and shops in the cities and towns that came into being as part of the new industrial movement or that grew out of some demand connected with the distribution of agricultural or mechanical products. The settlement of the West was a dispersion of families over a great space of territory; the building up of the cities of the Northeast was the concentration of men and women in limited areas.[1] As the latter development progressed the

[1] New England towns grew or declined in most astonishing fashion. Oftentimes the territorial extent of a town would diminish, but the population would increase owing to the establishment of some industry. Another town might lose almost all its inhabitants owing to some sudden migration of industry and workers. About all that can be said is that, in general, agriculture declined and manufacturing increased in the older settled parts of the Northeastern States in the years covered in this volume. Samuel Forbes of Canaan, Litchfield County, Connecticut, was an admirable example of a New Englander of diversified modes of bread winning. He was one of the earliest iron masters in the United States, kept a flourishing general store, and loaned money to his neighbors. Dr. Percy W. Bidwell's essay on "Rural Economy in New England in 1800" (*Transactions* of the Connecticut Academy of Arts and Sciences, xx, 241–399) gives an admirable picture of the conditions of life in that sec-

demand for clerks and shop hands in the commercial service, for operatives in the factories, and for domestic help in the household became stronger and stronger.[1] This increase of the farming area and this building up of centres of commerce and manufacture depended upon the development of transportation and this in turn created a demand for labor; but the steamboat and the railroad made it possible to feed, house, and warm large groups of people in contracted spaces. At the same time the constantly broadening market for manufactured goods and the increasing area from which the manufacturer could draw his supply of raw material rapidly led to manufacturing in larger units and thereby separated the owner and manager from the working men and women. The growing ease of movement also tended to make labor mobile: on the one hand, the worker could go from place to place; on the other hand, any particular body of workers became liable to an inundation from outside of those who were as skilled as themselves or could become so after short periods of instruction. The revival of immigration from Europe also provided the manufacturers with operatives who oftentimes were more skilful than the native American and were accustomed to work for smaller compensation. Not infrequently groups of these workers were imported from Great Britain to aid in the establishment of some new manufacturing industry, or to provide a supply of cheaper labor, — and these also brought to their new homes the social prejudices and theories of their old places of habitation.

tion at the beginning of the new era. A more definite picture of the old life can be obtained from a perusal of the opening pages of W. H. Francis's *History of the Hatting Trade in Danbury, Conn.* (1860), which practically is repeated in Bailey's *History of Danbury*, ch. xxxi. Three chapters in F.

Morgan's *Connecticut as a Colony and as a State*, iii, bring the facts together in a convenient form.

[1] *The Columbian Centinel* of Boston for July 29, 1809, has an advertisement of an "Intelligence Office" at number 10 State Street.

According to the above analysis, the rise of manufacturing in the United States depended upon mechanical inventions that were common to Western Europe and the United States and to the development of transportation facilities in America and throughout the world. In those days, government protection through the tariff was regarded as an important element in the successful operation of American mills and of other manufacturing establishments where handworkers were employed in great numbers in proportion to the total product.[1] Imposts had been laid upon foreign manufactures ever since the formation of the government under the Constitution; but they had not amounted to much in the way of protection. The embargo of 1808, the commercial war that followed it,[2] and the armed conflict that succeeded had provided a very efficient stimulus to the establishment of industries. After the close of the war, Congress sought to limit the influx of goods from outside by the passage of the Tariff Act of 1816. This law was followed by others in 1824, 1828, 1832, and 1833. This last act provided that the duties then levied by law should be gradually reduced during a period of ten years. In 1842, however, the condition of the treasury made more revenue necessary and the tariff was again increased to be lessened

---

[1] By 1816, even Jefferson had begun to believe that some encouragement was necessary to build up the manufactures of the United States: — "Experience has taught me," he wrote, "that manufactures are now as necessary to our independence as to our comfort." Jefferson's *Writings* (Memorial ed.), xiv, 392; also quoted in *The Soundness of the Policy of Protecting Domestic Manufactures*, issued by the Philadelphia Society for the Promotion of American Manufactures, in 1817. See also Jefferson's letter to D. Lynch, Jr., of June 26, 1817, in *A Narrative of a Tour . . . by*

James Monroe (Philadelphia, 1818), p. 61.

A good protective argument is J. S. Young's *Address to Congress on the Protection of American Labor* (Portsmouth, N. H., 1849).

The "Tariff Acts" are printed at length in *Senate Report* No. 2130, 51st Cong., 2nd Sess. and in *House Document* No. 562, 55th Cong., 2nd Sess. For a modern statement of the facts see Frank W. Taussig's *Tariff History of the United States* (6th ed., New York and London, 1914).

[2] See the present work, vol. iv, ch. xiv.

in 1846. Some manufacturers and some students maintained in those days and have ever since, that special duties were necessary to equalize the cost of high-priced American operatives and the "pauper labor" of Europe. Others have argued that this end would be more certainly gained by stimulating American invention and efficiency of operation by the exposure of American industry to active competition from outside. Fortunately, it is no part of the historian's duty to determine which of these two views is correct, or how much or how little of truth there was — and is — in either of them, because down to 1850 there was not enough fixity to tariff legislation to do much in the way of building up manufacturing industry. Moreover, there were many other factors that exercised an unquestionable influence on manufacturing. One of these was the abundance or the lack of loanable capital in America and Europe that accompanied eras of prosperity or rising prices, or eras of depression or falling prices, — for industry on a large scale can be carried on only by the use of borrowed funds. With much of the ups and downs in the demand for manufactured goods and abundance or dearth of capital, conditions in America and the precise percentage of "protection" had next to nothing to do. Iron and textiles were the most important manufacturing industries at that time. The development of the iron industry grew out of the new and urgent demands that were created by the new methods of transportation and by the introduction of machinery actuated by water or steam power in the new mills and factories. It is much more difficult to account for the enormous growth of the textile industry because the yardage of manufactured cloth increased out of proportion to the growth of population, — and the amount of cotton cloth exported was only a small fraction of the total production.

It would seem probable in this instance as in many others that the supply of cheap and attractive fabrics created a demand. The same thing is true as to innumerable small articles of utility, convenience, or ornament, — their production on a large scale and at low cost created a demand that had hitherto been lacking or dormant. Bearing in mind all these considerations, it is difficult to see what effect, if any, was produced by an ever-changing protective policy.

The impulse to manufacturing was general throughout the country, — Southerners and Westerners were as anxious to partake of the benefits of the new movement as were the Northeasterners. In the South, factories were established at Richmond, Spartansburg, Columbia, Atlanta, Natchez, and at many other places. The extent and development of manufacturing in that section, apart from bare statements like the above, are impossible to discover and describe owing to the absence of printed records and reports and to the destruction of quantities of manuscript material in the course of the War for Southern Independence. In itself there would seem to be no reason why manufacturing should not have flourished there in slavery days as it undoubtedly has prospered in the years of freedom. It has often been said that slavery and manufacturing could not live together, but there does not seem to be any good reason for this opinion. In the States where slavery existed in a non-intensive form, it was no uncommon thing for the poorer planters, or farmers, owning only a few slaves to work with them in the field. Possibly free whites and black slaves could not work together in a textile factory, but surely the slaves might have done the hard labor while the whites tended the machinery, — the two sets of workers being in separate parts of a building or in different buildings.

In iron manufacturing, negro slaves certainly were used. The payroll of the Tredegar Iron Works at Richmond indicates the employment of several hundred negroes;[1] and the negroes belonging to the Nesbitt Manufacturing Company[2] of South Carolina brought seventy-five thousand dollars at a sale of the company's assets. Probably it was not the existence of slave labor that interfered with the prosperity of Southern manufacturing; it was the fact that there was more than ample employment for all Southern capital in the cultivation of the cotton plant.

Iron had been worked up in Virginia from an early time and in 1800, there were several furnaces and forges in operation in the Old Dominion. Coal was also mined near Richmond. It was not until the establishment of the Tredegar works at that place that iron manufacturing beyond the rougher stages was carried on on a commercial scale. Those works went on prospering through the decades and in the War proved to be of great utility to the Confederacy. The Nesbitt Company was a South Carolina corporation that numbered among its stockholders some of the most prominent men of that State. It owned valuable beds of iron, scattered over some eight thousand acres of land; and also possessed water power, limestone, and forested tracts. The company procured machinery and workmen from New York and arranged to borrow one hundred thousand dollars from the Bank of South Carolina, but it seems never to have had the use of the full amount, owing to the financing of the Louisville, Cincinnati, and Charleston Railroad Company of South Carolina by the State through the bank. Owing to various difficulties, among which were trans-

[1] Miss Kathleen E. Bruce very kindly placed at my disposal the notes of her research on the Iron Manufacture in Virginia.

[2] A Compilation of All the Acts . . . in Relation to the Bank of the State of South Carolina, 297.

portation troubles and the impossibility of securing skilled workmen, the company could not repay the money that it had received and mortgaged its lands, buildings, and one hundred of its most valuable slaves through the bank, and later all its property was put up at auction and bid in for one hundred and twenty-four thousand dollars, three-fifths of the assets being scheduled as negroes. It appears in this case as in the case of other Southern manufacturing and transportation corporations, subscribers to the capital stock oftentimes paid in the form of slaves,[1] and it may be that the fact that three-fifths of the capital stock of the company was invested in labor may have had something to do with its lack of success. After the sale a new corporation was formed which agreed to pay seven per cent on the loan annually for five years, and thereafter to pay one-fifth of the debt yearly until the entire amount was paid; but what happened to the Nesbitt Company after that is unknown.[2] Very little has been written about early Southern cotton mills. Half a dozen or so were in operation in 1825 and at one time there had been a good deal of enthusiasm created over the establishment of cotton mills near the cotton fields. There was abundant labor of the same class of poor whites that formed the mainstay of the later mills in their earlier years. It is said that no mill that was founded in the South before 1826 was financially successful and after 1830,[3] the advocacy of manufacturing in the Cotton States was looked upon locally as more or less treasonable in that it implied some slight belief in tariff and the rightfulness of protection.

[1] From the "Elmore Manuscripts" it appears that shareholders contributed negro slaves to the Nesbitt Company instead of money to the total amount of $34,000, — forgemen being valued at $2500 and blacksmiths at $2000.

[2] *A Compilation of all the Acts . . .*

in Relation to the Bank of the State of South Carolina, 541–544, 643.

[3] See Victor S. Clark's *History of Manufactures in the United States, 1607–1860;* August Kohn's *Cotton Mills of South Carolina* (Columbia, S. C., 1907); Robert Mills's *Statistics of South Carolina*.

In the Northwest, in the country beyond the Pennsylvania boundary line, manufacturing had been begun in the towns on the Ohio River and its affluents. The cost of transportation to and from the Eastern commercial cities was well nigh prohibitive: Cincinnati people paid about double Philadelphia prices for manufactured goods and were obliged to sell their flour and pork for about one-half the amount those commodities would bring at Philadelphia and Baltimore, owing to the high freights by way of the New Orleans route.[1] The saying was that it required four bushels of corn to buy at Cincinnati what one bushel would purchase at Philadelphia. It was under these circumstances that saw mills were erected for fashioning the material for frame houses, grist mills for grinding wheat and corn grown in the neighborhood, and mills for spinning wool and weaving cloth. There were also some factories for working up iron, many breweries, and a few distilleries. In 1810, the prospect of disseminated manufacturing in the Western country was very good; but road, canal, steamboat, and locomotive brought the high-priced labor of the newly settled country into competition with the lower-priced labor of the Northeast with the result that the budding manufactures of the Western country either died or experienced a very slow development.

Manufacturing began in the Northeast at the very earliest time and progressed through the colonial and Revolutionary periods, practically without a break. After the Revolution, when reports of the new English manufacturing processes began to reach the country, efforts were made to reproduce them in America and make the United States independent of the Old World. Hamilton and Duer were at the head of

---

[1] These statements are taken from a valuable article by F. P. Goodwin in the *American Historical Review* (xii, 768). He cites two local papers, *Liberty Hall* and the *Western Spy*, as his authorities.

what was to be a great manufacturing enterprise in New
Jersey; on the Hudson there were active iron factories and
in Pennsylvania and Connecticut there were many others.
Woollen mills and cotton mills were in operation in all of
these States and also in Rhode Island. There were many
obstacles in the way of the successful prosecution of these
designs. There was lack of capital, lack of accurate knowledge of modern machinery, very little skilled labor, and
great difficulty in procuring raw material. It appears in the
case of a Hartford mill that the cost of the cleaning and preparation of the wool for the spinning machines frequently destroyed the profits. Indeed, one manufacturing enterprise
after another was established, only to fall a victim to one
or more of these adverse factors. The founding of the
modern textile business was due to Samuel Slater,[1] an Englishman, and Francis Cabot Lowell, an American. They
practically reinvented the machinery with which Slater had
been familiar in the old country and which Lowell had examined there, while on a visit. The Jeffersonian commercial
policy and Madison's War of 1812 gave American spinners
and weavers their first great opportunity, but it was not
until the 1820's that the American textile industry really
began its successful career. Thereafter, there were many
serious setbacks due in great measure to financial disturbances throughout the world, but taking year in and
year out there was a constant development. The "Census"
of 1840 gives a rough idea of the progress of manufacturing
in the United States; according to this there were nearly
eight hundred thousand people employed in it and they
produced about two hundred and forty million dollars' worth
of commodities in one year.[2] It is noteworthy that New

[1] George S. White's *Memoir of Samuel Slater*, 71–78; and see the present work, vol. iii, 423 and fol.

[2] George Tucker's *Progress of the United States in Population and Wealth* (1st ed., pp. 137, 195).

England and the Middle States had about two-thirds of the total number of persons engaged in manufacturing and produced nearly four-fifths of the total value of commodities made in the United States. Furthermore, it is significant that of the rest of the country, the Northwestern section produced more than the Southern and Southwestern sections put together.

The growth of commercial and manufacturing cities and towns was phenomenal in these years. In the Mississippi Valley, there were New Orleans, St. Louis, Cincinnati, Louisville, and Pittsburg, to which might be added Mobile although that town is not within the limits of the Mississippi watershed. The introduction of steam navigation on the Mississippi and its affluents built up the business of New Orleans, which became a distributing centre for imports, as well as a place of concentration for up-river products designed for exportation. New Orleans also shared with Mobile in forwarding the cotton grown on the rich lands of Mississippi and Louisiana and it handled great quantities of tobacco from Kentucky and of sugar from Louisiana. To New Orleans also came immigrants from Europe bound for Texas, or for points up the Mississippi. St. Louis was the centre of the mid-Mississippi commerce and of the fur trade of the western country except that which found an outlet through Canada. It also was the shipping point for the products of the lead mines of the upper river and was the centre of the steamboat traffic engaged in collecting the grain and hog products from the shipping ports of the Mississippi and its navigable affluents. Cincinnati and Louisville performed similar functions for the Ohio. The importance of these four centres of river steamboat traffic in the thirty years before 1850 can hardly be overstated, for in those years practically all the commerce of the Mississippi Valley gained access to the outer world by way of New Orleans and the Gulf of Mexico. Mobile was almost entirely dependent upon cotton for its commercial life and its period of great prosperity did not begin until the opening of the Indian lands in Alabama and Mississippi provided fields of great richness for the cotton planter.

Pittsburg has a most astounding history.[1] Politically, it belongs to Pennsylvania and the East, but geographically it is in the Mississippi Valley, standing at the edge of the mountains that separate the Atlantic seaboard from the interior basin. The National Road reached the Ohio River at Wheeling in western Virginia, but the steamboat traffic of the river still made its headquarters at Pittsburg. The Portage Railway connected it with Philadelphia and other routes gave it access to the Genesee Valley and the Erie Canal. It was inevitable that manufacturing should begin at an early date in such a centre of human effort, and grist mills, wood-working establishments, and distilleries were founded there or in the vicinity at an early time. Pittsburg stands in a region rich almost beyond comparison in coal and iron. In 1803 Zadok Cramer stated that upwards of $350,000 worth of manufactured articles were made at Pittsburg in one year. Of this amount $56,000 represented manufactures of iron ranging from axes to cowbells; another $13,000 was given as the value of manufactured glass, some of which was said to be equal to any cut in the states of Europe. Then there were nine hundred barrels of beer and porter, five thousand pairs of shoes, "segars, snuff, and pig tail tobacco" to the amount of $3000, five thousand yards of striped cotton and ninety dozen chip

---

[1] See J. N. Boucher's *A Century and a Half of Pittsburg*, i, chs. xxi and fol., and the books cited therein, especially Fortescue Cuming's *Sketches of a Tour*, ch. xxxvii. I. Harris's *Pittsburgh Business Directory, for the Year 1837* gives a complete picture of the town at that time.

hats.[1] Even in 1807 the Pittsburg atmosphere was described as filled with soot. Anne Royall, that notorious, early, strong-minded female, visited Pittsburg in 1828 and gave a most interesting account of the town and its people.[2] She was greatly impressed with "the polite, chaste and gentlemanly deportment of her [Pittsburg] workmen and mechanics . . . they, as a body, are the only gentlemen in the city." She devotes thirty-eight pages to describing Pittsburg factories, including those in what were then the suburbs of Birmingham and Manchester. She spent two weeks wandering around them. It is quite evident that the growth since 1803 had been very great, although it is impossible to state any comparative figures from her description. It appears, however, that the value of the castings made by the Pittsburg Foundry in 1828 was approximately as much as the value of all similar products turned out in the city in 1803. In 1850 Samuel Fahnestock estimated the total business of Pittsburg, — manufacturing and forwarding — to "not fall short of $50,000,000 annually."[3] There were then thirteen rolling mills, thirty large foundries, five cotton factories, eight glass factories besides countless other establishments of one sort or another, — and yet Pittsburg was only at the threshold of her career.

Of cities of the Atlantic Coast — and of the country as

[1] G. H. Thurston's *Pittsburgh As It Is* [1857], p. 81, quoting Cramer's *Almanack* for 1804. An enumeration of the manufactures in 1810 is in Cramer's *Navigator* (9th ed.), p. 53 and fol. A table of manufactures in 1818 is in Fearon's *Sketches*, 205. Charles W. Dahlinger's *Pittsburgh . . . Its Early Social Life* (New York, 1916) is a readable account of the early development of the town with matter quoted from newspapers.

[2] *Mrs. Royall's Pennsylvania, or Travels Continued in the United States,* i, 49–132. Other works by Mrs.

Royall are: *The Black Book*; *Southern Tour, or Second Series of the Black Book* giving descriptions of Washington society in the Jacksonian time; *Letters from Alabama;* and *Sketches of History, Life, and Manners, in the United States.* S. H. Porter's *Life and Times of Anne Royall* gives a not uninteresting sketch of this woman, who was greatly and justly feared by her contemporaries.

[3] N. B. Craig's *History of Pittsburgh*, 311. See also J. N. Boucher's *Century and a Half of Pittsburg and her People,* i, ch. xxv.

a whole — New York stood foremost in 1850. The Revolution left it in distinctly a second place, being inferior to Philadelphia in population and in business. At once its period of phenomenal growth began.[1] It grew faster than Boston or Philadelphia and soon outstripped them in population and commerce and, later, it exceeded Philadelphia in manufacturing. Then came the Erie Canal, tremendously accentuating New York's commercial business. By 1830 it had acquired the incontestable primacy in population and wealth, and had grown from a small town on the southern end of Manhattan Island to occupy about one-fifth of its present area. As the century advanced New York absorbed more and more of the distributing business of the Northeast. It became an American counterpart of Liverpool as a collecting and forwarding commercial centre. It is inevitable that when a town gains a certain commercial position, it absorbs to itself business that had formerly belonged to its rivals, at first those near by and then slowly those farther and farther off. Commerce is attracted to such a port by the certainties of securing conveyance to the destination; vessels, railroads, and steamboats likewise seek it because of the certainty of freight money both ways. Finally, such a centre of commerce, manufacturing, and

[1] The *Census* of 1850 (p. lii) shows the growth of leading cities : —

Cities	1790	1800	1810	1820	1830	1840	1850
Boston . .	18,038	24,937	33,250	43,298	61,392	93,383	136,881
New York .	33,131	60,489	96,373	123,706	202,589	312,710	515,547
Philadelphia	42,520	69,403	91,874	112,772	161,410	220,423	340,045
Baltimore .	13,503	26,114	35,583	62,738	80,625	102,313	169,054
Charleston .	16,359	20,473	24,711	24,780	30,289	29,261	42,985
Mobile . .				1,500	3,194	12,672	20,515
New Orleans			17,242	27,176	46,310	102,193	116,375

For other estimates, see Tucker's *Progress*, 128, and *Census* of 1880, vol. ii, "Manufactures," p. xxii, and below, p. 411 *n.*

distribution becomes naturally a centre of finance, and New York from about 1840 distinctly assumes the position in America which before that time had been held by Philadelphia. The accumulated wealth of New York had become very great compared with Philadelphia and Boston and the other cities on the seaboard. But when one speaks of it as the financial centre of the country, one means that the business of collecting funds — money and credit — and exchanging them for commodities and labor all over the United States centred at that point. Philadelphia and Baltimore grew steadily. Each of them made great efforts to retain the business that had once been theirs. In a measure they succeeded in extending their influence into that part of the western country that was not distinctly tributary to the Great Lakes, the Erie Canal, and New York City; but it was not until after 1850, when railroad connection was made between those seaports and the Middle West, that they were able to divert much of the western trade from New York and New Orleans to their own wharves and warehouses. Boston found itself seriously menaced by the commercial augmentation of New York and the utmost that it could do only deferred the loss of ocean-borne commerce. The New Englanders, thereupon, turned their abundant capital and energy into other directions. They built up great manufacturing enterprises and handled most of the commerce dependent on them; but as the years went by the tendency grew more and more to concentrate the commission and forwarding business of New England at New York.

The story of the old colonial towns of the South is a melancholy one. Williamsburg almost disappeared, but Richmond, owing to its nearness to coal and iron, not only kept its place, but slowly developed although the project of making it accessible to sea-going vessels was defeated. With the growing years, Charleston and Savannah slipped backwards; Charleston absolutely, and Savannah relatively to the other shipping ports. The new cotton country except a part of western Georgia was tributary to the Gulf; trans-Atlantic vessels no longer sought the Southeastern harbors because they could be assured of freight both ways by going to New York. Charleston became hardly more than a port of call for coastwise commerce, and its population actually declined. Had Robert Y. Hayne's project of a great railroad line connecting Charleston with the mid-Ohio Valley not been defeated,[1] owing partly at least to the efforts of Calhoun, it is quite possible that a large part of the business of the Middle West might have gone to Charleston, instead of to Baltimore and Philadelphia, — and thereby might have altered the course of American history.

In the ways described in the preceding paragraphs there grew up great centres of human activity in different parts of the country. In some places, owing to advantageous positions on lines of commerce, to nearness to iron and coal, or to proximity to abundant water power, commercial cities and manufacturing villages and towns came into existence. On the Great Lakes there were Detroit, Cleveland, Buffalo, and Chicago; in Pennsylvania, Lancaster and Wilkesbarre; in New Jersey, Paterson and Newark; Rochester and Geneva in New York; Meriden and Willimantic in Connecticut; Providence and Pawtucket in Rhode Island; Lynn, Lowell, and Fall River in Massachusetts; and innumerable others scattered throughout the Middle States and New

[1] See T. D. Jervey's *Robert Y. Hayne and His Times* and his *The Railroad the Conqueror* (Columbia, S. C., 1913) and the authorities therein cited; and see also *Proceedings of the Fourth Convention . . . Held in Charleston, S. C., April 15, 1839, for the Promotion of the Direct Trade*, especially p. 24.

England. Some of them were old towns revived to new uses; others, perhaps most of them, owed their existence to new manufacturing enterprises. In great commercial centres like New York and Philadelphia there were always large numbers of workers who were not connected directly with the commercial business of the place. And the larger the city the greater was the supply of non-commercial labor. It was natural, therefore, that manufacturing enterprises should develop there, especially those forms of manufacture that required comparatively large amounts of hand work, as was the case with the making of shoes and clothes before the days of the development of mechanical sewing. On the other hand, enterprises that utilized water-power necessarily grew up from the beginning near the rapids or falls of some river.

Of all the towns that have been mentioned in the preceding paragraphs, none have more interesting beginnings than the cotton mill cities of Lowell and Fall River. The former owes its origin to the half dozen men who had made a successful beginning of cotton spinning and weaving at Waltham in Massachusetts.[1] Francis Cabot Lowell was the master spirit of this enterprise. Being in England in 1811 and possessing a mathematical and mechanical turn of mind, he studied with great care all the cotton machinery he could see and gathered information as to that which he could not see. Returning home in 1813, he duplicated from his memory and notes of conversations the power loom which he had not seen in England or in Scotland, and he and his as-

[1] Nathan Appleton's *Introduction of the Power Loom and Origin of Lowell* is the basis of all accounts of the establishment of the city of Lowell. Of the later books James B. Francis's *Lowell Hydraulic Experiments* (Boston, 1855, 2nd ed., New York, 1868) contains a great deal of interesting information and Samuel Batchelder's *Introduction and Early Progress of the Cotton Manufacture in the United States* has some definite information by a contemporary.

sociates worked out readjustments and improvements in the
other machines used in the making of cotton cloth and performed all the processes in one establishment.   At first there
was a prejudice against American machine-woven cotton
cloth and it was difficult to dispose of the early products of
the Waltham mill.   Within half a dozen years the enterprise
outgrew the space and water-power at Waltham.   It was
suggested that the associates should buy the Pawtucket Canal
Company, which had constructed a canal around Pawtucket
Falls of the Merrimac River, not far above the entrance of
the Concord.   This enterprise had never paid and the Waltham people were able, therefore, to buy up the stock at a
low figure.   They also secured practically all the land on
the river front below the falls for what might well be termed
a nominal sum.   They also purchased the "rights necessary
to control" the outlet of Lake Winnepesaukee, a large lake
in central New Hampshire, which furnished most of the
water to the Merrimac River.   They formed the Merrimac
Manufacturing Company, deepened and widened the canal,
erected the necessary buildings and machinery and, in an
astonishingly small space of time, the first Merrimac mill
was turning out cotton cloth.   The associates then established a separate corporation for the management of the
water-power and disposal of factory sites in their new town,
which they named Lowell in honor of the founder of the
Waltham enterprise, who was no longer living.   They
disposed of their surplus water-power to others at extremely
reasonable rates.   The first steps in acquiring the stock of
the old Pawtucket Company were taken in 1821.   By 1839,
there were twelve distinct manufacturing corporations at
Lowell with a combined capital of twelve million dollars,
and the town which had only a few hundred inhabitants in
1820 had over twenty thousand in 1840, and over thirty-

three thousand in 1850.[1] One thing that had greatly contributed to the growth of manufacturing at Lowell was the
introduction of cloth printing by machinery and soon "Merrimac prints" had a country-wide reputation. The first
cotton cloth made at Waltham was thirty-seven inches wide
and was sold for thirty cents a yard; in 1843 the price
had gone down to six and a half cents a yard. In the beginning the old style breast water-wheel was employed;
later the French turbine, greatly improved, was introduced,
thereby raising the percentage of power utilized from sixty
or seventy-five per cent with the old wheels to eighty-eight
per cent with the improved turbine. The establishment
of manufacturing at Lowell is the best example of the diversion of commercial capital and experience from navigation
and trade to an entirely new venture. Fall River had a
much more normal origin and development, although the
circumstances of its existence were in themselves quite out
of the ordinary run.

For a hundred years, more or less, Massachusetts and
Rhode Island had contended for lands on the northeastern
side of Narragansett Bay. When an agreement was finally
reached, most of these lands were given to Rhode Island,
but a bit of territory known as Freetown and bounded by
the Fall River was assigned to Massachusetts. This river,
as it is called, is really a natural canal two miles long with a
granite bottom. It drained a succession of small lakes or
ponds and had a total fall of more than one hundred and
thirty-two feet in less than half a mile. So narrow was the
channel that it was possible to construct mills across the
stream, the wheels being placed in the current of the river.
The first cotton mill was erected to utilize this water-power

[1] See *Census* of 1850, p. lii. For   David Stevenson's *Sketch of the Civil*
statistics of Lowell mills in 1837, see   *Engineering of North America*, 319.

in 1813 ; but it was not until 1821 that the rapid development of manufacturing began with the establishment of the Iron Works Company which played a part in Fall River something like that of the Canal Company at Lowell. In 1820, there were about five hundred people living at Fall River and in 1840 nearly seven thousand.[1]

Before 1820 the growth of cities and towns that has just been described was retarded by the difficulty of housing, feeding, and caring for large numbers of human beings in restricted areas. By that year new transportation systems had become sufficiently developed to bring food and fuel to designated places with some degree of certainty and despatch. In those days, people had no idea of hygiene and sanitation and no laws curbed the money-making desires of landlords. Moreover, the construction of dwelling houses was primarily for the single family. Occasionally there was much overcrowding with resultant loss of vitality and earning power. Bacilli and bacteria were unknown and the mode of treatment of acute disorders was such that they frequently ran into chronic stages. Under existing conditions it was dangerous to gather people within a limited space, but it was impossible to disseminate them over a large tract of ground as there was no system of public urban transportation that would enable the working man, the clerk, or the professional man to get from his dwelling to his place of employment, if it were more than three to six miles away. Moreover, those were the days of riotousness and boisterous conduct ; there was a spirit of intolerance of individual opinions ; and there was a continuous drinking of distilled liquor, morning, afternoon, and evening.

By the close of the first quarter of the century, improved roads, canals, and steamboats had all contributed to bring

[1] Orin Fowler's *History of Fall River* (ed. 1841), 28, 29.

food and household supplies from distances of twenty or
thirty miles to centres of population. Sometime before 1828
Asa Hall established an omnibus line running from Wall
Street in New York City to the neighborhood of the State
Prison in Greenwich Village. In 1828, the service was
improved by the addition of more stages, the fare at that
time being twelve and a half cents. By 1850, there were
four distinct lines of omnibuses and the fare had been cut
in half. Most of the early omnibuses had been drawn by
two horses, but on some of the busier routes larger vehicles
with four horses and a boy collector of fares in addition to
the driver were employed. It took something over one
hour to run three miles through the crowded parts of the
city.[1] The first omnibus appeared in Philadelphia [2] in
1831 but other towns waited some years before the establishment of public urban stage-coach lines.

Philadelphia was the first city to supply any large proportion of its inhabitants with water from outside the city
limits. As early as 1791 or 1792, the introduction of Schuylkill River water into the city for household purposes was
advocated, but it was not until 1799 that the matter was
taken up in earnest. Steam pumping engines were then
installed and water was raised from the river to a reservoir
and thence distributed through log pipes to a limited
portion of the city. In 1819, the project was taken up
again and by 1822 the Fairmount Water Works were
opened.[3] In this system the water was taken from the
Schuylkill about a mile and a half from what was then the

---

[1] These details are drawn from
Charles H. Haswell's *Reminiscences
of New York*, 229, 231, 538.

[2] Scharf and Westcott's *History
of Philadelphia*, iii, 2199. See also
George L. Vose's "Notes on Early
Transportation in Massachusetts" in
the *Journal* of the Association of En-

gineering Societies for December, 1884,
and George G. Crocker's *From the
Stage Coach to . . . the Street Car.*

[3] See *Annual Report of the Watering
Committee . . . 1836 . . . of Philadelphia: to which are prefixed the Report
for . . . 1822 and . . . 1823*, pp. 1, 5,
10, etc.

occupied part of the city. It was raised by the surplus water-power of the river and was distributed through nearly forty thousand feet of iron pipes, most of which had been made in America. In New York the house pump and cistern were the main reliance until the nineteenth century was advanced. The Manhattan Company, that much berated corporation which was mainly devoted to banking, raised a large amount of water by a pumping engine from a well within the city limits and distributed it through log pipes buried in the streets. This water supply was plainly inadequate and various projects were put forward to supply the rapidly growing city.[1] As early as 1798, it was suggested that water might be obtained from the Bronx River, but nothing was done. In 1833, it was proposed that Croton River water[2] should be brought into the city through an aqueduct. The actual work of construction was begun in 1837 and in 1842 the works were so far completed that water could be turned into the city mains for the use of the inhabitants, which was done with nearly as much ceremony as when the waters of Lake Erie had been united with those of the Atlantic Ocean. By that time all the larger cities were supplied with water by artificial means.[3]

Until after the close of the War of 1812, lard and whale oil lamps and candles were the only means of lighting houses and streets after sundown. Hydrogen gas or some other chemically produced illuminant had been used in experiments and in pyro-technics. In April, 1816, Charles Willson

[1] See Charles H. Haswell's *Reminiscences of New York by an Octogenarian* using index under "water," "Manhattan Company," and "Croton."

[2] Charles King's *Memoir of the . . . Croton Aqueduct*, 90, 125, 140, 144, 225. The important reports and official documents were brought together by the Common Council of the City of New York in 1847.

[3] An interesting account of American water works in 1837 is in David Stevenson's *Sketch of the Civil Engineering of North America*, ch. x. The "Introduction" to the *Manual of American Water-Works* contains details of water systems in all parts of the country.

Peale advertised that his museum,[1] a renowned institution of Philadelphia, would be lighted by "lamps burning without wick or oil" and using "carbonated hydrogen gas"; and the Chestnut Street theatre was illuminated in a similar manner in the following November. New York seems to have been the first city to undertake the public lighting of the streets by gas. By 1830 the use of some form of illuminating gas was common in the larger cities, not without serious disasters in its train.

In the preceding pages the enormous social changes wrought by the westward movement and by the migration into urban areas have been suggested rather than described. In the new western homes, conditions were not essentially unlike those of the parental estate except that after toilsome beginnings, it was possible to produce much more generously on the rich soils of Transappalachia than could be done on the gravelly farms and worn-out plantations of the Original Thirteen States. The case was very different with those who sought the mill town or the commercial city. There the farmer boys and girls found themselves surrounded by entirely new conditions of life and thought. This produced an awakening that was as remarkable as that engendered by the long journey to the farms of Ohio, Indiana, and the other Western and Southwestern States. It is interesting to consider for the moment the relation of literary and scientific activity to density of population. This has been worked out by several investigators with somewhat different results as to details, but in general

[1] Scharf and Westcott's *History of Philadelphia*, i, 514, 583, especially 586, 643–646; William Dunlap's *History . . . of the Arts of Design* (ed. 1918), ii, 189; *Lecture delivered at the Centenary Celebration of the First Commercial Gas Company to sell Gas as an Illuminant* (Easton, Pa., 1912), pp. 12–14; and Victor S. Clark's *History of Manufactures in the United States*, 494 and footnotes. Thomas Cooper published at Philadelphia in 1816, *Some Information concerning Gas Lights*.

the agreement is remarkable.[1] From one of these estimates it appears that of 978 Americans born before 1851 who achieved distinction in letters, no fewer than 803 were born in the Middle States and New England. Also, it may be remarked how persistently men of literary and scientific attainments reside in the largest cities, and the same thing is observable of business men and of the foremost lights of the learned professions. Many of these are reared on the farm or in the small town, but they seek the great centres of industry and commerce because there they find the greatest chance for the exercise of their talents. All this concentration of industry, commerce, and business within the limits of a comparatively small number of cities and towns gave rise to new problems that the people living in the thirty-five years from 1815 to 1850 strove most vigorously and conscientiously to solve.

[1] Edwin L. Clarke's "American Men of Letters; their Nature and Nurture," 57, in Columbia University's *Studies in History*, vol. lxxii; George R. Davies' "Statistical Study in the Influence of Environment" in *Quarterly Journal of the University of North Dakota*, iv, 232; James McKeen Cattell's "Statistical Study of American Men of Science" originally printed in *Science*, New Series, xxiv, and reprinted as Appendix to the 2nd ed. of his *American Men of Science, a Biographical Dictionary* (New York, 1910), pp. 537-596. Clarke summarizes his work in chapter iv by saying that while social environment appeared to be one of the most potent influences; geographic environment was very important, and a disproportionate number of Literati had been born in large cities. The majority had been college trained. Economic security and early religious surroundings also exercised an influence. He concludes that Galton's proposition that nature is much more powerful than nurture may well be questioned, and that his third proposition that differences in the achievement of nations due to the difference of natural ability does not hold good.

NOTE

Industrial Conditions. — Professor F. W. Taussig in the first two chapters of his *Tariff History of the United States* has given a succinct view of industry in the first thirty years of the century.[1] The student who wishes to go further will find a mass of instructive and useful information in the " Reports of Committees " to the General Convention of the Friends of Domestic Industry that assembled at New York in October, 1831. Especially interesting are the reports on the manufactures of cotton, iron, and steel. Of course the members of the convention were distinctly influenced by their protective views, but the figures that they brought together are not easily duplicated elsewhere. Earlier statistics are to be found in Gallatin's *Report . . . on the Subject of American Manufactures* of April 17, 1810, and in Tench Coxe's *Statement of the Arts and Manufactures of the United States . . . for the year 1810* which was printed at Philadelphia in 1814. This is provided with elaborate tables of statistics which were gathered from official sources. The later period is illustrated in George Tucker's *Progress of the United States . . . to 1840;* the edition of 1855 carries the story down to 1850. Much larger, but not more useful for the first half of the century, is *Eighty Years' Progress of the United States* [2] which was published at New York in 1861, and reprinted in 1864. The first edition of this work contains a useful set of illustrations showing the progress of industry and transportation at the time of publication. Professor Rolla M. Tryon's *Household Manufactures in the United States, 1640–1860* contains interesting material gathered from all kinds of sources and illustrated with helpful tables laboriously compiled. Chapters vi and vii describe the process of household manufacturing and the transition to the factory system.

[1] All accounts of this earlier time are based largely on J. L. Bishop's *History of American Manufactures from 1608 to 1860,* vol. ii. Recently, Victor S. Clark has gone over much of the same ground from a different standpoint and using more material in his *History of Manufactures in the United States.* The *Reports of the Secretary of the Treasury* from 1790 to 1849 were printed at Washington in seven volumes in the years 1828–1851,

and contain a mass of information on the material side of our development that has as yet been only partially worked up. Much of this material for the earlier years is also given in *American State Papers* in the volumes on "Finance."

[2] Midway in point of time is R. S. Fisher's *Progress of the United States,* published by Colton at New York in 1854.

CHAPTER IV

THE FIRST LABOR MOVEMENT

In colonial days outside of the distinctly Slave States there were no classes in the producing part of the community. In the Middle States and in New England, ministers, lawyers, doctors, and a few men of means had lived somewhat apart from the rest of the people; but otherwise there had been a marked homogeneity in the population. Markets were very restricted, but there was a good deal of household manufacturing, commodities being made in limited quantities by the family, the hired help, and indentured servants. These goods were mainly sold in the neighborhood except such as were carried by sea to other colonies or to other parts of the world. In each town there were a few mechanics who worked for wages and in the seaports there were ship carpenters who built and repaired vessels. In some places, shoes, instead of being made on the farm as a home industry, were manufactured in shops, the employer and his operatives working side by side. This condition of affairs was true also as to a few other trades, but everywhere the master worked with his men and apprentices, and those of his employees who were not married boarded with him. Roughly speaking there was no wage system, labor being performed by apprentices and indentured servants and hired help who were compensated on a yearly basis. With the quickening of business life that followed the establishment of the government under the Constitution, with the widening of markets that was brought about by the breaking down of local financial systems and by the development of transportation, these conditions changed. For one thing, indentured service disappears as an institution in the first quarter of the century [1] except as to apprentices and the number of these constantly and rapidly diminished. There are countless instances of apprentices who did not serve out their time ; they ran away from their masters and worked for other employers, — half-journeymen, they were sometimes called. If the apprentices, after a few years of service, were desirous of leaving their masters, the masters seemed to be equally desirous of getting rid of their apprentices. The laws of most States held the master responsible for the pecuniary obligations of an apprentice, unless he gave notice that an apprentice was no longer in his employ. This the masters frequently did by advertising in the newspapers. There was, for example, James Van Valkinburgh, Jr., of Canaan, New York. He offered "one old shoe" and no charges paid for the return of "Annonias Gillet," an apprentice boy.[2] A Baltimore paper of the same year, 1808, announced a reward of five cents and ten lashes to any one bringing home a runaway apprentice girl named Catharine Fowler.[3] Probably the servants and apprentices

[1] Apparently the latest advertisement of the sale of indentured servants was in 1817 in a Philadelphia paper and two months later, these men or some of them were still unsold. In the same year a reward of thirty dollars was offered for the return of a redemptioner. This is the latest date of an advertisement offering a real reward for the return of an indentured servant. Albert Matthews noted an instance of the purchase of indentured servants "as late as 1817," presumably in Philadelphia, in his paper on "Hired Man and Help" in Colonial Society's *Publications*, v, 232, note. For "indentured" service in the earlier times,

see the present work, vol. ii, 367–376.

[2] The *Republican Crisis* (Albany), September 16, 1808.

[3] *American* (Baltimore), August 24, 1808. Other instances are as follows : *The Western Star* of June 26, 1797, a Massachusetts paper, offered "Two Pence Reward!" for the return of an indentured apprentice of eighteen ; the *Aurora* of January 17, 1800, offered "Six Cents Reward" for the return of an apprentice, and the same paper for May 16, 1800, offered two cents reward for the return of a "young bound white girl," — most of the advertisements adding "no charges paid." Contrast these with the reward of $100

yearned to escape from their bonds and thought they could make more as free workers, although with the low wages then prevailing, one would have supposed they would have been better off in their masters' families; and the anxiety of the masters to escape the performance of all the obligations of care in sickness and in health of the apprentice system and, instead, to pay wages points in the same direction. By 1815, in all the States north of Maryland, slavery as an effective producing institution had disappeared. There were slaves in New York and Pennsylvania, but the system of gradual emancipation was rapidly putting an end to the institution in all the old Northern States where it still had a legal existence. By 1820, it may be said that in the Middle States and in New England the wage system was established.

Wages in those days were low when measured in dollars and cents, the hours of labor were long, and the conditions under which the operatives worked were unsanitary and arduous. In 1800, eighty cents had been the ordinary daily wage for partly skilled labor in rural New England and a few cents less had been paid in the Middle States. This amount had increased to an even dollar or thereabouts in a decade and by 1830 to one dollar and a half. The ordinary laborer received a few cents less and in 1820 his wage may be set down at an even dollar, with possibly twenty-five cents more on government work.[1] In 1815, there was printed in "Niles's Register," which was published at Baltimore, a rather elaborate series of calculations intended to show that the laborer was much better off in America

offered for the return of a negro boy (*The Mirror*, July 14, 1808, a Kentucky paper) and $20 for the return of a dark brown horse and roan mare (*Western Star*, June 26, 1797).

[1] See the present work, iv, 10–14.

These later figures are taken from various sources as the "Wendell Manuscripts" which were kindly placed at my disposal by Professor Barrett Wendell.

than he was in England. In this article the daily wage of the
laborer in America is given at eighty cents with the qualification that most city laborers received from one dollar
and a quarter to one dollar and a half. The price of wheat
was stated at one dollar and a half for a bushel of sixty
pounds and beef was priced at six cents a pound. From
this and other calculations it appears that from eight to
twelve cents a day would purchase food for one adult and
one day's labor would provide food for three days for a
family of father, mother, and four children.[1] Running
through the decades, it would not be uninteresting to observe
how the "real reward" of bone and muscle in terms of daily
food has remained singularly constant, notwithstanding the
fluctuations in both wages and commodity prices. The
rise in real reward has accompanied the change from mere
bone and fibre expenditure to the training of muscle and to the
use of the mind. In other words the increase in the "real
reward" of the operative classes has come about by the
constant advance in skill and in the utilization of mind and
nerve for the operation of machinery, and not from any
marked rise in the real reward of any one class in the laboring community. As to the skilled workman in the olden time:
in 1806 it was testified in court that a Philadelphia cordwainer could earn six or seven dollars a week on piece work
and a very good and rapid worker as high as ten or even
twelve dollars.[2]

As to hours and condition of employment, these were
taken directly from the custom of the farm, where men and
women, and children too, worked from sun to sun — from
sunrise to sunset. Those engaged on piece work as shoemakers and tailors oftentimes labored for twelve, thirteen,

---

[1] Niles's *Weekly Register*, ix, 230.   [2] John R. Commons's *American Industrial Society*, iii, 83, 106.

or fourteen hours a day, much of it by the light of a candle, or a whale oil, or lard oil, lamp. When mills and factories were established and the working man went from his own home or bench to a place in his employer's shop, or a girl came from the parental farm to a factory in a mill town, the accustomed hours of labor were naturally kept up. As to the conditions of employment, no one in those days knew anything to speak of about hygiene, or the effects of poor ventilation on the human body and mind. In point of fact a closed and hot room was regarded as rather in the nature of a luxury, in the winter time, at any rate. In those days, also, very little attention was given to the purity of drinking water, and the minor human ailments, that are now recognized as a breeding ground for germs of serious disorders, were not cared for at all. The light that was provided in factory and shop was scanty and harmful to the working people. Furthermore many of those employed in mills were children, — as they worked on the farm, why should they not labor in the factory? In 1801, Josiah Quincy, on the beginning of a trip through southeastern New England, visited Pawtucket and gained admittance to the "cotton works." All the processes of cleaning, carding, spinning, and winding the cotton fibre were performed by machinery actuated by water wheels and "assisted only by children from four to Ten years old, and one superintendent." There were more than one hundred children employed in the factory and they were paid from twelve to twenty-five cents a day. Quincy pitied those "little creatures, plying in a contracted room, among flyers and coggs, at an age when nature requires for them air, space, and sports. There was a dull dejection in the countenances of all of them," [1] —

[1] Massachusetts Historical Society's *Proceedings*, Second Series, iv, 124. See also Robert Collyer's *Some* *Memories*, 15. In 1853, the *Report of the Commissioner*, appointed to ascertain the truth as to child labor

their condition must have resembled that of Robert Collyer as he describes his boyhood in England.

As population became dense in the commercial cities and towns and in the factory villages, working people came together in larger and larger groups. Associating in shop and boarding house they began to compare notes as to their wages and as to the wages paid in other shops and other trades and in other towns, for, as transportation facilities increased, there was more and more migration of the working people from one town to another in the same State or in separate States. Moreover, as factories were established it became necessary to import workmen from abroad, especially from England and Scotland, to operate machinery that was sometimes imported or, at all events, was strange to the people of the neighborhood in which the new factory was established, and these people brought ideas as to trade societies that had been worked out in their old homes. Three trades, — the cordwainers or shoemakers, the tailors, and the printers — were the first to become conscious of class distinctions for in them first of all the employer left his bench by the side of his workman and sat apart in an office busy with the affairs of money, of buying materials, of selling his goods, of getting payments, of enlarging his market. As the number of working men increased one of them was appointed to overlook the rest and became a foreman or a forewoman. A group system of employment in these trades first appeared in Philadelphia and New York and it is in those cities that one finds what appears to be the beginning of the movement of organized labor to se-

in Rhode Island, provided some facts for contemplation : — in some mills work began in the winter at 5.30 A.M., making more than thirteen hours' labor in the shortest days, and the only relaxation that great numbers of mill children enjoyed was due to the occasional stopping of the mills on account of low water or for repairs to the machinery.

cure more wages, shorter hours, and better conditions of working.

There may have been a few strikes of shoemakers in colonial days, but the evidence for them is very vague, and it is possible that the printers in one office in Philadelphia "turned out" in the 1780's, but the evidence for this is even more indistinct.[1] The Philadelphia cordwainers formed a society in 1794 and "turned out" in 1798 and again in 1799, but the strike of 1805 is the first of which we have ample evidence and this is owing to the fact that in 1806 the leaders in the movement were indicted for criminal conspiracy and the trial in the Mayor's Court, at which were present the mayor, three aldermen, and the recorder, was fully reported.[2] It appears that a working man, a journeyman cordwainer, Job Harrison by name, who worked for Mr. Bedford, had been making shoes or dress shoes at nine shillings a pair, side lining them with silk. In 1805, the cordwainers struck to secure larger wages for the making of boots. Harrison refused to turn out with the rest, partly because he had a sick wife and several children to support and needed all the wages he could get and partly because he could not understand why he, who was satisfied with the price he was getting for the making of shoes, should strike to enable the boot makers to get more for their work. He was still a member of the Cordwainers' Society, but he turned "scab" and continued to work. A committee of the working men

[1] In 1791, the Philadelphia carpenters struck for better conditions of labor; but the accounts of this strike are dim and little is known of the organization.

[2] Thomas Lloyd's *The Trial of the Boot & Shoemakers of Philadelphia*, pp. 3, 5, 6, 13, 91, 141, 142, 147, 149. This pamphlet, which was published at Philadelphia in 1806, is reprinted in *A Documentary History of American Industrial Society*, edited by John R. Commons and others, vol. iii, 59–250. This latter publication contains much matter of great value, — without the material thus made accessible, the present chapter could not have been written. Earlier, Professor Commons used the evidence given in this trial as the basis around which to build an article on "American Shoemakers" in the *Quarterly Journal of Economics*, xxiv, 39–81.

called on Mr. Bedford and demanded the discharge of
Harrison. Upon Bedford's refusal, the other journeymen,
fifteen to twenty in number, walking out, "scabbed"
Bedford's shop, leaving only Harrison and three or four
other men at work. The strikers refused to board at the
same house with any of Bedford's employees, and appointed
a "tramping committee" to watch his shop. In an interrup-
tion in the court proceedings a person in the room was
heard to say that "a scab is a shelter for lice," whereupon
he was fined ten dollars "for this contempt of court in
interrupting a witness." The strike, or turn out, or stand
out was against all the employers in town who had not
acceded to the higher wage list for boot making. The
evidence is minute in many particulars, showing that every
journeyman who came to Philadelphia was expected to join
the society. If he did not the shop in which he might find
work was scabbed until he was discharged or until he joined
the society, after paying a fine. Money was given by the
society to needy members out of work. Scabs were called
upon by two or three of the strikers and were evidently
frightened, although in 1805, it does not appear that actual
violence was used. Bedford, the employer, testified that
the strikers would come by his house and abuse him and that
they broke his windows by throwing through them potatoes
which had pieces of broken shoemakers' tacks in them,
but violence was not the policy of the society. He said that
he had lost four thousand dollars in business by the strike.
Another employer stated that the strike had cost him two
thousand dollars in the export business alone.

The lawyers made their addresses on both sides and then
Moses Levy, the recorder or judge, made his charge to
the jury. He stated the law which he said was "the will
of the whole community . . . and the most imperious duty

demands our submission to it." It was of no importance
whether the journeymen or the masters were the prose-
cutors, whether the defendants were poor, or rich, or their
numbers small or great, or whether their motives were to
resist the supposed oppression of their masters, or to insist
upon extravagant compensation, the question is whether the
defendants are guilty of the offences charged against them.
" If they are guilty and were possessed of nine-tenths of the
soil of the whole United States, and the patronage of the
union, it is the bounden duty of the jury to declare their
guilt." The indictment charged the defendants with
having combined unlawfully to increase the prices usually
paid and that they did unlawfully assemble and "corruptly
conspire, combine, confederate, and agree together that
none of them . . . would work for any master or person
whatever, who should employ" any workman who broke
any "of the said unlawful rules, orders or bye laws, and that
they would by threats and menaces and other injuries"
prevent any other workmen from working for such master.
Recorder Levy said that a combination of workmen to raise
their wages might be either to benefit themselves or to injure
those who do not join their Society. The contemporaneous
report made by Thomas Lloyd states that the recorder
declared all such combinations to be unlawful. One of
his successors who presided at the trial of the Journeymen
Tailors in 1827, stated that Recorder Levy declared that
"a combination to resist oppression, not only supposed but
real, would be perfectly innocent; where the act to be done,
and the means to accomplish [it] are lawful, and the object
to be attained meritorious, combination is not conspiracy." [1]
Levy closed his charge by telling the jurymen that if they

[1] M. T. C. Gould's *Trial of Twenty-
four Journeymen Tailors* (Philadelphia,
1827), p. 160; reprinted in vol. iv of
Commons's *American Industrial Society*.

could reconcile it with their consciences to find the defendants not guilty, they would do so, otherwise they must bring in a verdict of guilty. The defendants were convicted and fined eight dollars apiece and costs of the suit.

In the following years there were labor contests in New York, Baltimore, and elsewhere and these brought about prosecutions which usually turned upon the question of conspiracy. In 1842, in the case of the Commonwealth against Hunt and Others, Chief Justice Lemuel Shaw of Massachusetts ruled that it was a criminal offence for two or more persons to confederate to do that which is unlawful or criminal. This rule, he said, was in equal force in England and in Massachusetts; but it depended upon the local law of each country to determine whether the purposes sought to be accomplished by the combination or the means used by the confederates were unlawful or criminal in the respective countries. He defined a conspiracy as concerted action to accomplish some criminal purpose or by the use of criminal and unlawful means to accomplish something that was not in itself criminal. He went on to say that the inducing all those engaged in the same occupation to become members of an association is not unlawful unless the avowed object of the association is criminal. Even the purpose of an association that had a tendency to impoverish another person might not be criminal and unlawful; but, on the other hand, might be "highly meritorious and public spirited. The legality of such an association will therefore depend upon the means to be used for its accomplishment." [1] In this case as in many others, Chief Justice Shaw furnished the precedent that was followed, not only by the courts in Massachusetts, but in other States as well.

[1] Theron Metcalf's *Reports of Cases . . . in the Supreme Judicial Court of* *Massachusetts,* iv, 121–137, especially 134.

From 1805 to 1820 there were labor contests in different parts of the country but the times were against agitation for higher wages or improved conditions. Beginning with 1820 and more particularly after 1825, a new chapter opened. The regeneration of the second United States Bank following the transfer of the control from Langdon Cheves to Nicholas Biddle marked a new era of prosperity and growth which was reflected in great activity in building roads and canals and in general business. All this created a demand for labor and gave laboring men their chance to coerce their employers. At first the great point at issue was the shortening of the old hours of labor, from sun to sun, to ten hours a day. The march of democracy had placed the franchise in many States within the reach of considerable numbers of working men and in other States where the property qualification had been merely nominal, as in Pennsylvania, arrangements had been made to make political action easier. The working men argued that they should have more time for educational purposes, that they should have leisure to study and to consult about political matters which they could not do at the end of a thirteen-hour day. Of course in winter in many trades, where work was performed out of doors, working men had ample leisure in the long evenings to study and to contemplate; but with the cheapening of artificial illumination, with the introduction of gas into Philadelphia and New York and with the more common use of whale oil as an illuminant everywhere, the hours of indoor labor had become more constant throughout the year. As long as the hours of labor had been short in the winter months and indeed in the early spring and late autumn it had seemed not unreasonable to even up matters by utilizing to the full measure the long hours of daylight of the other five or six months of the year; but, now, when labor was pro-

longed throughout the year, it seemed reasonable to recover
the average yearly time by reducing the length of the work
day as a whole.   In June, 1827, several hundred Philadelphia
journeymen carpenters "struck out" or "stood out" for the
ten-hour day.[1]   The movement spread to other trades and
to other cities, but was not widely successful at that time,
and, indeed, it was not until the oncoming of the War for
Southern Independence that ten hours became the standard
of a day's labor in the mechanic trades throughout the
country.

The ten-hour movement appealed more strongly to working men as a whole than the earlier contest for wages.   The
mere fact that all working men — except agricultural
laborers and other distinctly unskilled outdoor laborers —
were now fighting for some one thing undoubtedly had a good
deal to do with the extended character of this movement.
At all events all kinds of trades established organizations
and, as all were struggling for the same end, the different
trade organizations naturally came together to concert
measures of coercion.   This led to the entrance of labor
into the political field, to the establishment of working
men's parties in Pennsylvania and New York, and elsewhere.
For several years the Working Men placed candidates in the
field ; but they were no match for the professional politicians
and succeeded only as they were able to combine with one
or another of the political parties.   In New York, the
leaders of Tammany Hall promptly adopted the cause of
the "workies."   But after a period of moderate success, the
labor movement divorced itself from politics.

These were years of reformations.   New York City seems
to have vied with Brook Farm in the presence of radi-

---

[1] John R. Commons' *Documentary History of American Industrial Society*, v,
75, 80–84.

calism.[1] Among the New York reformers was Thomas
Skidmore, who had an idea that every citizen should enjoy
in society the rights that belonged to him in a state of
nature, although possibly in order to create any society
some portion of man's natural rights had to be abandoned.
He argued for true equality among men and advocated the
taking away of all property from individuals and its pro-
rata division among all adults. Another radical New York
reformer was George Henry Evans, who, like so many of
the would-be remodellers of the American social organization,
was an immigrant from England. He had somewhat definite ideas as to the best mode to parcel out property
among the people. The prominence of these reformers,
combined with the machinations of the Tammany Hall
politicians, killed the political labor movement in New
York, as it gave the more conservative elements in the community the chance to stigmatize the Working Men's Party
as contaminated by association with the irreligious and the
levellers and with those of anarchical disposition.

The financial measures of 1830 and the next few years

[1] At a labor convention held in
Lowell, Massachusetts, March, 1845,
Mr. Ryckman of Brook Farm introduced the following resolution which
was most enthusiastically received
and secured him an election to the
presidency of the New England Workingmen's   Association : — "Resolved,
that this Convention recommend to the
N. E. Association to organize as
promptly as possible, a permanent Industrial Revolutionary Government
. . . to direct the legal political action
of the workingmen so as to destroy the
hostile relations that at present pre-
vail between capital and labor, and to
secure to all the citizens without exception the full and complete development of their faculties." *American Industrial Society*, viii, 104.
  Eli Moore, the labor Representative in Congress from New York, speaking in the House on April 29, 1836,
declared that the laboring classes were
"friends of freedom, in favor of equality
of political franchise . . . and opposed to monopolies of all kinds. . . .
The history of the aristocracy, through
all ages of the world, was a continued
series of rapine, plunder, villany, and
perfidy, without a single ray of honor,
virtue, or patriotism." See the *Congressional Globe*, under date.
  Seth Luther, an itinerant labor
agitator who lectured in the New
England mill towns in 1832, declared
that "while music floats from quiver-
ing strings through perfumed and
adorned apartments . . . of the rich;
the nerves of the poor woman and
child, in the cotton mill, are quiver-
ing with almost *dying agony*, from
excessive labor to support this splen-
dor."

brought on a period of terrific speculation. Everything went up in price — houses, lands, food, and clothing — and the working men felt that they, too, must get more money for the only commodity they had to sell, the labor of their hands and bodies. For a time the ten-hour movement gave way to demands for increased wages.[1] In this era of "prosperity," as it was called, trades unions, or labor societies, were organized and reorganized by the tens and twenties. No less than one hundred and fifty trade societies[2] appeared in the four cities of New York, Baltimore, Philadelphia, and Boston, in the four years from 1833 to 1837; and in 1834, at the beginning of the movement, there were twenty-five thousand trade unionists in those cities.[3] In the same years in the country as a whole there were one hundred and sixty-eight strikes.[4] Of these one hundred and three were for higher wages and twenty-six for a ten-hour day. All kinds of trades struck, the carpenters, bricklayers, masons, plasterers, and painters — those engaged in the building trades — to the number of thirty-four times; the shoemakers or cordwainers twenty-four times, and the rest scattered among all kinds of employment, tailors, hatters, bakers, sailors, rope makers, printers, mechanics, and so on. Among the unions of especial interest were those of the seamstresses, female factory hands, female book binders, shoe binders, and umbrella makers. These had unions of their own or formed branches of a union,

---

[1] An interesting article on this period is Evans Woollen's "Labor Troubles between 1834 and 1837" in *Yale Review* for May, 1892.

[2] See list prepared by Edward B. Mittelman in Commons and Associates' *History of Labour*, i, 472.

[3] They were distributed as follows:

New York and Brooklyn	11,500
Philadelphia	6,000
Boston	4,000
Baltimore	3,500
	25,000

American Industrial Society, vi, 191. See also *The South in the Building of the Nation*, v, 145.

[4] Commons and Associates' *History of Labour*, i, 478–484.

but where there were only a few women employed in some one trade in one locality, both men and women joined in one union. Another interesting item is that the factory operatives had begun to strike, the carpet weavers at Thompsonville, Connecticut, for higher wages, the cotton factory hands at Paterson, New Jersey, for an eleven-hour day, and the operatives at Lowell, Massachusetts, against a reduction in wages. A few of these strikes were against the use of apprentices, and one, that of the Boston printers, was against the employment of girls. The last of these strikes was in November, 1837. Then financial panic and hardness of the times resulting in lack of employment, put an end to all sorts of striking and also caused the disruption and disintegration of the trades unions.

Among all these strikes, the one that took place at Philadelphia in the summer of 1835 is particularly interesting. Seventeen trades took part in this movement, the house builders and shoemakers being joined by the leather dressers, plumbers, carters, saddlers, cigar makers, printers, and bakers. The movement was almost entirely for the ten-hour day, or for higher wages in connection with the ten-hour day. The bakers did not ask for a ten-hour day but demanded the discontinuance of baking on Sundays. This time the "workies" had the sympathy of the professional classes, — lawyers, physicians, and politicians joining them in their meetings. The politicians were so much impressed with the power of the workers that they provided that city employees should work only from six to six in the summer, allowing one hour for breakfast and one for dinner. There was no particular disorder at Philadelphia, but in some other places there was more intimidation and physical coercion than had been the case in previous years. The employers, too, were better organized and in some places and in some trades made use of the black list. The strike of the weavers at Thompsonville in Connecticut, in 1833, had one or two features out of the ordinary run. The carpet mills at that place had been recently started, operatives had been imported from Britain to work the new machinery and the owners of the mill had established a schedule of wages that, according to their own account, proved to be more than was paid for similar work in other establishments. When they tried to rectify this matter, the workmen struck, refusing even to finish the carpets that were in the looms. The leading operatives then wrote to friends in other places and to the keeper of the Blue Bonnet Tavern at New York, which seems to have been the rallying point of British operatives in this country. These letters simply stated that the operatives at Thompsonville had turned out and asked their correspondents to use all their influence to keep others from coming to Thompsonville until the strikers' object had been attained, and also to give them support in their undertaking. Certainly influence was used to keep men from going to Thompsonville and those that did get there were urged by the strikers not to work at the mill. The operatives in other factories also sent money to the strikers.[1] The most interesting case of these years — 1833 to 1837 — was that of the Geneva shoemakers, for the ruling of the Chief Justice of the New York Supreme Court in that case was the precedent followed by the New York courts for some years.

The trouble at Geneva originated in the attempt of the bootmakers and shoemakers to compel one of the employers to discharge a workman who was willing to labor for less than the price demanded by the society. The leaders of the society were thereupon indicted for a conspiracy in

---

[1] For an account of the Thompsonville weavers, see *American Industrial Society*, vol. iv, *Supplement*.

obstructing the business of boot and shoemaking to the injury of the trade of New York. A clause defining conspiracy as combining to commit an act injurious to public morals or trade had been included in a recent codification of the laws of New York. The case was carried from the lower court to the State Supreme Court where the Chief Justice laid down the law as required by the clause in the Code of 1829. If, he declared, the working people of Geneva demand so high wages that Geneva-made boots and shoes cannot be sold in competition with those made elsewhere, it was an act injurious to trade. Moreover, while one man might refuse to work for any particular wage, he had no right to say that others should not work for that amount of money and if one man did not possess such a right a number of men could not possess it. This case was decided in 1835.[1] In that year also the tailors of the City of New York, having already formed a society, increased the rate of wages demanded for its members and in 1836 the masters also formed a society. The journeyman society had compelled an increase in prices given for its work; but the organized masters, when the dull season came on, reduced the wages and the employees struck. The evidence in this case is quite as voluminous as was that of the Philadelphia cordwainers, thirty years before. There was now blacklisting, picketing, and coercion. The leaders of the striking tailors were indicted for conspiracy. The jury found them guilty and the judge, after a week's intermission, sentenced them to pay heavy fines or go to jail. In his charge and again in sentencing the convicted journeymen, the judge declared that the law governing the case was an act of the State legislature which not only had reënacted the provision

---

[1] Commons and Associates' *History of Labour in the United States*, vol. i, 405–408.

of the Common Law but had added to it a provision that an
act must be performed by one or more members of the
combination to bring the combination within the scope of
the law. Every individual was master of his own act, the
judge said, but he could not encroach upon the rights of
others. He might work or not as he pleased, but he "shall
not enter into a confederacy with a view of controlling
others, and take measures to carry it into effect." [1]

The Panic of 1837, in relation to the amount of business
of the country, was the severest that we have ever experienced, especially as one wave of depression followed
another for eight or ten years. Masters and working men
were both affected. In such circumstances the struggle
became one for existence, rather than for higher profits
and greater wages. There was great misery in many parts
of the country and this aroused the attention of the humani-
tarians and social panaceists. The decade beginning with
1840 was replete with plans for the making over of society
to secure justice for all.[2] Association, coöperation, agrarian-
ism followed one another and merged into each other.
Horace Greeley led in the attempt to reconstruct society,
giving space in his paper, the "New-York Tribune,"
lending money to what seemed to be promising ventures, and
using his personal influence for their establishment. The
story of the attempt to transplant Fourierism and Icarianism
from the Old World to the New is briefly told in another
chapter.[3] Here it need only be said that American working
men, whether native born or foreigners, who had been in
the country for several years, did not take kindly to any
of these experiments in socialism or communism. What

---

[1] J. R. Commons's *American Industrial Society*, iv, 319-333.
[2] See for example E. G. Squier's
Lecture on the . . . Laboring Class of
America, Albany and New York,
1843.
[3] See below, ch. xv.

they wanted was more wages for a given amount of labor. What these people offered them was no wages and living under social conditions that did not in the least appeal to them. It is easy to see why all the schemes of association failed: some men will work as hard without supervision as they will under direction, but these soon become masters; other men will do as little work as possible for "a living wage." Moreover, the early community experiments were not carried on on a sufficiently large scale for one thing and came into direct competition with more effectively managed private business enterprises for another. Exactly the same thing happened as to coöperation. This was of two general types, productive coöperation and distributive coöperation.[1] It would seem, at first glance at any rate, that one hundred workmen joining together and subscribing from their savings or borrowing from Horace Greeley or some other friend of labor enough money to purchase or hire a factory and procure the necessary materials could utilize their skill and knowledge so advantageously as to be able to undersell a competing work carried on in the usual way with comparatively large overhead expenses. In other words the elimination of the employer with the consequent elimination of the profit required by him would enable the working men's factory to pay good wages and live. On trial, however, it proved to be quite otherwise, for what is every man's business is no man's business and where the combining and overseeing faculty is absent, things are not done that should be done, or in the way they should be done, or at the time that they should be done. In distributive coöperation, there seemed to be much greater hope. The idea was that numbers of persons should each subscribe a small

[1] The constitutions and laws of half a dozen coöperative bodies were printed by Charles Sully in his *As-* *sociative Manual; Part I* (New York, 1851).

amount of money which should be used to procure a few goods that would be sold to members for the actual cost of purchase plus their share of the actual cost of distribution and, possibly, plus a moderate amount that might be used for enlarging the business. The plan seemed to offer great possibilities and one could point any doubter to the famous Rochdale system that had been worked out in England. Undoubtedly coöperative buying and selling had and has great advantages for the consumer; but these advantages are often overestimated and are more often very difficult to secure. These attempts, with the exception of a very few that were either peculiarly fortunate or were much more efficiently managed than the rest, and also always excepting a few of the community settlements, all came to early and untimely ends. One of the points that attracts attention in the distributive coöperative organizations of the 1840's was the difficulty that was experienced in apportioning the increased price that should be charged for store management. In one plan, it was provided that the person in charge should add to each article sold the exact amount of time consumed by him in the distribution of that particular purchase, — quite forgetful of the possibility that the amount of time consumed in the marketing of a yard of tape might well have been longer than that required in the disposal of a pair of back-strap boots.

A variant of the coöperative community plan was devised by Josiah Warren, who had been a foremost follower of Robert Owen, but had relapsed into excessive individualism. He devised a scheme by which every one would be spurred on to labor, but there would be no money and no wages.[1] In his plan there would be no laws or regulations, no one would have any power over another, and all intercourse

---

[1] Josiah Warren's *Equitable Commerce* (2nd Ed., Utopia, Ohio. 1849).

between human beings would be voluntary. In the transaction of business, everything would be done upon "the principle of an Equal Exchange estimated by the Time employed on the service." This was to be done by ascertaining the average amount of time required to produce various staple articles. These estimates when completed were to be hung up where every one could see them. Any man or woman producing any commodity and bringing it to the common store would be given a "Labour Note" for the number of hours required to produce the commodity. This note could be exchanged at the store or "magazine" for any goods requiring the same amount of time to produce. This plan was tried more or less completely in several places, but seems never to have produced satisfactory results.

The founders of some of the first factory towns, recognizing that the establishment of spinning and weaving machinery actuated by water-power would deprive the women of the farms of their chance to labor at the distaff and the hand loom, sought to make the life in the new mill town attractive to the operatives that would be drawn to them from the countryside. At Waltham, and later at Lowell,[1] wages were offered that attracted young women and the life was so guarded that the young women and their parents had every confidence in their change from the farm

[1] Harriet H. Robinson's *Loom and Spindle, or Life Among the Early Mill Girls* and her "Early Factory Labor in New England" in Massachusetts Bureau of Statistics of Labor's *Fourteenth Annual Report;* Henry A. Miles's *Lowell, As It Was, and As It Is;* and William Scoresby's *American Factories and their Female Operatives* (Boston, 1845). The superiority of the Lowell labor system is adverted to in the evidence given in the *Report* on *Manufactures* presented to Parliament in 1833, p. 121, where an English banker stated that the founders of the American factory system thought that great care must be taken of the young women who worked in their mills in order that such employment might be considered more respectable than ordinary housework. See also the evidence of James Kempton in *ibid.*, p. 147.

house to the factory village. Boarding houses were established near the mills which were kept by respectable women,
who were generally widows with children, and they were
subsidized by the mill corporations to the extent of twenty-
five cents per week for each man and half as much for each
woman operative. The board and lodging charged the
workers was $1.75 per week for a man and fifty cents less
for a girl.[1] At Lowell in 1848, the men operatives averaged
$6.05 a week, the women $3.45. The agent of the Lawrence
Manufacturing Company estimated that after paying for
board and clothing, the latter costing fifty-two dollars a
year, the male operative would have a weekly profit of
$3.30, and the woman of $1.52.[2]

The hours of labor at Lowell and in the other manufacturing towns were long. The operatives reported for duty
at five in the morning and worked until seven at night with
time off for breakfast and for dinner. In the early days
the work was not intense. The children who took the full
bobbins off the frames and replaced them with empty ones
worked only about fifteen minutes in every hour. They
occupied the rest of the time in study or play and sometimes
went home and helped their mothers in these intervals.

[1] John Aiken's *Labor and Wages,
At Home and Abroad* (Lowell, 1849),
p. 13. On p. 29, he remarks that
since 1800 men's wages had increased
50 per cent and women's from 200 to
300 per cent. In 1832, the New York
Convention of the Friends of Domestic Industry gave the weekly wages
of Massachusetts factory hands at
$2.25 besides board and lodging, Com-
mons and Associates' *History of Labour*,
i, 422. There is much information in
the "Minutes of Evidence taken before the Committee on Manufactures" in December, 1827, and January,
1828 (*House Report*, No. 115, 20th
Cong., 1st Sess.). In 1837, Stevenson estimated that the average wage
of the woman worker at Lowell was
$2.00 a week "clear of board"; that of
men .80 per day also "clear of board."
There were then 6085 females and 1827
males employed in these factories.
*Sketch of the Civil Engineering of North
America*, 319, 320.

[2] The Lawrence Manufacturing Company at Lowell had ordinarily paid
on the average about eight per cent
in dividends. In 1848, there were three
hundred and ten shareholders, one hundred and fifty-three of them having
only one or two shares apiece, the value
of the share being one thousand dollars, and the largest stockholder having
seventy-five shares. Aiken's *Labor
and Wages, At Home and Abroad.*

The speed of the machinery was slow, although it was faster than in England and the number of machines tended by any one operative was not large. Certain it is that notwithstanding the long hours, the Lowell factory girls of the thirties and the forties had time, strength, and inclination for intellectual improvement. Books were abundant and girls came to Lowell and worked in the mills because there they also had opportunity to read. In 1840 an "Improvement Circle" was organized and, later in the same year the publication of a magazine — "The Lowell Offering" — was begun.[1] The articles were written by the women operatives, although a man's name was given as editor for the first couple of years so as not to arouse the hostility of the public. "The Offering" was issued for five years or so and we have Charles Dickens's authority for the statement that it would "compare advantageously with a great many English annuals." Of its contributors Lucy Larcom,[2] alone, attained more than local fame. Lowell, indeed, in these early days seems to have been a species of money-making Brook Farm.[3]

About 1850 a new chapter opened in the history of Lowell and of other New England manufacturing enterprises, as it did in many of those in New York, New Jersey, and Pennsylvania. The founders of these manufacturing establish-

[1] *The Lowell Offering; a Repository of Original Articles, written exclusively by Females Actively Employed in the Mills* (Lowell, 1841–1845). For an account of this magazine, see Harriet H. Robinson's *Loom and Spindle*, ch. vi and fol.

[2] Lucy Larcom's account of her life is contained in her *New England Girlhood* and her poem, *An Idyl of Work*. See also Daniel D. Addison's *Lucy Larcom, Life, Letters, and Diary*.

[3] The Hopedale experiment differed from either of these; it had elements of community life that never existed at Lowell; and lacked entirely the literary stimulus of Lowell and Brook Farm. It was a religious, social, and economic experiment. It was ultra-idealistic. J. H. Benton calls these Hopedale dwellers "religious visionaries" who "claimed all the benefits of citizenship, while they refused to perform any of its duties." See "Argument" of J. H. Benton, Jun. in *Draper Corporations against the People of Milford*, 3.

ments were no longer living or had withdrawn from active business. Instead of being in the hands of a few men of established fortune, the mills were now owned by numerous stockholders and were managed solely for purposes of gain.[1] The first type of operative also no longer entered their gates. Lowell had been an educational force in fitting women for clerical work; now the farmers' girls stayed at home or went directly to the counting-rooms of the cities and their places in the mills were taken by immigrants. The looms were speeded up, more machines were allotted to each operative, wages were reduced, and so also were the hours of labor. The work became harder and more intense as the decades went by, labor agitators at length obtained a hearing there, and Lowell ceased to be unlike other centres of manufacturing industry.

By 1850, business had picked up again; the trade societies that had gone out of existence or those that had led a lingering life were resuscitated or reorganized and a new contest between labor and capital began. By this time the railroads had influenced production and distribution, both of which were carried on in larger units by men possessed of greater means or banded together in corporations with considerable capital. The earlier unions had been usually temporary societies, largely governed by idealism as the desire for greater educational opportunities, or the shortening of the hours of labor for hygienic reasons; the new unions were devoted purely and simply to the task of getting higher wages and they were much more effectively organized and fell under the direction of abler men who made the management of the union their sole occupation. Then the unions in several cities combined to form a central representative

---

[1] The agitation for a ten-hour law in Massachusetts is traced by Charles E. Persons in S. M. Kingsbury's *Labor Laws and their Enforcement with Special Reference to Massachusetts*, ch. i.

body and in some cases the separate trades unions throughout the country became more or less closely combined into
national organizations. Strikes again became the order of
the day ; but while there was vigor displayed, there were no
new methods employed. Then came the Panic of 1857
and before it had run its course, the firing on Fort Sumter
brought to the front new problems and new conditions. In
the sixty years since 1800, labor had won many distinct
triumphs ; it had secured the ten-hour day and the right
of organization with the power to compel attention to its
behests, and it had secured a constantly rising rate of wages.
How far this increase in compensation corresponded to the
ever improving conditions of American life is quite another
question and may well be reserved for later volumes. It
may also be a question for debate as to whether it is correct
to say that the right of organization was admitted, but it
certainly is correct to assert that it was viewed with much
greater tolerance by the law-makers and by those whose
business it was to enforce the laws than it had been in the
earlier time.

NOTE

Bibliography. — Professor Richard T. Ely of the University of Wisconsin became interested in the labor movement in America when he was Associate in Political Economy at Johns Hopkins University. In 1886, he published a book entitled *The Labor Movement in America* which broke the ground for all future discussions on the subject. Of course, as a first attempt in a difficult and unexplored field, this book has been very largely superseded, but Professor Ely brought together materials and students and thus laid the foundation for future studies of the subject. In 1887, George E. McNeill, himself a labor leader, published a book entitled *The Labor Movement: the Problem of To-day.* In this undertaking he had the aid of many other persons, as Terence V. Powderly, Edmund J. James, Henry George, and leading men in the movement. This book is very useful for the later time. It was not until the publication of *A Documentary History of American Industrial Society* in 1910 (10 vols. with a " Supplement " to vol. iv) that it became possible to study the history of labor in the years covered in the present volume without going through the same amount of work that was performed by Professor John R. Commons and his associate editors and researchers. The " General Introduction " to volume i of this publication was written by Professor J. B. Clark of Columbia University; it is a luminous exposition of the evolution of industrialism that might well be read by every student of American history. The *History of Labour in the United States* in two volumes by Professor Commons and Associates (New York, 1918) points the way through a maze of happenings and theorizings of the period. Frank T. Carlton's *Organized Labor in American History* (New York, 1920) contains in brief compass and in readable form the leading facts of this earlier labor movement.[1]

McMaster, in the volumes of his *History* covering this period, has printed a mass of useful information on the labor movement, see the indexes to the separate volumes — a consolidated index to the whole work would add greatly to its value.

[1] Other compendious works dealing with the labor problem are Arthur W. Calhoun's *Social History of the American Family*, ii; Edith Abbott's *Women in Industry, a Study in American Economic History*. Appendix A to the latter deals with "Child Labor in America before 1870," which is reprinted from the *American Journal of Sociology* for July, 1908.

CHAPTER V

THE PLANTATION SYSTEM AND ABOLITIONISM

THE humanitarian impulse that has just been described in relation to the new labor problem of the North also found expression as to the new labor problem that had grown up in the South. We have always been accustomed to think of slavery as slavery, as practically the same thing throughout the course of American history;[1] in reality, there was a great change in the slave system in the first forty years of the nineteenth century, — a change entirely analogous to that which has just been described as to the industrial system of the North. In the South, in the Revolutionary epoch, slavery was distinctly on the wane. The great Virginians — Washington, Jefferson, Henry, Madison, Monroe, and John Randolph of Roanoke — all condemned it. Patrick Henry stigmatized it as an "abominable practice" and declared it to be a "species of violence and tyranny" that was repugnant to humanity, was inconsistent with religion, and was destructive of liberty.[2] Washington and Randolph provided by will for the emancipation of their slaves, and Jefferson to the end of his life argued for the adoption of a system of gradual emancipation combined

---

[1] For slavery in the pre-Revolutionary days, see the present work, vol. ii. 376–398, 512–515.

[2] *The Commercial Register* (Norfolk, Va.) August 30, 1802; reprinted from "a Philadelphia Magazine." The same passages — somewhat differently worded — are printed in Tyler's *Henry*, 346, from "Bancroft, ed. 1869, vi, 416–417." See also on the general subject George Livermore's "Historical Research respecting the Opinions of the Founders . . . on Negroes as Slaves" in Massachusetts Historical Society's *Proceedings* for August, 1862.

with deportation. The South Carolinians on every occasion defended most vigorously their rights to their property, but for years a South Carolina law prohibited the importation of slaves into that State. This act was repealed in 1803 and for a few years until the federal law of 1807 went into effect there was a vigorous importation of fresh negroes from Africa into Charleston.[1]

The persistent and ever increasing demand for cotton fibre, the improvement of the cotton-gin, and the discovery that the short staple, green seed cotton plant throve marvellously in the uplands of South Carolina and Georgia and in the black belt to the westward, changed the whole course of economic and social existence in the South and, indeed, governed the course of history of the United States down to the year 1865. In so far as Eli Whitney's perfection of the cotton-gin contributed to the cultivation of the upland cotton plant on a great scale it was a curse to the South, to the United States, and to humanity. In the earlier time by far the greater number of Southern slaveholders possessed only a few slaves each. In the families of professional men living in the towns, there would be one or two to do the household work. In the rural districts, the smaller farmers likewise owned one or two slaves, or a slave family or two, and the whites and blacks worked together in the fields, the farmer or his grown-up son often setting the pace for the negroes. Not infrequently, the remnants of a once well-to-do family owned a few slaves who were "hired out" to a neighboring planter, their wages providing the old ladies with food and clothing for the last years of their lives.

[1] McCord's *Statutes of South Carolina*, vii, 449. By this law former acts prohibiting the importation of slaves from Africa and other places were repealed; but the importation of negroes from the West Indies and of adult negroes from the "sister States" was forbidden. See also the present work, vol. iv, 432 n.

Next in the order of evolution from the old Southern slave system to the plantation system of the cotton era was the production of cotton or tobacco in larger units. The larger planter possessed from ten to one hundred slaves. With these he conducted a plantation, growing tobacco or cotton for sale and sufficient foodstuffs and animals to maintain his family and his slaves, — clothing, tools, and luxuries being procured from outside with the proceeds of the staple crops. In 1790 there were twenty thousand families in the country owning one slave apiece, somewhat more than fifteen thousand owning from five to nine slaves each, and only two hundred and forty-three families possessing more than one hundred slaves each, and of these families only thirty-three lived outside South Carolina and Virginia.[1]

As the production of cotton became more and more profitable plantations increased in size, the number of slaves on each estate increasing accordingly, and the "gang system" replaced the older and less organized modes of production. On the great plantations, the slave was not in any sense a member of his owner's family, he was simply a producing unit in a larger agricultural machine. Even Southerners recognized this. Henry A. Wise, who passed his boyhood on a small plantation of the old type in eastern Virginia, on visiting friends who operated a large plantation in the southwestern part of the State noted how different were the lives of master and slave and the attitude of the one

[1] *Century of Population Growth,* 136. See Phillips's article on the "Origin and Growth of the Southern Black Belts" in *American Historical Review,* xi, 798–816. In the last pages of this essay Professor Phillips makes an interesting study of typical counties in the cotton States and in Virginia and Maryland, showing the growth of slaveholdings in the cotton region, especially in the newer plantation country, and the decline or stationary status of slaveholdings in the older cotton region and especially in the tobacco States. A table showing the distribution of the negro population, 1810-1860, is in *The South in the Building of the Nation,* v, 111 note. The volume on "Agriculture" of the eighth *Census* contains the number of slaveholders and slaves by counties.

to the other in the two regions. As was the case with the development of the factory system of the North, so with the growth of the plantation system of the South, the employers and masters no longer worked side by side with their laborers and slaves, but lived their lives apart and developed new ways of thought and of action. Quantity production either in factory or plantation could perhaps be carried on in no other way at that time, but it is in this new social order or disorder, that one sees much of the cause of labor discontent in the North and of the rise of a demand there for the immediate and total extinction of the slave system throughout the country.

The life on one of these great plantations must have been monotonous in the extreme. It was one ceaseless round of looking after the slaves, keeping them in health, seeing that they did not steal or run away, and superintending the superintendents or overseers. The slaves had to be adequately fed and clothed or they would lose their bodily vigor and become unprofitable, but at the same time there were great opportunities for waste and peculation of both food and clothing and the details of purchase and distribution had to be most carefully and continuously looked into. The negroes, especially in the newly cleared country, were liable to disease and in the first half of the nineteenth century there were epidemics of small-pox and of fevers that were more especially prevalent in the Mississippi Valley.[1] On some occasions one-third of the slaves on a plantation were carried off by one of these epidemics within a few weeks, and in other parts of the country slaves had to be moved every year from the low lands to the high lands to keep their health from deterioration.[2] Then there

[1] See *Account of the Epidemic Yellow Fever . . . in New Orleans, . . . 1833* by Dr. Edward H. Barton.

[2] For instance the "Stock and Crop Book" of Silver Bluff Plantation in South Carolina states that in 1833 a

was the question of discipline. It was very necessary to maintain good order and strictness, for the planter, his wife, and his children were often living miles away from any other white family and surrounded by hundreds of blacks with only two or three white overseers to aid them in case of trouble. On the one hand, discipline must be severe enough to impress the necessity of obedience and regularity on the minds of the slaves and yet not be so severe as to limit bodily strength or in any way to lower their working capacity, — for a non-working slave was an actual burden upon the plantation finances. Finally, there was the question of overseers and this seems to have been the most troublesome problem of all for the owner of a great plantation. They were difficult to procure and more difficult to keep, for if an overseer had the faculty of raising a good crop and keeping the slaves healthy and contented, he was in great demand and if he lacked either of these qualities, he was of little use as an overseer. On the great plantations. elaborate rules were laid down for the guidance of overseers ; they were often distinctly limited in the amount of labor which they could exact and in the amount of punishment they could inflict. One planter, to get away from the harassments of slavery, employed a gang of Irish and German immigrants to work on one of his plantations ; they struck in the midst of the picking season and the experiment cost that planter ten thousand dollars.[1] All in all, the troubles and vexations of plantation life must have detracted immensely from the pleasures of existence and to this must be added the burden of debt that often hung over the owner of

"fresh" ruined part of the corn on the plantation so that there was barely enough left for the needs of the year and in the same twelve months, fourteen slaves died from illness and there were only five births. "Ham-

mond Papers" in Library of Congress.

[1] Charles Lyell's *Second Visit to the United States*, ii, 126, quoted by Phillips in *American Industrial Society*, ii, 183. Lyell's visit was made in 1846.

thousands of acres and hundreds of slaves. In fact, the great planter of the Cotton Belt had all the business cares of the prosperous Northern manufacturer or man of commerce with a multitude of petty human details thrown in. It is by no means improbable, as one Southern writer has intimated, that the slaves were often happier than their masters.

A constant cause of anxiety on the part of the slave owner was the propensity of the negroes to run away. This was oftentimes due to excessive severity and sometimes it was the result of an inborn desire for freedom, especially on the part of those slaves who had a large admixture of white blood in their veins. In other cases, it was due to the desire of a slave to rejoin a wife or child who had been sold away from the plantation. There had been runaways in colonial days, when slavery existed by law in every colony, and a clause in the New England Articles of Confederation of 1643 had provided for the return of fugitives escaping from one of the confederated colonies to another. At the time of the Revolution, there were many free negroes living in Philadelphia and other parts of Pennsylvania and also in New York, but how far these were fugitives from the South, or their children, is impossible of determination. At all events there was a strong feeling in the distinctively Slave States that runaways should be returned as a matter of interstate comity. This led to the insertion in the Constitution of a clause providing that a person held to service in one State,[1] escaping into another "shall be delivered up on Claim of the Party to whom such Service or Labour may be due." In 1793 Congress passed a law to carry out this constitutional provision, but the machinery provided in the act was so vague that it was difficult for

[1] Article iv, § 2, third paragraph.

masters to secure the return of their runaways.[1] As pointing to the difficulty of securing runaways under this law an incident that comes out in the "Jefferson Manuscripts" is interesting. It appears that a mulatto slave named Joe, who had worked for ten years at the blacksmith trade at Monticello and had never received a blow or had a word of difference with any one had run away and gone toward Washington. Jefferson, writing from Monticello to his manager at the President's House in Washington, directed him to use all possible diligence in searching for the runaway and to have aid to take him for he was strong and resolute. Jefferson's surmises were correct and his directions were followed to the letter, for four days later the fugitive was seen in the President's "yard," was apprehended, and the next day was on his way back to Monticello.[2] This instance has been given at length partly because it shows Jefferson's administrative power, but more especially because it is a bit of presumptive proof against the efficacy of the Act of 1793 and exhibits Jefferson's attitude toward his own slaves.

There was undoubtedly a small but steady stream of fleeing slaves from the South, but the losses from this cause in the Cotton Belt were much more than made good by the constant inflow of slaves from the Border States.[3] This traffic was looked down upon by many people in the South

---

[1] See W. H. Smith's "The First Fugitive Slave Case" in *Report* of American Historical Association for 1893, p. 93. See also *ibid.*, 1895, p. 393, and W. H. Siebert's *Underground Railroad* (New York, 1898).

Until 1836 visiting slave owners brought their body servants into Massachusetts, held them there in bondage, and carried them away. In that year Chief Justice Shaw set free such a slave practically on the ground of Somerset's case. See Frederic H. Chase's *Lemuel Shaw*, 164; the case was that of the Commonwealth *vs.* Aves, and the slave's name was Med. See also B. R. Curtis's *Memoir of Benjamin Robbins Curtis, LL.D.*, i, 85 and fol. For Somerset's case, see the present work, vol. iii, 555.

[2] "Jefferson Manuscripts" in the Cabinet of the Massachusetts Historical Society under date of August 3, 1806.

[3] *The South in the Building of the Nation*, iv, 217–226; W. H. Collins's *The Domestic Slave Trade of the Southern States.*

and its conductors were outside the pale.[1] The history of it, therefore, is indistinct. On the one hand, it is necessary to discount largely the stories told by abolitionists and travellers; on the other hand, it is equally necessary to place slight reliance upon the disclaimers of Southern writers. The mortality of the negroes on the rice plantations and in the newly cleared cotton lands of Alabama and Mississippi was very great, owing in part to the severity of the labor and in part to the adverse climatic conditions. The birth-rate was very high, but the death-rate seems to have counterbalanced it in those sections as the mortality, especially among children, was very great. In the northern tier of the Slave States the conditions of climate and of living were distinctly favorable to the negro, and there was a constant surplus of servile black laborers for sale to the Cotton Belt. Marital relations between the blacks were very flexible, even in Virginia and Kentucky. Undoubtedly, too, miscegenation was by no means rare.[2] From time to time it is not unusual for men to argue that the white race and the black race are different and that they are incapable of amalgamation. This may all be true as to the ultimate merging of the two races,[3] but miscegenation was common in

---

[1] The attitude of a typical Virginia planter of the olden time is seen in a letter from J. F. Mercer to James Madison informing him that he "must notwithstanding the repugnance you will suppose, sell a parcel of human beings who have been born and bred in the family and on the soil which they will leave with the greatest reluctance." "Madison Manuscripts" in the Library of Congress, under date of November 14, 1799. Virginia slaves were advertised for sale at New Orleans in 1808, *Courrier de la Louisiane*, December 12, 1808. South Carolina by law restricted the importation of slaves from other States in 1816; the act was repealed in 1818 and an attempt to reënact it in 1822 failed. Jervey's *The Railroad the Conqueror*, p. 6.

[2] Rhodes's *United States*, i, 334 and fol. See also Arthur W. Calhoun's *Social History of the American Family* (vol. ii, Cleveland, 1918).

[3] See John Bachman's *Doctrine of the Unity of the Human Race* (Charleston, 1850); Jervey's *The Railroad the Conqueror*, p. 13; Robert B. Bean's "Some Racial Peculiarities of the Negro Brain" in *American Journal of Anatomy*, v, 353; and an article on "Present British Opinion on the Negro Problem" in *Littell's Living Age* for August 2, 1919.

the Slave States before 1861, although it may be going too far to assert that it was a distinct menace to the integrity of the white race. Certain it is that black children and mulatto children were born in great numbers in the Border States and multiplied so greatly that the land under the existing modes of cultivation could not support them. To the masters the only way of escape from bankruptcy was to sell off a portion of their human chattels and there was an eager market for them in the Cotton Belt.[1]

The external slave trade ostensibly came to an end in 1808,[2] but there are many indications of the importation of foreign negroes into the United States for years after that time. Opinions differ as to the extent of this traffic. It had to be carried on in a very clandestine manner, especially after European nations had combined to put an end to the exportation of slaves from Africa and the United States had declared the slave trade to be piracy and had joined with Great Britain in maintaining a fleet on the African coast to capture slave-running vessels. The profits were so great, however, that the traffic was going on in one way or another, directly or indirectly, through all these years.[3] Taking the external slave trade at the very greatest estimate of those who have argued for its existence, it could have

[1] Professor Dew had "no hesitation in saying, that upwards of 6000 are yearly exported to other States. Virginia is, in fact, a *negro* raising State for other States; she produces enough for her own supply, and six thousand for sale." *The Pro-Slavery Argument,* 359.

[2] See W. E. B. Du Bois's *Suppression of the African Slave-Trade* (*Harvard Historical Studies,* i) with a lengthy bibliography of books printed up to 1904. From Eugene C. Barker's article on "The African Slave Trade in Texas" (*The Quarterly* of the Texas State Historical Association, vi, 145)

it would appear that the number of slaves illegally imported by way of Texas has been greatly exaggerated. On the other hand, the fact that an agent to receive all slaves brought into the State of Alabama in violation of the federal laws prohibiting the slave trade was authorized by the legislature would seem to point to the fact of large and constant infractions of those laws. *Digest of the Laws of . . . Alabama* (1823), p. 643.

[3] See *House Report* No. 59, 16th Cong., 2nd Sess., and *House Report* No. 348, 21st Cong., 1st Sess.

supplied but a very small part of the new negroes required in the rapidly developing production of cotton and sugar. The rest of them must have come from the natural increase in the negro population of the Cotton Belt and Louisiana and from importation from the Border States.

The probability of a large exportation of slaves from Virginia comes out in the average valuation set upon "prime field hands" by the State authorities in conformity with laws that provided for the compensation of all masters whose slaves were executed for crime.[1] In 1802, the value was set at $400 and reached the first high point of $800 in 1818. In the hard times that followed the crisis of 1819, the value went back to $400; but in 1837, it was fixed at $1000. In 1843, it went down to $500 and then gradually rose until 1860 when it was fixed at $1200, — the highest point it ever reached. These extreme prices must have been a powerful spur to the owner of surplus slaves to dispose of them to the interstate dealers. Indeed, the mere fact that this rise and fall in the price of negro slaves in Virginia synchronizes so closely with the prosperity and dulness of cotton growing in the South is in itself suggestive of the close connection between slave breeding in the Old Dominion and the development of plantations in the Cotton Belt. Of course Virginia tobacco culture had its ups and downs with the general prosperity of the country and of the world; but owing to the competition of Kentucky and North Carolina in the production of tobacco it is impossible to conceive of there being any such keen demand for field hands in the Old Dominion as the highest of these figures indicates.

[1] *American Historical Review*, xix, 813, xx, 340; *The South in the Building of the Nation*, v, 127; and *American State Papers, Foreign Relations*, vi, 339. In the years noted in text the April price of Upland cotton at Boston was as follows: — 1802, 25 cts. per lb.; 1818, 32 cts.; 1819, 25 cts.; 1837, 17½ cts.; 1843, 9 cts.

Side by side with the slaves in the South and with the free white workers in the North, but not of them, were the free blacks. These were most numerous, comparatively speaking, in Charleston, South Carolina, and in Richmond and Norfolk, Virginia, in the Slave States, and in Philadelphia and New York, in the free States. In the North, the free blacks were largely the offspring of legislative emancipation,[1] but some of them were refugees from the South and still others were Southern negroes who had been emancipated by their masters or had purchased their freedom by working extra hours and had been obliged to leave the State of their birth. Many of them, of course, had been born free in the North, — the children of those who were themselves free. However they had become free, they were looked upon with suspicion by the white laborer of the North and with dread by the slave owners of the South. Northern farmers did not want them on their farms and Southern planters would not permit them to live near their plantations if they possibly could help it. One of the most interesting stories of the hardships of the free blacks is that of the slaves emancipated under the will of John Randolph of Roanoke. The freedmen could not remain in Virginia, as the laws of that State required every emancipated slave to leave the State within twelve months or be sold for the benefit of the "literary fund."[2] The executors of Randolph's will, therefore,

[1] A very helpful list of the State emancipation laws is in E. R. Turner's *Slavery in Pennsylvania*, 80 and note. Slavery was done away with in Massachusetts by the judicial interpretation of the Bill of Rights (see the present work, vol. iii, 559) and also in New Hampshire by judicial interpretation. The history of the gradual abolition of slavery in Pennsylvania is well told in E. R. Turner's *The Negro in Pennsylvania*, 78 and fol. Slaves were bought and sold at Troy,

N. Y., as late as August 9, 1808, according to the *Farmers' Register* of that date.

[2] See H. N. Sherwood's "Settlement of the John Randolph Slaves in Ohio" in *Proceedings* of the Mississippi Valley Historical Association, v, 39–59; *Revised Code of . . . Virginia* (1819) i, 421–444, §§ 53, 61, 65; and "Was John Randolph a Lunatic" in *The South Atlantic Quarterly* for January, 1913.

procured land in central Ohio and transported the freed blacks thither. But when they reached their destination by boat, the white settlers of the neighborhood refused to permit them to land. As no free negro could be brought into Virginia under the penalty of $333.33 for each negro, the executors were in a quandary. In the end the freedmen found employment in various places in Ohio and some of them were even permitted to settle on the lands that had been purchased for their benefit.

The laws of Virginia as to free blacks were very strict. Those who were free in 1819 were permitted to remain in the State, but all who were freed after that date were obliged to leave within twelve months under penalty of being sold into slavery.[1] Every free negro who was permitted to live in Virginia must be registered under penalty of going to jail and must always have his registration paper with him, which must be renewed every three years. If a registered free negro permitted a slave to use his paper, he could be imprisoned for from one to ten years, and any one harboring an unregistered negro was liable to a fine of five dollars. Moreover, free blacks were to pay an annual tax under penalty of being hired out at a very low rate until the amount of the tax was earned. Otherwise, they were subjected to the laws governing slaves. They could not carry a weapon without a license, administer medicine to a white person, have any commercial dealings with any one, or assemble with the slaves of the neighborhood.

The District of Columbia, as the meeting point of the routes of transportation from north to south and as the place of abode for Southerners, was necessarily occupied more or less permanently by a considerable free black population. Some of these people were actual residents of the

---

[1] *Revised Code of Virginia* (1819), i, 436.

District, their status being governed by the laws of Virginia, if they lived in the portion of the District that lay south of the Potomac, or by the laws of Maryland, if they resided in Washington City or Georgetown. Then there were free blacks who came to the District on their own account, either for some business purpose or to search for a lost relation, and there were persons claiming to be free in the bands constantly passing through the District under the guidance of slave dealers from Delaware and Maryland to the slave markets of the South.[1] As might be expected, there was much confusion and undoubtedly a good deal of injustice and Congress seems to have been singularly remiss in not providing clear and definite rules for the guidance of the law officers of the District. The best known case, as pointing to the possibilities of injustice to the free blacks, was that of Gilbert Horton. He was a free negro from New York who came to Washington on business in 1826 and was arrested and confined as a runaway until he could obtain evidence of his freedom from New York and, as this was slow in coming, he was advertised to be sold in payment of the jail fees. It was this case that aroused the interest of William Jay of New York and led him in a somewhat dramatic manner to stir the governor of that State to write to the President on the subject. The case aroused so much com-

---

[1] In the Slave States the presumption of law, one might say, was in favor of a person of color being a slave, — the burden was upon him or her to prove his or her free status. No doubt many free blacks were sold into slavery for jail fees or because they could not prove their freedom. It is also undoubtedly true that the high price set on a slave tempted unprincipled slave dealers to kidnap free persons of color in the Border States and conduct them to Southern slave markets. The stock example of this is found in Charles Ball's *Slavery in the United States: A Narrative* (1836); but how much reliance can be placed on this and other narratives supposed to have come from the pens of persons of color may well be doubted. The best evidence as to the existence of the practice is to be found in the laws of the Border States prohibiting it, as, for example, the laws of Virginia and Kentucky, which provided a jail sentence of from one to ten years for selling a free person as a slave.

ment that a congressional committee was appointed to inquire into it. It appears from the report of this committee that the negro, being seen wandering about the wharves without any evidence on his person of his being a free man, was arrested and committed as a runaway by a justice of the peace. The officers immediately wrote to the persons in New York mentioned by Horton and it appearing that he was a free black, he was set at liberty without being subjected to any charge or expense. About two months later, he was again arrested as a runaway, but was at once discharged, and apparently continued to live unmolested[1] in Washington.

In the Northeastern States, in Massachusetts, New York, and Pennsylvania, there was the same jealousy and dread of the free black population that there was in the Southern States. The " Census " of 1800 gives the free black population of Massachusetts at over six thousand. Many of these were old and helpless and the town authorities were dismayed at the prospect before them. The free negroes committed crimes out of all proportion to their numbers[2] and insanity was not at all uncommon.[3] They also congregated in the towns and aroused the fears of their neighbors. In 1788, the Massachusetts legislature provided by

[1] See Mary Tremain's "Slavery in the District of Columbia" in the *Seminary Papers* of the University of Nebraska, No. 2, p. 42; B. Tuckerman's *William Jay*, 29; and *Niles's Register*, xxxi, 345. In default of federal law for Washington City the laws of Maryland applied there; in 1806 the Maryland Assembly enacted that no free negro or mulatto should come into the State to settle under penalty of a fine of ten dollars for each week that he remained in the State — after the first two and should be sold for time sufficient to pay costs and fines. Maxcy's *Laws of Maryland*, iii, 293.

[2] Boston Prison Discipline Society's *Annual Reports*, i, 23, 24; ii, 45. On p. 86 of *An Account of the State Prison . . . in the City of New York* it is stated that the "blacks constitute less than *one twenty-eighth* part of the whole population of the State, yet they form nearly *one-third* of the whole number of convicts."

[3] See Edward Jarvis's "Insanity among the Coloured Population of the Free States" in the *American Journal of the Medical Sciences* for January, 1844 — also printed separately.

law that no African or negro, other than a citizen of some one of the United States and bringing with him a certificate from the Secretary of that State, should tarry within the limits of the Commonwealth longer than two months under penalty of being "whipped not exceeding ten stripes" and this law was still in force in 1823.[1] There were more negroes in Philadelphia than in any Massachusetts town and the jealousy and the dislike of them on the part of the whites was very marked. Between 1790 and 1800, the black population of Philadelphia county increased from 2489 to 6880 and there were at the last of these two dates, no less than eleven thousand free blacks in eastern Pennsylvania.[2] Those in Philadelphia herded together in one part of the city. In 1804, there were riots in which groups of negroes marched through the streets, knocked down one or more white men, and declared they would "show them San Domingo."[3] In 1834, a white mob drove hundreds of free blacks out of Philadelphia, across the Delaware River to New Jersey, where their presence at once aroused apprehensions on the part of the white inhabitants.[4]

In South Carolina, the most intense slave State of the older time, the free blacks, curiously enough, were in places exceedingly numerous. As they became emancipated, for one reason or another, they gravitated to Charleston where they were able to find employment about the wharves or in mechanic trades. In 1820, there were over three thousand of them in the city in comparison with 1680 in 1810, — the increase being about eighty-five per cent in ten years in comparison with an increase of the white population of

[1] *Laws of . . . Massachusetts* (1801), i, 413; *General Laws of Massachusetts* (1823), i, 324.

[2] W. E. B. Du Bois's *The Philadelphia Negro* in the *Publications* of the University of Pennsylvania,

p. 17, and the *Census* of 1800, page a.

[3] *The Freeman's Journal, and Philadelphia Daily Advertiser* for July 9, 1804.

[4] *American Industrial Society*, ii, 159.

only fourteen per cent.[1] Already in 1806 the Charleston
city council had endeavored to limit the congregation of
free blacks in the city. They evidently thought that the
practice of slave owners in hiring out their mechanically
expert slaves to city employers was the cause of the constantly increasing numbers of free blacks, as these hired-out
slaves when they had accumulated enough money bought
their freedom. They provided, therefore, that no slave
should occupy a house in the city without a ticket from his
owner; they were not to assemble together to more than
the number of seven unless some white person was present;
they were not to exercise any mechanic employment, own
any boat, or carry on any trade without a license, — all
under penalty of whippings and fines.[2] By 1819, their
numbers had so increased that the city council again undertook their regulation. In 1822, the Denmark Vesey
attempt at insurrection in Charleston[3] again aroused the
apprehensions of the whites. Vesey was an exceedingly
intelligent colored man from the West Indies who had so
devised his attempt that success might well have attended
it, for the moment, at any rate, had not a faithful slave
disclosed it to his master. Leading men of Charleston drew
up a memorial[4] reprehending severely the habit of slaveholders of hiring out their slaves or permitting them to hire

---

[1] "Memorial of the Citizens of
Charleston" to the South Carolina
legislature in *American Industrial
Society*, ii, 103–116. The United States
Census for 1810 (p. 79) and for 1820
(p. 26) give quite different figures for
the free colored population of Charleston.

[2] *Digest of the Ordinances of Charleston* (1818), p. 178, and "Appendix,"
p. 32.

[3] On the Denmark Vesey plot,
see L. H. Kennedy and T. Parker's
*Official Report of the Trials of Sundry
Negroes* (Charleston, S. C., 1822);

*Negro Plot. An Account of the Late
Intended Insurrection . . . Published
by the Authority of the Corporation of
Charleston* (Boston, 1822); T. W.
Higginson's *Travellers and Outlaws* (Boston, 1889), p. 215, and bibliography
on p. 332; and A. H. Grimke's "Right
on the Scaffold or the Martyrs of
1822" in the American Negro Academy's *Occasional Papers*, No. 7.

[4] *American Industrial Society*, ii,
103–116. While this statement is
one-sided, it shows the reality of the
fears of the whites.

themselves out, or allowing them to work overtime for
wages which were sometimes paid by the owner or more
often by a neighbor. These "hired-out" slaves were
ordinarily mechanics. They had a good deal of spare time,
lived under no supervision except when actually at work,
competed with white mechanics and tradesmen, and were a
menacé to the institution of slavery in many ways. For
these reasons, the memorialists thought the practice should
be absolutely forbidden by law. This memorial and the
excitement attendant upon the Vesey plot induced the
Charleston city council to provide a municipal guard of
one hundred and fifty men to protect the roads leading into
Charleston and the water front by day and by night, whenever necessity should seem to require it. To defray the
expenses of this guard an annual tax of ten dollars was levied
on all houses inhabited by persons of color within the city
and a further tax of ten dollars upon all free male persons
of color exercising any mechanic trade within the patrol
limits.[1] A few years later, the council provided that every
ticket giving permission to a person of color, whether slave or
free, to go about after dark should designate the name of the
street, of the owner of the premises from which such person
had permission to go, the place of destination, and the permission to return, if return were contemplated. Any
person of color apprehended without a ticket, after the
guard was set, should be dealt with according to law. The
State legislature also took up the matter, and passed law
after law [2] designed to limit what seemed to them to be a

[1] A Collection of the Ordinances of
Charleston (1823), p. 48; see also T. D.
Condy's Digest of the Laws of . . .
South-Carolina . . . relating to the
Militia; with an Appendix, containing the Patrol Laws; The Laws for the
Government of Slaves and Free Persons
of Colour (1830); The Militia System of South Carolina . . . A Digest
of Acts (Charleston, 1835); Digest of
the Ordinances of . . . Charleston (1818);
and Collection of the Ordinances of . . .
Charleston (1832).

[2] Cooper's Statutes . . . of South
Carolina, vii, 461–474.

grave menace to the white people of the State and to the institution of slavery. By these laws free blacks were forbidden entrance to the State by sea and by land, were made liable to several taxes, and were forbidden to carry arms. Moreover, a "guardian" might be appointed for a free black [1] on very slight pretext and the patrol laws for the State as a whole were extended and invigorated. Notwithstanding all these attempts at restriction, the free blacks in the State and in Charleston steadily increased in numbers. In 1859, three hundred and fifty-five "free persons of color" living within the city limits paid a tax of $12,342.02 on two hundred and seventy-seven slaves, worth about fifty-five thousand dollars, and on other property, almost wholly real estate, valued at $778,423.00. These two hundred and seventy-seven slaves were owned by one hundred and eight "free persons of color." [2]

Throughout the country, in the North and in the South, the presence of free persons of color was regarded as undesirable. In looking about for a method of escape, the idea of deportation occurred to many people and the American Colonization Society was founded in 1817. The plan was to purchase a piece of land on the western coast of Africa, or to get a part of a West Indian Island, and to deport

[1] According to a South Carolina act of 1822, every free male negro above the age of fifteen was compelled to have a guardian, a white freeholder, and by a law of 1823 no free person of color could come into the State in any manner, not even as a cook on board a vessel. Cooper and McCord's *Statutes of South Carolina*, vii, 462, 463.

[2] *List of the Tax Payers of the City of Charleston for 1859* (Charleston, 1860), pp. 383–405. For a somewhat different statement, see *The South in the Building of a Nation*, ii, 49. Maria Weston, the largest tax payer among the "free persons of color," paid $675.63 to the city of Charleston in 1859 on $41,575 worth of real estate, 14 slaves and one horse; while Richard E. Dereef, another free black, paid a tax of $431.00 on $25,000 worth of real estate, 12 slaves, one horse and $400.00 worth of "commissions." The tax on real estate was $1\frac{1}{2}\%$ and the tax on slaves was three dollars each: *List of the Tax Payers of the City of Charleston for 1859*, pp. 403, 387, 407. The *Census of . . . Charleston . . .For the Year 1861*, p. 9, places the total free colored population at 3785, taking it from the *United States Census* of 1860.

thence such free blacks as were willing to go without any expense to them.[1] To the Northerners, this seemed to be a feasible mode to get rid of the constantly increasing free black population in the cities and towns. To the Southerners, the additional argument presented itself that the deportation of free persons of color would stimulate emancipation, especially in the Border States, but there were people in the Far South who were anxious to emancipate their slaves and were only kept from doing so by the inadvisability of adding to the free black population. Among the founders of the Colonization Society were many of the leading men of the country and Bushrod Washington was its first president.[2] As a class, Robert Goodloe Harper said the free blacks [3] were "a burden and a nuisance"; but in a proper situation might become a virtuous and happy people. The idea appealed to philanthropically minded persons throughout the country. State auxiliary societies were founded and county and city societies were established to aid them in collecting funds. State legislatures and Congress also fell in with the idea and appropriated. public money to further the scheme. The British already had established the negro state of Sierra Leone on the African coast and the American Colonization Society procured a

[1] Jefferson had advocated colonization as early as 1776 and had elaborated a plan in his *Notes on Virginia* (ed. 1782, p. 251). In 1811, he returned to it (American Colonization Society's *Reports*, i, 6) and the idea formed an integral part of his latest plan of gradual emancipation. John H. T. McPherson's "History of Liberia," chs. ii, iii, in *Johns Hopkins Studies*, ix, 487–539, has a good and concise account of the colonization movement. With this should be read William Jay's *Inquiry into the Character and Tendency of the American Colonization, and American Anti-Slavery Societies*,

p. 11. R. C. F. Maugham's *The Republic of Liberia* (London, 1920) gives the first adequate account of the African settlement.

[2] He was an associate justice of the Supreme Court and a nephew of General Washington. See Niles's *Weekly Register*, xi, 296. A good repository of the more important documents relating to the Colonization Society is the "Appendix" to *House Reports*, 21st Cong., 1st Sess., No. 348. Among the vice-presidents were Crawford, Clay, and Andrew Jackson.

[3] American Colonization Society's *Reports*, i, 16.

tract of land farther south and separated from the British
settlement by no great distance. Up to this point, all went
well, but then difficulties gathered in the path of the colo-
nizationists.[1] The amounts of money collected, while seemingly large, were totally inadequate to so great a venture.
The bit of country procured, named Liberia, proved to be
exceedingly unhealthy, not only to the white people who
conducted parties of negroes thither, but also to the blacks
themselves, for in the course of generations on a different
soil they had lost much of the acquired immunity of the
negro race to African diseases. Moreover, the American
negroes did not want to leave the United States and a large
section of Northern philanthropists felt that the blacks
had gained the right to residence in the United States, and
that immediate emancipation of the whole negro population
and not the deportation of a small portion of it was the only
way to deal with the problem. Finally, the Southerners
themselves came to look down upon the scheme and were
able to point to the fact, as were the Northern abolitionists,
that in fifteen years of effort, the Colonization Society had
deported from America only as many negroes as were born
into slavery in five days and a half.[2] In 1862, President Lincoln addressing a delegation of men of color, whom he had
invited to confer with him, stated that Congress had placed

[1] American Colonization Society's
Reports, xi, 94. See also H. N. Sherwood's "Paul Cuffe and his contribution to the American Colonization
Society" in Mississippi Valley Historical Association's *Proceedings*, vi
and the works cited therein; and his
"Movement in Ohio to Deport the
Negro" in Ohio Historical and Philosophical Society's *Quarterly Publications*, viii, No. 1; and *Minutes* of the
State Conventions of the colored citizens of Ohio, 1850–1860.

[2] William Jay's *Inquiry*, 78. See
also Garrison's statement that the
number of slaves annually smuggled
into the South was "seven times as
great as that which the Colonization
Society has transported in fifteen
years" in his *Thoughts on African Colonization* (Boston, 1832), p. 160.

For later statistics see American
Colonization Society's *Reports*, xxxiv,
pp. 82–84. The last emigrants were
sent out in 1907: these were Edward A.
Caesar, his wife Louise Caesar, and
their daughter, Mary Emma Caesar,
aged two. Even now, 1920, sub-
scriptions are being solicited in aid
of the settlement in Liberia.

at his disposal a sum of money for the purpose of aiding the colonization of people of African descent, outside the limits of the United States, and had made it his duty, as it had for a long time been his inclination, to favor that mode of action. This he did because "You and we are different races. We have between us a broader difference than exists between almost any other two races. . . . Your race suffer very greatly, many of them, by living among us, while ours suffer from your presence." [1] Therefore, the two races he thought should be separated.

By 1830 the profits that were coming in from one cotton crop after another were driving all thoughts of emancipation from the Southern mind; and the planters of the Border States, who could not then produce cotton, were finding an eager market for their surplus slaves in the far South. In 1834, a case was argued in a North Carolina court that shows something as to the condition of the Border State mind at about the beginning of the period of aggressive abolitionism. It appears that a slave named Will,[2] being pursued by the overseer of his master's plantation and having been shot at, drew a knife and stabbed wildly about him, inflicting fatal wounds upon the overseer. At the trial, Bartholomew Figures Moore, Will's counsel, asserted that fear of death so far justified the slave in resistance as to take away all presumption of malice or premeditation and therefore converted murder into manslaughter. In other words a slave, circumstanced as Will had been, might resist seizure without fear of the hangman. The argument so affected the court and jury that the accused was convicted of manslaughter only.

[1] Nicolay and Hay's *Works of Abraham Lincoln*, viii, 2. See also Charles H. Wesley's "Lincoln's Plan for Colonizing the Emancipated Negroes" in *Journal of Negro History*, iv, 7.

[2] *Historical Papers of Trinity College*, of Durham, N. C., Series ii, 12–20.

Meantime, in the fifteen years before 1830, there had certainly arisen in the South a distinct feeling against the action of Northerners in promoting the flight of slaves from the plantations to the free States and in placing obstacles in the way of capturing fugitives under the provisions of the Constitution and the law of 1793. Many of the earlier settlers of Ohio and Indiana were Southern people who had left their homes to get away from contact with slavery. In Ohio, they joined anti-slavery societies and welcomed fugitives from across the Ohio River and passed them along on their journey toward Canada. Some Ohio men even went into Kentucky and incited slaves to leave their masters. In those earlier days, however, Pennsylvania was the most hospitable of all the States to fugitive slaves. Its proximity to Maryland and Virginia made it easy for them to reach free soil and Philadelphia, because of its size, afforded fairly secure hiding-places not only for those who came overland from the neighboring States, but also for those who came by water from the Carolinas. The federal fugitive slave law of 1793 was indistinct as to the agencies for its enforcement and relied on State officials and State facilities for the capture and detention of the alleged fugitives. This led to jealousies between Maryland and Pennsylvania. Maryland commissioners visited Pennsylvania to try to secure aid from the legislature of that State. The result was the passage of a law [1] in 1826 that appeared to make it easier for slave owners to capture alleged fugitives. In reality, under the guise of preventing kidnapping, the new law made it more difficult to recover fugitives. In 1842, the Supreme Court of the United States apparently gave some kind of standing to the idea that State officials could not be required to aid

---

[1] G. M. Stroud's *Sketch of the Laws relating to Slavery in the Several States of the United States*, 173.

in the enforcement of federal laws.[1] By this decision, the Pennsylvania act was annulled, but a dictum gave legislators of many States some justification for passing laws practically nullifying the federal act of 1793. In this same period North Carolina expressed the growing uneasiness of the Southern States by making it felony to steal a slave for the purpose of sending him out of the State or to aid a slave to escape.[2]

The last notable Southern attempt to do away with slavery occurred in Virginia in 1832. A few years earlier, in the State constitutional convention of 1829–30, a debate sprang up as to representation and taxation, — whether these should continue to favor the eastern portion of the State or not. The question of slavery and emancipation inevitably found its way into the arguments of the principal speakers, among whom were James Monroe and Benjamin W. Leigh, who a few years later was Virginia's commissioner to the South Carolina nullifiers.[3] Nothing came of this discussion and not much of the convention; but in 1832 a most important and significant debate was held in the Virginia Assembly. In the preceding year a negro slave, Nat Turner by name, had

[1] Marion G. McDougall's *Fugitive Slaves (1619–1865)* forming *Fay House Monograph*, No. 3, pp. 24, 28, 107, 108, and *Annals of Congress*, 17th Cong., 1st Sess., vol. i, 553. Because of the inefficiency of the old law, the Border States took the matter largely into their own hands. In 1822, an act was still in force in Kentucky that had been passed in 1798. It provided that any person might apprehend a runaway servant or slave, take him to a justice of the peace, and receive ten shillings reward and one shilling for every mile of his journey with the runaway; *Digest of the Statute Law of Kentucky* (1822), ii, 1105. It further provided that no ferryman or other person shall put over the Ohio River, any slave without the owner's consent on the penalty of a fine of two hundred dollars.

[2] J. S. Bassett's "Slavery in North Carolina" in *Johns Hopkins Studies*, xvii, 331.

[3] Charles H. Ambler's *Sectionalism in Virginia*, ch. v; Carter G. Woodson's doctoral thesis on "The Disruption of Virginia," ch. vii (unpublished); and *Proceedings and Debates of the Virginia State Convention of 1829–1830*. For somewhat similar movements, see Ivan E. McDougle's "Slavery in Kentucky" in *Journal of Negro History*, iii, 211; Asa E. Martin's "Anti-Slavery Movement in Kentucky prior to 1850" being No. 29 of the Filson Club's *Publications;* Oliver P. Temple's *East Tennessee and the Civil War*, chs. v and vi.

organized and led a series of attacks on the whites in Southampton County,[1] riding from house to house until fifty or
sixty white people were killed. Had not Governor Floyd
acted promptly the movement might well have assumed
wide proportions. At the next session of the Assembly a
committee was appointed to inquire into the policy of introducing anti-slavery legislation at that moment. The
committee, to avoid debate, reported that it was "in-
expedient"; but at once a member moved to substitute
the word "expedient," and still another moved as a substitute that provision should be made for the immediate
removal from the State of all negroes, then free, or who
should thereafter become free, and this substitute was
adopted by the House of Delegates by a vote of 65 to 58.
Following this, a plan for deportation of free blacks was
passed by the House and defeated in the Senate by only
one vote.[2] It was in the course of this discussion that
one member referred to slavery as "the *heaviest* calamity
which has ever befallen any portion of the human race,"
and another declared that slavery was "a curse upon him
who inflicts as upon him who suffers it."[3] On January 21,
1832, before the matter had been finally disposed of, Thomas
Jefferson Randolph, grandson of the writer of the great
Declaration, brought forward his grandfather's plan of
gradual emancipation in a concrete form.[4] He proposed

[1] See S. B. Weeks in *Magazine of American History*, xxv, 448, and William S. Drewry's *Southampton Massacre* (Washington, 1900). A bibliography is on p. 198. John W. Cromwell's "Aftermath of Nat Turner's Insurrection" in the *Journal of Negro History* contains some new statements mainly from "the recollections of old men."

[2] B. B. Munford's *Virginia's Attitude toward Slavery and Secession*, 47. Governor John Floyd's *Diary* (Dec. 26, 1832–Jan. 25, 1832) has some significant entries from which it appears that the interest in the matter was mainly sectional and that the slave owners who lived to the eastward of the Blue Ridge did not wish to give up their slaves and that it was the westerners, who had no slaves, who favored abolition.

[3] See the "Debate on Emancipation, in the Virginia Legislature, in 1832" in Goodloe's *Southern Platform*, 43, 47.

[4] *Speech of Thomas J. Randolph (of Albemarle) . . . on the Abolition of Slavery: . . . Jan. 21, 1832*, p. 5.

that no slaves born after the year 1840 should be permitted
to live within the Commonwealth after reaching maturity.
If the master had not removed them by that time, the State
should remove them, "the expenses . . . to be remunerated
out of the property itself." In the next year Madison,[1]
writing to President Dew of William and Mary, stated his
belief that the extinguishment of slavery would be easy
and cheap by a combination of deportation with emancipation and, especially, if the State were to purchase all
female children at their birth and deport them as soon as
they had earned the charge of their rearing and deportation.
The idea underlying the deportation plans was that it would
encourage private emancipation. Whether the scheme
would have worked out as its promoters believed it would
can only be a matter of surmise, but one excellent observer,
Charles Bruce of Charlotte County,[2] Virginia, expressed his
opinion and that of many other Virginians that had the
Colonization Bill of 1831 not been defeated, as it was by a
single vote, the fire that lurked in the slavery question
would have been drawn off by redoubled exertion on the
part of the Virginia anti-slavery men and that, if this had

At the end are two letters from Jefferson, one written in 1814, the other in
1824 advocating some such plan as
that proposed by his grandson. See
also *The Speech of John A. Chandler
. . . of Virginia with respect to Her
Slave Population*; *Speech of Charles
Jas. Faulkner*; *Speech of James M'-
Dowell, Jr.*; *The Letter of Appomattox
to the People of Virginia: exhibiting
a connected View of the Recent Proceedings in the House of Delegates* (Richmond, 1832) ; and Jesse Burton Harrison's *Review of the Slave Question
. . . Based on the Speech of Th: Marshall*. The last was first printed in the
American Quarterly Review for December, 1832, was reprinted separately
at Richmond in 1833, and is included
in *The Harrisons of Skimino*, 337–440.

[1] Madison's *Writings* (Hunt ed.),
ix, 498.

[2] In reaching an understanding of
this contest I am greatly indebted to
William Cabell Bruce, Esq. of Baltimore, whose little book — *Below the
James* — first drew my attention to
the importance of this debate. See
also Munford's *Virginia's Attitude
toward Slavery and Secession*, p. 46, and
"Anti-Slavery Sentiment in Virginia"
in *South Atlantic Quarterly*, i, 107.
The opinion of one of the best of Virginians on what he regarded as "one
of the heaviest calamities" is to be
seen in the Right Rev. William Meade's
*Pastoral Letter. Religious Instruction
of Servants*, delivered in 1834 and
printed at Richmond in 1853.

so fallen out, Virginia would not have seceded in 1861.
Confirmatory of this general view is the opinion of D. R.
Goodloe that had the abolition plan carried in Virginia,
it would have been repeated in North Carolina. If that
had been done, the sectional balance in the federal Senate
would have been broken and "secession would have been
blighted ere it had sprouted." [1] As it was, the failure of the
anti-slavery movement in Virginia in 1832 heartened the
extreme slave advocates in that State,[2] enflamed the abolitionists at the North, and pushed the two portions of the
country farther apart.

Until about 1830, the anti-slavery people generally had
favored gradual emancipation in one way or another,[3]
usually in connection with some form of deportation and
colonization. In 1816, George Bourne published "The Book
and Slavery Irreconcilable." [4] In this he argued for the
immediate abolition of slavery throughout the country
regardless of compensation of any kind whatsoever to the
slave owners. This plan was sometimes called "immediatism." The scheme of immediatism was later combined
with gradual abolitionism, proposing that this should be
immediately put into practice, — this was called "immediate gradualism." All these schemes were distinctly

[1] Quoted by J. S. Bassett in "Slavery in North Carolina" in *Johns
Hopkins University Studies*, xvii, 325.

[2] Two years later — 1834 — "prospective abolition" was seriously considered in the Tennessee constitutional convention of that year: see
Journal of the Convention, 85, 87, 98,
223, etc., and W. L. Imes in *Journal
of Negro History*, iv, 262.

[3] For sundry plans of emancipa-
tion, see Alice D. Adams's *Neglected
Period of Anti-Slavery*, using index.
For the earlier time, see Mary S.
Locke's *Anti-Slavery . . . [before] 1808*
(*Radcliffe College Monographs*, Nos.

14 and 11). The later abolitionists
thought that the Missouri Compromise was largely responsible for the
"paralysis" that fell on the anti-
slavery sentiment of the country.
Garrisons' *Garrison*, i, 89, 90 note.

[4] Other publications by or attributed to George Bourne are *Pictures
of Slavery in the United States of America*
(Boston, 1838); *A Condensed Anti-
Slavery Bible Argument; By A Citizen of Virginia* (New York, 1845);
*Slavery Illustrated in its Effects upon
Woman and Domestic Society* (Boston,
1837).

passive. They were advocated warmly, sometimes, but not in any savagely aggressive or militant spirit.[1] One of the earliest of the new type of abolitionist was David Walker, a free person of color who was living in Boston. The title of his book was an "Appeal in Four Articles . . . to the Colored Citizens of the World." It was issued at that place in 1829. The language was sometimes rude and was often inflammable, as was natural considering that he was a colored man writing to his own people. He could hardly "move" his pen, so deeply was he affected by the miseries of his race. The whites have always been "an unjust, jealous, unmerciful, avaricious and bloodthirsty set of beings," he wrote. He expected they would try to put him to death "to strike terror into others and to obliterate from their minds the notion of freedom." The whites wanted slaves and they wanted the blacks for slaves, "but some of them will curse the day they ever saw us. As true as the Sun ever shone in its meridian splendour, my colour will root some of them out of the very face of the earth." It was this book that aroused the Southerners to a full sense of the insecurity of their social fabric and, appearing not very long before the Southampton massacre, they naturally put the two together, and began to look with abhorrence upon all anti-slavery propaganda.

One might fill a volume with quotations and abstracts from books and articles that were written by the emancipationists before 1830,[2] but enough has been said to show

[1] Another early anti-slavery tract was published at Philadelphia in 1819. It was entitled *Free Remarks . . . Respecting the Exclusion of Slavery from the Territories and New States . . . By a Philadelphian.*

[2] To Bourne's and Walker's books should be added two tracts printed in Transappalachia: James Duncan's *Treatise on Slavery* which was printed at the "Indiana Register" office at Vevay, Indiana, in 1824, and John Rankin's *Letters on American Slavery* which were printed at about the same time and reprinted again and again after 1833. Two earlier books should also be mentioned: these are Thomas Branagan's *Avenia: or a Tragical Poem on the Oppression of the Human Species* which was published at Phila-

that many persons in different parts of the country disliked
and disapproved the slave system and that some persons
held very strong ideas on the subject.   One of these deserves
mention here because of his later public labors.   This is
John Quincy Adams.   In 1820, at the time of the Missouri
Compromise, he made several entries in his diary on the
subject.   The first of these recorded a conversation with
President Monroe, who had declared that the slavery question would be "winked away by a compromise."   Adams
thought, on the contrary, that it was destined "to survive
his [Monroe's] political and individual life and mine."
A month later, Adams had a conversation with Calhoun on
the subject and, after stating his disagreement with the
Secretary of War, he wrote that if the dissolution of the
Union should result from the slave question, it would
shortly afterwards be followed by universal emancipation.
And again, toward the close of the year, he made another
entry to the same effect that secession "for the cause of
slavery" would be combined with a war between the two
portions of the Union and that "its result must be the
extirpation of slavery from this whole continent."[1]

With the establishment of "The Liberator" by William
Lloyd Garrison in 1831, the anti-slavery agitation took on a
new form, passing from the mere advocacy of emancipation
to demands for immediate abolition.   Garrison on some
occasions quoted Bourne and other early writers and on
other occasions he paraphrased their sentences.   He seldom
exceeded Bourne and Walker in vigor of language or strength

delphia in 1805 and *The Penitential
Tyrant; or, Slave Trader Reformed*
(2nd ed., New York, 1807).   Branagan
was an Irishman, born in Dublin,
who had "crossed the ocean and experienced the Christian religion."   The
cut on the title page of the latter book
representing a kneeling and praying
negro with manacled hands and the
legend "Am I not a Man, and a
Brother?"   may have suggested a
similar cut to the later abolitionists.

[1] J. Q. Adams's *Memoirs*, iv, 503,
531; v, 210.

of advocacy. Now, however, the constant and prolonged agitation was greatly assisted by the formation of societies and by the activity of the abolitionists on the lecture platform. "The Liberator" found readers in every part of the Northern States and kept alive the movement whenever it seemed to be slackening. William Lloyd Garrison [1] was the son of parents who came from the Maritime Provinces to Newburyport some months before his birth. His forbears were English or Irish, only one branch having ever lived within the limits of the United States. On all sides his ancestors were strong, determined people, as one might expect from Garrison's own career. Moreover, with the improvements in transportation that came so rapidly after 1825, Garrison was able to organize the new movement on a much larger and more permanent basis than had been possible in the earlier time. The New England Anti-Slavery Society was formed in 1832. In December, 1833, the American Anti-Slavery Society was organized and by October, 1835, there were three hundred anti-slavery societies with one hundred thousand members, more or less, in a more or less active existence. The constitution of the general society declared that slaveholding was "a heinous crime in the sight of God" and should be abandoned immediately. The "Declaration of Sentiments," that was adopted at the same time as the constitution, maintained [2] that the cause for which the emancipationists were striving was vastly greater

[1] Lindsay Swift's *William Lloyd Garrison* in the *American Crisis Biographies* is a perspicuous study of the career of the abolitionist leader and has a bibliography at the end, and Oliver Johnson's *William Lloyd Garrison and His Times* affords a lifelike glimpse of the man and the movement. For the family account see *William Lloyd Garrison, 1805–1879: The Story of his Life told by his Children* (4 vols.). The chapters describing Garrison's ancestry and boyhood first appeared in *The Century Magazine* for August, 1885. The joint authors were Wendell P. Garrison and F. J. Garrison. They placed at the head of the title-page Garrison's own sentiment: — "My country is the world: my countrymen are all mankind."

[2] See *Platform of the American Anti-Slavery Society and its Auxiliaries* published by the society at New

than that for which the Revolutionary fathers had fought, for they "were never slaves — never bought and sold like cattle." The slaves enjoyed no constitutional or legal protection; for the crime of having the dark complexion they suffered hunger and brutal servitude. The anti-slavery people maintained that no man had a right to "enslave or imbrute his brother," that it was as great a sin to enslave an American negro as an African, and that every American citizen who retained a human being in "involuntary bondage" was a man-stealer. This being so all persons of color are entitled to the same rights as others, and no compensation should be given to the planters on emancipating their slaves, because they were not the "just proprietors of what they claim" and that freeing the slaves is not depriving them of property, but restoring it to the rightful owners; that if any compensation was to be given to anybody, it should be given to the outraged and guiltless slaves; and that any scheme of expatriation was delusive, cruel, and dangerous.

The influence of Garrison and of "The Liberator" may perhaps best be gathered by some quotations from the actual text. Many abolitionists having objected to the harshness of his writings, Garrison addressed them in the first number, saying that there was cause for severity and that on this subject he did not wish to think, or speak, or write with moderation. "Tell a man whose house is on fire, to give a moderate alarm; . . . tell the mother to gradually extricate her babe from the fire . . .; — but urge me not to use moderation in a cause like the present.

York in 1855. The best that can be said for the abolitionists as a body is in John F. Hume's *The Abolitionists, together with personal memories of the Struggle for Human Rights, 1830–1864;* but so far as it is reminiscent it par- takes of the disadvantages of recollections of old men as a source of history, — and a great deal of other matter about the abolition struggle is of that character.

I am in earnest — I will not equivocate — I will not excuse — I will not retreat a single inch — AND I WILL BE HEARD." And whatever one may think of Garrison, or of his methods, or of immediatism, one must admit that he lived up to his asseverations. In one of the early numbers of the paper, he printed a group of advertisements taken from other journals of slaves wanted and for sale and asked, "Is this the occupation of the inhabitants of the world of wo — and this their punishment, to prey upon each other, with the inconceivable ferocity of demons, throughout eternity? . . . O no! . . . They are — hear, O earth! and be astonished, O heaven! — American men — American women! . . . Blush for your country, and pity the poor slaves!" In the opening remarks in the first number of the second volume of "The Liberator," which was issued on January 7, 1832, Garrison declared that "We are a nation of blind, unrelenting, haughty, cruel, heaven-daring oppressors." He stated that sixty to one hundred thousand infants were born to slave mothers in each year and asked whether it was not "as atrocious a crime to kidnap these, as to kidnap a similar number on the coast of Africa?" Indeed, "negro thief," "negro stealer," and "negro driver" were the mildest epithets employed by him. In the seventeenth number of the paper the plain heading was replaced by a wood-cut depicting a horse sale and a slave auction in combination with the federal capitol with a liberty pole in the background and a slave being flogged at the stake. Later, other inflammatory illustrations appeared as the headings of departments: throwing a slave over the side of a ship, selling negro children, and a half-naked black woman on her knees with manacled hands upraised and the legend "Am I not a Woman and a Sister?" The Southerners declared "The Liberator" to be an incendiary publication inciting their laborers to rebellion, and it must be said that if the slaves could not read the text, they certainly could understand the lesson taught by these illustrations, — if they should see them.

The New Yorkers were not far behind the Garrisonians of Boston. They, too, established a paper called "The Emancipator" that competed with "The Liberator" in the vigor of its verbal appeal. On March 23, 1833, for example, it reprinted from another paper "A Negro's Soliloquy on the Ten Commandments." In this a slave is represented as commenting on the commandment "Honor thy father and thy mother." The negro asks who "dey be? . . . suppose him see driver flog his fader, what can he do? — suppose him see driver throw down his moder, flog her, lick her; — she cry — she bleed; — negro say one word, he too be throw down; . . . Oh Lord, tell his massa, let poor negro alone, to honor his fader and moder; — Oh Lord my God, what land gave dou me? gave all land to massa; — he live long, — me die soon." And in the same number there was the following from a sermon to ministers who held slaves: " 1. Colored people are not accounted as human beings. 2. They are treated in all respects as if they were an inferior order of cattle. . . . 3. It is considered the greatest insult in the world . . . to take any notice of a gentleman's killing a Negro." [1] Indeed, one reading the abolitionist literature of this and succeeding decades would come to the conclusion that the people of the South were all man-stealers and kidnappers, and that the swish of the lash was constantly heard south of Mason and Dixon's line from the beginning of the year to the end thereof. Many good people, thousands of them, hundreds

[1] Stated in slightly different language in George Bourne's *Slavery Illustrated in its Effects upon Woman*, 41.

of thousands of them, believed this word picture to be true.
No wonder, then, when the editor of "The Emancipator"
saw in a Southern paper a query as to whether the abolitionists preferred "a perpetuity of slavery, or a dissolution
of the Union?" he unhesitatingly answered "The latter,
we say, by all odds." [1] Garrison, as was his wont, assumed
a more aggressive attitude and some years afterward went
so far as to declare that the Constitution of the United
States was "a covenant with death and an agreement with
hell."

The mass of the people of the North did not in the least
agree with the aggressive abolitionists. They loved the
Union; slavery was afar-off, it had come down from colonial
time, it was an evil, perhaps, but no more so than drinking
intoxicating beverages, gambling with cards, or with dice,
or through the medium of lotteries. Many of them, especially the working people, believed the slaves to be better
off than themselves. The Southerners, too, were very good
customers and the "business interests" of the North were
distinctly opposed to anything that would interrupt Southern
prosperity and, therefore, trade. Southern gentlemen and
gentlewomen habitually visited Northern summer resorts,
bringing some of their personal slaves with them; they did
not in any way resemble the monsters of iniquity that were
described in "The Emancipator" and "The Liberator"
and by Garrison and Thompson and other anti-slavery
orators on the platform. Nor did the slaves seem unhappy
or show marks of the lash or of blows. In short, labor,
business, and society were opposed to aggressive abolitionism.[2] At Philadelphia, a mob attacked the anti-

---

[1] *Selections from the Letters and
Speeches of the Hon. James H. Hammond, 24.*
[2] The slaveholders and the anti-

abolitionists frequently stigmatized the
Garrisonians as "amalgamators" or
persons who favored the amalgamation
of the whites and the blacks. This

slavery people and drove free negroes out of the city.; at
New York, mobs broke up meetings and attacked anti-
slavery agitators. An especial object of wrath was George
Thompson, an English anti-slavery propagandist, who
came to the United States to correct the morals of the
American people and build up a better social state in this
country, — and he was only one of many British visitors who
saw much to blame in the American republic. In 1835, the
announcement that Thompson was to address the Massachusetts Female Anti-Slavery Society at Boston appeared
to the anti-Garrisonians to be a good opportunity to settle
matters, once for all. Warned in time, Thompson did not
attend the meeting, but the advance guard of the rioters
discovered Garrison there. The mayor of the city appeared
in the hall and advised Garrison to leave and suggested that
the ladies should also depart.[1] The latter were permitted
to march safely away, but the news that Garrison was
accessible inflamed the mob. He had withdrawn at first
to his office and then had found shelter in a near-by carpenter's shop, being concealed by the carpenter under a
bench behind a pile of boards. He was found there by the
vanguard of the rioters, taken to the window, and slid down
to the ground on a board, a rope having been made fast

charge was fiercely resented by the
anti-slavery advocates, especially by
those living in Pennsylvania and
New York. Some of the Massachusetts abolitionists seem to have felt
differently on this subject as they were
constantly agitating for the repeal of
the "tyrannical section" of the act of
the Massachusetts legislature of June
22, 1786, which provided a fine of fifty
pounds for any one celebrating a marriage between a white person and a
negro, Indian, or mulatto. See *The
Liberator* for Feb. 5, 1831, and Jan.
21, 1832, etc.; and the Garrisons'
William Lloyd Garrison, i, 254, 255.

[1] The family account of this episode
is in Garrisons' *Garrison*, ii, 1–72.
Mayor Lyman's statement of his own
doings that day is in *Papers Relating
to the Garrison Mob*, edited by Theodore Lyman, 3rd. There is other
matter in C. F. Adams's "Memoir
of Theodore Lyman" in the *Proceedings* of the Massachusetts Historical
Society for March, 1906, p. 169. Years
later, Ellis Ames wrote out an elaborate
series of "Reminiscences" on the
episode which moved Edward L.
Pierce to deliver a paper on "Recollections as a Source of History" (*ibid.*,
for February, 1881, and March, 1896).

around his body, presumably to prevent too rapid a descent. He was rescued by the mayor and committed to the jail for safe keeping.

In the Western country the aggressive anti-slavery movement lagged for a time. Large portions of the States of the Old Northwest were settled by Southerners who did not believe in destroying the property rights of their cousins in the old home and who knew that a great deal that was proclaimed by the abolitionists did not represent the actual existing fact. It is instructive to notice how slowly the movement made its way into the religious organizations that were strongest on the frontier. For years the Methodists refused to join in the movement and the fact that a candidate for the ministry was an abolitionist was good cause for his rejection.[1] Notwithstanding, the New England Methodists formed anti-slavery societies, the New Yorkers followed, and then the whole church became rent in twain into the Methodist Church and the Methodist Church South. Under these circumstances the formation of anti-slavery societies in the Old Northwest was slow and difficult and was made to the accompaniment of mobs and assaults of all kinds. As was natural, the conflict was especially severe in Kentucky and Missouri and anti-slavery men, driven from those States, found refuge in Ohio, Indiana, and Illinois where some of them continued to carry on their missionary labors by means of newspapers and tracts. The refugees were not welcomed by the dwellers on the Northern side of the Ohio and the eastern bank of the Mississippi. In 1837, Elijah P. Lovejoy, a clergyman who

---

[1] William W. Sweet's *Circuit-Rider Days in Indiana*, 86, 87, and index under "slavery"; see further his *Methodist Episcopal Church and the Civil War*, 15–46. For the official action of the Presbyterians in the early years see *A Digest; Compiled from the Records of the General Assembly* (Philadelphia, 1820, pp. 338–357).

had edited an anti-slavery paper in St. Louis, was obliged
to leave that city and essayed to carry on his work from the
town of Alton in Illinois. The people there destroyed one
printing press after another, and finally, when Lovejoy and
his friends undertook to defend his property by arms, they
killed him and another man and wounded several more.[1] On
December 8, 1837, an assemblage gathered in Faneuil Hall in
Boston to take action on the Lovejoy murder. The attorney-
general of the Commonwealth spoke advising the people to
be calm, for the mob of Alton had done nothing more than
pre-Revolutionary rioters at Boston had done. It was then
that Wendell Phillips, a young man and unknown, made
his way to the platform, and, with voice and manner that
for forty years charmed and aroused his countrymen, said
that when he heard the words of the attorney-general placing
the Alton murderers side by side with Hancock and Adams,
he thought [2] "those pictured lips [pointing to the portraits
in the hall] would have broken into voice to rebuke the
recreant American, — the slanderer of the dead."

Another form that Northern dislike of the abolition movement assumed was violent opposition to the education of
colored children of the free blacks. In Canterbury, Connect-

[1] A letter from W. S. Gilman, a
participant, dated the day after the
event is printed in *The Mississippi
Valley Historical Review*, iv, 492.
Contemporary accounts of the Alton
riots are Joseph C. and Owen Lovejoy's *Memoir of the Rev. Elijah P.
Lovejoy* and William S. Lincoln's
Alton Trials; both of these books were
printed at New York in 1838. Henry
Tanner's *Martyrdom of Lovejoy . . .
By an Eye-witness* and his brief paper
on the *History of the Rise and Progress
of the Alton Riots* (Buffalo, 1878) are
both written by one who took part in
the defence of Lovejoy's printing
press, but long after the event which
they describe. Edward Beecher's

Narrative of Riots at Alton was written
by a man who had some part in the
earlier stages of the trouble and it was
printed at Alton in 1838. Possibly
the best brief connected account is
contained in chs. x and xi of Harvey
Reid's *Biographical Sketch of Enoch
Long* (Chicago Historical Society's
Collections, ii). The best extended
modern account is N. D. Harris's
History of Negro Servitude in Illinois,
chs. vi, vii. A contemporaneous anti-
abolition account is in Henry Brown's
History of Illinois, 459.

[2] Wendell Phillips's *Speeches, Lectures, and Letters* (Boston, 1863), p. 3,
and Carlos Martyn's *Wendell Phillips: the Agitator*, 96.

icut, Prudence Crandall, a Quakeress, undertook to convert a private school that she had recently opened for white girls into a mixed school for both whites and blacks. The white parents at once removed their children and she then essayed to carry on the school for blacks exclusively. From the beginning, the townspeople objected to Miss Crandall's project of teaching colored people; the neighbors visited her and remonstrated; the selectmen came and remonstrated; and the Canterburyites held a town meeting. All was in vain, for urged on by Garrison and other abolitionists, although perhaps she did not need any urging, Miss Crandall persisted. In the spring of 1833 the school opened with "a dozen or so quiet little colored girls" and Miss Crandall immediately found herself the object of legal proceedings. In the interval, the Canterbury townsmen and other freemen of Connecticut had petitioned the legislature for protection and the legislature had replied by enacting a law that no person should set up any institution for the instruction of "colored persons who are not inhabitants of this state" nor teach in any school, or board any colored person who is not an inhabitant of "any town in this state" without consent in writing previously obtained of magistrates and selectmen.[1] Miss Crandall was haled into court and the lawyers talked on both sides: whether a free colored person was a citizen of the United States, whether the act was constitutional or unconstitutional; and they went from one court to another until they came to a court of appeals, when the judges ruled that the "information" under which the trials were held was insufficient, and therefore reversed the decision of the court below and put an end to the legal contest. The townspeople of Canterbury then intervened in their own manner. Already they had visited the Crandall

---

[1] *Public Statute Laws of the State of Connecticut* (Hartford, 1835), p. 321.

premises; now they smashed in the windows of the house. Before this time, a month or so, Prudence Crandall had married the Reverend Calvin Philleo, a Baptist clergyman of Ithaca, New York, and this fact may have made the closing of the school less painful, pending Mrs. Philleo's removal to her new home.[1]

The Prudence Crandall school affair is the best known exhibition of Northern dislike of providing educational facilities for the free colored people, probably because of the notice given to it by Garrison, May, and other literary abolitionists. There were many others, however, before and after 1833. Two years earlier, great excitement had been aroused at New Haven. The Reverend Simeon S. Jocelyn, a clergyman in that town, and Arthur Tappan had conceived the plan of establishing there, alongside of Yale College, a seminary of learning for colored people which was also to give them instruction in the mechanical arts and was, in short, to be something like a modern manual training school.[2] Subscription papers were opened and the approval of the anti-slavery people was obtained when the townsmen and freemen of New Haven met and condemned the project in no measured tones by the vote of some seven hundred against and the Reverend Mr. Jocelyn and three others in

[1] See Bernard C. Steiner's "History of Slavery in Connecticut" (*Johns Hopkins University Studies*, xi, 415–422). From the abolitionist point of view, the best account is in Garrisons' *Garrison*, i, ch. x. Much the same is in Ellen D. Larned's *Windham County, Connecticut*, ii, 490–502. See also *Report of the Trial of Miss Prudence Crandall, . . . August Term, 1833*; *Report of the Arguments of Counsel in the Case of Prudence Crandall . . . July, 1834*; Andrew T. Judson's *Remarks to the Jury . . . Superior Court, Oct. Term, 1833*, which also contains the judge's charge to the jury and the report of the committee of the General Assembly on which the act of 1833 was founded; and Samuel J. May's *Letters to Andrew T. Judson, Esq. . . . Relative to Miss Crandall and her School for Colored Females* (Brooklyn, 1833).

[2] See *Niles's Register*, October 1, 1831, p. 88, from the *New Haven Palladium* and *Poulson's American Daily Advertiser*; Clarence W. Bowen's *Arthur and Lewis Tappan*; and Garrisons' *Garrison*, i, 259, 260. Jocelyn's own account is in a pamphlet entitled *College for Colored Youth* that was printed at New York in 1831.

favor. In New Hampshire, too, in Canaan, in Grafton County, the sturdy farmers met and with sundry yokes of oxen hauled a small building designed for a school house for colored children into a neighboring swamp.[1] In Boston, after the Revolution, colored children — some of them — attended the town schools with the other children. In 1800, some colored people petitioned for the establishment of a separate school for their children. This petition was refused, but a separate school was organized by the blacks and their white sympathizers, and was partly supported by the public authorities after 1806. In 1835, a separate school building was erected near by and there the school was kept in successful operation for years. In 1846, an agitation began for the abolition of the separate school for colored children and their transferrence to the common schools. This question was given to a committee to examine and the majority reported decidedly against it, and in favor of continuing the existing arrangement of separate schools. But there was a minority report which argued, with some interesting evidence from other Massachusetts towns, for the inclusion of the colored children in the regular educational system. The principle of perfect equality was stated to be the vital principle of the common school system and negro children were lawfully entitled to the benefits of the free schools. The minority seem to have thought that exclusion from the white schools was akin to the expulsion of the negroes "from the cabins to the fore-decks of steam-boats, from the first class to the jim crow cars"[2] and from churches, theatres, and other places.

[1] Albert Bushnell Hart's *Slavery and Abolition*, 245, citing the *Boston Morning Post* for August 18, 1835.

[2] See *Report to the Primary School Committee, June 15, 1846* (*Boston City Documents, 1846*, No. 23); *Report of the Minority of the Committee of the Primary School Board on The Caste Schools* (Boston, 1846); Thomas P. Smith's *Address in Opposition to the Abolition of Colored Schools, December 24, 1849* (Boston, 1850); and the majority and minority reports on the same subject in 1849.

Nevertheless, it was some years before the colored race attained an equality with the whites in the public schools of that city. These instances of Northern opposition to the abolitionists might be largely extended; but enough has been said to show how prevalent it was. Unquestionably, the mass of the people of the North — before 1850 — did not regard the negro as "a man and a brother." On the contrary,[1] very many of them thought that he belonged to a distinct race and that the racial distinctions were not at all agreeable.

The Southern slaveholders in the earlier part of the century had grave doubts, to say the least, as to the advisability of the slave system. This opinion continued in the northern tier of the Slave States until 1830, but the profits to be derived from slave-grown cotton were so great in the southern group of the planting States that the people there before 1830 had come to regard slavery as the very basis of their prosperity, arguing that great crops of cotton could not be produced by white labor and that slavery could not be eradicated without doing great injury to the whites. To all the slaveholders in both tiers of States, the call of the "immediate abolitionists" came as a challenge and a reproach. They resented being stigmatized as man-stealers. Their peculiar institution had come down to them from "the fathers"; it had come to them from colonial days when it was universal throughout the colonies that formed themselves into the Thirteen Original States. It had become economically unsound in the Northern States and had either died out there or was dying out. But the Southerners could not understand why their prosperity should be attacked, because slavery was no longer profitable in the

[1] See for example Richard H. Colfax's *Evidence against the Views of the Abolitionists, Consisting of Physical* and *Moral Proofs of the Natural Inferiority of the Negroes* (New York, 1833).

North, when it was not only profitable in the South, but was necessary for the well-being of a large portion of the Southern whites. The language of the Garrisonians alarmed them and aroused all their fighting instincts. Moreover, South Carolina had come triumphantly out of the nullification contest. The other Southern States had not joined her at that time, but the arguments which justified nullification justified resistance to any Northern attack upon their institutions. Furthermore, the means adopted by the abolitionists to propagate their ideas — their papers and their printed illustrated posters — seemed to the planters to be distinctly dangerous, and they were being disseminated far and wide throughout the South.

In the year 1835 a wave of indignation rolled through the Southern States. At a meeting at Charleston resolutions were passed condemning abolitionism in the severest terms and demanding the exclusion of incendiary publications from the mail. Then the people proceeded to destroy by fire the abolition papers that were in the post-office and they also closed the schools for the free colored population of the city.[1] J. H. Hammond expressed the thought of very many Southerners in a letter to Mordecai M. Noah, a New York newspaper editor: the "Northern Fanaticks," he wrote, must not expect to find in South Carolinians the unrepresented subjects of an arrogant monarchy; they were freemen, they knew their rights and strength, and intended to stand upon them. The abolitionist leaders could be "silenced in but one way — *Terror-death*."[2] The non-slaveholding States must give up Garrison and the rest, and this alone could save the Union. Another South Carolinian — a Mr. Bellinger —

[1] See *Proceedings of the Citizens of Charleston, on the Incendiary Machinations, Now in Progress against the Peace and Welfare of the Southern States* (Charleston, 1835).

[2] Letter of August 19, 1835, in "Hammond Papers" in Library of Congress.

addressed a public meeting of the citizens of Barnwell District on the subject of slavery. He declared that slavery was "a blessing to both master and Slave," that the Southerners were living within their rights, and the Northerners would better keep their hands off.[1] In Alabama, the people took official action when the grand jury of Tuscaloosa County returned a true bill against the editor of "The Emancipator" of New York, for circulating papers of a seditious and incendiary character tending by gross misrepresentations and illicit appeals to excite the slaves of Alabama to insurrection and murder. The Governor of Alabama transmitted the indictment to the Governor of New York and demanded that the obnoxious editor be arrested and confined until he could "dispatch an Agent to conduct him to Alabama"; for, although the offender was not in the State when the crime was committed, he had "evaded the justice of our laws"[2] and therefore should be delivered up for trial within the State as a fugitive from justice.

Already the Southerners were beginning to feel the reproach cast upon them by public opinion outside of the United States, and the emancipation of the slaves in the British West Indies in 1833 had excited their apprehensions of interference from outside. They, themselves, constantly referred to the lamentable condition of the laborers of England; but they did not at all relish having English antislavery people advocate abolitionism in the United States. Daniel O'Connell had referred to the deplorable condition

[1] Edmund Bellinger's *Speech on the Subject of Slavery* (Charleston, 1835). The tone of the meeting may be gathered from the resolutions that were unanimously adopted. The second reads "That we view with *abhorence* and *detestation* the attempt to deluge our State with Incendiary publications; and that we consider the authors of such attempts no more entitled to the protection of the Laws than the *ferocious monster* or *venomous reptile*."

[2] *Gulf States Historical Magazine*, ii, 26.

of the Southern laboring class and had stigmatized the masters as "felons of the human race" doomed to extirpation by the avengers of African wrongs. This aroused "The Charleston Mercury" to protest against the Irish agitator's attitude.[1] In closing the writer asked, why will the South fight phantoms at such a time? "Why sleeps her patriotism, her instinct of self-preservation? Let her rally her sons under one banner — 'Southern rights and Southern safety' — and defy 'A World in arms.'"

The Southerners were by no means content to stand on the defensive. On the contrary they assumed an aggressive anti-abolitionist attitude. They declared that slavery came from God, that it was the ideal social condition, and was for the benefit of the blacks and of the whites. Somewhat later, Rabbi Morris J. Raphall stated the biblical argument in favor of slavery in its baldest form. There, in the Ten Commandments given on Mt. Sinai, he wrote, "There where His finger scorched, the tablet shone." The fourth commandment brought rest to all including "Thy male slave and thy female slave" and the Lord forbade a man to covet his neighbor's house or "his male slave, or his female slave, or his ox, or his ass." And Abraham and Isaac, who themselves talked with God, were slaveholders. Why then invent a new sin not known to the Bible, and thus exasperate thousands of God-fearing, lawabiding citizens of the South? In 1919, a former slave of one of the best-known South Carolina families was "laid to rest" in "the God's Acre" on the old plantation [2] and his former mistress gave a third of a column of a local paper to his obituary, telling how in a time of lawlessness "this wise

[1] *The Charleston Mercury* of July 31, 1835. This was copied for me by Mr. D. Huger Bacot of Charleston.

[2] *The Charleston News and Courier* for March 28, 1919.

and faithful man" had kept his sense of affection for those who had previously done everything for him; and to the end gave faithful service to the family to whom he and his ancestors had belonged. It was an echo from the past.

Thomas Roderick Dew, Professor of History, Metaphysics, and Political Law in William and Mary College in Virginia, and later its president, came forward in 1832 as the opponent of the Virginia anti-slavery men. He declared that it was wild to think of doing away with slavery in Virginia by any process of gradual emancipation as that advocated by Thomas Jefferson and his grandson. Besides, slavery was good for the blacks and for the whites. It was a benign institution to be encouraged and not destroyed. In 1836, Professor Dew delivered an address "On the Influence of the Federative Republican System of Government upon Literature and the Development of Character."[1] In an ordinary condition of society, he said, the dependent classes will be driven forward by their employers or, becoming discontented, will look with eyes of cupidity upon the fortunes of the rich and plunder them by legislative action. In a slaveholding country, political power is removed from the hands of those who might abuse it and the moral effects of the system are striking. In the South, the relation between capital and labor is kinder than anywhere else on earth. The slave is happy, except when "the very demons of Pandemonium" come and destroy his happiness. The negro slave compares himself with his own race; he does not covet the wealth of the rich, but identifies his interests with those of his master. He is free from care and from that constant feeling of insecurity that haunts the poor men of other countries. There are no riots in the South, no

[1] *Southern Literary Messenger*, ii, 261-282.

breaking of machinery, no scowl of discontent, no midnight murders.[1] The master is attached to his slaves by interests and by sympathy; he does not work them sixteen hours a day and turn them adrift without money upon a cold and inhospitable world when their labor will not support them. To the oft repeated argument that slavery was not only wrong, but was uneconomical, was wasteful in comparison with the wage system, another Virginian — George Fitzhugh — replied that that could only be because the employer of the free laborer secured a larger part of the produce of the wage earner than the master did of his slave. Free laborers, he declared, had not a thousandth part of the rights and liberties of negro slaves. By 1845, the Southerner had come to look upon himself as a superior being; and this was not confined to the slave owner, but was held by the Southern non-slave owners, and one might almost say that the slaves were actually superior to white wage earners because when dangerous and excessively laborious work was to be undertaken, Southern plantation owners sometimes employed white wage earners in order that the lives, the health, and the strength of their negro slaves might be conserved. Indeed, according to Fitzhugh,[2] the plantation system was a "beautiful example of communism, where each one receives not according to his labor, but according to his wants."

Before many years had passed away, the Southern planters began to think of themselves as an aristocracy. According to Gideon Welles, they read Sir Walter Scott's romances and in their "diseased imaginations" fancied themselves

---

[1] This speech was delivered four years after the Nat Turner insurrection.

[2] George Fitzhugh's *Sociology for The South, or the Failure of Free Society* (Richmond, 1854), p. 29. See also his *Cannibals All! or, Slaves without Masters* (Richmond, 1857); and Toombs's defence of slavery in 1853 in Phillips's *Robert Toombs*, 162; and Jeremiah Smith's *Is Slavery Sinful?* (Indianapolis, 1863).

"Cavaliers," [1] or the descendants of the Cavaliers of England of the seventeenth century in evident contradistinction to the offspring of the Puritans! [2] Governor J. H. Hammond of South Carolina, whose words have frequently been drawn upon, declared that "God created negroes for no other purpose than to be the subordinate 'hewers of wood and drawers of water' — that is, to be the slaves of the white race." He wished to see negro slaves on every spot of the earth's surface where their labor would be beneficial to the whites. [3] Southern slaves were much better off than thousands and thousands of operatives in English factories and mines. There was no wretchedness on Southern plantations comparable with that of English peasant life, where workers lived in filthy hovels with their pigs or in cellars with a family in each corner and where children of four years of age worked below ground. It was true that slaves were flogged, but so were the sailors and soldiers of England ; [4] and if an English laborer stole a lamb, he might be transported for life. As to the abolition of the slave trade, Hammond thought that was an impossibility. Before its ending had been decreed in 1787, forty-five thou-

---

[1] *Diary of Gideon Welles* (Boston, 1911), ii, 277, 312. A similar idea was expressed by Professor William E. Dodd in his stimulating article on "The Social Philosophy of the Old South" in the *American Journal of Sociology* for July, 1917, p. 742.

[2] See the present work, volume i, 145 note.

[3] *Selections from the Letters and Speeches of the Hon. James H. Hammond, of South Carolina*, p. 338. The quotation is from the speech which he delivered at Barnwell Court House on October 29, 1858. It is interesting to observe that the tenth rule for the guidance of Governor Hammond's overseer at his Silver Bluff Plantation commanded that "the sick must be treated with great tenderness."

[4] Flogging of American naval seamen was not abolished until 1850. The rules of Silver Bluff Plantation provided that the negroes must be flogged as seldom as possible and never kicked or struck, except in self-defence, and "the highest punishment must not exceed fifty lashes in one day." For the rules as to slaves in typical States, see H. Toulmin's *Digest of the Laws of . . . Alabama* (1823) using index under "slaves," "negroes," etc.; the *Revised Code of the Laws of Virginia* (2 vols., 1819) ; Littell and Swigert's *Digest of the Statute Law of Kentucky* (2 vols., 1822) ; and the *Civil Code of . . . Louisiana* (1825). For a comparison with earlier conditions, see the present work, vol. ii, 376–394.

sand Africans were carried in each year across the Atlantic with the loss of only five or ten in every hundred; but in 1840, if Sir Thomas Fowell Buxton's figures were right, the number of Africans annually transported across the sea had increased to one hundred and fifty thousand and the mortality had risen to twenty-five or thirty in each hundred.[1]

The Southerners now carried the fight into Congress and demanded the passage of a law excluding incendiary publications from the mails and the silencing of the abolition appeals to Congress for the stoppage of the slave trade in the District of Columbia, which the extremists of the North were constantly demanding of Congress. A bill was introduced to carry out the first demand, but it met with many difficulties and was defeated. In fact it was not necessary, because Amos Kendall, the postmaster general, aided and abetted his subordinates in taking the necessary action themselves. He had no power to prescribe rules for the exclusion of matter from the mails or to direct the non-delivery of any mail matter, he wrote; but if he were a local postmaster, he should act on his own responsibility. It really made very little difference whether such a law was passed or whether Amos Kendall wrote or did not write to his subordinates, for the Southern whites were determined that the flow of inflammatory papers, posters, and books to their plantations and people should cease. If the local postmasters did not do their duty, as the Southerners saw it, they themselves took possession of the mails [2] and destroyed whatever they listed.

[1] Hammond's *Two Letters on Slavery in the United States* (Columbia, 1845), p. 4.

[2] *Proceedings of the Citizens of Charleston on the Incendiary Machinations now in Progress against the Peace and Welfare of the Southern States* (Charleston, 1835). The seventh resolution declared that the citizens of Charleston were "united as one man in the fixed and unalterable determination to maintain our rights, and defend our property against all attacks, — be the consequences what they may." And the City Council, on its part, resolved that the Committee of

By 1836 the flood of anti-slavery petitions to Congress had reached a very high point. Ordinarily, the number of such petitions would have been very small; but the mere fact that the Southerners seemed to dread their coming incited the abolitionists to great exertions. Daniel Webster in the Senate and John Quincy Adams in the House were the members through whom chiefly these papers proceeded. They both presented them by the fifties and the hundreds, — on one occasion Adams put in as many as 511 at one time. Some of these petitions were signed by thousands, very many of the signers being women. Calhoun was deeply affected by this manifestation of Northern feeling for he had now come to be the champion of the plantation system in the Senate. Many Northern Democrats saw the danger of limiting the right of petition and Buchanan warned the Southerners that if it were once understood that the right of petition and the abolition of slavery must rise and fall together the consequences might be fatal. It was in the House, however, that the most dramatic scene occurred for there was John Quincy Adams, the venerable ex-President. All his earlier life, with the exception of a short time in the national Senate, had been passed in the diplomatic service or in administrative positions. He speedily learned the art of debating and soon gained a knowledge of parliamentary practice that with his fearlessness, vast learning, and mental alertness, even in these later years, made him one of the most dangerous opponents that the House of Representatives has ever known. It was practically impossible to stop him when he once got started and it was practically impossible to prevent his getting possession of the floor. If one attempt was blocked, he made another. In May,

Citizens appointed at this meeting be of mails and see that they are in-
instructed to attend the arrivals spected.

1836, the House adopted a rule that all petitions and papers relating in any way to the subject of slavery should, without being printed or being referred to committees, be laid on the table and no further action be taken thereon.   When his name was called for his vote, Adams refused to vote saying that he held "the resolution to be in direct violation of the constitution of the United States, of the rules of this House, and of the rights of my constituents." [1]   It was in the course of one of these debates that Adams informed the House (May 25, 1836) that the instant the slaveholding states become the theatre of war, civil, servile, or foreign, from that "instant the war powers of Congress extend to interference with the institution of slavery in every way," — to sustain it, or to abolish it, or even to the cession of a Slave State to a foreign power. [2]   The irritation became so great that the House adopted a further rule that petitions relating to slavery should not be received at all.   In February, 1837, Adams presented a petition purporting to come from twenty-two slaves and asked the Speaker if it could be received.   The Southerners stormed with fury.   They demanded that he should be censured and expelled.   After two days of vituperation, Adams gained the floor and stated that he doubted the genuineness of the document; and whether it was fraudulent or not, the petitioners asked that the Northerners should cease offering emancipation petitions and that the members who persisted in presenting them should be expelled. [3]

[1] *Journal of the House of Representatives*, 24th Cong., 1st Sess., p. 889; *Register of Debates*, xii, Pt. iv, 4062; and Adams's *Memoirs*, ix, 287. As showing Adams's place in the esteem of his fellow members, in 1839 for eleven days at the beginning of the session he presided over the House without any other authority than the good will of his fellow representatives. See J. T. Morse, Jr.'s *J. Q. Adams*, 291,

and Adams's *Diary* under date of December 2, 1839.

[2] The best description of J. Q. Adams's opinions on the effect of martial law on slavery is in the *Proceedings* of the Massachusetts Historical Society for January, 1902, p. 440.

[3] *Letters from John Quincy Adams to his Constituents of the Twelfth Congressional District in Massachusetts* (Boston, 1837), pp. 6, 7, 10–14; *Journal*

In December, 1844, Mr. Adams had the satisfaction of having the "gag rule" rescinded on his motion.[1]   Otherwise, up to this time, the abolitionists had accomplished nothing, except to arouse the fiercest resentment of the cotton planters of the South and to make them fear for the continuance of their prosperity and their peculiar form of society.

of the House of Representatives, 24th Cong., 2nd Sess., p. 350 and fol.; and *Register of Debates*, xiii, Pt. ii, col. 1586 and fol.

[1] Adams's *Memoirs*, xii, 115; *Journal*

of the House of Representatives, 28th Cong., 2nd Sess., p. 10 (Dec. 3, 1844); and *Congressional Globe*, xiv, p. 7.

NOTES

I. Bibliography. — The papers printed in the first two volumes of the *Documentary History of American Industrial Society* are valuable for an insight into the slave system.   The Introduction to this material by Professor Ulrich B. Phillips, the editor, is the best brief survey of the system that has been written.[1]   A longer account is Phillips's *American Negro Slavery* (New York, 1918).   The secondary title of this book is " A Survey of the Supply, Employment and Control of Negro Labor as Determined by the Plantation Régime," which well describes the contents ; but it also deals briefly with town slaves and free blacks.   It is based on much more material than that which is printed in the *Documentary History*.   Of the older books, R. F. W. Allston's *Essay on Sea Coast Crops;* F. L. Olmsted's *Journey in the Seaboard Slave States;* Charles Lyell's *Second Visit to the United States;* Frances Kemble's *Journal of a Residence on a Georgian Plantation in 1838–1839;* J. D. B. DeBow's *Industrial Resources . . . of the Southern and Western States* and the successive volumes of his *Review* are all instructive.   Of the more recent books, the first volume of James Ford Rhodes's *History of the United States since the Compromise of 1850* and Albert Bushnell Hart's *Slavery and Abolition, 1831–1841* in the "American Nation " series present the results of prolonged studies by Northern men.   There is a brief bibliography of secondary works on slavery in the *Documentary History*, i, 105, and a more extended list at the end of Professor Hart's volume.   The subject may be easily followed in the footnotes to Phillips's *Negro Slavery* and to Rhodes's chapters.

II. The Moderates. — William Jay of New York and William Ellery Channing, the Unitarian minister of Boston, trod the middle path that satisfies no one, but sometimes is the path of wisdom.   Jay was an early member of the American Anti-Slavery Society ; but he resigned from it when it advocated and encouraged measures that

---

[1] A list of Professor Phillips's writings on slavery follows this introduction ; of these the articles on "Southern Black Belts" in *American Historical Review*, xi, 798–816, and "The Economic Cost of Slaveholding" in the *Political Science Quarterly* for June, 1905, are the most suggestive.   Some of the most significant matter in the documents in the *American Industrial History* first appeared in the form of footnotes to these articles and Professor Phillips's contributions to *The South in the Building of the Nation* give his ideas in somewhat different form.

were directly against the Constitution of the United States.[1] Channing, in a tract entitled "Slavery," that was published at Boston in 1835, aroused the resentment of the Garrisonians by condemning the system of agitation adopted by them which had alarmed the considerate, had alienated multitudes, and had stirred up bitter passions. The abolitionists proposed to convert the slaveholders by exhausting on them the vocabulary of abuse, " and he has reaped as he sowed." Defences of slavery have been sent forth in the spirit of the dark ages and "something has been lost to the cause of freedom and humanity." Channing had lived on a Virginia plantation as a tutor in his early life and he resented the abusive tone of the abolitionist papers which gave the impression that the slave's abode was " perpetually resounding with the lash, and ringing with shrieks of agony." He thought that it was of the highest importance that emancipation should be followed by friendly relations between the whites and the blacks and that there was no power in the United States to remove slavery but the slaveholding States themselves.

[1] See Bayard Tuckerman's *William Jay and the Constitutional Movement for the Abolition of Slavery.*

CHAPTER VI

SOCIAL READJUSTMENTS IN THE FIRST HALF OF THE CENTURY

UNTIL the War of 1812 the people of the United States were occupied — apart from the necessary bread winning — with the resettlement of the political fabric after the separation from the British Empire. There had been reformers and philanthropists before 1783, but their voices had been those of individual men and women crying in the wilderness.[1] Of these the most interesting were Anthony Benezet and Benjamin Rush, both of Philadelphia. The former, under the sobriquet of "A Lover of Mankind," published a book in 1774 with the descriptive title of "The Mighty Destroyer Displayed, In some Account of the Dreadful HAVOCK made by the mistaken USE as well as ABUSE of DISTILLED SPIRITOUS LIQUORS." Benezet declared that the excessive and increasing use of liquors in America must be highly displeasing to the Creator who must see "his favourite creature man thus debased, disgraced, and destroyed both in body and soul." The curiously wrought human frame had been abused and disordered, so Benezet wrote, by irregularities of many kinds, "but never before to the enormous degree that it has of late years arrived at by the excessive abuse of these fermented, distilled spirituous liquors, which, by their mischievous effects, seem to claim Satan himself for their

[1] Mr. T. F. Currier, Assistant Librarian of Harvard College, has greatly assisted me in collecting material for this chapter by searching through and sorting out by topics the unplaced pamphlets in the Harvard Library.

For drinking habits and lotteries in earlier times, see the present work, vol. iv, 16 and 24.

author." Dr. Rush was Physician General to the Military
Hospitals of the United States in the early years of the
Revolutionary War.[1] In the performance of his functions,
he drew up "Directions for Preserving the Health of Soldiers." This tract was published first in the "Pennsylvania
Packet" in 1777, and republished as a small pamphlet by
direction of the Board of War. Thirty-one years later in
1808 it was reprinted in Cutbush's "Observations on the
Means of Preserving the Health of Soldiers and Sailors"
and a century later was reproduced in facsimile. Another
of Dr. Rush's temperance publications was entitled "An
Inquiry into the Effects of Spirituous Liquors on the Human
Body."[2] This was even more popular than the earlier essay
and was still being reprinted in 1823. Rush thought that
rum, instead of abating the effect of heat and cold, increased
them and left the body languid and more liable to be affected
by heat and cold afterwards. Horses, he affirmed, performed their labors with no other liquor than cold water
and the soldiers of ancient Rome carried vinegar in their
canteens instead of spirits. One of the most effective and
revolting pictures of drunkenness to be found in the temperance literature is in Rush's "Inquiry." He declared

[1] The first third of Harry G. Good's
*Benjamin Rush and his Services to
American Education* (Berne, Indiana,
1918) is in reality a sketch of Dr. Rush's
career.

[2] This was written in 1784, but the
earliest edition that I have seen was
printed at Boston in 1790. The quotations in the text are taken from the
8th edition, which was printed at Boston in 1823 with the following title. —
*An Inquiry into the Effects of Ardent
Spirits upon the Human Body and
Mind.* Either in whole or in part
this essay was repeated again and
again in temperance publications of
one sort or another.

"A Moral and Physical Ther-

mometer" appears either at the end or
the beginning of the "Inquiry." It
met with such favor that it was reproduced widely in temperance publications. It is noteworthy that Rush
held that "small beer" led to serenity
of mind, reputation, long life, and
happiness, and that cider, wine, and
beer, when taken in small quantities
and at meals conduced to cheerfulness,
strength, and nourishment. Punch and
drams were all below zero and led to
the debtor's prison or to the gallows.
Attempts were also made to express
the dangers of intemperance by cartog-
raphy, as in the "Temperance Map"
by C. Wiltberger, Jr.

that the drunkard resembled a calf in folly, an ass in stupidity, a tiger in cruelty, a skunk in fetor, and a hog in filthiness. The drunkard's houses were gradually stripped of their furniture, their windows shattered, their barns had leaky roofs, and "their children [were] filthy and half clad, without manners, principles, and_morals." The good doctor's idea that opium and water would be a good cure for the rum habit is rather appalling to twentieth-century practice.[1]

With the close of the Second War with England, the American conscience seemed to awaken to the evils of everyday social practices and this awakening process went on with redoubled vigor every decade down to 1860. It does not by any means follow that there was any looser sense of moral obligations in 1820 than there had been in 1800 or in 1770. The concentration of the population in commercial cities and industrial towns brought poverty, crime, and intemperance to the notice of the people, for one drunkard apiece in ten towns of one thousand inhabitants each would arouse little thought, whereas ten drunkards in the public square of one town of ten thousand inhabitants would excite animadversions. The rapid fluctuations in the means of existence that were concomitant with embargo, war, and financial panic possibly increased poverty and riches at the extremities of the social scale. There may have been more drinking in these classes and there certainly was a development of crime in some directions, as in counterfeiting; but this was the result of the tremendous increase in paper money. The recent improvements in transportation brought people together and made possible association for carrying on this or that social readjustment.

[1] In December, 1790, the physicians of Philadelphia — presumably at Dr. Rush's instigation — memorialized the federal government to restrict the use of spirits as beverages by imposing heavy duties upon them. See *American State Papers, Miscellaneous*, i, 20.

Societies were organized, committees appointed, and reports made as to social matters in much the same way that earlier local political affairs had been reformed. The net result of all this inquiry, consultation, and agitation was a conviction on the part of large numbers of very good and earnest persons that the modes of treating misfortune and crime that had come from England by way of the colonies required most thorough reformation, and that the labor system of the North and the South needed radical readjustment.

Whether the considerations contained in the preceding paragraph are true or false there can be no question whatever that the first half century under the Constitution saw a most appalling consumption of alcoholic stimulants throughout the country and among all classes of people,[1] clergymen, women, and even children, on occasion joining the mass of mankind in this custom. Lyman Beecher, in his "Autobiography," describes the scene at a Connecticut ordination: how the sideboard was set with decanters, glasses, sugar bowls, and lemons. The ministers stepped up again and again to get a drink, and as the day wore on the sideboard "with the spillings of water, and sugar, and liquor, looked and smelled like the bar of a very active grog-shop."[2]   Liquor was served at funerals, to the mourn-

---

[1] Hamilton in his report on the "Public Credit" of January 9, 1790 (*American State Papers, Finance,* i, 22) states that the consumption of ardent spirits, partly because of their cheapness, "is carried to an extreme which is truly to be regretted, as well in regard to the health and morals, as to the economy of the community." Should the increase of duties that he suggested tend to a decrease in the consumption of spirits, the effect would be desirable in every way.

[2] Lyman Beecher's *Autobiography* (New York, 1864), i, 245. A readable and probably exaggerated account of the drinking habits of the second quarter of the century is in P. S. White and E. S. Ely's *Vindication of the Order of the Sons of Temperance* (New York, 1848). Beecher in 1812 asserted that five gallons of distilled spirits per capita was the ordinary yearly consumption. By 1840, it appears that the per capita consumption had fallen to about one-half of that of 1810. See Beecher on the *Reformation of Morals,* 9; Tench Coxe's *Statement of the Arts and Manufactures of the United States, . . . 1810,* Tabular Statement, Pt. i, 22; *Permanent Temperance Documents,* i, 493; American Temperance Society's *Second Annual Report,* 48; *Cyclopaedia of Temperance and Pro-*

ers, sometimes repeatedly. In some of the prisons, as in Massachusetts, beer was served to the inmates. The idea prevailed that no strenuous labor could safely be performed without alcoholic stimulation. It was the custom, therefore, to provide large quantities of crude liquor for the workers in the haying fields and on the wharves. At house raisings, where the friends and neighbors gathered to assist, spirits were consumed so freely that it was desirable to have a doctor in attendance to set the limbs of any one who should fall from plate, rafter, or ridgepole. In those days it was customary in some places to "vend" the poor to the highest bidder, that is to the man who would pay most for the services of those able to work and charge least for the care of the aged and impotent; in some towns this practice was made still worse by the custom of furnishing rum and other spirits free to the bidders.[1] In some parts of the country, whiskey took the place of money and ministers and teachers received their compensation in the form of gallons of spirits; and there were cases where clergymen dealt in alcoholic beverages.[2] There were towns where the "settled" minister was entitled to a free dram before he began the Sunday services.[3] Drinking was not by any means confined to the

hibition, 129; Tucker's Progress of the United States, 163; and J. D. B. De Bow's Statistical View, 182. For another estimate see Circular Addressed to the Members of the Massachusetts Society for Suppressing Intemperance (Boston, 1814).

[1] Levi W. Leonard's History of Dublin, N. H., 26, 269. It is worthy of remark that in 1842 a Washingtonian Society was formed at Dublin and in 1844 the town went "no license" and since then no liquor has been legally sold within its limits. The practice of vending the paupers and of supplying the bidders with drink, was common in those days as in the neighboring town of Peterborough: see its History by Albert Smith, p. 179.

[2] In 1816 the General Conference of the Methodist Episcopal Church resolved "That no stationed or local preacher shall retail spirituous or malt liquors without forfeiting his ministerial character among us." Daniel Dorchester's Liquor Problem in All Ages, 193; and Journals of the General Conference of the Methodist Episcopal Church . . . 1796–1836, i, 168. See also Sweet's Circuit-Rider Days in Indiana, 69, and Ohio Church History Society's Papers, vi, p. 8.

[3] See T. S. Griffiths' History of Baptists in New Jersey, 513; on the other hand the Baptist church at Bordentown resolved in 1832 to admit only total abstainers, ibid., 511.

Before coffee and tea came into

northern part of the country, for Moncure D. Conway relates that in Falmouth, Virginia, there was a "rough corner"
where whiskey was abundant; on Saturday nights many of
the country folk depended on the sobriety of horse or mule to
get them safely home.[1]   In short, in the dearth of recreations
— of athletics and of the motion picture — the people
drank rum in New England and whiskey in the South and
in the West, — and alcoholic stimulants were so cheap that
it was said " a man could get drunk twice in America for six-
pence."

The growing poverty of large portions of the people led
men and women, some of them gathered into societies and
others working independently, to scan closely the causes of
pauperism and crime.   In Philadelphia and in New York,
they came to the conclusion that intemperance and in-
discriminate charity were the chief causes of distress and
wrong-doing.   Societies made reports and the churches took
action.   In the West and in the South, the Methodist Church
became a temperance society[2] and in New England the
Congregational Associations took up the matter.   In
Connecticut, where the temperance movement was vigorous,
the Association recommended that church members should
exercise vigilance,[3] should cease to use ardent spirits ordinarily in the family, and should substitute palatable and
nutritious drinks for liquors for their employees, giving them

[1] Moncure D. Conway's *Autobiography, Memories and Experiences*, i,
14; Arethusa Hall's *Life and Character of Sylvester Judd*, 315. White
and Ely's *Vindication of . . . the Sons
of Temperance* (New York, 1848)
contains an excellent *ex parte* account

common use as a matutinal stimulant,
it was the general practice in England as well as in America to take a
"morning draught." See, for example,
the numerous entries to this effect in
the diary of Samuel Pepys.

of this early crusade against the use of
alcoholic beverages.

[2] On the attitude of the Methodists toward temperance see W. W.
Sweet's *Circuit-Rider Days in Indiana*,
69, 147; E. J. Pilcher's *Protestantism
in Michigan*, 130; A. H. Bedford's
Western Cavaliers, 83; and innumerable other books of the same general
character.

[3] See *Intemperance. An Address,
to the Churches and Congregations*
(Hartford, 1813).

additional compensation, if necessary, instead of the customary dram.[1] Like all earnest persons, temperance reformers saw only one side and described in trenchant phrases what they saw or what they thought they saw. To read some of their descriptions of American life in the first thirty years of the century, one would suppose that the country was on the edge of dissolution instead of actually girding up its loins for the work that "Destiny" had provided for it. An article in "The Clergyman's Almanack" for 1812 after dealing with the evils of intemperance sums up the whole matter in an answer to the inquiry as to "Who hath wo"? and who in the morning of life has an impaired memory, a bloated face, and a broken constitution by saying that it is "*they* who greedily swallow *liquid fire*, and are 'never satisfied.'" Falsehood, fraud, theft, and profanity are the result of the "cup of intemperance." In 1826, Lyman Beecher of Litchfield, Connecticut, preached "Six Sermons" which inaugurated the new temperance movement that culminated in the legislation of the middle of the century.[2] He had been impressed with the evils of intemperance in his earlier residence as pastor of a Long Island parish and things that he had seen after his return to Connecticut had in no way softened the impression. Daily drinking, he declared in one of his "Six Sermons," generated a host of bodily infirmities and diseases: "loss of appetite — nausea

[1] The reform found favor with the owners of merchant vessels for it did away with a distinct item of expense, as Dana noted in his *Two Years Before the Mast*, which describes a voyage made in the years 1834–1836. The serving of grog to crews of naval vessels lasted much longer and was not finally done away with until 1862. See Allen's "Introduction" to the *Papers of . . . Dallas (Publications* of the Naval History Society, viii), p. xxiii. In 1831, however, by order of the Secretary of the Navy, all persons in the naval service might commute their spirit ration for money payment; *Writings of Levi Woodbury,* i, 454.

[2] Beecher relates the circumstances of the writing of these sermons in his *Autobiography*, ii, ch. v. They were first printed in 1827 and reprinted over and over again in the following years. The full title is *Six Sermons on the Nature, Occasions, Signs, Evils, and Remedy of Intemperance.*

at the stomach — disordered bile — obstructions of the
liver — jaundice — dropsy — hoarseness of voice — coughs
— consumptions — rheumatic pains — epilepsy — gout —
colic — palsy — apoplexy — insanity," — these were the
results of moderate tippling according to this clerical
diagnostician. Looking about him, Beecher was dismayed
at the difficulty of the minority's enforcing laws in the teeth
of the opposition of the majority; he asserted that the
magistrates could not put a stop to the drinking of ardent
spirits amid a population who are in favor of free indulgence.
Even associations to support the authorities were ineffectual
because the efforts required to keep up their energy never
had been and never would be made. The only efficacious
course to pursue was to associate for the special purpose of
superintending the reformations of the people's habits.
In this Beecher was no doubt mistaken, for it seems certain
that a nation's habits can be markedly changed by legislation which, in the course of years, sets up a new standard
in men's minds and consciences. The license system aroused
the indignation of the temperance people because it seemed
to give the sanction of the community to the selling of
liquor and gave the holder of a license a feeling that he had
some vested rights which could not be interfered with. Another mode of dealing with the problem was to place so heavy
a tax upon the distillation and sale of spirits that only the
well-to-do could use them, and a third method had much the
same idea at bottom. This was to prohibit the importation or sale of rum, whiskey, or brandy in smaller quantities
than fifteen gallons or twenty gallons or ninety gallons.[1] Of
course all expedients of high taxes and limited sales bore
heavily upon the common people, while leaving the rich un-

[1] See the interesting *Argument of Peleg Sprague, Esq.* before a com- mittee of the Massachusetts legis- lature, February, 1839.

touched. None of these plans found favor with the new temperance reformers. Limited drinking, license systems, fifteen gallon laws, were about as bad to their minds as absolute freedom. What they wanted was prohibition, pure and simple.

Societies were formed in several States and an educational propaganda was carried on by means of the press and of the lecture platform. Mason L. Weems's "Drunkard's Looking Glass" was published in 1812 and recited vividly the evils of excessive drinking as did Peter Parley's "Five Letters" and Sargent's "Temperance Tales." [1] In 1833, the National Convention of Temperance Workers was held at Philadelphia. Four hundred and forty delegates attended from the local societies and adopted resolutions to the effect that it was the duty of all men to abstain from the use of ardent spirits as morally wrong and that pure water was the only substitute. Within twenty years seven Presidents or ex-Presidents of the United States acceded to a declaration that the drinking of ardent spirits was not only needless, but hurtful and that its discontinuance would be for the good of the country and the world. [2] The man who by indomitable

[1] Among Sargent's twenty-one *Temperance Tales* in seven volumes may be mentioned "Kitty Grafton," "The Stage Coach," and "Margaret's Bridal." G. B. Cheever's *True History of Deacon Giles' Distillery* and *The Dream: or The True History of Deacon Giles's Distillery, and Deacon Jones's Brewery*, also by Cheever, were landmarks of the movement, but offended the supposed Deacon Giles and led to a trial for libel and to *A Defence in Abatement of Judgment* by Cheever. These seem rather forced nowadays as also do Peter Parley's *Five Letters to my Neighbor Smith, touching the Fifteen Gallon Jug,* and *The Cracked Jug, or Five Answers to My Neighbor Parley's Five Letters . . . by "Neighbor Smith."* In lighter vein and not so effective was *The Evils of Intemperance, Exempli-* fied in Poetry and Prose with Engravings that was published at Boston in 1829. For some years a *Temperance Almanac* was published by the Massachusetts Temperance Union; the numbers for 1841 and 1842 have some striking illustrations and the number for 1843 has an article by Nathaniel Hawthorne entitled "A Rill from the Town Pump." Among the most effective short pieces were Thomas Herttell's *Exposé of the Causes of Intemperate Drinking and the Means by which it may be Obviated* which was first published at New York, in 1819 and Professor Edward Hitchcock's *Essay on Temperance, addressed particularly to Students* and printed at Amherst in 1830.

[2] See "Thirteenth Annual Report," p. 37, in *Permanent Temperance Documents,* iii.

will and strong physique made possible the passage of actual prohibitory legislation was Neal Dow of Portland, Maine. He had been led to interest himself in the matter by the misfortunes of a neighboring family which were due to the intemperance of the father. Total abstinence to him seemed to be the only goal to gain. At first he tried to reach it by persuasion, by inducing those around him to become total abstainers. He travelled up and down the State speaking everywhere with great effect and supported by a band of lecturers and by literary propaganda. The Washingtonian movement also came to his aid. This was started by a group of half a dozen steady drinkers at Baltimore, who had themselves been greatly stirred by a temperance lecturer, Matthew Hale Smith, by name. They pledged themselves not to drink any spirituous or malt liquors, wine, or cider. These reformed drunkards immediately began making converts at home; soon they travelled over the country securing attention by reason of their past histories, more, perhaps, than by their eloquence. But there were temperance lecturers outside of the Washingtonians who possessed power to attract and convert their fellow men and women, as John B. Gough, although he gained his end rather by the vigor of his utterance than by the use of his mind. In 1849, Father Mathew, the Irish Catholic temperance reformer, landed in New York and received a great ovation.[1]

In 1846, Neal Dow induced the Maine legislature to pass the first law in our history designed to absolutely prohibit the sale of liquor as a beverage. It proved to be difficult to enforce this law. In 1851, Dow drew up a measure which he thought would be effective and would not arouse the extreme opposition that the earlier act had excited. He

[1] See J. F. Maguire's *Father Mathew*, 460–518.

took this bill with him to the State capital and by his own efforts prevailed upon the legislature to pass it.[1] This was the famous "Maine Liquor Law" which became the model for all similar legislation. By it the sale of intoxicating liquors and the manufacture of them were prohibited, except for medicinal and mechanical purposes, under reasonable but increasing penalties. At first these were fines, but for the third offence a jail sentence of from three to six months was provided in addition to the fine and in every case the seized liquors were to be destroyed. Dow, himself, was mayor of the city of Portland. Proceeding home he gave the liquor dealers a limited time in which to transport their goods out of the State and then he seized and destroyed whatever remained. The passage of this law marked the beginning of the incoming tide of temperance legislation. Some years before, in 1839, the Ohio legislature had provided for partial prohibition; in 1850 it prohibited all retail trade in spirits for beverage purposes and in 1851 an amendment of the State constitution forbade the establishment of any system licensing the sale of liquors within the State. In 1851, the Illinois legislature by law prohibited the sale of spirituous liquors to be drunk on the premises. By the end of 1856, indeed, thirteen of the existing States had more or less thoroughly abolished the sale of spirituous beverages.[2] In all these States, however, cider made from apples grown within the State limits was permitted and from the ex-parte accounts of the reformers, there was about as much drunkenness in the "cider-growing States" as there was before the passage of the prohibitory legislation. In running over the list of the States, one is impressed with the fact that not

[1] *Reminiscences of Neal Dow*, ch. xiv. The act was entitled "An Act for the Suppression of Drinking Houses & Tippling Shops" and is printed in the collected statutes of Maine and separately.
[2] For a convenient summary of this legislation, see Woolley and Johnson's *Temperance Progress*, 138–141.

one of them below Mason and Dixon's line prohibited the
sale of liquor by State law and that only two of those north
of that line, one east and one west of the Appalachians, did
not enact prohibition. Maine, New Hampshire, and Vermont have continued prohibition from 1860 down to the
present day; but the other States by positive enactment
or by judicial action restored freedom or local option
in the matter of making and selling alcoholic beverages.
In 1868, the Massachusetts prohibition law was repealed
largely in consequence of the efforts of John A. Andrew,
the "War Governor" of that State, who held that no government had the right to restrain a man's rational liberty to
regulate his private conduct and affairs [1] or "to punish one
man in advance for the possible fault of another." Prohibition was reënacted in 1869, but in 1870, the sale of fermented
liquors was allowed. In 1875, a local option law by which
the voters of each town decided each year whether they would
have license or prohibition was enacted. In the same year
Michigan repealed her prohibitory law and Connecticut had
already restored the license system. Indeed, at the close
of that year only three States were constant to the temperance ideals of 1860. In all the discussions of these laws,
the difficulty of enforcing them was constantly brought
forward and the impolicy of having laws on the statute
book that could not be carried out was reiterated.

The philanthropists and reformers were united in regarding intemperance in the use of alcoholic beverages as the
predisposing cause of poverty and crime. This they were
all agreed on, but nowadays students would attribute much
of the excess in pauperism and wickedness to the social unrest
that is the concomitant and follower of periods of war.
However this may be, it is certain that in whatever direction

---

[1] *The Errors of Prohibition* by John A. Andrew.

the American investigator turned his eyes — and the same thing was true of the European reformer — he was appalled at the conditions of the prisons and of the prisoners. In the olden time the American colonists had simply reproduced the penology of their English forbears.[1] That had been brutal, as it was contemporaneously in the continental countries of Europe. Death met the convicted perpetrator of every serious crime, and the rest were treated with pitiless publicity combined with bodily pain, — flogging, mutilation, branding, and exposure to the taunts and missiles of the populace. The non-payment of a debt in "those good old days" was looked upon as practically equivalent to theft. In the course of long exposure to new conditions, there had been some changes in the old rules for dealing with crime and some of those that had not been changed by legislation had been seldom if ever actually used in practice in the colonies. With the Revolution began a new outlook, although it must be said that such amelioration as there was was slow and sporadic. The number of capital crimes was greatly diminished and the punishment of those that did not bring death was changed from pain and humiliation to imprisonment.[2] Before this time, the prison had been looked upon as a place of detention for those owing money and for persons accused of crime while awaiting trial; when convicted of felony or misdemeanor the punishment was not another period of detention in prison, but some form of summary punishment or execution.

With the changed ideas, the prison became the instrument of punishment and of hoped-for reformation, but the early prisons were far from filling either of these require-

[1] See the present work, volume i, index under "crime"; ii, 392–394; iii, 570–572.

[2] In 1829, the Boston Prison Discipline Society reported that there were then twelve capital offences in Massachusetts to one in Pennsylvania. In the Southern States death was provided for numerous offences on the part of a slave (pp. 31–54).

ments.[1] In them the prisoners were confined in large rooms, there being ten, twenty, thirty inmates in each.[2] These were indiscriminately assigned to whichever room was then filling up — poor debtors, murderers awaiting execution, accused persons awaiting trial — all placed together — men, women, children, white and black, sane and insane. These early prisons were sinks of iniquity and schools of corruption and crime.[3] There was no attempt made to warm them, or ventilate them, or keep them clean; the inmates slept on the floor or on mattresses if they had money to procure them, and in some cases hammocks were used when the floor was filled. Attempts were occasionally made at classification, placing the poor debtors by themselves and relegating the insane to the cellar; but in these early days women were regarded as equals of men and treated accordingly without any favors. In some cases, as with the poor debtors, the inhabitants of the early prisons were permitted to labor in the daytime, but by sundown were locked up in the night rooms. The Pennsylvanians and New Yorkers were the

[1] For a summary of prison conditions up to 1828 or 1829, see Boston Prison Discipline Society's *Fourth Annual Report* (2nd ed.), pp. 265-288; especially pp. 285-288. Gamaliel Bradford's *State Prisons and the Penitentiary System Vindicated* (Charlestown, 1821) is an illuminating essay from several points of view. See also Harry E. Barnes's *History of the Penal . . . Institutions of . . . New Jersey* (Trenton, 1908). *New York City Document No. 29* contains a survey of the old penal institutions with recommendations for their betterment.

The old copper mine prison at Simsbury, Connecticut, has received altogether undeserved notoriety owing, probably in part, to Walter Bates's *The Mysterious Stranger; or Memoirs of . . . William Newman* (New Haven, 1817). The copper mines were used for a time as prisons and Tories were confined there for a few months, but they proved to be undesirable and the mines, in later years, were used only as sleeping rooms for the prisoners who were employed in a building on the surface in the daytime. See Noah A. Phelps's *History of Simsbury, Granby and Canton* (Hartford, 1845), ch. x; and an illustrated article in the *Magazine of American History*, xv, 321. E. A. Kendall visited Simsbury in 1807 and described the prison in his *Travels*, i, ch. xxi, which is repeated in Barber's *Connecticut Historical Collections*, 95.

[2] Boston Prison Discipline Society's *Reports*, i, 38, 39.

[3] Counterfeiting was very prevalent in those days. The *Second Report* of the Boston Prison Discipline Society (1827, p. 40) enumerates "237 different kinds of counterfeit bills on the banks of 18 different States and Canada." It is said that the art was regularly taught in some prisons — also lock-picking and pocket-picking.

first to try to inaugurate a better state of affairs. As the existing prisons were seminaries of sin where experts in crime taught counterfeiting, lock-picking, and other evil things to attentive audiences, one way out seemed to be to compel solitude, which would have the further advantage of providing time for contemplation and possibly for self-reformation. Another plan was to secure all the advantages of solitude by confinement in single cells at night and a gang system of labor during the day in absolute silence. These came to be known as the Pennsylvania and the Auburn systems of prison management, or sometimes as the solitary and congregate systems.[1] The solitary system was seen at its best in the Eastern Pennsylvania Penitentiary at Philadelphia.[2] There each convict occupied a single cell of good size, communicating with an exercise yard into which he was permitted to go for an hour or so a day. At first it was not intended that the prisoners should engage in labor, but should spend their whole time in solitary contemplation. These cells were lighted from above, provided with water and drainage, and were heated. In this system no attempt whatever was made to punish or reform by bodily torments or deprivations. Everything was to be accomplished by solitude, by enforced and absolute solitude. Before the prison was opened, a change was made in the plan by which labor in the cells was provided. This change had been brought about by an experiment that had been made on eighty selected convicts at Auburn, New York, by direction of the State legislature in 1821. In this case cells were constructed of moderate size, the convicts were placed in their cells and there remained under constant observation

---

[1] See Note II at the end of chapter.
[2] See *Description of the Eastern Penitentiary* published by C. G. Childs, Engraver at Philadelphia, in 1829 and *A Vindication of the Separate System of Prison Discipline from the Misrepresentations of the North American Review, July, 1839* (Philadelphia, 1839).

without work and not allowed to speak or, during the daytime, to lie down. The consequence was that in less than three years' time, they had so declined in health, had died from consumption, or had become insane that the governor pardoned the survivors.[1] In the Eastern Pennsylvania Penitentiary labor was combined with solitude, the prisoners making shoes or textiles, each in his own cell. As years went by the austerity of the system was relaxed, instruction was introduced to a degree, more books were permitted, visitors became more frequent, and the convicts were permitted to raise flowers in their little yards.

The Auburn system was developed by Captain Elam Lynds. The central idea was solitude gained by solitary confinement at night in small cells, only a little longer and wider than the cot on which the prisoner slept, and hard labor during the day. At daybreak, the wardens unlocked the doors, the prisoners, each with his pail and mush-kid, "locked marched" to the shop, depositing his utensils on the way. At the appointed hour they locked marched to the eating room where they breakfasted sitting back to back, then again to the shop and, later, to dinner and then back to the shops. At night, after labor hours, they locked marched to the water supply where they got their pails, to the kitchen where they received their kids of mush and molasses, and then to the cell, where they were locked in for the night. At nine the bugle announced the time of retirement and all went to bed. Discipline was enforced, partly by corporal punishment at once on the slightest infractions of the rules or, in serious cases, by flogging in the presence of the higher officers. More especially, however, it was enforced by the remarkable power of Elam Lynds,

[1] G. Powers' *Brief Account of the . . . New-York State Prison at Auburn*, 32–36.

who is said to have gone among the convicts absolutely unarmed. It was a system of terrorism, but the actual amount of bodily punishment inflicted per convict was very small. Moreover, the labor of the convicts was so profitable that several prisons conducted on the Auburn plan actually brought in money to the State.[1] The success of the Auburn system depended in great measure upon the construction of the prison. The cells were built in five tiers back to back in the centre of a building eighteen to twenty feet wider than the combined length of two cells. A platform three feet wide ran around each tier, leaving five or six feet next to the side of the building unoccupied from floor to ceiling.[2] Escape was practically impossible and the slightest noise was at once heard.[3] The building was warmed by stoves on the ground floor and there was a ventilation pipe in the back of each cell. Commendable efforts were made to keep the cells clean. At Auburn, the atmosphere seems to have been fair, but at Sing Sing and at other prisons which were constructed on the same plan as Auburn, the dampness of the surrounding country, or some other cause, made the conditions of the night cells unfavorable to health.[4]

The two systems of prison discipline had scarcely got into working order when disputations began between the advo-

[1] See Beaumont and De Tocqueville's *Penitentiary System in the United States*, 279–285; Boston Prison Discipline Society's *Second Annual Report* (1827), p. 97, and *Fourth Annual Report* (1829), p. 94.

[2] In the State Prison, at Thomaston, Maine, the night rooms were cellars or pits, entered by ladders through trap doors in the ceiling as one entered a ship's hold through a hatchway. This arrangement had been designed for solitary perpetual confinement but was never used for that purpose; it proved unwieldy in the hard labor, solitary night system and especially so when the crowded condi-

tion of the prison compelled the confinement of two prisoners in one of these pits. Boston Prison Discipline Society's *Second Report* (Boston, 1827), pp. 81–83.

[3] See *Report of Gershom Powers, Agent and Keeper of the State Prison at Auburn* (1828) and *Letter of Gershom Powers . . . in relation to the Auburn State Prison* (1829).

[4] The difficulty of heating a prison of this type is brought out in the *Minutes of the Testimony . . . [on] the Condition of Connecticut State Prison* (Hartford, 1834), pp. 4, 10, 68, etc.

cates of one or the other of them. Societies for the study
and improvement of prison conditions were founded in
Pennsylvania, New York, and Massachusetts. Of these the
Massachusetts society was active in printing and most of its
officers were ardent advocates of the Auburn plan. It will
be seen, therefore, that easily available statistics usually
point to the success of that system and the failure of the
Pennsylvania plan. In reality, the statistics are so constructed that it is impossible to reach any valid conclusion
from a study of those that can be found, and the arguments
of those who wrote on the one side or the other appear to be
extremely prejudiced. It would seem to be clear that almost
any plan of prison administration and treatment of convicts
works well in the beginning, — as long as the buildings are
new and the administrators enthusiastic. In time the
buildings become overcrowded and insanitary, inferior
persons are employed as underkeepers, and the psychological
glamour of the earlier years is replaced by a general penitentiary gloom. Where once there was health there now is
disease; where once there was more or less cheerful acquiescence there now is friction. In the history of all experiments
of the continuous solitary system, consumption, dementia,
and insanity supervened and so shocked the community
that modifications had to be made. The Auburn system at
first was carried on by fear: the new-comer was completely
"curbed," to use Captain Lynds's expressive word; a
wink or a whisper brought a blow from the keeper and
"stripes," which was a politer word than flogging, awaited
any further resistance. Corporal punishment by the cowskin
whip or the cat o' nine tails was going out of fashion as the
middle of the century approached,[1] and as soon as the nature

---

[1] In the latter part of the eighteenth
century, petty larceny was punished
in Indiana by not exceeding fifteen
lashes on the bare back (Esarey's
Indiana, i, 148). Massachusetts did
away with whipping as a punishment

of the method by which discipline was enforced in prisons of the congregate system became public by some distressing example, it was inevitable that opinion would turn against it as it had earlier turned against the solitary system. Both plans, therefore, were modified. The inmates of solitary prisons were given more human companionship and more opportunities for relaxation, and the inmates of congregate prisons, like the Massachusetts State prison, were permitted to talk while at work, so that the difference between the two became simply one of laboring alone or in company.[1] The keepers of the prisons of that time seem to be fairly united in doubts as to the reforming of any considerable number of convicts. The solitary plan was believed to give abundant opportunity for introspection and for the making of good resolutions; but the number of reconvictions under this system seems to have been sufficiently large to cast doubts on its efficacy in this respect. On the other hand, the Auburn system in its pristine vigor was not supposed to reform, but to habituate a man to obedience and labor; it is certain, however, that either of them was preferable to the old plan of promiscuous herding in idleness. When the prisoner's term of service was over or upon his pardon, he was given a new suit and three or

for crime in 1813 (*Public and General Laws of . . . Massachusetts*, Boston, 1816, iv, 341). The Harrison County whipping post in western Virginia was hewed down in 1810 according to Mr. E. C. Smith of Clarksburg, West Virginia. In 1831, Levi Woodbury, who was then Secretary of the Navy, informed the commanding officers that the President and the Department wished them to substitute fines, badges of disgrace, and "other mild corrections" for whipping, whenever the laws permitted (*Writings of Levi Woodbury*, i, 454). Owing to the persistent endeavors of Senator John P. Hale of New Hampshire, flogging in the navy was abolished in 1850 by act of Congress (*Statutes at Large*, ix, 515). As a rule the reformers of those days were more solicitous of the backs of convicts and slaves than they were of the backs of free American citizens. On the general subject, see *An Essay on Flogging in the Navy*, reprinted from the *Democratic Review* for 1849, and Gardner W. Allen's "Introduction" to *The Papers of . . . Dallas* (Naval History Society's *Publications*, viii), p. xxiii.

[1] For an account of this prison see Gamaliel Bradford's *Description and Historical Sketch of the Massachusetts State Prison* (Charlestown, 1816).

five dollars in money. Some keepers added good advice and in some places there were societies for the aid of discharged prisoners. The number of reconvictions was disheartening, taking the country through, although it should be said that those who had experienced the Auburn system in its first days preferred to commit the next crime outside the limits of New York State.

In the preceding paragraphs the treatment of persons convicted of crime has alone been considered; but there were four or five poor debtors to one regular criminal in the prisons of the Northern and Middle States. In a period of eight months and eighteen days from June, 1829, to February, 1830, 817 persons were imprisoned for debt in the city of Philadelphia alone. Of these 30 owed less than one dollar each and 233 between one dollar and five dollars. Nearly six hundred of the total number owed less than twenty dollars and only 98 over one hundred dollars. In Rochester, New York, in the year 1830, 24 persons were imprisoned in the county jail for debts of less than one dollar, ranging from six cents to ninety cents apiece.[1] Imprisonment for debt takes us back to the England of Fielding and Smollett and Daniel Defoe. The Fleet Prison, with its great halls filled with helpless, hopeless human beings had its replica in Philadelphia, New York, and other American cities and towns. The theory underlying imprisonment for debt was that the unlawful conversion of another man's property to one's own use was criminal. It was also held that one way to secure the payment of the debt was to imprison the debtor and thereby arouse the active interest of his family and of all those who were likely to be called upon to

[1] See Boston Prison Discipline Society's *Reports*, v, 38, 50, and vi, 57. A powerful indictment of the existing system was published at New York in 1818 under the title of *A Disquisition on Imprisonment for Debt as the Practice exists in the State of New York. By Howard.*

take any part in his support to bring about his release and, thereby, enable him again to take up the business of family bread winning. Many of the imprisonments for small amounts are said to have borne the character of spite persecutions; but it is difficult to understand how a man would take forethought and loan a proposed victim twenty-five cents for the purpose of afterwards imprisoning him. There is no question, however, as to the multitude of imprisonments for less than twenty dollars, and the position of these small debtors was peculiarly hard, because in most of the States they could not claim a hearing before a regular judge, but could be imprisoned upon an execution obtained from an exiguous magistrate. From such statistics as one can procure and such other indications as there are, it would seem that the first third of the nineteenth century was the heyday of prosecutions for debt. There may have been more poor debtors, more poverty stricken persons in those times of rapid financial changes, or it may be that in the recurrent financial crises, creditors found it more necessary to secure the moneys that were due them. The prisons were overflowing with poor debtors and the scandalous conditions attending their incarceration aroused the attention of philanthropists and legislators. Already, the poor debtor's oath had been devised by which a confessed bankrupt, on giving up all his property, with certain trifling exceptions,[1] and swearing that he had none concealed, could be released from all obligations to his creditors. As time went on, the amount that the person taking the poor debtor's oath could retain was constantly increased. The labor societies also added to the protection of the laboring classes by securing the passage of laws giving mechanics a lien on the products of their labor and thereby made the path of the dis-

[1] See the present work, ii, 416-420.

honest employer more difficult.[1] In the early days of the
poor debtor law administration, the debtor was obliged to
maintain himself in prison, but it was customary to grant
him considerable enlargement, sometimes even permitting
him to live and work anywhere within reach of the jail.
As the years of the nineteenth century went by, the tendency was to restrict him more and more to the prison walls
and to compel the creditor to contribute to his support.
In some States, the authorities maintained the debtor for
a specified time; when this expired, he would be discharged unless the creditor came forward and assumed the
burden. As the years went by also, there is observable a
general tendency throughout the States to limit the amount
of debt under which a person could be imprisoned to twenty
dollars and this did away with much of the petty persecution.

With the development of the credit system throughout the
country, with the rapidly changing conditions of buying and
selling, and with the rise of cities and towns, tremendous
changes occurred in the modes of carrying on business.
There were recurrent panics and demi-panics and the legislators of State and nation were obliged to act to enable the
business of the country to go on. In the olden time, bankruptcy had been a matter of special legislation for each individual or for a group of cases. One of the earliest American
bankruptcy laws was that of Maryland, under which James
Greenleaf had obtained a discharge from prosecution by his
creditors in 1798. In 1800, Congress passed a federal bankruptcy act by virtue of which Robert Morris obtained his
freedom.[2] These and other similar laws related to persons
who were engaged in trade or business; they did not relieve
ordinary individuals from the penalties of statutes relating

[1] *American Industrial Society*, v,   *Congress*, 6th Cong., 1452; see also the
28, 29, 121, 160, 161.   present work, iv, 111–113.
[2] *Statutes at Large*, ii, 19; *Annals of*

to debt. Even with these limitations, they do not seem to
have worked well, and the federal act and some of the others
were repealed. The Panic of 1837, and the widespread
commercial distress that followed it, again brought the
question before the country. In 1841, Congress passed
another general bankruptcy law,[1] but this like the earlier
one proved to be unsatisfactory in many respects and was
repealed not long afterward and no more general legislation was attempted until after the close of the War for
Southern Independence.

Of all the unfortunate and incapacitated persons who
come down to us in the pages of history, none so arouse our
sympathies as those who were afflicted with some form of
insanity; but in the older time they aroused no sympathy
whatever. In America, as in England, demented persons
were regarded as guilty of having done something wrong,
although what it was that they had done no one could
tell. In colonial days deranged and crazy persons were cared
for by their families and neighbors in isolated rooms in the
house or, if dangerously violent, they were confined, sometimes in chains, in an outhouse or in a cellar. Poor and
lonely insane persons who "came on the town" were treated
in a similar manner, confined by themselves in the almshouses or otherwise secured. At the beginning of the prison
era, they were handed over to the keepers of the prisons and
jails, who often were extremely unwilling to accept them, but
could not help themselves. Occasionally a committee from
a philanthropic society or a legislative body would visit a
prison or two and describe a most distressing condition of
affairs; but no one thought of doing anything, probably
because no one had any idea of what could be done. In
December, 1837, the directors of the Ohio Lunatic Asylum

---

[1] *Statutes at Large*, v, 440, 614.

quoted from a report [1] that a committee of the New Hampshire legislature had drawn up with a view to explain the reason for there being so many more lunatics in that State than had been expected. It appears from this report that many persons "laboring under an inoffensive hallucination of mind" had been found wandering about the country the sport of unthinking boys and unprincipled men. Others had been found in close confinement, some were in cages made for the purpose, others in outbuildings or garrets or cellars in private houses; and still others had been found in the county jails, incarcerated with felons; and a few had been discovered in the cellars of almshouses that were "never warmed by fire, or lighted by the rays of the sun." In one prison in Massachusetts,[2] an investigator found a man confined in a dark room in a cellar where he had lived for seventeen years; he had protected himself against the cold by stuffing hay into the cracks of the door, his food being passed to him through a wicket.

The Pennsylvanians appear to have been the first to try to alleviate the lot of the insane, for as early as 1751, some provision was made for them in the hospital at Philadelphia. But the first public institution that was devoted exclusively to the care of the insane was the Eastern Lunatic Asylum that was opened at Williamsburg in Virginia in 1773.[3] In 1801, the commissioners of the poor of Charleston,

---

[1] Directors of the Ohio Lunatic Asylum's *Third Report* (December, 1837), p. 4.

[2] For innumerable instances of harsh and negligent treatment of insane persons, see Dorothea L. Dix's *Memorial to the Legislature of Massachusetts* which is dated January, 1843, and subsequent memorials to the legislatures of Kentucky, Tennessee, Pennsylvania, and other States. For denials of many of her statements as to Massachusetts institutions, see *A Memorial to the Legislature of Massachusetts* signed by the "Overseers of the Poor" of Danvers and dated February 10, 1843. One of Miss Dix's most remarkable reports was a *Review of the Present Condition of the State Penitentiary of Kentucky* which was printed at Frankfort in 1845.

[3] See the present work, vol. iii, 571.

South Carolina, were given the care of "all lunatics, or persons disordered in their senses" who might be confined in the poor house.[1] Little more seems to have been done for the care of the mentally unbalanced until the era of the War of 1812. In 1813, members of the Society of Friends in Philadelphia associated for the purpose of establishing an asylum for the relief of persons deprived of the use of their reason.[2] In 1814, Dr. George Parkman of Boston issued a pamphlet entitled "Proposals for Establishing a Retreat for the Insane" and followed this in 1817 with another on the "Management of Lunatics with Illustrations of Insanity" and in 1818 with "Remarks on Insanity."[3] Mainly as a result of the interest in the treatment of the insane that is indicated in these and other writings the McLean Asylum for the Insane was founded in 1818 by private benefaction and placed under the charge of the management of the Massachusetts General Hospital, a privately supported institution at Boston.[4] State legislatures slowly recognized the obligations of the community to provide proper care and surroundings for the insane poor, and several State institutions were established in the third

---

[1] *Ordinances of the City Council of Charleston* (1802), p. 229. This ordinance was amended in 1819 by authorizing the wardens of the city to commit to the "Asylum for Lunatics" attached to the city poor house "persons laboring under insanity" brought to the guard house or found strolling in the streets or otherwise incommoding the citizens; see *A Collection of the Ordinances of the City Council of Charleston* (1823), p. 7. South Carolina established a State lunatic asylum in 1822, R. Mills's *Statistics of South Carolina*, 213.

[2] The "Annual Reports" (1813–1848) of this institution give an excellent idea of the progress of the treatment of insanity in the earlier days.

[3] Dr. J. L. Hildreth's *Public Care of the Insane in Massachusetts* (Cambridge, 1897) is a brief and readable essay.

[4] See R. C. Waterston's *Condition of the Insane in Massachusetts* (Boston, 1843); Morrill Wyman's *Early History of the McLean Asylum for the Insane*. For an account of John McLean's bequest, see N. I. Bowditch's *History of the Massachusetts General Hospital* (Boston, 1872), pp. 64–67. Reports of the McLean Asylum are contained in the Massachusetts General Hospital's *Annual Reports*. For a hostile view of the McLean Asylum, see *An Account of the Imprisonment and Sufferings of Robert Fuller, of Cambridge*.

decade of the century.[1] The Ohio Lunatic Asylum was opened in 1839 and proved to be a very creditable establishment for that time, because the managers had taken advantage of all the earlier experiments, the failures as well as the successes.[2] The Massachusetts State Asylum at Worcester, which was opened in 1833, was regarded by contemporaries with a good deal of admiration, partly because it was built within the appropriation, which seems to have been an unusual occurrence even in those days. The advocates of better methods for the treatment of insane persons had argued that many cases of insanity were curable. In the early years, however, the number of "cures" was not large because, so it was said, the early groupings of lunatics comprised the most deplorable cases to be found. More than one-half of those who were taken to Worcester in the first year came from jails and almshouses and the majority of them had already been confined for more than ten years.[3] When the incoming flow of patients represented the normal amount of insanity, a considerable portion would be cured, so it was expected, but up to 1850 or 1860, these expectations had not been fulfilled.[4]

The philanthropists and reformers had traced much of the crime and distress that was to be found around them to the habit, that was quite widespread in those days, of pur-

[1] See *The North American Review,* xliv, pp. 91–121; Edward Jarvis's *Insanity and Insane Asylums;* John M. Galt's *Essays on Asylums for Persons of Unsound Mind* (Richmond, 1850) and "Second Series" (Richmond, 1853); and George L. Harrison's *Legislation on Insanity . . . Lunacy Laws . . . of the United States to . . . 1883.*

[2] See Directors of the Ohio Lunatic Asylum's *Reports,* iii (December, 1837); Directors and Superintendent of the Ohio Lunatic Asylum's *Reports,* iii (December, 1841).

[3] *Reports and Other Documents relating to the State Lunatic Hospital at Worcester, Mass.* (Boston, 1837), especially p. 37 and fol. Part of this report is in Boston Prison Discipline Society's *Reports,* ix, 299.

[4] Beginning with 1840, the federal censuses contain information on the defective and dependent classes; see E. C. Lunt's *Key to the . . . Census,* § K. George Tucker's *Progress of the United States* (New York, 1855), ch. ix, and "Appendix," ch. vi, has useful information on the subject compiled from the censuses.

chasing shares in lotteries.[1] Ill success had driven men to drink, had induced them to steal, and had even deranged their intellects. Success, however, did not reward the readjusters so soon in this matter as it had in others. Indeed, until the multiplication of stocks and bonds provided an outlet for speculative desire, lotteries maintained their place despite reformers, legislatures, and courts of law. The truth of the matter seems to be that legislators in those days hesitated to use the taxing power and preferred to raise funds for schools and colleges and internal improvements by means of lotteries,[2] for, whatever might be said against them, it was certain that money raised in this way was always "cheerfully paid." It was an expensive process, for, generally speaking, for every hundred thousand dollars paid by the public for lottery tickets, about one-half went to the managers of the enterprise and to the ticket brokers and sellers and of the other half about one-third went to the beneficiary and the other two-thirds to the buyers of tickets in the form of prizes. No tax ever brought in so small a net percentage as a lottery.

Moreover, the practice of "insuring" or betting that a number would be lucky or unlucky encouraged gambling to a greater extent than any other device that ever claimed respectability. And there were very serious charges

[1] In 1830, the Grand Jury of the City of New York "presented" the great and growing evils of lotteries. They found that from August 12 to November 10, fourteen lotteries had been drawn in the city, comprising five hundred thousand tickets that were sold for nearly two and one-half million dollars or at a yearly rate of nearly ten million dollars. See G. W. Gordon's *Lecture before the Boston Young Men's Society on the Subject of Lotteries* (Boston, 1833), Appendix, Note 11.

[2] Job R. Tyson on page 29 of his *Brief Survey of the . . . Lottery System* (Philadelphia, 1833) states that there were about four hundred lottery schemes then going on in nine States, the yearly amount of prizes in them being something over fifty-three million dollars. There were then two hundred lottery offices in Philadelphia, alone. Thomas Doyle's *Five Years in a Lottery Office* (Boston, 1841) contains much curious information.

made of fraud, although in many cases the preparing the numbers and the drawing them from the wheel was all done in the presence of some high official as a Secretary of State, a mayor, a governor, and the public. The two decades following the crisis of 1819 that saw so great an advance in manners and customs of the people in one way or another also witnessed the greatest development of lotteries in our history. They were no longer confined to the construction of churches, to the aid of privately endowed colleges, or to helping corporations to dig canals. Now, they often formed part of the regular financial system of the State, as the Literature Fund of New York and the so-called national lottery for the building of a court house, a penitentiary, schoolhouses and other public buildings in the District of Columbia.[1] Between the close of the war and 1820 several States passed acts forbidding the sale of "foreign" lottery tickets within the State limits, prohibiting private lotteries, and licensing the sellers of legal lottery tickets.[2] The machinery for enforcing these laws seems to have been very ineffective as a rule, but one case, that of Philip J. and Mendez Cohen against the State of Virginia, worked its way into the Supreme Court and secured immortality through a decision made by Chief Justice Marshall. By 1835 lotteries had been forbidden in most of the Old Thirteen States, but the selling of tickets in lotteries outside of these States went on, apparently, as merrily as ever, and it was not until half the century was passed that any real impression had

[1] W. Bogart Bryan's *History of the National Capital*, ii, 38, 81.

[2] A. R. Spofford collected much interesting information in his "Lotteries in American History" in American Historical Association's *Report* for 1892, pp. 171–195. More information can be found in John H. Stiness's "Century of Lotteries in Rhode Island" in Rider's *Rhode Island Historical Tracts*, Second Series, No. 3, and in A. F. Ross's *History of Lotteries in New York*. The evidence presented in the *Report of the Trial of Charles N. Baldwin* (New York, 1818) will repay perusal by any one who wishes to get an actual insight into an institution of a by-gone age.

been made on this most demoralizing institution. With this exception, however, the first fifty years of the nineteenth century saw more progress in the reconstruction of American morals than all the years that had preceded since the first settlement at Jamestown in Virginia.

NOTES

I. The Temperance Movement. — Chapter xxxvii of the fourth volume of McMaster's *History* is by far the best collected account of the social readjustments of the first part of the century; but the author's love of the picturesque sometimes leads a reader to get an overdrawn impression.

The nine *Annual Reports* of the American Temperance Society from 1827 to 1836, were printed at Boston and were followed after 1838 by the *Reports* of the Executive Committee of the American Temperance Union. The fourth to the sixteenth *Reports* of the Society were printed in three volumes at New York in 1852 and 1853 under the title of *Permanent Temperance Documents.* This last publication taken by itself gives the best generally accessible account of this early temperance movement. In addition there were State societies and local societies. Some of these printed reports and others did not. *The Panoplist,* from 1810 to 1820, contains much material on the earlier time. Besides Beecher's *Autobiography* may be mentioned John B. Gough's *Autobiography,* Neal Dow's *Reminiscences,* L. A. Biddle's *Memorial . . . of Dr. Benjamin Rush,* and John Marsh's *Temperance Recollections* which were jotted down in his old age and published at New York in 1867. A digest of State laws is in *The Cyclopædia of Temperance and Prohibition,* 275–360. Of the compendious books, Daniel Dorchester's *Liquor Problem in All Ages* is, perhaps, the most useful, but Woolley and Johnson's *Temperance Progress of the Century* is usable and accurate. George F. Clark's *History of the Temperance Reform in Massachusetts* is clear and concise and of wider interest than the title implies.

II. Prison Discipline. — The *First Annual Report* of the Boston Prison Discipline Society was published in 1826, and for some years thereafter succeeding reports came regularly from the press. The early reports attracted so much attention and were so valuable that they were reprinted several times, partly at public expense. The first report contains a summary of the actual conditions of the old style prisons,[1] the second report contains details of the new prisons

---

[1] An earlier account is C. G. Haines's *Report on the Penitentiary System in the United States, Prepared under a Resolution of the Society for the Prevention of Pauperism, in the City of New* York (1822). A later account of the Auburn system is *Crime and Punishment* by Blanchard Fosgate, at one time physician at that prison.

that were then in process of building with diagrams showing the arrangements. In later reports the question of imprisonment for debt is taken up at length. The news of these experiments in America spread to Europe and attracted four sets of explorers into the doings of the trans-Atlantic people. Two of these visitors, De Beaumont and De Tocqueville, wrote a remarkable report which was translated by Francis Lieber — with considerable annotation — and was published at Philadelphia in 1833.[1] In the " Appendix " to this book (p. 187) is a series of notes on conversations with prisoners in the Eastern Pennsylvania Penitentiary and on page 199 notes of a striking conversation with Captain Lynds to which may be added a note on him printed on page 156. These researchers were attracted by the Auburn system, partly perhaps on account of its cheapness. Another investigator, also of power and eminence, Miss Dorothea L. Dix, published in 1845 *Remarks on Prisons and Prison Discipline in the United States*, which might almost be described as a report on the condition of affairs in that year. She favored the Pennsylvania system as it had been worked out, mainly because of her dislike of the terrorism that was required by the congregate system, if it were really to amount to anything.[2] Of publications that came directly from the prisons is *A Brief Account of the Construction, Management, & Discipline, etc., etc., of the New York State Prison at Auburn*. This was written by Judge Gershom Powers, agent and keeper of the prison and a remarkable man. The " General Regulations and Discipline " are printed on pages 1 to 21. Chapter viii of Frederick H. Wines's *Punishment and Reformation*[3] contains the only compendious account

---

[1] The title is *On the Penitentiary System in the United States, and its Application in France* by G. De Beaumont and A. De Tocqueville, translated by Francis Lieber.

[2] For a favorable view of the unmitigated solitude plan, see George W. Smith's *Defence of the System of Solitary Confinement of Prisoners adopted by the State of Pennsylvania*. This was first published in 1829 and was republished in 1833 by the Philadelphia Society for Alleviating the Miseries of Public Prisons. The pros and cons were summed up in Dr. S. G. Howe's *An Essay on Separate and Congregate Systems of Prison Discipline*

(Boston, 1846), Francis C. Gray's tract on *Prison Discipline in America* (Boston, 1847), F. A. Packard's *Inquiry into the Alleged Tendency of the Separation of Convicts, . . . to produce Disease and Derangement. By a Citizen of Pennsylvania* (Philadelphia, 1849), and in George Combe's *Remarks on . . . Criminal Legislation, and . . . Prison Discipline* (London, 1854).

[3] The full title is *Punishment and Reformation. An Historical Sketch of the Rise of the Penitentiary System.* The first edition was published in 1895. The book was revised by the author in 1910 and "a new edition

of this phase of penological adjustment by an expert on the general subject.

revised and enlarged " by Winthrop D. Lane was printed with an abbreviated title in 1919. In both of these later editions ch. viii on "The Pennsylvania and Auburn Systems" was left as in the original edition and so was the bibliographical paragraph at the end of the original preface.

CHAPTER VII

THE CHANGING RELIGIOUS SCENE

IN colonial days Church and State had been more or less intimately connected, no matter whether the religious body was termed "established" or simply recognized by the rulers as the dominant religious organization.[1] With the separation from England hierarchical control disappeared for the moment: Roman Catholic laymen enjoyed some of the privileges of congregationalism and the Episcopalians also managed their own affairs. Then, too, the contest for the political rights of man temporarily overshadowed the necessity of providing for the spiritual care of the soul and the intense idealism of the day gave other means of satisfying the desire for a future life. Religious systems seemed to have broken down. This opinion may reflect only the feelings of the older clergy that people no longer listened to their ministrations but went off in search of strange gods, — gods that to us, nowadays, appear to be quite as regular as the old ones. Thomas Jefferson represented as well as any one this radicalism of belief. In 1820, he wrote to a friend that he hoped the "genuine and simple religion of Jesus" might be restored, for it had become so "muffled up in mysteries" that it was concealed from the vulgar eye. He wished that now men would use "the talent of reason" that God had confided to them.[2] In the preceding year William Ellery

[1] See the present work, vols. i, ii, and iii, using the index under "religion" and the several sects.

[2] Buffalo Historical Society's *Publications*, vii, 28.

204

Channing in a sermon at Baltimore had expressed somewhat similar ideas. That sermon was in the nature of a
declaration of independence on the part of the Unitarians
and an exposition of their beliefs.[1] The Scriptures, he
said, were "the records of God's successive revelations to
mankind, and particularly of the last and most perfect
revelation of His will by Jesus Christ" who is the only
"master of Christians"; and whatever He taught "we,"
meaning Unitarians, "regard as of divine authority."
Forty years later, on the eve of the War for Southern Independence, Theodore Parker, the foremost Unitarian minister
of that time, stated that the New Testament contained four
doctrines [2] that had been "taught even by Jesus of Naz-
areth" and that he, Theodore Parker, took "neither him
nor the New Testament" for his master. What was good
in both he used and he tried to lift up men whom he saw
"bowed down before the superstition of the Protestants."
On the other hand, Dr. Lyman Beecher and his daughter,
Harriet Beecher Stowe, held vigorous opinions of Unitarianism, even of the earlier type. The latter declared
that the Unitarian denomination was "a whole generation
in the process of reaction," while her father regarded it as
"the deadly foe of human happiness," for its direct tendency
was to prevent true conviction, stop revivals, and leave men

[1] This sermon may most easily be
found in *The Works of William E.
Channing* issued by the American
Unitarian Association in 1875, p. 367.
It has also been printed in many other
forms. Dr. Fenn's article on Unitarianism in *The Religious History of
New England: King's Chapel Lectures*, pp. 77–133, is distinctly interesting. Thomas Cooper, writing to
J. A. Hammond in 1836, said, "Channing is not an original writer — his
language is good, and his religious
opinions liberal, but he has no ideas of
his own. He is not a Spring, but a

Reservoir. He can pour out what he
has recd. but he has no permanent
sources of Ideas; and he writes for
popularity." "Hammond Papers" in
Library of Congress.

[2] Theodore Parker to Mrs. S. B.
White, May 22, 1858; Manuscript
in the Massachusetts Historical Society. The four doctrines enumerated
by Parker are "(1) *total depravity*,
(2) a *wrathful God;* (3) the *Salvation* of a few by the *merits of Jesus*,
& (4) the *eternal damnation* of the great
Mass of Mankind."

bound hand and foot under the power of the adversary.[1]
In 1825 he prophesied that at no distant day Unitarianism
would "cease to darken and pollute the land," but even
Lyman Beecher's life was not to cease without charges that
he himself had weakened somewhat on one of the cardinal
beliefs of the old New England Calvinists.[2] Moreover,
the fact that Channing's sermon was preached at Baltimore,
the first city of Maryland, is in itself significant of the religious change, for it was Maryland that had provided in the
"good old colonial days" boring of the tongue, branding
of the forehead, and death on the scaffold for him who
announced his disbelief in the Holy Trinity.[3]

As the century advanced change succeeded change; new
doctrines, new disciplines, new modes of procedure are
everywhere to be discerned.[4] To a twentieth century
historical onlooker it is oftentimes difficult to comprehend
what some of these differences really were and even more
difficult to understand how men were willing to sacrifice
themselves and their families for what seem to have been
distinctly doubtful matters or matters of small moment.
But so it was, and however much difficulty one may have
in understanding, there is no question whatsoever that the
earnestness of purpose and tenacity of belief of the holders
of any one of these hundred or more religious divisions
deserve the most earnest and respectful consideration.[5]

---

[1] Lyman Beecher's *Autobiography*, ii, 56, 110.

[2] *Trial of Lyman Beecher, D.D. before the Presbytery of Cincinnati, on the Charge of Heresy* (New York, 1835).

[3] See the present work, vol. ii, 430 and note.

[4] Chapter x, Part Second of Chapman and O'Neal's *Annals of Newberry*, South Carolina, contains a detailed account of religion in that one county that was representative of a type of settlement.

[5] Census Bureau's *Special Reports, Religious Bodies: 1906*, Pt. i, especially pages 99 and fol., which give the date of organization. In the "Introduction" there is a comparative analysis of the *Censuses* of 1850 and 1860. John Hayward's *Religion Creeds and Statistics* (Boston, 1836) gives details of the existing denominations of the earlier time.

Among the Baptists there were a dozen different bodies: there were the regular Baptists, the Seventh-day Baptists, the Free Baptists, the Free-will Baptists, the General Six Principle Baptists, and the Two-Seed-in-the-Spirit Predestinarian Baptists and there were three colored Baptist bodies. There were also a dozen or so Methodist bodies: the Methodist Episcopal Church was the regular organization and then there were the Methodist Protestant Church, the Congregational Methodist Church, the New Congregational Methodist Church, and the Independent Methodist Church. The regular Methodist organization was divided on the slavery and anti-slavery question into the "Church" and the "Church South" and the colored Methodists worshipped by themselves and formed their own church bodies, as the African Methodist Episcopal Church, the African Union Methodist Protestant Church, the Union American Methodist Episcopal Church, the African Methodist Episcopal Zion Church, and the Reformed Zion Union Apostolic Church, and as many more. The Presbyterians were not so thoroughly subdivided, but there were half a dozen kinds of them, as the Presbyterian Church in the United States, the Presbyterian Church in the United States of America, and the United Presbyterian Church of North America. Then there was the Welsh Calvinist Methodist Church which was a Presbyterian body. Some of the Presbyterian Churches were divided by the line between freedom and slavery, and there were also colored Presbyterian Churches. Besides these numerically strong Protestant organizations, there were isolated sects as the Adventists, who were grouped under half a dozen names: the Shakers or United Society of Believers as they termed themselves, the Rappists, the Dunkers or German Baptist Brethren in four forms, the Quakers in four forms, the Latter-

Day Saints, or Mormons as they are usually termed, in three forms, a dozen kinds of Mennonites, among them the Amish and the Old Amish, the Moravians in two forms, and the Schwenkfelders, the Campbellites, and the Millerites. Indeed, with the coming of the German and Scandinavian immigrants in the middle of the century, there was a further addition to the minor sects; but if the Reverend James W. Alexander was right in his assessment of them, nine-tenths of the German Protestants [1] in New York City were infidels and radicals, and the German Reformed Church itself was mad after a "delusive transcendentalism"; but very likely he was ill informed and generalized on insufficient premises.

The multiplicity of sects did not imply a lack of religious fervor among large portions of the people.[2] Alexander's own career in New York showed that there was opportunity for evangelical preaching and teaching. After a preliminary settlement of some years, he left New York for a time, but was recalled by the same congregation. For his second administration a great church was built and the sale of pews in it before the edifice was completed brought in enough money to pay the cost of the building and of the land on which it was situated. To provide more room the organ was moved from its usual place to the wall behind the pulpit and the additional pews were sold before they were finished. Alexander seems to have been appalled at the size of his audiences. He always wished to try the experiment of a free church and he had endeavored to secure a number of free pews in the new building. To satisfy his longings his people erected a mission chapel for him where he preached once a week to all those who came to him. And Alexander

[1] *Familiar Letters of James W. Alexander*, ii, 173, 176.
[2] See, however, "Plain Truth," published at Canandaigua, N. Y., in 1822 and 1823, Ohio Church History Society's *Papers*, vi, 1–22.

was only one of many strong, eloquent, and earnest preachers who gave joy and hope to hundreds of thousands of men and women.

As the years went by, the activities of the churches widened. The religious people began to look after the affairs of the body and before long devoted so much time, strength, and resources to the founding and maintaining of schools, hospitals, and recreative organizations that the modern observer sometimes finds it difficult to discriminate between those that may well be looked upon as religious and those that are mainly concerned with physical and mental welfare. The Quakers had always supervised the worldly doings of their members and so had the early New England Congregationalists; but neither of these bodies had gone outside of their own denomination. Now, the churches became seized with a missionary spirit to send devout men and women into the hidden recesses of the great cities and into the wildest regions of America, Africa, and Asia,[1] to preach the word of God and to teach the proper care of the mind and body to those of other ways of thinking on religion and possessing different ideas as to the duty of man to himself and to his neighbor. Alexander envied the Episcopalian, Dr. Mühlenberg, because he had only a free church; but he also records, possibly not with entire approbation, that Mühlenberg had on his staff an apothecary who

---

[1] The history of the American Board of Commissioners for Foreign Missions may be easily traced in Rufus Anderson's *Memorial Volume of the First Fifty Years* that was issued by the Board in 1861. The first two *Annual Reports* of the American Board give the details of its organization. This association represented slaveholders as well as other persons. Those who favored missionary enterprises and abhorred slavery formed other societies which united in 1846 in the American Missionary Association. See Lewis Tappan's *History of the American Missionary Association* (New York, 1855). The missionary spirit is vividly shown in the *Memoirs of the Rev. Samuel J. Mills* by Gardiner Spring (New York, 1820) and in the lives of Adoniram Judson by his son, Edward Judson, and by Francis Wayland.

administered to all free of charge and four Sisters of Mercy who in one year had cared for twelve thousand persons. Had Alexander's life been prolonged, it would have been interesting to read his comments on the Episcopal sisterhood and St. Luke's Hospital founded by Mühlenberg. How it all appeared to the Reverend James Dixon, an English Methodist, who visited Boston in 1848, is interesting. He noted that the Sabbath there was strictly observed, but it was a painful reflection to him — nevertheless — that the churches should be "occupied by a race who preach a diluted kind of Socinianism" and that the bold, broad, deep faith of the original settlers [1] should be replaced by "the meagre and flimsy philosophy now announced in their pulpits."

Territorially there was a somewhat free distribution of religious bodies. Louisiana — the old Louisiana — was peculiarly the abode of the Roman Catholics as was natural from its early history; but they were strong in the homes of the Irish immigrants, — in New England, New York, and Philadelphia, — and there was the old Catholic population of Maryland.[2] Among the Evangelical sects the Presbyterians were strong in the old Northeastern States, but there the Methodists and Baptists were competing vigorously with them. Transappalachia, however, was the harvesting place for the Methodists and the Baptists, for their beliefs and modes of procedure were peculiarly fitting to the wilderness and to the pioneer. This mingling of religious sects was made possible by the breaking down of the old barriers and requirements.[3] New York had had a constitutional requirement that made it impossible for the Roman Catholic immi-

[1] James Dixon's *Personal Narrative . . . with notices of the History and Institutions of Methodism in America* (New York, 1849), p. 23.
[2] In 1792, the Maryland Assembly passed a law permitting property,

both real and personal, to be held for the benefit of the Roman Catholic Church: *Digest of the Laws of Maryland* (1799), p. 466.
[3] See the present work, vol. iii, 560–566.

grant to acquire citizenship or to hold office, but this was
done away with in 1821.[1]　North Carolina retained the word
"Protestant" in her constitution until 1835 and then only
extended the limits of office-holding [2] to "Christians."　In
Massachusetts, in Connecticut, and in New Hampshire [3]
the general rule had been that every one must worship the
Creator and that all tax payers must contribute to the
support of the public Protestant "teacher of piety" in his
town.　Those who did not attend or support the regular
organization were obliged to secure a certificate from the
town clerk and then their contributions would go to their
own parson or priest and they themselves could worship
in their own church, provided they were Christians.　Office-
holding, however, was confined to Protestants.　Under
this scheme a Quaker or a Roman Catholic might worship
in his own way and hold office — except in New Hampshire,
where Roman Catholics were debarred; but, unless there
was a society of the tax payers' own kind in their own town,
their religious taxes went to the support of the regular public
minister.　Oftentimes, also, there was a good deal of trouble
experienced in securing certificates and in applying their
share of the taxes to their own minister, when there was
one, — in one case it is said that it cost one hundred dollars
to collect four dollars from a town treasurer for the use
of a Baptist clergyman.　Moreover, owing to the peculiarities of the Methodist organization, its ministers were
not "settled" and, therefore, could not secure for their own
use any of the town tax money paid by their own communicants.　In 1811, "voluntary societies" of Protestants were

[1] See the present work, vol. iii, 564;
*Journal of the Convention of the State of
New-York . . . 1821*, pp. 314–332, 462–
464; L. H. Clarke's *Report of the . . .
Convention . . . of August, 1821*, p. 70, etc.;
and Poore's *Constitutions*, Pt. ii, 1346.

[2] *North Carolina Booklet*, viii, 105.
[3] For the general condition of
religion in New England in this period,
see Paul E. Lauer's *Church and State
in New England*, ch. v.

recognized by law in Massachusetts. This relieved the situation for the less closely organized Protestant societies, but did not in any way help the Roman Catholics. These had to wait until the constitution was amended in 1833 before they were freed from the obligation of contributing to the support of the regular Protestant minister as well as of their own priest;[1] but after 1821 Roman Catholics might hold office in Massachusetts.[2] The requirement that the Governor and State legislators should be Protestants was not removed in New Hampshire until 1877, and the requirement that the "teacher of religion" supported by public contributions must be a Protestant was also omitted at the same time. In Massachusetts what might be called local option in religion had been established by a decision of the State supreme court in 1820.[3] Under the State constitution and laws, the voters of a town had the ultimate right of choosing the town minister. In the old days the more devout of the townspeople had formed the "church" and had selected the minister, but the confirmation of the appointment and arrangement as to compensation belonged to the voters in town meeting. In 1818, the voters of the town of Dedham decided to choose a minister of the Unitarian persuasion, notwithstanding the fact that all but two or three members of the regular town religious organization were Orthodox Trinitarian Congregationalists. These seceded, demanded the town ecclesiastical property and, being denied it by the town authorities, sued them

[1] In 1819 the old colonial system was done away with in New Hampshire by a law that was known popularly as the "Toleration Act." At least one man felt called upon to protest against any person being required to support public worship in a pamphlet entitled *Some Remarks on the "Toleration Act" of 1819 . . . By a Friend to the "Public Worship*

of the Deity" (Exeter, N. H., 1823).
[2] See oath of governor and members of the legislature in *Constitutions of the United States, and of the Commonwealth of Massachusetts*.
[3] *The Constitution of New Hampshire as amended by the Constitutional Convention . . . 1876* (Concord, 1877), pp. 2, 9, 11, 15.

for it. The court decided that the property and goods of the town religious organization belonged to the town — or to the parish which was the town or a part of the town in its ecclesiastical form. It made no difference how many of the church members seceded, the religious edifice and all the religious property, even the communion service, belonged to the town [1] and not to the old "church." In a few years the eastern part of the State was about equally divided between the Orthodox and Unitarian Congregationalists [2] and it was this revolution in religion that led to the destruction of the old Massachusetts ecclesiastical system by the amendment to the constitution that was adopted in 1853.

The establishment of religious toleration and religious freedom is best seen in the growth of the Roman Catholic Church within the limits of the Old Thirteen States. In common with the two other hierarchically controlled religious organizations, the Episcopal Church and the Methodist Episcopal Church, the Roman Catholics had been seriously affected by the severance from the British Empire. In the case of these and especially of the Episcopal Church, it could hardly be expected that the revolutionists, whether Catholic or Protestant,[3] would recognize or tolerate the English connection. Indeed, the Revolution had been undertaken in part to limit the exercise of power by the Episcopal authorities. The Roman Catholics had no

[1] Edward Buck's *Massachusetts Ecclesiastical Law*, chs. ii–v. There is a list of cases following the index. This decision was made by Chief Justice Parker, who had recently presided over the deliberations of the constitutional convention of 1820 that had refused to alter the religious laws, see *Journal of the Debates of the Convention of 1820–1821*, using index under "Declaration of Rights."

[2] At the close of the period covered in this volume there were about 130 Unitarian congregations in Massachusetts as a whole and more than 250 Orthodox churches. George Burgess's *Pages from the Ecclesiastical History of New England*, 121.

[3] See John Gilmary Shea's *Life and Times of the Most Rev. John Carroll* (New York, 1888) forming vol. ii of Shea's *History of the Catholic Church within the Limits of the United States*.

connection with the English government, but the control
of the church in English America had been exercised through
persons domiciled in Great Britain. At once the Roman
Catholic laymen in Maryland and Pennsylvania took
possession of the church property and established a system
of trustees in whom the title of the property was legally
vested.[1] Bishop Carroll felt himself obliged to assent to the
establishment of this system, and in the time of his immediate successors, the Roman Catholic laymen even undertook to exercise some option as to the choice of their priests.
The liberality and quasi-independence of the Church in
America at this time attracted to it many members of the
old colonial families in Boston, New York, and Philadelphia.
In Massachusetts, the Catholics rejoiced in the presence of
two remarkable men, Francis A. Matignon and John
Lefebvre Cheverus. Like so many of the Roman Catholic
priests of that time in America, they were Frenchmen born
and were men of culture.[2] Under their administrations,
Roman Catholics in Boston, who had numbered about one
hundred in the first year of the century and about seven
hundred in 1808, increased to over two thousand in 1820.[3]
In New York the opposition to the Roman Catholics in the
early decades of the century was very marked. They
belonged to the church of the old French invaders and the
memories of Dutch contests with Spanish Catholics in the
Netherlands was still a matter of vigorous tradition. But
with the accession to power of Bishop Hughes a period of
rapid development set in. In the years after Bishop

[1] Thomas O'Gorman's *History of
the Roman Catholic Church*, 269.

[2] There are some interesting notes
on the beginnings of Roman Catholicism
in New England and references to other
books in *American Catholic Historical
Researches* for 1887, pp. 12–18. See
also James Fitton's *Sketches of the*
*Establishment of the Church in New
England* (Boston, 1872) and Hamon's
Life of Cardinal Cheverus translated by
E. Stewart.

[3] For other estimates see *American
Catholic Historical Researches* for 1887,
p. 18.

Carroll's death in 1815 the Catholic churches in Philadelphia and New York had become almost congregational societies. In Philadelphia, Father Hogan, of St. Mary's parish, even celebrated mass contrary to orders from Rome, for which he was excommunicated by the church authorities.[1] In the end the trustees and congregations in Philadelphia and New York and elsewhere were obliged to give way and ultimately, throughout the country, the local Catholic authority, or the bishop of the diocese, has come to be recognized as the legal holder of the church property. In the early part of the nineteenth century an interesting case came up for settlement in New York as to the responsibility of a priest for the revelation of knowledge that had come to him in the confessional. Father Anthony Kohlman, who was then administering the diocese, being questioned on the witness stand, refused to reveal anything that had been said to him in the confessional. He was ready to do his duty as a private citizen, he said, but as a priest his conscience and his duty would prevent him from stating what he had learned in the discharge of his clerical functions.[2] To do otherwise would make him a traitor to his church, his ministry, and his God. It would render him "guilty of eternal damnation" and he would go to prison or to instantaneous death before endangering his soul. The court through its president, De Witt Clinton, thereupon decided that a priest could not be compelled to testify as to what had come to him only through the confessional.

[1] "Documents Relating to the Case of Rev. William Hogan, and the Schism in St. Mary's Church, Philadelphia" are in *Works of the Right Rev. John England* (Baltimore, 1849), v, 109–213. A copy of the excommunication of Father Hogan is on page 485 of W. Oland Bourne's *History of the Public School Society of the City of New York;* see also p. 495 for an earlier form of excommunication.

[2] Thomas O'Gorman's *History of the Roman Catholic Church in the United States,* 313, 314, and J. G. Shea's *History of the Catholic Church,* iii, 165–167. The trial is printed in *The Catholic Question in America* reported by W. Sampson (New York, 1813).

The first great accession of Roman Catholics came with the purchase of Louisiana which brought into the religious population of the country about one hundred thousand communicants of that faith. With them came also a contest that had been raging for some years between the regular church authorities of Louisiana and the Capuchins. The latter maintained that they had had certain proprietary rights in the province in the Franco-Spanish days. Ultimately they were obliged to yield, but not until the dispute had greatly hindered the prosperity of the Catholic Church in the Mississippi Valley. With the annexation of California and New Mexico in the course of the Mexican War, other historic bodies of Roman Catholics came into the American commonwealth; but the great accessions to the northeastern part of the United States were Irish immigrants from the old country across the Atlantic. These began coming in large numbers in the 1840's. They settled in the commercial cities of the seaboard for the most part. Soon English and continental clerics gave place to Irish priests and the church rapidly drifted away from the old population of the country. It became an immigrant church and its rapidly growing strength alarmed many persons. Moreover, as it increased in size its rulers became more and more insistent upon acquiescence in their demands and especially in freedom to carry out the established features of their faith. In New York, Bishop Hughes conducted a manful fight to bring about a diversion of a part of the public school fund for the support of Roman Catholic schools. Objections were raised to the books used in the schools that were then under the care of the Public School Society. This was a private corporation that had been established by benevolent persons to provide better instruction for the poor children of the city. Originally, most

of its members had belonged to the Society of Friends, but
by 1840 it included members of many evangelical faiths.
This society had built up a great organization that was probably one of the best bits of pedagogical enterprise in the
country. When the Roman Catholics objected to the books
used in their schools the society met them with a friendly
spirit and blotted out passages that were objectionable as
one in Maltebrun's "Geography" animadverting on the
influence of the Roman Catholic clergy in Italy; but it soon
appeared that concessions of this kind were not at all what
were wanted. In 1841, the Roman Catholics cast enough
votes in the New York City election for members of the
State Assembly to attract the attention of the politicians
and to bring from Governor Seward an earnest message.
The result was the passage of the School Law of 1842 which
established a public Board of Education for that city and
diverted the public money to it from the School Society.
For some years two sets of schools were maintained; but
this was a condition of things that could not last and in 1853
the School Society turned over its property to the public
authorities and went out of existence.[1]

As the century advanced and the Roman Catholic numbers increased, fear of them became acute. They had established convents and houses of refuge for men and women in
different parts of the country, and around them all kinds
of stories gathered. These finally became associated in the
minds of many people with the so-called confessions of
Maria Monk, who was supposed to have been an inmate of a
Catholic institution at Montreal. Escaping from this
place, according to her story, she fell into the hands of
persons who realized what an effective use might be made

[1] W. Oland Bourne's *History of the
Public School Society of the City of New
York*. The greater part of this volume
is occupied with this contest, giving
long extracts from documents on both
sides.

of her. Soon the "Awful Disclosures of Maria Monk" appeared.[1] They created a tremendous stir and led to further confessions by herself and by others.[2] Later a thoroughly competent historical student went over the Canadian convent, book in hand, and proved the whole story to be false.[3] The tale, however, had served its purpose by adding to the suspicion and dread of the Roman Catholic conventual houses held by very many Protestants. In 1844, there were several riots in Philadelphia directed against the Irish and the Roman Catholics. In a few days buildings were burned in that city and neighborhood, the militia and public officials standing idly by.[4] The most spectacular of these aggressions on the Roman Catholics was the burning of the Ursuline Convent at Somerville near Boston by a band of people from that city in August, 1834. A former occupant of that institution, Rebecca T. Reed, had related stories about it greatly to its prejudice.[5] In 1834, one of the nuns living there had a nervous breakdown and wandered away. The next day she was brought back by the Catholic bishop of the diocese, for the convent was the best place for her. Everything was on a perfectly friendly footing and she was at entire liberty to leave at any time that she wished. The story, however, assumed the form of an account of an imprisonment of a woman and a Boston mob set out to rescue her.[6] She met her would-be

[1] First printed at New York and reprinted at Philadelphia, San Francisco, and elsewhere. See also the *Works of the Right Rev. John England* (Baltimore, 1849), v, 347–418.

[2] See *Confessions of a French Catholic Priest* edited by S. F. B. Morse (New York, 1837).

[3] See William L. Stone's *Maria Monk and the Nunnery of the Hotel Dieu* (New York, 1836).

[4] McMaster's *People of the United States*, vii, 375–383; *Address of the*

Catholic Lay Citizens of . . . Philadelphia . . . in Regard to the Causes of the Late Riots; and the tracts listed in the note to p. 383 of McMaster.

[5] Later these were collected into a book and printed as *Six Months in a Convent* (Boston, 1835). For a Roman Catholic view see *An Answer to Six Months in a Convent by the Lady Superior* (Boston, 1835) and the *Works of the Right Rev. John England*, v, 232–347.

[6] See *Report of the Committee, relating to the Destruction of the Ursu-*

liberators at the door of the convent; but nothing she could do or say could convince them that she was safe within its walls. They compelled all the inmates of the building to leave, although some of them were ill. They searched the house thoroughly, plundered it effectively, and set it on fire. The religious and racial jealousies that had been aroused by the occurrences that have just been noted assumed a political form with the rise of the Native American Party.

Statistics of the churches are more vague and untrustworthy than those of population and industry, — which is saying a good deal; but if we make large allowances and do not draw too fixed conclusions from them the figures are worth putting together and setting down. The population of the United States in 1850 was a little over twenty-three millions and there were something over fourteen million "aggregate accommodations" in all churches, according to the "Census" of that year, by which must be understood seating capacity.[1] Of this total, nearly seven hundred thousand was set down by the census takers of 1850 as belonging to the Roman Catholics and fifteen thousand to the Jews,[2] leaving the rest to the Protestants. It has been often claimed and is no doubt true that it is difficult to put

---

line *Convent* (Boston, 1834); Massachusetts Historical Society's *Proceedings*, 2nd Series, iii, 216; *An Account of the Conflagration of the Ursuline Convent* (Boston, 1834); *Trial of John R. Buzzell . . . for Arson and Burglary in the Ursuline Convent* (Boston, 1834); *The Trial of the Persons charged with Burning the Convent* (Boston, 1834). For other titles, see James F. Hunnewell's *Bibliography of Charlestown*, 58.

[1] These figures are taken from the *Census* of 1850, pp. ix, lvii and fol., 1016 and fol. The figures of "accommodations" in this census are repeated in the *Compendium of the Ninth Census*, 516, 517.

[2] In 1818, Mordecai M. Noah estimated the number of Jews in the United States at 3000; in 1848, there were 50,000 according to M. A. Berk; see *United States Census, Special Reports, Religious Bodies; 1906*, Pt. ii, 320. Up to 1919 the Jews have published little valuable historical material for the *Publications* of the American Jewish Historical Society are largely argumentative. Ezekiel and Lichtenstein's *History of the Jews of Richmond* gives promise of better things.

the Roman Catholic figures side by side with the Protestant, because in the Catholic Church several persons may use one accommodation on one or every Sunday of the year; whereas, in the Protestant churches, in the old settled regions, one sitting per church attendant would be the rule, but in the newer settled country and in the church of some popular city preacher the number of attendants greatly exceeds the number of sittings and far exceeds the number of communicants. Probably it would not be far out of the way to set down three-quarters of the inhabitants of the United States as belonging to some Christian organization in 1850, or at all events, as considering themselves within the Christian fold.

Proceeding now to an endeavor to trace the growth of some of the Christian bodies, the total number of Roman Catholics in the United States in 1800, before the purchase of Louisiana and the accession of Mexican territory, is generally given as one hundred thousand in round numbers,[1] and the number of Roman Catholics in 1850, after these accessions and the first wave of Irish immigration, is set down as one and one-half millions, — each Roman Catholic sitting accounting for two or three communicants. Sorting out, adding, and multiplying the numbers of "accommodations" as given in the "Census" of 1850, it would appear, therefore, that not far from three hundred thousand Roman Catholics were added to the population of the United States by reason of the acquisitions of the first half of the nineteenth century. Making every allowance for the increase of the native Catholic population since 1800, it would appear that the great mass of the Roman Catholic communicants in 1850 were immigrants, mainly from Ireland, and their children. Most of

[1] O'Gorman in his *History of the Roman Catholic Church*, p. 293, gives the number of Catholics in the United States outside of Orleans Territory at 70,000.

the remainder were of Spanish or French origin; in other words the great mass of the Roman Catholics in the United States had not grown up in the midst of American political institutions.

Apart from the Roman Catholic exotic growth and from the increase in the isolated faiths — Unitarians, Universalists, and others — the interest in religious development centred about the Baptists, the Presbyterians, and the Methodists; for these were the three great frontier religious organizations that grew with the growth of Transappalachia. From the best figures attainable, the Presbyterians increased in the fifty years from forty thousand to one-half a million, the Baptists from one hundred thousand to eight hundred thousand, and the Methodist Episcopal Church in all its branches from sixty-five thousand to over one and one-quarter millions.[1] Of course some of this growth occurred in the "Old Thirteen" and there it represented a withdrawal from the two religious bodies that might well be called established, the English Episcopalian or Anglican Church and the Congregational connection.

Conditions on the frontier — in the mountainous regions of the older States and in the newly settled regions of the Mississippi Valley — were favorable to the peculiar influences and modes of procedure of the Baptists and the Methodists and to a less degree, of the Presbyterians. All these represented religious proceedings in which every one could take part and the manifestations of faith had something tangible in them and emotional. Among "historical sources" of the nineteenth century few are better worth reading than the reminiscences, letters, and journals of

[1] These figures as to the strength of religious organizations are taken from Daniel Dorchester's *Christianity in the United States*, p. 615 ror the Roman Catholics, and pp. 733–735 for the Evangelical faiths. Dr. Dorchester put a great deal of labor into this compilation and under each entry gives a definite citation to his authority.

Asbury and his followers and of the Baptist[1] and Presbyterian ministers. The activities and accomplishments of the itinerants are startling. It is estimated that Asbury, the Methodist Bishop, preached more than sixteen thousand sermons, ordained more than four thousand preachers, and travelled on horseback or in carriages nearly three hundred thousand miles at a period when travelling was difficult and oftentimes dangerous.[2] His salary was sixty-four dollars a year and the conditions of his life were such that he could not think of marriage. He might well be described as the greatest of the circuit riders, although he never rode what was technically called a circuit ; but the careers of the actual circuit riders were full of human interest, and besides carrying the religious impulse to the uttermost parts of the land, they bore with them the elements of education.

The astonishing growth of the Methodist, Baptist, and Presbyterian sects in the newer part of the country dates back to the Great Revival of 1800 in eastern Kentucky. The people living there were of the primitive type, working and sleeping in the midst of danger and lacking everything but the bare necessities of existence. Moreover, they belonged to the Scotch Irish race, which, for the most part, was singularly impressionable. James McGready appears to have been the first moving force, but it was not until the coming of the brothers McGee, William and John, one a Methodist and the other a Presbyterian, that the movement assumed the proportions of a religious revolution. Twenty

---

[1] The hardships and the spirit of the life of a Baptist minister are well illustrated in the *Memoir of Elder John Peak, written by himself* (Boston, 1832) and P. Donan's *Memoir of Jacob Creath, Jr.* (Cincinnati, 1872).

[2] This computation is from J. M. Buckley's *History of Methodists in the United States*, 345. See for details of a journey or two W. P. Strickland's

Pioneer Bishop : or, The Life and Times of Francis Asbury, chs. vi, ix. An idea of the extent and variety of Asbury's labors may be had from *The Heart of Asbury's Journal*, edited by E. S. Tipple in 1904 or from H. M. Du Bose's *Francis Asbury, A Biographical Study* (Nashville, Tenn., 1916).

years later, the latter set down his recollections of the revival
in a letter [1] that has been widely reprinted. The two went
to the Red River settlement in Kentucky in 1799, drawn
thither by curiosity to witness McGready's methods of
exhortation, about which they had heard a great deal.
After he and two other ministers had preached and the day
was drawing to a close and the other ministers had left,
the McGees remained with most of the people. William
sat down on the floor of the pulpit, but the power of God
was upon John. He told the people that he was appointed
to preach; he exhorted them to let the Lord God reign in
their hearts and their souls should live. A woman suddenly
broke silence and "shouted tremendously." McGee left
the pulpit to go to her, but hesitated for a moment. Then
"the power of God was strong upon me," so he asserted
twenty years later. He turned again, and, losing sight of the
fear of man, went through the house "shouting and exhorting
with all possible ecstasy and energy." The floor was soon
covered with "the slain"; their screams for mercy pierced
the heavens and mercy came down.[2] Soon afterward, the
McGee brothers were instrumental in instituting the first
great camp meeting, where thousands of people came
together from "far and near" to enjoy their ministrations.

[1] A. H. Redford's *History of Methodism in Kentucky*, i, 267–272, citing
the *Methodist Magazine*, iv, 189–
191.

[2] D. L. Leonard's "Kentucky Revival of 1799–1805" is a very lifelike and not sympathetic account of
this event (*Papers* of the Ohio Church
History Society, v, 44–71). A much
longer account is Catharine C. Cleveland's *The Great Revival in the West,
1797–1805*. A fairly complete bibliography is at the end of the second of
these books, but Leonard gives a brief
list of available works. W. P. Strickland's *Autobiography of Peter Cart-*
wright, the Backwoods Preacher and
Richard M'Nemar's *The Kentucky
Revival; or a Short History of the Late
Extraordinary Outpouring of the Spirit
of God in the Western States of America*
are most widely used by writers.
M'Nemar's book was printed originally in 1807 and therefore has the
merit of contemporaneousness. Robert Davidson's *History of the Presbyterian Church in Kentucky* contains
criticisms of the doings of the re-
vivalists which are vigorously answered in the last half of F. R. Cos-
sitt's *Life and Times of Rev. Finis
Ewing*.

At one time, night came on and the task was not finished, so they made what shelter they could and remained — whole families, day after day and night after night — until their food was exhausted and they had to leave. One can imagine the scene as darkness fell, with the camp-fires blazing and the sound of song rising and falling and the preachers, often of different faiths, two or three of them exhorting at one time. The people "fell" by the hundreds, and those who continued prostrate were conveyed to the neighboring meeting house or to a tent and there laid away until they came to. Many of them had the "jerks," which were involuntary hysterical movements, by which the head swayed from side to side and sometimes the body bounded over the ground. At one great camp meeting, one in six of those present were numbered among the "slain." Possibly the best description of the "working of the Lord" in one of these gatherings was written by a New Yorker who went to a Methodist camp meeting in Maryland some years later. For some time he himself had been wrestling with the spirit. On this occasion "the Holy Ghost as a mighty rushing wind" came into his soul. He rose from his seat, gave "two or three jumps" and fell upon the ground. Then the preacher leaped from the stand "as a giant exhilarated with wine and went through the congregation shouting and exhorting, and the holy fire seemed to run amongst the stubble with a perfect blaze." [1] Revivals were not by any means confined to the frontier or to the Southern and Middle States, they were also a regular part of the Congregational and Presbyterian religious system in New England. Lyman Beecher led strenuous revivals in Litchfield, Connecticut, and later in Boston. They brought many converts

[1] *Incidents in the Life of George W. Henry* (Utica, 1846), pp. 200–203.

to the church, but they lacked the picturesqueness and the hysteria of the frontier.[1]

In the three-cornered contest for converts between the Presbyterians, Baptists, and Methodists, the last-named sect was most successful, although all three added greatly to their numbers in the first forty years of the century. The success of the Methodists was due to their doctrinal liberality in comparison with the Presbyterians and to their wonderful mechanical organization as a sect in comparison with the Baptists. There are, indeed, not many volumes of proceedings of religious bodies that offer more interest to the student of institutions than do those of the Methodist conferences. Asbury and a few missionaries came to America before the Revolution under authorization from Wesley, himself. They made converts, perhaps not as many as they expected to make; but when the Declaration of Independence was signed most of them returned to England. Asbury, himself, and one or two others, remained. After the Revolution, the connection with England was only slowly and haltingly resumed. Wesley recognized Asbury, but sent Dr. Coke to act with Asbury as joint superintendent of the church in the United States. Asbury maintained his actual hold on the organization and Coke's position was finally recognized both by himself and by the conference as untenable.[2] Within the church Asbury was equally successful in maintaining the right of the bishop to rule. The clergy in their conferences would gladly have arranged the appointments, but Asbury was firm on this point and

[1] Calvin Colton in his *History and Character of American Revivals of Religion* (London, 1832) defends revivals as a regular part of religious exercise and declares that the evil things connected with them are no worse than what happens out of them. See on this general subject H. C. Mc-

Comas's *The Psychology of Religious Sects*, chs. viii-xi and Frederick M. Davenport's *Primitive Traits in Religious Revivals*.

[2] See Samuel Drew's *Life of the Rev. Thomas Coke, LL.D.*, New York, 1837, pp. 71-147.

won. In the early years the Methodist minister was an itinerant unless ill health incapacitated him from movement, in which case he was given a superannuated charge or was "located." Remaining stationary, however, was a mark of feebleness and removed one from the possibility of doing great service to the church in making converts. The appointments were made at the close of the yearly conference after all the business was done; the horses were ready for their riders when the bishop announced, one at a time, the appointment of each circuit for the coming year. There was no appeal, the only thing to do was to accept the appointment and do the best that one could. At every conference the "characters" of the members were passed in review. Every year a man's doings were canvassed by his fellows, and failure met its speedy reward as did success, — the latter leading to ever greater tasks and greater opportunities. As long as this militant discipline was maintained, the church grew under the most adverse circumstances that one can well imagine.

As the century advanced, the sects became more closely organized and supplemented their personal efforts by a strong printed propaganda. Each of them had its publishing arrangements, sometimes independent of all other printing establishments, but sometimes two or three of them united for some special purpose or some particular line of action. Of these, possibly the most active was the American Tract Society which was the successor of the New England Religious Tract Society that had been founded in 1814. In 1825, the different tract societies were merged into a national organization which lasted until 1859. It issued leaflets and books of from four to sixteen pages each, which were gathered into twelve volumes. It was a child or a replica of the Religious Tract Society that had been instituted at London in 1799. It repeated many of the English tracts, using the same illustrations, but oftentimes employed an English cut for a purpose unlike that of its original use. In 1826, the directors of the society stated that they had already issued more than two and one-half million tracts, and their efforts had only begun.[1] The Bible societies, denominational, State, and national, worked together and at one time were merged into one organization. The ambition of the leaders in this enterprise was to see to it that every family in the United States possessed a Bible. They also supplied hotels and prisons so that in the United States from 1830 to 1860, the Bible was everywhere accessible in the settled parts of the country. Several of the sects possessed their own publishing houses. Of these the earliest and best known was the Methodist Book Concern that may be said to have gone back to 1788.

One of the most interesting contests in the denominational history of the first half of the nineteenth century was over slavery and abolition. The Methodists were very strong throughout the South, as were the Baptists and the Presbyterians. Life in that part of the country was dependent upon the slave system. Farming and housekeeping, except on the humblest scale, demanded the ownership of one or more negro slaves, because they were the only farm and domestic labor to be had. Oftentimes, also, slaves would come to a clergyman through inheritance of himself or his wife, for in many Southern States it was practically impossible to emancipate a slave. In the first decades, these churches were either silent as to slavery or were pro-slavery. The Methodists omitted from their discipline Wesley's prohibition of the ownership of man and for a long time the

---

[1] Instances of wonderful effects of tracts are in *Eighth Annual Report* of the American Tract Society, pp. 60–67.

opposition to slaveholding on the part of clergy and laity was confined to New England and to New York.[1] Indeed, the language of other conferences was hostile to "the mad-running Garrisonian abolitionists." By 1840, one begins to be conscious of a great change in the Northern conferences. The matter came to a head over the case of Bishop James O. Andrew of Georgia, who had inherited a slave and had married a woman who was a slaveholder and in both cases it was impossible to free them owing to the laws and to the conditions under which they had been inherited. In 1844, however, the General Conference voted that Bishop Andrew must either get rid of his slaves or cease to exercise the functions of a Methodist bishop. The adoption of this vote was the signal for the withdrawal of the Southern conferences and in 1845 they set up for themselves as the Methodist Episcopal Church South.[2] They sent representatives to the General Conference the next year, but these were not admitted within the bar. For the next few years there was a vigorous contest between the two Methodist church bodies for the possession of the Border States. In the course of this struggle the people often took the law of God and man into their own hands and abused and even, occasionally, tarred and feathered cleric and layman, who were not sympathetic on the slave question.

The Sunday School or Sabbath School system,[3] as it has

[1] W. W. Sweet's *Methodist Episcopal Church and the Civil War*, 15–18; chapter x of this book contains an excellent bibliography on the "Slavery Struggle in the Church." Rev. John Wesley's "Thoughts upon Slavery" are added to Rev. O. Scott's *Grounds of Secession from the M. E. Church* (New York, 1851), pp. 193–229.

[2] See H. B. Bascom's *Methodism and Slavery* (Frankfort, Ky., 1845).

[3] See Marianna C. Brown's *Sunday-School Movements in America* (New York, 1901) and the works mentioned in her footnotes and in a bibliography on pp. 246–257; C. S. Lewis's *Work of the [Episcopalian] Church in the Sunday School;* and Lewis G. Pray's *History of Sunday Schools and of Religious Education* (Boston, 1847), chs. xxi, xxii. A. D. Matthews's "Memory Sketch of Early Sunday-School Work in Brooklyn, New York" in the Appendix to E. C. Matthews's *A. D. Matthews' Autobiography* has the interest of personal recollection.

been worked out in the Protestant religious organizations in the United States, has a two-fold origin. On the one side it is a duplication of the effort made in England to provide some kind of education for the children who worked during the week, or most of it, in the factories and in the mines.[1] This was the well-known Raikes system as it was called from its founder. Otherwise, it grew out of the necessity of providing religious instruction for children in a country where Church and State are absolutely separated. In the Roman Catholic system religious instruction is as much the duty of society as secular education, and, indeed, more so, and is given on week days and supplemented by the catechism on Sunday. In the United States the Roman Catholics necessarily were forced to provide the religious instruction themselves and where they wished to combine it with secular education, as in European countries, to establish and maintain schools of their own where all instruction should be under the direction of the priests. On the other hand, they insisted that all religious teaching should be taken out of the schools supported by taxation and that the Bible should not be read there. In these ways the Protestant churches were forced themselves to provide religious instruction and this they did by the establishment of the Sunday School. These began a vigorous existence in the 1820's and became organized and systematized as the years went by. Moreover, as to these there seems to have been a tendency towards common effort on the part of the sects, as was

[1] In 1781, Robert Raikes of Gloucester, England, gathered the very poor children together twice on Sunday for two hours to instruct them in reading and learning the catechism and to lead them to the church. His plan does not seem to have been strictly religious, but these destitute children worked during the week and on the Sabbath were idle and mischievous. See William B. Tappan's *Sunday School*, 22. A school on this model was established by Samuel Slater in 1793 for poor children who worked in his factory in Pawtucket, Rhode Island. See W. R. Bagnall's *Textile Industries of the United States*, i, 161, 162, and George S. White's *Memoir of Samuel Slater*, 117.

shown by the joining of the Congregationalists and Baptists and other of the evangelical sects into school unions like the Massachusetts Sunday School Union, which was an auxiliary of the American Sunday School Union. In a table giving a summary of Sunday Schools in 1829–1830, the total number of "scholars" in the whole world is given as one and a half million, no less than one-third of them being in the United States.[1] These figures are another attestation of the fact that has already been noticed that the splitting up into groups of religious believers, which is so marked in the first third of the century, did not in any way mean a lessening of religious desire. Another indication of the same trend is in the stiffening of the Sunday laws that one associates with these years.

The early strictness of Sunday observance in New England is familiar to every one, largely on account of the publication of the bogus Blue Laws of Connecticut. Throughout New England — except in Rhode Island — no one was permitted to labor or transact business of any kind or to travel or be present at any public diversion on the Lord's Day. On the contrary, every one must apply himself, publicly and privately, to the duties of religion and piety and not disturb public worship under severe penalties. There was a difference of opinion as to the length of the Lord's Day, as to its beginning and its ending. In Massachusetts, in 1823, it legally extended from the midnight preceding to the following setting of the sun, but no one should be present at any music or dancing or be entertained at a tavern on the evening preceding or succeeding the Lord's Day, or should travel except when engaged in a work of necessity or charity.[2]

[1] This table was compiled by Daniel Dorchester, partly from the *American Quarterly Register* for 1829–30 and partly from official sources and printed in his *Christianity in the United States*, 429.

[2] *General Laws of Massachusetts* (1823), i, 407; *Public Statute Laws of . . . Connecticut* (1821), p. 385.

Moreover, at a little earlier time, no vessel should unnecessarily depart from any of the harbors of the State of Connecticut and no vessel, anchored in the Connecticut River within two miles of a place of public worship, should weigh anchor between morning light and setting sun on that day, unless to get nearer to the place of public worship.[1] These laws and laws like them have generally been regarded as peculiar to New England and to Congregationalism, but in 1822 the laws of the State of Georgia were approximately the same. There was to be no working or selling of goods on the Sabbath in that State and no sports as bear-baiting, football playing, and horse racing, and the public houses were to be closed, except to those actually living within them. In Alabama, in 1823, no worldly business, shooting, sporting, or gaming was to be practised on Sunday, no store to be open, no wagoner to ply his trade. Similar laws — but a little milder — were to be found in Kentucky and in the States northwest of the Ohio River,[2] where the influences of the various bands of immigrants combined to bring about a cessation of worldly employments on the Lord's Day. Of course, it is doubtful how much vitality any one or all of these laws had at any one time or at any one place, or in the country as a whole. There are evidences, however, that the tendency was toward a greater strictness of the observance of the Sabbath as we find petition after petition presented to Congress, or at any rate drawn up, praying for the cessation of work by federal law, as for example the carriage of the mails, within those hallowed hours. In 1828, a union was formed to promote the observance of the Sabbath, and

[1] *Statute Laws of . . . Connecticut*, Book I (1808), p. 579.
[2] *Digest of the Laws of . . . Georgia* (1822), 510, 511; *Digest of the Laws of . . . Alabama* (1823), 216; *Digest of the Statute Law of Kentucky* (1822), ii, 997; *Acts of a General Nature . . . of Ohio* (1824), xxii, 196; *Revised Laws of Indiana* (1831), 194.

in 1844, a convention was held at Baltimore for that purpose which was presided over by John Quincy Adams.[1] The progress that was made may be judged from a report to the effect that in 1850 forty railroad companies had stopped the running of their cars on the Sabbath on about four thousand miles of road. Another evidence of the religious earnestness of the time is to be found in the establishment of educational institutions by the different sects at their own cost throughout the country.

It seems to be agreed that a college education was a positive disadvantage to the camp meeting converter or the circuit rider. In one case that came before the Indiana conference where two men, one a college graduate, the other not, rode the same circuit, the non-college man "shouted" louder than his companion, sympathized with the women, and received nearly all the gifts, which he generously divided with his rival. The situation reminds one of the New Englander who said that one of the elders in his church never prayed without breaking all the rules of syntax, but that he would rather have him pray "than any of the best preachers in New York." Readiness in repartee and earnestness in conviction and in demeanor were of more importance to the missionary type of preacher, whether in the city or in the forest, than polished manners or a college training, — and religion was in the missionary stage in America in these early years of the nineteenth century. It was recognized, however, that other things being equal, a knowledge of commentators on the Scriptures and of Bible history was not amiss, especially in debate with one who was a peer in argument, but did not possess book learning. Then, too, it appeared that the laity was being debarred from temporal

[1] See *An Account of Memorials presented to Congress* (New York, 1829); J. Q. Adams's *Memoirs*, xii, 110–114; Dorchester's *Christianity in the United States*, 476–477.

education, because people of one faith did not like to send
their sons to colleges where they would not be under suitable
denominational influences and enjoy the ministrations of
their own clergymen.   The State universities that came into
being in these years did not supply the need for either
minister or layman, — a non-sectarian institution was not
what was wanted, but one that would be under the un-
disputed control of Methodist, or Congregationalist, or
Roman Catholic.   Seminaries came into existence in numbers and colleges for the education of one kind of religious
youth and of others, if they wanted to attend, also were
founded.   Many of these institutions led most painful
existences and many of them, in the fulness of time, disappeared altogether, but their establishment is a witness
to the genuineness of the beliefs of their founders and to
their desire that the coming generations should have better
facilities for gaining knowledge than they themselves had
enjoyed.   And some of these colleges and universities are
today among the strongest spiritual and educational influences in the country.

The intense, long-continued introspection, so charac-
teristic of the old type of Congregationalist and of those
who were near to him, as the Baptists and the Presbyterians,
and the protracted communing with the invisible power,
together with the strictness of daily life, led to tremendous
reactions when public religious control was slackened or
removed.   These manifested themselves in reformations of
all kinds, from redeeming one's neighbor from the rum habit
to rescuing Southern society from the curse of negro slavery ;
and they led to the greatest literary efflorescence in our
history, and to most extraordinary religious seekings.   Of the
religious readjusters, Alexander Campbell, Joseph Smith,
and William Miller are the most interesting.   The last two

sprang originally from the New England soil, but did not bear fruit until after transplantation to New York and even to the Western Reserve in northern Ohio.[1] Alexander Campbell was not a New Englander, but the son of a Scottish immigrant. He had grown up in Presbyterianism, but had broken away from it and had adopted "the primitive Christian faith."[2] He seems to have been a born religious controversialist and the result of his religious debating was the conversion of a very large portion of the Baptist population of the Western Reserve. They abandoned their covenants and beliefs and followed Alexander Campbell. William Miller began his labors in New York and Vermont. He studied the Bible persistently and took it literally from one cover to the other. After making the most elaborate calculations, which can be followed in a chart appended to his "Evidence . . . of the Second Coming of Christ, about the Year 1843,"[3] Miller prophesied the ending of the world within the twelve months after March, 1843. The number of his followers was extraordinary — more than extraordinary — because any one who sincerely followed him must be prepared on a certain moment of time to abandon all earthly things and with the others of the faithful commune in the ether with the Lord at his second coming. Some of them closed their business well in advance and sat down awaiting the second advent. Others kept on, because the Lord had commanded them to "occupy" until his coming.

[1] Mrs. L. A. M. Bosworth's "A Stormy Epoch, 1825–1850" in *Papers of the Ohio Church History Society*, vi, 1–22 is a brief, well written account of the religious life of the Western Reserve in the Campbellite–Millerite–Mormon period. The religious spirit of the time and place is well seen in J. A. Williams's *Life of Elder John Smith* (Cincinnati, 1870).

[2] Thomas W. Grafton's *Alexander Campbell, Leader of the Great Reformation of the Nineteenth Century* (St. Louis, 1897) states the main facts in brief compass and in readable form. Campbell's method can be gathered from a perusal of a section of his *Debate on Christian Baptism, between The Rev. W. L. Maccalla . . . and Alexander Campbell* (Buffaloe, 1824).

[3] Miller's *Evidence* was printed at Troy, N. Y., in 1838.

When nothing in particular happened in 1843, it was found that errors had been made in the calculation, which could hardly have failed to be the case considering the intricacies of the computations and combinations.[1] When nothing happened on the later appointed time, believers began to fall away.

The Church of Christ of the Latter-day Saints or the Mormon Church, as it is usually called, had its rise in the imaginings and business capacity of a very remarkable man, Joseph Smith. He came of a family that had been long on the New England soil. He, himself, was born in Vermont and when ten or eleven, removed to New York State. His early life was unsuccessful from the usual point of view. In the autumn of 1823, when not quite eighteen years of age and living at Manchester, Wayne County, New York, he received a visit from a "Messenger of God" who warned him that the preparatory work for the second coming of the Messiah was about to begin and that he had been chosen as an instrument in the hands of the Lord to bring about some of the purposes of this dispensation. In 1827 the "Angel of the Lord" delivered to him certain plates that had the appearance of gold. The plates were seven inches wide by eight inches long and the package was nearly six inches through—each plate being about the thickness of tin. "With the records was found a curious

---

[1] James White's *Sketches of the Christian Life and Public Labors of William Miller* (Battle Creek, Mich., 1875) and William Miller's *Evidence . . . of the Second Coming of Christ about the Year 1843* (also in the "Advent Library") taken together will exhibit to the ordinary reader the thoughts and theories of the great Adventist preacher. At the end of the 1841 edition of the *Evidence* is a "Chronological Chart of the World" that shows more clearly than the lectures the results of Miller's study and cogitation. Those who wish to go farther can read in the "Second Advent Library" in eight volumes and in *Advent Tracts*, especially No. 2 in vol. ii entitled "First Principles." The "Appendix" to Ellen G. White's *Great Controversy between Christ and Satan* is a clear statement of Miller's views as to the time of the second advent.

instrument, called by the ancients the Urim and Thummim, which consisted of two transparent stones, clear as crystal, set in two rims of a bow"; with these was a breastplate and a sword. The plates were covered with marks. These "by the gift and power of God" and by the use of "Urim and Thummim" Joseph Smith translated and dictated to a scribe, — and in this way the Book of Mormon was written down and the plates were then borne away by the "Angel of the Lord." "The Book of Mormon" was first printed in 1830.[1] It describes the coming of a colony to America from the Tower of Babel and its history in the New World. The language closely follows that of the Old Testament in the King James version and the story told in it is a variant of the Old Testament narrative. As originally printed there were many errors of grammar, some New York provincialisms, and some paraphrases of the New Testament. Critics, then and since, have marvelled that the Lord should have used such phrases in the "Golden Book of Cumorah," that chroniclers before the Christian era should have been familiar with the New Testament, and should have repeated the phrasings of the King James Bible. To this it has been answered that "the highest interpretation" was a reflex of the Prophet's mind and that Joseph Smith, therefore, in dictating, repeated phrases with which he was familiar. It has also been argued that the "Book of Mormon" is an adaptation from a manuscript written by Solomon Spaulding. He was a graduate of Dartmouth, had once been a clergyman, had later failed in business, and had solaced his declining years by writing a supposititious history of the American Indians in Biblical language. The Spaulding manuscript has never been produced, but it is averred that somehow it came into the hands of Joseph Smith and

[1] For a bibliography of Mormonism, see Note IV at end of chapter.

by him was used as the basis for the "Golden Bible" or
"Book of Mormon."

. At first, as is always the case in religious movements,
the gathering of disciples proceeded slowly. It was not until
Smith removed to Kirtland in Ohio, some twenty miles
to the eastward of Cleveland and in the centre of the Campbellite country, that converts flocked to the new dispensation. Smith introduced into the new life an element of
communism by which the Latter-day Saints lived very
much by themselves and conducted their own business
operations apart from those of the outer world. This won
for them the hostility of the neighbors who used the first
legal means that came within reach to eject Smith from
their midst. He and his followers removed to Missouri
where they increased in numbers, but again aroused the ill
will of those around them. They were most inhumanly
driven out of the State and settled in Illinois at Nauvoo,
just above the Des Moines rapids on the Mississippi River.
There they again increased in numbers, again aroused the
enmity of the neighbors, and again fled, but not until after
Smith himself had been murdered and his place taken by
another remarkable man, also of New England stock,
Brigham Young. From this time on Mormonism lost some
of its missionary character and became partly, at any rate,
a community experiment and a very successful one in the
heart of the Rocky Mountain region. Today (1920) it is
supposed that the Church of the Latter-day Saints numbers
more than half a million adherents in the regular church in
Utah and its mission establishments throughout the country
and in the dissenting Mormon faiths, as the "Reorganized
Church" of Joseph Smith, Jr., which is established again
at Kirtland on the property of the original church.

In this brief survey of the changing religious scene, it has not been possible to follow the stories of the Episcopalians, the Baptists, the Univeralists, and others among the sects. Enough has been said, however, to show that seldom in history have men and women developed a more widespread and active religious life than they did in the United States in the years that followed the great wars of the French Revolution and of Napoleon.

· NOTES

I. General Works. — Daniel Dorchester's *Christianity in the United States* (New York, 1889) traces religious activities from the earliest time to 1887. It is the result of long research and is distinctly usable. Containing such a mass of details it is necessarily unreadable and should be used as a cyclopædia of religion. There is no bibliography but the footnotes point the way to the best authorities. The *American Church History Series* contains denominational histories published under the auspices of the American Society of Church History. The thirteenth volume is Leonard W. Bacon's *History of American Christianity*. It is a literary survey rather than a cyclopædia and distinctly reflects the author's religious views. Robert Baird's *Religion in America* (New York, 1844) was written to exhibit the condition of Christianity in the United States to people of the countries of continental Europe, who found it difficult to understand how a " Church " could live without a close connection with the temporal power. It is even today the best brief statement of the religious condition of the American people in the first forty years of the century.

II. The Roman Catholics. — The best brief book is the *History of the Roman Catholic Church in the United States* by Thomas O'Gorman, Professor of Church History in the Catholic University at Washington, which forms volume ix of *The American Church History Series*. The bibliography prefixed to this work, while brief and incomplete, is useful. John Gilmary Shea's *History of the Catholic Church within the Limits of the United States* in four large volumes is a work of scholarly research. Volume i relates to colonial times; volume ii bears the sub-title of *Life and Times of the Most Rev. John Carroll* and brings the story down to 1815. Volumes iii and iv carry it on to 1866. This work is abundantly supplied with footnotes, but has no formal bibliography. Thomas Hughes's *History of the Society of Jesus in North America* contains a mass of documentary material that throws most interesting lights here and there. *The American Catholic Historical Researches*, the *Records of the American Catholic Historical Society of Philadelphia*, and the *American Catholic Quarterly Review* contain much important historical material; but most of the articles in the last named are argumentative rather than historical.

III. The Methodists. — *The Journal of the Rev. Francis Asbury . . . from August 7, 1771, to December 7, 1815* (3 vols., New York, 1821) is necessarily the foundation on which all extended accounts of the rise of American Methodism are based. W. P. Strickland's *Life and Times of Francis Asbury* follows it closely. J. M. Buckley's *Methodists* in the *American Church History Series* has a useful bibliography and is a good book in itself. The best way, however, to gain an insight is to read in the journals of the conferences as, for instance, the *Journals of the General Conference of the Methodist Episcopal Church;* the first volume brings the story down to 1836. Of the separate conferences, the " Minutes of the Indiana Conference, 1832–1844 " forming part ii of W. W. Sweet's *Circuit-Rider Days in Indiana* is most useful in throwing light on the early Methodist spirit, and part i, which is an historical summary, is very helpful.[1] It may be supplemented by the volume on the North Indiana Conference by Professor Sweet and H. N. Herrick that relates the history of the Methodist church in northern Indiana down to the present century. An earlier book, J. C. Smith's *Reminiscences of Early Methodism in Indiana*, contains biographical sketches of members of this conference and there are also separate and more detailed biographies of many of them. A. H. Redford's *History of Methodism in Kentucky* in three volumes is serviceable, bringing the story down to 1832. An extremely hostile examination of Methodism is J. R. Graves's *The Great Iron Wheel; or, Republicanism Backwards and Christianity Reversed*, to which a reply was made by W. G. Brownlow, the " Fighting Parson," in *The Great Iron Wheel, Examined,* and by Francis Hodgson, in *The Great Iron Wheel Reviewed* (Philadelphia, 1848). The cut showing " Methodism Mechanically Illustrated " facing p. 160 of the first of these books is a forcible illustration of the discipline of the Methodist church.

IV. The Latter-day Saints. — There is no adequate bibliography of Mormonism. *The Book of Mormon: An Account Written by the Hand of Mormon . . . By Joseph Smith, Junior, Author and Proprietor* was published at Palmyra, N. Y., in 1830. The second edition

[1] Greenough White's *An Apostle of the Western Church* is an interesting account of religion in the Western States woven around the life of Bishop Jackson Kemper. Other useful books are Rev. Charles Elliott's *South-Western Methodism* and Rev. A. M. Chreitzberg's *Early Methodism in the Carolinas.*

— the one now in use — was published at Kirtland, Ohio, in 1837. This is conveniently found in the volume issued by the Mormon Church in 1907 which also contains *The Doctrine and Covenants* and *The Pearl of Great Price, a Selection from the Revelations, Translations, and Narrations of Joseph Smith*. Nowadays, the Church seems to rely for spiritual guidance more on the last two than it does on *The Book of Mormon*. The "Articles of Faith" are printed at the end of *The Pearl of Great Price*. C. W. Penrose's "*Mormon*" *Doctrine, Plain and Simple* published by the Missions of the Church (3rd ed., 1917) is a brief plain statement of its doctrines at the turn of the century.[1] George Q. Cannon's *Life of Joseph Smith, the Prophet* (Salt Lake City, 1888) states the case for Mormonism as does B. H. Roberts's *Defense of the Faith and the Saints* that was printed in 1907–1912. The other side is set forth by Charles A. Shook in *The True Origin of The Book of Mormon* and *Cumorah Revisited*. Neither of these volumes has a bibliography, but the citations at the foot of the pages will take the student as far as he wishes to go.[2] An extremely hostile contemporaneous account by an inhabitant of Palmyra or its vicinity is in O. Turner's *History of . . . Phelps and Gorham's Purchase*, 212–217. Possibly the best way to get at the spirit of Mormonism is to read a volume or two of their serial publications[3] in combination with fifty pages or so of *The Pearl of Great Price*.

[1] The official account of the origin of the sect is the *History of the Church of Jesus Christ of Latter-day Saints* in six volumes. It was published at Salt Lake City in 1902–1912. The portion covering the story to 1844 is said to have been written by Joseph Smith, the Prophet. A series with the same title was issued by the "Reorganized Church" at Lamoni, Iowa, in four volumes in 1897–1908. The first two volumes contain the history of the Church to 1844; the last two the later history of the "Reorganized Church."

[2] This matter was re-examined by James H. Fairchild in 1886 (Western Reserve Historical Society's *Tracts*, iii, 187).

[3] From 1832 to the present day the Mormon Church has used the serial publication as a vehicle: — *Evening and Morning Star* (Independence, Mo., and Kirtland, Ohio, 1832–1834); *Latter Day Saints' Messenger and Advocate* (Kirtland, 1834–1836); *Elders' Journal* (Kirtland and Far West, Mo., 1837–1838); *Times and Seasons* (Commerce and Nauvoo, Ill., 1839–1846). *The Latter-Day Saints Millennial Star* has been printed in England by the missionaries there from 1841 to the present time.

CHAPTER VIII

EDUCATION

THE first third of the nineteenth century is usually regarded as the most barren in the educational history of English America;[1] yet that was the precise time when the reading habit was the most widespread among our people, when the writing of verse and prose was most common, and when our greatest writers were doing their best work or securing their mental stimulus. It is true that there were few public secondary schools outside of the largest towns; but their places were taken for a portion of the population by the academies. These were day schools or boarding schools or mixed day and boarding schools that were supported in part by public endowments which were largely supplemented by private gifts and fees. Oftentimes, too, pupils worked for their board and sometimes for their board and tuition. Besides the academies, there were private schools supported entirely by payments of the pupils. In the Southern States, academies and private boarding schools were not at all infrequent[2] and many of the richer families employed private tutors to teach their sons and the sons of their friends. Oftentimes, everywhere in the coun-

---

[1] For accounts of earlier times, see the present work, vol. ii, ch. xvi and iii, 566–570.

[2] Many of the academies admitted girls and there were many academies and schools that admitted girls only. These were numerous and active in the South. See Mrs. I. M. E. Blandin's *History of Higher Education of Women in the South Prior to 1860* (New York, 1909) and the memoirs of Southern men and women.

try, a cultivated maiden aunt exercised a distinct influence over the children of a family. Moreover, the colleges of those days were hardly more than secondary schools, boys habitually entering them at from thirteen to fifteen years of age. If the object of education is to produce scholars, the educational system of that time was singularly successful. But its influence was not widespread. The mass of the people had very slight educational opportunities and most of them, indeed, had no educational opportunities beyond the ungraded schools. These were small institutions, having one teacher and from a dozen to thirty pupils, and they were open only from three to five months in the year. To them came children and young men and women from five to seventeen years of age. They brought with them whatever text-books their homes afforded and proceeded to study whatever they could under these circumstances. Given a born teacher, one can hardly conceive of a more fruitful field for the display of pedagogical talents. Undoubtedly in many a town and district there was such a teacher and the young people who came under his or her influence must have been mentally stimulated and educated in the truest sense of the word, — far beyond what they can gain in the excellent graded schools and with the admirable text-books of our own time.

In the closing years of the eighteenth century some colleges had been founded and schools established and important legislative measures had been enacted that were to bear fruit eventually; but the unrest of those years gave an excuse to the handlers of public money to divert whatever funds they could get hold of to other uses. In 1789, the Massachusetts State legislature seriously impaired the old colonial school system by providing that the towns, which had formerly been obliged to establish secondary

schools whenever the number of families within the town
limits reached the one hundred mark, should in the future
be obliged to provide those facilities only when the number
of families had increased [1] to two hundred. In New York,
Pennsylvania, and other States many laws were passed
between 1790 and 1820 dealing with general education; but
very little public money was provided for education in any
of these States. In the Southern States, or in some of
them, "Literary Funds" were established. These generally
were based upon lotteries or on some peculiar financial
source. For example, in Delaware, in 1796, the legislature
provided that the money that came into the State treasury
in the next ten years from marriage and tavern licenses
should be devoted to the establishment of local schools
where children should be taught English and arithmetic
free of cost, but none of this money should be used for academies or colleges. This generosity to education continued
for only a year when the legislature provided that the money
arising from these sources should be devoted first of all to
paying the salaries of the judges and then what was left
over should be given to the cause of free education.[2] In
some of the States, especially in the newer ones, money
arising from the public lands was devoted to the education
of the people, either by the voluntary action of the State,
as in the case of Connecticut, or by reason of the conditions
of the grant as in the States organized on the public domain.[3]
In Virginia the money derived from the sale of the Church

[1] *Laws of . . . Massachusetts* (1807),
i, 469–473; see also, the present work,
vol. i, 432–434; vol. iii, 566–570.
[2] *Laws of . . . Delaware* (1797), ii,
1296–1298, 1352–1354. Delaware invested her share of the surplus deposits of 1837 in bank stock and in
railroad bonds; the income she devoted to her schools, and was still
doing it in 1880. E. G. Bourne's
History of the Surplus Revenue of 1837,
p. 52.
[3] See Clement L. Martzolff's "Land
Grants for Education in the Ohio
Valley States" in *Ohio Archæological
and Historical Quarterly*, xxv, 59;
Frank W. Blackmar's "Federal and
State Aid to Higher Education" in
Bureau of Education's *Circular of
Information, No. 1, 1890*.

lands and from some other sources was to be paid into the "Literary Fund." [1] This was to be used for the education of the poor and for such other purposes as the legislatures might direct. In Kentucky a similar fund was established from the profits of the Bank of the Commonwealth.[2] Elaborate provisions were made in the laws in some of these States for education, but many of them did not amount to very much. In 1796, the Virginia Assembly provided that all free children, male and female, should receive tuition free for three years and after that as much longer "at their private expense" as "their parents, guardians, or friends, shall think proper." The electors in each county were to choose three of their best men to be termed "aldermen" to divide the county into sections, provide school houses, and pay the teachers;[3] but not a single county had carried the plan into effect by 1801.[4] Of the States west of the Appalachians, Alabama is in some ways the most interesting. Her land grant was well managed and provided an appreciable revenue for education. The income was to be used for the support of the University and academies, and township schools were to be established, so that each school district should contain between thirty and forty pupils.[5] It is a most interesting paper educational project; but the speedy conversion of Alabama into a cotton-producing State and the consequent dispersal of the white population made impossible the carrying out of any such plan. The academies, however, grew and flourished and the University for

[1] *Revised Code of . . . Virginia* (1819), i, 89.

[2] *Digest of . . . Law of Kentucky* (1822, vol. ii, p. 871). North Carolina also had a "Literary Fund," see *South Atlantic Quarterly*, xiii, 270, 361.

[3] *Collection of Acts of the General Assembly of Virginia* (1803, p. 354, 355).

[4] Governor James Monroe to the Virginia Assembly in his *Writings*, iii, 309.

[5] These laws were enacted in the years 1818–23, see *Digest of the Laws . . . of Alabama* (1823), 543, 547, 552, 570, etc.

some years was remarkably successful, ranking number thirty-nine in the list of collegiate institutions in 1850, out of a total of one hundred and twenty-one.

Of the States organized on the territory northwest of the Ohio River, Ohio and Indiana made the most progress toward a free school system of any of the newer States in the first half of the century.[1] Professor Calvin E. Stowe of Lane Seminary in Cincinnati, who married Harriet Beecher, seems to have given the direct stimulus to the establishment of common schools in Ohio. His attention had been attracted to the German system of education. In 1831, Victor Cousin had been sent by the French Minister of Public Instruction to report upon the educational machinery of Germany.[2] His report was printed at Paris in 1833 and in English at New York in 1835. It aroused great interest in America as well as in France. Cousin declared that in 1831 there was not a single human being in Prussia who did not receive an education "sufficient for the moral and intellectual wants of the laborious classes." Moreover, secondary education was well attended to there, normal schools for teaching the teachers were abundant, and over all was the university, — the whole establishment from bottom to top, or from top to bottom, being under the control of the central governing authority. In 1836 Professor Stowe delivered an address on the "Prussian System of Public Education and its Applicability to the United States." He then sailed for Europe to buy books for Lane Seminary and to investigate the school systems there for the State. On

[1] President Butler (*Monographs on Education in the United States*, i, p. vii) tells us that land greater in area than New England, New York, New Jersey, Maryland, and Delaware all put together has been set apart at one time or another for educational purposes.

[2] M. V. Cousin's *Rapport sur L'État de L'Instruction Publique dans Quelques Pays de L'Allemagne, et Particulièrement en Prusse* (new ed., Paris, 1833) and translated into English by S. T. Austin as *Report on the State of Public Instruction in Prussia* (New York, 1835).

his return he delivered a report [1] to the Legislature that was most favorable to the German system and was adopted as the basis of the educational fabric of Ohio. The legislature at once established a fund for the purpose of free education and decreed that profits to be derived from the canal system and bonuses that might be received from the State Bank should be paid into it.[2] It was under these circumstances that the free common school system of Ohio was established in 1837.[3] Indiana managed her public lands with a thrift that was not usual. By laws passed in 1824 and 1831, a complete system of education was provided, including a university or two, primary schools, academies, and free common schools. Funds came in slowly, however, and succeeding legislatures were lax in passing laws for which there was no urgent demand on the part of the voter. It happened, therefore, that there was really no system of free schools above those of the district grade before 1850 and, owing to the strength of the religious sects in the State, the public university did not get the support that it deserved.[4]

---

[1] Calvin E. Stowe's *Common Schools and Teachers' Seminaries* (Boston, 1839), pp. 5–64. His "Report on Elementary Public Instruction in Europe" was made to the 36th General Assembly of Ohio, on December 19, 1837.

[2] Two acts were passed for the support of common schools in 1831. These were altered and extended in 1833, 1834, and later years and in 1838 a State superintendent of public schools was appointed. See *Acts of a General Nature . . . of the State of Ohio* (Columbus, 1831), vol. xxix, pp. 414, 423. For the later laws see *ibid.*, vol. xxx, p. 4; vol. xxxi, p. 24; vol. xxxii, p. 35, etc.; *Statutes of . . . Ohio* (1841), 819–845, etc.; A. D. Mayo's "Development of the Common School in the Western States from 1830 to 1865" forming chapter viii of *Report* of the United States Commissioner of Education for 1898–99, vol. i; E.

O. Randall and Daniel J. Ryan's *History of Ohio*, iii, 367–396; and Caleb Atwater's *History of the State of Ohio* (2nd ed.), 298.

[3] According to the first *Annual Report* of Samuel Lewis, Superintendent of the Ohio Common Schools issued in January, 1838, there were 468,812 children in Ohio between the ages of four and twenty-one years (242,518 males; 226,294 females). Of these only 146,440 attended school in the preceding year and of them 84,296 attended for less than four months.

[4] See *Revised Laws of Indiana* (Corydon, 1824), p. 379, Act of January 31, 1824, and *Revised Laws of Indiana* (Indianapolis, 1831), p. 463, Act of February 10, 1831. For a good, brief summary of early education in Indiana, see A. D. Mayo's "Development of the Common School," 373–380, in United States Commissioner of Education's *Report*, 1898–1899, vol. i.

In fact these paper educational systems, based on federal land grants and on adventitious financial sources as tavern licenses, do not seem to have had much life in the early days and it was not until the people began to pay for them as tax payers — direct or indirect — that they began to take an effective interest in them. The best example of the deadening effect of education without cost to the voters is seen in the case of Connecticut, where the funds derived from the sale of lands in the Western Reserve obviated the necessity of public grants by the State and local units. As far as this money went,[1] the school system was well provided for, but as the population grew and systems increased in cost, Connecticut lagged behind her two great neighbors.

The schools, such as they were, were "free" in the sense only that no white person was excluded from them by reason of poverty or position in the social scale. Ordinarily, the local school unit was authorized to levy a moderate tax upon the inhabitants of the school area for educational purposes. This was usually inadequate for the payment of the teacher's wages, small though they were. The balance was made up by the teacher's "boarding round" — staying in each family so many days, according to the number of children that came from that house to the school. Fuel was provided by the families according to the number of pupils in each household. Whatever money had to be raised by the district to pay the teacher's wages and to repair the school house was divided among the families, also, according to the children of school age. This was called the rate bill, and in many States the assessors were authorized to excuse from the payment of the school rate those persons

[1] See an act of the General Assembly, dated May, 1795, which provides that if two-thirds of the legal voters in any town wish to use their share of this fund for religious purposes, they may do so; *Acts and Laws of . . . Connecticut* (1796), p. 31.

who were unable to pay it. Their children could go to school, but they were referred to officially as "pauper pupils" or "charity pupils."

A good example of the working of the charity school system is to be found in Pennsylvania. The constitution of that State of 1790 directed the legislative body to provide education for the poor gratis, as soon as convenient.[1] Naturally, nothing was done for some years. In 1812, however, provision was made for the free education of poor children, but it was done in such a way as to put a stigma upon the child, as the recipient's name was entered upon a special list as a poor person. The working people looked askance at the system: they wanted their children to be educated, but were not able to pay for it, or thought they were not, and felt that the tax-paying part of the community ought to provide for the education of the children of the "workies" in common with their own.[2] In answer, the Pennsylvania legislature established a permissive system of common schools at public expense so far as the different portions of the State wished to have them. Not very much was accomplished under this law, partly because of the racial distinctions that prevailed in the different parts of the State.[3] In 1801, the legislature of New York authorized

[1] *Constitutions of Pennsylvania* (Harrisburg, 1916), p. 194, article vii, sec. 1. The second section provides that "The arts and sciences shall be promoted in one or more seminaries of learning." These two provisions were repeated verbatim in the constitution of 1838. It was not until the constitution of 1873 (article x, sec. 1) that a direct provision was made in the fundamental law of the State for the maintenance of a system of public schools (see *ibid.*, p. 57).

[2] See Commons and Associates' *History of Labour in the United States*, using index under "education," especially vol. i, 223–230. Many docu- ments relating to this subject are printed in *American Industrial Society*, vol. v.

[3] *Proceedings and Debates of the Convention of the Commonwealth of Pennsylvania* (Harrisburg, 1838), v, 183. For further debates on educa- tion, see *ibid.*, vols. xi, xii, and xiv, using the indexes, and pp. 297–305 of Isaac Sharpless' *Two Centuries of Pennsylvania History*. In 1837, the Secretary of State reported that the "public cost of education" amounted to $585,000 for primary instruction, acad- emies had received $106,900 and land worth $135,000, and colleges had been paid in money and land $260,000. Moreover, a school house fund of nearly

the raising of one hundred thousand dollars by four successive lotteries for the promotion of literature. A part of this money was to be given to institutions of a higher grade,[1] but a part was to be paid over to those who were actually educating the children in the common schools of the State and there, as in Philadelphia, the work was being done by private societies. And there, as in Philadelphia, the working people thought that their children should be educated by the public without any expense to the parents.

The leaders in this movement for free public schools in the two great industrial States were Robert Dale Owen and Frances Wright. Owen had been a pupil of Fellenberg's at Hofwyl in Switzerland. Their plan was worked out in the "Sketch of a System of National Education" by Frances Wright.[2] According to this plan the State should be organized into districts. All the children within each district from two to sixteen years of age should be gathered into public schools in three groups, the middle group comprising those from six to twelve years. The parents were to be allowed to visit the children at stated times, but were not to interfere in any way with them. The pupils were to be instructed in every branch of knowledge, intellectual and operative, or vocational. The produce of the labor of the older pupils would in time exceed the cost of their own training and the surplus could be devoted to the maintenance of the others. For the rest, the parents were to pay something in money, labor, produce, or domestic manufactures, and whatever other expense there was should be met by a progressively increasing tax on property. From the age of

half a million had been expended, *Proceedings and Debates of the Convention . . . of Pennsylvania* (1837), iii, pp. 6, 7.
[1] *Laws of . . . New York passed . . . in the year 1801* (Albany, 1887), v, 299.

[2] *Popular Tracts*, No. 3 (New York, 1830). For a substantial account of her, see G. B. Lockwood's *New Harmony*, 186 and fol.

two years, the children would be under the care of the
State. No inequality of any kind would be allowed, they
would be clothed in a common garb, "uniting neatness with
simplicity and convenience" and would eat at a common
table and exercise common duties. This nationalization of
children did not commend itself to any large number of
persons at that time, 1830; but something similar to it
was tried in more than one of the "communities" which
were so frequent in the first part of the century.[1]

Resulting partly from the work of semi-professional
agitators and partly from the widespread reformatory
spirit of the time, legislatures and those interested in education pushed forward the establishment of common schools.
These were schools above the primary grade that were free to
all and entirely supported by public money, and in which
the studies taught were modernized by the dropping of
Greek and Latin and better facilities were provided for the
comfort of pupils and teachers.[2] The person who had
most to do with the practical bringing to pass of the changes
in the school system was Horace Mann of Massachusetts.
Largely owing to his efforts, a State Board of Education
was established in Massachusetts, in 1837, thus introducing
the Prussian system of educational organization.[3] Mann
became secretary of this board. He travelled all over the
State examining schools and drew up reports that put an
end forever to the old idea of local control of educational

---

[1] See below, ch. xv.

[2] See "Report" of the Committee
on Education of the Massachusetts
House of Representatives, presented
January 29, 1827, *Massachusetts House
Reports*, 1826–27, Nos. 29 and 34.

[3] Jefferson, in 1820, speaking of the
influence of the old Massachusetts
school system, said that although
that State was the twenty-first State
in point of size and only one-tenth

the area of Virginia "it is unquestionable that she has more influence
in our confederacy than any other State
in it. Whence this ascendancy? From
her attention to education, unquestionably. There can be no stronger
proof that knowledge is power, and that
ignorance is weakness." *Early History
of the University of Virginia, . . .
in the Letters of Thomas Jefferson and
Joseph C. Cabell*, 193.

institutions. New standards were set up and the schools, not only of Massachusetts but of other States, felt it necessary to come up to them or to approach them at any rate. Horace Mann also brought about the establishment of a few normal schools for the training of teachers.[1] This meant the formation of a class of professional pedagogues, — for up to that time teachers, apart from the keepers of "dame schools," had been college students in the seven weeks winter vacation or students of law, physic, or theology.[2] There was great opposition to these changes by the old timers and their influence was so strong with the legislature that Horace Mann, although a public official, was at one time obliged to rely upon the contributions of rich men to keep the new system alive. In 1847, he resigned his office to become a member of Congress, but in ten years he had directed the tide of interest in educational matters towards improved, free, secondary schools of an unsectarian character.[3] In time free high schools were superadded to this system which in its perfected form was intended to provide free instruction of the old collegiate grade for every child in the State. As a part of the general movement, state-aid was taken away from academies and the old

[1] See Putnam's *Primary and Secondary Education in Michigan,* 136.

[2] In 1804, commencement was usually at the end of August, the winter vacation seven weeks from the third or fourth Wednesday in December, and two weeks in May and four weeks after commencement, *Columbian Almanack* for 1804, p. 43.

[3] Mrs. Mary Peabody Mann's *Life and Works of Horace Mann* (3 vols., Boston, 1865–68). His educational papers are included in these volumes, which were later enlarged and reprinted by his son, Horace Mann, in 5 volumes in 1891. A strong criticism of Mann's methods and his defence of them will be found in *Remarks on the Seventh Annual Report of the Hon. Horace Mann* (Boston, 1844); his *Reply to the "Remarks"* (Boston, 1844); Leonard Withington's *Penitential Tears; or a Cry from the Dust, by "The Thirty-One,"* *Prostrated and Pulverized by the Hand of Horace Mann, Secretary, &c.* (Boston, 1845); and George B. Emerson's *Observations on a Pamphlet entitled "Remarks."* Much interesting information is to be found in the reports of the "Visiting Committees" of the Boston schools as that for 1845 forming "City Document" No. 26 for that year.

colleges, which in the future had to rely on private bene-
factions and tuition fees for support.

The tax payers and the well-to-do generally were against
any scheme of the kind such as Horace Mann and his fellow
laborers wished to see established. They paid for the
education of their own children and failed to see why they
should also pay for the education of the children of their
neighbors. As the century advanced and an industrial
class came into being and as the number of immigrants increased an entirely new outlook was presented. It was
then easy to argue that with the extension of the franchise
and the establishment of a laboring class, education would
be a species of insurance against attacks on property,
pauperism, and crimes of violence. Jefferson, with his
keen insight, asserted that the establishment of a free public
educational system at the cost of the tax payers would be a
direct benefit to the rich man. It would people his neighborhood with "honest, useful, and enlightened citizens, understanding their own rights, and firm in their perpetuation."
Moreover, within three generations, the rich man's descendants would themselves be poor and would benefit by the
free public school system that had been established by their
grandfathers' money.

It is truly remarkable how slight America's contribution
had been to the practice and organization of teaching. Our
school system comes from Prussia, our pedagogics down
to 1860 at any rate from Switzerland, from Pestalozzi,
Emanuel Fellenberg, and Louis Agassiz. The ideas seem
to have been those of Pestalozzi, but their first practical
exemplification was by Fellenberg, his disciple or follower.
According to this idea instruction, instead of being a matter
of memory and of acquisition, should be the result of thought
and of analysis. Children should be employed in all kinds

of work and play and these should be frequently changed so as not to become wearisome; they should study languages and mathematics under competent direction, engage in games under supervision, and cultivate the soil under proper guidance. Fellenberg's "Institutions" were at Hofwyl in Switzerland. They provided for the children of both the rich and the poor. These did not live together, but the surplus fees of the rich were used to augment the instruction of the poor who were taught scientific farming by actual practice. It is difficult to arrive at any exact conclusion as to the success of the Hofwyl experiment.[1] Most of the information that we have about it is controversial and comes from sympathizers, but one thing is certain that, owing in part at least to the conditions of the times, no long life attended Fellenberg's Institutions.

In the establishment of free education, whether by private societies or by public means, the question of expense always came forward. One way of economizing that enjoyed great prosperity for a while was to have the older pupils teach the younger. This system was devised by

[1] According to Fellenberg, education should "develop all the faculties of our nature, physical, intellectual, and moral, and to endeavor to train and unite them into one harmonious system, which shall form the most perfect character of which the individual is susceptible; and thus prepare him for every period, and every sphere of action to which he may be called." As an example of his method in teaching mineralogy, he called upon the pupil to use his own senses to describe the color and form of the mineral presented, to observe its weight, and to test its hardness, and to compare it with other objects and other minerals, and then he is given the name. The best description of the Hofwyl Institutions is in the *Letters* written by William C. Woodbridge and printed in the *American Annals of Education* in 1831 and 1832, and also as the Appendix to *Letters from Hofwyl by a Parent* (London, 1842), pp. 225 and fol. For a brief account of Hofwyl see *Edinburgh Review* for December, 1818 and *Educational Institutions of Emanuel de Fellenberg by his son*, Wilhelm de Fellenberg (London, 1859). See also *Lettre de M. Ch. Pictet*, published at Paris in 1812; and other works of Pictet have other matter relating to Hofwyl. An interesting engraving showing the Hofwyl Institutions is in J. K. Bellweger's *Die Schweizerischen Armenschulen nach Fellenberg'schen Grundsäken* (Trogen, 1845). There is a lifelike glimpse of Hofwyl in Robert Dale Owen's *Threading My Way*, 146 and fol.

Andrew Bell or by Joseph Lancaster [1] or by both of them. The idea is said to have come to Bell in India by observing the children of a Malabar school writing with their fingers on the sand. As the system was worked out, the children sat at tables covered with fine sand on which they wrote with rattan styluses. An older pupil, or monitor, wrote a letter or a syllable on a blackboard and pronounced it; the pupils copied it on their sand tables and then repeated the sound in unison. The method at once found favor in England and even greater favor in America. Primary education in New York [2] and Philadelphia was then in the hands of private societies which were maintained largely by the Quakers. These naturally adopted Lancaster's system because that was supported by the English dissenters while Bell's plans had been adopted by the Established Church people. With the advancing decades the system became more and more elaborate, until the teachers were really more than older pupils, being paid and partly trained. As far as numbers went, the Lancasterian schools were very successful. They spread from New York and Philadelphia as far west and south as Detroit and Cincinnati, Louisville and Baltimore, and there was a "monitorial school" in Boston in 1823.[3] This was conducted on the "united plans of Lancaster and Pestalozzi"; there were seventy-five pupils, their ages ranging from five years to eighteen.

[1] See Note II at end of chapter.

[2] See "Sketch of the New-York Free School" prefixed to the American edition of Lancaster's *Improvements in Education* (New York, 1807); J. F. Reigart's "Lancasterian System of Instruction in the Schools of New York City" (*Columbia University Contributions to Education*, No. 81); and C. C. Ellis's *Lancasterian Schools in Philadelphia*. This and the preceding essay contain helpful bibliographies.

Wm. Oland Bourne on pages 14–24 of his *History of the Public School Society of the City of New York* prints De Witt Clinton's address of 1809, which is one of the very best brief accounts of the introduction of the monitorial system in America.

[3] W. B. Fowle's *First Biennial Report of the Trustees and Instructer of the Monitorial School, Boston* (Boston, 1826).

So well thought of were the Lancasterian schools that in 1819 the Massachusetts Peace Society declared the abolition of war would provide, among other things, for the establishment of such schools "over the globe," in which all the children of the world could be constantly taught! On the other hand, one of the enemies of the system, referring to the fact that neither paper nor slate was necessary, because the characters were written by a rattan stylus in sand sprinkled on a table — declared that the Lancasterian system "was cheap, very cheap! Sand and rattan were its chief outlay, and . . . sand and rattan were its chief returns."

The colleges in point of numbers and in scholastic quality were poorer off in 1800 than they had been in 1750; but they began to arouse themselves in the early years of the century. The governing boards of Harvard College provided that the conditions of admission must be higher than heretofore. Besides both Greek and Latin translation and grammar and the turning of English into Latin, students in the future were to be examined in addition and subtraction and other branches of arithmetic and in some approved "Compendium of Geography." [1] Within a few years the instruction in the college itself was considerably modified and in the 1830's, it looked for a time as if the German influence would bring about an extension of the curriculum, or even the establishment of something approaching an elective system. A similar tendency toward change and experimentation was shown in the reorganization of the governing board. Until 1800 Harvard was practically a State university and was so recognized in the constitution of 1780. Its governing board included the principal State officials and certain Congregational ministers. In 1810,

[1] *Boston Independent Chronicle* for February 6, 1804.

provision was made for the election of fifteen Congregational ministers and fifteen laymen by the existing Board of Overseers in addition to the principal political officers of the State. In 1812, this arrangement was overturned and the old colonial organization restored. But two years later in 1814, the act of 1810 was restored with the addition that the members of the State Senate should be added to the Board of Overseers. In 1834, the requirement that the clergymen should be Congregationalists disappeared, and in 1851 the requirement that any of its members should be ministers was abandoned. In 1865, State officials ceased to sit on the Board and the election of Overseers was given to the alumni. In the early days the colony had provided a large part of the funds for the support of the college. Its financial interest in the institution declined, however, and after the Revolution practically ceased.[1] Tuition fees and salaries were diminutive in the first half of the nineteenth century. In 1828 fifty-five dollars and forty cents were paid for board, tuition, and breakage for a boy at Harvard for a term. This amount was excessive in comparison with M. M. Strong's quarter bill at Middlebury College in the preceding year, which was only nine dollars and eighty-eight cents for tuition, lodging, and the use of the college library, and thirty-eight cents for repairs.[2] Scholastic desire, however, was in the air and boys of fourteen read wide and deeply, far beyond the requirements of their teachers and became the scholars of the century.

The list of studies in those days included no science or technical subjects. Professor John Winthrop had given

[1] *General Laws of Massachusetts* (ed. 1823), ii, 251, 312, 347, 405, etc.; *Massachusetts House of Representatives Reports* for 1827, No. 28. The annual *Catalogue* of Harvard University reprints the official documents relating to that institution.

[2] Strong Mss. in the library of the Wisconsin Historical Society. On the other hand he paid six dollars for a copy of "Jones's Lexicon."

some lectures on astronomy and scientific matters in the preceding century but he seems to have had no immediate successor. In 1788, the Harvard Corporation authorized Dr. Benjamin Waterhouse, who had been lecturing on natural history at Providence for a year or two, to deliver annually a course of lectures on this subject "to such students as shall obtain permission, under the hands of their Parents or Guardians" at one guinea for each hearer. Waterhouse lectured for years,[1] drawing his information from the best writers of the time and stimulating many persons to the study and endowment of science.

Philadelphia was the first seat of American science, partly no doubt because it had for years sheltered Benjamin Franklin and David Rittenhouse. As far back as 1728, Franklin had instituted a scientific society that in 1769 was refounded as the American Philosophical Society [2] with himself as president. The University of Pennsylvania had recognized the desirability of scientific instruction and in 1800 possessed a professor of chemistry,[3] mineralogy, and physics. His name was James Woodhouse and his lectures served to pass on the scientific learning of one generation to the next. More important in every way was Robert Hare.[4] He was the son of a brewer and watch-

---

[1] In 1803, Waterhouse began the publication of articles on botany and other scientific themes in the *Monthly Anthology and Boston Review*. These articles greatly enlarged were gathered into a book entitled *The Botanist. Being the botanical part of a course of lectures* (Boston, 1811). He also dabbled in literature, writing a romance entitled *A Journal, of a Young Man of Massachusetts, . . . on Board An American Privateer* and printed a substantial volume on *Junius and his Letters* (Boston, 1831). There is a sketch of the life of Dr. Waterhouse in a book entitled *The Harvard Medical*

School, 1782–1902 edited by Dr. Harold C. Ernst and published at Boston in 1906, pp. 15–20.

[2] For the early history of this organization see *Laws and Regulations of the American Philosophical Society* (Philadelphia, 1833), pp. 27, 28.

[3] John Penington's *Chemical and Economical Essays* published at Philadelphia in 1790 was the first book to be printed in America devoted entirely to chemistry.

[4] See Edgar F. Smith's *Life of Robert Hare, an American Chemist* (Philadelphia, 1917) and his *Chemistry in America* (New York, 1914), ch. viii.

ing the processes of brewing may have incited him to inquiry. While still a mere lad, he made the first workable oxy-hydrogen blow-pipe, although possibly he cannot be regarded as the discoverer of it. His development had been influenced greatly by Priestley and later as a professor in the University, he devoted himself mainly to electricity. The popularization of science, however, is connected with Yale College and with the names of Timothy Dwight and Benjamin Silliman. The former was a Congregational clergyman of stupendous industry, wide range of learning, and remarkable judgment. He published many books and his posthumous "Travels in New-England and New-York" [1] can be read with profit, even now. At the age of forty-three and in the year 1795, Dwight became president of Yale College. He redirected the course of that institution into the orthodox path, but, besides, was happily inspired with the thought that the students might well be somewhat weaned from the classics and theology and given a taste of science. There was no one in America who could do what he wished and he hesitated to import a foreigner. Looking about him, he selected Tutor Silliman for the job. This young man was then twenty-one years of age, was teaching the ancient languages and studying law, and was as innocent of science as any man in Connecticut. Dwight's plan was that a "chair" of chemistry and natural history should be established, that Silliman should be appointed to fill it, and should then study the subject at the expense of the college. After some hesitation Silliman agreed to the plan, the trustees ratified the scheme, and the new professor departed for New York and Philadelphia. He got little help at the first-named place, but in the latter he

---

[1] This was published in four volumes at New Haven in 1821-22. An edition appeared in London in 1823.

listened to Woodhouse, conversed with Priestley, and worked
with Hare. Returning to New Haven, he lectured on science
with illustrative experiments and won an audience at once.
His apparatus was crude and, according to his own account,
his lectures were less scientific than his experiments.[1] The
college authorities were so well satisfied with him that they
sent him to England to buy apparatus for his laboratory and
books for the college library, — paying him his salary and
giving him a percentage on the money expended for apparatus and books. At London and Edinburgh, Silliman made
good use of his opportunities for scientific study. Returning to New Haven, he renewed his college lecturing and
sought wider opportunities of service. In 1818, he established "The American Journal of Science and Arts" and
edited it so well that in a few years it became self-supporting.
He also lectured to the people of New Haven and neighboring towns and gradually sought larger centres until he became a well-known figure on the platform. As a student,
and as an inciter to the acquisition of knowledge by others,
Benjamin Silliman's life was one of the most striking in
our annals.

Apart from the awakening of the older collegiate institutions in response to the intellectual movement of the age of
Emerson, the foundation of the Universities of New York
and of Virginia and the opening of the Southern and Western State Universities are points of interest. The origin
of the New York University is confused.[2] Some people

[1] See George P. Fisher's *Life of Benjamin Silliman*, especially vol. i, chs.
iii and iv and Edgar F. Smith's *Chemistry in America*, ch. ix.

[2] For accounts of the University
of the State of New York, see Franklin B. Hough's *Historical and Statistical Record of the University of the
State of New York . . . 1784 to 1884*
(Albany, 1885) and Sidney Sherwood's

*University of the State of New York,
Origin, History and Present Organization* forming *Regents' Bulletin*, No. 11,
January, 1893 or "Appendix 3" of the
106th Annual Report of the Regents.
The statutory condition of education
in New York, both primary and higher,
may most easily be seen in the *Revised
Statutes of the State of New-York* (1829),
chap. xv.

have argued that the intention was to found something like an English University composed of a group of semi-independent colleges under one management, the difference being that the colleges instead of being within the limits of one town as in England would be within the limits of one State of the American union. The other theory is that the New York legislature was influenced by French ideas, by the thought of combining all education within the State limits under one governing board. In 1784, the State legislature established the Regents of the University of the State of New York. They had the right of visitation of all incorporated institutions of learning in the State and such secondary schools as they should take into their care. They were authorized to hold property to the amount of an annual income equal to the value of forty thousand bushels of wheat and were to apportion whatever funds came to them from the State among the institutions under their charge according to rules of scholastic efficiency to be laid down by them. At first the history of the new university was hardly more than the story of a contest between the State authorities and King's College, which changed its name to Columbia.[1] The law establishing the Regents of the University has been modified from time to time and the control of primary and secondary education has been entrusted to a separate board; but, when all has been said, it is still true that this institution has played a very great part in the history of the development of education in New York and in the United States.

The University of Virginia was peculiarly the child of Thomas Jefferson and still lives[2] with many of the dis-

---

[1] *Laws of the State of New York* (Albany, 1886), i, 686; Van Amringe (editor), *Historical Sketch of Columbia College . . . 1754–1876*, especially the "Appendix."

[2] The best account of the founding of the University of Virginia is in the *Early History of the University of Vir-*

tinctive features that he looked upon as of great importance, and in the first thirty or forty years of its existence it produced a most remarkable set of men. In 1817, Jefferson drew up a plan for the division of Virginia into districts, in each of which there should be a free public school providing primary and secondary instruction. Grouping these districts together into nine collegiate divisions, he proposed to provide a college for each, so that no house in the State should be more than a day's ride from a college. Above them all, at some central point, there should be a university at which every branch of learning should be taught. He and his friends found their way beset with difficulties. The genius of Virginia society was opposed to any such scheme of primary and secondary education. Moreover, the religious bodies were unfalteringly hostile to the establishment of non-sectarian collegiate institutions and a State university, especially by the expenditure of public money, while they themselves were struggling hard to keep their own colleges alive. When Jefferson had once put his hands to the plough, it was difficult to make him turn back, although he might seem to be diverted from his purpose. In

ginia, as contained in the Letters of Thomas Jefferson and Joseph C. Cabell (Richmond, 1856). Cabell was Jefferson's right hand man and, indeed, deserves to be called the co-founder of the University. This volume, in a series of Appendices, contains nearly all the original matter relating to the subject. A brief account largely founded on this book is J. S. Patton's *Jefferson, Cabell, and the University of Virginia* (New York, 1906). The "Memorial Association's" edition of Jefferson's *Writings* contains practically all the Jefferson material. Herbert B. Adams's *Thomas Jefferson and the University of Virginia* (U. S. Bureau of Education's *Circular of Information*, No. 1, 1888) is an elaborate account of the founding and later history of the institution. Possibly the most interesting thing that has been written on the subject is P. A. Bruce's "Background of Poe's University Life" in *The South Atlantic Quarterly*, x, 212, and the first part of D. M. R. Culbreth's *University of Virginia* (New York, 1908) is a readable account of the early time. There are some interesting glimpses of the institution in its earliest days in Edward Warren's *A Doctor's Experiences in Three Continents*, pp. 92, 100, 115. In May, 1810, Jefferson had outlined a part of his ideas as to a university in a letter to Hugh L. White, in which he refused to sell lottery tickets for the benefit of East Tennessee College ; — *American Historical Magazine*, i, 296.

this case no opportunity escaped him to forward his plan, although for a time his interest appeared to be torpid. He turned an inchoate Albemarle Academy into what he called Central College and then, in 1819, secured an appropriation from the Virginia legislature for the conversion of that college into his long-hoped-for non-sectarian University of the State of Virginia. Already, he had provided elaborate plans for university buildings. These would cost a great deal of money, but would constantly instil culture into those who lived in them and used them. A rotunda, one-half the size of the Pantheon, would serve as a library and a centre. Stretching from it was a range of pavilions and cloisters. The pavilions were to be occupied by professors who were expected to be bachelors at appointment and to remain so, and the cloisters and the cells opening on them were for the students. As the buildings progressed and the demands for money became an annual feature, public opinion turned against the project. Then Jefferson struck his last blow. Virginia was sending her sons to Princeton and to Harvard, he wrote, where they were learning anti-Missourian principles and were imbibing ideas absolutely opposed to those held by the people of the State in which they were born and in which they must pass their lives![1] Why not provide an institution within the State that would give them a better education, or at any rate as good a one? The university was opened in 1825 and immediately overflowed with students.[2] The sectarians were more alarmed than ever, for Jefferson had made no provision for a professor of theology and some of the professors that he had drawn from abroad were free thinkers. In reply, he suggested that each religious sect should appoint

---

[1] *Early History of the University of Virginia . . . Letters of . . . Jefferson and . . . Cabell*, 201.

[2] See *Enactments relating to the Constitution and Government of the University of Virginia* (Philadelphia, 1838).

and maintain a professor of its own kind or establish a college on the outskirts of the university. With his liberality as to administration, he provided that the students should govern themselves, most of them being of the mature years of from thirteen to sixteen.[1] It is sad to think that the last year of his life and of his career as Rector of the University was troubled by the ill behavior of a few of the first set of students to whom scholastic freedom, such as Jefferson prescribed, was not comprehensible.

Of the collegiate institutions in the country west of the mountains, Transylvania University at Lexington in Kentucky had possibly the most interesting history in the early time.[2] It was originally in the hands of the Presbyterians, but in 1818 Dr. Horace Holley, then pastor of the Hollis Street Church at Boston and a Unitarian, became president. The next few years saw a most astonishing growth in the medical as well as in the academic departments. Holley was soon driven out on the ground that he was a Socinian and taught "morality and the beauty of nature and not Christ crucified"; his enemies declaring that the gospel was "of more value to the western country than all the science upon the earth." The attendance soon fell off, there being only two hundred and seventeen students in the academic department in 1842. Numbers, of course, mean very little ordinarily in assessing the value of educational effort; but in this case they certainly seem to show that there was an urgent demand for good non-sectarian

---

[1] Massachusetts Historical Society's *Collections*, 7th Series, i, 356–360.

[2] See Robert and Johanna Peter's *Transylvania University* (*Filson Club Publications*, No. 11). This and all other books on the history of the University down to 1828 are largely based on Charles Caldwell's *Discourse on the Genius and Character of the Rev. Horace Holley* (Boston, 1828) containing an "Appendix" by "several pens." Jefferson Davis attended Transylvania in 1821–1824 and W. L. Fleming's "Early Life of Jefferson Davis" in the *Mississippi Valley Historical Review* for April, 1917, has a few pages on the institution and a bibliography.

instruction in Transappalachia at that time. In fact, after 1840, the educational impulse in the Southwestern country distinctly diminished. In 1854, the trustees of the University of Alabama directed the faculty of that institution to draw up a plan for the establishment of the system of the University of Virginia at Tuscaloosa. This led to the presentation of a remarkable report by Professors F. A. P. Barnard and John W. Pratt. This is in some ways the best survey of higher education in the United States in 1850 to be found in print. The comparative numbers of students in the universities of Virginia and Alabama convinced them that there was no demand among the people of the latter State for an institution of the Virginia type. The demand was really for the opportunity to study anything that one chose. It was impossible for the University to provide instruction in any branch that any Alabama boy or man, regardless of his previous training, might desire, and it was absurd to turn the University into a sort of ungraded higher institution of learning. The real underlying objection of the people to the University seems to have been that they wished for vocational training, while it thought only of disciplining the mind. Barnard and his colleague [1] closed the discussion by stating that after leaving college one might forget his Greek and Latin and retain the mental discipline that he had derived from the study of the classics which he could apply to the prosecution of any business in which he might happen to engage, — to the practice of the law, or of medicine, or of theology, or to the prosecution of any technical work, or to the pursuit of any career.

In 1800, there were no technical schools in the country

[1] See *Professor Barnard's Report on Collegiate Education* (New York, 1854). On the general subject of education in Alabama, see Willis G. Clark's monograph forming United States Bureau of Education's *Circular of Information No. 3, 1889*, and also Dr. Alva Woods' *Literary and Theological Addresses* (Providence, 1868), p. 64.

and few schools for training in the learned professions. There were medical schools in Philadelphia and in New York. The Harvard Medical School was already established at Cambridge [1] and within a few years the College of Medicine opened its doors at Baltimore. Jefferson provided for law and medicine in his University and there were schools of law and medicine attached to Transylvania. In fact, by 1830, the study of medicine was generally prosecuted in some special school. With law, the case was different. The lawyer's office maintained its position as the best place for legal training although Judge Gould's Law School at Litchfield, Connecticut, was flourishing in the first quarter of the century. The charge for tuition at this school was high, being one hundred dollars for the first year and sixty for the second.[2] In most of the universities there were lectures given on law, or constitutional law, or "natural law," or on the Common Law.[3] But this instruction was intended to be additional to the more important work in the lawyer's office. Theology, alone, of the learned professions was well taken care of. Each one of the leading sects had one or more seminaries that were well attended and vigorous institutions.

Near the close of the eighteenth century several associa-

[1] Thomas F. Harrington's *Harvard Medical School* in three volumes (New York, 1905) is almost a history of medicine in the United States in the earlier time. *Some Account of the Medical School in Boston* that was printed in 1824 gives one a glimpse of those days of small things, but of high aspirations. An extremely useful publication is *The Harvard Medical School 1782–1906* issued in 1906.

[2] For accounts of this school, see the reprint of 1900 of *The Litchfield Law School* which contains a catalogue of the pupils from 1798 to 1833; the "Moses M. Strong Manuscripts" in Madison, Wis.; Pease and Niles's *Gazetteer of . . . Connecticut and Rhode-Island*, 233; and *Life of Horace Mann, By His Wife*, 30.

[3] The Harvard Law School was founded in 1817. Its early years were feeble, but in 1829 with the accession of Joseph Story to its staff, it at once assumed the foremost place that it has since held. For a dozen years, from 1833 to 1845, it had only two professors, Story and Simon Greenleaf, but those two gave to it a distinction that few Law Schools have had before or since. See *The Centennial History of the Harvard Law School, 1817–1917.*

tions of men of learning were founded; the oldest was the American Philosophical Society that was instituted in Philadelphia [1] in 1769. The next was the American Academy of Arts and Sciences which was founded at Boston in 1780, and thereafter associations of the kind were established in different parts of the country.[2] West Point Military Academy and the United States Coast Survey bred a remarkable succession of men for technical service in civil life. No technical schools of the modern type were established until after 1820. The earliest were the Rensselaer Polytechnic Institute at Troy, the Sheffield Scientific School at New Haven, and the Lawrence Scientific School at Cambridge. Otherwise, engineers and men of science got their training in Europe or were Europeans by birth, or were taught in the school of experience in America.

One thing that took the place of professional and technical education — to a very limited degree, however — was the lecture platform. This was the epoch of lecturing when the foremost men in letters, and art, and science in the country sought to enlighten and stimulate their fellow citizens by the spoken word. Courses of lectures were promoted by professional organizers and institutes were endowed by philanthropists for the enlightenment of their countrymen. Of them all the most remarkable was the Lowell Institute. It was in 1835 that John Lowell, Jr., amidst the ruins of Thebes, completed the happy idea of establishing by bequest an Institute in Boston for the dissemination of knowledge among the people of his native

[1] G. Brown Goode printed a most serviceable essay on the origin of the "National Scientific and Educational Institutions" in the *Papers* of the American Historical Association for April, 1890. For the organization of these national technical schools, see pp. 109, 110, 130–135.

[2] The Massachusetts Historical Society was founded at Boston in 1790. At first it collected and studied both human and natural history, but after a time the natural history collections were transferred to another society; and since then it has devoted its attention entirely to human history.

town and State. Some of the provisions of his bequest
are peculiar and deserve notice: — none of the money
was to be put into bricks and mortar for the Institute's
purposes, although it might be invested in productive real
estate or mortgages; the care of the property and the conduct of the Institute were confided to a single trustee whose
first business was to nominate his successor, if possible, from
those who bore the name of the donor.[1] Furthermore, no
more than the equivalent of two bushels of wheat could ever
be charged for the privilege of attending any one course of
lectures or instruction. Mr. Lowell's idea was to give practically free instruction in technical subjects to mechanics
and other persons whose labors prevented attendance at the
usual schools and institutions; and to provide lectures
by leading men for the instruction of the serious minded
in the best thought and practice of the day. The Institute
was opened in 1839. One of the first persons to whom the
trustee turned was Benjamin Silliman, who in four successive years gave a series of twelve lectures, repeating the
course for those who could not get seats for the original
lectures. For years the Lowell Institute has performed a
service that is almost without parallel in alluring by high
payments the foremost men of the world to stimulate the
minds of the people of New England. In its success, its
practical freedom from tuition fees, and its absence of
"plant," the Lowell Institute stands alone as a tribute
to its founder and to those who have managed its interests.

The early connection between portrait painting, invention, and the study of natural history was very marked.
Fulton was an artist before he studied the application of
steam to navigation; Morse supported himself and his

[1] Harriette K. Smith's *History of the*   Edward Everett's *Memoir of Mr.*
Lowell Institute (Boston, 1898) and   *John Lowell, Jun.*

family by portrait painting while he was putting together the various parts of the telegraph; and Audubon provided whatever sustenance he did provide for his family by the same means. The three earliest students of natural history in the field devoted themselves mainly to the study of birds and they were all foreigners by birth; but they may well be regarded as American by reason of long habitation within the United States. These were Alexander Wilson, Charles Lucian Bonaparte, and John James Audubon. Wilson was a Scot and had been apprenticed to a weaver. He came to America in 1794, travelled the country over, especially the Southwestern part of it, and published at Philadelphia, in the years 1808–1814, nine volumes entitled "American Ornithology."[1] He had been aided on the botanical side of his research by William Bartram, and Bonaparte added four volumes to Wilson's nine as a sort of appendix. Considering the infancy of the country and the difficulties of book making, this work must be regarded as supremely creditable, but it was so superseded by Audubon's "Birds" that few persons out of the ornithological walks have ever heard of Wilson.

John James Audubon was born in Haiti, April 26, 1785. His father was a French sea officer and his mother a creole of San Domingo. Audubon's own youth was passed in France.[2] Coming to America, like most men of genius he

[1] *American Ornithology; or, the Natural History of the Birds of the United States. Illustrated with Plates* (9 vols., Philadelphia, 1808–1814). Unfortunately Wilson died before the 8th volume was printed and his friend George Ord edited the last two volumes, prefixing a brief sketch of the life of Wilson to the 9th vol. In 1825, Ord printed a *Supplement* to the 9th volume containing a much enlarged account of Wilson's life and birds which were omitted from volume ix.

Charles Lucian Bonaparte supplemented this work by printing an *American Ornithology; . . . of Birds Inhabiting the United States, not given by Wilson* (4 vols., Philadelphia, 1825–1833); thus making fourteen volumes in all.

[2] For accounts of Audubon, see Lucy Bakewell Audubon's *Life of John James Audubon* (New York, 1869) and Maria R. Audubon's *Audubon and his Journals with . . . Notes* by Elliott Coues (2 vols., New York,

thwarted the paternal plans and failed in business. He lived
for long periods in the wilderness, and painted birds ˙and
plants in colors wonderfully like the originals.   In 1826,
he went to England, made friends there and secured enough
subscribers to permit the beginning of the actual work of
making the engravings from his own portraits of birds in
their natural surroundings.   The plates were engraved at
first in Scotland at Edinburgh and afterwards at London,
the coloring being done by hand and the execution of the
work was spread over a number of years.[1]   Naturally,
therefore, there is great difference in the plates and in the
colorings ; but the work still stands apart as a masterful
expression of the verities of nature.

In 1840, the census takers, for the first time, inquired into
the scholastic condition of the people and into the machinery that had been provided for their enlightenment.
From the resulting tables, it appears that there were 173
colleges and universities in the whole country, more than
3000 academies and grammar schools, and over 47,000
primary schools. As to pupils there were 16,000 in the
colleges, 164,000 in the secondary schools, and about 2,000,-
000 in the primary schools. In other words, over eight-
tenths of the people had no schooling beyond the primary
grade.[2]   In 1840, also, there were half a million white persons over twenty years of age who could neither read nor

1897). These and all other works
are now superseded by Francis H.
Herrick's *Audubon the Naturalist* (2
vols., New York, 1917).

[1] *The Birds of America; from
Original Drawings by John James
Audubon* (London, 1827–1838). It was
originally published in double ele-
phant folio, measuring 39½ by 29½
inches untrimmed, and issued in 87
parts at 2 guineas a part, costing
more than $100,000 to produce (see
F. H. Herrick's *Audubon*, i, 358 and

fol.). A copy was recently sold in
Philadelphia at over $4000. An edi-
tion in royal octavo in seven volumes
was published at New York and
Philadelphia in 1840–1844, entitled
*The Birds of America, from Drawings
made in the United States and their
Territories.*

[2] See Tucker's *Progress of the United
States* (New York, 1855), pp. 144 and
145. His figures are taken from the
Census of 1840 (p. 475) but differ from
it slightly in one or two cases. The

write. These figures were bad enough; but the "Census" of 1850 shows a very slight lengthening of the school period and the number of white illiterates had nearly doubled in ten years owing to the great increase in foreign immigration. Up to that time, therefore, it would seem that the educational movement of the first half of the century had produced very little result. There were more colleges and more secondary schools in proportion to the total population than there were in 1800 or in 1820, but so far they do not seem to have greatly affected the average intelligence of the American people, and it was the education of democracy and not the breeding of scholars that underlay the whole educational movement of that time. Indeed, by 1860, the golden age of American scholarship was passed.

table on p. 145 deals entirely with white pupils and shows the percentage of pupils in each class of schools:

College students .... 0.8 per cent
Scholars in grammar schools .... 8.1 per cent
Scholars in primary schools............................... 91.1 per cent
　　　　　　　　　　　　　　　　　　　　　　　　　　　　100. per cent

See also the *Census* of 1850, p. lxi; the white illiterates formed about $\frac{1}{11}$ of the total population of the United States in 1840, and $\frac{1}{12}$ in 1850.

NOTES

I. Bibliography. — The successive *Reports* of the United States Commissioner of Education, which began in 1868 with Henry Barnard's survey of the field, contain masses of historical detail. In 1887 the Bureau began the publication of a series of " Contributions to American Educational History " under the editorship of Herbert B. Adams that opened new fields of historical investigation. Similar reports of the State commissioners, especially those of Illinois, New York, and Massachusetts, are store-houses of facts. Beginning with the publication of the *American Journal of Education* [1] at Boston in 1826, there have been almost continuous serial educational publications which reflect the changing educational ideals of successive decades. Of bibliographies, the Columbia University *Library Bulletin*, No. 2, " Books on Education " is useful although divided into small groups. Elmer E. Brown's *Making of Our Middle Schools*, Edwin G. Dexter's *History of Education in the United States,* and G. H. Martin's *Evolution of the Massachusetts Public School System* bring together within small compass the results of prolonged study.

McMaster's statements as to the paucity of Southern educational facilities in the first volume of his *History* aroused interest on the subject in the South and led to the publication of numerous articles. Of these General McCrady's " Education in South Carolina " was first in point of time and is still interesting. Stephen B. Weeks has a very useful article on " The Beginnings of the Common School System in the South " in the *Report* of the United States Commissioner of Education for 1896–97, ch. xxix.

II. Bell and Lancaster. — Dr. Andrew Bell's principal writings are : *An Analysis of the Experiment in Education, made at Egmore, near Madras* (3rd ed., London, 1807) ; *Instructions for Conducting a School Through the Agency of the Scholars themselves* (4th ed., London, 1813) ; and *Mutual Tuition . . . or Manual of Instructions for conducting Schools through the Agency of the Scholars themselves* (7th

---

[1] This was followed by the *American Annals of Education and Instruction* (Boston, 1831–1834) ; the *Quarterly Register and Journal of the American Education Society* that was published from 1829 to 1846 with slightly varying titles ; and the *American Journal of Education* edited by Henry Barnard, which began in 1856 and continued under various editors and various forms to the present day. The *Introductory Discourse & Lectures . . . assembled to form the American Institute of Instruction* has continued with somewhat different titles from 1830 into the twentieth century.

ed., London, 1823). The second volume of the Southeys' *Life of the Rev. Andrew Bell* (London, 1844) relates to the Indian portion of his career. A shorter and more usable work is J. M. D. Meiklejohn's *An Old Educational Reformer, Dr. Andrew Bell* (Edinburgh, 1881).

The *Epitome of Some of the Chief Events . . . in the Life of Joseph Lancaster . . . Written by himself* (New Haven, 1833) is perhaps the best account of Lancaster's career; but the shorter account by David Salmon (London, 1904) is sufficient for most students. The best known of Lancaster's pedagogical writings is *Improvements in Education as it respects the Industrious Classes of the Community* (1st ed., London, 1803). There are some interesting pictures showing this system in Reigart's *Lancasterian System* and in the *Manual of the System of Primary Instruction, pursued in the Model Schools of the British and Foreign School Society* (London, 1844).

CHAPTER IX

LITERATURE

GREAT as were the changes in the outlook of the people of the United States that have been noted in the preceding chapters, it is in the domain of literature that the renaissance of the American mind is most noticeable. Before the Revolution there was no literature or very little that can be so accounted and the Revolutionary epoch itself was taken up from the literary side with the production of a series of most remarkable political papers that reach their highest point in "The Federalist." With the turn of the century the production of works of fiction, poems, and essays proceeded on an ever increasing scale, both as to quantity and as to quality until it culminated in the literary efflorescence that is associated with the names of Emerson, Hawthorne, Thoreau, and the others of the New England group. Fifty thousand separate books, pamphlets, and periodicals, and probably more, were printed in the United States in the thirty years after 1800, and some of them went through several editions.[1] Included in this list are works on law and politics, reprints of foreign books, and translations of French and German romances.[2] Considering the comparative

[1] For this estimate I am greatly indebted to Mr. Charles Evans of Chicago, whose *American Bibliography* has already facilitated the work of the literary historian.

[2] On the other hand, the works of many American writers, Irving, Cooper, Paulding, and others were translated into German. Dr. S. A. Green in his *Journal kept by Count William de Deux-Ponts, 1780–81,* p. xi note, points out that during "the American Revolution, it was not uncommon for books published in Paris to bear the imprint of Boston or Philadelphia."

smallness of the population, these figures seem to show that the demand for works of literature and for technical books was great. There were a few proprietary libraries at Charleston, South Carolina; Newport, Rhode Island, and Philadelphia and New York. Then, too, the booksellers loaned copies from their stock upon the payment of a small rental or subscription; but the circulating library, as it exists today in England, never gained any large measure of popularity in America, owing probably to the opening of public libraries, supported by taxation and free to every one. In 1827 there was a project for the establishment of libraries of valuable books in each State which was to be financed by means of a lottery.[1] Whether this scheme ever amounted to anything is not known. It is certain, however, that the second third of the century saw the founding of a multitude of subscription and free public libraries, and libraries open to particular classes of people.[2] It may well be that the presence of these collections of books easily attainable by the people led to a great change in the reading habit, and that books by 1860 ceased to be regarded as prizes to be acquired by effort and privation and preserved as heirlooms in the family.

Whatever truth there may be in this surmise that the establishment of public libraries put an end to the private accumulation of books, it seems certain that book buying was much more general and on a much larger scale in those

---

[1] Letter from "Sam Brown" to Andrew Jackson, dated Philadelphia, Nov. 23, 1827. In it he refers to the generous support that Jackson had "already given to the cause of literature in aiding the University Lottery."

[2] In 1876 the Bureau of Education issued a large report written by several hands entitled *Public Libraries in the United States of America, their History, Condition, and Management.* A convenient list of books relating to American libraries is appended to C. K. Bolton's "Proprietary and Subscription Libraries" in the *Manual of Library Economy*, ch. v (Chicago, 1912). Of the books mentioned by Bolton, Lindsay Swift's "Proprietary Libraries and Public Libraries" in the *Library Journal* for 1906 is the most useful.

days than now. The "Columbian Centinel" for March 7, 1810, contains a list of over five hundred books for sale at "The Sign of Franklin's Head," Court Street, Boston. Among them were Cruden's "Concordance," Anderson's "History of Commerce," Fourcroy's "Philosophy of Chemistry," and Ossian's "Poems," besides the books that one would ordinarily associate with New England in those days as Knox's "Sermons." Another list of books is appended to Bason's "Country Almanack" for 1821, which was published at Charleston, South Carolina. This list includes seven hundred title:. Among them are "Abelard and Eloisa," "The Arabian Nights" in four volumes, and "The Abbot, a New Novel by the Author of Waverley." There was also Clarkson's "Slave Trade" in two volumes. The "Western Spectator," published at Marietta, Ohio, in October, 1811, contains an advertisement of two hundred and forty books for sale. Among them were the "Art of Contentment," "Beddoes on Consumption," Lemprière's "Classical Dictionary," and Weems's "Washington."[1] In 1816, the editor of an almanac estimated that about twelve hundred tons of paper were made and consumed annually in the United States, six hundred tons of it being used for newspapers and the rest for books; and the compilers of these statistics averred that twenty-two million newspapers were annually printed in the country. With

[1] Other interesting lists are in the *Kentucky Gazette*, published at Lexington, on February 28, 1807. Besides a lot of law books, this list contains "Edwards on Redemption," "Hunter on the Blood," and Hume's *History of England*. In July, 1798, the *Political Focus*, published at Leominster, a small inland village of Massachusetts, contained a list of 72 books offered for sale; among these was the usual assortment of sermons and other books of an entirely different cast, as Milton's *Paradise Lost*, Cook's *Voyages*, *Adventures of Baron Trenck*, *Life of Belisarius*, and Duncan's *Cicero*.

The five thousand and fifty-seven titles enumerated in the *Catalogue* of the Charleston Library Society that was printed in 1826 give a very good idea of the scholarly taste of that time, and may be supplemented by the titles in the *Catalogue of the John Adams Library* issued by the Boston Public Library in 1917.

the high cost of postage that prevailed in the earlier years of the century, it was an expensive matter to send books and papers from one part of the country to another. The number of small presses scattered throughout the country was very large and one constantly comes across books printed in most unexpected places. Looking at the matter from another point of view, it appears that Franklin H. Elmore of South Carolina in the year 1836 bought among other books "Humphrey Clinker," "Lives of the Necromancers," Hill's "Reports," Earle's "Medical Companion," and "Paulding on Slavery." John Quincy Adams had five thousand books in his library in 1809 and Jefferson's library contained 6488 volumes; among them were 222 on moral philosophy, 304 on religion, 210 on zoölogy, and 208 on poetry. In 1829, two hundred and thirty-eight books from Timothy Pickering's library were offered for sale; the list included Sterne's "Sentimental Journey," Anson's "Voyage," Scott's "Napoleon," and many of his novels, Boswell's "Life of Johnson," and editions of Virgil and Horace.[1] Certainly the reading habit was widespread in those days.

The fifty thousand separate works that were printed in the first thirty years of the century were published widely over the country and were often written near the place of publication. Some of them belonged to the great men of American literature as Irving and Cooper, but most of these books were the work of writers whose names are unknown now and have been for half a century. They chose morbid themes, — death and destruction, unrequited love and shipwreck;[2] but some of them have distinct historical merit.

---

[1] "Pickering Manuscripts," vol. 55, fo. 290, in the cabinet of the Massachusetts Historical Society. The list of Jefferson's books is on the back of folio 94 of the same volume.

[2] A child's weekly of four pages duodecimo was begun at Salem, Massachusetts, in September, 1828. It was named *The Hive* and was as full of death, tragedy, and gloom as the magazines and books designed for the older folk.

There was the Reverend Jonathan Farr's "Sunday School Teacher's Funeral," which was published at Boston in 1835. At first sight it seems to be painfully lacking in every quality that gives life to most literature; but it is one of the most effective bits of writing in the English language and whoever reads the opening page will be reasonably certain to go on to the end. Captain M'Clintock's "John Beedle's Sleigh Ride, Courtship, and Marriage," which was published at New York in 1841, deals with love to be sure, but the manner of treatment is amusing rather than tragical. George Tucker's "Voyage to the Moon" is in an entirely different vein and is, even now, somewhat readable in parts.[1] John Peck's poem entitled "The Spirit of Methodism" is really a political screed and contains moreover a good stroke at the Presbyterians. William C. Foster's "Poetry on Different Subjects" that was published at Salem in New York in 1805 is of the time: in one hundred and twenty-eight pages there are seven poems on death, five on love, and five on Washington; but the rest are in lighter vein as "The Bachelor and Cat," and "The Washing Day." Of these second class writers, Mason L. Weems probably stands first. He created the Washington of tradition and gave us Francis Marion. He attempted to do the same thing by Franklin but the latter's fragmentary autobiography has rescued him forever from the pen of the Maryland romancer. Weems also wrote many reformatory tracts exhorting drunkards, gamblers, and celibates to mend their ways. Well over a million copies of his books have appeared. An edition of his "Washington" was printed in 1918 and ranks with "The Federalist" and

[1] The full title is *A Voyage to the Moon: with some Account of the Manners and Customs, Science and Philosophy, of the People of Morosofia, and other Lunarians. By Joseph At-* terly (New York, 1827). The plan of the book is directly borrowed; but there are some pleasing suggestions scattered through it.

Franklin's "Autobiography" as possessing the longest life of any American book. As a "Maker" of history, Mason L. Weems vies with the household poets.[1]

The geographical distribution of writers, readers, and students shows that all sections of the country were interested in literature, using that word in its widest meaning. In the South, the whites, whom it must be remembered formed but a portion of the total population, were divided between farmers and those interested in the government of the country. These devoted to public work talents that in the North were more often directed to what is sometimes called polite literature; but the state papers that they produced were of a high order of merit. Moreover, there were few men in the country who had a greater knowledge of the literature of the past than John Randolph of Roanoke. From the youth of South Carolina and Georgia, the famous Waddell school turned out many brilliant scholars. Of these John C. Calhoun easily stands first and his "Disquisition on Government" is one of the most memorable books on politics that this country has yet produced. There were poets without number in the South, nearly all of them now forgotten, and many writers of prose fiction.[2] Of these William Gilmore Simms alone stands in recollection today, but he resided for a large part of his working life in the North. Simms is not in the first rank, but his "Yemassee" and his "Partisan" and one or two others of his books are still readable.

---

[1] See William S. Baker's *Bibliotheca Washingtoniana*, 31. The Washington of Weems undoubtedly comes as near to historic fact as large portions of Bancroft's *United States*, the *Myles Standish* of Longfellow, or the *Barbara Frietchie* of Whittier; and the book has had equal or greater influence on succeeding generations of Americans than any of these. See also the present work, vol. iv, p. 57.

[2] Many of these Southern literary productions have been gathered into the *Library of Southern Literature* in sixteen volumes, with a collective index in volume xvi and with sketches of the lives of nearly two hundred and fifty Southern authors.

The earliest school of literature was localized in Connecticut and is known as the "Hartford Wits." The most attractive of this group, which included Trumbull and Dwight, was Joel Barlow.[1] On leaving Yale College, he set out to be a poet; but his lack of means and love for a lady impelled him to other exertions. He served as a chaplain in the Revolutionary Army, was admitted to the bar as a practising lawyer, and was sent abroad by Duer and Craigie in the capacity of land agent. While serving as chaplain, he had married the lady of his choice without the consent of her father. At Paris his land activities were somewhat unfortunate, — to those who bought of him; but his own foolhardy or fortunate investments in French securities — before the rise of Napoleon — made Barlow a rich man for the rest of his life and enabled him to indulge his poetical fancies. He had an idea that the history of America was as deserving of verse as the siege of Troy or the settlement of Rome, and he carried his idea into effect in a most sumptuous volume, entitled "The Columbiad." It appeared in 1807 in a quarto of four hundred and forty-eight pages with a dozen engravings at the cost of twenty dollars a copy. In the last "vision," Columbus sees a general congress of nations settling their affairs by arbitration, and inaugurating perpetual peace, till at last they grasp fraternal hands in union o'er the world! More worthy of remembrance is the mock heroic and pastoral poem singing the praises of hasty pudding, for which Barlow had searched in vain in Paris "that corrupted town" and in London "lost in smoke and steep'd in tea." It begins

> " Ye Alps audacious, thro' the Heavens that rise,
>   I sing not you "

[1] See Charles B. Todd's *Life and Letters of Joel Barlow, LL.D.*

but the charms of hasty pudding which he had unexpectedly come across in Savoy. Barlow was not the only one to praise food in rhyme for an anonymous poem entitled "The Buckwheat Cake" in some ways is not left far behind by Barlow's masterpiece. The American epic was not an uncommon form of poetic expression in those days. It was in 1827 that Dr. Richard Emmons of Philadelphia and Great Crossing, Kentucky, delivered himself of four volumes entitled "The Fredoniad : or Independence Preserved," which, strangely enough, went through three editions as did Barlow's "Columbiad." In 1833, Thomas H. Genin published "The Napolead" at St. Clairsville, Ohio, in three hundred and forty-two duodecimo pages. "The Nosiad ; or the Man of Type and the Major Domo" by Icabod Satiricus gives an idea of the heavy humor of 1829, which may also be seen in Miss Mary Elizabeth Talbot's "Rurality," which is a collection of "desultory tales" that also deals with the common subjects of the day, as shipwrecks and duels.

From the mass of third and fourth rate authors, there step out, as one runs them over in recollection, four Allens. There was Benjamin, first of all, who signed himself "Osander" and again "Juba" and wrote "The Death of Abdallah"; Benjamin, Jr., who printed "Urania . . . a Poem"; Mrs. Brasseya Allen, who published "Pastorals, Eligies, and Odes" at Abingdon in Maryland in 1806; and Miss Elizabeth Allen, who affixed her name to a singularly mis-entitled book of poems, "The Silent Harp," at Burlington, Vermont, in 1832. The poem on "Soliloquy" in this volume is the most stilted bit of writing except possibly Harrison Gray Otis's "Eulogy on Alexander Hamilton."

The possibilities of printed political propaganda seem to have first been realized by those who were intent upon pushing the fortunes of Andrew Jackson. As early as 1817, books appeared reciting the events of his life up to the date of publication, so far as these would appeal to the favorable prejudices of the voters and those who influenced them. Within ten years there were eight or ten books of the type. The most interesting of them is the "Civil and Military History" of Jackson by an "American Officer." It was published at New York in 1825 and the account of the "Day of Thanksgiving and Praise" for the victory obtained by the "Hero of New Orleans" has seldom been surpassed in our campaign literature.[1] In 1829, Jackson appeared in the Gift Books, — "The Jackson Wreath, or National Souvenir." This is a good example of a book of the kind. It contained a well-written memoir, a dirge to the memory of Mrs. Jackson, a bit of music entitled "Jackson's Grand March & Quick Step," some excellent engravings, and a map of the United States of high historical value at the present day.

The newspaper literature of the South was fully as vigorous and as influential as that of the North, and of as great value to the historical student. The "Richmond Enquirer," published and edited by Thomas Ritchie, was as influential in moulding political opinion in the Old Dominion for nearly half a century as any paper that has ever been published in the United States. The magazines which were so plentiful at the North in those days were not so largely duplicated in the South. In 1834, the first number of "The Southern Literary Messenger" appeared at Richmond. It was noteworthy as having for a short time been edited by

[1] The following extract from the opening paragraph of chapter xvii of this book will show the style of the time: — "The attention of the reader is now to be called from scenes of carnage, wounds, death, defeat, and victory . . . from those appalling scenes, which, if tears are permitted to soil the purity of heaven must make the angels weep, to one which must make them rejoice."

Edgar Allan Poe and as having lived for a considerable
period. It was originated as a protest against "vassalage
to our Northern neighbors"; but its contents were mainly
an echo of the magazines that were printed at Philadelphia
and New York. In 1845, Simms published at Charleston
"The Southern and Western Monthly Magazine and Review" which was to release the South from the Northern
literary yoke. Twelve numbers satisfied him and the subscribers and the periodical was merged in "The Southern
Literary Messenger." All in all, the Southerners were
eager for books and for the exercise of literary expression,
but so many of them were engaged in growing cotton and
governing the country that the few who were left with
leisure and learning produced little of actual literary work
before the era of the War for Southern Independence.

The case was very different with the Middle States,
for Philadelphia and New York were the literary capitals
of the country for a generation. The close connection between commercial prosperity and literary outlook has been
oftentimes adverted to, but is still difficult of explanation,
for it would seem that the pursuit of gain would be un-
congenial to the effort of the literary mind. It has been
said, however, that the leisure provided by the business
success of a community or a family has enabled the fortunate
idlers to produce works of literature. It is true that many
examples can be found, as those of James Fenimore Cooper
and William Hickling Prescott, where absence of necessity
has led to literary expression. But, on the other side, one
finds men of poverty, as Emerson, Thoreau, and Hawthorne,
winning the foremost places in the works of the mind.
Possibly, a market for literature is a necessity of its production and this is provided by the dense population of a
commercial community. Whatever the reason for their

prominence, it is certain that the two great commercial cities of the Middle Atlantic States occupied the first place in our literary history for many years. Authors and would-be authors flocked to them from the East and the West and the South. Of those from across the Appalachians, Alice and Phœbe Cary alone won extended fame before 1860.[1] The magazines naturally made their homes in the largest cities, for in those days of high postage rates periodical publications necessarily found their subscribers within reasonable distances from the printing office. For years Hezekiah Niles's "Weekly Register," published at Baltimore, Mathew Carey's "American Museum" and Dennie's "Portfolio," both published at Philadelphia, occupied the first place among American magazines and deservedly;[2] but the "North American Review" after 1820 began to fill in part the field once held by these publications and to add an element of scholarly criticism that one had formerly associated with the British quarterlies. These serials are filled with original poems and tales and also with serious articles partly of an historical and scientific character. In 1830, the New York newspapers began to occupy a prominent place. The names of the early editors, Bryant, Greeley, George Ripley, Henry J. Raymond, and Mordecai M. Noah, are familiar in the political history and literature of the second third of the century.

[1] W. H. Venable's *Beginnings of Literary Culture in the Ohio Valley* (Cincinnati, 1891). The other Western names that are associated in one's recollection with this period are Timothy Flint and James Hall. Flint's *Arthur Clenning*, published at Philadelphia, has some of the characteristics of the modern novel; Hall's works are a mine of facts and traditions of his adopted country; and Alice Cary's *Clovernook or Recollections of Our Neighborhood in The West* takes one into the very heart of the pioneer's home. The *Western Literary Magazine, and Journal of Education, Science, Arts, and Morals* was published at Columbus, Ohio, in 1853 and well represents the community of artistic and literary desires of the people living on both sides of the Appalachian Mountains.

[2] Algernon Tassin's *The Magazine in America* (New York, 1916) is a useful and gossipy book; chs. ii–viii relate to the earlier time.

The Philadelphia and New York authors of that day enjoyed great reputations among their contemporaries. Of these, Charles Brockden Brown serves as a sort of standard for writers on American literature, partly because he was the first to devote himself professionally to the literary art. Irving and Cooper easily stand first of this group. Washington Irving was born of British parents in New York. In 1809, he put forth anonymously "A History of New York, from the Beginning of the World . . . by Diedrich Knickerbocker." It may be regarded as the earliest American work of imaginative literature. After an interval, he published the "Sketch Book" in which foreign folklore is adapted to the scenery of the Catskills. From this point, Irving fell more and more under foreign influences. His "Columbus" and his "Conquest of Granada" might as well have been written by an Englishman, born and bred. The middle period of his life, Irving passed in England and Spain, engaged in business and diplomacy and in gathering materials and impressions for his books. After his return to the United States and in his last years, he wrote the historical work that best gives him his place, the "Life of George Washington," the fifth volume of which was published only a short time before Irving's death in 1859 at the age of seventy-six. Cooper came of old colonial ancestry and was born in New Jersey. His father moved to a wilderness section of New York when Fenimore was a child. The future author grew up therefore on the frontier and in his truly great "Leatherstocking Tales" repeats his boyhood impressions of scenery and of men. Being dismissed from Yale College, Cooper followed the sea for a few years and thus gained the knowledge of ships and of seamanship that made him easily first of marine romancists. He also ventured on history and wrote on the "Navy of the United

States" with so much vigor and honesty that he speedily became embroiled with some of those whose deeds or misdeeds he had described. Like Irving, Cooper spent a large portion of his middle life in Europe and like Irving, also, reserved his historical labor for his later life. Irving and Cooper took so prominent a place among the writers of the Middle States and occupied it for so long a time that they may fairly be said to have eclipsed their contemporaries. In the second rank were J. K. Paulding and Herman Melville. In the third rank, there was a crowd of competitors. The selection is dangerous, but John Lofland's "Harp of Delaware; or, the Miscellaneous Poems of the Milford Bard" remains in memory as an example of the ordinary versification of the Middle States of America in 1828. The poem to "The Mother" is expressive of deep feeling, that on "Fame" evinces the horror of war that was even then deep in the heart, and his lines on the 19th of April, 1775,

> " In Lexington the sons of Freedom form
> On the green square, and wait the coming storm "

reveal the quiet courage of that gallant band.

Typical books of that day were "Queechy" and "The Wide, Wide World" by Elizabeth Wetherell, who really was Susan Warner. The latter is a long-drawn-out tale of petty female persecution and love mingled with religion. It was first printed in 1849, saw a fourth edition in 1851, was reprinted in England, and again and again in America, as late indeed, as 1895. If a permanence of half a century entitles any novelist to glory, it certainly does Susan Warner. Moreover, it represents the type of book that men and women of that time were eager to read, but now seems intolerable. Is it that our taste has become blunted and can be satisfied only with intense, blood-curdling novels?

Is modern life, itself, so strenuous that the account of quiet humdrum existence of a village no longer satisfies? Is life so rapid, nowadays, that one can no longer read books like "The Wide, Wide World"? Possibly it is that we require double the action for every thousand words that our fathers did.

The Middle States were the homes of magazines and "Gift Books" and Annuals. Of the first none enjoyed long life or great reputation. "The Knickerbocker," which was published at New York, was perhaps the most popular and the most permanent. These serials contained the first attempts at the American short story, which were really nothing more than replicas of English tales with an American dressing and like the poems of that early time dealt with love, disease, and death, mainly with the last. By 1850 the public mind was beginning to tire of this form of entertainment, if the publishers of "Wright's Casket" had good business sense in beginning publication of a monthly paper that should contain "no silly love tales, or other *deleterious matter*." The publication of magazines was still widespread and the smaller towns produced them as well as the great commercial cities. An example of these, and a very good one, is "The Rural Repository" that was published at Hudson, New York, for several years beginning with 1824; about one-eighth of the contents was poetry, most of it original, but a good deal of the prose matter was taken from other publications as the "American Monthly Magazine," "The Emporium," and "The New-York Statesman" and some of it was translated from the French.

The Gift Books begin in 1824, but are most numerous in the late 40's and early 50's.[1] Their popularity may be

[1] F. W. Faxon in his *Literary Annuals and Gift-Books* has listed one thousand and twenty-two separate books as having been published in America. He has prefaced his list with an interesting article on the books

seen from the fact that in one year no less than sixty separate works of the kind were published in America. They ranged from duodecimo to quarto and were bound in ornately decorated cloth or leather with heavily gilded edges. Many of America's best-known men and women of letters found their way to public notice through the pages of these books, or, having achieved reputation, acquired money by contributing to them. Some of these books were beautifully illustrated by the best engravers who have flourished in America, as John Cheney, A. B. Durand, and the elder Sartain. It is these engravings, as Sartain's "The Mother" in "The Diadem" for 1847, or Cheney's "Viola" in "The Gift" for 1844, or Durand's representation of "The Duchess and Sancho" in "The Atlantic Souvenir" for 1832 that give the Annuals and Gift Books their greatest attraction. The last named engraving was an illustration of Miss Leslie's poem with the same title. One verse of this has interest even now :

" The wreath of the warrior has faded and gone,
 While the laurel of genius is green in the land ;
 And the fight of Lepanto will only be known,
 As the fight where Cervantes was maim'd of his hand."

The demand for good literature and fine illustrations that was shown by the continuing publication of these very expensive books is one of the most interesting indications of the condition of the American mind of this time, more especially in the Middle States.

A genius who has no geographic bounds was Edgar Allan Poe. He was born in Boston, Massachusetts, and published his first book there,[1] but his father was a Marylander

themselves; he shows, among other things, that many of these titles were repetitions and where that was not the case, old articles and old plates were used in different combinations.

[1] This work was entitled *Tamerlane and Other Poems* and was published in 1827.

and his mother an English actress who happened to be per- forming in the Puritan capital at the time of his birth. They soon migrated to Richmond where John Allan, a Scotch merchant of the Richmond tobacco exporting firm of Ellis and Allan, took the child into his family.[1] Poe's early youth was passed in Virginia and in England and he spent a brief space at the University at Charlottesville, when gambling and drink forced his removal. Later he edited "The South- ern Literary Messenger" at Richmond for a time, but his working years were mainly passed at New York as a literary critic and writer of prose, none of which is read now except by professors of English and their pupils. It is upon the three poems "The Raven," "The Bells," and "Annabel Lee" that Poe's reputation rests[2] and makes the world forget the insanity and debauchery that were so closely associated with his life.

Philadelphia and New York were the centres of the ex- pression of the dramatic art, whether by writing or by acting. The production of dramas was widespread, almost as much so as the writing of poetry, both being in those days a com- mon form of expression and not confined to a more or less professional class. The plays, like the poems, dealt with the tragic side of love and with death. The actors on the stage, the principal actors I mean, were almost entirely from England, although a few Americans like Edgar Allan Poe's father had drifted into the theatrical profession. There were stock companies at Philadelphia and at New York and these, after a "season," travelled into New England and

[1] Poe's undated letter to "Mr. Wm. Poe" gives details as to his family history (*Gulf States Historical Maga- zine*, i, 281).

[2] "The Raven" appeared in 1845, "The Bells" in 1849, and "Annabel Lee" in the same year, — they are all associated with the closing period of Poe's life. "Appendix C" at the end of vol. ii of Woodberry's *Life of Edgar Allan Poe* is a bibliography with notes. Susan A. Weiss' *Home Life of Poe* (New York, 1907) contains the Rich- mond traditions set down by a lady in her old age, who had known the Allans in Poe's childhood.

southward to Richmond and even to Charleston. After 1825, New York may be regarded as the centre of the theatrical profession, having by that time outstripped Philadelphia in that respect, as in literature and in commerce. In 1820, there seems to have been only one theatre in New York, but play-houses multiplied after that time.[1] The "pit" was still the pit, not having yet become the parquet, and a restaurant and a bar were usually included within the theatre walls. In the later theatres, these features disappeared. Another form of amusement was connected with what were called "gardens" as Niblo's Garden. This establishment included a hotel, a theatre, and a garden, the last being provided with walks, flower-beds, and summer-houses. But before long it became a theatre, pure and simple. Outside of New York there was horse-racing, bull-baiting, and cock-fighting and in New York there were exhibitions of curiosities. In 1825, an Italian opera company appeared in "The Barber of Seville" which seems to have been the first professional operatic performance in the United States. In the next year Mme. Malibran received six hundred dollars for each appearance in opera; but it was not until twenty-six years later that the first "long run" took place when Edwin Forrest played "Damon" for sixty-nine consecutive nights. A French danseuse appeared at the Bowery Theatre in February, 1827, and from that time on dancing was a favorite form of entertainment, Mlle. Celeste, Madame Vestris, and a child, Emma Wheatly, six years of age, all appearing within two years; and this culminated in 1840 with the appearance of Fanny

---

[1] See Charles H. Haswell's *Reminiscences of New York*, using index. This is an invaluable book for the tracing of social history, as it is for the coming and development of public utilities and manners and customs.

William Dunlap's *History of the American Theatre* is a contemporary view down to about 1830. There is a good bibliography of "The Early Drama" in *The Cambridge History of American Literature*, i, 490–507.

Elssler before an enormous audience in "La Cracovienne."
Of the famous actors of those days, besides those that have
been mentioned, there were James H. Hackett, Charles Kean,
Charles Kemble and his daughter, Fanny, Tyrone Power,
and Junius Brutus Booth, to mention no others. Theatres
were not numerous, perhaps, taking the country through and
the performances were not numerous, but judging by the effect
produced upon the audiences and the permanence of their
fame, the actors then must have been of a very superior order.

Literature, common and polite, does not owe as much
to foreigners as did the theatre, but its debt is very great,
nevertheless. The first newspapers of political moment
after 1789 were edited by recent immigrants, and law, theology, and science owed a great deal to outside stimulus.
Of the early newspapers, those edited by Callender, Chee-
tham, Duane, and John Binns achieved remarkable notoriety and had enough influence to arouse the wrath of the
rulers. Of the fugitives from England, Joseph Priestley and
Thomas Cooper, his devoted friend, had the most influence
in scholarly directions. The latter was a lawyer by training, but had dabbled in politics and the natural sciences.
His radicalism compelled his departure from England and
brought him within the scope of the Sedition Act in America.
Jefferson recognized his scholarly qualities and secured for
him an appointment as professor of chemistry and law in
the newly established University of Virginia.[1] Objections
being raised to his religious radicalism, he never entered

[1] He resigned before the University
was open for students. See *Early
History of the University of Virginia
. . . Letters of Thomas Jefferson and
Joseph C. Cabell*, 88, 164–172, 234 n.;
Herbert B. Adams's *Thomas Jefferson and the University of Virginia*,
106–109; Colyer Meriwether's *History of Higher Education in South
Carolina*, 143–156; Edwin L. Green's
*History of the University of South Caro-
lina*, 34–55, 332–343; and Edgar F.
Smith's *Chemistry in America*, 128–
146. Cooper wrote to J. A. Hammond in 1836 that the "Idea of these
New England theologians, that their
notions of religious duty are to super-
cede all law, is quite inconsistent with
the well being of civil Society & it
elevates every ignorant fanatic into an

upon the discharge of his duties there. Shortly afterwards he became the head of the University of South Carolina and rendered a great service to that State by collecting its laws into one series of printed volumes. In his last years he became one of the most ardent advocates of States'-rights to be found anywhere, and did a great deal towards building up public sentiment in favor of Southern nationalism leading up to the nullification episode. Priestley was a clergyman by profession, but was by nature a man of science. His radicalism also compelled him to leave England. In America he joined in the distrust of Washington and Adams, who cordially distrusted him. He corresponded with men in different parts of the country, promoted the scientific activities of Robert Hare and James Woodhouse, and published scientific articles.[1] Among the productions of his later years was "A Comparison of the Institutions of Moses with those of the Hindoos and Other Ancient Nations" and "The Doctrine of Phlogiston established; with Observations on the Conversion of Iron into Steel." William Thornton, who was a West Indian by birth, won the Magellanic Gold Medal of the American Philosophical Society in 1793 for a most stimulating scientific paper entitled " Cadmus : or, a Treatise on the Elements of Written Language." He proposed to simplify the alphabet and thus lay the foundation for an American language that would be as

irresponsible dictator," — a dictum which unfortunately he did not apply to himself. The "Hammond Papers" in the Library of Congress.

The Case of Thomas Cooper, M. D. (Columbia, S. C., 1831); Letter of a Layman to Any Member of Congress; and Reply to Censor give an idea of Cooper's methods and of the condition of thought in South Carolina at the time.

[1] See Memoirs of Dr. Joseph Priestley to the Year 1795, written by himself:

With a Continuation . . . By his Son (2 vols., London, 1805); John Corry's Life of Joseph Priestley (Birmingham, 1804); "Memoir" by Dr. Aikin in Lucy Aikin's Memoir of John Aikin, 460. Self-revealing letters of Priestley to George Thacher are in the Massachusetts Historical Society's Proceedings, 2nd Series, iii, pp. 13–40. Edgar F. Smith's Chemistry in America (New York, 1914), ch. v describes his influence upon science in Pennsylvania.

distinct from the languages of Europe as government in America was free from "the dangerous doctrines of European powers." As a part of this work he wrote an essay upon the proper method to teach the deaf and dumb to speak. These should be induced to imitate the efforts of a hearing child to speak, studying the motions of one's own vocal organs in a looking glass and noting in a book the proper arrangement of those organs for any given word.[1] The great buildings at Washington were the work of foreigners, Thornton, Latrobe, and Hoban, and the plan of the city came from the mind of another foreigner, L'Enfant.[2] There was no technical skill whatever among native Americans and for every public work engineers had to be imported until native born Americans could become trained, or train themselves in the school of experience. Among the foreigners was Clodius Crozet, who had served in the armies of Napoleon, had taught engineering at West Point, had written a "Treatise on Descriptive Geometry," and had then become the State engineer of Virginia. While thus acknowledging our indebtedness to those who came to our aid from outside, it must ever be kept in mind that it was the grandeur of the imagination of Washington and Jefferson and other Americans that made possible the construction of such great works as the City of Washington, the Erie Canal, and the Portage Railway system.

[1] The actual education of deaf mutes in America is associated with the name of Thomas H. Gallaudet, who visited Europe to study the methods in use there. The beneficence of Amos Kendall led to the establishment of the national institution at Washington. See Edward A. Fay's *Histories of American Schools for the Deaf* (3 vols., Washington, 1893) and E. M. Gallaudet's *Life of Thomas Hopkins Gallaudet* (New York, 1888).

The education of the blind likewise comes from Europe. In America its beginning is associated with the name of Samuel G. Howe, who for years was at the head of the Perkins Institution for the Blind at Boston. See the *Address of the Trustees of the New-England Institution for the Education of the Blind* (Boston, 1833) and the *Annual Reports* of the Institution which became the Perkins Institution in 1840.

[2] See the present work, vol. iv, 106–108, 112.

The school books used in America in the Revolutionary epoch were of European authorship, although many of them were printed in the United States. To provide books more suitable to American needs attracted the attention of three remarkable men of Connecticut: Noah Webster, Jedidiah Morse, and Samuel Griswold Goodrich, who is much better known under his pen name of "Peter Parley." Noah Webster [1] was given a Continental note for eight dollars by his father in 1778 and sent out into the world to fight for himself. He became a school master and, impressed with the poverty of the existing books for the teaching of English, set out to make better ones. The book that afterwards became known as "The American Speller" was published at Hartford in 1783 as Part I of "A Grammatical Institute of the English Language." A few years later, Morse's "American Geography" [2] found its way to the printer, delayed, as was Webster's work, by the struggle to obtain recognition by law for the production of a man's brains.[3] The almost instant popularity of these books shows how great was the need for them and how well their authors had judged the necessities of American pedagogics at that period. In all fifty million copies of the "Speller" are said to have been printed and sold. To it more than to any other one thing is due the uniformity of the spoken and written English language throughout the United States, — but whether this is an indication of strength or of weakness may well be questioned.

[1] This account is largely drawn from Ford and Skeel's *Notes on the Life of Noah Webster* (2 vols., New York, 1912).

[2] His *American Geography* was first printed at Elizabeth Town, N. J., in 1789; his *American Universal Geography* at Boston in 1793; and his *Gazetteer* in 1797. He was also the author of *A Compendious and Complete System of Modern Geography* (Boston, 1814) and of smaller works and of innumerable revised editions of the above. See W. B. Sprague's *Life of Jedidiah Morse*, ch. iv.

[3] See *Copyright Enactments, 1783–1900* (Library of Congress, Copyright Office, Bulletin No. 3).

For a time Webster edited a paper in New York City and gained considerable credit as a political writer. Ultimately the profits from the sale of his school books enabled him to devote his whole time to the carrying out of a long-cherished plan of making a dictionary of the English language.[1] For ten years he resided at Amherst in Massachusetts, but his life is mainly associated with New Haven. He sought the aid of others, even going to Europe to gain it. He met with little success in this endeavor and was forced to rely upon himself. The picture of this solitary scholar perambulating the periphery of a table made in the form of a hollow circle and covered with dictionaries in Greek, Hebrew, Arabic, and all the known languages, working steadfastly for twenty-eight years at one object and succeeding in his self-imposed task, is one of the most inspiring in the annals of American literary endeavor. The "Dictionary" was originally published in 1828 in two quarto volumes of more than one thousand pages each. It contained twelve thousand words and thirty thousand definitions that had never before been in any dictionary of the English language. Since that time it has passed through innumerable editions and printings and editings until today the dictionary based on Webster's work is the standard among all English speakers, the world over. Like all reformers and men of positive ideas, Noah Webster had some crotchets that have given comfort to carping critics in his own day and since. Noting that many English spellings of the early Middle Ages were no longer used by any one, he thought it would be well to omit letters that no longer had any significance in pronunciation as the *u* in honour, or the final *e* in fugitive. Moreover, it was a matter of the greatest difficulty to decide

[1] See Ford and Skeel's *Notes on the Life of Noah Webster*, ii, 116; his conceptions of his task are given in a letter to Judge Dawes on p. 65. Volume ii of this work deals mainly with the *Dictionary*.

on the proper pronunciation of words and on the proper spelling of them. Webster desired help in deciding these questions, but was denied it, and he had to make up his own mind as between the pronunciations of different sections of the United States and of different strata of English society. The permanence of the greater part of his work and the enormous influence that it has had and now possesses is proof of the general catholicity of Webster's judgment and of the certainty and sweep of his scholarship.

Goodrich belonged to the next generation. Although born in Connecticut, he passed his working life mainly at Boston, where, for fourteen or fifteen years he edited "The Token," one of the most successful and creditable of the annual Gift Books. In 1827, he published the first "Peter Parley" book under the title of "The Tales of Peter Parley about America." A later book, "Peter Parley's Method of Telling about Geography," in its various forms had enormous popularity, two million copies having been sold. In all Goodrich estimated that seven million copies of his books were sold in the thirty years after 1827. Unfortunately, he had parted with all right: to the "Geography" at the time of its publication.[1] He died in poverty, leaving behind him "Recollections of a Lifetime" that has permanent value. The "Peter Parley" books were not literary masterpieces, nor were they works of deep scholarship, but they were precisely adapted to the needs of the schools that were becoming common throughout nearly all parts of the

[1] Goodrich or "Peter Parley" was the author or editor of "about one hundred and seventy volumes — one hundred and sixteen bearing the name of Peter Parley." At least twenty other American productions were falsely attributed to him, and no less than twenty-eight English ones. For an interesting account of Samuel G. Goodrich, see his *Recollections of a Lifetime* (2 vols., New York, 1856) and the "Appendix" to vol. ii for a complete list of his publications. Nathaniel Hawthorne collaborated with Goodrich for a time and, indeed, wrote *Peter Parley's Universal History on the basis of Geography. For the use of Families* (Boston, 1837).

country and they rank with Webster's "Speller" as an educational force in the nation.[1] Another native of Connecticut greatly to influence the education of American youth
was Emma Willard. She was a believer in the education
of women. In 1819, she appeared before the New York
legislature in advocacy of "A Plan for Improving Female
Education." She argued that the improvement of the
education of the daughters of the enlightened citizens of
America was a worthy object in itself and that the raising of
"the female character . . . must inevitably raise that of
the other sex." So far female education had been left to
"the mercy of private adventurers." "Feminine delicacy"
required that girls should be taught by their own sex. The
best way to do this was in boarding schools where the pupils
should be properly classed and provided with libraries and
philosophical apparatus, all of which, so far as Mrs. Willard
was concerned, she hoped would be subsidized by the State
of New York.[2] As in the case of Webster, Mrs. Willard
was impressed with the poverty of American text-books,
which were entirely unsuited to her methods of teaching.
She set to work, therefore, to provide better books in
history and geography. Her first "History of the United
States" was printed at Hartford in 1828 and reprinted in
different forms again and again, and translated into "pure
Castilian" to answer the call for it from Spanish America.
Her other books[3] were connections between history and
geography, as her "Guide to the Temple of Time."

[1] Two brothers, Jacob and John
S. C. Abbott, performed a somewhat
similar service in the production of
The Franconia Stories, The Rollo Books,
and The History of Napoleon.

[2] Mrs. Willard was not successful
in this, but in 1821 she opened the
Troy Female Seminary, as a private
enterprise. Mt. Holyoke College,
which is associated with the name of

Mary Lyon, followed in 1837. For
the higher education of women in the
early time, see ch. i of Sarah D. Stow's
History of Mount Holyoke Seminary.

[3] Ancient Geography as connected
with Chronology (Hartford, 1822, forming a volume of W. C. Woodbridge's
Universal Geography) and Geography
for Beginners: or the Instructer's Assistant, in giving First Lessons from

Literary men of that day owed much to the protracted study of the great writers of England of the preceding century. English books also had a great circulation in the United States,[1] largely in copies printed in America. In the teaching of the history of England, an abridgment of Oliver Goldsmith's "History of England . . . to the Close of the Reign of George II" was printed in a dozen editions, at Philadelphia, New York, and also at Alexandria, Virginia, and Hallowell, Maine. Young's "Night Thoughts on Life, Death, and Immortality" was even more widely used for instruction in the English language. Two dozen editions were printed in America, at Troy in New York, Exeter in New Hampshire, Brookfield in Massachusetts, and elsewhere. Possibly as better showing the universal acknowledgment of English leadership was the reprinting — with adaptations — of Thomas Cook's "Universal Letter Writer" at Baltimore, in 1819.

Perhaps in no way was the influence of England and of Europe more marked on the working out of American ambition than in building up a school of painting. John Singleton Copley,[2] Gilbert Stuart,[3] Edward Greene Malbone,[4] Benjamin West, John Trumbull, Washington Allston, and John Vanderlyn were none of them of the first rank, or possibly

---

Maps in the style of Familiar Conversation (Hartford, 1826). See John Lord's *Life of Emma Willard* (New York, 1873) and the memoir prefixed to *Emma Willard and her Pupils* which was published by Mrs. Russell Sage at New York in 1898. It should be added that Mrs. Willard's *Series of Maps*, which was prepared to accompany her *History of the United States*, would do credit to a modern historical cartographer.

[1] One of the early protesters against this literary vassalage was J. W. Simmons. America stood to Europe, he thought, in much the same way that Rome stood to Greece, which was a misfortune, — to his mind. See his "Observations on American Literature" in a volume entitled *The Maniac's Confession* (Philadelphia, 1821, pp. 105–164).

[2] Martha B. Amory's *Domestic and Artistic Life of John Singleton Copley, R. A.* and A. T. Perkins's *Sketch of the Life . . . of John Singleton Copley.*

[3] George C. Mason's *Life and Works of Gilbert Stuart.*

[4] For an account of Malbone, see William Dunlap's *History of the . . . Arts of Design in the United States* (New York, 1834), ii, 14–29.

of the second; but it would be difficult to duplicate so good a group of artists in any other country at any one time.[1] Of them all, Benjamin West stands first in point of worldly success and influence on his brethren, — he was an artistic Franklin whose wilderness beginnings commended him to London "society."[2] West was of English-Pennsylvania-Quaker stock, but he was not born a Quaker and never became one. He passed most of his life in England painting a few noteworthy pictures — and many others — and training a school of American artists. His first important work was a representation in color of "The Death of Wolfe" on the Plains of Abraham. Instead of depicting the dying general in classic robes, as was then the custom, he clothed him in the uniform of a British general and defended this barbaric innovation by saying that historic painting, no less than historic writing, should be true to the facts. This statement may possibly be in itself quite unhistorical, but the picture represents what West believed to be the fact. His other important large paintings were "Penn's Treaty with the Indians," "Christ Healing the Sick," and "Death on the Pale Horse." "Penn's Treaty" and the "Wolfe" have done more to form pseudo-historical tradition than almost anything of the kind, but West's other two large pictures had, if possible, greater popularity. They were copied time and time again and exhibited all over the United States. West found favor also with the British nobility and with George III and became president of the

---

[1] Samuel Isham's *History of American Painting* (New York, 1905); there is a general bibliography on p. 565 and fol. See also Dunlap's *Arts of Design* and Henry T. Tuckerman's *Artist-Life: or Sketches of American Painters* (New York, 1847). On Trumbull, see John F. Weir's *John Trumbull, A Brief Sketch of His Life.*

[2] Charles H. Hart's *Benjamin West's Family . . . Not a Quaker* (Philadelphia, 1908). For the old time traditional view of West and his place in the history of art, see John Galt's *Life, Studies, and Works of Benjamin West, Esq.* (London, 1820). The "Appendix" gives a list of four hundred and ten of West's pictures.

Royal Academy, — a career that has seldom been surpassed. Most of the artistic work of that time was in portraiture. Artists travelled from town to town in America, reproducing with more or less faithfulness the lineaments of almost countless men and women. Oftentimes they charged small prices for their services and spent little time at the work; but they perpetuated for us the faces and forms of their generation of American men and women. The silhouettists and the fabricators of wax portraits also helped to preserve the features of our ancestors. From 1810 to 1840 was the period in which the silhouette makers flourished.[1] The most remarkable of them was Auguste Edouart, who came to America from France by way of London. He and some of the others delineated family groups and some of these are among the most striking representations of the figures of the past.

Ordinarily, having procured a little money by portrait painting, an artist sought the other side of the Atlantic and almost inevitably found himself in West's studio in London. Returning to the home land, he painted more portraits of greater artistic merit, though perhaps of not greater historic truth, and then yielded place to younger men. Of them all, the career of Washington Allston possesses the greatest attraction as showing the progress of the American mind. Allston[2] was born in South Carolina in 1779, passed his boyhood in Rhode Island, which even then was sought by "the most fashionable influential Characters from Maryland to Georgia,"[3] and entered Harvard College in 1796. There, the coloring of Symbert's copy of Vandyke's portrait of

---

[1] Charles Henry Hart in *The Outlook* for October 6, 1900, has an interesting article on "The Last of the Silhouettists." The best work is Ethel S. Bolton's *Wax Portraits and Silhouettes* (Boston, 1915). See also E. Nevill Jackson's *History of Silhouettes* (London, 1911).

[2] Jared B. Flagg's *Life and Letters of Washington Allston* (New York, 1892).

[3] G. L. Rives's *Correspondence of Thomas Barclay*, 144.

Cardinal Bentivoglio attracted him and did much to turn his attention to art. He studied with West at London, spent four years at Rome, and at one time or another passed seven years in England. Finally returning to America, he devoted his last years to the remaking of a large picture of " Belshazzar's Feast " and died before the work was done. Allston delivered a series of lectures on art which were the first of their kind in America and even now are interesting. He protested against " faithful transcripts." Art should be characterized by originality, by poetic truth, by imagination, and by unity. The difference between nature and art is that one is " the work of the Creator, and the other of the creature." Washington Allston also printed a volume of poems and a rather striking work of fiction entitled " Monaldi," which is worth reading even now. And five lines of his poetry linger in the memory :

> "'Tis sad to think, of all the crowded Past,
> How small a remnant in the memory lives !
> A shadowy mass of shapes at random cast
> Wide on a broken sea the image gives
> Of most that we recall."

The earliest chronicler of the painters and the actors was William Dunlap, himself an artist, a theatrical manager, and a dramatist, besides being the writer of two distinctly useful books, a " History of the American Theatre " and a " History of the Rise and Progress of the Arts of Design in the United States." The latter was published in New York in 1834 when many of those who are memorialized in its pages were still alive and able to contribute to the work. Dunlap quoted largely, but he rejected many of the stock anecdotes that came to him from Galt's biography of Benjamin West. Dunlap painted partly from memory and partly from sketches[1] replicas of West's large pictures. These, with some of his own productions, he exhibited all over the country, in Transappalachia as well as in the Old Thirteen States, and his series of exhibitions was only one of many. Doubtless the artistic merit of many of the pictures and of other objects, as Hiram Powers's " Greek Slave " in marble, was not great, but the fact that thousands of people wished to see them and were willing to pay for the privilege is an indication of a quickened artistic sense. Powers's " Greek Slave " and Greenough's " Washington " pall on the modern taste.[2] The latter was designed for the interior of the Capitol and in its half-clothed condition out of doors the figure of the seated Washington strikes modern observers as somewhat bizarre. There have been critics who have been rude enough to suggest that the fame of the Greek Slave was largely due to its being the first unclad life-size female figure to be exhibited in America ; but the further assertion that it was simply a copy of a second-rate antique and not the result of a frontier genius is unjust to Powers, who lived for years in Cincinnati, although he was born and nurtured in Vermont, and did most of his work in Italy.

Whence come genius and talent ? Do they arise from the soil, come from one's parents, from one's early environment, or from the circumstances of one's working career ? In the preceding pages care has been taken to note all four of these points, partly with a view to illustrating this very matter. Recently, attention has been drawn to the comparative influence of " nature and nurture " in forming men's lives, partly as a test of Galton's famous thesis. Edwin L. Clarke has tabulated the birth-places[3] of four

[1] See Oral S. Coad's *William Dunlap, A Study of his Life* and Dunlap's own account in his *Arts of Design*, i, 243–311.

[2] See Lorado Taft's *History of American Sculpture* (New York, 1913), Pt. i.

[3] Edwin L. Clarke's *American Men of Letters ; their Nature and Nurture*, 80.

hundred and sixty American Literati born before 1851.
Of these 218 were born in New England, 140 in the Middle
States, 48 in the South Atlantic States, 44 in all the rest
of the United States, and 8 in Canada. At first sight it
would appear that there was some peculiar quality inherent
in the rocks and sands of New England, so that people born
there were influenced by the geographic character of the
place, by its soil and its climate. Looking a little farther
Clarke placed these 460 literary persons according to the
religious surroundings of their families. It appears that
119 were " trained " as Congregationalists, 73 as Presbyterians, 49 as Unitarians, 7 as Universalists, and 20 as
Quakers, or 268 in all belonging to the religious faiths that
had been prominent in early New England. When one
considers the relative size of the population served by these
religious faiths, the picture is startling; but when one
goes beneath the surface a bit and looks into the circumstances of the careers of these men, or of the most famous
group of them, one finds that it was not so much their
religious training as it was a revolt from the ideas of their
fathers and grandfathers that influenced them. The greatest of them produced their most effective works in New
England in the second third of the century.[1] It was the
time when Church and State were separated, when the
old ideas suffered a most severe shock. Emerson tells us

[1] The following dates are associated
with the names of the foremost members of the New England group:
1821, Bryant's *Poems;* 1830, Holmes's
"Old Ironsides," 1858, *Autocrat of the
Breakfast Table;* 1831, Whittier's *Leg-
ends of New England,* 1841, *Voices of
Freedom;* 1836, Emerson's *Nature,* 1838,
The American Scholar; 1837, Hawthorne's *Twice-Told Tales,* 1850, *The
Scarlet Letter;* 1839, Longfellow's *Hy-
perion,* 1847, *Evangeline;* 1841, Greeley's New York *Tribune* begins; 1848,
Lowell's *Fable for Critics* and the
Biglow Papers; 1849, Thoreau's *Week
on the Concord and Merrimack Rivers,*
and 1854, *Walden.* Of the historians,
the first volume of Bancroft's *United
States* appeared in 1834; Prescott's
Ferdinand and Isabella in 1837; Parkman's *Conspiracy of Pontiac* in 1851;
and Motley's *Rise of the Dutch Republic* in 1856.

to think for ourselves; Thoreau to see for ourselves; Channing to interpret the Bible for ourselves; and Hawthorne gives a picture of the older time that makes one's flesh creep even now. Longfellow and Whittier objurgated the preceding generations in verse, and Holmes gently chided his ancestors and their companions as the New England Brahminical class. All of them threw precedents to the winds and in their mental revolt they broke away from the old social order and inaugurated a period of freethinking. It was not the New England soil and climate, it was not any physical or mental peculiarity of the old New England stock, it was not any particular schooling that bred these men, it was the reaction of the period and the place from the old conditions and the bounding forth into a new and freer life that produced them. Moreover, the idea that family scholasticism was an essential element in the production of the New England literary school does not seem to be borne out by the facts of these men's nurture. Emerson and Holmes were sons of Congregational ministers, but Thoreau and Whittier were farmer boys, and Hawthorne's father was a merchant, and whenever one approaches this particular theme, the career of Abraham Lincoln at once comes to mind as controverting all theories on nature and nurture. It may well be that the simplicity of existence in that time gave men and women opportunity to turn from bread and luxury winning to affairs of the imagination.

Ralph Waldo Emerson was the clearest thinker that America has yet produced and one of the clearest thinkers that the world has ever seen, and his English is of the kind that is eternal. Thoreau in his lifetime was not at all appreciated, but as the years have gone by and people have come to know him better, especially through the publication of his "Journal," it is clear that, in some respects, he has had no equal in this country and few anywhere. Hawthorne, curiously enough, had little fame in his lifetime compared with that which has since visited him. It is interesting to think of these men as Americans who drew their inspirations from America, who in their formative years never went far from their boyhood homes. Besides the poets and essayists who have been enumerated in the preceding paragraphs, New England produced a quartette of historians who enjoyed great vogue in their lives and whose fame is not yet dead. Of these, George Bancroft was the earliest in point of time and represents for America the doctrinaire historical writer, and it is as a protest against the theory of the aristocratic march of American history that his work can still be used. Prescott and Motley had none of the usual equipment of the successful historical student: they were not poor, they were not teachers, they had no scientific training. They were subject to the English historical method and sought by literary expertness to make historic scenes and events appeal to their readers, — and they succeeded. The fourth in the list, Francis Parkman, combined careful scientific historical investigation with great literary charm. No historian can hope to live as can a poet or an essayist, because new facts will constantly arise to invalidate his most careful conclusions; but these four men have enjoyed a life beyond that generally awarded to historians. In short, this half-century in the United States in poetry, in fiction, and in history stands apart, — it is without an equal since the days of Shakespeare, Francis Bacon, and John Milton.

NOTE

General Bibliography. — The bibliographies at the ends of the first two volumes of the *Cambridge History of American Literature* are of great value to the student and include, not only works of " pure " or " polite " literature, but also sections on travels, newspapers, and orators.[1] Histories of American literature have been written by Barrett Wendell, Bliss Perry, Thomas Wentworth Higginson, William P. Trent, and George E. Woodberry;[2] but they are all mainly concerned with " the Augustan Period of American Literature " or the " Renaissance of American Letters," meaning thereby the period of New England literary flowering.[3] Earl L. Bradsher's *Mathew Carey, Editor, Author, and Publisher* (New York, 1912) is one of the few essays to give a view of the American non-classical literature.

[1] A comprehensive list of the writings of Southerners is at the end of vol. xvi of the *Library of Southern Literature.*

[2] *A Literary History of America* by Barrett Wendell; *History of Literature in America* by Wendell and C. N. Greenough; *The American Mind* by Bliss Perry; *A Reader's History of American Literature* by T. W. Higginson and H. W. Boynton; *The Cambridge History of American Literature* edited by W. P. Trent and others;

America in Literature by G. E. Woodberry; C. F. Richardson's *American Literature* (2 vols., New York, 1887); D. D. Addison's *Clergy in American Life and Letters.*

[3] William B. Cairns's essay "On the Development of American Literature from 1815 to 1833" (*Bulletin* of the University of Wisconsin, Literature Series, i, No. 1) is almost the only attempt to give an adequate place to the literary activity of this early time.

CHAPTER X

THE PRESIDENCY OF JAMES MONROE

POLITICALLY and superficially the ten years from 1815 to 1825 were years of calm within the boundaries of the federal government. They have often been termed the Era of Good Feeling and are usually regarded as having no interest and as being of little importance. In reality they were a formative period in our political history and in our international history of the greatest interest and of the highest importance. It was in that time that forces were taking shape that were to determine the history of the United States down to the year 1865. The Southerners consolidated their grip upon the government of the country and developed the solidarity of society to the southward of Mason and Dixon's line that was to become apparent to every one in 1850. John Quincy Adams noted the general high ability of the Southern congressmen and government officials in comparison with that of the Northerners with whom he had to do in Washington. A leisured class had developed in the South; its members were only slightly interested in "reforms" or in literature, but they were absorbed in politics. This was not confined to the very rich men, because many well-to-do planters, who were actively engaged in the management of their plantations, were able to leave their fields and slaves to the care of overseers and managers and attend the meetings of the State legislatures and of the federal Congress. In the North the members of the leisured classes were either engaged in reforming the abuses that had come down from colonial times, or were devoted to literature; and the strong men of affairs were so immersed in business that they could not enter public life; and, in the newer country of the Northwest, the farmers were obliged to stick to their ploughs. There were exceptions to this rule as to any other, — John Quincy Adams, himself, was a most marked exception; but, generally speaking, political matters in the North were left to the professionals whose horizons were bounded by petty offices and personal advancements. One could enumerate twenty-five or fifty men in the South in this period whose abilities could not be matched by more than a dozen Northern politicians. It is true that, with its rapidly growing population, the North was steadily outstripping the South in Congress — notwithstanding the working of the federal ratio, but so far the Southerners by combining with the democratic elements in the Northern population had been able to keep their grip on the federal government. In 1816, James Monroe,[1] a Virginia planter like Jefferson and Madison, had been elected President by 183 electoral votes to only 34 for his Federalist opponent, Rufus King of New York. In 1820, there was no Federalist candidate at all and Monroe was reëlected President, receiving all but one of the electoral votes. That single vote was given by William Plumer of New Hampshire to John Quincy Adams, because he thought that Monroe had shown "a want of foresight and economy."[2]

One department alone had resisted the triumph of the

---

[1] The *Writings of James Monroe* were edited by S. M. Hamilton and published in seven volumes in New York in 1903. These volumes reproduce the most important part of the papers purchased from Monroe's heirs in 1849. These manuscripts are in the Library of Congress and have been listed by W. C. Ford in a volume entitled *Papers of James Monroe.*

[2] William Plumer to William Plumer, Jr., January 8, 1821, in the "Plumer Mss." in the Library of Congress, and in the *American Historical Review*, xxi, 318.

Republicans, the federal judiciary as represented by the Supreme Court of the United States. It is true that by 1820, all but two of the judges were Republicans and the Chief Justice himself was a Southerner. But that Chief Justice, John Marshall, was a Virginian of the George Washington type. In point of fact, in some respects he strongly resembled that great man. Like him he was not deeply versed in the minutiæ of learning, but like him he had steadfastness of purpose and the power of commanding the learning of those who worked with him. Decades came and decades went; for thirty-five years Marshall remained at the head of the national judiciary, and for thirty-five years he remained a Federalist. Moreover, as one of the old Federalist justices after another died and his place was filled by a Republican appointed by one of the Virginia Republican Presidents, he fell immediately under the overwhelming influence of the Chief Justice. In seven leading cases spread over the twenty-one years from 1803 to 1824 Marshall and his colleagues announced the supremacy of the federal government over the States of the Union so far as powers had been delegated to it by the sovereign people through the medium of the Constitution.[1] In Marbury *vs.* Madison, the earliest decision in point of time, the supremacy of the Supreme Court over the federal legislature was enun-

[1] The cases are as follows: Marbury *vs.* Madison, 1803; Fletcher *vs.* Peck, 1810; Martin *vs.* Hunter's Lessee, 1816; M'Culloch *vs.* Maryland, 1819; Cohens *vs.* Virginia, 1821; Osborn *vs.* Bank of the United States, 1824; Gibbons *vs.* Ogden, 1824. These cases may be most conveniently consulted in J. B. Thayer's *Cases on Constitutional Law*, in *The Writings of John Marshall*, and in the "Reports" of the Supreme Court. Albert J. Beveridge's *John Marshall*, in four volumes, is one of the most illuminating of American biographical works and the "Letters" of Marshall to Judge Story, printed in the *Proceedings* of the Massachusetts Historical Society for November, 1900, throw a flood of light on the personal and mental characteristics of the great Chief Justice and his ablest supporter.

Monroe — when governor of Virginia — wrote to Jefferson in 1801: "Each govt. [federal and State] is in its sphere sovereign, so far as the term is applicable in a country where the people alone are so." *Works,* iii, 282.

ciated. In the last of them, Gibbons *vs.* Ogden, in 1824, the supremacy of the Constitution over State constitutions and laws was set forth in a decision that navigation, so far as it could be included within the phrase "regulate commerce" between the States, was within federal control. In the case of Cohens *vs.* Virginia in 1821 and in Martin *vs.* Hunter's Lessee in 1816, the Supreme Court actually had the temerity to issue orders to Virginia State courts. In M'Culloch *vs.* Maryland and in Osborn *vs.* the Bank, the power of the United States government to regulate the financial concerns of the several States and practically of every individual within the United States was laid down with undeniable distinctness. It is true that the persons and powers directly affected by some of these decisions paid little attention to the orders of the federal Supreme Court; but the orders and the principles and the reasoning upon which these decisions were based remained and remain to this day practically the supreme law of the land. In death, indeed, the Federalist party triumphed.

One of the most distinctive features of the Hamiltonian policy had been the concentration of the control of the finances of all the people of the United States within the grasp of a great financial institution that had been incorporated by act of Congress in 1791 and had been more thoroughly hated than any other creation of the Federalists. In 1811, the charter of the Bank of the United States had expired by its limitation. For several years one attempt after another had been made to prolong its life by a new charter embodying some peculiarly favorable features so far as the central government was concerned.[1] All had

<hr/>

[1] See *Report of the Secretary of the Treasury on the Subject of a National Bank* (March 2, 1809). Gallatin's later ideas are to be found in his *Con-siderations on the Currency and Banking System of the United States* (Philadelphia, 1831). A vigorous and virulent attack on the Bank was made by

been in vain. The Jeffersonians had aroused the jealousies of the people against centralized financial power, the Jeffersonian government had sold bank stock belonging to the United States to English capitalists through the Barings of London,[1] and Albert Gallatin, who was still Secretary of the Treasury, had aroused the anger and distrust of politicians and local financiers partly by his insistence on things that were good in themselves and partly by an ignorance of the ordinary methods of business transactions,[2] — and besides he was of foreign birth. His enemies combined with those Congressmen who naturally distrusted banks and with the anti-British people to defeat every attempt to renew its existence. When the war came, the difficulty of collecting government funds and paying them out was greatly increased by the lack of a central financial institution, and from time to time it became almost impossible to provide the money to purchase supplies in distant parts of the country. Gold and silver disappeared from circulation, except in New England. This was mainly due to the vicious banking systems of other parts of the country, but it was helped on by the exportation of seven million dollars in specie to pay the foreign holders of the stock of the first United States Bank at the precise moment that gold and silver were most needed in the United States.[3] Moreover, the demise of the old bank had been followed by the chartering of in-

Jesse Atwater in *Considerations on the Approaching Dissolution of the United States Bank* (New Haven, 1810).

[1] See "Letter from the Secretary of the Treasury" dated January 23, 1811, in which he says that three-fourths of the shares of the Bank of the United States were held by foreigners.

[2] See the present work, vol. iv, 403.

[3] Henry Clay's speech against the rechartering of the old Bank in 1811 (*Annals of Congress*, 11th Cong., 3rd Sess., 219) shows in a graphic way the feeling of a large part of the American public against the Bank. In view of this it is rather curious to reflect that Clay's salary, as one of the Commissioners at Ghent, and the salaries of the other diplomatic representatives abroad were paid through the Barings of London — in time of war between the United States and Great Britain. See American Historical Association's *Report* for 1913 (ii, 210 and note).

numerable State banks which had been created without any restrictions on their doings. These had naturally issued paper money, practically without stint, and loaned funds oftentimes on very slight security. At the time of the ratification of the Treaty of Ghent, the financial condition of the United States was desperate.

Alexander J. Dallas [1] was Secretary of the Treasury in 1815. He thought that the establishment of a national bank was the best method to adopt to rehabilitate the federal finances, restore the currency, and revive public and private credit by controlling the excesses of the local State banks. There was a great deal of opposition to the plan, but in April, 1816, the second Bank of the United States was incorporated by act of Congress.[2] In many ways, it resembled the old Hamiltonian institution. The government was to subscribe to a portion of the capital stock and was to appoint five of the twenty-five directors. The government funds were to be deposited in the Bank unless the Secretary of the Treasury should think it was inadvisable so to do; but if he did not so deposit them, he was to state his reasons to Congress as soon as possible. The Bank was to transfer the public funds from one part of the country to another without any expense to the government, but it was not to pay interest on the public money. The capital stock of the Bank might be largely composed of government securities, the institution was to perform certain functions in the handling of government loans, and the Bank was to pay a bonus to the government of one and a half million dollars in three payments within four years

---

[1] Like Morris, Hamilton, and Gallatin, Dallas was born outside the limits of the United States, — on the island of Jamaica.

[2] The charter is printed in full in *Annals of Congress*, 14th Cong., 1st Sess., col. 1812; *American State Papers, Finance*, ii, 892; and in Appendix i to R. C. H. Catterall's *Second Bank of the United States*.

after its organization. The Bank might establish branches in different parts of the country and it could issue circulating notes which must be signed by the president and cashier of the Bank. In opposing the adoption of the charter John Randolph of Roanoke prophesied that the Bank would become "an engine of irresistible power in the hands of any administration" and an instrument by which the federal executive could hurl the whole nation to destruction.[1] His financial ineptitude was as glaring as that of any man in the country; but he forecasted future events with painful accuracy, in this case, at least. Other financial legislation that was passed at about the same time looked to the resumption of specie payment within twelve months.[2] The subscription to the stock of the new national Bank proceeded slowly, but at length it opened its doors. For the first four or five years, it was badly managed. Numerous branches were established, especially in the South and the West where there were many State banks and where paper money had been issued in the greatest abundance. Undoubtedly the attempt to bring about deflation in so short a time and by means of a national financial institution was most unwise and accounted for the great unpopularity of the Second Bank in large portions of the country; and also did something at least to bring about the hard times of the next few years. In 1820, William H. Crawford was Secretary of the Treasury. He declared that the demands for gold and silver coin that were constantly made by the United States Bank and its branches led people to ascribe to it all the evils that had been suffered from the rapid contraction of the currency; but in bringing this about the Bank had really been only a passive agent in the hands of the government.[3]

---

[1] *Annals of Congress*, 14th Cong., 1st Sess., 1110.

[2] Act of April 30, 1816; *Annals of*

Congress, 14th Cong., 1st Sess., 1919.

[3] *American State Papers, Finance*, iii, 508. These sentences are at the

What would have happened to the country without this financial legislation cannot be stated. The Bank did a great deal towards stabilizing business and Dallas's masterful policy aided powerfully the reëstablishment of sound financial methods. But the times and seasons and conditions throughout the world were most unusual in this period of reaction after the European struggle against the domination of Napoleon and of France. Harvests were bad in England and on the Continent and riots and outrages were common. In America, the condition of affairs was even more attended with danger than in Europe. One season of bad harvest succeeded another. Year after year there were droughts, hot spring weather, cold summer weather, and crop-devouring insects.[1] From 1816 to 1819 and to 1821, farmers were unable to buy goods, or to pay for goods that had already been purchased. With the reopening of the ocean routes and of the ports of the United States, European commodities were sent from the eastern side of the Atlantic and sold for what they would bring. Factories were closed, employment reduced, and wages lowered, so that the purchasing power of the working people was everywhere diminished. Letters and diaries of prominent men of that time are filled with statements showing how impossible it was to meet the ordinary financial obliga-

end of the report, but the whole document, which begins on p. 494, and Crawford's later report on "Banks of Deposite" on pp. 718–782 deserve thoughtful reading.

[1] In August, 1818, Charles Ellis, writing from Richmond to John Allan, who was then in London, noted many failures in Virginia and that property would only bring as many hundreds as it would have commanded thousands eighteen months earlier. Eastern banks, he said, were calling loans and Western banks were closing their doors. In February, 1819, there were more failures, and in the following March a "general curtail" took place. Negroes were unsalable and the hard times continued in parts of the country as late as 1825, when Vincent Nolte's firm failed at New Orleans. See Nolte's *Fifty Years in Both Hemispheres*, p. 329. It is also worth noting that the cashier of the New York Branch foretold failures in New York, Philadelphia, and Baltimore, as far back as October, 1818.

tions of everyday life, and year by year the Bank incessantly
called for payment of debts that were due to it, and its
example was necessarily followed by the State banks so
that men found it difficult to look ahead from one season to
another — whether they were mill owners, or farmers, or
retailers of merchandise. The manufacturers appealed to
Congress for aid and in 1816 a tariff act was passed with
the direct intention of giving them assistance.[1] By this
act moderate duties were laid on the principal commodities
that were or could be made in the United States, and "a
minimum duty" was provided on cotton cloth [2] by enacting
that all imported cottons should be valued at twenty-five
cents per square yard at the lowest, for the purpose of cal-
culating the import duty. This impost was twenty-five
per cent ad valorem until 1819 and twenty per cent thereafter. It may well be questioned whether this law provided any efficient "protection" for the languishing manufactures; but it assuredly was the beginning of the new protective period and of the "minimum" principle. About
both of these many fierce political battles were to be waged
in the coming years, — and about them there was to be

---

[1] *Annals of Congress*, 14th Cong.,
1st Sess., 1870.

[2] This part of the law was aimed
against the importation of low-priced
India cottons. Some of these cost
as little as six cents a square yard, at
which price American manufacturers
could not hope to compete. By ap-
praising these cheap cloths at twenty-
five cents a yard and levying a duty
of one-quarter or one-fifth on this
appraised value, the price of these
imported Indian cottons was raised to
a figure at which American manufacturers could compete and thus
provided a market for Southern grown
cotton. The Southerners seem to
have been entirely unaffected by the
argument that this arrangement

created a new demand for their cotton;
they argued, on the contrary, that the
greatly increased price of cotton
cloth, which was due to this legislation, was equivalent to compelling
them to pay a duty of seventy-five
per cent on the cloth they purchased
for their slaves. Moreover, the price
of cotton was fixed at Liverpool and
depended upon the prosperity of
English manufacturers of hardware,
etc. Anything, the American tariff
for instance, that interfered with this
prosperity lowered the price of cotton
at Liverpool and on every plantation
in America. See Governor Hammond's "Message of November 26,
1844."

much argument as to who paid the tariff duty and who received the benefits from it, and whether they lived in the South, or the North, or the West.

The improvement of the transportation facilities of the country, or of portions of it, at the general expense or at the expense of one or two colonies or States was undertaken even in colonial times when a passable route from Portsmouth in New Hampshire southward to Baltimore was opened.[1] With the establishment of the government under the Constitution, it was generally recognized that the defence of the country as a whole and the building up of the economic and social welfare of the people would be greatly facilitated by better means of transportation overland and by water through the sounds and bays and up and down the rivers that separated and at the same time connected different parts of the country. During the Federalist regime, Congress and the administration had been so busily occupied with matters of primary organization that they had no time to devote to schemes of internal improvement. And, besides, if Martin Van Buren can be trusted, Hamilton thought an amendment of the Constitution would be necessary to authorize the general government to open canals through the territory of two or more States.[2] Gallatin thought otherwise and on his advice Congress included in the act admitting Ohio to the Union as a State a provision that one-twentieth part of the net proceeds of the sale of the public lands within the limits of the new State "shall be applied to the laying out and making public roads" from the sea-

[1] The economical and social aspects of internal improvements have been treated in ch. i.

[2] In the "Van Buren Papers" at Washington is a paper given by Hamilton to Senator Drayton advocating such an amendment, partly because the making of these improvements by the federal government would be "a useful source of influence"; but how this paper, if it is genuine, came into Van Buren's possession is not stated in the endorsement upon it.

board into and through the State of Ohio, "such roads to be laid out under the authority of Congress with the consent of the several states through which the road shall pass." [1] The act containing this clause was approved by President Jefferson, — such was the origin of the Cumberland Road. In 1807, the matter of internal improvements again arrested Gallatin's attention. He caused a friendly Senator to call for a report from him on the general subject of internal improvement and replied with the report of April 4, 1808, which has been already mentioned.[2] About a year earlier, February 10, 1807, a bill authorizing the survey of the coast had been passed by Congress and approved by Jefferson, although no organization was effected until 1816.[3] Thus the policy of internal improvements by federal action, including the surveying and protecting of the coasts, the deepening and betterment of rivers and harbors, and the making of national roads belongs in its first phase distinctly to Gallatin and to Jefferson.

Although Jefferson fell in with Gallatin's desires as to physical improvements by the national government, he thought an amendment to the Constitution would be necessary to legalize such proceedings, — thus agreeing in this with Hamilton. In his Annual Message to Congress in December, 1806, Jefferson states that there will soon be surplus revenues.[4] He asks, shall the government avoid collecting more money than it needs for current expenses

[1] *Statutes at Large*, ii, 173. See also Adams's *Gallatin*, 350 and the *Writings* of Albert Gallatin, i, 78.

[2] See above, p. 9.

[3] See *Laws of 1807, 1832, and 1843, relating to the Survey of the Coast of the United States*; *Statutes at Large*, ii, 413; and in the *Centennial Celebration* of the Coast Survey, p. 175.

[4] *Annals of Congress*, 9th Cong., 2nd Sess., 14. It is interesting to note that ten years earlier, Jefferson had looked upon any kind of internal improvement as "a source of boundless patronage to the executive, jobbing to members of Congress & their friends, and a bottomless abyss of public money. . . . It will be a scene of eternal scramble among the members, who can get the most money wasted in their State; and they will always get most who are meanest." *Writings* (Ford ed.), vii, 63.

and the discharge of the public debt by suppressing the imposts and giving just so much "advantage to foreign over domestic manufactures," or shall it apply the surplus to "public education, roads, rivers, canals, and such other objects of public improvement as it may be thought proper to add to the Constitutional enumeration of federal powers"? Although Jefferson doubted the constitutionality of internal improvements without an amendment to the Constitution, he signed the bills for the survey of the Cumberland Road and the rivers and harbors on the coast.[1] The early Presidents seem to have discerned some constitutional difference between spending money on surveys and on construction that is not now comprehensible. The embargo and the War of 1812 interfered with the prosecution of these designs as it did with so many others; and it was not until 1816, when the prospect of receiving some ready money from the new Bank of the United States awakened fresh interest in the subject. On the 16th day of December in that year John C. Calhoun of South Carolina declared that the auspicious circumstances under which the subscription to the stock of the National Bank had begun made it desirable to consider whether the course of internal improvement was a proper direction to give to the national profits to be derived from that institution. He moved for the appointment of a committee to inquire into the expediency of setting apart these profits as a permanent fund for internal improvements.[2] The committee was appointed and, as its chairman on December 23, 1816, Calhoun introduced a bill, "to set apart and pledge, as a permanent fund for internal improvements" the profits received from the Bank. In the debate that followed John Randolph of

---

[1] *Statutes at Large*, ii, 357, 375, 413.

[2] *Annals of Congress*, 14th Cong., 2nd Sess., 296, 361.

Roanoke declared that the old States ought to have a share in the "sunshine of government" and that the navigation of the Roanoke, the Catawba, and the Yadkin rivers ought to be improved, as well as that of the Tombigbee. The bill passed and went to the President and on March 3, 1817, on the last day of his public career, James Madison vetoed it, being "constrained," he wrote, "by the insuperable difficulty" of reconciling the bill with the Constitution of the United States. Having thus killed the measure, Madison stated that he fully realized the great importance of roads and canals and improved navigation, but that no power to provide for internal improvements was given by the Constitution to the National Legislature or could be deduced from any part of it without "an inadmissible latitude of construction." He hinted that an amendment might well be made authorizing such expenditures. Monroe in his first message declared that he, likewise, was convinced that Congress did not possess the right to construct roads and canals and he also suggested that an amendment should be adopted to make it possible.

It was at this point that Henry Clay stepped into the arena and made the subject of internal improvements a cardinal point in his policy for the next dozen years. Clay believed that Congress had ample power to do what he desired and that no amendment to the Constitution was necessary. Before long the question of internal improvements at the expense of the nation became commingled with the maintenance of a protective tariff, — the combination being termed the "American System." With his marvellous powers of speech and boldness of purpose, Clay took the leading part in the formulation of this programme; but, as is not infrequently the case, the statement of the scheme was made in a more usable form by persons of talents distinctly inferior to his. One of these was Andrew Stewart, a member of Congress from Pennsylvania, who was very well regarded by many people of that time. The true American policy, according to him,[1] was to cherish national industry so as to secure at home an abundant amount of food, clothing, housing, and articles of defence. The articles of luxury consumed by the rich should be taxed for revenue purposes, but the necessaries of life that were consumed by the poor and all articles that could not be produced in the United States should be free from all taxation. Whatever surplus revenue might accrue should be used for national improvements, — those of a local character being left to the care of the States. Economy should be pursued in public expenditure that financial burdens might be lightened and the rewards of labor increased. To this general outline of the American System should be added the contribution to the internal improvement fund of the money received from the sales of the public lands. In its most optimistic form this system, so it was said, would render the United States independent of the world, would promote the manufacturing interests of the Northeast and the agricultural interests of Transappalachia, and would bind together by arteries of commerce and by ties of mutual benefit the different parts of the country. It certainly was a grand conception. Unfortunately, the interstate commerce clause of the Constitution had not then been interpreted, not even by John Marshall, to authorize the federal government to do whatever it wished, so long as its wish stepped over a State line. Monroe vetoed every bill that came before him that involved federal construction in a State; but, in 1822, he sent a very long dissertation[2] to Congress on the

[1] See his *American System*, 322–343.
[2] See "Views of the President of the United States on the Subject of Internal Improvements" in *Messages and Papers of the Presidents*, ii, 144, and "Annual Message," pp. 185–195.

subject of internal improvements and, later, he again recommended the adoption of an amendment to the Constitution authorizing the national government to make
internal improvements at the national expense. The
Cumberland Road, or the National Road, was built to the
Ohio River and further on the western side of that stream
according to the earlier laws; but every effort that was
made to repair that highway or to improve it was sternly
resisted although Monroe signed his name to an act for
surveying the extension of the road to the Mississippi.[1]

Curiously enough although the repair of the National
Road was regarded by many persons as beyond the constitutional power of the federal government, river and harbor
improvements in the earlier days did not strike the same
constitutional snags,[2] although there were not wanting signs
of doubt in the executive mind as to whether these were
within the purview of the fundamental law. Thus matters
stood when Monroe laid down the reins of office and John
Quincy Adams and Henry Clay came into power as President
and Secretary of State and proceeded to do whatever they
could to push on the American System, but without much
success. Years after, James K. Polk, when President,
could see no difference between harbor and river improvements and canal digging and road making by the federal
government. Whenever such a measure came before him, he
vetoed it and explained to the members of Congress that a
thing that is convenient is not always "necessary and
proper" and therefore constitutional. Like Jefferson, Madi-

The "Views" may be found also in
Monroe's *Writings*, vi, 216–284.

[1] *Statutes at Large*, iii, 604; Act
of May 15, 1820.

[2] On May 24, 1824, Monroe signed
the act to improve the navigation of
the Ohio and Mississippi rivers: *Annals*
of *Congress*, 18th Cong., 1st Sess., vol.
ii, 3227. Jackson, who was then in
the Senate, voted for this bill as he
did for the Survey Bill of the same
year: Sioussat's "Memphis as a Gateway to the West" in *Tennessee Historical Magazine*, March, 1917.

son, and Monroe, President Polk recognized somewhat grudgingly the need of providing "aids to navigation" that were immediately connected with foreign commerce and were for the protection and security of American naval vessels. He thought that when one advanced a step beyond this point, it was extremely difficult to know where to stop. As long as he was President, no river or harbor or part of a river or harbor above a port of entry or delivery had any chance of improvement.   Polk even anticipated the possible passage of such a measure by writing out a veto message in advance, so as to have it in readiness in case Congress should pass a river and harbor bill in the very last hours of the session.[1] He thought that if Congress had power to improve a harbor, it had power to deepen inlets and to make harbors where there were none ; and in the scramble for the contents of the Treasury the true interests of the country would be lost sight of and the most artful and industrious persons would be the most successful.[2]   It will be interesting, before dropping this subject, to see how Jefferson felt toward public ownership and management in general. He thought that the only way to secure good and safe government was to divide and subdivide the administration until every one managed his own affairs. "The generalizing and concentrating all cares and powers into one body" has destroyed liberty and the rights of man in every government that had ever existed. This was written in 1816. In 1825 he actually drew up a "solemn Declaration and Protest of the commonwealth of Virginia" against the internal improvement policy, but it was not approved of by his two presiden-

[1] The idea that a President had ten days after the close of a session of Congress to consider measures passed by both Houses had not then been invented.

[2] See *Diary of James K. Polk during his Presidency* (4 vols., Chicago, 1910) using index under "Harbor," "Internal Improvements," and "Message, veto."

tial friends and was never acted upon.[1] It is worth noting, however, as having been drawn up by Thomas Jefferson in the next to the last year of his life.

It was in 1803 that the United States had come into possession of the French-Spanish province of Louisiana. The southern part of this province was erected into the Territory of Orleans and later was admitted to the Union as the State of Louisiana; the northern part was for a time fastened to the Territory of Indiana forming a district, which came to be known as the District of Louisiana and later as the Territory of Missouri. Negro slavery had existed in Louisiana as a French Province and as a Spanish Province. The Louisiana Purchase Treaty had distinctly provided that the inhabitants of the ceded province should be protected in their liberty, property, and religion. How many slaves there were in Upper Louisiana in 1804 is not precisely known;[2] but there were presumably somewhere near a thousand of them within the limits of the settled part of what are now the States of Missouri and Arkansas. Soon after the delivery of the province, Captain Amos Stoddard, an officer of the United States army and first Civil Commandant at St. Louis, was approached by a committee of the leading citizens of that place. They were anxious, so they said, as to the conduct of their slaves in the altered condition of affairs. Stoddard replied that he

---

[1] *Early History of the University of Virginia*, pp. 54, 55; Jefferson's *Writings* (Ford ed.), x, 349-352.

[2] In 1799, there were 883 slaves in Upper Louisiana (*American State Papers, Miscellaneous*, i, 383); in 1810, there were 3011 (*Aggregate Amount of . . . Persons within the United States, . . . in the year 1810*, p. 84); in 1820, there were 10,222 (*Census* for 1820, under Missouri, and Viles's "Missouri in 1820" in *Missouri Historical Review*, xv, 36–52). According to Professor Viles (*ibid.*, v, No. 4) the total slave population of the Missouri settlements in 1803–1804 was 1349 or a few more. Trexler (*Slavery in Missouri, 1804–1865*, p. 9) makes the number of slaves in 1803 to be between two and three thousand. Viles's figures are based largely on Amos Stoddard's *Sketches of Louisiana*, 211, 214, 217, 221, 224.

would enforce such rules as "appear necessary to restrain
the . . . slaves and to keep them more steadily to their
duty." Rules were drawn up and submitted to Stoddard,
were accepted by him, and were promulgated over all Upper
Louisiana.[1] Captain Stoddard's actions were never directly
disavowed by the authorities at Washington, and therefore
it would seem that slavery was recognized by the national
government as an institution in that part of the Louisiana
Purchase. In all of the fundamental laws establishing the
territorial and district governments in Upper Louisiana
that have just been enumerated, there is no mention whatever of slavery, and in 1818 there must have been between
two and three thousand slaves in that country. Nevertheless, in 1818, when the people of Missouri applied to Congress for admission to the Union as a State and the question
of the passage of an enabling act came up for debate in
Congress, General James Tallmadge of New York, then
serving his one term in the national House of Representatives, moved to amend the bill by prohibiting the further
introduction of slaves into Missouri and by providing that
all children of slaves born after the admission of Missouri as
a State should become free at the age of twenty-five years.[2]
The precise meaning of the Tallmadge amendment was not
clear then and is not now, because as it was never adopted

[1] Houck's *History of Missouri*, ii, 375.

[2] The words of the Tallmadge amendment as printed in the *Journal of the House of Representatives*, 15th Cong., 2nd Sess., p. 272, are as follows:

"And provided also, That the further introduction of slavery or involuntary servitude be prohibited, except for the punishment of crimes, whereof the party shall be duly convicted; and that all children of slaves, born within the said state, after the admission thereof into the Union, shall be free but may be held to service until the age of twenty-five years."

In the *Annals of Congress* (15th Cong., 2nd Sess., i, 1170–1214) the last phrase is altered to read "shall be free at the age of twenty-five years," and the words "of slaves" after "children" are omitted. Greeley's *Text-Book of 1860*, p. 55, gives the words of the amendment correctly. The *Speech of the Hon. James Tallmadge, . . . on Slavery* [on his amendment] was printed as a "separate" at Boston in 1849; it does not contain the words of the amendment.

it has never received any interpretation except at the hands
of political debaters. It has been stated that the amendment did not propose " to interfere with the rights of property in that Territory." [1] Probably those who used this
argument were thinking of Rufus King's contention that the
wording of the Louisiana Treaty was " the common formula
of treaties . . . to secure such inhabitants the permanent or
temporary enjoyment of their former liberties, property, and
religion ; leaving to the new sovereign full power to make
such regulations respecting the same, as may be thought
expedient, provided these regulations be not incompatible
with the stipulated security." Senator King[2] argued that the
term property in its common meaning does not include
slaves and, therefore, if the makers of the treaty had intended to include slaves in the word " property " they would
have said so. Of course, these niceties of interpretation were
confined to lawyers and other professional arguers. The
plain people of the North seem to have thought that as
slavery had been prohibited in the territory covered by the
Northwest Ordinance of 1787, in some way this prohibition
had projected itself or had been extended across the Mississippi River and that admitting Missouri to the Union as
a Slave State meant the enlargement of slave territory ; but
as a matter of fact slavery had existed in the trans-Mississippi
region ever since its settlement by Europeans, and to any
Southerner, as to Monroe, one of the negotiators of the treaty
of 1803, the word " property " plainly included slaves, —
indeed, they formed the bulk of the movable property of
the richer people in the South. At all events, to them the
Tallmadge amendment seemed to be a blow directed at their
peculiar institution, and they attacked the aggressors with

[1] American Historical Association's
Report for 1893, p. 256.
[2] See *Substance of two Speeches*
. . . *on the Subject of the Missouri
Bill. By the Hon. Rufus King* (New
York, 1819), pp. 16, 24.

all the vigor and fury that they were capable of.[1] In 1847
David Wilmot asserted, without reservation of any kind,
that the Missouri controversy was " a struggle . . . to
abrogate the law of slavery." [2]

The Missouri question has been treated in the preceding
paragraph from the social point of view ; it also had a
political significance, and many people at the time and since
have regarded its political significance as outweighing its
social. At the time of the making of the Constitution,
the North and the South had been political equals. Since
that time the industrial advance of the North and the movement of settlers into the Old Northwest had so increased
the population and power of the North — of the free North
— that it had gained a majority in the federal House of
Representatives. The only way that the South could protect itself from attack on the slave system was to possess
a majority in the Senate and, therefore, possess a veto on
federal legislation. In 1818, the free States outnumbered
the slave by one, but Alabama and Missouri were asking
admission and the admission of Alabama as a Slave State
was inevitable. The further admission of Missouri as a
Slave State would give the South a majority in the Senate.
It happened that in 1819 the people of the northeastern part
of Massachusetts applied for admission to the Union with

[1] Jefferson's letter to John Holmes,
Representative from Massachusetts,
dated Monticello, April 22, 1820, contains the well-known fire bell statement and also a keen prophecy : —
"A geographical line, coinciding with
a marked principle moral & political
once conceived and held up to the
angry passions of men, will never be
obliterated." *Writings of Jefferson*
(Ford), x, 157 and in many other places.
In 1821, Calhoun, writing to Charles
Tait, a Virginian then living in Alabama, stated that the Missouri question "was got up by a few designing
politicians in order to extend their influence and power; and that the
tendency of the question was of the most
mischievous character, being such as
was well calculated to alienate the
affections of the people of one section
from the other. . . . The North considered it as a single question involv-
ing only the extension of slavery."
The *Gulf States Historical Magazine*,
i, 103.

[2] *Proceedings of the Herkimer Mass
Convention of Oct. 26, 1847*, p. 13.

the consent of that State as a separate and free State. Under these circumstances the question of the admission of Missouri as a Slave State lost some of its political significance, for coming in with Maine the equality of power would be preserved in the Senate,[1] and the North would continue to have the greater number of the members of the House of Representatives, notwithstanding the tremendous extension of cotton growing in the Southwest. No doubt there was an apprehension on one side and a feeling of hopefulness on the other that the development of Alabama, Mississippi, and Louisiana with the help of the federal ratio and the slowing down of industry in the North — which was plainly visible — might give the Slave States a majority of the members of the House of Representatives. It was to this that Rufus King alluded when he asserted that Congress possessed complete power over slavery in purchased territory and objected to the further extension of slave territory while the federal ratio operated to give slaveholders representation in the national House and in the electoral college in proportion to the number of slaves they owned "so that five free persons in Virginia have as much power in the choice of representatives in congress, and in the appointment of presidential electors, as seven free persons in any of the states in which slavery does not exist." Finally, as Representative Timothy Fuller of Massachusetts asserted,

---

[1] Some inhabitants of Maine objected to her being "a mere *pack-horse* to transport the odious, anti-republican principle of slavery into the new State of Missouri, against reason and the fundamental grounds of the great fabric of American liberty." This sentence is from a letter of George Thacher of Biddeford, Maine, to John Holmes and dated January 16, 1820, undoubtedly expressed the belief of many Northern men. It is printed in Massachusetts Historical Society's *Proceedings* for 1878, p. 180. In the preceding October, Francis Corbin of Virginia had written to Madison that this "Union must snap short at last where Liberty ends, and Slavery begins. The Missouri Question is bringing on the Crisis." *Ibid.*, vol. 43, p. 261. There is an article on "The Separation of Maine from Massachusetts" in *ibid.*, June, 1907.

Congress had made conditions in 1812 at the time of the admission of Louisiana to the Union and might make conditions now.

Eventually the Missouri-Maine matter took on the form of the admission of both States to the Union without conditions; but slavery should be forever prohibited in all the remainder of the Louisiana Purchase north of the parallel of thirty-six degrees and thirty minutes of north latitude, which was, as a matter of fact, the southern boundary of Missouri for the greater part of its length. It was in this way that Missouri and Maine entered the Union.[1] This settlement is always spoken of as the Missouri Compromise and it is generally supposed to have put off the "irrepressible conflict" for a generation and therefore to have been justifiable from the anti-slavery point of view. There is another way of looking at it. This attempt of the Northern politicians and Northern abolitionists, or both, to limit the power of the South by destroying the institution of slavery in Upper Louisiana aroused the whole slaveholding popu-

[1] When the Missouri bill came before Monroe, he asked the opinions of his constitutional advisers in writing. These were given after a considerable discussion had been had and they were filed away in the archives of the State Department. See *Memoirs* of J. Q. Adams, v, 5–14, and Hart's *American History Told by Contemporaries*, iii, 452.

When the proposed constitution of Missouri came before Congress and the question came up of counting the electoral vote of Missouri in the presidential election of 1820, there was renewed excitement, for the constitution provided that the State Legislature should pass a law "to prevent free negroes and mulattoes" from coming into the State. This was clearly contrary to the clause of the Constitution of the United States guaranteeing the rights of "citizens," but the makers of the Missouri consti-

tution presumably did not regard colored persons as coming within the purview of citizenship. The language used by members on both sides and the threats that were bandied forward and backward were beyond anything that Congress had known up to that time. Finally, the matter was "compromised" by admitting Missouri and counting her electoral vote provided that the clause in question should never be construed to authorize the passage of any law. Curiously enough in making this demand and in all the subsequent history of the matter the wrong part of the section of the Missouri constitution was referred to; but no attempt was ever made to pass any such law. See the books on the Missouri Compromise and the *Proceedings* of the Massachusetts Historical Society, for February, 1900, p. 448.

lation of the South to defend their rights, — as they saw them. At the moment the South and the Southern leaders acquiesced in the settlement from a sense of the value of the Union and from a sentimental attachment to it.[1] But from that moment may be dated the beginning of Southern section-nationalism. It developed slowly at first, but by 1825 it threw off disguise in South Carolina and by 1830 had acquired considerable solidarity, although not enough to bring the other slaveholding States to the side of South Carolina. In reality, therefore, the Missouri Compromise of 1820 marked the ending of one epoch in our history and the beginning of another.

Following on the Peace of Ghent and the overturn at Waterloo, the world passed through a series of years of revolution and unrest and of coercion, either singly by the authorized rulers of this country or that, or by the league of nations that in those days went by the name of the Holy Alliance. In these years, the position of the United States was full of danger. She stood alone without a friend in the world and with debts to collect and matters to settle with the leading military powers of Europe. Fortunately, at the head of her affairs were several remarkable men and these were guided in great measure by the two Virginia ex-Presidents, Thomas Jefferson and James Madison. James Monroe, who succeeded Madison in 1817 as chief executive and remained in office for eight years, until 1825, was not a great man. Nobody would have called him so, except possibly himself and a few devoted friends and relatives, but he was a man of experience in the management of public affairs and in the paths of diplomacy, — and this experience had been gathered in pain and humiliation and, therefore,

---

[1] For example J. W. Barbour wrote to J. C. Crittenden in February, 1820, that the proposed compromise was "a lesser evil than dividing the Union, or throwing it into confusion." Coleman's *Crittenden*, i, 41.

was all the more valuable. Monroe's Secretary of State for the whole time of his administration — except the first few months — was John Quincy Adams. Adams was not a lovable man nor a companionable man and he had eccentricities of temper and awkwardnesses of action that concealed his real capacities and aroused enmities where none need have existed. But very few men have ever controlled the foreign affairs of a great country in an exceedingly critical time who possessed the power of the younger Adams to appraise a difficult situation and especially to deal with it with a courage and a tenacity almost unsurpassed. In friendly union with Monroe's cautiousness and the almost childlike acumen of the venerable Jefferson and Madison, the United States was carried triumphantly through.

In Great Britain starvation and rioting were not infrequent in these years and her own poverty and critical condition induced or even compelled those who guided her destinies to stand up for what they conceived to be her best interests and to endeavor to bring into British coffers every penny of profit that could be garnered. Moreover, George Canning was still prominent and toward the close of this period again occupied the British Foreign Office, — and no more ill-omened secretary ever occupied it, not even Palmerston, so far as the United States was concerned. Stated in brief, and to state it in any other way would take one too far afield, the British policy towards the United States was to close the British West Indies and the British Maritime Provinces to our shipping, to absorb as much as possible of the oceanic trade to and from the United States, and to secure every possible relaxation of American laws restricting the entry of British goods into the American republic. On our part, of course, we wished to do just the opposite. We wished to have free trade with Great Britain,

with the British West Indies, and with the Maritime Provinces, to exclude British ships absolutely from our coasting trade, and to shut our ports to the introduction of
every manufactured commodity that we could make in
our own factories. Then, too, there were questions as to
boundaries : the northeastern boundary, the northern boundary of New York, the northern boundary west of the Lake of
the Woods, the possession of Oregon, and the question of
the policing of the Great Lakes. All these questions were
full of unpleasant possibilities, and the attempt to coerce
Great Britain in any one direction was so certain to bring
reprisals in another that it was very difficult to know which
way to turn or what to do. And possibly the only way to
accomplish anything was to let the whole matter alone until
time and circumstance should so increase the economic and
military powers of the United States that even the authorities
at Downing Street would think twice before they aroused
the resentment of the American people. The story of the
trade relations is so intricate and so little came out of it
that it is hardly worth while to more than mention the few
things that were settled before the end of Monroe's term, in
March, 1825. In 1818, a treaty was signed and promptly
ratified that made the forty-ninth parallel from the Lake
of the Woods to the crest of the Rocky or Stony Mountains,
the dividing line between the United States and British
America.[1] It seems to be a little bit incongruous to apportion a vast wilderness between two nations by an imaginary
line ; but in this particular case the settlement proved to be

---

[1] On August 26, 1719, the British
Board of Trade instructed its representatives at Paris that from a certain point "where the said Line shall
cut the 49th Degree of northern Latitude, another Line shall begin, & be
extended westward from the said Lake
upon the 49th Degree of Northern
Latitude" to the southward of which
the French should not pass. Professor
O. M. Dickerson copied this entry
for me from the "Board of Trade
Journal," xxix, 135. Apparently it
is the first mention of the 49th parallel
as a boundary line.

very happy. As to the country to the westward of the mountains, as no agreement could be reached it was arranged that it should be "open for the term of ten years . . . to the vessels, citizens, and subjects of the two Powers"; but this "joint occupation," as it has generally been termed, was not to be construed to the prejudice of any claim of either of the two parties or of any other power or state.[1] In 1817, an arrangement had already been entered into by which the British and American governments agreed to limit the naval forces on Lake Champlain and the Great Lakes to one vessel each on Lake Champlain and on Lake Ontario and two on the Upper Lakes, none of the vessels to exceed one hundred tons burden or to carry more than one eighteen pound gun.[2] In this time, too, one question after another was submitted to arbiters for settlement or to joint commissions for investigation or report;[3] but all these attempts met with delays and when reports or decisions were rendered they were evaded or not accepted by one or both countries concerned. In all there were half a dozen treaties negotiated with Great Britain in the eight years of Monroe's presidency,[4] but with the exception of the northern boundary treaty they made slight impression on our development as a nation — the greatest disappointment of all being, possibly, that no other arrangement could be made as to commerce except a mere renewal of the Treaty of 1815. With France the case was no better, for the condition of affairs in that country, and in Europe, was so critical that no government could agree to make any payment of money

[1] See *Treaties and Conventions* (ed. 1873), p. 351. This whole subject is admirably treated by J. C. B. Davis in "Notes" appended to this volume, p. 1022.

[2] See J. M. Callahan's "Agreement of 1817" in American Historical Association's *Report* for 1895, pp. 367-392.

[3] The first part of vol. i of J. B. Moore's *International Arbitrations* contains the official papers on these arbitrations and commissions.

[4] *Treaties and Conventions* (ed. 1873), pp. 348-362.

for spoliations by the rulers of France before 1815, — and hope to live. It is with Spain that the main interest lies in these years, for the fate of her American colonies was inextricably commingled with that of the United States.

Ever since the occupation of the Iberian Peninsula by Napoleon and the French, Spanish America had been restless and one revolution had succeeded another. Most of these insurrections were successful, for succeeding governments in Spain could not maintain themselves, much less reconquer distant colonies. The declining power of Spain and Portugal in America and the constantly increasing strength of the insurgents opened the way for great irregularities on the sea and on the adjacent shores. Piratical bands seized Spanish territory that was contiguous to the United States, and established there a so-called republic with which President Madison had had to deal. This he had done by seizing Amelia Island, driving off the pirates or insurgents, and returning it to the jurisdiction of Spain. Amelia Island is scarcely more than an anchorage within the mouth of the St. Mary's River. Its position made it a favorite spot for illicit traders. There they could anchor in Spanish waters and at the same time be within a few cables' lengths of the American boundary and could covertly slip in goods by the boatload, without paying duties, or tonnage dues, or in any way complying with the commercial laws of the United States. Every now and then, a French, or a Spanish, or a Portuguese, vessel would be seized by irritated and zealous United States officials, with the result of compelling Adams to hold many conversations with foreign representatives in this country and to write many letters to them and also to our own diplomatic officers abroad ; but without accomplishing very much, except to keep things as they were. Privateers, commissioned by Spanish American revolutionists, appeared upon the ocean and entered American ports for the purpose of fitting or re-fitting their hulls and armaments and getting needful supplies.[1] These vessels carried crews of several nationalities and could appear as American vessels or as South American, or French, or Spanish, as the occasion might demand. Many people at Philadelphia, Baltimore, and Norfolk and also at Charleston found profit in equipping these vessels and doubtless sympathized with the warfare that they carried on against other than American seafarers. Attempts of United States officials to put down this practice and the difficulty of dealing with these seagoers in any lawful manner added greatly to the labors of the administration and also to its embarrassments. At length the Portuguese minister, the Abbé Correa de Serra, worn out with age and worry, informed Adams that United States judges were not doing their duty ; but, on being pressed for names and specifications, he took his departure for Rio de Janeiro,[2] — the only time that an official animadversion had been made against the national judiciary up to 1820. There were also numerous trials of American citizens on charges of piracy and not a few executions, much against the will of the President.

Even more serious was the inattention of the Spanish authorities in Florida to their obligations under the treaty of 1795.[3] By this Spain had bound herself to be a good neighbor to the United States and not to permit her lands and her

---

[1] As early as 1798–1799, American vessels were in the River Plate. See documents collected and edited by C. L. Chandler in *American Historical Review*, xxiii 816–826.

[2] *Writings, of John Quincy Adams*, vii, 68, 73 and footnotes. There are many entries relating to the general subject in his *Diary*, and much useful and out-of-the-way matter has been brought together in Lockey's *Pan-*

Americanism and in ch. vii of Fuller's *Purchase of Florida.*

[3] *Treaties and Conventions* (ed. 1873), p. 776. On the Floridas, see John L. Williams's *View of West Florida* (Philadelphia, 1827) and his *Territory of Florida* (New York, 1837). Official papers are printed in connection with the President's "Messages" of Feb. 22, 1817, March 14, 1818, and Nov. 17, 1818.

ports to be made use of by the enemies of the American republic. Spain's position was one of great difficulty. Every soldier that she could transport across the Atlantic was needed in the attempt to preserve her colonies. As Florida was one of the few that did not rebel, it was denuded of troops and the Spanish officials were helpless, — they could not perform the plain requirements of the treaty. Moreover, its northern borders became the place of refuge for runaway Southern slaves and hostile Indians from the United States. These frequently recrossed the boundary and stole and murdered where they could. To put a stop to these outrages General Gaines was directed to pursue hostile bands across the boundary to the limits of the Spanish posts. As he accomplished nothing the task was handed over to Andrew Jackson, the original orders to Gaines being repeated to him. Jackson pursued the Indians across the border, followed them into the Spanish towns of Pensacola and St. Mark, and took possession of those posts in April, 1818. When Monroe learned of these doings and of the execution of two British subjects — Alexander Arbuthnot and Robert C. Ambrister — in the course of the campaign, he was greatly disturbed. The orders had not been perfectly clear and the President felt that Jackson must have acted on facts that were unknown to the administration. When the matter came before the Cabinet, Adams was the only member who justified Jackson's doings as being compatible with the dictates of international law. Of the other members, Calhoun, who was then Secretary of War, thought that Jackson's " conduct " ought to be " the subject of investigation before a military tribunal "[1] and Crawford agreed

[1] See *Correspondence of John C. Calhoun*, p. 285, forming vol. ii of the American Historical Association's *Report* for 1899. Much other matter on this same subject is in this volume. See also Monroe's *Writings*, vi, 54–61; vii, 209–213, 225–230; J. Q. Adams's *Memoirs*, iv, 107–119, and his *Writ-*

with him that the general should be sternly dealt with. Monroe handled the matter in his own way. He wrote to Jackson [1] that he had acted on facts unknown at Washington, but that the Constitution gave the power to declare war to Congress and not to the Executive. It followed, therefore, that the posts must be handed back to Spain; but as the ill-faith of the Spanish authorities had made his actions necessary, it was for the Spanish government to punish its own officials and also to perform its treaty obligations. Reviewing the evidence given in the trials of Arbuthnot and Ambrister and having in mind the facts stated by Adams in his correspondence with our ministers at London and at Madrid,[2] one cannot help coming to the conclusion that Jackson's doings in Florida were amply justified. The politicians in Congress thought differently. They moved resolutions and made speeches, but after an acrid debate nothing was accomplished, except to arouse the fierce anger of Andrew Jackson.

Meantime, Adams had been engaged in a long and trying negotiation with Don Luis de Oñis,[3] the Spanish minister at Washington, and in the Spaniard's periods of ill-health with Hyde de Neuville, the French minister, who acted the part of friend to both the United States and Spain. Beside

---

ings, vi, 474–502. Professor Bassett, in his *Life of Andrew Jackson*, i, 266 and fol., gives an excellent account of the whole affair with citations to original material.

On July 20, 1818, Calhoun wrote to Judge Charles Tait that the "taking of Pensacola . . . was unauthorized." *Gulf States Historical Magazine*, i, 93.

[1] See Note II at end of chapter.

[2] Ford prints Adams's letter of Nov. 28, 1818, to G. W. Erving, our Minister to Spain, in the *Writings* of J. Q. Adams, vi, 474–502, with citations to *American State Papers*.

[3] The final section of Don Luis de Oñis's *Memoria sobre las Negociaciones entre España y Los Estados-Unidos de América* (Madrid, 1820) relates to the actual negotiations of 1795 and 1819 and is followed by an exceedingly valuable "Appendix" of documents including the text of the treaties of the retrocession of Louisiana, etc.; but only this single document is repeated in the translation by Tobias Watkins of this memoir that was printed at Baltimore in 1821, — which also lacks the extremely interesting map that accompanies the original.

the Floridian troubles, there were old claims against Spain
for spoliations that had been more or less connected with her
in the period of the French Wars,[1] and there was a conflict
over the boundaries of Louisiana. Adams asserted that
that province, as the United States had acquired it, extended
to the Rio Grande del Norte, or the Rio Bravo, as it was
often called in those days.[2] The Spaniards maintained, on
the contrary, that the western boundary of Louisiana was
the Mississippi as far north as the Red River. As to
Florida, the United States, for one reason or another, had
seized it as far east as the Perdido River,[3] which it claimed
was included in the old Louisiana. Finally, to the west of the
Mississippi and north of the Red River, the United States
had "taken possession" of the country as far west as the
Stony Mountains, and, indeed, had exercised some sort of
control or jurisdiction even farther west to the shores of the

[1] Yrujo secured the opinions of five
leading lawyers against the validity
of these claims; *American State Papers
Foreign Relations*, ii, 604. Madison's
opinion of this proceeding is in *ibid.*,
ii, 615, and is worth reading. These
citations were given to me by Mr. J. P.
Harley of Los Angeles, California.

[2] On April 20, 1818, Adams wrote
to G. W. Erving, then American
minister at Madrid, "of our unquestionable right to the Rio Bravo as the
western boundary." Again in June,
in thanking Joseph Hopkinson for
calling his attention to Moll's *Atlas*
of 1720 giving the Rio Bravo as the
western limit of Louisiana, Adams
stated that he had "so thoroughly
convinced" himself of the justice of
that boundary that with his good will
no further offer should be made to
Spain of any other western boundary.
See *Writings of J. Q. Adams*, vi, 307,
345; and the present work, volume
iv, 320 n., 332.

[3] According to the American view,
the United States had acquired by the
Louisiana Purchase Treaty of 1803

a complete title to all of the old French
Louisiana as far east as the Perdido
River and, in one way or another, it
had taken possession of that territory.
The Spaniards maintained, however,
that the Louisiana of the retrocession
was bounded on the east by the old
western boundary of West Florida, or
included only the island on which New
Orleans stands. On the whole matter,
see H. B. Fuller's *Purchase of Florida;*
P. J. Hamilton's *Colonial Mobile;*
and the present work, volume ii, 596,
iii, 20, and iv, 304, 348, 415.

For the St. Mary's River as the
boundary between British East Florida
and Georgia, see Lawrence Shaw Mayo's
The St. Mary's River. A Boundary.

Extracts from the official documents are brought together in *American History Leaflets*, No. 5, from
Martens and Cussy's *Recueil des Traités*,
i, 30; *The Annual Register* for 1763,
pp. 208–213; Bioren and Duane's
Laws of the United States, i, 450–452;
and *Treaties and Conventions between
the United States and Other Powers*, 315.

Pacific Ocean. The rightfulness of this occupation had
been in some measure recognized by the British when they
"restored" to the United States the fur-trading post of
Astoria at the mouth of the Columbia River in conformity
with the provision of the Treaty of Ghent that all places
taken during the war should be restored by both parties.
The propositions that underlay the negotiations of 1818 were
that the Spaniards should give up all claims to territory on
the North American continent east of the Mississippi River
and also to the territory on the Northwest Coast north of
California.[1] In exchange the United States would give up
all claims to Texas or to the country between the Rio Grande
and one of the Texan Rivers, — the Colorado, the Sabine,
or some other — and in addition pay five million dollars to
its own citizens to extinguish claims that they were supposed
to have against the Spanish government for spoliations
committed on American commerce during the French wars.
Jefferson had some objections to any bargain that would
restrict the western extent of the United States. Monroe
answered him that the boundary in that wilderness could be
easily arranged with whatever new government might be
formed in Mexico, — which seemed to be on the point of

---

[1] On March 12, 1818, John Quincy
Adams, writing to Don Luis de Oñis
laid down three rules for the regulation of land titles in America which he
said were "sanctioned alike by im-
mutable justice and the general practice
of the European nations" interested
in the American colonization:

"First. 'That when any European
nation takes possession of any extent
of seacoast, that possession is understood as extending into the interior
country to the sources of the rivers
emptying within that coast, to all
their branches, and the country they
cover, and to give it a right in exclusion of all other nations to the same.'

"Secondly. 'That whenever one

European nation makes a discovery
and takes possession of any portion of
this continent, and another afterwards does the same at some distance
from it, where the boundary between
them is not determined by the principle above mentioned, the middle
distance becomes such of course.'

"Thirdly. 'That whenever any
European nation has thus acquired a
right to any portion of territory on
this continent, that right can never
be diminished or affected by any
other Power, by virtue of purchases
made, by grants or conquests of the
natives within the limits thereof.'"
*American State Papers, Foreign Rela-
tions*, iv, 470.

seceding from Spain. He maintained, moreover, that the immediate settlement of our western boundary was necessary for the internal peace of the country.[1] The negotiations dragged on and on, until Adams was thoroughly tired. His general proposition was to take Florida and give up all territory west of the Texan Colorado and south of the forty-first parallel; De Oñis, on his part, proposed the Sabine River and the forty-third parallel. Finally, somewhat against his will, but in conformity with the wish of the President, Adams compromised on the Sabine and the forty-second parallel. The treaty was signed on February 22, 1819, the American ratifications were handed over and the documents were sent to Spain.[2]

Adams had scarcely written a joyful sentence or two in his diary over the completion of the Florida negotiations when doubt arose as to the completeness of the settlement. The treaty had provided that all grants of land made by the Spanish authorities before January 24, 1818, should be regarded as valid; it now appeared that some very large grants which the negotiators had in mind in selecting this date were, as a matter of fact, actually dated January 23, and therefore had been validated by the provision of this treaty which had purposely been drawn to exclude them.

[1] See Jefferson's letter of May 14, 1820, in *Writings* (Ford ed.), x, 158, and Monroe's reply in *Writings*, vi, 119.

[2] *Treaties and Conventions* (ed. 1873), p. 785. At the moment the acquisition of Florida was very dear to the Southern heart. Monroe had practically forced the treaty on Adams and Andrew Jackson heartily approved it. Later, it became the Southern fashion to reprobate Adams for his weak concessions to Spain. In the course of the discussion, use was made of a letter written by George W. Erving, who had been our minister to Spain at the time. At first he had been in charge of the negotiations, which had been transferred to Washington, retransferred to Madrid, and transferred back again to Washington. In the course of this correspondence Erving stated that if he had been let alone, he could have secured the Colorado limit, and this assertion was gleefully laid hold of by Adams's enemies. See J. L. M. Curry's "Acquisition of Florida" in *Magazine of American History*, xix, 286; documents in the *Proceedings* of the Massachusetts Historical Society for October, 1889; Adams's *Memoirs*, xii, using index under "Erving."

Adams at once addressed De Oñis. The Spaniard appeared to be shocked and signed a statement that the validity of these land grants was not recognized in the treaty.[1] Before many months passed away, further mortification appeared in the shape of the refusal of the Spanish government to ratify the treaty at all. Possibly, some one in authority at Madrid wished to barter ratification for a recognition of these land grants; but it is more likely that the Spanish government hoped that by withholding ratification it could postpone the recognition of the Spanish American republics, perhaps indefinitely.[2] The six months provided for the exchange of ratifications passed away and then came a revolution in Spain that made the king a constitutional monarch and deprived him of the power to alienate Spanish territory. As the probability of the ratification of the treaty faded away, its value became more manifest to American eyes. Monroe and Jefferson and Adams were one in condemning the actions of the Spaniards. It was even suggested that the United States might be justified in taking possession of Florida without any ratification; but before anything was done, the Spanish Cortes and the king decided to ratify and the transaction was completed at Washington on February 22, 1821, two years to a day [3] after the actual signing of the instrument by Adams and De Oñis.

The ratification of the treaty did not put an end to the

---

[1] J. Q. Adams's *Memoirs* using index under "Spain"; his *Writings*, vi, 535, 537; and *American State Papers, Foreign Relations*, iv, 650 and fol.

[2] For information on the general subject see Frederic L. Paxson's *Independence of the South American Republics*.

[3] By this time Mexico had become free from Spain, but the limits of Texas laid down in the Florida Treaty were ratified by the United States and Mexico by a treaty concluded in January, 1828, and ratified in 1832. In 1836, Webster, Livingston, and Joseph M. White declared in so many legal opinions that one of the grants mentioned above was legal notwithstanding the fact that in the Spanish ratification of the treaty it had been expressly stated that the grants were invalid; see *Legal Opinions of the Honorable Joseph M. White*, etc. (New York, 1836) and *Treaties and Conventions* (ed. 1873), p. 794.

friction between American officials and the Spaniards. The
treaty obliged the latter to hand over the province within
six months after the exchange of ratifications and to deliver
up the forts and the archives. The archives had been removed to Havana, for Florida had been under the administration of the governor general of Cuba. An American
officer was sent to Havana, but after many delays he came
away without the papers. Then, too, questions arose as to
whether forts included artillery and whether the obligation
of the United States to transport Spanish officials and employees and their families from Florida to Cuba included
feeding them on the voyage. Adams declared that a fort
included artillery and the Spaniards insisted that transportation included provisions. Monroe sent Andrew Jackson to take possession of the ceded province and govern it,
until other arrangements should be made. Congress had already provided that for a limited time the officers appointed
by the President to take possession of Florida should have
all the powers that the Spanish authorities had exercised ;
and, as they had exercised practically all powers, Jackson's
authority was unlimited by law or usage.[1] Jackson proceeded to Pensacola, " took possession," issued decrees
and orders, and then, in the somewhat naïve language of his
biographers, was waited upon by a daughter of a deceased
Spanish official. She declared that the Spaniards, who had
not yet gone, were taking with them papers that were necessary to prove her title to land and property in Florida.
Jackson at once sent an officer to demand the papers and
upon these being refused, he directed them to be seized and
also that Colonel Callava, the recalcitrant official, should
be brought before him. This was done and, after some
debate, Jackson sent him to prison (1821). It was at this

[1] Annals of Congress, 16th Cong., 2nd Sess., 1809.

point that Eligius Fromentin, whom Monroe had appointed judge in Florida, ordered Callava to be produced bodily in his court, which led to Fromentin's being summoned into Jackson's presence. From this point, the matter diffused into letter writing and Jackson soon after resigned his appointment and retired to his Tennessee plantation.

The other important diplomatic occurrence of the administration of James Monroe and the occupation of the office of Secretary of State by John Quincy Adams was the enunciation of what was known then and has been known ever since as the Monroe Doctrine. The relations of the United States to the rebellious Spanish colonies was one of the most delicate questions that ever came before the rulers of the United States : too early recognition meant war with Spain and her European friends; too late recognition meant the hostility of the new republics. The question as to when and how these should be recognized was one on which the responsible officials and members of Congress might easily take sides : Monroe and Adams were obliged to walk warily no matter what their sympathies were; while Clay and other eloquent members of both Houses could express their sympathies openly without any fear that the government would carry their wishes into execution at the cost of war to the country. It is interesting to read Adams's official correspondence with different foreign ministers at this time and his remarks upon the subject in his diary. The question was not entirely one of sympathy with the oppressed, for the plain dictates of international duty played some part in the management of the affair. Had there not been so many causes of friction between the United States and Great Britain, the two powers whose interests and sympathies in these matters were very close might have marched hand in hand ; but before 1822, there were so many causes of irritation between them that this was quite impossible. By that year, however, three-quarters of the causes of dispute had been done away with and both countries were in a frame of mind to approach with some degree of cordiality, or coöperation, the menacing attitude of continental European governments. In August, 1822, George Canning succeeded Castlereagh at the foreign office. For a few weeks, he was friendship itself. He fairly startled Richard Rush, our minister at London, by suggesting that Great Britain and the United States should sail abreast in their dealings with Spanish-American revolutionists, declaring that if they did so, nobody else would have much of anything to say and it would not make much difference what they said or did.[1] At the moment, Canning was disturbed by the proposed action of the Holy Alliance, which had given a mandate to France to set the Spanish monarch on his throne again, and there was some probability of Continental intermeddling with Spanish-American affairs. Under ordinary circumstances, Canning suspected American republics and especially any league of them under the guidance or guardianship of the United States, but possibly it would be worse to have France interfering in American affairs than to have the United States asserting its foremost position in the Western

[1] W. C. Ford's "Genesis of the Monroe Doctrine" in Massachusetts Historical Society's *Proceedings*, 2nd Series, xv, 373–436; Richard Rush's *Memoranda of a Residence at the Court of London* (ed. 1845), 414–423, 429–443. The bibliography of Rush's works is somewhat confused. The first edition of the *Memoranda* was printed at Philadelphia in 1833; a second edition, revised and enlarged, was issued at the same place in the same year, but by a different publisher and a different printer. Another volume, published at Philadelphia in 1845, with a similar title, *Memoranda of a Residence at the Court of London . . . from 1819 to 1825. Including Negotiations on the Oregon Question* is practically a continuation of the earlier volume. In 1873, at London, Benjamin Rush published a new edition of his father's later work under the title *The Court of London from 1819 to 1825; with Subsequent Occasional Productions, now first published in Europe;* the last sixty pages of this work contain four chapters from another book of Richard Rush's entitled *Occasional Productions, Political, Diplomatic, and Miscellaneous* (Philadelphia, 1860).

World. Rush had no instructions on this precise point and all that he could reply was that he would lay the matter before his government. After a few more conversations between the two, Canning visibly lost interest,[1] probably because he had used such assertions as Rush had felt himself willing to make on the general theme of French interference in America to coerce the French government into holding its hands or, at all events, into not doing anything.

Side by side with these important conversations and suggestions were equally important suggestions and conversations from and with Russian representatives. The authority of the Czar in the preceding half century had gradually extended eastwardly across Siberia to Bering Strait and Sea and to America and to the exploitation of the fur trade on the Northwest Coast.[2] The Russians had established posts at Bodega Bay to the northward of the Golden Gate, and on the Farallones at the entrance to San Francisco Bay. Not much was known of these endeavors at Washington until Baron Poletica, in February, 1822, trans-

[1] Canning's own account of this episode is contained in a letter dated January 22, 1824, to Charles Bagot, formerly British minister to the United States, but now ambassador at St. Petersburg (Josceline Bagot's *George Canning and his Friends*, London, 1909, vol. ii, p. 215) ; and see also pp, 222, 232, and 274 ; and Augustus G. Stapleton's *The Political Life of George Canning*, ii, ch. viii. In the idea expressed in his famous phrase of calling in the "New World to redress the balance of the Old," Canning had reference to trade and not to politics, except as these reflect economic conditions. James Workman writing in 1797 seems to have anticipated him in this when he suggested that an equivalent for the lost trade of the Netherlands might be found in Louisiana,

La Plata, Mexico, and Peru. See Workman's *Political Essays* (Alexandria, 1801), p. 138 and Rush's *Occasional Productions*, 188.

[2] See F. A. Golder's *Russian Expansion on the Pacific, 1641-1850;* Irving B. Richman's *California under Spain and Mexico*, using index under "Russia"; Greenhow's *Oregon and California, and the . . . North-west Coast;* Joseph Schafer's *History of the Pacific Northwest;* and the *Alaska* volume of H. H. Bancroft's *Pacific States*. The main facts from Adams's "Diary" and the State Department Archives are brought together in John C. Hildt's "Early Diplomatic Negotiations of the United States with Russia " (*Johns Hopkins Studies*, xxiv, Nos. 5, 6).

mitted to Adams an ukase [1] of his imperial master. It was dated September 4, 1821, and ordered all non-Russian vessels, including American, to keep away from the coast of Russian America to the distance of one hundred Italian miles. Later, Baron Tuyll, Poletica's successor, informed Adams that he had been instructed to announce to the American government that the Russian Czar would never receive a diplomatic representative from the revolutionized Spanish-American provinces.[2] Then followed most interesting letters between Monroe and the two ex-Presidents and between Richard Rush, Baron Tuyll, and John Quincy Adams. As these have come to light the whole genesis of the Monroe Doctrine has slowly found its way to the printed page. Adams thought that the British advances should be declined, because he believed that Canning wished to separate the United States from the Spanish-American republics and that, at any rate, the United States would better sail alone than be a cock-boat [3] in the wake of the British man-of-war. As to his former friend, the Czar Alexander, he proposed to read him a lesson in the principles of government and to suggest that his doings did not comport with the Christian spirit of the Holy Alliance. Finally Adams declared that the time had come to suggest that the American continents were no longer open to new European colonizers. Monroe hesitated, but in the end he outstripped his masterful Secretary of State and together they elaborated the paragraphs in the presidential message of December 2, 1823, that announced in well-known phrases that the

---

[1] *American State Papers, Foreign Relations*, iv, 857–864. The *Writings* of J. Q. Adams, vii, 212, 214 also prints Adams's letters. See also *American Historical Review*, xviii, 309–345 and *Memoirs* of J. Q. Adams, vi, 157.

[2] *Writings* of James Monroe, vi, 343, the letter itself is on p. 390; *Memoirs* of J. Q. Adams, vi, 201; Massachusetts Historical Society's *Proceedings* (January, 1902), p. 378.

[3] *Memoirs* of J. Q. Adams, vi, 179.

American continents were closed to future colonization by Europeans, that the United States did not propose to interfere with European affairs,[1] and that any interference with the independence of the Spanish-American republics would be regarded as "the manifestation of an unfriendly disposition toward the United States."

Russia was the first to see the meaning of the plain speaking of the American President. She had contended that the Russian territory on the Northwest coast extended as far south as the fifty-first parallel. When Adams and Tuyll took up the debate, Adams restricted the Russian claim to latitude fifty-five.[2]   After a short negotiation, the

---

[1] The exact words are as follows: " . . . The occasion has been judged proper for asserting, as a principle . . . that the American continents, by the free and independent condition which they have assumed and maintain, are henceforth not to be considered as subjects for future colonization by any European powers." As to intervention Monroe said: " . . . The citizens of the United States cherish sentiments the most friendly in favor of the liberty and happiness of their fellow-men on that side of the Atlantic. In the wars of the European powers in matters relating to themselves we have never taken any part, nor does it comport with our policy so to do. It is only when our rights are invaded or seriously menaced that we resent injuries or make preparation for our defense. With the movements in this hemisphere we are of necessity more immediately connected, and by causes which must be obvious to all enlightened and impartial observers. The political system of the allied powers is essentially different in this respect from that of America. This difference proceeds from that which exists in their respective Governments; and to the defense of our own, which has been achieved by the loss of so much blood and treasure, and matured by the wisdom of their most enlightened citizens, and under which we have en-

joyed unexampled felicity, this whole nation is devoted. We owe it, therefore, to candor and to the amicable relations existing between the United States and those powers to declare that we should consider any attempt on their part to extend their system to any portion of this hemisphere as dangerous to our peace and safety. With the existing colonies or dependencies of any European power we have not interfered and shall not interfere. But with the Governments who have declared their independence and maintained it, and whose independence we have, on great consideration and on just principles, acknowledged, we could not view any interposition for the purpose of oppressing them, or controlling in any other manner their destiny, by any European power in any other light than as the manifestation of an unfriendly disposition toward the United States."

This text is taken from Monroe's *Writings* (Hamilton ed.), vi, 328, 339, 340. Other copies of the message, differing slightly in spelling, capitalization, and punctuation, are *Message from the President of the United States . . . December 2, 1823* (Washington, 1823) and *Annals of Congress*, 18th Cong., 1st Sess., vol. i, 14, 22, 23.

[2] Adams to Middleton, July 22, 1823, in *American State Papers, Foreign Relations*, v, 436.

two came together by agreeing that latitude 54° 40′ should
be the southern boundary of Russian America.   This instrument was signed in April, 1824 ; [1] on the 4th of the following
March, 1825, John Quincy Adams took the oath of office as
the sixth President of the United States.

[1] *Treaties and Conventions* (Washington, 1873), 733.

NOTES

I. The Missouri Compromise. — The best works on the Missouri Compromise are Floyd C. Shoemaker's *Missouri's Struggle for Statehood, 1804–1821;* James A. Woodburn's "Historical Significance of the Missouri Compromise" in American Historical Association's *Reports* for 1893, pp. 251–297; Frank H. Hodder's "Side Lights on the Missouri Compromises" in *ibid.* for 1909, pp. 153–161; Harrison A. Trexler's *Slavery in Missouri, 1804–1865 (Johns Hopkins Studies,* xxxii, No. 2); Louis Houck's *History of Missouri,* iii, ch. xxix; *Annals of Congress,* 15th Cong., 1st Sess., vol. i, 591 and the six following volumes, using the indexes; and *Niles's Weekly Register,* vol. xiii, p. 176 and following volumes through vol. xx, p. 388, using indexes. Some interesting entries on this subject are to be found at the end of the fourth and the beginning of the fifth volumes of the *Memoirs* of J. Q. Adams. *Free Remarks . . . Respecting the Exclusion of Slavery From the Territories and New States . . . By a Philadelphian* (Philadelphia, 1819) which is attributed to Robert Walsh, is a well-sustained argument from the Northern point of view.

The True History of the Missouri Compromise and its Repeal by Susan B. Dixon, the widow of Senator Dixon (Cincinnati, 1899) and James C. Welling's article entitled "Slavery in the Territories Historically Considered" in the *Magazine of American History,* xxvii, throw some new light on the general question.[1]

II. Jackson and the Seminole War. — Jackson's doings in Florida in the campaign against the Seminoles and the executions of Arbuthnot and Ambrister led to such important results for Jackson and other participants in the affair, that much material is to be found in the books without shedding very much light upon the matter. The official papers are printed in the Congressional documents;[2] Monroe's

---

[1] The Missouri question produced several fictional productions. Madison took up his pen and in *Jonathan Bull & Mary Bull* drew a parallel between a family conflict and this political struggle (Hunt's *Writings of Madison,* ix, 77 and also separately). Two other publications of larger size were *Fragments of the History of Bawlfredonia . . . by Herman Thwackus* (copyrighted in Maryland) and *Pocahontas; A Proclamation by*

"The High and Mighty, the Burgesses of the Royal State of Virginia" (copyrighted in Connecticut).

[2] *Message from the President . . . transmitting Information in Relation to the War with the Seminoles* (March 25, 1818) in *State Papers,* 15 Cong., 1st Sess., No. 173; *House Executive Documents,* 15 Cong., 2nd Sess., No. 14, forming also No. 35 of papers printed by order of the Senate, 15 Cong., 2nd Sess. Many of these documents are

Writings, vi, 54, 74, 75; *Writings* of J. Q. Adams, vi, 386, 409, 434, 474, 511, 545; *Memoirs of John Quincy Adams*, iv, 31–248, 274. What is known as Jackson's " Exposition " is printed in Benton's *Thirty Years' View*, i, 169–180. The supposed letter to Monroe of January 6, 1818, is there printed and has been reprinted in Parton's *Jackson*, ii, 433 and J. S. Bassett's *Life of Andrew Jackson*, i, 245 and elsewhere. This letter led to what is known as the Rhea affair. The last original document in the story is in Monroe's *Writings*, vii, 234, a " Denunciation " of Rhea's story made by Monroe on his death bed and witnessed by two attendants. Summations of the affair have been made by Professor Bassett in his *Jackson*, i, 245–250, especially the note on page 249 and by James Schouler in *The Magazine of American History*, xii, 308–322.

III. The Monroe Doctrine. — The standard account of the genesis of the Monroe Doctrine is by Worthington C. Ford in the *Proceedings* of the Massachusetts Historical Society for January, 1902. This may well be supplemented by H. W. V. Temperley's paper on " The Later American Policy of George Canning " in *American Historical Review*, xi, 779–796. A succinct and useful summary is in Hart's *Monroe Doctrine*, 20–68. The leading documents are brought together in Ford's article; but most of them may be found in the published writings of Monroe, Adams, and Jefferson and in the *American State Papers, Foreign Relations* and the *British and Foreign State Papers*. The careful student will wish to read the " Correspondence of the Russian Ministers in Washington, 1818–1825 " in *American Historical Review*, xviii, 309–345, 537–562; " The Papers of Sir Charles Vaughan " — the British minister at Washington, 1826–1833 — in *ibid.*, vii, 304–328, 500–533; and " Protocols of Conferences of Representatives of the Allied Powers respecting Spanish America,

also printed in the *Annals of Congress*, 15 Cong., 2nd Sess., vol. ii, 1629, 2136; and a few of them are collected in the *Correspondence between Gen. Andrew Jackson and John C. Calhoun, . . . in the Seminole War*, printed by Duff Green (Washington, 1831). In connection with the President's messages of November 16, 1818 (usually cited as of November 17, the day of reception) and of February 22, 1819, see *American State Papers, Military Affairs*, i, 681–769. These papers sadly need correlation. See also *The Trials of A. Arbuthnot & R. C. Ambrister* (London, 1819) and John D. Lawson's *American State Trials*, ii, 862, 891, and *Memoirs of General Andrew Jackson, together with the Letter of Mr. Secretary Adams, in vindication of the execution of Arbuthnot and Ambrister, and the other Public Acts of Gen. Jackson, in Florida* (Bridgeton, N. J., 1824). Many of these documents are printed in *Niles's Register*, xv.

1824–1825 " in *ibid.*, xxii, 595–616. See also W. S. Robertson's article on " The United States and Spain in 1822 " in *ibid.*, xx, 781–800. Even now — 1920 — it would be well if some one would correlate and analyze this material more carefully than has hitherto been done.[1]

[1] A. F. Pollard's article on the Monroe Doctrine in *History, The Quarterly Journal of the [English] Historical Association* for April, 1919, is a penetrating analysis of the general situation in 1823 from the point of view of an English student of European history; Frederic L. Paxson's *The Independence of the South American Republics* (Philadelphia, 1903), chapter ii, describes the South American policy of the United States and iii the British relations with South America. Herbert Kraus's *Die Monroedoktrin in ihren Beziehungen zur amerikanischen Diplomatie und zum Völkerrecht* (Berlin, 1913), is preceded by a useful bibliography. W. F. Reddaway, in a small volume entitled *The Monroe Doctrine* that was published by the Cambridge Press in 1898, states the English idea of the matter in a brief compass.

CHAPTER XI

EVER since his early days John Quincy Adams had been in the service of his country. In 1778, at the age of eleven, he accompanied John Adams, his father, to France. Soon after his arrival there he resolved to keep a diary and informed his "Honoured Mamma" that although the journal of a lad of eleven could not "be expected to contain much of Science, Litterature, arts, wisdom, or wit, yet it may serve to perpetuate many observations that I may make." He began the actual diary some months later and continued it, at times spasmodically, and sometimes with regrettable breaks to within a few months of his death. The journal certainly perpetuated many of John Quincy Adams's observations to the dismay of the descendants of some of his contemporaries, and oftentimes to the confusion of kings, Congressmen, and Presidents. In 1794, when not quite twenty-seven years of age, he was appointed by President Washington, minister to the Hague, and three years later was transferred to Berlin. In 1801, he returned to Massachusetts and the next year was elected a member of the Senate of that State. In 1803, he took his seat in the Senate of the United States and, espousing the side of Jefferson, voted for the embargo. Being defeated for reëlection, he was appointed minister to Russia and was one of the Commissioners at Ghent. As John Adams was the first minister of the United States to Great Britain after the

Revolution, so his son was the first American minister at the Court of St. James after the War of 1812, and it may be added that his son, Charles Francis Adams, was our representative there during the extremely critical years of the War for Southern Independence. In 1817, John Quincy Adams returned to his native land to take up the office of Secretary of State, and was performing the duties of that high station when he was elected President. After his four years in the White House, he returned to Quincy, his birthplace, to pass his declining years in seclusion. It was not so to be, for a year later, some of the voters of his congressional district waited upon him and inquired if he thought it would be beneath the dignity of one who had exercised the presidential office to serve in the national House of Representatives. Adams replied that he thought it would be entirely proper for him to serve in any office to which he might be chosen by the voters,[1] even that of a selectman of a town. Accordingly, he took his seat in Congress in 1831 and for seventeen years thereafter upheld the rights of his countrymen and fought for liberty, until he fell senseless from his chair to the floor of the House in 1848.[2] Hardly anything in the twelve printed volumes of his "Diary," not even the characterizations of his contemporaries, so impresses the reader as the reiterated expressions of his gratitude for the confidence that his countrymen, from humble voter to President Washington, had given him in this long series of years. He never stood higher in public esteem than he did on the day of his death, and his funeral was a pageant without example up to that time in the City of Washington.

[1] *Memoirs of John Quincy Adams,* viii, 238–240.
[2] Possibly the best way to gain an insight into Adams's method and an understanding of the fear and respect in which he was held by his enemies is to read one of his speeches, as the one delivered in June and July, 1838, on the annexation of Texas.

In Monroe's Cabinet were four of the dozen most eminent men then in active life: Adams, John C. Calhoun, William H. Crawford, and William Wirt. The last named, who occupied the office of Attorney General, was wedded to the law;[1] but the others had immediate presidential aspirations. Crawford had been a candidate against Monroe in 1816, when they had both been members of Madison's official family; but he had consented to continue to hold the office of Secretary of the Treasury in the administration of his successful rival and eight years later sought to succeed him in the White House. William H. Crawford enjoyed great reputation in Georgia, his native State, and Southern writers always speak of him in eulogistic terms; but it is difficult to understand wherein his greatness consisted.[2] Apparently, in those days, Georgia and South Carolina were overflowing with "distinguished and celebrated lawyers" and among them, such as they were, Crawford attained high place. As Secretary of the Treasury, he made no great mark. Indeed, the principal thing associated with him was the passage by Congress of an act providing that the greater number of presidential appointees to office should hold their places for four years only and should be removable at pleasure.[3] This has always been regarded as an electioneering device on Crawford's part to secure subserviency to himself among the treasury officials throughout the country; but it is not unlikely that he

[1] Wirt occupied the Attorney General's office for twelve years until Adams's exit in 1829, but two years later Wirt, himself, was nominated for the presidency by the Anti-Masons.

[2] J. E. D. Shipp's *Giant Days; or the Life and Times of William H. Crawford* (Americus, Georgia, 1909). There is much to be read about Crawford and there are many of his letters to be found in the *Annals of Congress*, in the *State Papers*, and in the correspondence of Adams, Clay, Calhoun, and others, including an interesting letter from Nathaniel Macon in *James Sprunt Historical Monographs*, No. 2, p. 67.

[3] Act of May 15, 1820, *Statutes at Large*, iii, 582; *Annals of Congress*, 16th Cong., 1st Sess., vol. ii, 2597. It affected district attorneys, collectors and surveyors of the customs, receivers of public money, paymasters, etc.

pushed it forward to make it possible to rid the service of inefficient employees without hurting their feelings and arousing resentments among the voters.[1] For the last year or two he had been ill and by 1824 he had been "bled to the verge of death, defitalised into fits, and ptyalized to infantine helplessness."[2] With this chronic ill health upon him, Crawford made a good fight for the presidency; and, had he been well, would probably have been elected.

Another member of Monroe's Cabinet, John C. Calhoun, also desired to be his successor in the White House. Calhoun was one of the most remarkable men of his day. He stands second only to Franklin in power of analysis; many of his papers are models of reasoning and expression. Nevertheless he was not a man of extensive learning.[3] Entering Congress, he at once took a prominent place and he showed administrative ability in the office of Secretary of War. In the course of his long career, Calhoun made many enemies, and his life was not free from contradictions. It is easy to attribute his change of attitude as to internal improvements and nationalism to ambition, but Southern leaders generally shifted at the same time, and it might well be that they were convinced, in common with many other Southerners, that the action of Northern political leaders and of Northern manufacturers was impoverishing the South and especially South Carolina. The most difficult thing in Calhoun's

[1] See Carl Russell Fish's "The Crime of W. H. Crawford" in *American Historical Review*, xxi, 545.

[2] "Van Buren Mss." in Library of Congress. Gales and Seaton to M. Van Buren, September 15, 1824.

[3] At one time Calhoun was interested in a Georgia gold mine in the Dahlonega district near a little village which was named at his suggestion Auraria. From time to time, these gold deposits have been exploited to considerable advantage. See Charles T. Jackson's and William P. Blake's "Reports" in the volume entitled *The Gold Placers of the Vicinity of Dahlonega, Georgia* (Boston, 1859) and Yeates's report of 1896 forming *Bulletin No. 4-A* of the Geological Survey of Georgia. The discovery of gold was made in 1829 and by 1879 fourteen million dollars' worth had been produced by the Georgia mines.

career to reconcile with his personal honor is his permitting Andrew Jackson for years to look upon him as having been his defender in the Cabinet at the time of the Seminole War;[1] but possibly it is not necessary for a politician to go out of his way to make enemies. The other Cabinet member who aspired to the presidential succession was John Quincy Adams. Reading his "Diary," one would come to the conclusion that Crawford and Calhoun were persistent presidency seekers, while he, Adams, was simply and solely "in the hands of his friends." There can be no doubt that the two first were more active in their efforts to secure the coveted honor. They dallied with newspapers and possibly appointed to office some persons who might be politically useful to them. It is certain that Adams refused to purchase newspaper support and he had very few offices at his disposal for any purpose; but if he had had them, there is no reason whatever to believe that he would have used them for his own personal advancement.

Outside of the Cabinet, there were two formidable aspirants for the presidency, — Henry Clay[2] and Andrew Jackson. Like Calhoun and Crawford, Clay had been long in political life. He was a Virginian by birth, but had moved to Kentucky when a young man and since that time technically had resided there. Clay had been one of the Commissioners at Ghent, but his career had been identified with the national House of Representatives over which he had presided with brief interruptions for fourteen years. He had borne a foremost part in bringing on the War of 1812 and, more recently, had been the leading advocate of

[1] See the present volume, pp. 334–336.

[2] For an informing account of Clay, see Carl Schurz's *Life of Henry Clay*, 3 vols.; Greeley's edition of Epes Sargent's *Life and Public Services of Henry Clay*, p. 322 to the end of the volume is Greeley's own account and deals with the years after 1848.

internal improvements.   But he and his fellow-workers
were far ahead of their time, for any such scheme demands
a community spirit on the part of the people of the several
sections of the country and all the signs at that moment
were pointing to an era of sectionalism and of the upbuild-
ing of the community spirit in the South apart from the
rest of the Union.   Andrew Jackson, the fifth figure in this
group of presidency seekers, was a Carolinian by birth,[1]
but a Tennesseean by reason of residence and land ownership.   His military career is most familiar to us, but he had
served in the national Senate for parts of two terms and in
the House for part of a term.[2]   He had had no civil administrative experience, but conducting the business of an army
had brought out very strong executive qualities in him.

Of the five candidates for the presidency, Adams was the
only one from the North.   It was reasonably certain that
he would carry New England and might carry New York,
— these together would give him seventy-three electoral
votes.   The eighty-eight Southern votes would be divided
somewhat among the four Southern candidates.   Considering this fact, it seemed fairly certain that the election would
turn on the twenty-eight votes of Pennsylvania and the
twenty-four votes of the Northwestern States.[3]   In some
manner that is not at all explicable from accessible books
and manuscripts, Jackson appealed to the democracy of

---

[1] In *The North Carolina Booklet*,
ix, 232, Bruce Craven argues that the
McKemey cabin in which Jackson
first saw the light of day was in Meck-
lenburg County, North Carolina, and
not on the South Carolina side of the
line, as Jackson himself thought, but
a man has slight personal knowledge of
his birth-place.

[2] Jackson served in the House
from 1796 to 1797, and in the Senate
from 1797 to 1798 and again from
1823 through 1825. *Annals of Congress*, 4th Cong., 2nd Sess., 1589;
5th Cong., vol. i, 470; 18th Cong.,
1st Sess., vol. i, 24; *Register of Debates*, 18th Cong., 2nd Sess., Appendix,
p. 1.

[3] A convenient table showing the
apportionment of representation according to the *Census* of 1790 through
the *Census* of 1840 is in Tucker's *Progress*, 123.

Pennsylvania and his adherents in that State were much better led than were the partisans of any other candidate. As the election of 1824 drew nearer, it became increasingly evident that Calhoun had no chance whatever, for there appeared to be little doubt that the vote of New York would be divided between Adams and Crawford and that Jackson would get the better part of the twenty-eight Pennsylvania votes. Calhoun, therefore, accepted a practically unopposed election to the vice-presidency. After the withdrawal of Calhoun, Crawford would naturally have absorbed most of the strength of the South, but long continuance in office and long-continued intriguing for the presidency had greatly diminished his hold upon workers and voters. As it was, he received the twenty-four votes of Virginia and the nine of Georgia. Besides he had five from New York and three others or forty-one in all. Clay received the fourteen votes of his own State, Kentucky; the sixteen of Ohio, four of New York and three of Missouri, making thirty-seven in all. Adams received the fifty-one votes of New England, twenty-six of the thirty-six cast by New York and seven scattering, or eighty-four electoral votes in all. Jackson stood at the head of the list with ninety-nine votes, receiving twenty-eight from Pennsylvania, all of the Carolinas and all of Tennessee and Mississippi, Alabama and Indiana and some others.[1] As no candidate had received a majority of the electoral vote as demanded by the provisions of the Twelfth Amendment, the actual choice of the President for the next four years lay with the House of Representatives, voting by States and confined to the three highest on the list.[2]

[1] *Journal of the Senate*, 18th Cong., 2nd Sess., p. 149. See also *Niles's Register* for February 12, 1825, p. 382. The vote for the President in the House immediately follows.

[2] This election led to renewed interest in the proposition to elect the President directly by districts and to take away the election from Congress. See H. V. Ames's *Proposed Amend-*

As soon as the way in which the members of the electoral college would cast their votes become known at Washington, rumor and scandal became rife in the capital. Clay was out of the running, being a low fourth. He had polled the votes of Kentucky, Ohio, and Missouri. Adding these States to the seven that were almost certain to vote for Adams would give him the votes of ten States and as he needed only thirteen, it would probably mean his election. Under these circumstances, the friends of the several candidates busied themselves and rumors flew rapidly through the corridors of the capitol and around the rooms of the mess-houses.[1] If Jackson were chosen would he make Clay his Secretary of State? Or, if Adams were elected, would he likewise offer this position to Clay? No conjectures of the kind were made as to Crawford, because his relations with Clay were not at all cordial and his health was such that it was difficult to approach him. The three candidates were in Washington, Jackson being a Senator from Tennessee. A coalition between Jackson and Clay was entirely out of the question, for Clay had openly attacked Jackson and no one who had done that had ever been forgiven. On the other hand, it was entirely natural for Adams and Clay to coalesce: they both believed in the American System, they both distrusted Crawford, and neither of them had much faith in Jackson's administrative capacities. It

ments to the Constitution of the United States, 89, and the speeches of McDuffie, Everett, Polk, and others delivered in the course of a six weeks' debate in the House of Representatives in 1826.

[1] As showing the spirit of the time and also the difficulty of reaching a conclusion at the present day it is interesting to note that Willie P. Mangum wrote to Bartlett Yancey in December, 1824 (James Sprunt Historical Publi-

cations, x, 51) that the practical equality of votes in Illinois enabled Daniel P. Cooke to vote for Adams although he had agreed to vote with his State and two of her three electoral votes had been given to Jackson and only one to Adams. Duff Green, writing in old age but doubtless repeating the stories of his early years, gives some interesting gossip (Facts and Suggestions, New York, 1866, p. 25 and fol.)

happened, therefore, that Adams was chosen on the first ballot. Adams and Jackson had been on very good terms owing to Adams's defence of the General's Florida deeds in 1818,[1] and it is said that on meeting Adams soon after the vote in the House, Jackson congratulated him and declared that he was better fitted for the place than himself. Some of the far-seeing manipulators, however, determined to arouse Jackson's enmity. At the moment, it was supposed that if the General were elected, he would serve for only one term and therefore that the office of Secretary of State would be as good as a nomination for the presidency in 1828. In January, 1825, an "unsigned letter" appeared in the newspapers, stating that Clay and Adams had made a bargain by which Adams was to be elected and was then to appoint Clay his Secretary of State. Shortly afterward, George Kremer, an insignificant Representative from Pennsylvania, acknowledged the authorship of this letter. Thereupon Clay took the floor of the House and called for an inquiry, but Kremer refused to appear either as accuser or as a witness.[2] Two years later Jackson, himself, reiter-

---

[1] "We thenceforth heard the praises of Mr. Adams sounded throughout the military camp." Jesse Benton's *Address to the People of the United States* (Nashville, 1824). This is a good — and readable — example of the political pamphlets of the times.

[2] See the *Condensed Speech of Hon. Linn Boyd, of Kentucky . . . April 30, 1844;* Colton's *Life of Henry Clay,* chs. xiv–xviii; and Clay's "Address to his Constituents, March 26, 1825" in Colton, Reed, and McKinley's *Works of Henry Clay,* v, 299. This address was originally printed at Washington in 1825 with the title "To The People of the Congressional District composed of the Counties of Fayette, Woodford, and Clarke, in Kentucky." The most interesting of these papers is *An Address of Henry Clay, to the Public; containing Certain Testimony in Refutation of the Charges against him, made by Gen. Andrew Jackson.* This was printed by Peter Force at Washington in 1827.

The Buchanan side of the case is stated in Curtis's *Life of Buchanan,* i, 49–56 and *Works of James Buchanan,* i, 260–271, viii, 444. The episode is also treated at length in Bassett's *Andrew Jackson,* i, 356–368 and Schurz's *Clay,* i, 241. The Jacksonian side of the controversy was set forth at length in the "Reply by the Jackson Corresponding Committee of the District of Columbia" which was printed in the *United States Telegraph,* vol. i, Nos. 10–12; and see also "Calendar of Jackson-Lewis Letters" in *Bulletin* of the New York Public Library, iv, 292.

ated the charge and then upon investigation it appeared
that the velvet hands of James Buchanan of Pennsylvania
had pushed Jackson forward, but that the latter had misunderstood his astute manager in the Keystone State.
Altogether it was a discreditable piece of business for all
concerned, but it exercised none the less a baleful influence
on the lives of two good men, for unfortunately Adams,
looking upon Clay as the ablest man for the secretaryship
of state, offered the place to him and Clay felt obliged to
accept it so as not to give color to the charge.[1] Possibly
the reason for the lack of the highest success in political
warfare on the part of these two men may be seen in this
incident.

Whatever his failings, John Quincy Adams possessed
honesty of mind and of purpose. Replying to the committee that notified him of his election, he said that as one
of the other candidates had had "a larger minority of the
primary electoral suffrages" than he had, he should not
have hesitated to decline the presidential office, could
his refusal have given "an immediate opportunity to
the people" to express again their wishes. As it was he
necessarily accepted the result of the election by the House
of Representatives. The greatest part of Adams's Inaugural
Address was devoted to the achievements of the American
Republic [2] up to that time; but he made some suggestions
as to the future. The prosecution of internal improvements,
he thought, would bring down upon the heads of those
who made them the blessings of "unborn millions of our

[1] In 1850, according to Henry S.
Foote (*Casket of Reminiscences*, 27)
Clay declared that if he were to live
his life over again he would not accept from Mr. Adams the Secretaryship of State. "By doing so I injured
both him and myself; I placed myself in a false position before the country, and often have I painfully felt that
I had seriously impaired my own capacity for public usefulness."

[2] Richardson's *Messages and Papers
of the Presidents*, ii, 292-299.

posterity." As to the constitutional objections that had been raised to the prosecution of this design, he thought these might be obviated by friendly deliberations; but no consideration should induce Congress "to assume the exercise of powers not granted . . . by the people." In his first message to Congress, he reiterated this desire for internal improvements and coupled other subjects with it, as the founding of a national university.[1] Congress was deaf to all appeals of the kind and paid no attention to them.

In the Inaugural, Adams had also stated that the new Spanish-American republics had invited the United States to send representatives to a meeting of Congress to be held at Panama for consultation and action as to objects of common interest.- He had accepted the invitation and commissioners would be sent to take part in the conference so far "as may be compatible with that neutrality" from which the United States does not intend to depart. On the 26th of December, 1825, he sent a message to the Senate repeating the invitation from the Spanish-American republics. He added that although the acceptance of this invitation "was deemed to be within the constitutional competency of the Executive" he had not taken any step in it and wished to ascertain whether his opinion of its expediency would be agreed to by both Houses of Congress. With the message there were documents and also nominations of commissioners.[2] This Panama Congress had been summoned by Bolívar and both the United States and England had been invited to it. In respect to foreign policy, the administration of John Quincy Adams was hardly more than a continu-

---

[1] "Message from the President of the United States . . . December 6, 1825": *House Documents*, 19th Cong., 1st Sess., vol. i, No. 1, pp. 6, 15.

[2] *Executive Proceedings of the Senate . . . Congress at Panama* (19th Cong., 1st Sess., No. 68); also printed separately at Washington in 1826.

ation of that of Monroe, and the Panama Congress was expected to be a capstone to the Spanish-American revolutions. Had everything gone well, it is conceivable that a league of American nations — North, South, and Central — might have been formed then that would have powerfully affected the progress of the world. The United States would naturally have taken the lead and this would have been most distressing to George Canning who was then at the head of the British government, for he had determined to prevent the United States assuming such a position and also to prevent the absorption of Cuba and Porto Rico by France or by the United States. Moreover, he wished to bring the great American Republic within the scope of European politics.[1] Adams was equally determined to keep his country out of the European entanglements, to facilitate the voluntary incorporation of Cuba and Texas with the United States, and to have all the American powers adopt the principles of that republic as to the freedom of the seas. The sources of political opposition to the participation of the United States in the Panama Congress are not easy to fathom. Possibly the Jacksonian partisans may have looked upon its defeat as a blow dealt at Jackson's rivals. Possibly, also, they may have thought opposition to it would place their candidate distinctly at the head of the Southern party. Some of the subjects that would necessarily come up for debate at Panama would have to do with negro slavery and with the future of the colored races in America. At all events a most factious opposition to Adams's plan appeared in the Senate. It must be confessed that Adams's action was weak and ill considered ; he had accepted the invitation and then had asked

[1] Temperley's "Later American Policy of George Canning" in *American Historical Review*, xi, 779 and fol. ; and his *Life of Canning*, ch. x.

the Senate if the United States should be represented. He had declared that the appointment of commissioners was within the power of the Executive and had then asked the consent of the two Houses to such appointments. The Senate committee, to whom the subject was referred, doubted the constitutional authority of the government to negotiate with foreign nations for the purpose of settling and promulgating principles of internal polity or abstract propositions. By strict observance of their old course of policy, the United States had grown up in happiness, so the committee asserted. Were they now to embark upon an unknown ocean, directed by little experience and with no certain destiny, and especially since in such a voyage the dissimilarities of language, religion, customs, and laws would generate discords? It was true that the Senate might reject any agreements that were entered into; but long experience had shown that it was difficult and sometimes impossible to escape from the embarrassment of the mere act of entering into the negotiations. The Senate confirmed the nominations, nevertheless, and the House voted the necessary funds. One of the United States delegates died and the other did not go to Panama. There was an English diplomatic representative there and possibly two or three other Europeans. Probably nothing would have come of the enterprise had the United States been represented at Panama and it may have been for the best that no such league of American nations was formed. The one thing that strikes the observer in reading the available documents is that both Canning and Bolívar succeeded in their policy [1] in so far as they prevented the United States

[1] See H. W. V. Temperley's "The Later American Policy of George Canning" and his *Life of Canning* (London, 1905); and also E. J. Stapleton's *Some Official Correspondence of George Canning*, i, using the table of contents.

For Bolívar's views on the Con-from taking the position of leadership that should have belonged to it. Bolívar failed, however, in his plan of establishing a Spanish-American league in close agreement with Great Britain. But had Adams and Clay been given hearty support by their own countrymen, the United States might even then have taken the foremost position in a League of Nations of the American continents.

Another critical and disappointing episode of these years had to do with the partly civilized Indians of western Georgia and the neighboring counties of Alabama. These were the Cherokees. In 1791, President Washington had entered into a treaty with them by which they were assured that they would never be driven from their lands.[1] In 1802, Gallatin, on behalf of the federal government and as a part of the Yazoo land settlement, had agreed to put Georgia in possession of the Indian lands within her limits.[2] Christian missionaries also had sought out the Cherokees, had converted some of them to Christianity, and had taught them something of the arts of civilization.[3] Administration followed administration and the Georgians who needed more lands for cultivation of the cotton plant were kept out of the acres that they regarded as rightfully theirs. In

gress of Panama, I am indebted to Professor Julius Klein, who kindly placed at my disposal some printed notes from an unpublished manuscript in the archives at Caracas that were presented at the second Pan-American Scientific Congress that was held at Washington in 1916. For a somewhat different view see W. R. Shepherd's "Bolívar and the United States" in *Hispanic American Historical Review*, i, 270.

[1] *American State Papers, Indian Affairs*, i, 124, art. 7; "The United States solemnly guaranty to the Cherokee nation, all their lands not hereby ceded."

[2] *Ibid., Public Lands*, i, 126, art. 4;

see also the present work, volume iv, 290 note. The later documents are printed in *House Reports*, No. 98, 19th Cong., 2nd Sess.

[3] On the general subject of the removal of the Indians see Miss Annie H. Abel's "Indian Consolidation West of the Mississippi" in American Historical Association's *Annual Report* for 1906, i, 233 with an extensive bibliography on pp. 413–438. Joseph Hodgson's *Cradle of the Confederacy* (ch. viii) and G. L. Sioussat's "Tennessee and the Removal of the Indians" in the *Sewanee Review* for July, 1908, have been especially useful.

Monroe's administration, matters were greatly compli-
cated by personal and political hostilities between Governor
Troup of Georgia and the federal Indian Agent which were
not at all allayed by the bad feeling on the part of the governor toward the missionaries and between the missionaries
themselves, for they were of different sects.[1] Troup addressed communications to the heads of the federal departments in the language of a sovereign commanding his
servants; but he gained nothing at the moment. Adams's
weak administration seemed to the Georgians to be the
appointed time, and they marched into the coveted lands,
notwithstanding the utmost opposition that the Washington
government could make. It was one of the most unfortunate episodes in the history of the presidency.

The election of 1828 marked the breaking down of the
old system and the coming into power of the democracy
of the next thirty years that was ushered in by the triumphant election of Andrew Jackson to the presidency. There
is something peculiarly interesting about Jackson and his
political and presidential career, fully as interesting in its
way as the story of his earlier military performances. He
seems to have had slight desire in the beginning for high
executive place and in 1825 to have welcomed Adams, and,
indeed, they had been on friendly terms. He was put forward
for the presidency by a group of active and aspiring politicians, of whom William B. Lewis and Amos Kendall were
the ablest. Lewis was a neighbor of Jackson's and for
some years had acted as a literary friend, putting the
General's roughly written communications into the forms
in which we possess them.[2] How early Jackson's friends be-

---

[1] *Report of the Select Committee of
the House of Representatives, March
3, 1827* (19th Cong., 2nd Sess., H. of
R. No. 98); E. J. Harden's *Life of
George M. Troup*, chs. ix-xii.

[2] S. G. Heiskell in his *Andrew Jackson and Early Tennessee History*
(Nashville, 1918) has a few interesting
paragraphs on Lewis, pp. 441-446.

gan to put him forward as a public character is not quite clear, but they conducted a skilful propaganda, certainly as far back as 1817, when John Henry Eaton completed a biography that really was a campaign document.[1] By 1826, it was evident that Crawford was out of the presidential race. Thereupon Calhoun was led to believe, or came to believe, that continuing in the vice-presidency through Jackson's term, provided the General were elected to the chief magistracy, would make him, Calhoun, the Jacksonian candidate for the first place in 1832. It is impossible to prove that any definite proposition of the kind was made to Calhoun, or that any categorical statement of Jackson's determination to serve only one term was ever made. But it is evident that for some reason best known to themselves, Calhoun and his friends thought that it would be wise for him to continue in the second place. Crawford and Calhoun being thus removed from the presidential race, the only other Southern competitor was Henry Clay, and systematic efforts were at once begun to blast his reputation and make his candidacy impossible.

Rumors of bargain and corruption had been rife in 1824 and John Randolph of Roanoke had given them a place in popular imagination by stigmatizing the coöperation of Adams and Clay as the "coalition of Blifil and Black George, — the combination, unheard of till then, of the Puritan with the blackleg,"[2] and by fighting a duel, a bloodless one, with Clay. The story was brought up again in 1827 and led to letters and pamphlets. From them it appears that Jackson thought or was made to say that he thought that,

[1] *The Life of Andrew Jackson . . . Commenced by John Reid, . . . Completed by John Henry Eaton.* It was published by Carey at Philadelphia in 1817 "For the Benefit of the Children of John Reid." Reprinted with Eaton's name alone on the title-page at Philadelphia in 1824 and later.

[2] Schurz's *Clay*, i, 273; Garland's *Randolph*, ii, 254.

in 1824, he had been approached and been told that if he would not appoint Adams Secretary of State the presidential contest would at once be decided in his favor. Upon demanding the name of the person who had made this offer, Jackson replied that it was James Buchanan; but Buchanan declared that what he said was if Jackson would agree not to continue Adams in the Secretary of State office, the Clay men would vote for him, Jackson, and thus decide the contest.   Buchanan said he had no idea that he could have been mistaken for a representative of Clay and, if one can believe him, he appears to have undertaken the mission out of a simple desire to bring about Jackson's election and without having any authority whatever from Clay.   The latter now secured written testimony from his adherents in the House of Representatives in 1824 and published it with private letters of his own, written at the time, with a view to making it clear that he and his friends had voted against Jackson and for Adams from the highest motives of duty.   Nothing was of any avail.   The more Clay protested, the more firmly his countrymen disbelieved him, and he was definitely put out of the presidential running for the time being.   The Southern vote was, therefore, secure for Jackson and probably the twenty-four votes of the Old Northwest would also be given to him.   These would not be enough and it would therefore be necessary to gain electoral votes in Pennsylvania and New York to make the result certain.

In 1824, Jackson had had only a small following in New York, for the politicians of that State and their followers supported Crawford, and the other voters generally stood behind Adams.   The two principal leaders in New York at that time were William L. Marcy and Martin Van Buren. The former was a politician of that time and place, but Van

Buren cannot be so easily dismissed, partly because he himself achieved the presidential office, but more especially because he was unjustly dealt with by his contemporaries and has been even more so by historical writers since. He grew up a poor boy at Kinderhook, New York. He made his own way in the world, standing up for the humble and downtrodden, and gained influence by reason of his clearness of thought and cogency of utterance. He was a wirepuller, like nearly every one else in public life and, being one of the ablest men of the day, he was one of the ablest wirepullers of New York and Washington. Van Buren and Marcy and others of inferior abilities formed the Albany Regency, as the ruling body of a portion of the old Republican Party of the State was called. Among the minor New York politicians was Churchill C. Cambreleng, who might be described as Van Buren's lieutenant. Together they travelled through the South, visiting Crawford in Georgia and other politicians along the route. It was at this time that Van Buren probably entered into some kind of alliance with the Jackson forces because Jackson's name, as a candidate for the presidency, appears in the Van Buren papers for the first time in October, 1826. Writing to Thomas Ritchie in January, 1827, Van Buren advocated a political combination between the planters of the South and "the plain Republicans of the North," and not long afterwards he practically took charge of the Jackson campaign in New York. In 1827, the Jackson Republicans secured most of the assemblymen from the city of New York, which greatly encouraged them not only within the State but also without; and the sudden death of Governor De Witt Clinton in February, 1828, removed from the political field the anti-Jacksonian whom Van Buren most feared. In the end, with exceeding craft and cunning [1] he secured for Jackson twenty of the thirty-six votes [2] of the Empire State and the governor's office for himself.

From Revolutionary days western Pennsylvania and Philadelphia had been the homes of the most advanced American democrats. They had troubled Washington, and Jefferson had not fully appreciated them. Now, for the first time, they could exercise political power commensurate with their numbers because the electoral system of the State had been so changed that it was possible for the country voter to record his vote without undue expenditure of time and strength. Henry Clay had had a strong following in Pennsylvania because of his championship of the tariff and Adams also had had many friends in the State, especially among the Germans, or "Pennsylvania Dutch." To break down the hold of Clay and Adams on the Pennsylvania people all kinds of stories were put into circulation: — the election of Adams in 1824 had defeated the "will of the people"; [3] Adams and Clay had been

[1] Two letters from Van Buren to Jackson in the Library of Congress throw light upon the relations of the two men as early as September, 1827, and also give some information as to election methods. In the first, Van Buren assures Jackson that he will have "a very decided majority" of the votes of New York, if nothing turns up to change the present aspect of things. Pennsylvania, also, looks more hopeful, as of the fifty Republican papers in that State, all but three have come out for Jackson. "All that is necessary to rout the enemy is that he [Van Buren] be left alone" and that Jackson make no statements or explanations. Again, about six weeks later, Van Buren urges "quiet."
There is no fitting life of Van Buren. Edward M. Shepard's book in the *American Statesmen* series is very good for its size, but is necessarily

brief. The political history of New York must be studied by any one who wishes to understand this period, but it is most difficult to comprehend. Jabez D. Hammond's *History of Political Parties in New York* in 2 vols. and D. S. Alexander's *Political History of New York* in 3 vols. pave the way; and the perusal of R. H. Gillet's *Life and Times of Silas Wright* will fill in a portion of the picture.

[2] *Journal of the Senate*, 20th Cong., 2nd Sess., p. 120.

[3] The Twelfth Amendment to the Constitution provided that the person having the greatest number of electoral votes for President shall be the President, if such number were a majority of the whole number of electors; but if no person had such a majority the House of Representatives voting by States shall choose immediately by ballot the President

guilty of bargaining and fraud; and the Adams administration was corrupt. More especially, to shock the economical sense of the German farmers, Adams was accused
of having received enormous sums of public money, — the
amount being calculated by adding together all the salaries
and money for expenses that had been paid to him in the
thirty years of his political career. Finally, the moral sense
of the Presbyterians was assailed by charging Adams with
having bought a billiard table with public money and having
installed it in the President's Palace.[1] It was of no use to
point out that Adams, by faithful and prolonged service,
had earned all the money that had been paid to him, or to
demonstrate that of the twenty-five thousand dollars that
Congress had voted for the rejuvenation of the White House,
only six thousand had been spent,[2] or that the billiard table
had been purchased with the President's own money.
Almost never in our history have reputations been so un-
warrantedly attacked and so successfully as were those of
Henry Clay and John Quincy Adams in this campaign.[3]

"from the persons having the highest
numbers not exceeding three on the
list of those voted for as President."
In voting the representation of each
State should have one vote, two-
thirds of the States should constitute a
quorum, but "a majority of all the
States shall be necessary to a choice."
From this it is clear that the Representatives were entitled to pick the
President from the three highest on the
list without defeating the will of the
people or doing anything of the sort;
otherwise the amendment makers and
ratifiers would have provided that the
person receiving the highest number of electoral votes without any regard to its being a majority should be
President.

[1] S. G. Heiskell, the Tennesseean
biographer of Andrew Jackson (p.
306) states that Jackson was devoted
to the game of billiards.

[2] An "Inventory of Furniture in
the President's House, taken the 24th
day of March, 1825" (*House Documents*, 19th Cong., 1st Sess., No. 2).

[3] One of the most interesting charges
levelled against an opponent was that
he had been a Federalist at some
anterior time, particularly in 1808.
Theodore Lyman, Junior, having in-
advertently said something of the
kind as to Daniel Webster, was charged
with criminal libel. See *A Notable Libel
Case*, by Josiah H. Benton, Jr. (Boston, 1904). It is interesting to read
in a letter from a well-known politician to Van Buren, dated June 18,
1827, to the effect that in 1824, Webster had come to him and had said if
Adams were not chosen on the first
ballot, he had a letter to show him
stating that Adams could not do
justice to the old Federalists by admitting them "to a proper share in the
influence of his administration."

Moreover, it must be admitted that the anti-Jackson campaign was very poorly conducted. It had been suggested
that Adams should attend a large meeting of the Pennsylvania Germans and address them in their own language,
but this he refused to do on the ground that it was not becoming the holder of the chief magistracy to harangue on his
own behalf.[1] He also refused to do anything to prevent
holders of federal offices from taking part in the election and
attacking him in unmeasured terms. And, indeed, it
would seem that Adams's ultra-sensitive attitude as to the
offices, however right it may have been, harmed him greatly
because his managers could hold out no hope to any one
who took his part in the campaign of securing any pecuniary
advantage whatever. Finally, Jackson's interests in Pennsylvania were most ably managed by James Buchanan and
his lieutenants.

One of the most difficult feats that was performed by
the Jacksonians was to appear to disapprove of a protective
tariff in the eyes of the Southern supporters and at the
same time to appear to further the wishes of the Pennsylvania protectionists; but the Jacksonians accomplished
the apparently impossible by bringing about the passage of
the abominable tariff of 1828. As it was certain that the
New Englanders would vote for Adams, in any event, and
equally certain that the Pennsylvanians would desert any
man who destroyed the protection of iron, the policy of the
Jackson men was fairly clear. The tariff must appear to be
the work of the Northeasterners and then be amended in
such a way that all protection should be taken from the
textile manufactures. It was expected that this would
cause the New Englanders to vote against the bill and

---

[1] In 1843 Calhoun refused to take
the stump in his own behalf because
he was "adverse to being made a
spectacle, or considered an elec-
tioneerer." Jameson's *Correspondence
of Calhoun*, 541.

thereby defeat it, make the Pennsylvanians hostile to
Adams and favorable to Jackson, and preserve the good
will of the Southerners.[1] This scheme is generally attributed
to Martin Van Buren, but there is little evidence to connect him with it, and Van Buren was not the man to show
his hand to contemporaries or to posterity. At all events
the plan succeeded too well, which is another reason for
supposing it was not the work of Van Buren. The New
Englanders voted for it, because they were certain that before
long they could secure changes favorable to themselves,—
and, meanwhile, the bill prolonged the life of the protective
system. It passed and Adams approved it. The Pennsylvanians voted for Jackson and the Southerners necessarily voted for him, too; but there was added hatred in
their hearts toward the federal government that persisted
in taxing them for the benefit of others, — according to
their mode of thinking.

It must not be supposed from what has been said in the
preceding paragraphs that the Adams men were free from
reproach in their campaign. Adams, himself, was above
blame. To every doubtful suggestion, he invariably said
"No!" He declared that he had never sought public
office and was not going to begin to seek it at his time of
life. His adherents, however, were bound by no such
scruples. There is a curious collection of letters that passed
between Edward Everett and John McLean whom Adams
had retained in office, although it was fairly certain that

[1] John Bailey, writing to J. B.
Davis from Washington, May 10,
1828, stated that the tariff bill "was
engendered between the avowed anti-
tariff men of the South, and the *pro-
fessed* tariff Jackson men of the middle
states, and framed most pointedly so
as to bear heavily and injuriously on
New England, in the hope that it
would thus be defeated." Massachusetts Historical Society's *Proceedings* for February, 1916, p. 212. The
ideas of the time as to the relation of
manufacturing and farming and the
justification of the tariff question may
be seen in George Tibbits's *Essay on
the Expediency and Practicability of
Improving or Creating Home Markets
for the Sale of Agricultural Productions* (Philadelphia, 1827).

McLean favored Jackson and was even working in his interests. Everett criticised severely the giving of a contract to carry the mail to Isaac Hill, a New Hampshire newspaper man and Jacksonian politician, for it was a condition of the contract — as of other contracts to carry the mail — that the contractor could transport his own products free. This enabled Hill to carry on an intense printed propaganda against Adams among the farmers of New Hampshire. McLean insisted that a contract must be awarded to the lowest bidder, and that no discrimination as to terms could be made. Also replying to Everett he declared [1] that Adams could not have made changes in the offices because the hostile Senate would not have confirmed his new appointments. Adams refused to give money or place to secure newspaper support, but some newspaper editors supported him, nevertheless. One of these was John Binns, an Englishman who had successfully conducted a paper in Pennsylvania in opposition to the Duane Republicans. Binns had hit upon the scheme of pictorial propaganda and had prepared posters depicting the most distressing incidents in Jackson's career, some of them resting on mere rumor. One of the things that it was thought would excite hostility against Jackson was the shooting of militiamen to preserve discipline. The Revolutionary device of coffins at the head of a handbill containing the printed particulars of the deed that was denounced was again brought into requisition.[2] Binns also printed posters

---

[1] Massachusetts Historical Society's *Proceedings* for February, 1908, p. 391. There is an interesting letter from Isaac Hill to Henry Lee, dated "Concord, N. H., Sept. 16, 1828" in *ibid.*, for October, 1909.

[2] The handbills were entitled "Some Account of some of the Bloody Deeds of GEN. JACKSON." Facsimiles are not uncommon in the larger libraries. The two copies of the original posters in the Library of Congress vary in important details. See also *Official Record from the War Department* and the *Orders of General Jackson for Shooting The Six Militia Men . . . showing that these American Citizens were Inhumanly and Illegally Massacred* (Concord, 1828).

and handbills after the manner of tombstones, reciting in "Monumental Inscriptions" the misdeeds of General Jackson, and reprinted them as a pamphlet; but the "Binns Coffin Hand Bills," as these were called, do not seem to have stirred the Pennsylvania farmers as they were expected to.

The Adams men established a political paper, "Truth's Advocate and Monthly Anti-Jackson Expositor." [1] It was published at Cincinnati and charged Jackson with speculating in western public lands and also printed the old tales of his pre-marital relations with Mrs. Jackson. The land speculations were indignantly denied and there is no proof whatever that Jackson had "speculated" in western lands before 1828; but while he was President he tried to buy lands in Mississippi and failed to do so owing to the high prices at which they were held, — of course this was before the issuing of the "specie circular." The fact that he tried to buy lands and failed does not of course prove that he speculated in lands at an earlier period, but it would seem to indicate no great feeling of delicacy on his part. Finally, some of the Jackson leaders thought — whether justly or not is unknown — that the Adams men had in mind a scheme to report Jackson as dead just before the election, to prevent people voting for him, as had been done in the case of Governor Snyder of Pennsylvania twenty years earlier.[2]

[1] A good way to get an idea of the spirit of the presidential election of this year is to read consecutively *Truth's Advocate*, pp. 4–20, 117–119; and twenty or thirty pages in the Jacksonian paper, *The United States Telegraph* . . . *Extra* published at Washington by Green and Jarvis.

[2] William B. Lewis to Martin Van Buren, September 27, 1828, in the "Van Buren Manuscripts" in the Library of Congress.

In the *Petersburg Intelligencer* for October 18, 1808, is a despatch from Philadelphia announcing the murder of Simon Snyder with a circumstantial account of finding the corpse. An editorial comment says that this is impossible as no mention was made of the fact in Philadelphia papers of a later date, — and Snyder was elected Governor soon after. For a still earlier instance of the same manœuvre, see the *Richmond and Manchester Advertiser* of November 8, 1796.

All together the story of the presidential campaign ending in 1828 is one of the most woful in our annals.

When the votes were counted, it appeared that one hundred and seventy-eight electoral votes had been cast for Andrew Jackson of Tennessee and only eighty-three for John Quincy Adams of Massachusetts.[1] This was hailed by the Jackson men as a great popular triumph and it did mark the beginning of a new era in our history. None the less, it is worth while to analyze the figures a bit before acceding to this or any other assertion. Jackson received the electoral votes of every State south of Maryland and of the three Northwestern States. He also received the twenty-eight votes of Pennsylvania, and twenty of the thirty-six votes of New York. The one hundred and five Southern presidential electors who had voted for Jackson received two hundred and four thousand votes, while John Quincy Adams received over three hundred and fifty thousand popular votes. The four and three quarters millions of free people in the North in 1828 had one hundred and thirty-seven votes in the electoral college, while the two and one-half million Southern whites possessed one hundred and five electoral votes, each Southern presidential elector representing twenty-five thousand free people, while each Northern presidential elector represented not far from thirty-five thousand free persons.[2] This was due to the working of the federal ratio.[3] Indeed, Jackson was really chosen to

[1] The electoral vote of 1828 is in *Journal of the Senate*, 20th Cong., 2nd Sess., p. 120.

[2] Taking a definite case, New Hampshire and South Carolina each had 244,000 free inhabitants according to the *Census* of 1820. But New Hampshire had only 8 presidential electors to 11 for South Carolina. Again: in 1810 Virginia and Georgia together had a total white population of 729,319 while Massachusetts, alone, had a white population of 700,745. By the working of the federal ratio Virginia and Georgia had thirty-three votes in the national Senate and House of Representatives to Massachusetts' twenty-two votes. At the same time Massachusetts was paying into the federal revenue $2,774,226.34 while the two Southern States together were paying $596,428.26.

[3] See *Census* for 1820 (Washington, 1821). The tables of population are

the presidency by the solid South, as was quite proper as he was a Southern man, a slaveholder, and a cotton grower. At the same time, he could not have received a majority of the electoral votes, even adding the twenty-four electoral votes of the Western States to his Southern votes, without the aid of Pennsylvania and New York, for if we subtract the forty-eight votes received in those States from Jackson's one hundred and seventy-eight and add them to Adams's eighty-three, Jackson would have received one less electoral vote than Adams. Finally, the twenty-four votes of the Northwestern States in this election, as things were, practically counted for nothing because if they had all been given to Adams, and the Pennsylvania and the New York votes had remained as they were, Adams would have had only one hundred and seven electoral votes to 148 for Jackson.[1] Indeed, however one manipulates the figures, it would seem that Jackson was raised to the presidency by the over-representation of the South combined with the employment of most unjustifiable methods by his partisans in Pennsylvania and in New York. On the whole, possibly it was more honorable to have been defeated in 1828 than to have been elected.

summarized at the beginning. Practically the same figures are given in Edwin Williams's *New-York Annual Register for . . . 1830*, p. 335.

Williams's *Politician's Manual* (New-York, October, 1832) contains the vote for presidential electors in 1828 and for the nearest local election, making it useful for purposes of comparison with the above. *Ibid.*, for 1834 gives additional local figures. McMaster (*History of the . . . United States*, v, 518) gives slightly different figures, but does not state his authority. The figures given in Williams's *Annual Register for . . . 1832* (p. 387) seem to be most carefully compiled and are repeated in the *Politician's Manual* (p. 4); they are somewhat different from those in the *Annual Register for . . . 1830* (p. 344).

[1] Nevertheless, Professor Paxson in the *Mississippi Historical Review* (ii, 3) states that "the political revolution of 1828 opened a period of twelve years in which the Mississippi Valley . . . controlled the destinies of the United States" and Professor McLaughlin has told us that with the entrance of Jackson to the White House "the West took the whip hand" in driving forward the United States.

NOTE

Democracy, Historically Considered. — In its ordinary definition, " democracy " implies the direct rule of the people; but the term people is susceptible of many definitions.[1] As it was used by ancient philosophers and by the " Fathers " it denoted the aggregation of persons who shared in the rule of the community, city, or state that was under discussion. In its widest meaning, it would include every man, woman, and child from birth to death — the babe, the senile man and woman, the criminal, the pauper, the hard-working laborer, and the long-houred brain worker. Obviously, all these cannot take part in the direct rule of the state. There must be some limitations, but the approximation to direct rule marks the steps toward the realization of democracy. In Washington's time the franchise was limited by law and even more limited by the geographical difficulty of exercising it. Government was on a republican basis. The voters represented the community and deputed some of themselves to represent them and those whom they, in turn, represented.[2] The development from this republican form of government to that of an absolute democracy, where every one takes a direct share in the government, is marked by the enlargement of the franchise, the providing greater facilities for exercising it, and the remodelling of the apportionment to do away with advantages of wealth or of political and financial corporations.

[1] Professor W. S. Ferguson of Harvard University has given me the following definition of "democracy" in ancient days: "Democracy among the Greeks meant the rule of the *demos*. The *demos* in a strictly technical sense was the legally constituted citizen body whether it included a few only or the many. In popular usage it meant the supremacy in this legally organized body of the middle and lower classes. Democracy always implied the settlement of all important political questions by the citizens met in a general assembly;" Moreover, the *demos* did not include women, children, slaves, or ineffectives, so that the *demos* itself represented human kind within the geographical limits of the state, — in much the same way that "the voters" represented the whole mass of human beings in the period of limited suffrage.

[2] In the Virginia Convention of 1829–1830, Mr. Leigh of Chesterfield asked the members to observe "how generally the introduction of Universal Suffrage has been followed by the caucus system of nomination . . . or convention to make a regular nomination of candidates, to discipline parties, to whip in all who hope [to gain] a share of the loaves and fishes in their turn, and to whip out all who show a disposition to rebel against 'regular nomination.' . . . The elective body, in fact, is the caucus. . . The freeholders of Virginia . . . want no ballot-box to hide their votes from their neighbours, and to screen them from the indignation of others." *Proceedings and Debates of the Virginia State Convention of 1829–30* (Richmond, 1830) p. 406.

CHAPTER XII

PRESIDENT JACKSON

ANDREW JACKSON of Tennessee was inaugurated President
of the United States on March 4, 1829. Fifteen or twenty
thousand persons listened to his address which, according
to one favorable hearer, was "excellent, chaste, patriotic,
sententious, and dignified." To others who were not so
favorably inclined to the new President, it appeared to have
nothing in it. This variety of opinion was more than usually
marked as to Jackson. George Livermore,[1] a Massachusetts
man who later became a strong abolitionist, described Jackson as "gentle and affable in private conversation." On the
other hand, Jefferson refused to appoint Jackson to office
in 1804, declared him to be "rude, malignant, and muddy
headed" in 1809, and warned Monroe years afterward not
to send the "Hero of New Orleans" to Russia, for if he did
Jackson would get the United States into trouble within
one month. To the American people at large Jackson
seemed to be a radical and was acclaimed as such by some
and dreaded by others. In reality, at this period of his
life, whatever he may have been at other times, Andrew
Jackson was distinctly a conservative and used the powers
of his high office to restrain rather than to excite.

The older writers, who were mostly from the North, and
James Parton, an Englishman by birth, have usually de-

---

[1] Massachusetts Historical Society's *Proceedings* for 1867–1869, p. 420.

scribed Jackson as a man of small mentality, slight knowledge of books, unversed in affairs, and having a frontiersman's illiterate roughness. All these statements have some truth in them, but the general expression of this truth is greatly exaggerated. It is true that Jackson was in the habit of having his letters copied for him and of using state papers prepared by others, but so was Washington, our first President, and no one would assert that he was unversed in affairs or illiterate. In the "Jackson Papers" at Washington there are many letters in Jackson's unmistakable handwriting. In them there are errors in spelling and in punctuation, but not more than one finds in the productions of high school graduates and many college undergraduates of the present day, none of whom can be spoken of as "illiterate." In point of fact, Jackson's spelling belonged to the generation before Noah Webster placed such things in the cast iron jackets that Jefferson refused to respect and that many good people of our own time have tried to modify under the guise of "simplified spelling." For vigor of expression and cogency of reasoning, Jackson's rough drafts are distinctly creditable. In the New Orleans campaign and in the crises of his presidential career his judgment was rapid and extraordinarily certain. It is true that he had slight knowledge of books, but he had read the Bible or had stored in his memory what he had heard others read of that great example, and he sometimes used Shakespearian expressions. He was no scholar or man of books, but he probably had read a few of them and had pondered somewhat those that he had read. He came into office at the moment when the Hamiltonian republican form of government was changing to the more democratic institution of the middle of the nineteenth century. Jackson was placed by circumstances at the head of this movement, and being there, he fought for it as intelligently and as strongly as he had fought for his country at New Orleans. Moreover, he was not only the representative of the rising democracy of Pennsylvania and New York and of frontier radicalism, he was more particularly the representative of the cotton planters. To harmonize Southern agricultural and Northern democratic interests was no mean task and, whether we like Jackson and his policies or detest him and them, it must be conceded that from his own point of view he performed the task that came to his hand exceedingly well.

Jackson's administrations form so interesting an epoch in our history that it will be well to look for a moment at the statistical and industrial condition of the people of the United States in those years. In 1830 the total population of the country was between twelve and thirteen millions. These figures [1] include not only the whites but the free colored persons and slaves. Of the thirteen millions nearly two of them lived in New England, three and one-half in the Middle States, and three and one-quarter in the Old South. West of the mountains and south of the Ohio River there were two millions more and in Missouri one hundred and forty thousand. Ohio, Indiana, and Illinois numbered nearly one and a half millions and in the Territories and the Dis-

---

[1] The exact figures of the population in 1830 are hard to get at, as the tables in the official *Census* of 1830 are somewhat crude in arrangement. The numbers in the text have been reached by combining and by adding and subtracting the figures given in this volume (pp. 162, 163) and the figures given in S. N. D. North's *Century of Population Growth* and George Tucker's *Progress of the United States in Population and Wealth in Fifty Years*. The first edition of this valuable work was published at New York in 1843; an edition that was printed at the same place in 1855 has an "Ap-

pendix" that carries the story through the *Census* of 1850. The figures are as follows:

	POPULATION IN 1830
New England	1,954,717
Middle States	3,664,412
Old South	3,251,282
The Southwest	2,031,498
Missouri	140,455
Old Northwest	1,438,379
Territories (Michigan, Arkansas, Florida)	96,757
District of Columbia	39,834
	12,617,334

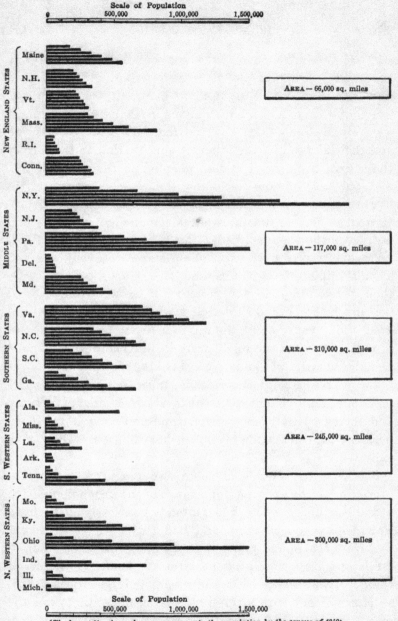

Scale of Population

(*The lowest line in each group represents the population by the census of 1840;
the next line above, the population by the census of 1830 and so on.*)

From Tucker's *Progress*, p. 126.

trict_of Columbia there were one hundred and thirty-six thousand. Grouping the figures somewhat differently, we find that there were nine millions in the States on the seaboard and three and a half millions in Transappalachia. If we draw the line a third way, putting the free soil on one side and the slave soil on the other, it appears that in the former there were over seven million people and in the latter five and one-half millions including the slaves. Some thirty-five hundred of the population of the free States were returned as slaves, for the gradual emancipation plans had not yet borne their full fruit; in the Slave States and Territories there were over two million slaves to over three and a half million free whites and free blacks. There were then three hundred and nineteen thousand free colored persons in the United States as a whole, of whom one hundred and seventy-eight thousand were in the Slave States; of these more than one-half were in Maryland and Virginia and the District of Columbia. Looking forward to 1840, it is noticeable that in this decade, notwithstanding the tremendous abolition agitation, the total free colored population had increased only sixty-seven thousand or about twenty per cent, which is certainly much less than one would have expected.

Studying the figures of these two censuses, one is impressed with the growing importance of the urban population of the North. New York had already hopelessly outstripped Philadelphia and Boston, and had become a great manufacturing centre and point of distribution for products of all kinds and from nearly all parts of the country. South of the Potomac and the Ohio, there were no large cities in 1830, — New Orleans with forty-six thousand inhabitants was the only city that could compete in size with Northern commercial ports. In the next ten years, owing to the prosperity of the cotton and sugar plantations that were tributary to the Mississippi River, the population of New Orleans increased one hundred and twenty-one per cent. It had outstripped Boston and was very nearly as large as Baltimore.

The "Censuses" of 1820 and 1840 contain figures as to the number of persons engaged in agriculture, commerce, and manufacturing, and the "Census" of 1840 gives the value of the year's products in dollars. The science of statistics was then quite rude and probably these figures are not exact in any respect, but they afford an interesting glimpse of what the people were doing, — which is sufficient for the present study. In 1820, two and a third million persons were returned as engaged in industry in the whole United States; and of them over two million (83.4%) were employed in agriculture, three hundred and forty-nine thousand (13.7%) in manufactures, and over seventy-two thousand (2.9%) in commerce. In 1840 the number of agriculturists had increased to nearly three and three-quarters millions (80.4%) but the percentage had declined. On the other hand the number engaged in manufacturing had increased to over three-quarters of a million, while the proportion of those engaged in commerce remained almost stationary. Looking at the matter now from the point of value of products, it appears from the "Census" of 1840 as interpreted by Professor Tucker [1] of the University of Virginia, that the value of the total annual production of the United States was one billion sixty-three million dollars. Of this six hundred and fifty millions were agricultural products, two

---

[1] See his *Progress of the United States*, pp. 135-142, 150-201, especially the table on p. 195. The *Census* of 1840 gives no values of annual productions of manufactures and commerce, but Tucker deduced his figures by estimating the annual products as the equivalent of twenty-five per cent of the capital employed. He thought that the inaccuracies and inconsistencies would correct one another. His figures may be used, however, in the rough way in which they are in the text of the present volume without any pretence to exactness.

hundred and thirty-nine millions manufactures, and only seventy-nine millions commerce. The distribution by geographical sections is particularly instructive. It appears that the free-soil North produced three hundred and forty-two million dollars' worth of agricultural products to only three hundred and twelve million dollars' worth for the Slave States as a whole, including in this latter designation, Maryland, Delaware and the District of Columbia. As to manufacturing, New England and the other States north of Mason and Dixon line and the Ohio River, not including Missouri, produced manufactures to the annual value of nearly two hundred millions, while the whole South is credited by Tucker with the production of only forty-two millions. His figures as to commerce include in that designation the marketing of commodities at home as well as external commerce and navigation. He credits the North with a commerce of sixty-one millions and the South with a commerce of thirty-five millions, and he gives the annual product of the "Fisheries" at nearly twelve million dollars, and of this nine and one-half millions are allotted to New England and over one and a quarter millions of the remainder to New York.

Governmental institutions were still on the Jeffersonian model in 1830 and remained so substantially for some years thereafter. Jefferson's idea, as has already been stated, was that the less government there was the better, that the qualities of each individual should be developed to the utmost, and that as little as possible should be taken from the people by taxation, reasoning that all such exactions ultimately fell upon the working man in the form of increased rents and increased prices for commodities — the clothing and food and fuel for himself and family. This had been the good old New England idea, although never so for-mulated. In the South, too, each great plantation formed a little community by itself, and the functions that were left for the State governments were distinctly limited. Apart from the transportation of the mails, the federal government did not engage in any social function. State ownership and operation of some public utilities, as canals, and also the attempt to absorb some of the profits derived by capital through the partnership in State banks, was marked at this time, but a few years demonstrated to the voters all over the country that the State governments and the federal government were not then equipped to carry on such enterprises. The army and the navy were both very small, and the year 1840 may be regarded, perhaps, as the acme of inefficiency of both these branches before 1860. The task, therefore, to which Jackson set himself was something so unlike that to which Presidents after 1860 were obliged to address themselves that it is rather difficult to realize his point of view and his reasons for action.

Jackson came to Washington armed with a "Rough Draft" of an inaugural address written in his own hand.[1] It deserves close attention, although for reasons of political expediency it was thoroughly made over before delivery. The rough draft is Jackson's own. In it he says that he has been called to administer the affairs of a government "whose vital principle is the right of the people to controul its measures." Among the important duties of the presidency is the filling of the offices with "individuals uniting as far as possible the qualifications of the head & heart,"

---

[1] A convenient collection of the *Messages of Gen. Andrew Jackson* was published at Concord, New Hampshire, in 1837. The "Rough Draft" is among the "Jackson Papers" in the Library of Congress and is printed in Bassett's *Andrew Jackson*, ii, 425–430. In the first form of this paper Jackson had written "protection high enough to insure," but in the copy taken to Washington he had changed the phrase to read "Judicious Tariff imposing duties high enough to insure."

for the demand for moral qualities should be superior to that of talents, as in a republic fidelity and honest devotion must be the first qualification. The general safety must be provided for, which implies the provision of "those internal supplies which constitute the means of war." A "Judicious Tariff" insuring against the lack of these supplies will meet with his coöperation; but beyond this point laws affecting "the natural relation of the labour of the States are irreconcilable to the objects of the Union, and threatening to its peace and tranquility." The national revenue should be applied to the payment first of the national debt and for the support of the government and for the safety of the Union. The necessity of conforming to this principle "is illustrated by the dissatisfaction which the expenditures for the purposes of improvement has already created in several of the States." No line can be drawn between the powers granted to the general government and those reserved to the States and to the people, and the settlement of such a line must be governed by the good sense of the nation in a spirit of compromise. In the last paragraph Jackson states some of the topics intimately connected with the prosperity of the country, as the liquidation of the national debt, the observance of the strictest economy, a judicious tariff, "combined with a fostering care of commerce & agriculture," just respect for States'-rights as the best check to the tendencies to consolidation and the distribution of the surplus revenue amongst the States for purposes of education and internal improvement. It will be interesting to observe how closely Jackson's career as President followed the prescription of the inaugural. It is noteworthy also that the only things not mentioned that were to arouse great controversy in the next eight years, were the Bank and the currency.

Jackson's first task was to select his official advisers, and in the performance of this duty he was not fortunate. As a military man, he naturally wanted persons about him who would be efficient in the administration of their own departments, would not be officious in giving advice, and would be men in whom he had every confidence. As it turned out, he abandoned the sage politicians of the old school, either because he was in a condition of tutelage or because he distrusted their motives. Instead he appointed personal friends and politicians whose fortunes were closely bound up with his own.[1] One of them was Major Eaton, who was almost a member of his family. To him he gave the office of Secretary of War. The one good appointment was that of Martin Van Buren to be Secretary of State; for, however much confidence Jackson felt in his own ability to manage home affairs, he wanted a strong man to stand between him and foreign powers. Van Buren was not a great man, but he had principles, and at this time his principles were in harmony with those of Jackson, although later his anti-slavery attitude was not at all pleasing to the Southern cotton growers, among whom Jackson must always be reckoned. Native ability combined with long experience in dealing with men and situations, not always in a wire-pulling sense, had made Van Buren an expert politician, and he soon acquired a very strong influence with the new President. In treating of Jackson's administrations, one always writes of "the Kitchen Cabinet," which was a name given by his enemies to a group of confidential advisers who had served Jackson long and faithfully and were men of

---

[1] Charles H. Ambler's *Life and Diary of John Floyd*, 97 and 123. Floyd had done everything possible to promote Jackson's election and was keenly disappointed at not receiving an appointment to some high office. The *Diary* runs from March, 1831, to February, 1834, and in its vigor and vituperation of Jackson and his minions rivals that of J. Q. Adams.

peculiar abilities as William B. Lewis and Amos Kendall. These were given minor offices and Jackson sought their advice, as he had in the case of Lewis for some years and of Kendall for a shorter time, and they essayed to direct the presidential steps in the ways that seemed best to them. The whole proceeding was unusual, but has received undue opprobrium. The phrase "Kitchen Cabinet" conveys an entirely wrong impression, as its inventors, who hated Jackson, doubtless meant it should. It is pleasing to look upon another picture of his life in the "Palace," as the White House was often called, even as late as 1830. We can picture him sitting with his nephew's family, with the children playing about. It was in one of the larger parlors with an open fire and Jackson was smoking, a habit which was not nearly so common among men in those days as it was later, for then most male tobacco users, especially in the South, chewed rather than smoked, and probably it was for this reason that Jackson's smoking attracted attention. We may imagine Van Buren, Lewis, or Kendall as being announced, and when the visitor appeared, he and Jackson would sit together in front of the fire or, if there was anything very private to be considered, would retire to a corner of the room or perhaps to an adjoining apartment, and there consult together. At this stage of his career, Jackson was distinctly a gentleman and, when undisturbed, an agreeable companion. A most unfortunate situation arose in connection with Major Eaton. In January, 1829, he had married a rather too well-known Washington woman. Almost at once, a furious feud arose between the wives of the other Cabinet officers and Mrs. Eaton, who was energetically upheld by the President.[1] Stories had circulated

---

[1] Bassett's *Jackson*, ch. xxii. Governor John Floyd constantly recurs to this subject in his *Diary*.

about his and Mrs. Jackson's premarital relations. He insisted that there was just as little truth in the Eaton scandal as there had been in the earlier Jackson scandal, and that was none at all. The principal person to profit by this situation was Martin Van Buren, who was a widower and therefore able to recognize Mrs. Eaton without a household insurrection, while Calhoun, the Vice-President, on the other hand, was absolutely incapable of doing anything to placate Jackson. It was a condition that could not continue, and was terminated by the disruption of the Cabinet [1] and the appointment of new heads of departments who were greatly superior to the first. Van Buren went to London as minister, and some time later Eaton went to Madrid as American representative there, taking his wife with him — and the first doubts had been planted in President Jackson's mind as to the uprightness of Calhoun's character.

Apart from the Eaton Affair, the first noticeable incident in the Jacksonian administration was the removal of a large number of office-holders and the appointment of good "Jackson men" to their places. As Andrew Jackson had been the choice of the "solid South," there were naturally very few changes among the officers in that section, for they were all Jackson men [2]; by far the greater part of the

---

[1] William T. Barry, the Postmaster-General, was retained — although he offered his resignation. There are some interesting and inconsequential letters from him to his daughter in the *American Historical Review*, xvi, 327–336.

[2] On March 24, 1830, Postmaster-General Barry reported the number of deputy postmasters removed between March 4, 1829 and March 22, 1830 at 491, of whom 63 were in the South. See *Senate Documents*, 21st Cong., 1st Sess., No. 106. This table is repeated in *Niles's Weekly Register*, xxxviii, 105. It is given also in Fish's *Civil Service and the Patronage*, 126,

and in Lucy M. Salmon's "Appointing Power of the President" in American Historical Association's *Papers*, i, 347. In his "Removal of Officials by the Presidents" in American Historical Association's *Reports* for 1899, i, 74, Fish gives a list of presidential offices vacated at this time. He suggests that the figures in this latter table mean very little because only heads of departments are included, but the change of one of these officers might mean the discharge of many old employees and the appointment of other persons. It is impossible to do better, because the "Executive Journals of the Senate" for the first three

removals were in New England, New York, Pennsylvania, and Washington City, where the offices were largely occupied by Adams men. Up to Jackson's accession in 1829, public office-holding had been looked upon as one of the more aristocratic modes of bread-winning and the offices had been filled with people from the so-called "upper walks of life." Moreover, office-holding had been looked upon as a permanent occupation, — a man, once in a custom-house job or a post-office place, expected to continue in it as long as he lived, or, at all events, as long as he could work or make a pretence of so doing, and the chances were good that he would pass on the office to his son or his son-in-law, or a nephew, perhaps. In 1829, there were in the departments officials whose appointments bore the signature of President Washington. The office-holders at the capital and throughout the country had acquired house property and lived on a scale commensurate to their salaries, expecting that these would continue. They looked upon government jobs as the holders of business places regarded their positions in those days, — the duties of the place were to be discharged faithfully and to the best of a man's abilities, and that being done the position would be his as long as he could carry on the work. In Pennsylvania and in New York, more especially perhaps in the latter, a system had grown up of distributing the local State offices among the members of the party in power. The system was based upon the idea that the offices belonged to the victors. This development was partly due to the extraordinary pre-Revolutionary conditions that had prevailed in Pennsylvania, where practically all power had been centred in a very small portion of the people living in one geographical unit. The rest of the

years of Jackson's administration are peculiarly irritating in the vagueness of the information therein given.

people of Pennsylvania had had no share in the management of the affairs of the province. They were divided geographically and racially, and the subsequent political contests became very bitter. It was quite natural that the Pennsylvania common people when they gained control of affairs should look upon salaries paid by the State as part of that control, and when they in turn became divided into two parties it was likewise perfectly natural that whichever party was successful should regard the offices as belonging to itself. In New York, the case was somewhat different — somewhat worse, if possible. The first constitution of that State had given the appointment of State officers to the governor and four senators sitting as a Council of Appointment. Any political party that could capture this Council and a legislative majority had the whole political patronage of New York at its disposal, and, under the circumstances, the easiest way to keep in power was to use the public offices as a fund with which to reward or punish one's political friends or political enemies. "To the victors belong the spoils of victory," which was attributed to Governor Marcy of New York, simply stated the truth as to that State. It was natural and inevitable that the New Yorkers and Pennsylvanians and the people of the Transappalachian Northwest — who agreed with them in political methods — should carry those methods into national politics, and this they now proceeded to do.

For more than a quarter of a century one political party had occupied the national offices, for Jefferson, Madison, and Monroe were all of one political family and John Quincy Adams regarded himself as their natural political successor. There had been no political changes in the offices for twenty-eight years, and it is remarkable how well the government had been administered in that generation. Methods that

had come down from colonial times and had been imported
originally from England had been gradually changed to
adapt themselves to early nineteenth century conditions.
There were still great vagaries in accounting and the Third
Auditor of the Treasury and after him the Comptroller
reported the unpaid balances year after year. Some of
these statements are worth a moment's notice. For years
an unpaid balance was reported due from John Adams, even
as late as 1837, eleven years after his death, of over twelve
thousand dollars of an appropriation that had been made
for the "accommodation of his household" at the time of the
removal to Washington, because the Auditor of the Treasury
and the President's steward had not agreed as to the form of
voucher.[1] Another case was that of Benjamin Austin, also
of Massachusetts, who was for years returned with an unpaid
balance against him of over two thousand dollars, which
appears to have arisen out of a conflict between the federal
and State governments as to whose business it was to support the incapacitated soldiers of the War of 1812. In
1818, Nicholas J. Roosevelt was debited with thirty thousand dollars on a contract for manufacturing copper.
Roosevelt and one of his sureties had been imprisoned and
had been released by order of a former Secretary of the
Treasury, presumably for good reasons, — but the unpaid
balance was carried on the books. The clerks of the House
of Representatives as custodians of the contingent fund
fared ill because of differences of opinion with successive
auditors; in 1819, John Beckley's executors were charged
with over five thousand dollars for which a judgment had
been obtained. Charles Pinckney was charged with an
unpaid balance of over twelve thousand, as minister to

[1] The following details are taken
from the "List of Balances" transmitted with the "Letter from the
Comptroller of the Treasury . . . February 16, 1820," *House Documents,*
16th Cong., 1st Sess., No. 80.

Spain years before, but he alleged that the United States owed him a great deal more than that. It seems to be certain that Edmund Randolph still owed fourteen thousand of the original forty-nine thousand for which judgment had been entered against him for money unaccounted for on his resignation from the office of Secretary of State in 1794. It is evident that any one adding up all these figures and taking as proven every statement made by a treasury official could make out a very bad case against the administrations from Washington to J. Q. Adams, and that detailed analyses of them, showing that pretty much everything could be explained, would have no effect upon the popular mind. At all events, the holders of public office in 1829 were looked upon as "rascals" by those who wanted to be their successors. The few cases of actual fraud that were found were treated with a ferocity that showed how difficult it was to justify the actual division of the spoils of victory among the victors.

The Jackson men thronged to Washington and demanded jobs. One man asked for anything that would yield anywhere from three hundred to three thousand dollars a year, except a clerkship. Upon being pressed for his reasons for the exception, he acknowledged that he could not write. Some of the friends of the new government advised that all the applicants should be sent to their homes. This would give the excitement a chance to subside and the whole subject could be taken up in the coming autumn. But it was not so to be, and the proceedings of the next few months as to the offices turned out to be one of the greatest scandals in our history, although probably the enemies of the new regime greatly exaggerated the hardships of the displaced officials and the number of them. One man, who wanted a scientific berth in an exploring expedition, repaired to the capital. He wrote that when the office-seekers had long faces he began to conceive hopes of the "General" because the new President might have done as he pleased, if he had "kicked his pretended jackals to the devil, but it seems that every Jackson dog and cat, born and unborn, is to be provided for." [1] Like all great soldiers, Jackson had unbounded faith in himself and every confidence in his friends, — and appointed them to office without any regard to their capacities and experience. One of these men was Samuel Swartwout, who had attracted Jackson's attention at the time of the Burr trials in Richmond by the courage and pertinacity with which he maintained himself. Swartwout went to Washington to get anything that he could pick up "in the general scramble for plunder." Somewhat to his surprise, he was given the most profitable job in the whole range of the federal offices, the collectorship of customs at New York. In a few years time he was a defaulter to the extent of one and one quarter million dollars and a fugitive in a foreign country; but it is not unlikely that he was the victim of the bad conduct of those under him [2] and of his own

[1] Letter of William Oakes dated March 17, 1829, in the possession of Mr. Walter Deane of Cambridge. Oakes was a distinguished early New England botanist.

An example of the thoroughness of the Pennsylvania politicians is the Findlay or Finley family; of them, five members of one generation were in office in 1830; "Torrence Papers" in Ohio Historical and Philosophical Society's *Quarterly*, i, 80 note, and there is a good deal of other similar illustrative matter in the same number.

It is noticeable that in August, 1828, John McLean wrote to Edward Everett that it was impossible to believe that Jackson would "lend himself and the powers of his office, to the miserable caterers for office, who look upon the Treasury of the Union as spoil won by their efforts." On the contrary, McLean thought that the General would exhibit evidences of magnanimity which would "flush the cheek of his bitterest enemies." It is worth noting that McLean, refusing to dismiss postmasters, was made a judge of the Supreme Court. Massachusetts Historical Society's *Proceedings*, 3rd Series, i, 386.

[2] Walter Barrett's *Old Merchants of New York City*, third series, 255. Fish (*Civil Service and the Patronage*, ch. vi) has brought together a mass of information as to the defalcations of this period. He is very severe on Swartwout and writes that he "passed the evening of his days abroad." According to Barrett he died peacefully in New York City in 1856, which would seem to confirm the statement that the government ultimately lost nothing

inability to distinguish between good men and bad. The number of actual removals from office and the proportion of the removals to the total number seems to have been greatly exaggerated in the minds of historical writers. Of some six hundred and twelve presidential officers, only two hundred and fifty-two were removed, and the highest estimate of the number of deputy postmasters removed was six hundred, and there were then about eight thousand deputy postmasters in the country.[1]

Apart from the reconstruction of the public service, where Jackson's ideas closely followed Northern radicalism, he showed himself to be distinctly conservative. As to the tariff, he had to tread very warily, because his supporters in the different parts of the country had very different ideas on protection, and they came near splitting the Union over their differences. As to internal improvements, however, Jackson felt himself strong enough to put an end to that part of the American System; and, if the tariff had to be continued and produced a surplus revenue, he suggested that after the debt was all paid, the surplus should be distributed among the States according to the federal ratio and be by them expended in internal improvements[2] or otherwise as each State might determine for itself. While in the Senate, Jackson had voted for the Survey Bill of

by Swartwout. The latter with his father had for a long time been engaged in reclaiming low-lying lands in the vicinity of New York City, and these were turned over to the government (see "Annual Report of the Solicitor of the Treasury," November, 1843, in *House of Representatives Documents*, 28th Cong., 1st Sess., No. 35, p. 63). Samuel Swartwout's wife was the niece of Cadwallader D. Colden. This report of the solicitor of the treasury deserves careful analysis. From another entry it appears that the late John P. Timberlake, the former husband of Mrs. Eaton, was indebted to the treasury to the amount of over fourteen thousand dollars, and that no suit had been entered against her father's estate as a surety because the district attorney had "inferred" that he had died insolvent. See for a somewhat different account the *Diary* of John Floyd, 215–220.

[1] Fish's *Civil Service and the Patronage*, 125.

[2] Richardson's *Messages and Papers*, ii, 452.

1824 and also for the bill to improve the navigation of the
Ohio and Mississippi rivers,[1] the first river and harbor bill in
our history ; and his ideas on the subject seem to have been
as confused as those of President Monroe who had accepted
the principle that Congress could vote money for an internal
improvement, but could not undertake the actual construction of such an improvement.

The test came suddenly over a bill that passed both Houses
of Congress to authorize the federal government to subscribe to the stock of the "Maysville, Washington, Paris,
and Lexington Turnpike Road Company." Great systems
of internal improvements had been brought forward.[2]
Among these was the establishment of a line of communication from the Great Lakes to the Gulf of Mexico. One
idea was to open a road from Buffalo to Washington City ;
thence to follow the Cumberland Road to Ohio and so on in
a general southwestwardly direction to New Orleans.
Another project called for a road through the western parts
of New York and Pennsylvania to the National Road and
thence across the Ohio River to the Gulf. It was planned
that either of these lines would cross the Ohio River at

[1] See St. George L. Sioussat's
"Memphis as a Gateway to the West"
(*Tennessee Historical Magazine*, March
and June, 1917). This paper has a
much broader interest than the title
indicates.

[2] There is a good deal of uncorre-
lated information on internal improvements, both from the economic
and political aspects in the printed
public documents, doubtless,
much more in manuscript. Among the
printed reports are a "Letter from the
the Post-Master General" dated
November 28, 1803, giving details
as to unprofitable post roads. Another report dated March 21, 1806,
gives an estimate of the probable
expense of opening a "Horse Road"
between Athens, Georgia, and New

Orleans. On March 18, 1828, a "Report of the Reconnoissance of A Route
for a National Road from Zanesville,
Ohio to Florence, Alabama" was
transmitted to Congress (*House Documents*, 20th Cong., 1st Sess., No. 209).
This was followed on December 21,
1830, by "A Statement of Disbursements" made since 1789 for fortifications, light-houses, pensions, and internal improvements (*House Documents*, 21st Cong., 2nd Sess., No. 11).
From this it appears that $5,310,930.11
had been spent for internal improvements, rivers, and harbors. In the
same period over thirteen million dollars had been spent for fortifications,
three millions for light-houses, twenty
millions for pensions, and one hundred
and eighty millions for the public debt.

Maysville and thence run to Lexington, Kentucky. From that point the road would proceed by one of several routes through Tennessee. The bill was abruptly brought forward and passed without adequate discussion. What the anti-Jackson men had in their minds can only be surmised; but, knowing Jackson and Jackson's power as we now do, it seems almost inconceivable that even so maladroit politicians as Henry Clay and his followers should have selected an internal improvement confined to the State of Kentucky to test Jackson's sincerity and power. Possibly the fact that the next portion of the road would be through Tennessee suggested to them that it might meet with his favor. Martin Van Buren was one with his chief on this subject. He saw with glee the chance that the bill gave him. He at once told the President what was going forward. They were riding out together on the Tenallytown Road. Jackson listened intently and asked his friend to put his ideas into writing. Thereupon Van Buren pulled a written document from his pocket and handed it to the President. Jackson took it home with him and said nothing about it for several days. The friends of the measure, not liking the delay, visited the President to persuade him to approve the bill; but Jackson remained firm, and on May 27, 1830, sent in his first veto message,[1] and thus he put an end for a generation to the building up of a land transportation system at federal expense.

[1] Richardson's *Messages and Papers of the Presidents*, ii, 483; Bassett's *Andrew Jackson*, ii, 475–496.

On January 30, 1854, Van Buren wrote to F. P. Blair.

"You & I can never forget the ardor with which Genl Jackson pursued such objects & the world knows the success which crowned its efforts. I think I have pointed out to you the spot in the vicinity of Washington, where the Maysville veto was decided upon, & I had the most amusing scenes in my endeavors to prevent him from avowing his intentions before the bill passed the two houses. My apprehension being, that if Mr. Clay could be made to believe it possible that the Genl would dare to veto an Int Imp Bill in the then state of public opinion, he would change its character from a local to a general object."

For this quotation and many valuable citations, I am indebted to Mr. B. M. Hulley of De Land, Florida.

Other most interesting achievements of Jackson's time were the securing access to the British West Indies and the wrenching payment for spoliations from France. At first sight it would seem remarkable that Jackson, Van Buren, and Edward Livingston should have been able to achieve what experienced diplomatists like James Monroe and John Quincy Adams had failed to accomplish. Jacksonian historians have attributed it to the might of their hero coupled with the suppleness of Van Buren; but in reality these remarkable successes in the field of international politics were due to the march of events rather than to any skill on the part of the Jacksonians. The question of commercial relations with Great Britain is so full of turnings and twistings that one can read diplomatic papers by the hundreds of pages and fail to gain any clear understanding of it. American trade was confined mainly to trans-oceanic commerce — the greater part of which went to Britain, — to supplying the West Indians with food — taking their produce in exchange, — and to the coastwise trade of the United States itself. The New Englanders wished to reëstablish their commerce with the British West Indies, with the Maritime Provinces, and with Newfoundland. On the other hand it had become a cardinal principle of American policy to exclude all foreign vessels from the coastwise trade. The British, on their part, were perfectly willing to admit American shipping to the trans-oceanic trade, but they very much desired to build up the industries and commerce of the Maritime Provinces, Newfoundland, and Canada by giving them a monopoly of provisioning the British West Indies.[1] At the same time the British

[1] The official papers relating to the long-drawn-out contest as to trade between the United States and the British colonies are buried in the governmental documents. Of these may be mentioned the following: *House Documents*, 19th Cong., 2nd Sess., No. 2 (Colonial Trade); *ibid.*, No. 45 (British Statutes and Acts of Congress on Trade with the West

wished to retain the carriage of their West Indian products to Europe to their own vessels. This commerce in several of its branches, at any rate, would be greatly facilitated by allowing British vessels to take part in the coastwise commerce of the United States. We may suppose a British ship, sailing from London to Halifax, there leaving one cargo, taking on board another, and going to New York. Perhaps a cargo might be obtained at that port for Jamaica ; but undoubtedly it would often add greatly to the profits of the voyage if a part of a cargo, at any rate, could be taken from the Northern port of call to Charleston or Savannah, where more cargo might be obtained for Jamaica. Any such traffic between ports of the United States was prohibited by the provisions of the navigation laws. On the other hand, Americans were practically debarred from direct commerce with the Maritime Provinces and with the British West Indies. During a large part of this time, British-American international relations were largely in the hands of George Canning, Britain's foreign minister, and Stratford Canning, his cousin, the British representative at Washington. The persistent hostility of the first of these to the United States has already been sufficiently adverted to in the present work. Stratford Canning was a conscientious Englishman, who possessed rather more temper than did John Quincy Adams, then Secretary of State, — which is saying a good deal. It must not be supposed for one instant that either of these gentlemen had anything but the best interests of his own country at heart ; but they did not get on well together and Stratford Canning left Washington for another post. In 1827, George Canning died, and in 1829, Lord Aberdeen,

Indies) ; *ibid.*, No. 144 (Exports to and Imports from British American Colonies) ; *House Documents*, 21st Cong., 2nd Sess., No. 22 (Papers relating to the settlement of 1830) ; *British and Foreign State Papers*, vols. iv, v, xiv, xvii, xviii ; Edward Smith's *England and America after Independence*, ch. xvi, and Bassett's *Andrew Jackson*, ii, 656–663.

always conciliatory, was at the head of the British foreign
office. Van Buren instructed McLane, our representative
at London, to pursue an extremely conciliatory attitude
toward Great Britain on the ground that the United States
had too long and too tenaciously resisted the right of Great
Britain to impose protecting duties in her colonies and in
other ways. The British government on its part laid hold
of the words of Jackson's first Annual Message to Congress
that we might "look forward to years of peaceful, honorable,
and elevated competition" with Great Britain and "preserve the most cordial relations" with her. Moreover, Congress had authorized the Executive to dispense with some
of the requirements that had stood in the way of friendly
commercial relations. Under these circumstances it is not
to be wondered at that negotiations which for fifteen years
had been hopeless were now rapidly carried to a conclusion
by which both countries drew back somewhat from their
extreme pretensions and agreed to modify their commercial
regulations.[1] In the outcome, possibly the most interesting
feature of the whole matter was that when Van Buren was
appointed minister to England after his retirement from the
Cabinet, this nomination failed of confirmation by the
Senate because of what seemed, to many members of that
body, the pusillanimous attitude displayed in the instructions
to McLane. In the upshot, he became the Jacksonian candidate for the vice-presidency, and being elected enjoyed
the satisfaction, such as it was, of presiding over the body
that had refused to confirm his nomination.

[1] The papers relating to this negotiation are in *House Executive Documents*, 21st Cong., 2nd Sess., No. 22;
*British and Foreign State Papers,
1830-1831*, pp. 1181-1212. Edward
Smith's *England and America after
Independence . . . Their International
Intercourse, 1783-1872* (Westminster,
1900) gives a connected view of
the relations between the two countries from the British standpoint.
The Jacksonian case is stated at
length in Bassett's *Andrew Jackson*,
ii.

The other triumph of Jacksonian diplomacy was in securing payment from France for certain depredations that had been committed years before in the course of the Napoleonic strivings for world power, when the ordinary rules of international intercourse had been widely departed from. Monroe and Adams had tried their hands at the solution of this problem, also, but the question of its settlement had always been connected by the French government with the granting of favors to French commerce, and this had been out of the question. In 1830, a new revolution placed on the French throne the younger branch of the old ruling family in the person of Louis Philippe. Toward France, Jackson adopted a rather menacing attitude. Edward Livingston, who had been Secretary of State, went to Paris as American representative. The French government agreed to pay five million dollars in satisfaction of these old claims,[1] but before the legislative branch acted, knowledge of Jackson's aggressive language became known at Paris. Thereupon, the French Chambers refused to vote any money to carry out the agreement. In the end, they drew back, but not until the American minister had left France and all diplomatic intercourse between the two countries had been suspended. Ultimately the French, seeing in the President's later utterances something which they could regard as "an explanation," voted the money, and relations between the two countries were resumed and a long-standing cause of grievance against France was removed.

In all these matters, even as to re-allotting federal offices, dealing a master blow at Clay's American System, and bringing to an end foreign complications that had long threatened the continuance of profitable intercourse with America's two best customers, Jackson's administration

---

[1] Bassett's *Andrew Jackson*, ii, 663–673.

was successful beyond dispute. It may be said that the introduction of the "spoils system" should not be regarded as a cause of satisfaction, and it should not; but the change from the old colonial system of permanent official tenure to the more democratic mode of political rotation in the public offices was inevitable, and Jackson may fairly be said to have minimized the blow. The real interest of his administration lies in the relation between the federal government and the growing power of Southern sectionalism, as shown in the nullification episode and the rising spirit of capitalistic industrialism in the North as exemplified in the bank struggle and in the contest over national ownership and operation of public utilities. In the upshot, Southern ideas triumphed, although nullification and secession were laid at rest for a generation. It is curious to note in passing that it has been left for a later Democratic administration to go back behind the gospels of Jacksonism and reincarnate the system of national ownership and operation of public utilities that was so dear to the hearts of John Quincy Adams and Henry Clay

NOTE

Bibliography. — A very valuable " List of Publications " as to Jackson, his times, and contemporaries is prefixed to James Parton's *Life of Andrew Jackson* (3 vols., New York, 1860). The " list " was practically made by William Gowans, the best-known second-hand book dealer of that day. Bassett provides no formal bibliography in his *Andrew Jackson* (2 vols., New York, 1911), but his footnotes with Parton's " List " open wide the door to the researcher. Parton's " Life " was a remarkable book at the time of its publication, but so much material has been made accessible since that it is now superseded by Bassett's two-volume work. W. G. Sumner's *Andrew Jackson as a Public Man* in the " Statesmen " series deals especially with the financial side, and William G. Brown's *Andrew Jackson* in the " Riverside Biographical " series gives an admirable personal setting. J. Q. Adams's *Report on Manufactures* that was presented to the House of Representatives on February 28, 1833, is a most illuminating and caustic review of Jacksonism.

CHAPTER XIII

SOUTH CAROLINA AND NULLIFICATION

IN the early time, in the years following the Revolutionary War, there had been slight thought of the people of the Thirteen States forming a "Nation." Noah Webster, in 1783, in the introduction to the first edition of his "Spelling Book," unconsciously expressed this idea [1] when he wrote that the object of his book was to promote the prosperity of "the confederated republics of America." The makers of the Constitution refrained from using the word "nation" in that instrument, although the aim of some of them was to establish a consolidated government. One of the earliest changes in the Constitution was to take away from the federal Supreme Court the power to adjudicate disputes between a State and citizens of another State. In 1798 the States had been almost on the point of flying at each other's throats [2]; in 1803 and again in 1808 disunion had been rife in New England and in New York; and the hostile attitude toward the government at Washington by the New Englanders in the most perilous years of the War of 1812 had been almost heartrending. With the coming of peace in 1815, a distinct tendency toward greater unity set in. But there was not then and there is not now (1920) in the United States a true nationalism. The American people comprises many races and, while the English language has

[1] Skeel's *Noah Webster*, i, 61.
[2] E. P. Powell in his *Nullification and Secession in the United States*
gives a connected account of most of the early separatist movements.

been predominant throughout the country as a whole, other languages have held their places persistently. Nationalism in the United States means unity of aspiration and accomplishment, or, possibly, unity of social and political sentiments. In the first two decades of the nineteenth century, the national spirit was stronger in the South than in any other part of the country. In 1808, at the time of the Federalist secession movement in New England, the Virginia presidential electors who had voted for Madison dined together at Richmond with Spencer Roane at the head of the table, and drank to the toast, "*The Union of the States:* The majority must govern. It is treason to. secede." [1] In 1819 forty-six gentlemen of Charleston came together and founded the New England Society in memory of their common origin, and in the next year Calhoun and other Southern Congressmen voted for the Missouri Compromise rather than endanger the existence of the Union. Indeed, as late as 1824, the South Carolina House of Representatives voted that no power had been given to a State legislature to impugn the motives of the federal Congress [2]; but the next year the succeeding House passed resolutions of directly opposite tenor.

The Missouri Compromise marked the end of the first chapter in the history of nationalism. From that time for forty years, the whole spirit of our development was towards dualism, — for the Missouri Compromise practically marked the division of the country into two groups, having distinctly different economic interests. The first note of the new sectionalism was sounded in Virginia by Spencer Roane

[1] *Secession-Letters of Amos Kendall* (Washington, 1861), p. 20.

[2] Ames's *State Documents*, iv, 6. In a note he gives an extract from a speech of George McDuffie to the effect that the Federal Convention did not regard "the State Governments as sentinels upon the watch-towers of freedom."

and John Taylor of Caroline.[1] The last named had been for separation in 1799 and very likely had never given over the idea that Virginia would be better off without any alliance with the States north of the Potomac or of Mason and Dixon's line. He now took to the writing of essays, — "Construction Construed" (1820) and "Tyranny Unmasked" (1822).[2] He was especially excited by Marshall's opinions in the cases of Martin and Hunter's Lessee and Cohens against Virginia. In both of these the Supreme Court of the United States had taken to itself cases that had been adjudicated in the Virginia courts and had even issued commands to them. Roane wrote one series of communications after another. These were printed in the "Richmond Enquirer" that had been founded by him and was edited by his brother-in-law, Thomas Ritchie.[3] The most famous of the series was signed "Algernon Sydney" and was reprinted separately.[4] In these writings Roane sought to combat the pretensions of the federal Supreme Court by denying its supremacy and by exalting the constitutional rights of the State courts and through them the rights of the States. Possibly Marshall went too far when he wrote to Judge Story that Roane was "the champion of dismemberment" and not of States'-rights. However this may be, it would seem certain that

[1] Phillips's chapter on "The Economic and Political Essays of the Ante-Bellum South," in *The South in the Building of the Nation*, vii, ch. viii, brings together the main facts in brief compass and in an interesting way.

[2] Taylor also wrote *An Inquiry into the . . . Government of the United States* (1814) and *New Views on the Constitution of the United States* (1823). Taylor's writings had great influence among certain groups of Southerners; now they seem extraordinarily dull and quite commonplace. There is a long article on his life in *John P. Branch Historical Papers*, ii.

[3] See C. H. Ambler's *Thomas Ritchie*. In the Richmond *Times-Dispatch* of Dec. 1, 1913, President Lyon G. Tyler points out that Dr. Ambler is not a Virginian by birth and training and is out of sympathy with the eastern section of the State from which his forbears came. There is a mass of Ritchie's letters in the *Branch Papers*, iii, iv.

[4] The two sets of letters to the *Richmond Enquirer* signed "Hampden" and "Algernon Sydney" are reprinted in the *Branch Papers*, i, 357 and ii, 78.

to Roane belongs whatever honor or dishonor there may be in being the original Southern secessionist,[1] for one can trace the movement directly from him to Fort Sumter.

The administrations of John Adams and of John Quincy Adams, his son, fell within the closing years of distinct epochs in the history of the United States. The election of Jefferson in 1800 marked the ending of the Revolutionary epoch, and the election of Jackson in 1828 witnessed the assured dominance of cotton raising in the South and the rise of a spirit of unity there that was distinctly bounded by geographical lines. The modern history of cotton remains to be written. Few things in this world have so greatly influenced modern life as the fibre of the upland cotton plant. The development of the demand for cotton goods throughout the world is one of the extraordinary phenomena of the nineteenth century. People left off wearing garments that had been handed down by elder brothers and sisters, and from fathers and mothers, and clad themselves in clothing made of cheap and unenduring cotton fibre instead of the more expensive and longer wearing flax and wool. Families laid aside their linen sheets for those of cotton, and the sailing ships of the world — with the exception of men-of-war — ceased the use of linen duck in favor of cotton sail-cloth. And whole races of mankind and womankind, who before had been innocent of clothing, now attired themselves in yard upon yard of cotton cloth. This almost fabulous increase in the demand for cotton fabrics synchronizes with the development of machinery driven by water power or by steam for the spinning and weaving of these fibres into the cloth of everyday use. But he would be a courageous man who would say that the demand led to the invention, or

---

[1] Professor William E. Dodd has a readable article on Roane in the *American Historical Review*, xii, 776.

that the presence of cheap cotton cloth created the demand. In 1791 the United States produced about two million pounds of pure cotton, and in 1834 four hundred and fifty-seven million pounds. By 1830 cotton produced within the limits of the Un ted States had driven all other cotton fibres from the British mills, because, although labor was cheaper in India and Brazil whence cotton had formerly come, it was so inefficient that cotton could not be grown in those countries — in ordinary years — in competition with the slave-driven production of the Southern States, which was also more uniform in quality and of better color. Unfortunately, as the production of cotton increased, the price constantly declined, for the supply was overtaking the demand. In 1801, cotton brought at New York from thirty to forty-four cents a pound[1] for "middling uplands," and by 1832 had declined to seven cents. It is impossible to ascertain accurately what the planter received for his crop, but it was probably not far from one-half of the average yearly price at New York.

The tremendous increase in the size of the cotton crops that has been noted in the preceding paragraph was accompanied by a great change in the methods of cultivation, or new methods of cultivation led to a great increase in the total production. New plantations were opened in western Georgia and in the country to the westward as far as the Mississippi River and, decade by decade, the size of the cotton-producing unit increased. Soon the planters on the old uplands of Carolina and Georgia found themselves at a serious disadvantage in comparison with the planters on

[1] James L. Watkins's "Production and Price of Cotton for One Hundred Years" (Department of Agriculture publications, *Miscellaneous Series*, Bulletin, No. 9, pp. 7, 9, 10). The only figures available for the early time are the prices paid at New York and Liverpool, and these were often highly speculative.

the newer lands. The result was a constant movement of planters and slaves from the seaboard to the Black Belt.[1] The amount of fibre grown in the old seaboard States reached its highest point in 1826, when the price paid at New York was at the lowest point in the first third of the century. The increase in the amount of cotton produced in the Black Belt was startling. In 1801 only one million pounds were grown in the western country, — all of it in Tennessee; in 1826 no less than one hundred and fifty million pounds were grown there and in 1833 two hundred and forty million pounds.[2] By 1828 the Southwest had outstripped the Southeast. Moreover, the conditions of transportation[3] were such that the crops of the new country were exported from New Orleans, Mobile, and other Gulf ports and not from Charleston and Savannah. There is no means of proving it conclusively, but there seems every reason to believe that the Western planters were making money out of cotton, while those on the Atlantic seaboard, taking them together, were losing money every year, although the conditions were so peculiar that this fact was not known to many of those who were running into insolvency.[4]

[1] In this connection it is noticeable that the emigration from the old States north of the Potomac River was about replaced by the coming in of people from other States or from European countries. In the three States south of the Potomac precisely the opposite was the case. In 1850 there were 388,059 persons born in Virginia living in other States and only 76,210 persons were living in that State who were born outside of it whether in America or in Europe. The case was even worse as to South Carolina, for there were only 21,363 outsiders living in that State as against 186,479 South Carolinians living in other parts of the Union. In these figures can be seen a cause of unrest in the Old Dominion and in the Palmetto State.

[2] For more detailed figures, see Note at end of chapter.

[3] U. B. Phillips in his *History of Transportation in the Eastern Cotton Belt to 1860* shows not only how earnestly the two eastern cotton States were striving to secure for themselves as much of the traffic of the new cotton States as they could, but also how futile these efforts were, especially as to Charleston.

[4] See U. B. Phillips's "Economic Cost of Slaveholding in the Cotton Belt" in *Political Science Quarterly*, xx, 257-275.

Some extracts from the "Stock and Crop Book of Silver Bluff Plantation" in South Carolina, kept by J. H. Hammond and now in the Library of Congress, will be to the point. It ap-

Contemporaneously with the slipping backward of the agriculture of the Southern seaboard there was a distinct loss of trade at Charleston and other South Carolina ports that was patent to every one. New York had become the commercial metropolis of the Atlantic seaboard. This was due in part to the amount of business that was brought to her wharves by the Erie Canal route. It was also owing to the fact that that city had become the greatest manufacturing centre of the country and also because her merchants were absorbing the distribution of the products of mills in New England and New Jersey, and also the agricultural products of the whole Atlantic seaboard to the southward of the Chesapeake. A vessel sailing across the Atlantic from Liverpool and elsewhere and returning to some European port was reasonably certain to have full cargoes both ways, if she went to New York. If she sailed to Charleston her hold would be scantily filled with European manufactured goods on the westward trip. She might have a full cargo on the return voyage;[1] but the total freight money earned on a voyage, let us say, from Liverpool to Charleston

---

pears that there were in the 30's from 80 to 147 slaves on the plantation. The average expenses were worked out as $3,696.98; the average sales at $11,491.86. The expenses consisted in the salary of an overseer, which is given as about $500 a year, taxes on lands and on negroes, cost of negro cloths and shoes, salt, bagging, and rope used on the plantation and the wear and tear of tools and work animals. The family, overseer, slaves, and animals were subsisted from the plantation, except that the family purchased coffee, tea, etc., through the agent. The estimate includes no 'overhead" except the overseer's $500 and only a small amount for depreciation. Putting the master's and mistress' superintending care at $5000 a year, leaves less than $3000 a year as the annual net income from an investment of $92,000, plus increase in slaves and minus decreasing fertility of soil. A few other items are worth noting. It appears that cotton in those years brought from 12 to 16 cents a pound to the planter, which shows that the product of the Hammond plantation was of superior quality. The average profit per slave was $75 a year.

[1] S. S. Huebner, in *The South in the Building of the Nation*, v, 407, states that the tariffs of 1816 and on, by preventing the importation of slave cloths from England, led to a change in southern commercial currents. He attributes the unrest in the Old Cotton States to that cause, in combination with the decline in the profits from cotton growing.

and back was certain to be much less than that gained on a similar voyage from Liverpool to New York. Under these circumstances the cotton of the seaboard States found its way to European markets through New York, and the commerce of Charleston and Savannah was confined almost entirely to coastwise voyages. The tariff undoubtedly had something to do with building up the trade of New York and with the decline of Southern importations from England; but the combined movement was the result of much more vital factors than any or all of the tariff acts that were passed before 1828, — and that were enacted after that time. In 1830 there were one-quarter of a million human beings living on Manhattan Island, and twenty years later — in 1850 — the population of New York City was greater than that of the whole State of South Carolina.[1] These were surface conditions, but the delver into figures could easily find that while three million dollars worth of foreign merchandise had been imported directly into South Carolina ports in 1821, less than one-half of that amount had passed through the custom houses there in 1831, al-

[1] The following population figures, taken from the *Census* of 1910, "Population," vol. i, pp. 31, 80, 86, and from De Bow's *Statistical View of the United States* (1854), p. 192, give an interesting comparison:

	1800	1820	1830	1850
New York City	79,216	152,056	242,278	696,115
Rochester			9,207	36,403
Lowell			6,474	33,383
Charleston, S. C. . .	20,473	24,780	30,289	42,985
South Carolina	345,591	502,741	581,185	668,507
Virginia	880,200	1,065,366	1,211,405	1,421,661

In 1833 the Charlestonians, led by Joel R. Poinsett, issued a *Statement of the Comparative Advantages of Charleston* over the ports to the northward which completely evaded the real point in issue — the land connections of the several seaports. See also the *Proceedings of the Fourth Convention of Merchants and Others* (Charleston, 1839).

though the total value of the goods imported into the United States in 1831 was nearly double what it had been ten years earlier. Moreover, in that decade the registered tonnage of South Carolina had been cut nearly in halves, declining from thirty thousand tons in 1821 to a little over fifteen thousand in 1831, although the total registered tonnage of the entire country had nearly doubled in those ten years.[1] This decline in the commerce of the city that once had been the foremost mart of the South was perfectly clear to the importer and even to the simple city dweller in Charleston. The planter oftentimes was not aware of the seriousness of his own position or that of his neighbors. He kept looking forward to the next season when the climate and the rainfall would be more favorable to the development of the cotton plant, or his slaves would be in better health, or the new overseer would get more out of the worn acres and the slow moving negroes. Some Southerners attributed the recession of prosperity in the Old South to the deadening effects of the slave system; others thought that it was due to the persistent devotion to a single crop.[2] In reality it was the inevitable result of the competition of the old East with the new West. In the North the farmers of New England no longer tried to compete with those of the Northwest; instead they turned to trade and manufacturing on a large scale. The planters of the Old South, on the contrary, persisted in trying to compete with the planters of the richer lands to the westward, and they were continuously and insensibly consuming their capital.[3]

[1] Watterson and Van Zandt's *Tabular Statistical Views* (1828), pp. 104–113, and their *Continuation* (1833), pp. 152–155, 168–172.

[2] There is an interesting letter from Macon to Bartlett Yancey on these general themes in *James Sprunt Historical Monographs*, No. 2, p. 76.

[3] William Gilmore Simms (*The Southern and Western Monthly Magazine*, i, 142) wrote that "the devotion of our planters to the culture of cotton only, until they fail of food and clothing, is precisely that of the Virginians in their devotion to tobacco," and the policy of the North toward the

In the earlier years of the century, the South Carolinians had established many manufacturing plants. Some of these were successful for a time, but then were either shut up or went into bankruptcy. It was said that the reason why the Southern textile mills could not compete with those of the North was that each mill sought to produce many varieties of cloth, instead of being devoted to one staple article. Others declared that it was owing to the presence of slavery that manufacturing was not successfully carried on in the Cotton States.[1] Possibly a better explanation than either of these is to be found in the great profits that were derived from cotton raising in extraordinary years, — so great were they, indeed, that planters withdrew their slaves from all outside employments, such as grading railroads, and even sought to restrict the production of foodstuffs on the plantations, so as to put every available ounce of labor to the production of cotton. Whatever the cause of the decline of manufacturing may have been, it not only had declined, but, so keen had become the popular distaste, that to be a favorer of even local manufacturing and thereby to share in the federal protection of industry was anathema and was sufficient to ruin or retard a South Carolinian's political career. In one case, indeed, the fact that the brother of a candidate for office was interested in manufacturing was used by his opponents as a political asset.[2]

South is like that of James I and Charles II toward Virginia in the seventeenth century.

[1] C. S. Boucher's "Ante-Bellum Attitude of South Carolina towards Manufacturing and Agriculture" in *Washington University Studies*, iii, Pt. ii, No. 2. Victor S. Clark has given some attention to the material side of the problem in his *History of Manufactures in the United States* and has two pages on early South Carolina factories in *The South in the Building of the Nation*, v, 320, 321. August

Kohn's *Cotton Mills of South Carolina* republished from the *Charleston News and Courier* and issued by the South Carolina Department of Agriculture, Commerce, and Immigration in 1907 is by far the best essay on the subject. "Article ii." pp. 6–16, relates to the period before 1840. H. T. Cook's *Life . . . of David Rogerson Williams* has a few pages on manufacturing in South Carolina.

[2] Washington University's *Studies*, ii, Pt. ii, 243.

In 1822 the extreme view as to the harmfulness of manufacturing was expressed by John Taylor of Caroline in his
"Tyranny Unmasked." Manufacturing was an offering to
avarice, he wrote, and "the people" — presumably those
of the United States as a whole — are "worked" out of sixty
million dollars a year by the protective system and banking.
Governor Troup of Georgia stated the general view of his
section when he wrote that no evil is more to be dreaded
in the general government than the regulation of industry.
The example he gave was the duty of five cents per yard on
cotton bagging. This, he said, was levied to enable the
people of the Western States to supply it on their own terms,
but the proceeds would be used for internal improvements
in the North.[1] In 1826 a bill was brought into Congress by
the friends of the American Colonization Society for the
appropriation of a sum of money in aid of that enterprise.[2]
Originally the colonization scheme had been favored in the
Slave States. By this time, however, in South Carolina
the project had come to be regarded as an attempt to facilitate emancipation and thereby reduce the mass of available
slave labor. The "Charleston Mercury" of April 24, 1830,[3]
contained a fiery letter by Henry L. Pinckney. He asked
will Congress "violate the Constitution by legislating on a
subject with which it is expressly forbidden to interfere"?
Will it tax the people of the South for schemes leading to
their destruction and do this at the "imminent hazard of
rending the Union to atoms"? Men might remonstrate
about internal improvements "by which one section of
the country is drained and fleeced for the enrichment of

---

[1] Harden's *Troup*, 511.

[2] *House Reports*, 21st Cong., 1st
Sess., No. 348. This contains in an
"Appendix" a mass of material on
Liberia and on the slave trade that apparently attracted the attention of the
cotton planters to the dangers to be
apprehended from the successful carrying out of the project.

[3] Mr. D. Huger Bacot of Charleston kindly called my attention to this
letter and copied a portion of it for
me.

others"; but the proposed act would be so monstrous and the consequences so awful that the Southern States would "burst their bonds and, at all hazards, cast off a government" which could thus meditate their destruction. These are only a few examples that might be largely continued [1] to show the restlessness of the Carolinians under what they regarded as intolerable burdens and oppressions.

Of all the fomenters of discord, Thomas Cooper, an Englishman by birth and then connected with the University of South Carolina, might well be regarded as first in ability and in influence. In 1826 he published his "Lectures on the Elements of Political Economy." [2] In this book he declared that no government had ever interfered to regulate trade without doing mischief. Government was instituted to protect and not to direct, and every individual must judge for himself in these matters. In 1827, Cooper wrote

[1] See, for example, Robert J. Turnbull's *The Crisis: or, Essays on the Usurpations of the Federal Government. By Brutus* (Charleston, 1827), p. 53: — "What is it to us whether the great Cumberland Road be kept in repair or not? . . . Has the Government subscribed to our Santee Canal Company? . . . We are not yet sufficiently fleeced. The GREAT SOUTHERN GOOSE will yet bear more Plucking." And p. 112: — "As for myself, I cannot conceive a measure more fraught with permanent mischief and ruin to the Plantation States, than the Tariff. It is not simply to tax us to support our Northern brethren, but it is also to destroy all our means to acquire the ability to pay those taxes." He admits that the Northern manufacturers now furnished "some coarse fabrics cheaper than the English dealer," but he is protected by duties, — but the whole pamphlet should be read to understand one hundredth part of the South Carolina mind of that epoch.

See also the *Review of a Late Pamphlet, under the Signature of "Brutus."*

By Hamilton. First Published in the Charleston Courier (Charleston, 1828); *The Crisis: A Solemn Appeal to the President . . . on the destructive tendency of the present policy of this country on its agriculture, manufacture, commerce, and finance* (Philadelphia, 1823); the "Colleton Address of R. Barnwell Smith (Rhett)" in the *Charleston Mercury* of June 18, 1828; a "Letter" describing the feelings of the people of the interior of the State over the tariff in *ibid.*, for July 8, 1828; and Jameson's *Correspondence of Calhoun*, 403.

[2] Cooper's *Lectures*, 138, 139 and note, 142, 196. These *Lectures* and Cooper's *Manual of Political Economy* together with Thomas R. Dew's *Lectures on the Restrictive System* shaped Southern sentiment on the tariff and in general on the working of economic laws so far as they applied to the South. See also "Letters of Dr. Thomas Cooper" in the *American Historical Review*, vi, 725. H. M. Ellis has brought together the leading facts of Cooper's life in *The South Atlantic Quarterly* for 1920.

to Martin Van Buren that if the tariff bill, which was then being debated in Congress, should be carried, the South Carolina legislature would be ripe for a motion to recall the South Carolinians from Congress. And if the American System were persisted in, the State would separate and declare Charleston a free port, because the South could not exist under a system that transfers her money into Northern pockets without an equivalent.[1] Other writers elaborated this thesis and declared that imposts are in the nature of a bounty upon manufactures. Upon the "staple growing states" fell almost the entire burden of supporting the federal government, they asserted, but only one-twentieth of the revenue raised by the tariff was expended in that section.[2] A Southerner, indeed, was in contact with the "emblems of oppression," namely, tariff-stimulated Northern manufactures, from the time he went to bed at night until the close of the next day.[3] His sheets were from Northern mills and so was his clothing, and "the very light of heaven" came to him through "Boston window glass" that was heavily charged with "tributary taxation." One Georgia planter declared that he would rather sit in the dark than pay tribute to the Massachusetts manufacturers. With

---

[1] "Van Buren Manuscripts" in the Library of Congress under dates of July 5, and 31, 1827.

[2] See an article reprinted from the "Southern Review" in *The Free Trade Advocate*, i, 147. The "Cooper line of argument" was set forth with great clarity in a *Memorial of the [Charleston] Chamber of Commerce* presented to Congress in 1827. On p. 9 it is stated that "the present duty on woollens is equal to an assessment of three sixteenths per cent" on Southern capital and formed "an annual tax of between 60 and 70 thousand dollars" on slave cloths. Another clear statement of the theory is in "The Report of the Committee of Twenty-one" in the *Proceedings of the Fourth Con-*

vention of Merchants and Others at Charleston, April 15, 1839.

Governor Floyd of Virginia in his *Diary* under date of April 30, 1832, writes that the Northerners claim that Congress had the right to lay protective taxes upon importations. "Hence all the states to the South of the Potomac became dependent upon the Northern States for a supply of whatever thing they might want, and in this way the South was compelled to sell its products low and buy from the North all articles it needed, from twenty-five to one hundred and twenty-five per cent higher than from France or England."

[3] *The Free Trade Advocate*, i, 133, 134.

these ideas in their minds, the proposition that a surplus
revenue should be raised by means of tariff imposts to
pay for internal improvements mostly in the North seemed
to Southerners to be outrageous in the highest degree.[1]
This attitude was best expressed by Langdon Cheves some
years later when he wrote that resistance to the insufferable
and insulting oppression of the North was justifiable. He
believed that the threat of separation would bring the North
to terms; for without the agriculture of the South and the
Southwest, the grass would grow in the streets of the
Northern cities.[2]

The South Carolinians and Georgians had no objection
to government ownership and operation of public utilities
in themselves, but the only large schemes that aroused much
interest in the country had to do almost entirely with the
North and, according to their view, would be paid for by the
Southerners through increased prices for the clothing and
other necessary goods for their slaves and themselves.

The Southerners had no hostility to banks and banking,
and two of the most successful State-owned banks were in
Virginia and South Carolina. The opposition that arose in
that section to the Bank of the United States grew out of the

[1] The following figures have been
compiled from the "Letter from the
Secretary of the Treasury" of December 20, 1830 (*House Documents*,
21st Cong., 2nd Sess., No. 11) : —

DISBURSEMENTS FOR INTERNAL IMPROVEMENTS FROM 1789 TO 1830

Old North (including Md. & Del.)	$ 567,543.65
Old South	37,434.68
Old Northwest & Mich. Terr.	671,056.37
New South (including Ark. & Mo.)	224,704.40
Florida	102,955.16
Cumberland Road	2,443,420.20
Federal Subscriptions to canals	1,083,500.00
Improving Miss. & Ohio rivers	180,315.65
Total	$5,310,930.11

[2] Letter of Langdon Cheves in
*Southern State Rights, Anti-Tariff &
Anti-Abolition Tract No. 1.* There is
an interesting article on Cheves in the
Papers of the American Historical As-
sociation for 1896, p. 363.

erratic conduct of that institution. Under its early presidents, it had loaned freely, but after the change of management in the early twenties one curtailment succeeded another. As the mobile capital of the country was mainly in the North, the Southerners soon found themselves owing large sums of money to creditors on the other side of the Potomac. It is probable also that in this respect, as in others, it was a change in business methods that especially annoyed the South Carolinians. Formerly, their staples had gone directly to Liverpool from their own ports ; now they went through New York, and their business instead of being financed from England was largely arranged from New York; and the credits allowed by American bankers were much shorter than those that had been allowed by the Englishmen. For all these reasons it was not at all unnatural that Southern planters should look with hostile eyes upon Northern capitalists and oppose whatever schemes were brought into the federal Congress for the building up of Northern industry and navigation.

It happened most unfortunately that the hard times that began in 1818 and lasted over into the twenties impelled the Northern manufacturers to appeal to Congress again for assistance in the shape of increased protection to their industries. This movement resulted in the Tariff Act of 1824. It was not a high tariff in any way, but it was the first truly protective tariff in our history. The attitude of the Southerners may be gathered from the fact that of the fifty-six or fifty-eight members of the House of Representatives from Virginia and North Carolina and the five Cotton States to the southward, only one — Johnson of Virginia, from the Monongahela District — voted for it.[1] In 1827, a

[1] *Journal of the House of Representatives*, 18th Cong., 1st Sess., 428, 429; W. M. Meigs's *John Caldwell Calhoun*, i, 274; and Ames's *State Documents*, iv, 12.

convention of the Friends of Domestic Industry met at Harrisburg in Pennsylvania and called for more protection. This in turn excited the South Carolinians to renewed agitation, and the State legislature adopted a report and resolutions declaring that the Constitution of the United States was "a compact between the people of the different States with each other, as separate, independent sovereignties," and the view that the Constitution emanated from the people as a whole was a dangerous doctrine. Georgia and North Carolina also protested against the protective system. The actual passage of the Tariff of Abominations in 1828 gave the signal for more radical demonstrations. Governor Taylor of South Carolina, in a message to the legislature, advised that the act should be declared unconstitutional and that adequate measures should be taken to enforce the action of the State.

John C. Calhoun now comes to the front. In earlier years he had advocated internal improvements and protection to industry and had sponsored the act chartering the second Bank of the United States.[1] Apparently during Monroe's administration, he had seen nothing wrong in these policies; but now he took charge of the rhetorical campaign and used his great powers of analysis and of literary expression to put the best face possible upon the proposition that a State could refuse obedience to an act of Congress and at the same time not be in a condition of rebellion. Calhoun's change of front has naturally caused much trouble to his biographers and to students of the

---

[1] Calhoun's actions and early opinions on these matters are admirably set forth in *Measures, Not Men. Illustrated by Some Remarks upon . . . John C. Calhoun. By a Citizen of New York.* This was published in 1823 and judging by the subject matter was written by a Southerner. "Calhoun as Seen by his Political Friends, 1831–1848," in the *Publications* of the Southern History Association, vii, 159, 353, 419, is an interesting series of minutes of unpublished letters from Duff Green, D. H. Lewis, and R. K. Crallé.

nullification episode. Houston gives one the impression that he looks upon it as an instance of Calhoun's time serving and restoration of his political fences; Von Holst seems to regard it as the natural action of a slaveholder. It would seem that Houston was nearer right and that political considerations and not convictions caused Calhoun to assume leadership. After all, the dearest wish of his life was the attainment of the President's Palace. Seldom has a man succeeded in reaching that goal who has not had his State behind him, or, at all events, has not had the indorsement of his own political party in his own State. Calhoun wrote the report of the committee of the State legislature on Governor Taylor's message which was adopted in December, 1828, and made public early in 1829.[1] For a time, his authorship was kept secret, probably because it might have seemed ill-fitting for the Vice-President to affix his name to a document justifying the annulment of an act of Congress. Jefferson, in writing the Kentucky Resolutions of 1798, had done precisely this thing, but he, too, had carefully covered up the traces of his participation. The nullification doctrine, as one finds it in the "Exposition" of 1828 and in Calhoun's speech on the Force Bill in 1833,[2] rests on the assumption that the people of each State was sovereign at

[1] The "Exposition" and "Report" are printed in Crallé's *Works* of Calhoun, vi. According to the "Preface" these are copied "from the originals in the handwriting of the author. The first varies somewhat from the printed copy." The "Exposition" and "Report" are in *Niles's Register* and in the official publications of Congress and of South Carolina (Ames's *State Documents*, iv, 20). R. Barnwell Rhett, writing in 1854, stated that the "Exposition" was "greatly altered by the Committee. . . . Mr. Calhoun had nothing to do with these corrections and I know disapproved

of them." *American Historical Review*, xiii, 311. Probably Crallé's text best represents the thoughts of Calhoun. Sundry resolutions that were introduced into the legislature are printed in the Southern History Association's *Publications*, iii, 212.

[2] The 1833 speech may most conveniently be found in Calhoun's *Works*, ii, 197. Possibly the case is more clearly stated in Chancellor William Harper's address that was delivered at Columbia on September 20, 1830, and printed in 1832 under the title of *The Remedy by State Interposition, Nullification; explained and advocated.*

the time of the ratification of the Constitution and, in ratifying that instrument, acted in its separate and sovereign capacity. The Constitution, therefore, was a compact to which each State was a party and each one of them had a right to judge of its infractions and to interpose to maintain the rights of the people of the State within its limits. The general government is only "the joint agent of two distinct sovereignties" and the Union is "a union of States as communities, and not a union of individuals" and there is no immediate connection between individuals and the general government. It followed, therefore, that the people of a State in its sovereign capacity could declare an act of the federal government null and void and not binding on it, and could by legislative action protect the citizens of that State against the federal government. The scene of action now shifts to Washington and centres about the person of Daniel Webster.

The history of Webster's famous series of speeches which have come to be known collectively as the "Reply to Hayne" has never been written, although they were probably the most famous speeches ever delivered in the national Senate.[1] The usual story is that Senator Foote of Connecticut moved the adoption of a resolution which seemed to the Westerners to be part and parcel of a scheme to curb migration to that region. The Westerners objecting, the Southerners thought they saw the opportunity to separate the two groups of

[1] On Webster see Edward Everett's *Works of Daniel Webster* (6 vols., Boston, 1851); Fletcher Webster's *Private Correspondence of Daniel Webster* (2 vols., Boston, 1857); *The Writings and Speeches of Daniel Webster* (National Edition, 18 vols., Boston, 1903); Van Tyne's *Letters of Daniel Webster from Documents* (New York, 1902); G. T. Curtis's *Life of Daniel Webster* (2 vols., New York, 1870); E. P. Wheeler's *Daniel Webster, the Expounder* *of the Constitution* (New York, 1905); and Lodge's *Webster* in the *American Statesmen* series. Wheeler's book contains a good deal of legal information in an understandable form; but Lodge's *Webster* will satisfy the needs of nearly every one. Peter Harvey's *Reminiscences and Anecdotes of Daniel Webster* (Boston, 1877) is the tribute of an old friend; but oftentimes lacks vitality.

Northerners by joining forces with the West. In his first speech, Senator Hayne,[1] whose voice was described as like "morning's music on the air," confined himself to justifying the aggrieved feelings of the Westerners. It was then that Webster gently drew him away from that theme into setting forth the South Carolina doctrine of the sovereignty of the people of the States. Having achieved this, Webster fell upon him with all the might of his power of mind and of speech in sentences that have long thrilled the American heart and might well be repeated every Fourth of July after the reading of the immortal Declaration. He was really replying to Calhoun and the South Carolinians, and it may well be that the whole thing was a shrewdly devised scheme to provide a proper setting for the enunciation of the Union doctrine. The Constitution, Webster declared, was "the people's Constitution." The government was the people's government; "made for the people, made by the people, and answerable to the people. . . . The general government and the State governments derived their authority from the same source." In cases of conflict a method of relief had been provided in the Federal Judiciary, in frequent elections, and in the power of amendment. It cannot be overthrown by direct assault and will not be "evaded, undermined, nullified" if the representatives of the people conscientiously discharge the public trust committed to them.

Andrew Jackson held to the full the Southern ideas as to the undesirability of internal improvements at federal expense. He thought there was no justification to raise a surplus revenue by taxation of goods imported into the

[1] Theodore D. Jervey's *Robert Y. Hayne and his Times* (New York, 1909) and Paul H. Hayne's *Lives of . . . Hayne and . . . Legaré* (Charleston, 1878) give one a certain amount of knowledge of South Carolina hopes and fears, but Hayne deserves even more extended commemoration.

country. He distrusted banks and bankers and especially doubted the wisdom and good faith of many officials of the United States Bank. In all these matters, he agreed with the South Carolinians and with the other cotton planters. But there he stopped. He had saved the Union at New Orleans and he would brook no interference with it. To him the Union was sacred. He was a States'-rights man, like most other Southerners, but that dogma should never be used to justify action derogatory to the continuance of the Union. It is rather singular that the South Carolina leaders should not have realized what Jackson's real feelings on the matter were; but most of them had no conception of the strength of his affection for the Union or realized the length to which he would go in the performance of what he looked upon as his duty. The "Tariff of Abominations" had been a distinctly Jacksonian electioneering device, but the leaders of Charleston and Columbia refused to see in it anything but a Northern attempt still further to tax them for the benefit of the people on the other side of the Potomac. The election of Jackson was so probable, however, that they postponed action until he should be in the presidential mansion, when they could act with a freer hand.[1] For two years afterwards, there was a strange calm in South Carolina which was ended by the passage of the Adams Tariff of 1832. Meantime Jackson's feelings had been aroused against the chief of the nullifiers, or the person who seemed to be the chief of the nullifiers, John C. Calhoun, then Vice-President of the United States.

In 1818, at the time of Jackson's raid into Florida and

---

[1] In resolutions that were submitted to the South Carolina legislature in December, 1828, the "happy election" of Jackson is adverted to as holding out "a well-founded hope of a more just, moderate and impartial administration of public affairs"; Southern History Association's *Publications*, iii, 216.

the execution of Arbuthnot and Ambrister, Calhoun, who was then Secretary of War, had proposed in Cabinet meeting that the over energetic general should be placed under an arrest and brought before a military court of inquiry. President Monroe and the other members of the Cabinet, except the Secretary of State, had felt much the same way as had Calhoun, and it was John Quincy Adams who single-handed had defended Jackson against his chief and all the other members of the Cabinet, and had gained his point. It fell to Calhoun, however, to communicate the decision of the government to Jackson and the latter had concluded that it was Calhoun who had defended him. For years Jackson and Calhoun maintained the friendliest relations. Calhoun wrote to Jackson in 1826 that his name would be found in the future, "as it always has been on the side of liberty and your country," and Jackson, on his part, had toasted Calhoun as "An honest man — the noblest work of God." Some time after 1824, but exactly when cannot be stated, and, indeed, is immaterial, those around Jackson began to hear suggestions that it was Calhoun who had been Jackson's enemy in 1818. The first authentic information of this came to William B. Lewis indirectly from Crawford, and, although it was indirect, it was evidently worthy of credence. Lewis kept this knowledge to himself for a year or so until it seemed that the time had come to excite President Jackson's feelings against the Vice-President. Then it was done so craftily that the General could not fail to notice it, but at the same time was not in any way aroused to take Calhoun's part. The first information had come in a letter from John Forsyth, who merely reported what Crawford had said to him. Jackson declared that he could take no notice of the matter until information came directly from Crawford. Thereupon, he was written to and he replied in almost the

exact language of the letter to Forsyth. Jackson forwarded
Crawford's letter to Calhoun with a request for an explanation and received one or more [1] which, however, could not
explain what was unexplainable. Jackson now was fully
convinced of "the duplicity & insincerity of the man,
. . . the entire want of those high, dignified, & honorable
feelings which I once thought he possessed" and left him to
"the gnawings of a guilty conscience." And it would seem
on the surface that there was some reason for Jackson's
stigma, for when John C. Hamilton, who had Forsyth's
letter in his custody, asked Calhoun whether any motion
had been made in the Cabinet meeting at the time of the
Seminole affair to bring Jackson before a military court,
Calhoun had answered [2] that "no such motion had been
made." This was literally true, as Calhoun had only proposed or suggested that Jackson's conduct should be inquired into. One thing was certain, that Calhoun's hopes
of succession to the presidency or, indeed, to any leading
part in the Democratic organization, were entirely at an end,
until time should remove Andrew Jackson from his hold
on the party. What effect the rupture with Calhoun had on
Jackson's treatment of nullification is by no means clear.
It is natural to suppose that the irritation he certainly
felt toward Calhoun may have influenced him; but on the
other hand, it is absolutely clear, clear as anything is in
history, that Andrew Jackson would have done his duty
as he saw it, and long before this time his devotion to the

[1] See *Correspondence between Gen.
Andrew Jackson and John C. Calhoun, President and Vice-President
of the U. States* (Washington, 1831);
reprinted in the "Appendix" to Crallé's
Works of John C. Calhoun, vol. vi.
[2] *Niles's Weekly Register*, xl, p. 42.
This is Calhoun's own statement of
the conversation with Hamilton.

Hamilton's account which is printed
on the preceding page differs somewhat
in the phraseology, Calhoun denying
that the propriety of arresting General Jackson was "discussed." The
episode is treated at length in Meigs's
Calhoun, i, 401. Bassett in his *Andrew Jackson* (ii, 502–512) gives by
far the best account of this intrigue.

Union had been clearly expressed. Jackson's diction and grammar are not often those of the schoolmaster, but when his mind was excited, he could express himself so plainly that few persons could misunderstand him, notwithstanding faults of punctuation, spelling, and grammar. It was in a letter to his wife's nephew and his old comrade in arms, General John Coffee, that he wrote it was absurd to hold that "a state has a right to secede & destroy this union . . . or nullify the laws of the union. . . . The people are the sovereigns, they can altar & amend . . . but the moral obligations is binding upon all to fulfill the obligations. . . . Therefore, when a faction in a state attempts to nullify a constitutional law of congress . . . the ballance of the people composing this union have a perfect right to coerce them to obedience." [1] He had a passionate love for the Union, "The union must be preserved . . . I will die with the union." That his own people could have misunderstood him seems almost incredible; but Jackson had a sphinx-like capacity for concealing his thoughts until the time came to exhibit them. As he wrote to a friend in the midst of the bank contest, a military man keeps his army in reserve until the time comes to use it. Partly to discover his thoughts and partly to pledge him to themselves, the Southerners got up a banquet on the anniversary of Jefferson's birth and invited Jackson to be the guest of honor. He took his place at the table and when the time came stood up, and, to the dismay of his hearers, proposed a toast "Our federal union, — it must be preserved!" How any one could have misinterpreted his sentiment after that is a mystery, but they tried to explain his words to mean much the same as their own.[2] On May 1, 1833, Jack-

[1] *American Historical Magazine*, iv, 236, 237. Given in part with some changes in Bassett's *Andrew Jackson*, ii, 569, 570.

[2] Henry Barnard, writing in his journal at Beaufort, South Carolina,

son wrote to an humble relative who had not got the precise
office he had wished and having explained that, went on to
say something about nullification, for its "actors and
exciters" will be execrated by the people and "Haman's
gallows ought to be the fate of all such ambitious men,
who would involve their country in civil wars . . . that
they might reign and ride on its whirlwinds and direct the
storm." It was in this letter, too, that Jackson wrote that
the tariff was only the pretext for nullification, which had
disunion and a Southern confederacy as its real object;
the "next pretext will be the negro, or slavery, question." [1]

For a couple of years the nullifiers kept quiet until in
1832 the passage of the new tariff law seemed to give them
a chance to renew the agitation. The act of 1832 was probably the most equitable tariff law that had been passed for
twenty years; but owing to the necessity of securing majority votes in Congress its provisions were not such as would
commend themselves to any one political party or group.[2]
In other words, it was a compromise and, as a matter of
fact, had not gone far enough to satisfy those who dreaded
a surplus because of its effect on the morals of politicians.
Nor had it at all satisfied those who held what J. Q. Adams
was pleased to call the "Mulatto doctrine of political economy," [3] which was that two-thirds of the federal revenue

April 30, 1833, states that the "leading
men of this State had the surest
pledges that Jackson was with them
in their views of the Constitution.
. . . Their hatred of him amounts to
madness." *Maryland Historical Magazine*, xiii, 361.
   [1] Massachusetts Historical Society's *Proceedings*, viii, 172, and 2nd
Series, vol. xiv, 371.
   [2] See Massachusetts Historical Society's *Proceedings* for December, 1905,
and Brooks Adams's Introduction
to *The Degradation of the Democratic
Idea*. The ideas of the Northern free

traders can be best seen in *An Exposition of the Unequal, Unjust and Op-
pressive Operation of the present tariff
system in relation to Iron, Wool, Hemp,
Paper . . . by a Select Committee appointed by the Free Trade Convention*
(Philadelphia, 1832).
   [3] *American Historical Review*, xi,
340. The phrase "Mulatto doctrine"
refers to the "forty bale theory" of
McDuffie of South Carolina: — "If
the duties upon imports were levied
in kind, and the planters made their
own exchanges with the foreign manufacturers, without the intervention

being derived from a tax on imported goods, some of which were used in the Southern States, was really "a tax upon the *export* of Cotton!" It makes no difference whatever whether the law was harmful to Southern interests or not, a majority of the ruling class in South Carolina believed that it was injurious. When the legislature met, it was clear that the majority was distinctly on the side of State interposition.[1] With some difficulty, two-thirds of the legislature voted to call a State convention for the purpose of considering the condition of affairs and taking such action in the name of the sovereign people of South Carolina as seemed best in the circumstances. As the election of members of the convention was conducted on the same rules that prevailed as to the election of members of the legislature, it represented precisely the same mass of opinion. The Union men or anti-nullifiers took a lukewarm part in the election because the case seemed to be pre-judged. The nullifiers had a great majority and were able to carry their desires into action without very much discussion and

either of money or commercial agents, the most unreflecting would perceive that the import duties were direct taxes upon the productions of the planters. If, for example, forty bales of cotton were taken out of every hundred when it passed the customhouse, going abroad, it would be impossible for them to obtain any larger quantity of goods for the remaining sixty, in consequence of this levy; because the agents of the Government would carry the other forty into the foreign market, and, of course, the supply would be undiminished" (*House Reports*, 22nd Cong., 1st Sess., No. 279). An interesting critique of this report is the speech of Nathan Appleton of Massachusetts of May 30, 1832, in Gales & Seaton's *Register of Debates*, viii, Pt. iii, 3188; also printed separately. The extreme South Carolina view is succinctly set forth in *The*

Prospect Before Us; or Strictures on the Late Message of the President of the United States . . . By Aristides (Charleston, 1832). McDuffie's report should be read by every student who wishes to understand the Southern point of view and may be reënforced by a passage in one of Calhoun's letters in American Historical Association's *Report* for 1899, vol. ii, pp. 401–404.

[1] Various details — mostly of little historical value — can be found in Henry D. Capers' *Life and Times of C. G. Memminger* (Richmond, 1893, pp. 37 and fol.); W. J. Grayson's *James Louis Petigru. A Biographical Sketch* (New York, 1866); and "George McDuffie" in J. H. Carlisle, Jr.'s *Addresses of J. H. Carlisle* (Columbia, S. C., 1910) p. 208 and fol.

without any delay. The convention met November 19, 1832, and passed a Nullification Ordinance declaring the federal tariff act of 1832 to be null and void. They also called upon the State legislature to pass the necessary laws to protect the people in their disobedience to the federal law and to prevent the United States authorities from enforcing it. The legislature at once responded and passed a series of laws that were most comprehensive and well designed to produce the results that were aimed at. It authorized the raising of a volunteer military force and appropriated money for the purchase of arms. The legislature also adopted resolutions declaring it to be expedient "that a Convention of the States be called" to consider questions that had arisen "between the States of the confederacy and the General Government"; but this plan met with slight favor.

Senator Hayne now became governor of South Carolina and exchanged speech-making for the administration of the State in one of the three most critical times in its history. He took the necessary steps to enroll and train a military force, a portion of which consisted of mounted minute patrolmen. How effective this force was, or would have been had it ever been properly supplied with arms and trained, we cannot say.[1] We have definite information as to it, but as to the opposing forces provided by the Unionists, possibly in a more inchoate condition, we have no tangible information, except that the Union men were feared by the nullifiers. How much this was due to the fact that the Union men had the confidence of President Jackson is not perfectly clear. Jackson was in secret correspondence with Poinsett and some other leading Unionist

[1] "Letters on the Nullification Movement in South Carolina, 1830– 1834," in *American Historical Review*, vi, 736–765, vii, 92–119.

men in the State. He made provision for the assembling
of large forces and for providing them with arms, but also
insisted that these should be kept from sight until the time
came to act. He sent a few hundred soldiers to Charleston, an extra revenue cutter or two, a ship of war, and,
much more important than any of these, General Winfield Scott, who certainly performed a very useful task in
heartening the anti-nullifiers, making plans for military
movements, and in keeping the iron hand very well concealed within the military glove, — although the presence
of the military glove was quite evident. Nathaniel Jarvis,
a Massachusetts man, happened to arrive off Charleston
harbor in the Spanish brig *Hermosa* from Havana on the
first day of February, 1833. When within three miles of
the port, the United States revenue cutter *Alert* ran alongside and ordered the captain to drop anchor until he could
give bonds to secure the duties on his cargo or pay the probable amount in dollars. Jarvis describes the condition
of affairs at Charleston after his landing as "nigh rebellion
as one could well be without having made any overt acts." [1]

The other Cotton States showed slight sympathy with
South Carolina and no intention of following her into nullification. In Virginia the planters of the old tide-water
region seemed to agree with the nullifiers, but they were
held in check by the members of the legislature from the
western counties, and all that they could do was to secure
the appointment of a "commissioner" to go to South
Carolina and ask her to take more time. North Carolina
was opposed to both her neighbors, one of her leading men,
William Gaston, declaring that it would be better for her
to "personate the drowsy hero of Washington Irving, than

[1] *Journal* kept by Nathaniel Jarvis
of a trip to Havana and return by
way of Charleston. See also Charles
J. Stillé's *Life and Service of Joel R.
Poinsett.*

excite the mingled horror and ridicule of mankind by representing the combined characters of Captain Bobadil and
Cataline." [1] In January, 1833, Jackson asked for the passage of an act giving him powers adequate to meet the crisis,
and he had already issued a proclamation, December 10, 1832,
informing the people of his "native State," as he always
regarded South Carolina, that "Disunion by armed force
is *treason*. Are you really ready to incur its guilt? . . .
On your unhappy State will inevitably fall all the evils of
the conflict you force upon the Government of your country.
It can not accede to the mad project of disunion, of which
you would be the first victims. Its First Magistrate can
not, if he would, avoid the performance of his duty." [2] He
also suggested a modification of the tariff system. In point
of fact very many good people at the time were convinced
that protection had been carried too far and should be
abated. This opinion had been growing regardless of
South Carolina nullification, which, however, brought tariff
revision within the range of practical politics at that precise
moment. For once, Clay, Calhoun, and Webster acted
together; the first named to save what he could of the
American System, the second to rescue his fellow nullifiers
from the edge of Jackson's wrath, and the third to preserve
the Union. The result was that the Force Bill and Clay's
Compromise Tariff were passed at the same time and
approved by President Jackson.[3] And this was the end,

[1] *Records* of the American Catholic
Historical Society of Philadelphia, vi,
236.
[2] These exact ideas in different language may be found in Lincoln's First
Inaugural; see Richardson's *Messages and Papers*, vi, p. 11.
[3] F. L. Nussbaum has brought the
leading facts together within reasonable compass in *The South Atlantic
Quarterly* for October, 1912. The

"Compromise Tariff" provided for a
gradual reduction of duties spread over
ten years, one-tenth of the existing
duties above "twenty per centum on
the value thereof" to be taken off
every other year until 1841, when one-
half of the residue should be removed,
and in 1842, the other half, bringing
the tariff down to the horizontal rate
of twenty per cent. See *Statutes at
Large*, iv, 629. The other law was

for the South Carolina nullifiers, having achieved a part of their desire in securing an important modification of the tariff, held a somewhat informal meeting of the Convention, advised the executive officers not to enforce the nullifying ordinance, and substituted for it an ordinance nullifying the Force Act.[1] They undoubtedly agreed with Henry L. Pinckney that "the Genius of Carolina" had planted itself firmly upon the federal Constitution and with the Kentucky Resolutions in one hand and the palmetto banner in the other, had proclaimed resistance to the Washington government. "Yes, Volunteers, you have saved the State. Your firmness and constancy have given us the victory. The doctrine of Nullification, once the theme of ridicule, is now the theme of praise. The State of South Carolina, lately so fettered and degraded, is now honoured and respected, and, in saving her, you have saved the Constitution and the Union."[2] In the future, as another orator declared, South Carolina would come before Congress "not as a suppliant, but as an equal."

entitled "An Act further to provide for the Collection of Duties on Imports" (*ibid.*, iv, 632). It was commonly called the "Force Bill" and, like the preceding act, was approved on March 2, 1833. It gave great discretionary power to the President as to the details of collection and authorized him to use the forces of the United States practically in any way he saw fit to enforce the federal laws "until the end of the next session of Congress, and no longer."

[1] The most important of the Nullification documents were published in 1834 by the State of Massachusetts under the title, — *State Papers of Nullification.* The "Journal of the Convention" is on pp. 295–375: the "Report" or "Exposition" on p. 1; and the body of the book contains the answering resolutions of Maine and the other States, etc.

[2] *Oration . . . on the 4th of July, 1833* (Charleston, 1833), pp. 21, 54.

NOTE

Cotton. — The figures of production in the following table are drawn from Levi Woodbury's report [1] and the prices from Watkins's paper. [2]

COTTON CROP OF THE UNITED STATES IN MILLIONS OF POUNDS

STATE	1791	1801	1811	1821	1826	1833	1834
Va.		5	8	12	25	13	10
N. C.		4	7	10	18	10	9½
S. C.	1½	20	40	50	70	73	65½
Ga.	½	10	20	45	75	88	75
Total . . .	2	39	75	117	188	184	160
Ala.				20	45	65	85
Tenn.		1	3	20	45	50	45
Miss.				10	30	70	85
La.			2	10	38	55	62
Total		1	5	60	158	240	277
Fla.					2	15	20
Ark.					¼	¾	½
Total . . .					2¼	15¾	20½
Grand Total . .	2	40	80	177	348¼	439¾	457½
Price per lb. at New York . .	26	44	15.50	14.32	12.19	12.32	12.90

In 1848 the total production of cotton in the United States was over one billion pounds and in 1860 was over two billions.

See also diagram in Harry Hammond's *South Carolina*, 13.

[1] It is entitled "Cotton, Cultivation, Manufacture, and Foreign Trade of" and forms No. 146 of the *House Executive Documents* (24th Cong., 1st Sess.,) and is most easily used in the *Writings of Levi Woodbury*, iii, 248. Matthew B. Hammond's "The Cotton Industry" in the *Publications* of the American Economic Association (New Series, No. 1) is the result of great labor and is extremely useful.

[2] James L. Watkins's "Production and Price of Cotton for One Hundred Years" is in the publications of the Department of Agriculture, *Miscellaneous Series*, Bulletin No. 9. Very useful condensed tables showing both production and prices are in *The South in the Building of the Nation*, v, 211, 431–434.

CHAPTER XIV

THE BANK AND THE PANIC OF 1837

APART from the offices and the struggle with the nullifiers, the main interest in Jackson's administrations has to do with financial matters. It was inevitable that this should be the case because, by 1829, the country had recovered from the long period of depression that began with the embargo, and in every year of his term of office business activity was greater than in any preceding twelve months. A reaction from this period of agricultural and industrial expansion was inevitable, but it must be said that both the going up and the coming down were greatly hastened by the actions of the President. Jackson, himself, had never had anything that could be remotely termed a business education. He had a plantation and slaves, but his income for the most part had been derived from offices that he had held and especially in the later years from his position in the army. As a frontiersman, he regarded credit and banks as something provided by nature and the government for the benefit of the converter of new lands to the uses of civilization. There is something fascinating in the ingenuousness of the frontiersman in these matters.[1] He has no objection whatever to the establishment of banks by the State or by individuals and at once proceeds to borrow money, giving a mortgage on his crops and lands in return. As the people

[1] In the following analysis I have greatly profited by conversations with Professor E. E. Dale of Oklahoma University; but all errors of fact or statement in these paragraphs must be charged to me and not to Professor Dale.

434

come from the East, as the forest is cleared away and the ground brought under cultivation, his property will double, treble, or quadruple in value. To him it is worth not what he paid for it or what he could sell it for at the moment, but what he can obtain for it in eight or ten years' time, if everything goes well. To him time is no object : in the spring he plows and plants and through the summer and into the early autumn watches the forces of nature bringing the crops to fruition with a little hoeing or cultivating, now and then ; and in the autumn he collects the reward of his labor and of nature's work. As he joyfully ponders the affairs of his farm or plantation, it appears certain that if he can clear more land and employ more labor he will gain ever increasing returns. It is at this point that he goes to a banker to borrow money and finds the man of the counter possessed of a "horror of land," [1] for it is difficult to handle if taken on execution. Moreover the banker is ill appreciative of future land values. He will loan money only on a portion of the actual selling value of the land at the moment. And then the banker will sharply limit the duration of his loan to three months or possibly to six. Farm improvements mature slowly, and when the time for payment comes the frontiersman sees no reason for haste. The land is constantly improving in value, and the bank, therefore, is perfectly secure. The interest will go on, corn or cotton will be much higher in thirty days or in two or three months ; why not postpone the payment, therefore, especially as money is a little scarce at the moment, the demand for labor on the farm urgent, and travelling difficult? To the banker, the aspect of things is very different ; his obligations must be met on the moment and, therefore, if the debtor cannot or does not pay what he has promised, the only

[1] This is Biddle's phrase in a letter dated December 23, 1833.

thing to do is to take the property that was mortgaged as
security and sell it for what it will bring. There was thus
a wide gulf between the ideas of the farm and of the bank.
Furthermore there was little capital in newly settled regions
that was not already invested in land; the capital for new
enterprises necessarily came from the older settled parts
of the country. It seemed, therefore, as if a few capitalists,
living afar off, were consuming the fruits of the farmers'
labors. Jackson sets forth the frontier view in his letters.
He declared that banks are capitalistic institutions whose
sole function is to make money, and capitalists united in
corporations are devoid of ideals. In short, according to
him a bank is not a charitable institution as it should be,
but one where profit is the sole object even at the cost of
oppression to the people. Somewhat similar ideas as to
banks and bankers were held by most people throughout the
country, even in the Old Thirteen. To them there was something obscure in the workings of financial concerns and the
word "credit" possessed little meaning. A banker or a
bank opened an office, issued notes in exchange for mortgages or other collateral security, and demanded interest
oftentimes at a high rate, from twelve to twenty-five per
cent a year. The borrower took the notes and immediately
paid them out to the government for more land or to a
trader for more stock or slaves. It seemed as if nothing
had been transmuted into something, lands, cattle, or labor;
and the only person to profit immediately was the banker,
and thus he who had contributed nothing tangible was the
first person to be rewarded. It is true that the banker was
required by law to have on hand a certain amount of gold
and silver and oftentimes he was obliged to redeem in specie
all of his notes that were presented to him; but he issued
notes seemingly out of all proportion to the amount of specie

in his possession, six or eight times as much and frequently
more. The way for a frontier community to deal with this
problem was for itself to establish a bank, preferably one
that should be regulated by local law and would be responsible to local opinion. There were three general types of
banks: (1) private banks that lived solely on the credit
of the bankers, (2) local banks that were established under
some "free banking law" that involved some kind of supervision by the State government and, in some cases, were
more or less closely connected with the loan system of the
State by requiring State bonds as a basis of the bank note
circulation, and (3) a State bank that was sometimes a
part of the treasury organization and in other cases was
closely connected with the State fiscal system.[1] The State
banks often had branches in different parts of the State
and thus brought the benefits of banking to every one.

Of the banks described above, the first were the famous
"wildcat banks" which consisted of little more than a
banker or two, a valise or trunk filled with printed bank
notes of their own issue, and an office with the smallest
amount of furniture.[2] When one of these banks or institutions had achieved a moderate amount of success, it turned
into a more settled form of bank, and when it failed, the

---

[1] State ownership of banks north
of Mason and Dixon's line and east of
the mountains was confined to the
years 1789-1812; in the Old South
it continued until 1861; in the Northwest the greatest activity was between 1820 and 1857, and in the
Southwest from 1824 to 1840.

[2] See Logan Esarey's "State Banking in Indiana" in *Indiana University
Studies*, No. 15, — the "Bibliography"
at the end will point the way to a study
of state banking in general; and G.
W. Dowrie's "Development of Banking in Illinois, 1817-1863" in *University of Illinois Bulletin*, November

17, 1913. Gershom Flagg has something to say on the subject in Illinois
State Historical Society's *Transactions*, for 1910, p. 32. For Ohio, see
C. C. Huntington's article in the *Ohio
Archæological and Historical Quarterly*
for July, 1915. R. Hildreth's *Banks,
Banking, and Paper Currencies* (Boston, 1840) is a contemporaneous
account, and the sixth chapter of Sumner's *Andrew Jackson* is a lucid and
unsympathetic account of banking
in Kentucky and Tennessee. The
statement in S. Dean's *History of Banking*, 159 178, is clear and brief.

whole establishment disappeared. Of the banks that were more or less under State control some, as in Massachusetts, joined to put pressure upon any banks that were dilatory in redeeming their paper issues;[1] or, as in New York, they contributed specie to a safety fund that was administered by the State for the redemption of the notes of any New York bank that failed to redeem its paper;[2] or their circulation was founded on State bonds and administered more or less by a State functionary, as was the case in Indiana under the Bank Act of 1852. There was little to choose between these systems as systems, for their success depended upon the efficient administration of them by some officer or officers. The State banks, so called, were really parts of the State financial administration : they received the taxes and other public moneys, kept them, and paid them out on order of the proper official. Their capital was based on State loans besides the public funds, and in some cases they were to lend money on mortgage to land owners, generally in proportion to the political strength of the various parts of the State. The Bank of South Carolina had been founded to preserve the land owners of that State from ruin and had accomplished that design. From the beginning, it had as a rule been well managed, and, as was the case with the State bank of Virginia, remained an efficient institution down to 1861. One reason for the reëstablishment of these public banks was a feeling that the State as a political entity should reap some of the harvest to be gained from the use of credit facilities. This view left out of account entirely the fact that any

---

[1] This was called the "Suffolk Bank System" from the name of the bank that acted as agent. See Nathan Appleton's *Remarks on Currency and Banking* (Boston, 1841). The para-graphs as to the Suffolk Bank System are reprinted in Gouge's *Journal of Banking*, 34.

[2] D. R. Dewey's *Financial History of the United States*, § 69.

proper use of credit is simply the employment of the strength of a community for its good. The banker is simply a distributive agent for the community in securing the best employment of its faculties.

As one period of business inflation and of hard times succeeded another, the number of banks went up and down. The demise of the old Bank of the United States in 1811 led to the establishment of many local banks. The government was obliged to make use of these to carry on its financial business and in the extremely difficult years of 1814 and 1815 suffered heavy losses. It was to obviate these that the Second Bank of the United States was founded in 1816.[1] The federal government was to own stock in this institution, deposit in it all its receipts, and give over to the Bank the management of its loans and pensions. Besides managing these, the Bank was to keep the government moneys and pay them out on drafts from the proper officials and transfer the public funds from one part of the country to the other, — all without charge; but, on the other hand, it was to pay no interest on government deposits, — the cost of carrying on these government duties being regarded as approximately equal to the sum that might be gained from the use of that portion of the federal funds that was not held in the vaults for the purpose of honoring any calls made by the government. One of the principal motives for the establishment of the new Bank was to bring about a more reliable and more uniform currency. The notes of the State banks of one sort or another usually depreciated in proportion to the distance from the counter of the bank of issue. The United States Bank at once went into the business of transferring funds, public and private, from one

---

[1] For the act, see *Annals of Congress*, 14th Cong., 1st Sess., Col. 1812, and R. C. H. Catterall's *Second Bank* of the United States (ed. 1903), pp. 21, 479–488.

part of the country to the other; to do this, it established branch banks in important commercial centers. With the command of more funds than any other banking institution and with these antennæ branch banks, scattered all over the country, it was able to put pressure upon almost any State bank by collecting a bunch of the notes of that bank, presenting them for payment and refusing to take anything in exchange except specie.[1] In its first years, the Bank exhibited as many faults as the State banks and exhibited them on an extended scale owing to its large resources. When the hard times came in 1819, it was obliged to curtail and to change its management. The Bank carried out the process of deflation with an iron hand. Under the circumstances, doubtless, this was necessary for the safety of the Bank and of the country; but it was coincident with a period of falling prices and bankruptcies of banks and bankers, of farmers, merchants, traders, and planters.[2] Of course this was the inevitable result—as things were—of the preceding inflation and of the crude state of knowledge of the laws of finance; but, not unnaturally, the people laid it to the unwarrantable actions of the "monster bank" at Philadelphia which with its branches seemed to them to resemble a gigantic octopus, sucking the blood from the arteries of the toilers on the farm and in the shop.[3]

All the local banking institutions were regarded by the

---

[1] Ebenezer S. Thomas states that in 1816 he paid 28% premium for specie at Baltimore and that in two years' time the premium had disappeared. *Reminiscences of the Last Sixty-five Years*, ii, 84.

[2] As showing the severity of the crisis, it may be noted that in 1819 a pamphlet of 170 pages of double column was published at Albany containing a list of lands to be sold for arrears of taxes.

[3] On the other hand the "great bank" exercised a modifying influence on the tendency of the New York banks to combine and monopolize financial business. In 1825 it was stated that the City Bank of New York by means of interlocking directorates controlled twelve or fourteen "monied institutions" with a capital of six millions. See I. Lawrence to Biddle, June 9, 1825, in "Biddle Papers."

State legislatures as so many business establishments that could be taxed like any other business establishments, and they were ordinarily so taxed. When the Bank of the United States began to establish branches in the several States it did so without entering into any kind of negotiations with the State authorities or securing permission of any sort from them. When established, the branches at once competed vigorously with the local banks for the local business and took a large proportion of it away from the local banks. Then, too, the notes of the Bank of the United States came into general circulation and, being equally good in all parts of the country, supplanted the local issues, except in the commercial centers. For some reason a clause had been inserted in the charter, requiring all the notes of the bank to be signed by the president and cashier. Whether the object of this clause was to limit the circulation of the notes of the great Bank or was for some other reason, it certainly soon became evident that it operated to defend the local note circulation against a tremendously increasing United States Bank note circulation and Congress, therefore, absolutely refused to grant any modification. The Bank authorities then hit upon the expedient of branch drafts. These were drawn at any one branch on the parent Bank at Philadelphia, signed by the cashier of the branch, and drawn to the order of an employee. He endorsed the draft and it became, in effect, a circulating note which would be paid at any branch of the United States Bank and was really as good currency as there was in the country; but the device worked still further to lessen the profits of the local banks so far as they were derived from note circulation. As local business enterprises the State banks were subject to taxation as every other business concern, and the branches of the great Bank were likewise

taxed by the State authorities. It was at this point that
the federal Supreme Court interfered and decided that a
State could not tax a corporation chartered by the United
States, and thereby gave the Bank of the United States and
its branches still another chance to compete successfully
with the local banks.[1] Putting all these things together,
the great curtailment of credit in the early twenties, the
competition of the notes of the United States Bank with
the local note issues, and the freedom it enjoyed from local
taxation, it is easy to see why jealousies arose against the
"monster institution."

In 1823 Nicholas Biddle of Philadelphia succeeded to
the presidency of the Bank of the United States. He owed
his appointment primarily to James Monroe, who had become acquainted with him during his European diplomatic
residence. Biddle had had no business training, but he
was a man of strong administrative capacity. He was
not a good judge of men, he possessed the fatal gift of
literary fluency, and, in his attitude toward men and things,
he reflected the views of Philadelphia society and not at
all those of the "men of the street." Biddle and banking
circles watched with apprehension the rise of Andrew Jackson to the presidency and Biddle somewhat childishly
sought to ingratiate himself with the "Hero of New Orleans."
He might well feel apprehensive because Jackson had experienced to the full many of the evils of banks and of the
sordid character of many monied men. Tennessee and
Kentucky in his lifetime had gone through severe financial
struggles. Banks had come up and failed and relief meas-

---

[1] See E. L. Bogart's "Taxation of
the Second Bank of the United States
by Ohio" in *American Historical Review*, xvii, 312–331. In 1826 Biddle
wrote that the story that the agent
of the Bank in Ohio had threatened a
State official with ruin if he did not
secure the repeal of the hostile legislation was "nonsense."

ures of most questionable character had been adopted. Jackson, himself, had had an unpleasant experience with one of the branch banks which had refused to honor a draft of his except at a discount. In his First Annual Message [1] he called the attention of Congress to the approaching termination of the bank charter and suggested that the question of the continuance of its life should be taken up at an early day. It would seem that the question of recharter or demise was one to be worked out between the bank authorities and the government; but for some inconceivable reason Henry Clay thought that he saw in the question elements of political popularity, and took possession of it for the anti-Jacksonians. Of course this acted as a challenge to Jackson, which was about the worst possible thing that could happen. Biddle certainly did not manage this part of the business with discretion. He permitted himself to be drawn into a somewhat acrimonious correspondence with the Secretary of the Treasury in which he assumed an unjustifiable attitude of independence, and when he realized this, he had to retreat as well as he might; but a man of discretion and experience would never have permitted himself to be placed in so humiliating a situation. For a time, it seemed as if he would overcome Jackson's prejudices. He apparently was willing to accept a good part at least of Jackson's plan for a national bank of some kind provided the prolongation of the life of the existing institution was assured.[2] It was at this point that the politicians interfered and almost compelled Biddle to apply for a recharter in order that the Whigs might have some reason for political existence. This was in 1832 when the election was coming on. More than once Biddle wished to take the other tack

[1] Richardson's *Messages and Papers*, ii, 462.
[2] See the letters in McGrane's *Correspondence of Nicholas Biddle*, 142 and fol., and Catterall's *Second Bank*, 224–228.

and bring it about that the administration itself should pass a rechartering bill that Jackson would sign. But it was all in vain, and the reports of an investigating committee which was known from its chairman's name as the Clayton Committee,[1] while clearing the Bank of financial bad management, brought many things to light that were decidedly disadvantageous to the renewal of the life of that institution. Moreover, it distinctly appears that the resources of the Bank had already been used in ways that must have influenced political opinion, although it is by no means certain that in authorizing these transactions, Biddle had anything of the kind in contemplation. For example, there was a loan of twenty thousand dollars to General Duff Green,[2] the editor of the "Washington Telegraph," whose daughter had married a son of John C. Calhoun. This loan had been made originally, when Duff Green was a Jackson man, to enable him to undertake the public printing, for many preparations and much work had to be done before any payment would be received from the government. The matter was brought before the Bank authorities by Mr. Hemphill, a South Carolina congressman, who stated that the making of the loan would bring about no change in the political opinions expressed by Green's paper. To this Biddle replied that the loan was a mere matter of business and that no change in the newspaper's political attitude was desired. With Calhoun's fall from Jacksonian grace, the paper had turned and it is possible that it was Jackson's finding Duff Green's name among those to whom the Bank

[1] See Clayton's "Report on Behalf of the Majority of the Committee Appointed . . . to Examine into the Proceedings of the Bank of the United States" (*Reports of the Committees of the House of Representatives*, 22nd Cong., 1st Sess., No. 460). The three reports of this committee, that by Clayton and one by McDuffie (p. 297) for the minority, and a third by John Quincy Adams (p. 369) on behalf of himself contain a mass of material which any one who wishes to understand the bank business must read.

[2] *Ibid.*, No. 460, p. 109.

had loaned money that finally determined him to veto the
recharter bill,[1] for was it not evident that the Bank besides
being dangerous in itself was a Calhoun institution? Among
the "Biddle Papers" in Washington are letters showing that
the Bank had loaned forty-three thousand dollars to President
Monroe [2] and on March 1, 1825, three days before his exit
from the White House, had refused to lend him any more.
It also appears that McDuffie, the South Carolina Representative who had signed a report distinctly favorable to
the Bank, had secured a loan for Mr. Hampton, another
South Carolinian who offered his land as security. Biddle
at once replied that the Bank did not habitually lend on
mortgage and that the threat to withdraw the public deposits had induced it to confine its loan to terms of not over
ninety days. Nevertheless in this case the loan would be
made and authority be given to the cashier to renew the
notes as they became due.[3] Another example of the close
connection between the Bank and the politicians was the
case of Daniel Webster, who was Senator from Massachusetts, for three years a director of the Bank, and also
acted as its counsel. Webster was indebted to the Bank
as principal or endorser to the amount of seventeen thousand
dollars, and he asked for a renewal of his retainer as counsel;
but Biddle thought that the time was not opportune for
such "refreshment" and refused.[4] Another loan that has

---

[1] This was the rumor current at New
Orleans. See Vincent Nolte's *Fifty
Years*, 236, 237. There is a good
notice of Duff Green in Southern History Association's *Publications*, vii,
160.

[2] The exact amount was $43,605.97
minus $2500.00. Monroe was to have
reduced this total by the payment of
$1000.00 a month, but had not done
so. In Biddle's memorandum of 1837
(*Correspondence of Nicholas Biddle*,
p. 358) the loan is stated at $10,596, a

large part of it having been taken up
by the sale of Monroe's Virginia
property.

[3] Biddle's letter to McDuffie is
dated August 29, 1833.

[4] Biddle's letter is dated December
25, 1834; but the practice to which
it alluded was evidently of long standing. As Biddle thought the Washington post-office "faithless" he had
his letter addressed by another hand.
Incidentally, he remarked, that he
always burned what he was requested

certain elements of interest in it was one made to Asbury Dickins, Chief Clerk of the Treasury Department. It seems that in 1828 he owed the Bank twenty-five hundred dollars which he could not pay. The cashier of the Washington branch suggested that the demand for payment be not pressed and, indeed, that another twenty-five hundred dollars be loaned to Dickins to enable him to pay off his other debts. The printed correspondence does not say what happened, but the loan was probably made, as Dickins, who had "the management of the Bank accounts" for the Treasury Department, remained most amicably disposed toward the Bank.[1] All these loans, of course, may have been perfectly justifiable, as also may have been absolutely right those to Clay, Crawford, Calhoun, Livingston, Amos Kendall, W. B. Lewis, and J. H. Eaton; but it was inevitable in 1832 and still is that another construction would be placed upon the practice of attaching so many persons in high places to the interests of the institution.[2]

It is difficult to fathom the motives that led Henry Clay and his political companions to stake their success at the polls in the election of 1832 on the question of rechartering the Bank. The struggle between the Bank and the anti-bank men was really a part in the never ending contest between localism and nationalism; the question was as to whether the local banking system should flourish or should be destroyed by the institution which had been chartered by the federal Congress. Moreover, the sympathies of the

to burn. Curtis, in his *Life of Webster*, i, 493–500, devotes several pages to trying to clear Webster's reputation in this regard.

[1] R. C. McGrane's *Correspondence of Nicholas Biddle*, 53.

[2] The names of borrowers are noted in the reports of the Clayton committee and at the end of the *Correspondence of Nicholas Biddle* is a list of the members of Congress, newspaper editors, and officers of the general government "who have been or are responsible to the Bank as drawers or endorsers of notes during the last few years." As this was drawn up in 1837, the amounts and even the names do not always agree with the reports of 1832; but the lessons to be drawn from the different lists of figures are identical.

average man were distinctly opposed to the money lender,
dignify him as you please. The combination between the
localists and the ordinary voter proved to be irresistible.
Jackson received 707,217 votes to 328,561 given to Clay [1]
and two hundred and nineteen electoral votes to forty-
nine for Clay and eighteen for other candidates. As it
was, it was one of the completest victories in the history
of the presidency and impelled Jackson forward to the
prosecution of his design to put an end to the monster
Bank at Philadelphia and all its branches. The campaign
for justice to the Bank had about as much chance of success
as a campaign for "Justice to the Profiteers" of the present
day would have. The fact that they could save a little
on their loans and have a better currency with the Bank
than without it meant nothing to the localists; what they
wanted was that they and their neighbors should enjoy
whatever profits were to be secured from lending money or
loaning credit, and not contribute to the money-bags of
far-off capitalists at Philadelphia and New York.

The election over, Jackson turned his attention to the
next step in the warfare on the Bank; its demise as a national
institution being certain in 1836, by the provisions of the
charter, he seems to have come to the conclusion that its
death agonies would better be prolonged as much as possible in order that the shock to business might be lessened.
He expected to accomplish this by reducing its loanable
funds at once, by not placing any more government money
in the Bank. Moreover, it is not at all unlikely that Jackson, after reading all the evidence that is now accessible
and pondering other facts that were known to him, but
are now inaccessible, should have come to the conclusion

[1] Edwin Williams's *Politician's Manual* (New York, 1834), p. 35. The figures given in Greeley's *Po- litical Text-Book* (p. 239) are somewhat different; — 687,502 for Jackson and 530,189 for Clay.

that the public funds were not safe in the control of Biddle and the Bank men.[1] He proposed, therefore, to stop depositing the government moneys with the Bank and to withdraw in the ordinary course of business the funds that were already there. This turned out to be not so easy as one might have supposed it would be. Ever since the beginning of the government, the Secretary of the Treasury has occupied a peculiar position toward the President and toward Congress. He is nominated by the President, confirmed or rejected by the Senate and, except for the period of the tenure of office act, has been removable by the President. Unlike all other executive officials, however, the Secretary of the Treasury reports directly to Congress at the opening of each session, and his independence of the Chief Magistrate and dependence upon Congress were further accentuated in the charter of the Second Bank by prescribing that he should direct the bestowal of the government funds and, if these were not deposited in the Bank, to state the reasons to Congress.[2] Louis McLane was then Secretary of the Treasury. He was friendly to the Bank, could see no reason to question the solvency of the institution, and apparently thought that in the existing condition of affairs the public money would be much safer in the Bank than anywhere else. As he was a man of very considerable influence, Jackson evidently thought that it was better not to dismiss him. He appointed him Secretary of State in place of Edward Livingston, who went to France as our representative at Paris. McLane's place was given in 1833 to William J. Duane, who knew nothing of finance

---

[1] Jackson is reported as saying to a committee that went from Pittsburgh to Washington to protest against the removal of the deposits that he would never "return the deposits . . . I will protect the morals of the people

— see the large amount of the funds of the government applied to corrupt the press." B. A. Konkle's *Life and Speeches of Thomas Williams*, i, 59.

[2] Catterall's *Second Bank of the United States*, Appendix I, § 16.

or of the conduct of public business, but was the son of the
editor of the "Aurora," whose influence was still supposed
to be important in Pennsylvania. Apparently, Duane
was not informed as to what he was to do when he was
appointed. When he found out that he was expected to
"remove the deposits" and thereby kill the Bank at the
bidding of the President, he refused to obey.[1] He also refused to resign and made it necessary for Jackson to remove him. Jackson then transferred the Attorney General
to the Treasury Department, this time there being full
understanding as to what should be done. This man was
Roger B. Taney, a former Maryland Federalist who had
renounced his earlier political faith and was now a zealous
Jacksonian. Taney was one of the ablest lawyers in the
country, from whose advice Jackson had already profited.
He made no trouble and signed the order directing his
subordinates to cease depositing money with the United
States Bank or its branches on September 26, 1833.[2] He also
signed several drafts on the Bank for considerable sums,
sending them to Baltimore and Philadelphia to be used in
case the Bank should prove to be fractious. One of these
drafts for five hundred thousand dollars was sent to the
president of a Baltimore bank in which Taney himself was
a director. This particular draft was cashed at an early
day and the money used by the president of the Baltimore
bank for speculative purposes. The United States Bank
was naturally compelled to restrict its discounts, as the
withdrawal, gradual though it was, of nine millions of
government deposits could hardly fail to make such action

---

[1] See W. J. Duane's *Narrative and Correspondence concerning the Removal of the Deposites* (Philadelphia, 1838).

[2] Samuel Tyler's *Memoir of Roger Brooke Taney*, 206. For the other side of the story, see Calvin Colton's *Life and Times of Henry Clay* (2nd ed.), ii, chs. iii, iv. Taney's report of December 3, 1833 as to the removal of the deposits forms *House Document*, No. 2, 23rd Cong., 1st Sess.

necessary; but Jackson viewed this proceeding as quite unnecessary and as directed against himself.[1]

The later history of the Bank and its president is not pleasant reading. Biddle secured a State charter calling the new institution the Bank of the United States of Pennsylvania. It seems reasonably certain that this charter was secured by underhand means.[2] As the president of a State bank, Biddle threw caution to the wind and used the funds of the institution for speculative purposes. Had times remained good, these speculations might have succeeded. As it was, in the perilous years from 1837 to 1843, the Bank of the United States of Pennsylvania closed its doors again and again until the latter year, when it closed them forever. Nicholas Biddle, himself, died in 1844, while still in middle life, a broken man.

Whatever its shortcomings, the Second Bank of the United States had performed a very useful work in taking care of the public funds and in transferring the government money to points where it was needed in the transaction of business. The question as to what should be done with the public moneys when there no longer was a monster Bank with its branches all over the country proved to be a difficult matter to adjust. The government itself had no vaults for the storage of bullion or paper money. The only thing to do was to utilize the State banks, and this proved to be a matter of difficulty and of danger. The general idea of politicians was that banks should be of political service

[1] On the other hand, in September, 1833, Biddle described the Jacksonians as "the gang of bankrupt gamblers who now wield the executive power and who are aiming to throw the country into disorder in hopes of plundering during the confusion."

[2] See *Proceedings of the Senate of Pennsylvania, together with the Record of the Testimony . . . of the Alleged* *Attempt to Corrupt the Integrity and Influence the Vote of Jacob Krebs* (Harrisburg, 1836); *Record of the Testimony, Proceedings . . . of an Alleged Attempt . . . Corruptly to Influence and Bribe the Vote of Jacob Krebs, Esq.* (Harrisburg, 1836); and *Report of the Joint Committee of Investigation* (Harrisburg, 1842).

and likewise that successful party men should be of service
to the banks which favored them. In the Northeastern
States there were fairly sound State banks that were officered
and capitalized by Democrats that could be expected to
weather storms of ordinary violence. In the South and
West, however, most of the banks were organized on perilous
foundations and were already transacting business in a
hazardous manner. The government prescribed stringent
conditions as the price of receiving public deposits, but the
selection of the favored banks was distinctly a matter of
politics, like the appointment of treasury officials in Washington and financial officers elsewhere. And it was by no
means an easy task to differentiate between Democratic
banks. The banks selected were as good as could be found,
complying with the requirements of "sound politics" and
willingness to assume the responsibilities attached to the
holding of government funds; but it was inevitable that
these "pet banks," as they came to be called, should make
many bad loans and should loan money with a free hand
to their friends.[1]

The years of Jackson's second administration witnessed
the wildest speculation that had taken place in the United
States up to that time. Everybody was making money
and putting it into lands, banks, roads, canals, railroads,
buildings, factories, and cotton. The speculative activity
was not peculiar to any one part of the country; it obtained
in New England and New York, as well as in Wisconsin,
Tennessee, and Alabama. In New England the money
went into factories; in New York into farms, factories, and

---

[1] The reports of Levi Woodbury,
Secretary of the Treasury, of 1837
and 1841 have much information
about State banking and public deposits. See *House Documents*, 25th
Cong., 1st Sess., No. 2. A portion
of this report without the accompanying documents is printed in his *Writings*, i, 425. The report of 1841 is
printed in full in *ibid.*, i, 432, with the
documents in the "Appendix."

commerce; in Wisconsin into developing lands and mines; in Tennessee and Alabama into lands and slaves for the most part to increase the area of cotton cultivation. Rates for money advanced until in 1836 two and even four per cent a month was not unusual. In such circumstances unscrupulous men always come to the fore, and this time was no exception. "Paper towns" in Wisconsin were sold in New York [1] and Georgia gold mines were capitalized and put on the markets at one hundred or two hundred per cent above their value. New banks were organized and went into wild competition with their neighbors. There was not nearly enough capital in the country to finance these operations. The high interest rates prevailing in New York, Philadelphia, Boston, Charleston, and other commercial centers attracted capital from abroad, especially from England, so that by 1836 the country was heavily indebted to Europe. The reckless speculation in frontier lands aroused Jackson's attention and apprehension. He, himself, had caught something of the fever and had dispatched Alfred Moore to the Southwest to seek out and buy lands adapted to the growing of cotton. On March 6, 1836, Moore reported that the good unimproved lands in Alabama and Mississippi were in the hands of speculators and that the improved lands were held at prices at which it would be ruinous to purchase. For these reasons he had done nothing.[2] The increase of banking capital and loans in this period is startling. In 1830, the banking capital of the country was one

---

[1] On October 13, 1836, J. R. Dorr wrote from Detroit about the sale in New York of lots in the "City of Lafontain" and adds "our Banks will not discount a Dollar." See "M. L. Martin Manuscripts" in the cabinet of the Wisconsin Historical Society.

[2] See Moore's letter in the "Jackson Papers" in the Library of Congress. In the "Biddle Papers" under date of April 22, 1836, there is a letter from Henry Clay introducing his brother Porter Clay of Jacksonville, Illinois, to Biddle with a statement that he had formed "an association . . . to make investments, as agents for others, in the purchase of public lands." This was only one of multitudinous agencies that were operating in the Western country.

hundred and ten millions, in 1837, two hundred and twenty-five millions.[1] Whichever way one looks, one comes upon similar facts all pointing to the increasing strain on credit. Good observers thought that the crash would come in the spring or early summer of 1836; but, although there were great difficulties in that year, they were obviated for the moment.

Jackson and the treasury officials did what they could to stem the tide of inflation which they had partly set in motion by providing the "pet banks" with loanable funds. In April, 1835, the Secretary of the Treasury ordered his subordinates to receive no bank notes of denominations under five dollars. In July, 1836, he issued the "Specie Circular."[2] In this he directed government agents to accept only gold or silver or Virginia script in payment for public lands, except that until December 15 of that year actual settlers buying three hundred and twenty acres or less might pay for them as formerly. This circular stated that it had been issued in consequence of complaints that had been made of frauds, speculations, and monopolies which had been aided by excessive bank credits.

The last act in the Jacksonian financial drama was the distribution of the surplus government revenues to the States. Whether a national debt is a national blessing or not may be doubtful, but it is perfectly certain that a national surplus is a curse. One of Jackson's firmest convictions, in which he followed his great predecessor, Thomas

[1] Benjamin R. Curtis in *The North American Review*, lviii, p. 113.

[2] *Senate Documents*, 24th Cong., 2nd Sess., No. 15. The last paragraph states that the object of the measure was "to repress alleged frauds, and to withhold any countenance or facilities in the power of the Government from the monopoly of the public lands in the hands of speculators and capitalists, to the injury of the actual settlers in the new States, and of emigrants in search of new homes, as well as to discourage the ruinous extension of bank issues, and bank credits." The "Specie Circular" is also printed in Richardson's *Messages and Papers*, x, 104.

Jefferson, was that the national debt must be paid off at the earliest possible moment. Under ordinary circumstances, when this had been accomplished the government revenues could be reduced. But under the Compromise Tariff Act of 1833 the duties collected on imported goods could be reduced only by the amounts provided in the act.[1] The government paid off the final instalment of its debt in 1835, but until the year 1842 could not reduce its revenues to meet the demands of current expenses only. There was likely to be a large surplus in 1837, and what should be done with it was a difficult question. In other times it might have been used to pay for the completion of the Great National Road, or the construction of a line of canals along the coast; but Jackson's veto of the Maysville Bill made any such disposition of the surplus revenues impossible. The only thing that could be done was to deposit it with the pet banks or to distribute it to the States. No one seems to have advocated pouring any more money into the government banks, and there were grave doubts as to whether the Constitution authorized the federal government to collect money to pay over to the States. In the end this particular objection was euphemistically evaded by loaning the money to the States or depositing it with them, — every one being agreed that they would never be asked to pay it back. Another difficult question was how the money should be apportioned, whether it should be by population or by the federal ratio.[2] In the act as passed the latter method was chosen. The surplus funds were to be deposited in quarterly instalments; but when three of these had been made, the Panic of 1837 put an end to im-

[1] See ante, p. 431 and n.
[2] *Statutes at Large*, v, 55. The account in McMaster's *History* (vi, 319 and fol.) is detailed, and the subject is pursued into wearisome lengths in the biographies of Clay and other statesmen of that time and in the works on economic and financial history.

portation and to the surplus. Probably it is not going too far to say that three-quarters of the money paid over to the States in this way was wasted.[1] It does not seem, however, that the "distribution" contributed to bring on the crash of 1837, but it has often been so regarded. One observer, who was not unfriendly to Jackson in the main, declared that the increase of loanable funds due to the Jacksonian financial policy led to the panic and inflicted untold injuries upon the poorer classes — upon those who were least able to bear hardships and who had benefited very little by the inflation of the currency.[2]

The causes of the Panic of 1837 are by no means so simple of ascertainment as our historians have usually held. Jackson's financial misdeeds could not have had much effect in bringing on the crisis, because it was world wide. No doubt the tremendous inflation that had taken place in the United States did contribute materially to make the crisis more severe and more prolonged in America and in Europe. The word "speculation" is a hateful term and is easily used to discredit whatever one does not like. It connotes failure or cessation of development. Investments in lands, buildings, and industry, if they succeed, are included in the phrase "good business judgment" ; if they fail, they are stigmatized as speculation. The primal cause of the crash of 1837 was outside of the United States. The high interest

[1] Edward G. Bourne's *History of the Surplus Revenue of 1837* (New York, 1885) is a very useful compilation from the more accessible sources. The "Report of the Auditor of the State of Ohio, relative to the Surplus Revenue, February 3, 1837" forms Document No. 40 of *Documents, including Messages . . . made to the Thirty-Sixth General Assembly of . . . Ohio* (Columbus, 1837). By this it appears that the Ohio money was paid out to the several counties and by them was loaned to corporations and to individuals at seven per cent interest. Sometimes these loans were secured by mortgage; at other times by "other adequate security" or "personal security." Some of it was used to buy bank stock, some was loaned to transportation companies, and some was loaned to towns to use in erecting public buildings.

[2] See Henry Lee's *Letters to the Cotton Manufacturers of Massachusetts,* 128.

rates paid for the use of capital in America had attracted large loans from England. English capital, moreover, had been freely used to develop manufacturing enterprises at home, and English capitalists in order to finance these operations in Britain and America had drawn upon Europe for support. The earliest demand for the return of funds came from Europe. This impelled the great English banking houses to call upon their debtors for the repayment of funds advanced to them and to refuse to make further loans. This had fallen with heaviest weight on English bankers who were intimately connected with America, and had compelled them to take similar action at New York, Charleston, New Orleans, and other financial centers in America. The pressure from England came at the precise moment when there was already a great strain in America owing to the speculations in western lands and in the enlargement of the area of cotton production. Also a disastrous fire in New York in 1835 had destroyed a large amount of property and created a demand for funds with which to reconstruct. The Specie Circular no doubt drew gold and silver away from the Atlantic financial centers at the moment when British bankers were demanding the return of funds that had been loaned in America. On the other hand, the distribution of the surplus, that came after the crash, may have minimized its effects by providing the banks with loanable funds that would otherwise have been held inactive by the government.

The primal cause of financial disturbances which have followed each other with some degree of regularity may possibly be found in the workings of the forces of nature.[1]

[1] See for varying views, W. S. Jevons's *Investigations in Currency and Finance*, ch. vi; H. S. Jevons in the *Contemporary Review* for August, 1909; H. L. Moore's *Economic Cycles: Their Law and Cause* (New York, 1914); E. D. Jones's *Economic Crises*; Herbert Foster's *Trade Cycles*. The Pe-

Before everything else, human activities depend upon the
production of food stuffs.[1] A succession of bad harvests
reacts upon industry and upon finance. It is an interesting
fact that the crises of 1837 and 1857 synchronized with a
maxima of sun spots. Going back to Benjamin Franklin
and reading his letters to Cadwallader Colden of 1751
and 1752 and his papers on electricity [2] one is struck with
the resemblance between his ideas and the modern theory
of electron. It is not impossible that a diminution of solar
activity influences agricultural production and thus affects
all human activities. At all events the Panic of 1837 was of
world wide extent and the causes underlying it were so
widespread that one can attribute only a very small portion
of it to the financial vagaries of the Jacksonian Democracy.
In these discussions, students seem to have failed to differentiate between accumulated capital and credit. The
amount of accumulated capital at any one time in the
world is only a small proportion of the total amount of capital
used in production. Anything that impairs credit puts a
brake on the forces of productivity ; but the amount of accumulated capital remains practically the same. If this view
is correct, the amount of credit involved in all the enterprises that were going on in the United States in 1836 would
have sufficed to sustain those enterprises, if something had
not impaired its vitality. If these enterprises could have
sustained themselves for a few years, the country would
have caught up with them. And then, instead of condemna-

riodic Rise and Fall in Prices, Wages;
and C. Juglar's *Des Crises Commer-*
ciales et de leur Retour Périodique
(2nd ed., Paris, 1889). Jones's book
has a good bibliography down to 1900,
and later titles may be found in Moore's
Cycles.

[1] A. P. Andrew's "Influence of
Crops on Business in America" in

Quarterly Journal of Economics, **xx,**
323–351.

[2] Franklin's *Works* (Bigelow ed.)
ii, 251, and Franklin's *Works* (Sparks
ed.), v. See on Franklin's electrical
theories John Trowbridge's "Franklin as a Scientist" in the *Publications*
of the Colonial Society of Massachusetts, xviii, p. 1.

tion of speculation and of Jackson, historian after historian
would have marvelled at the sagacity of the Democratic
administration and at the shrewdness of the business men
and cotton growers of that day.

Martin Van Buren[1] had acquired the confidence of Andrew
Jackson in 1828 and years of association had in nowise
diminished it. He was the administration candidate for
President and no other Democrat had the slightest chance
of being nominated or elected in face of the opposition of
"the General." The Whigs, as the anti-democratic party
had come to call itself, put forward as their candidate
General William Henry Harrison of Ohio, a Virginian by
birth, and descendant, so it is said, of the Puritan Major
General Harrison, "the Fifth Monarchy Man" of Oliver
Cromwell's time.[2] They did this in the hope that another
military hero might overwhelm the cool-blooded lawyer of
Kinderhook, as General Jackson had defeated John Quincy
Adams, eight years before. The time was not yet ripe and
Van Buren was elected by good majorities.[3]

In the election of 1836 many new elements came to the
surface of political life. Some of these had been in existence
for years, but Jackson's popularity had then obscured every-

[1] There is no adequate account of
Van Buren's life and services. His
Jacksonian affiliations prejudiced him
with the Northern literary group and
his later anti-slavery convictions deprived him of the favor of the Southerners. Edward M. Shepard's *Martin
Van Buren* in the *American Statesmen*
series is the best book that has yet
appeared, but it is very brief. W. M.
Holland's *Life and Political Opinions
of Martin Van Buren* that was published at Hartford in 1835 is better
than most campaign biographies, and
its "authenticity" was admitted by
Van Buren himself. In later life the
ex-President prepared an autobiography which was published in 1920 by
the American Historical Association
under the editorship of John C. Fitz-
patricks. In 1910 the Library of Congress published a *Calendar of the Papers
of Martin Van Buren* which are in that
institution.

[2] See F. A. Inderwick's *Side-Lights
on the Stuarts* (London, 1891), p. 289.

[3] Van Buren received 170 or 167
electoral votes — as one included or
excluded Michigan — to 73 for Harrison. The popular vote was 761,549
for Van Buren to 736,656 for all
others. *Journal of the House of Representatives*, 24th Cong., 2nd Sess., pp.
357–360, and Greeley and Cleveland's
Political Text-Book for 1860, p. 239.

thing else. Of these the Anti-Masonic faction or party, as it later became,[1] was the most extraordinary and the most important. It grew out of the excitement over the disappearance of William Morgan, who was on the point of betraying Masonic secrets or had betrayed them. There is much doubt as to the story, but the exactness or inexactness of this detail or that is of slight consequence. The important fact was the discovery that in New York — and in some other States as well — practically all the State office-holders, including the judges, were Masons. So powerful was the order that it seemed to be impossible to ascertain the truth as to anything where a Mason was involved, or to bring any of them to justice. No doubt there was a great deal of exaggeration. As one man expressed it, anti-masonry was "a moral and political cholera." Nevertheless, the hue and cry against masonry gave a rallying point for discontented Democrats and Whigs. Another group of the politically restless was composed of radical reformers who suddenly came into prominence in 1836 and flourished so luxuriantly in some localities for short spaces of time that they caused dismay to regular party leaders. These people were called Loco-focos.[2] Then there were the labor candidates, but these were not formidable. The Loco-focos and the Anti-Masons were strong in New York and the perturbations and hopes of the politicians of that State were correspondingly strong. Van Buren was himself a good deal of a radical, but the Democratic party was distinctly conserv-

[1] See Note at end of chapter.

[2] See William Trimble's "Diverging Tendencies in New York Democracy" in *American Historical Review*, xxiv, 396–421, and the books therein cited, especially F. Byrdsall's *History of the Loco-Foco or Equal Rights Party*. The disreputable political scandal of the day has been preserved in *The Jeffersonian*, a paper that was edited by Horace Greeley and published at Albany in 1838. The Loco-focos attained this name through having provided themselves with loco-foco or self-igniting matches and also with candles to foil a plot by the regulars to destroy their meeting by turning out the lights.

ative. In the upshot, and largely because of his promise to follow in the footsteps of President Jackson, Van Buren was elected in 1836, but it was inevitable that the forces of unrest should gather around the opposition party in the next four years.

Van Buren was scarcely comfortably installed in the White House, when the panic swept over the country: everywhere the banks closed their doors,[1] the imports fell off, and with them the customs revenues and the dwindling receipts from the land offices stopped altogether. When three of the four instalments of the distribution had been made, the treasury was wholly empty and the government was unable to pay the salaries of the clerks in the departments. The Specie Circular had greatly diminished the demand for the notes of the "pet banks" and had also greatly lessened their business. The deposit of the surplus revenue had been badly managed. It would have been possible for the States to enter into some arrangement by which the federal money which they received could have been slowly transferred from the "pet banks" to the institutions that were used by the States or to the State treasuries. As it was, the depository banks were obliged to curtail credits and hold funds inactive in their vaults when they would have been usefully employed outside. The question at once came up for decision at Washington as to what could be done with the funds that were slowly dribbling in. They could not be deposited in the "pet banks," for many of them had closed their doors and most of the rest were preparing to do likewise and, of course, the successor of Jackson could not direct the deposit of

---

[1] F. H. Elmore, writing from Charleston on April 13, 1837, describes second hand "the crashing of the merchants [at New York]. The accounts are awful and every hour adds to the spread of ruin." "Elmore Papers" in Library of Congress.

federal money in the Biddle Bank at Philadelphia or in the undemocratic banks of the Northeast. The only thing that could be done at the moment was to direct the receivers of public funds to care for them as well as they could. When Congress met in the autumn in special session, Van Buren greeted it with a message advocating the establishment of a treasury system entirely independent of the business of the country.[1] In the future, according to this plan, all moneys, as they came in, should be deposited in the treasury at Washington, in the vaults of the mints at Philadelphia, New Orleans, or Dahlonega, or in subsidiary treasuries in the principal importing cities where vaults would be built. The Whigs fought the scheme with all their strength, but in 1840 there was a sufficient administration majority in Congress to pass the acts necessary to establish the Independent Treasury system. There were several weak points in the plan. While the necessary vaults were being constructed, it would have been perfectly feasible to deposit the federal monies in the vaults of existing banks where they could be held and drawn upon by the government without being in any way made the basis of loans. The act forbade the treasury officials to make any use whatever of the existing banking institutions. They could not receive the notes of any of them or receive payment in the form of drafts on them. In 1837 the government asked for authority to issue treasury notes to tide itself over the period until customs revenues should again begin to come in. This authority was granted and the country saw a government

[1] Message of September 4, 1837 (Richardson's *Messages and Papers*, iii, 324). It is interesting to read that Jefferson on December 13, 1803, had already suggested that the government should hold its own funds — "letting the treasurer give his draft or note for payment at any particular place which, in a well-conducted government, ought to have as much credit as any private draft, or bank note, or bill, and would give us the same facilities which we derive from the banks." *Writings* (Memorial ed.), x, 439.

that had recently been depositing millions with the States incurring new debts to pay its everyday expenses.

As one year succeeded another, the financial condition of the country did not improve, except, of course, in some localities and then only for brief periods. Some of the banks, especially in the Northeastern States, resumed specie payments after a few months, but most of them were again compelled to suspend. This process of alternately paying and not paying went on until many banks closed their doors forever. In this time of stress, people naturally laid the cause of their troubles upon the existing administration. It was the Whigs' opportunity; but instead of selecting their real leader, Henry Clay, to lead them to victory when victory was fairly certain, they again brought forward the "Hero of Tippecanoe," General William Henry Harrison. Undoubtedly there was a certain glamour surrounding a successful military personage and, possibly, the discontented would not have ranged themselves behind the banner of Henry Clay. For the candidate for the vice-presidency, the Whigs turned to John Tyler of Virginia, one of the few anti-Jackson Democrats to be found in the country.[1] The campaign began sluggishly until a Harrisburg politician chanced upon an ill-natured jibe of a Baltimore editor to the effect that if Harrison were given two thousand dollars a year, a log cabin, and a barrel of cider he would be perfectly happy for the rest of his life. The Harrisburger went at once to a sign painter and had him paint a log cabin and the accessories and paraded it before the ratification meeting that was held at that place.[2] The suggestion aroused en-

[1] Among the innumerable publications of the campaign may be mentioned *The Northern Man with Southern Principles* and *The Rough-Hewer*. The latter was published at Albany from February 20, 1840, to December 24 of that year. It purported to up-hold the principles of Jefferson: the first numbers were dignified in tone, but as the campaign progressed the tone became scurrilous.

[2] Richard S. Elliott's *Notes taken in Sixty Years* (St. Louis, 1883), p. 120.

thusiasm and thereupon began a campaign of "Hurrah!" and unreason that has never been paralleled in the United States. Log-cabins with a table and a jug of cider, with a coon skin nailed on the door, and a representation of the General sitting by and drinking out of a gourd, were dragged through the streets by thousands of men wearing "wide-awake" or soft broad-brimmed hats instead of the more formal stiff top hats that were now fitting only for Democratic aristocrats like Van Buren, who sat in a stuffed chair in the President's Palace and used a gold spoon wherewith to take his food. As the marching men proceeded, they burst into song,[1] the favorite being "Tippecanoe, and Tyler, too" to the tune of "The Little Pig's Tail":

> Tippecanoe and Tyler too,
> Tippecanoe and Tyler too!
> And with them we'll beat little Van, Van, Van,
> And with them we'll beat little Van —
> Oh! Van is a used-up man!

When the votes were counted, it was found that Harrison and Tyler, too, had been elected by large majorities in the popular vote and in the electoral vote.[2]

On March 4, 1841, President Harrison delivered his inaugural and took up his residence in the White House. Thousands had come to Washington to greet him and to secure

---

[1] Elliott's *Notes*, 125. A good account of the choral aspects of the campaign is C. B. Galbreath's "Song Writers of Ohio" in *Ohio Archæological and Historical Quarterly*, xiv, 62. Among the effective means of arousing enthusiasm was the propulsion of a gigantic ball by the campaigners from town to town and from State to State, accompanied by song: "Hail to the ball which in grandeur advances." According to Joseph H. Choate, the winning campaign cry was Harrison and "Two dollars a day and roast beef." E. S. Martin's *Choate*, i, 52.

[2] Harrison received 234 electoral votes to 60 for Van Buren. The popular vote was 1,275,011 for Harrison to 1,122,912 for Van Buren. It is worth noting that in addition James G. Birney, the abolitionist candidate, received 7059 votes. *Journal of the House of Representatives*, 26th Cong., 2nd Sess., pp. 251–254 and Greeley and Cleveland's *Political Text-Book for 1860*, p. 239.

offices, for the "rascals" were to be turned out and good men and true, who had voted the Whig ticket, given the jobs. The office-seekers filled the boarding houses and overflowed into the public spaces and some of them even slept in the doorways of the President's Palace. One of these office-seekers, who had played an important part in the election, went to Washington to see what he could get. He was well known and well recommended. Making little headway in his quest, he, too, sought out the President, was received graciously by him, and invited to dinner. The opportunity seemed to have come, but the President managed the conversation so skilfully that no mention of office was made during the whole time. However, this particular applicant ultimately procured an Indian agency from which there seemed to be hope of gain and departed with a somewhat different idea of the simple-minded old general than that with which he had entered the capital city.

In a month President Harrison was dead and, for the first time in our history, a Vice-President succeeded to the chief magistracy. The precise place that John Tyler ought to hold in our annals is very difficult to determine.[1] He certainly had the courage of his convictions, having opposed Jackson when such opposition meant apparently the loss of political position. He made so many enemies and we know so little of his inner life that one cannot say whether he was a high-minded man of principle or a weak-minded Virginian who broke his word for the hope of election to the presidency in 1844. The story, so far as it is known, is a simple one. Clay and the Whigs carried through Congress a bill to

[1] The family view is given in Lyon G. Tyler's *Letters and Times of the Tylers*. Armistead C. Gordon's *Address* at the dedication of the Tyler Monument in 1915 presents the Virginian estimate in brief and readable form.

charter a new national bank which lacked some of the objectionable features of the older ones, but when the bill was presented to Tyler he vetoed it. Then another bill was prepared, this time embodying what it was understood Tyler would approve; but it too was vetoed. Probably the exact truth in the matter has never been stated and possibly it never can be,[1] for subterranean negotiations are very difficult to trace and also many documents perished in the four years of the War for Southern Independence. The Whigs broke with the President, and the extraordinary spectacle was to be seen of a President without a party and an overwhelmingly victorious party without any control of the Executive which it and misfortune had placed in the chief magistracy. For the next few years the treasury got on as well as it could without any formally organized system of holding the national funds. In 1846, in the time of President Polk, the independent treasury system was reestablished and continued for over sixty years in vigorous operation, — until it was replaced in part by the Federal Reserve scheme of tying the whole banking organization of the country to the government at Washington.

[1] The anti-Tyler side comes out strongly in the "Diary of Thomas Ewing" in *American Historical Review*, xviii, 97-112.

NOTE

Anti-Masonry. — Henry Gassett prefixed an elaborate arraignment of Masonry to his *Catalogue of Books on the Masonic Institution in Public Libraries of Twenty-eight States of the Union* (Boston, 1852). The two sides of the controversy may be best seen in William L. Stone's *Letters on Masonry and Anti-Masonry* (New York, 1832) and John Quincy Adams's *Letters on the Masonic Institution* (Boston, 1847). Stone's book is really an answer to letters that Adams had written in 1831 which are collected and printed in the second of these volumes. William Morgan's *Illustrations of Masonry* published by David C. Miller in 1827 is sometimes attributed to Morgan. The second edition is a good deal fuller than the earlier one. Henry Brown's *Narrative of the Anti-Masonick Excitement* that was published at Batavia, New York, in 1829, and the *Narrative of the . . . Kidnapping and Presumed Murder of William Morgan* that was printed at Brookfield in 1827 give that contact with the actualities of the day that is so interesting to the historical student. Charles McCarthy's "The Antimasonic Party" in American Historical Association's *Report* for 1902, vol. i, 365–574, brings together modern information on the subject and has an excellent bibliography.

CHAPTER XV

WESTERN LANDS AND SETTLEMENTS AFTER 1840

In 1840 the population of Transappalachia was nearly seven millions; by 1850 this had increased to over ten and one-half millions and by 1860 to more than fifteen millions. Before 1840 the immigration from abroad had been small in comparison with the total population of the United States at that time or with the immigration of the next twenty years.[1] In the decade ending with September, 1829, only 128,502 foreign immigrants were noted by the officials; in the ten years ending June 1, 1840, over one-half million of them arrived in the United States. In the next decade the number rose to over one and one-half millions, and in the ten years ending in 1860 the number had risen to nearly three millions. In 1840 there could not have been many over three-quarters of a million persons of foreign birth in the country,[2] but by 1860 this number had risen to over four

[1] The figures in the text are taken from William J. Bromwell's *History of Immigration to the United States* (New York, 1856), p. 175; the *Census* of 1860, i, pp. xix, xxix; and Edward Jarvis's *History of the Progress of Population of the United States*, p. 9. Similar figures may be deduced from the *Statistical View . . . A Compendium of the Seventh Census*, p. 122. Jesse Chickering (*Immigration into the United States*, Boston, 1848) gives tables of the foreign passengers arriving according to the custom house returns. There can be little question but that all the estimates based on these returns are defective and much under the actual numbers. In

1872 Dr. Jarvis, using European emigration reports and estimating the number of natives of the British provinces who had come into the country by land, determined the number of immigrants arriving in the United States in the ten years ending in 1830 as 200,000, instead of 143,439 as given by Bromwell and repeated in the *Census* of 1860 (p. xix).

[2] In 1869, Friedrich Kapp estimated that in 1850 the descendants of the white and free colored population of the country in 1790 would have amounted by natural reproduction to 7,355,423. The population of the United States then, exclusive of slaves, was 19,987,563. From this it would

millions. Of the immigrants who came in the years before
1850 about one-half of them had remained in or near the
port of debarkation. A few of the new-comers sought the
Far South, but the great mass of those who did not stay on
the Northern seaboard could be found in the Old Northwest
and in the country just across the Mississippi.[1] In the
decade after 1850, the immigrants came in different proportions from different countries, but, after their arrival
in the United States, they went the same ways.

Of the groups of foreigners who came to the United
States,[2] the Scandinavians left their northern homes mainly
because of economic pressure, but religious beliefs had something to do with the migration of many of them. It was in
the year 1825 that the sloop *Restaurationen* sailed from
Stavanger for New York and in just under one hundred
days entered the latter port. She left Norway with fifty-
two passengers on board and reached New York with fifty-
three, for a child had been born on the voyage. These first
Norwegian pilgrims settled at Kendall in New York State
and cultivated their farms there for the rest of their lives;

appear that foreign immigrants since
1790 and their descendants numbered
in 1850, 12,632,140. Probably Kapp
underestimated the proportion of children born in new communities (see
his "Immigration" in *Journal of
Social Science* for 1870).

[1] The information on these subjects in the *Censuses* of 1830, 1850,
and 1860, and in the several com-
pendiums compiled from them, is
somewhat vague and not at all easy
to handle; but the following figures
have been compiled and are printed
here for what they are worth. In
1830 the total foreign population of
Transappalachia was 10,313. Of this
8005 were in the Old Northwest; in
1850 the total number had risen to
800,742, of whom 566,310 were in the
Old Northwest and Wisconsin and
Iowa. In 1860 the total number was

1,952,332. Of these no less than
1,451,905 were in the Old Northwest,
Wisconsin, Iowa, California, and Nevada; there being no fewer than 146,528
foreigners in California in that year.

Various means were tried to restrain immigrants from going to
Transappalachia; among them was the
issuing of a pamphlet entitled *To
Persons Inclining to Emigrate to
America* which showed the advantages of western Pennsylvania in
comparison with "the dangers of the
middle West."

Caroline E. MacGill has an interesting study of foreign immigration to
the Southern States in *The South in
the Building of the Nation*, v, 595, with
a list of books at the end.

[2] Rasmus B. Anderson's *First Chapter of Norwegian Immigration*, 54–
131.

but their descendants are scattered widely over the country, although few of them can be found south of Mason and Dixon's line. The letters that the "sloop" party wrote to their friends and former neighbors in the old land were copied and passed from house to house, being read by hundreds of persons. It was some time before the settlers in New York had much to write about their new homes, but by 1836 Norwegians and Swedes by the hundreds and thousands sailed across the Atlantic, passed through New York and over the Lakes to Illinois and Wisconsin. Some of them and many of their descendants went farther west, even to the Pacific. This later movement was greatly accelerated by the publication of Ole Rynning's "True Account of America for the Information and Help of Peasant and Commoner." [1] Rynning had come to America in 1837 and had settled with his party at Beaver Creek to the southward of Chicago, in Illinois. They suffered greatly from malaria, and most of those who survived removed to other parts of the State. Rynning's little book was written when he had been in America only eight months, but it was the work of a keen observer. The United States, so he wrote, was more than twenty times the size of Norway and contained all kinds of lands. It was so extensive that there was no danger of immediate over-population and the Americans welcomed industrious and moral people. Land could be easily obtained and, when paid for, belonged absolutely to the purchaser. There were many speculators who were accustomed to lie in wait for the stranger and cheat him. There is no king in the United States; but there is a man called "president," who "exercises just about as much

---

[1] This was printed at Christiania, in 1838, and is translated in full with a valuable introduction by T. C. Blegen in *Minnesota History Bulletin*, ii, No. 4, pp. 221–269. See also R. B. Anderson's *First Chapter of Norwegian Immigration*, 202–218.

authority as a king." There are laws and government and authorities in America, but everyone is free to engage in any honorable occupation and to go wherever he wishes without a passport. The author declared that he knew several bachelors, each of whom had saved two hundred dollars clear by ordinary labor in one year's time. Rynning's book and other accounts in writing and in print led to a greatly increased migration from Scandinavian lands after 1840.

The Norwegians and the Swedes came in groups composed of families that had lived as neighbors in the old land. At first the members of each group lived together; but their descendants scattered far and wide over the country north of the State of Arkansas. In later years more of them have remained in the Eastern States, especially in New York and in Massachusetts.[1] Of all the groups or colonies that came out from Sweden, none has attracted more attention than the community which followed Eric Janson to the New World and named their settlement Bishop Hill from Bishopskulla, his birthplace. Like some other religious enthusiasts, Janson believed that he represented Christ and that the glory of his work would "far exceed that . . . accomplished by Jesus and his Apostles."[2] In Sweden the Jansonist or Devotionalist movement at first attracted little attention. As its followers increased in numbers, persecution began and waxed stronger and stronger until they determined to migrate to America. To do this they were obliged to combine their worldly goods to provide for the emigration of the poorer families, but communism was not

[1] Kendric C. Babcock's *Scandinavian Element in the United States* (University of Illinois, *Bulletin*, xii, No. 7). There is a valuable bibliography at the end of this essay. G. T. Flom's *History of Norwegian Immigration to the United States* has some interesting tables in Appendix I, showing the growth and distribution of the Scandinavians.

[2] Michael A. Mikkelsen's "The Bishop Hill Colony" in *Johns Hopkins Studies*, x, No. 1, p. 25. At the end is a list of books on this settlement. See also W. A. Hinds's *American Communities* (ed. 1908), 340–360.

a part of Janson's religious plan. The Devotionalists began to arrive at New York in 1846. They slowly and painfully made their way thence to Henry County, Illinois, — some of them going on foot the greater part of the way. A part of Janson's plan was to convert all mankind to the blessings of the new dispensation. At once some of the younger men, filled with missionary zeal, set to work to learn English and soon departed from Bishop Hill to spread the new faith. After the Devotionalists had been in the country two or three years and were beginning to see some prosperity ahead of them, Janson was murdered by an American convert who had married a cousin of the prophet and later wished to abandon the faith and take his wife with him. She declined. Janson supported her in her refusal and the husband killed him. For a time the affairs of the colony prospered; but then misfortunes came upon the community and eventually the Bishop Hill colony went into the hands of a receiver.

The German migration to our country began in colonial days.[1] There were the Palatines, the Mennonites, and others who settled in Pennsylvania and Virginia and elsewhere. They and their children fought on the American side in the Revolution while their cousinry from Hesse Cassel and other German states fought for their British employers. After the Revolution, the Germans began coming again, but the history of the movement is indistinct before 1830. The statisticians assert that in the preceding ten years 6761 Germans and Prussians arrived in the United States by sea; but this number is too small. It probably does not include those who came by way of Quebec, or those who landed in Texas before annexation to the United States.[2]

---

[1] For books on the German migration, see Note I at end of the chapter.

[2] See Moritz Tiling's *German Element in Texas*, 125.

After 1830, the German migration greatly increased, and in the five years beginning with 1850 no fewer than 654,251 immigrants from German lands disembarked at United States ports.[1]

Individual Germans and some families had come to Texas before 1830. The first movement of any size began after the revolutionary activities in France, which filled many Germans with radical ideas, and it was stimulated by the publication in 1829 of Gottfried Duden's "Reise nach den westlichen Staaten Nordamerika's." [2]   Princes, dukes, and other German potentates arrested and imprisoned the radicals in their principalities and dukedoms, and those who escaped found it desirable to emigrate. Thereupon they hit upon the idea of founding a "German State" in the United States. It would have to be a member of the Union, but its existence would "assure the continuance of German customs, German language and create a genuine free and popular life . . . in order that a German republic, a rejuvenated Germany may arise in North America." Others had larger ideas and suggested founding several States which would be predominantly German in character and in language; and, if this were found to be impossible, would secede.[3] Emigration societies were formed in Germany and colonies were sent out to the newer parts of the United States and thousands of individuals came with their wives and children on their own resources. The societies died after a few years, and the settlers, while living together in towns or communities to a very great extent, gave up all expectation

[1] See Bromwell's *Immigration to the United States*, 177.
[2] K. F. W. Wander's *Auswanderungs-Katechismus . . . für Auswanderer . . . nach Nordamerika* that was published at Glogau in 1852 gives one an idea of what a German emigrant of that time was expected to do. An interesting account of the Germans, themselves, is in F. L. Olmsted's *Journey Through Texas* (New York, 1857) ch. iii.
[3] See Moritz Tiling's *German Element in Texas*, 15, and books cited therein.

of founding a distinctively German State. Probably Wisconsin came near to answering their expectation.[1] The climate there was suited to them and the conditions of agriculture were not unlike those of the Fatherland. In the period treated in this volume, the German immigrants were farmers for the most part; but in later times they gathered into certain cities until some of them, as Milwaukee, became practically German communities. Many of the Germans took an active part in local politics and some of them rose to eminence in the national government. In 1848 there was another revolutionary epoch in Europe. Again the movement was unsuccessful in Germany and led to a renewed migration, this time on a very large scale. Although the Germans never achieved the early ideal of founding a distinctively German State, they preserved their language and national customs by the formation of societies for social and cultural purposes, many of which have had long and vigorous lives.

Of all the German societies that were formed for the purpose of encouraging emigration to America, none was more interesting than the "League of the Nobility" or the "Mainzer Adelsverein." It was founded in 1842. The Duke of Nassau was honorary president, and among its twenty-one noble members were the Prince of Leiningen, Prince Frederic William of Prussia, the Prince of Solms-Braunfels, and Count Carl von Castell. Two members of the society came to Texas on a prospecting tour in 1842 and having secured a grant of land returned to Germany. The princely promoters then fell into the hands of unscrupulous speculators who sold them temporary rights of preëmption that were

[1] Kate A. Everest (afterwards Mrs. Levi) has studied the German immigration to Wisconsin with great care and embodied the results in three papers: in *Transactions* of the Wisconsin Academy, vii, 289; Wisconsin State Historical Society's *Collections*, xii, 299 and xiv, 341.

bought by the Germans on the supposition that they were grants in fee simple. In 1844 three vessels brought from four hundred to seven hundred Germans to Texas with their household goods. Prince Solms had preceded them and had made the unpleasant discovery that their land grant was already forfeited by reason of not having been used within the specified time. There was plenty of unoccupied land in Texas, however, and the authorities were eager for hard-working colonists. Slowly and painfully, the Germans made their way from Galveston to the interior. And in the next few years they were joined by at least six thousand more new-comers from the Fatherland. They had understood that the Adelsverein would provide for them until they could shift for themselves, but they were left practically to their own resources. Then came the Mexican War, which necessarily disturbed the ordinary course of colonization in Texas, and epidemics due to climatic changes and the turning up of the virgin soil also attacked the colonists. One thousand of them are said to have died in one year, and the Adelsverein went into bankruptcy and dissolved. A beginning had been made, and the Texas settlements continued to attract thousands of other Germans, and in 1850 they and their children are said to have formed one-fifth of the total white population of that State.[1]

In 1850 there were more than two million foreigners in the United States and in 1860 almost double that number.[2] In both years the immigrants from the British Empire greatly outnumbered those from the rest of the world ; but in each year the Germans greatly outnumbered those from the non-British countries. Of the new-comers from the

[1] German writers give this proportion : see Moritz Tiling's *German Element in Texas*, 125, and Gilbert G. Benjamin's *Germans in Texas*, 59. It is difficult to reconcile this with the figures of the *Census* of 1850, which gives the total German "born" in Texas as 8191.

[2] *Census* of 1860, "Population," p. xxviii.

British Empire, numbering nearly a million and a half in 1850, not quite one million had come from Ireland. Of the non-British immigrants and non-Irish immigrants, more than half a million were listed as of German birth in 1850 and more than one million and a quarter in 1860. It is easy to see from these figures that Irish and German immigrants formed the great mass of the foreign-born population of the United States in this period.[1] It will not be out of the way to note, perhaps, that in 1850 there were 758 persons

[1] SELECTED FOREIGN NATIONALITIES IN THE UNITED STATES IN 1850

SECTIONS	GREAT BRITAIN (ENGLAND, SCOTLAND, WALES)	IRELAND	GERMANY	SCANDINAVIAN LANDS (NORWAY, SWEDEN, DENMARK)
Atlantic seaboard north of Potomac	230,942	745,605	241,830	2,731
Atlantic seaboard so. of Potomac incl. District of Columbia . . .	9,509	22,714	10,693	234
Transappalachia, north of Ohio R. and east of Miss. R.	107,568	126,608	222,590	12,825
Transappalachia, south of Ohio R. and east of Miss. R.	7,221	17,673	16,907	179
Transappalachia, west of Miss. R., north of Arkansas to 109th meridian	11,578	19,890	51,645	870
Transappalachia, west of Miss. R. and south of Missouri to 109th meridian	6,425	26,475	26,429	818
Pacific Slope west of the 109th meridian . .	5,850	2,754	3,131	418
Totals	379,093	961,719	573,225	18,047

Besides the above enumerated immigrants from the British Empire, there were 147,711 from British America, most of whom probably were born within the dominions of the British king. The total number of all foreigners in the United States, including those enumerated above, in 1850 was 2,210,839. Of these 1,690,699 were in the States north of the Potomac and Ohio rivers and east of the Mississippi, and 85,130 south of the Potomac and Ohio rivers and east of the Mississippi River.

of Chinese birth in the country and that this number had risen to 35,567 in 1860.

The English, the Scots, and the Welsh were impelled to migration by economic distress, with the exception of those who followed Mormon missionaries to the New World and those who belonged to the Shakers or to some other of the sects. They spread all over the country. Some of them went to the South. Many of them went to Wisconsin and other Northwestern States, but possibly one-quarter of the whole number remained within the limits of the State of disembarkation. They were drawn to Wisconsin by the opportunities for farming there and by the mineral wealth of the southwestern part of the State. It is said that no less than seven thousand Cornish people settled around Mineral Point before 1850.[1] Of the farmers there was one named Samuel Skewes who came from the southern part of England. He sailed from Falmouth to Quebec, paying three pounds passage money for each member of his family. Arrived at Quebec, he left for Montreal on the steamboat and thence to Toronto and Lewestown. From that place he went by "rail carrs" to Buffalo and there took another steamer to Racine. The total time consumed on the journey from England to Wisconsin was two months and seven days. The Canadian route by Quebec was much frequented in those years in the months when the St. Lawrence was free from ice. Skewes had friends in Racine and in the neighboring town of Yorkville. He appears to have been a man of some means, as he at once acquired improved land and bought more unimproved land from the government. He prospered from the start and soon became a substantial

[1] T. S. Allen's *Directory of the City of Mineral Point for the Year 1859* contains an interesting historical sketch and some illustrative statistics and advertisements. The form of government of an early settlement in Wisconsin may be understood by reading the *Act of Incorporation . . . of Mineral Point* which was printed at that place in 1855.

citizen of his new home. Samuel Skewes must have been typical of the English farming class, but there are very few diaries that have been preserved that give us so interesting a picture as does his.[1]

A group of English settlers, who also came to Wisconsin, offers another study, fully as interesting, but very different. This enterprise was set on foot by the "British Temperance Emigration Society" which was organized at Liverpool, England. Apparently it was a money-making venture with philanthropic aspirations. There was stock which was subscribed for and the emigrants expected to pay rent for their lands in America as people paid rent for their farms in England. The Society, or some of its leading men, seem to have tried to cultivate the soil of the New World while they themselves lived in England. This colony was located at Mazomanie in Dane County, to the northwestward of Madison and not far from it. The first settlers came out in 1843, each one having eighty acres allotted to him. In the next eight years, about six hundred persons came to the settlement from twelve English counties, from Wales, Scotland, and the Isle of Man. They at once began to find fault with the scheme of rent paying, for no one around them paid rent. There was litigation between the company's agents and the farmers, and the later history of the enterprise is uncertain; but the Temperance Society was still in existence in 1851.[2]

There were many Irish men and women in America before the Revolution and they played their parts in that move-

---

[1] "Diary of Samuel Skewes, 1839 to 1870" (Mss.) in the cabinet of the Wisconsin Historical Society.

An interesting and much more elaborate account of a migration is to be found in "The Letters of Edwin Bottomley, 1842–1850" (Wisconsin State Historical Society's *Collections*, xxv).

[2] Manuscripts of the British Temperance Society are in the Library of the Wisconsin Historical Society. See also William Kittle's *History of the Township and Village of Mazomanie* (Madison, 1900).

ment; but the great Irish migration began in the 1840's and continued as prosperity or adversity visited the land of their birth or the country to which they came. The famine in Ireland in 1847 [1] and the following years has been ascribed to various causes, as the Union of 1800 and an excess of rainfall. Local sources of relief were speedily exhausted and England could do little for the sufferers because she also was in distress. As the months went by, beggars crept through the streets and lanes of the Irish towns; the starving and penniless lay half naked in their fireless and foodless cabins, counting the days to the inevitable death; and in no long time the dead became so numerous that they were laid away between two boards wound about with ropes of straw. There was nothing for the survivors to do but to leave the land of their birth and those who could did so. In 1841 the population of Ireland was a little over eight millions; in ten years time it had dropped to six and a half millions. [2] In 1840 there came to the United States 40,642 persons from the United Kingdom of Great Britain and Ireland. Ten years later in 1850 there were living in the United States 961,719 immigrants of Irish birth. [3] Unlike the English, the Germans, and the Swedes, the Irish came as individuals and families; there was no occasion for them to form themselves into colonies and communities, because their race and religion bound them together indissolubly. Some Irishmen took up farming lands in the West; [4] others

[1] See Asenath Nicholson's *Annals of the Famine in Ireland, in 1847, 1848, and 1849* (New York, 1851).

[2] J. D. B. DeBow's *Compendium of the Seventh Census*, 124, and *Census of 1850*, p. xxxvii. P. H. Bagenal (*American Irish*, 28) gives 58,043 Irish arriving in the United States in 1846; 111,984 in 1847; dwindling to 56,328 in 1855. But it is not clear whence the figures came. See also Edward Young's *Labor in Europe and America*, 241. See also Spencer Walpole's *History of England* (ed. 1890), v, 209 *note*, and "The Irish Crisis" in *The Edinburgh Review* for Jan. 1848.

[3] Cardinal Gibbons has an interesting and brief study of the numbers of Irish immigrants in his *Retrospect of Fifty Years*, i, 268 and fol.

[4] See O'Hanlon's *Life and Scenery in Missouri* (Dublin, 1890), ch. xxiv.

settled on vacant acres in the older States; but the great mass of them remained in or near New York, Boston, and Philadelphia. They had no technical skill to speak of or special mental aptitudes, but they had strength of body and the will to work. There was abundant labor for them; but their living together in cities and towns and their strong racial and religious feelings kept them for fifty years or so in the same places and positions that they were in in the first ten years of their coming. In church and politics, only, did the first generation or two shine conspicuously. The Irish have always demanded priests of their own race and everywhere have secured political position and power.

Some of the Germans and Scandinavians came through England, but for the most part they sailed the Atlantic in vessels of German or Scandinavian management and ownership. There were many heartrending stories of misadventure, especially in connection with the navigation of the western Gulf on the way to Texas. For the most part, however, their sufferings were as nothing compared with those of the Irish in the first years of the great migration. The movement caught English ship-owners and English authorities unprepared. Suddenly, tens of thousands of Irish men, women, and children crossed to Liverpool and demanded passage to America. They had no knowledge of the sea and very little money and were accompanied by old people, for their family ties were very strong. They were packed away on shipboard with very slight attention to health and even less to comfort. In the pressing demand for shipping of any kind, unfit vessels were made over for the emigrants and sent out ill-manned and ill-found. The passengers were supposed to provide themselves with food and other necessities, but a great many of them went to sea with very little in the way of food and very poorly supplied with bedding. Some of the vessels were obliged to return to port after weeks of buffeting the westerly gales of the Atlantic. Their cargoes of emigrants were transferred to the first ships that could take the seas, and it was on these that the greatest suffering occurred, for these emigrants were worn down with sickness and want before they started on their final voyage, and it was on these vessels that the "ship fever" found its largest numbers of victims. These conditions led to the passage of laws by the United States and by Great Britain for the regulation of the emigrant trade, and these laws were constantly improved in the next few years.[1] The amounts of deck space and air space were regulated and ship owners were obliged to provide enough food and water to insure the passengers against famine. After 1851 there was much less suffering than there had been and the situation was greatly improved when steamers began to be fitted for the carriage of steerage passengers across the Atlantic Ocean.

From 1825 to 1840 there was a distinct lull in the founding of new communities; but with the beginning of the fifth decade there was a renewed movement. The earlier communities had been primarily religious. With the publication in 1840 of Albert Brisbane's "Social Destiny of Man: or, Association and Reorganization of Industry," the founding of the Hopedale community, and the Brook Farm experiment, an era of gropings for an ideal future of mankind dawned upon the minds of many persons. Brook Farm embodied the aspirations of a band of idealists who

---

[1] Friedrich Kapp in his *Immigration, and the Commissioners of Emigration* (New York, 1870) has set forth with great distinctness the hardships of the voyage and of the first few days in the New World in the 1840's and '50's, as well as later.

The early important laws regulating the transportation of emigrants across the Atlantic were 15 & 16 Victoria, c. 44 (June 30, 1852), and 18 & 19 Victoria, c. 119 (August 14, 1855; *Statutes of the United Kingdom*, xxi, 61; xxii, 796), and the act of March 3, 1855 (*Statutes at Large of the United States*, x, 715).

expected to regenerate the world by establishing a coöperative farm. They were high-minded men and women and some of them possessed great intellectual capacities. They had slight knowledge of agriculture and its adjoining pursuits and their lands were worn out and unfertile.[1] After a few years of spectacular existence, the Brook Farmers became Fourierites and speedily dissolved, owing partly to a conflagration that destroyed their new phalanstery. Another enterprise on somewhat similar lines was Bronson Alcott's little brotherhood at Fruitlands, also in Massachusetts. His theories were akin to those of the "English Christians" who thought it wrong to slaughter animals and eat their carcasses, to drink milk from cows or goats, or to devour the eggs of hens. They hoped that it might not be necessary to employ animals to draw the plough. They set out to do all the work of the farm themselves with spade and hoe, and found competition with near-by farmers, who had no objection to urging forward the laboring ox, a difficult matter. Nevertheless, it is pleasant to think of Alcott and his friends sitting at eve after a toilsome day refreshed with "chaste supplies for the bodily needs" looking across the pleasant valley to the barren hills beyond.[2]

Brisbane drew his ideas from Charles Fourier, a Frenchman, and placed his master's thoughts in a form that men of usual understanding could comprehend. Fourier foresaw with prophet's eye many things that have happened since his death in 1837 : coöperation in buying, coöperation

[1] John T. Codman's *Brook Farm, Historic and Personal Memoirs;* Lindsay Swift's *Brook Farm, Its Members, Scholars, and Visitors;* a list of books is on p. 283. Hawthorne in his *Blithedale Romance* figures his experience at Brook Farm.

[2] For accounts of Fruitlands, see H. S. Nourse's *History of the Town of Harvard,* 275–284; Alcott's reminiscences of Fruitlands thirty years later in Sanborn and Harris's *A. Bronson Alcott,* ii, 385, 386; and Louisa M. Alcott's "Transcendental Wild Oats" in *Silver Pitchers* and in Clara E. Sears' *Bronson Alcott's Fruitlands,* which contains much new matter on this curious experiment.

in production through stockholding in corporations and trusts or otherwise named groups. He clothed his ideas in fantastic phrase and elaborated his illustrations to tiresome and phantasmal extreme. He was regarded as a semblant lunatic — harmless or vicious, according to one's point of view. His followers in America sought to do in 1840 what possibly may be practicable in 1940. Their failure showed their lack of sense and not the insanity of the master or the absurdity of his ideas. Had he written in smooth, didactic phrase with less confidence in his own infallibility, he would have died unhonored and unknown. As it was, he attracted the unprofitable and inefficient, and failure followed every conscious effort to carry out his ideas. He thought that the society of his day was out of joint — man and his environment were out of harmony. As God made man and man made the environment, the way to bring God and man into harmonious association and to use all the forces that God had given man was to change the environment. This he proposed to do by bringing men, women, and children into harmonious action, avoiding waste, and utilizing human desires to bring about greatly increased production with greatly lessened effort. Everywhere, advantage and inequality were to be found in man and beast, but man alone had no joy in the struggle for existence, no love of labor for its own sake. Fourier proposed to substitute the passions of humanity for wages, for as all passions were given to man by God they must be good; at any rate they could not be got rid of. By having every one do the work that was most pleasing to him, and by combining workers in one branch of industry in groups laboring side by side, the spirit of rivalry would be utilized to increase production. By changing employment after an hour or two, the desire for variety would make labor pleasant. By coöperation in housekeeping

great economies of woman's time and of the community's
stores would be effected, and there would be one place in the
world where woman's work would come to a definite diurnal
ending. He wished to eliminate hirelings and middlemen
and the ordinary standards of value. Capital would be
employed and rewarded in inverse proportion to the amount
invested by an individual; the holder of one share getting,
perchance, twenty per cent, while the holder of two hundred
shares would have to content himself with three or four per
cent. Every adult, whether man or woman, possessed the
vote in the Fourier state, but the government was representative. Each industrial group selected its chief and the
"serie," that was composed of groups, chose a representative
to the general governing body; thus the Fourier state
was not a democracy. In 1842, 1843, and 1844 more than
thirty Fourierite communities were established in America,
including the made-over Brook Farm.[1] There were seven
of them in New York, six in Ohio, six in Pennsylvania,
and others scattered over the land. The largest was the
Clarkson Industrial Association of New York, which had
four hundred and twenty members and lived for six months;
one of the smallest was the Marlboro Association of Ohio
which had twenty-four members and lived for four years.
The most successful was the Wisconsin Phalanx at Ceresco,[2]
but the one that we know most about was the North American Phalanx which was founded by New Yorkers in New
Jersey.

Fourier had designed to have his experiment tried by a
large number of persons with a capital of hundreds of thousands of dollars. When the North American Phalanx

[1] Commons and Associates (*History of Labour*, i, 505) speak of "at
least forty" Fourierite organizations
and Hinds gives a list of thirty (*American Communities*, 250). See also Hillquit's *History of Socialism in the United
States* (ed. 1910), ch. iii.
[2] See *Wisconsin in Three Centuries*,
iii, ch. vii.

issued its call for recruits and money, few persons came forward and little money was subscribed; dissatisfied laborers saw little relation between "association" and the adjustment of their grievances, and capitalists saw more profitable use for their money elsewhere. In 1843 the North American Phalanx began the great experiment with only half a dozen families and with less than seven thousand dollars,[1] of which they were obliged to pay five thousand dollars down on account of the purchase of seven hundred acres of land near Red Bank, New Jersey. At the end of three months, the members nearly came to blows over the conduct of their business affairs. At first they were obliged to hire a few working men, but after that they depended entirely on their own exertions. Each year the standard price of the ordinary day's labor was fixed by vote, but those skilled in administration were rated somewhat higher. Easy and attractive work was appraised at the lowest rate and each group assessed the performance of its members, there being no discrimination for sex or age. Every day each person set down on a public card the number of hours he or she had worked. These accounts were footed up monthly, the amount produced by each group was stated and the workers credited on the books of the association with the number of computed hours of labor. They were debited with the cost of lodging and of board and with goods procured at the general store. Before long the mechanics became dissatisfied with the system and declared that the workers of the neighborhood were receiving higher wages, and some of them removed from the Phalanx. Religious troubles also assailed the association. The members were of many sects, and those of their faiths outside, fearing

---

[1] Charles Sears' *The North American Phalanx, An Historical and Descriptive Sketch* (Prescott, Wis., 1886); W. A. Hinds' *American Communities*, 266–275; and Commons' *History of Labour*, ij, 204.

for their souls, visited the community and meeting with a
cold reception held it up to scorn in their papers. In 1855
the enterprise came to a sudden ending with the burning of
the grist mill which was stored with grain that had not been
paid for. When the question of what could be done was
discussed in general meeting it was voted to dissolve.
Brook Farm had broken up in a similar way and the Wisconsin Phalanx at a later time went to pieces almost as
rapidly. In all three cases it was probably discontent with
the life that led to dissolution. For a time ordinary people
can live on enthusiasm and the pursuit of an ideal; but it is
only extraordinary men and women who can keep up the
search for any length of time when others in "The World"
about them are tasting of forbidden fruits or drinks, are
accumulating capital, and are living in leisured luxury.
Besides, a too sheltered existence is irksome to many people,
especially in their early years. They like to contend with
the forces of nature and with their fellow men and women, —
the humdrum life of a community, where one has no thought
for his food or his shelter or his clothing, has slight attrac-
tions for such as these. If the world were thoroughly
fourierized there would be no forbidden drinks, no capitalists, no leisured class, — all would be on a dead level, or
within appreciable distance of it. It is interesting to look
about the world in which one lives and note how far the
law of association has come to be the measure of human
effectiveness, how far, indeed, we have progressed toward
Fourier's seventh state of civilization.

The community of the Inspirationists at Amana, Iowa,[1]

[1] See Bertha M. H. Shambaugh's *Amana, The Community of True In-spiration* (Iowa City, 1908); W. R. Perkins and B. L. Wick's "History of the Amana Society" in the Univer-sity of Iowa *Publications* (Historical Monographs, No. I) is briefer and has a bibliography. Charles F. Noe's "Brief History of the Amana Society" is the work of a member of the so-ciety (*Iowa Journal of History and Politics* for April, 1904).

and the surrounding villages has possessed the longest life of any American society, except the Shakers. The Inspirationists had their rise in eighteenth century Germany and were descended from the Pietists of the century before. They had their own ideas as to religion, were pacifists, and had peculiar beliefs as to education. They found Germany a difficult place to live in and many of them in 1842 removed to New York. Originally they had no communal ideas, but, in order to provide for the emigration of the poorer families among them, the richer were obliged to invest their property in the enterprise. They first settled in the vicinity of Buffalo, but in 1855, having outgrown their quarters there, removed to Iowa, taking ten years to wind up the affairs of one settlement and get the other into prosperous working condition. In 1900 there were seventeen hundred or more Inspirationists in their settlement. They employed a couple of hundred hireling laborers and did a good deal of mechanical work as well as cultivating their lands. They lived in families, although marriage was rather frowned upon, but they ate in common kitchen-houses. Unlike most of the communities, whether religious or not, there were no restrictions on the use of tobacco or alcoholic beverages and women did not hold office.

Another community that has had a long life, although a somewhat checkered one, is the Iowa settlement of the Icarians, as the followers of Etienne Cabet are usually called.[1] Like Fourier, Cabet was a Frenchman, but unlike Fourier, he was an extreme radical. The French Revolution of 1830 did not satisfy him and he was obliged to seek safety in England. In 1840, 'his "Voyage en Icarie" was published. It describes an Utopia where advantage and class injustice were no more. Before long groups of Icarians

[1] For a bibliography, see Note III at end of chapter.

appeared in France, Switzerland, and Germany, and established little communistic societies entirely against the wishes of those in power. Persecutions followed and it was determined to establish a colony in the New World. Cabet's desires were illimitable,—hundreds of thousands of people and large sums of money. Thousands of emigrants joined the movement and there was a substantial amount of capital. At first they thought of trying their experiment in Texas, but after many vicissitudes, in 1849, they pitched upon the deserted Mormon city of Nauvoo as a place of habitation. There the Icarians passed some years of communistic happiness, apparently being guided and governed by Cabet, himself. He then turned the community over to its members and two parties were immediately formed. The minority refused to work and was thereupon deprived of food by the majority. Cabet, himself, was expelled from his own society and died not long after in 1856. For nearly fifty years, bands of Icarians of one party or the other lived in communal settlements in Missouri, Iowa, and California, — for Nauvoo had to be abandoned. Sooner or later all of these settlements became individualized.

The Mormon movement to Utah in some respects was like other religio-communistic enterprises; but in size, success, and permanence, it far outstripped them.[1] Also it deserves

[1] The books on the Mormon migration are innumerable. A list of them preceeds H. H. Bancroft's *Utah* that was printed in 1889. Bancroft in this volume aimed to be fair to both sides, generally putting one side in the text and the other in the foot-note. He and Mrs. Bancroft went to Salt Lake City and personally interviewed some of the leading survivors of the early days and their wives. Nevertheless the work, so far as it is based on these reminiscences, partakes of all the imperfections of such books. An earlier book is Lieutenant J. W. Gunni- son's *The Mormons, or, Latter-Day Saints in the Valley of the Great Salt Lake.* This was published in 1852 and went through several editions. Jules Remy's *Voyage au Pays des Mormons* was published in two volumes at Paris in 1860 and appeared in an English dress in the following year. It is a singularly faithful account. From the Mormon point of view B. H. Roberts's *The Missouri Persecutions* and his *Rise and Fall of Nauvoo* and James A. Little's *From Kirtland to Salt Lake City* may be mentioned. Of the anti-Mormon books Thomas B.

treatment by itself as a leading factor in the acquisition of California, for the routes from the High Plains to the Sacramento Valley led through the Utah Basin, and Salt Lake City became a place of succor for successive bands of gold-seekers and pioneers.   The Mormons at first settled at Kirtland in Ohio, about twenty miles from Cleveland. Thence they went westwardly to the frontiers of Missouri, where they established several thriving settlements.   They aroused the hostility of their neighbors and were driven out in the middle of winter to Iowa.   They then recrossed the Mississippi River to Illinois and built a flourishing town, which they named Nauvoo.[1]   At that place they enjoyed a brief season of peace and prosperity before their neighbors turned upon them.[2]   By this time some of the leading men practiced polygamy, although whether this was known to outsiders is not clear.   The Mormons had their own ministers, settled their disputes among themselves without going to courts of law, and healed their sick by their own methods, — and thereby aroused the jealousies of ministers, lawyers, doctors, and politicians.   They were a "queer" people and the ordinary everyday American has always distrusted queerness in others.   It is probable, also, that the power of the Mormons to accumulate property aroused ill-feeling among the people round about them.   In 1844, Joseph Smith, the Prophet, and his brother Hyrum were

H. Stenhouse's *The Rocky Mountain Saints* and Mrs. Stenhouse's *"Tell It All": the Story of a Life's Experience* and Judge R. N. Baskin's *Reminiscences of Early Utah* will suffice for the needs of most persons.

[1] An interesting contemporaneous account of Nauvoo is in Henry Brown's *History of Illinois* (New York, 1844), pp. 395–403, 487–492. See also, Pooley's "Settlement of Illinois," ch. xii, and the books cited by him.

[2] One of the most interesting of the Mormon off-shoots was the colony that gathered around James Strang on Beaver Island in the Straits of Mackinac. Edwin O. Woods' *Historic Mackinac*, i, ch. xviii; H. E. Legler's *A Moses of the Mormons, Strang's City of Refuge and Island Kingdom;* and *Wisconsin in Three Centuries*, iii, 125–136.

murdered by a mob at Carthage, Illinois. Then followed
months of distressing conflict which compelled the Mormons
to undertake another pilgrimage.

On the death of Joseph Smith and his brother, Brigham
Young seized the reins of authority and until his death led
the Mormon host successfully in peace and in war. As a
"captain of industry" he ranks with the best of them. Somewhat earlier, foreseeing the trend of events, Joseph Smith
had prophesied that the "Saints would be driven to the
Rocky Mountains and would become a mighty people." [1]
He had even organized an expedition to explore that region,
but nothing further had been done before his death.[2] Brigham Young appears to have investigated carefully the routes
leading westward and to have counselled with those who had
already been in the mountains. In the early spring of 1846,
the bulk of the Mormons left Nauvoo and began their westward way, at first over the ice and snow, and then halted until
the growing grass provided food for the cattle, when the
march was resumed. On reaching the Missouri River, a
permanent camp was established not far from the present
Omaha. It was known as Winter Quarters and for some
years was the rallying point for successive Mormon expeditions. Seven hundred log cabins were erected, the lands
were cleared, and food crops raised. Before the end of the
year they were all settled there, but their sufferings in the
following winter were keen, as the roofs of their cabins
leaked and they had insufficient fuel. Often the women's
clothes were frozen stiff and remained so day after day
and one "could hear them rattle as they struck against
anything." [3] While at this place the Mormons entered into

[1] John Taylor's Ms. "Reminiscences," p. 13.
[2] Wilford Woodruff's Ms. "Reminiscences," p. 3.

[3] Mrs. Richards in her "Reminiscences" relates that the log huts at
Winter Quarters were just large enough
to hold two beds and two chairs, and

an arrangement with the federal government by which some five hundred of them enlisted in the "Mormon Battalion"[1] and followed Colonel Kearny to California by way of Santa Fé and thence after a year or so made their way eastwardly through the mountains to the Utah Valley.

In the winter of 1846 and 1847 about twelve thousand people, men, women, and children, old and young, well and sick, were gathered at Winter Quarters and vicinity. In April, 1847, Brigham Young led an advance party westward to find a place of settlement. They went through the South Pass to Fort Bridger and thence through the mountains until they looked down upon the valley of the Great Salt Lake. "This is the place," said Young. At once they picked out a site for their town, staked off the land, and began a system of irrigation.[2] On September 19, 1847, the van of the main expedition with five hundred and eighty wagons and over two thousand oxen besides other animals arrived, and at the end of the year there were four thousand settlers in the valley. The Utah Valley had been visited by trappers twenty-five years and more before, and there were a few settlers living there when the Mormons came. These bought out their rights and at once spread out over the land, taking stations at the mouths of the cañons, thus controlling the water supply of the whole region. Within the next few years the greater part of the fugitives from Nauvoo joined the original settlers in the Utah Valley. From the very beginning of their life as a distinct sect, the Mormons were active in missionary enterprises. They sent their young men and some of their leaders to different parts of

the roof was made of logs covered with marsh flags with the earth spread over them.

[1] See below (p. 586) for books on the Mormon Battalion.

[2] See C. H. Brough's *Irrigation in Utah* (Baltimore, 1898) and Hamilton Gardner's "Coöperation among the Mormons" in the *Quarterly Journal of Economics*, xxxi, 461. A list of books on the subject is in Brough's paper, p. xiii.

the United States and to European countries. They made converts in great numbers and it was difficult to bring them from the western settlements to the Utah Valley. In 1856 there were so many of them that the leaders hit upon the scheme of having the new-comers walk the whole way, drawing their supplies in handcarts. There were five companies in all. The first three fared well enough, but the last two, starting late in the year, did not reach the mountains until the snows began to fall. Many of them perished and the others were rescued by expeditions sent from Salt Lake City. One of the rescuers wrote that when they came upon them they saw "aged men and women, with children of both sexes pulling and pushing their hand-carts through the snow with their clothing wet to their knees." [1] Nearly two hundred and fifty of these two last handcart parties perished on the way. Otherwise, the conduct of the Utah migration was so successful that nature and man appeared to work for them in a way that they deemed miraculous. In 1849, the rush to California began and thousands of gold-seekers passed through the Utah Valley on the way to the Coast. They were generally short of food, but had many things that the Salt Lake people needed, and this gave to the Mormons a profitable market for their surplus grain and meat. From the beginning, Brigham Young set his face most sternly against his people engaging in mining enterprises, for he felt that agriculture was the only sound basis of permanent settlement. Whenever any of his people showed a desire to go to the mines, he told them they were free to go, but could never return. He also declared that it was better to feed the Indians than to

[1] H. H. Cluff's "Overland in Winter," p. 7; Ms. in the Bancroft Library at the University of California. For the use of this and other material in that library, I am greatly indebted to the kindness of Professor Herbert E. Bolton and his able assistants.

fight them, and the Mormons were always singularly free from the usual excitements of frontier life.

The Mormon state was a combination of almost unlimited democracy with an unlimited autocracy. It would appear as if the two elements were incapable of combination in one community, but they certainly seem to have been combined in Mormon Utah. As Prophet, Brigham Young was the direct representative of God to his people, combining in his own person supreme authority in Church and State. The working of the system was well described by the editor of the "Millennial Star" at a later period in 1867. According to him the utmost freedom of speech was permitted in the legislature; "but any measure that cannot be unanimously decided on, is submitted to the President of the Church, who by the wisdom of God decides the matter." [1] As the representative of the Almighty in ecclesiastical and temporal affairs, a man of the business capacity of Brigham Young exercised authority almost unknown in any modern state. The Prophet was assisted by two councillors, and these three with others formed the First Presidency, which was the chief legislative, executive, and judicial body in the community as well as the chief religious body.

At the other end of the line from the Prophet and the First Presidency were the "Bishop" and the "Ward." In early times the latter was the civic and ecclesiastical unit. Most Utah towns comprised one ward, but Salt Lake City had thirteen of them and more. The record book of the Thirteenth Ward has been preserved and deserves careful

---

[1] *The Latter-Day Saints' Millennial Star*, November 23, 1867. I am indebted to Professor Franklin D. Daines of the Utah State Agricultural College for calling my attention to this passage, and for much help in my study of Mormon institutions, in placing at my disposal an unpublished paper of his on "Separatism in Utah." It is one of the first attempts to study the history of the Mormon enterprise apart from religious bias.

perusal by students of institutions.[1] The Bishop presided
at the ward meetings, which were opened with singing and
prayer. In the year 1854 there were twelve ward meetings.
To these came all the male inhabitants of the ward, and they
determined by majority vote such business questions as
repairing streets, opening ditches, setting out shade trees,
fencing the school house lot, and appointing water masters,
practically as a New England town in colonial days had
managed its affairs. One of the ward meetings in 1854 was
a "Blessing Meeting" at which converts and children were
blessed on their entrance into the Church of Jesus Christ
of the Latter-day Saints. There were inspectors in each
ward who visited each house within its limits and reported
to the ward meeting all those who did not have family prayers
or who did not take proper care of their children and house.
Generally, the report was sufficient to bring compliance
with religious and civil rule; but in obstinate cases the ward
meeting voted to separate the culprit from the Church.
This seems to have been the highest penalty inflicted in
Mormon Utah; in the early days it was equivalent to death
by starvation. The Bishop held court at his own house
with two counsellors. At one of these Bishop's Courts one
man prosecuted another for assault. Each party stated
his side of the case. The Bishop and his counsellors then
conferred together and ordered the defendant to pay twenty-
five dollars to the plaintiff for having treated him with
violence. There were no lawyers, no rules of evidence, and
no speeches of any kind. In other cases, there were wit-
nesses and some attempts at explanation that might fairly
be termed speech making, but ordinarily the proceedings

---

[1] Professor Levi Edgar Young of
the University of Utah most kindly
placed at my disposal "Book B" of
the Thirteenth Ward of Salt Lake
City and has greatly helped me in the
elucidation of many points of Mormon
history.

were simple and rapid. Bishop Woolley of the Thirteenth Ward was a little overbearing at times and was criticized in general ward meeting. He asked for a vote of confidence from the meeting, which was given him.

In the records of the "Blessing Meetings" the names of the persons blessed are given with their birthplaces. There were rather more than one thousand blessed in the record book under examination. Of these no fewer than four hundred and seventy-one came from the dominions of the British king, about four-fifths being natives of England. One hundred and forty more came from outside the United States; of these ninety-six were from Sweden, Norway, and Denmark, and the converts were from places as far apart as Iceland and the Cape of Good Hope. Of the natives of the United States, one hundred and fourteen were born in Utah and Winter Quarters, belonging therefore to the second Mormon generation. Of the rest one hundred came from New England, another hundred from the Middle States, and seventy-six from the Old Northwest. The Thirteenth Ward may not have been typical of the rest of Salt Lake City and the other Mormon settlements; but these figures, such as they are, testify to the remarkable success of Mormon missionary labors and to the large number of children born in the first years after the migration. A list of the original band of pioneers, one hundred and forty-eight in number, has been preserved.[1] Nearly two-thirds of these were born in the United States. Moreover, they had little of the ordinary pioneer spirit of restlessness, as only thirty-three of them died outside of Utah.

---

[1] For this list of the "Original Band of Pioneers," I am indebted to Professor L. E. Young.

NOTES

I. The German Migration. — The first volume of Albert B. Faust's *The German Element in the United States* (Boston, 1909) gives a continuous historical outline of the German immigrations from the earliest time to 1900 in 591 pages and has an exhaustive bibliography at the end of the second volume.[1] The histories of the States, counties, cities, and towns in which the Germans congregated necessarily form isolated treatments of the movement. As is the case with the other nationalities, there is great need of correlation and literary treatment. Until this is done the Germans cannot hope to gain the place in United States history that their quality and numbers and services to the country entitle them to. Two serial publications have historical matter on this subject: *Deutsch-Amerikanische Geschichtsblätter* and the *German American Annals Continuation of the Quarterly Americana Germanica*. The former contains Ernest Bruncken's " German Political Refugees in the United States . . . 1815–1860 " (vols. 3 and 4); the latter contains G. G. Benjamin's " Germans in Texas " with a bibliography (new series, vols. vi, vii). Both of these articles are reprinted separately. Moritz Tiling's *History of the German Element in Texas* brings together in convenient form current knowledge of this part of the German migration and gives a brief bibliography on p. 183. Of biographies, the first volume of the *Works* of Charles Follen contains a memoir by his widow, Eliza L. Follen, and Carl Schurz's *Reminiscences* give an insight into the lives of two Germans of eminence in very different walks of life who came to America about a quarter of a century apart and exerted influences for good in their respective walks.

II. The Irish. — Several books have been published relating more or less to the Irish immigration to America; but none of them is satisfactory for this period, partly because of the lack of definite statistics. Possibly the best account of this early immigration is Edward E. Hale's *Letters on Irish Emigration* (Boston, 1852) Chapter iii of Philip H. Bagenal's *The American Irish and their Influence on Irish Politics* (Boston, 1882) contains some interesting but unauthenticated statistics. Hamilton A. Hill's paper on " Im-

[1] Gustav Körner's *Das deutsche Element in den Vereinigten Staaten von Nordamerika, 1818–1848* (Cincinnati, 1880), presents the story of the earlier German migration in a compendious form.

migration," read before the May, 1875, meeting of the American Social Science Association, has some interesting statements on this subject, but most of Hill's paper relates to a later time. The same thing may be said of Rev. Stephen Byrne's *Irish Emigration to the United States* (New York, 1874). All these authors refer to Edward Young's *Labor in Europe and America* (Philadelphia, 1875) which has been freely drawn on in several chapters of the present work. A list of "Books relating to the American Irish" is appended to H. J. Desmond's "Century of Irish Immigration" in *American Catholic Quarterly Review*, xxv, 528.

III. **The Communities.** — Part I of Morris Hillquit's *History of Socialism in the United States* (New York, 1903) is devoted to a clear and brief account of these forerunners of what is now termed "Socialism." Charles Nordhoff visited such communities as were still in existence in or about the year 1870 and described his observations in a readable book entitled *The Communistic Societies of the United States* (New York, 1875). It has a few illustrations somewhat after the manner of Lossing's *Field-Books* that really tell one a great deal, so far as they go. William Alfred Hinds, himself interested in communism, published a small volume at Oneida, N. Y., in 1878, entitled *American Communities: Brief Sketches of Economy, Zoar, . . . and The Brotherhood of the New Life.* A first revision of this work greatly enlarged was printed at Chicago in 1902, which was followed by a second revision, still larger, in 1908. This last has been of great use in preparing several paragraphs of the present volume. At the close of most of the sections of Hinds's second revision is a brief list of the books relating to the particular community treated in that section. This edition has an index and is continued practically down to date. An older book, but one still of service, is John H. Noyes's *History of American Socialisms* (Philadelphia, 1870).[1] *Selections from the Works of Fourier* with an Introduction by Charles Gide translated by Julia Franklin forms a number of the *Social Science*[2] series published

[1] There are a few pages on "Fourier and Association" in Commons and Associates' *History of Labour*, i, 496, and considerable extracts from official documents, etc., in *American Industrial Society*, vii.

[2] A list of Fourier's writings is on p. 44 of Gide's Introduction. What purported to be the *Œuvres Com-*

plètes de Ch. Fourier was published at Paris in 1841–1845 in six volumes (3rd ed., Paris, 1846–1848). Charles Pellarin's *Vie de Charles Fourier* was translated into English by Francis G. Shaw (New York, 1848), and C. T. Wood compiled from the French of Madame Gatti de Gamond a small work entitled *Fourier and his System* at London in 1901. The Introduction in forty-five pages gives a clear survey of Fourier's theories and the selections are admirably made and translated. Any one reading this book will readily understand the influence exercised by Fourier upon the intellectuals of the idealistic age. Albert Brisbane's publications in book form and in the newspapers of the day greatly influenced the people of the 1840's. Hinds likens his *Social Destiny* [1] in importance to Mrs. Stowe's *Uncle Tom's Cabin*. The most useful, as unfolding in consecutive and intelligible form the ideas of the master, is Brisbane's summation in English of Fourier's *Theory of Universal Unity*, but his *Concise Exposition of the Doctrine of Association, or Plan for a Re-Organization of Society* . . . (*based on Fourier's Theory of Domestic and Industrial Association*), the eighth edition of which was published at New York in 1844, is possibly more instructive. Gide's little Introduction, however, will serve the purposes of all but the most energetic student. See also M. Ferraz's chapter on " Charles Fourier et L'Attraction Passionnelle " in his *Étude sur la Philosophie en France au xixe Siècle* (Paris, 1877), ch. ii. Frederick A. Bushee in his useful article, " Communistic Societies in the United States " (*Political Science Quarterly*, vol. xx, No. 4), has a helpful list of these societies at the end.

Cabet and Icaria attracted attention only second to that of the Mormons, their predecessors at Nauvoo; but the literature concerning them is not great. Albert Shaw's *Icaria, A Chapter in the History of Communism* (New York, 1884) is extremely laudatory and has usually been drawn upon for descriptions of the Icarians. Lifelike details of the Nauvoo enterprise can be obtained from successive leaflets issued by the Icarians in Paris in the years 1856–1858. They were compiled by J. P. Beluze; of them possibly *Compte-Rendu de la Situation Morale et Matérielle de la Colonie Icarienne* is the most useful and the *Mort du Fondateur D'Icarie* is the most truly Icarian. Jules Prudhommeaux, in his *Icarie et son Fondateur Etienne Cabet* (Paris, 1907), has given a prolonged and satisfying account of this experiment and has illustrated it with some interesting photographs of Nauvoo as it appeared in the Mormon and Cabetian epochs and in 1900. The paragraphs in the text are based very largely upon

with a brief biography extracted from the *London Phalanx* (London, 1842).

[1] A keen criticism of Fourierism as interpreted by Brisbane is Donald C. M'Laren's *Boa Constrictor, or Fourier Association Self-Exposed* (Rochester, 1844).

a perusal of Cabet's *Colony, or Republic of Icaria in the United States of America; its History*, that was printed at the Icarian printing office, Nauvoo (Illinois), 1852.

IV. The Black Hawk War. — This Indian conflict played an important part in the opening of northern Illinois and southern Wisconsin to settlers. In the forces opposing the natives were Abraham Lincoln, Jefferson Davis, and Winfield Scott, and the war, therefore, always finds a place in biographies, books of reminiscences, etc. Black Hawk, moreover, produced an autobiography or something that passes as such.[1] Finally, the conflict between the soldiers of the regular army and the cholera is one of the dramatic bits of our military history. For these reasons the literature of the Black Hawk War is large. Reuben G. Thwaites has two brief articles on this subject with abundant citations in the *Magazine of Western History*, v, 32, 181, and in *Wisconsin Historical Collections*, xii, 217-265. An intelligible map by Mr. Thwaites precedes the latter article. Chapters xxxvi-xl of C. R. Tuttle's *History of the Border Wars of Two Centuries* (Madison, Wis., 1876) give a not uninteresting view of this conflict. The real reason for the conflict and other Indian wars comes out in Milo M. Quaife's chapter on "The Vanishing of the Red Man" at the end of his *Chicago and the Old Northwest*, and the preceding pages give some heartrending incidents of the struggle of Scott and his soldiers with the cholera.

[1] *Life of . . . Black Hawk* (Boston, 1834). There are numerous editions, the most useful being that edited by Dr. Quaife (*The Lakeside Classics*, Chicago, 1916). A contemporary account by an Illinois settler who took part in the war is John A. Wakefield's *History of the War between the United States and the Sac and Fox Nations* (Jacksonville, Ill., 1834). Frank E. Stevens's *Black Hawk War* published at Chicago in 1903 is a detailed account of the conflict and its genesis, but has no bibliography. The papers of General John R. Williams, edited by C. M. Burton, are in the *Collections* of the Michigan Pioneer Society, xxi, 313-471.

CHAPTER XVI

TEXAS, CALIFORNIA, AND OREGON

IN the thirty-five years after 1815 the United States acquired all the continent south of the forty-ninth parallel and north of the Rio Grande from the western limit of Louisiana and the line of the Florida Treaty to the Pacific Ocean. It is now (1920) included in the territory of a little over nine States with a total population of nearly twelve million human beings. It is a country of marvellous agricultural and mineral capacities, possessing rich forests and enjoying climates surpassing those of the most favored regions of the earth in either Eastern or Western hemispheres. The Spaniards had looked upon this farthest western country as their own,[1] but they had made little use of it because their eyes had been fixed on the greater immediate possibilities of Mexico and South America. All the people and strength of Spain had not sufficed for the utilization of the resources of those countries, but the Spaniards were as jealous of the possessions that they did not use[2] as they were of those that they did use. This farthest western country was divided geographically, politically, and internationally into four blocks: Texas, New Mexico, California, and

---

[1] The early history of this part of the United States is succinctly set forth in Bolton and Marshall's *Colonization of North America, 1492-1783* (New York, 1920) especially ch. xxi.

[2] An example of the inefficiency of Spanish colonial administration occurred as to the first voyage of the *Columbia*. Her appearance in the Pacific drew forth orders for her exclusion that reached their destination about one year after that famous ship had passed by. See Robertson's unpublished essay entitled "From Alcalde to Mayor," p. 36.

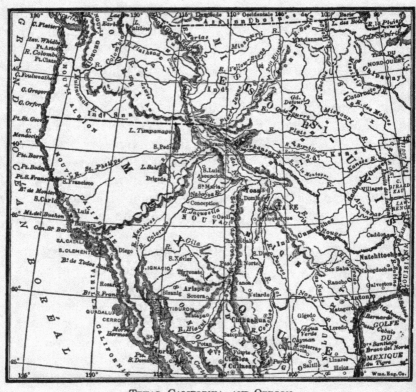

TEXAS, CALIFORNIA, AND OREGON
(From Map at end of Luis De Onís's *Memoria*)

Oregon. Eastwardly from California [1] and Oregon and
northwardly from Texas and New Mexico there was a stretch
of mountainous country that comprised the headwaters of
the rivers flowing eastwardly into the Mississippi, westwardly into the Pacific, and southwardly into the Gulf of
California or into the Gulf of Mexico. This land might
be regarded as pertinent to the Mississippi Valley and the
United States or to the regions claimed by Spain. Texas,
as a geographical phrase, included the lands between Louisiana and the Rio Grande, and New Mexico was the country
to the westward as far as California. The northward limit
of Texas and New Mexico was indistinct, but those geographical units included certainly the watersheds of the
Rio Grande and Colorado rivers. California was the coastal
land from Mexico to the forty-second parallel, and Oregon
was the region stretching northwardly from that parallel
for an indefinite extent. These names and boundaries
are used here in what might be called the ordinary geographical sense and not as accurately descriptive of political
countries at any one time.

Originally, that is to say, in the sixteenth and seventeenth
centuries, this whole extent of land had belonged to Spain
or had been claimed by her, so far as it had belonged to or
had been claimed by any one. Toward the end of the
eighteenth century, British and American fur traders had
anchored in the harbors along the coast and had established
a profitable commerce with the Indians.[2] The Russians,
crossing Bering's Strait, had likewise entered into the fur

[1] As to the origin of the name California, see Ruth Putnam and H. I.
Priestley's article in the *Publications*
of the University of California, for
December, 1917, pp. 293–365.

[2] Professor Joseph Schafer's *History of the Pacific Northwest* in its
revised form (New York, 1918) will
satisfy the needs of most readers.
G. C. Davidson's *North West Company* (University of California *Publications in History,* vii) sets forth in
great detail certain aspects of the
history of the Northwest with abundant citations.

trade of the Northwest and had founded stations at various places on the American shore.[1] In 1790, by the Nootka Sound Treaty,[2] Spain abandoned some of her pretensions to the northern part of the region in favor of Great Britain; but the precise terms of the treaty are of no service for the present purpose, because no two persons of different nationalities have ever interpreted them alike. Whatever they meant, they certainly clouded the Spanish title to the northernmost part of the coast and gave Great Britain vague rights of trade and possibly something more. In their voyages along the coast, whether on exploring expeditions or on trips to and from the Philippines, Spanish navigators had noticed breakers at a certain place south of the Strait of Juan de Fuca; but it was reserved for Captain Gray of the Boston trading ship *Columbia* to sail through this swirl of waters and enter the actual mouth of the river that still bears his vessel's name. This was in May, 1792.[3] Captain Gray was not in the service of the United States government, his ship was a private trading vessel, and the voyage had no official standing whatever; but in this instance these factors were overlooked. At the time that Gray was on the coast Captain Vancouver of the British navy was also there in command of an exploring expedition. He had recently passed by the mouth of the river without entering it; but, on being apprised of its existence by Captain Gray, he sent

[1] F. A. Golder's *Russian Expansion on the Pacific, 1641–1850* has a wider interest than the title indicates and is provided with an excellent bibliography. His *Bering's Voyages* in 2 vols. (1921) brings the story to American shores.

[2] See the present work, vol. iv, 118–123, and E. S. Meany's *Vancouver's Discovery of Puget Sound*, ch. iii.

[3] *House Reports*, 25th Cong., 3rd Sess., No. 101; Appendix F gives an extract from the log-book of the *Columbia*. See a following "Supplemental Report" also numbered 101. The log-book extract is repeated in Robert Greenhow's *History of Oregon and California*, 434; see also ch. xi of the latter book; Schafer's *History of the Pacific Northwest* (ed. 1918), p. 22; and H. H. Bancroft's *Northwest Coast*, i, 250, 258–260.

a boat party to verify the discovery. This expedition ascended the river sixty miles or more above the point where the *Columbia* had anchored.[1] In 1803, the United States acquired Louisiana and thereby may have gained some rights as to the region to the westward of the headwaters of the affluents of the Mississippi. It has been said that the French bishopric of Louisiana extended westwardly to the Pacific Ocean; but, if such a claim was ever made by the French, no official action of any importance was ever taken to make good such pretensions. On the other hand, French fur traders and trappers seem to have been ubiquitous. Mentions of their activities are constantly turning up, and no one would be bold enough to assert that any particular trapper was the first to carry his pack to the headwaters of any particular river in this western country or was the first to penetrate the secrets of any particular mountain pass.[2] It may well be, therefore, that the territory which can fairly be regarded as tributary to the St. Louis fur market covered a much greater extent than has formerly been supposed. Whatever claims these fur trading expeditions gave to France or to Spain, her successor in the ownership of Louisiana, passed to the United States in 1803. They were still in existence in 1840, except as they were limited by the Florida Treaty of 1819 and by subsequent agreements with Russia and with Great Britain.

In the winter of 1805–1806, Lewis and Clark, on their memorable exploring trip, had wintered in a camp not far

---

[1] *A Voyage of Discovery to the North Pacific Ocean . . . under . . . Captain George Vancouver* (3 vols., London, 1798) i, 422 ii, ch. iii. Professor Schafer has set forth the facts, with abundant citations, in the *Bulletin* of the University of Oregon, vi. The first volumes of H. S. Lyman's *History of Oregon* cover the period treated in this chapter.

[2] Harlow Lindley's "Western Travel, 1800–1820" in the *Mississippi Valley Historical Review*, vi, 167–191, is very useful in placing the early expeditions, and see also Bolton's "French Intrusions into New Mexico" in *The Pacific Ocean in History*, 389–407.

from the mouth of the Columbia River. In the spring of
1811, John Jacob Astor, a New York merchant who was
greatly interested in the fur trade, had established a post
at the mouth of the Columbia River and had named it
Astoria.[1] This post had been sold to the North West Fur
Company before its seizure by the British on December
12, 1813.[2] Nevertheless in 1818 it was restored to the United
States under the terms of the Treaty of Ghent, but the
North West Company was not disturbed in its trade.[3] In
1819, by the Florida Treaty, the Spaniards handed ove.
to the United States all their existing rights to the Northwest Coast, north of the forty-second parallel.[4] Five years
later, in 1824, another treaty was made, this time between
the United States and Russia, by which the latter agreed
to retire from the Pacific coast of America, south of 54° 40'
N. L.[5] In this way the United States and Great Britain
became the only two countries to have interests in the
region which was called Oregon. As neither of them could
make any effective settlement there for the time being,
they agreed in 1818 to occupy the country jointly for ten
years.[6] This agreement was renewed in 1827 to last until
one or the other party to it gave notice a year in advance
of the termination of this joint occupation.[7] At the moment,
the British were apparently in the better position to utilize
whatever rights might accrue under these treaties, as in
1821 the Hudson's Bay Company by the absorption of the

---

[1] Gabriel Franchere's *Narrative of a
Voyage to the Northwest Coast*, ch. xv;
H. M. Chittenden's *American Fur
Trade of the Far West*, i, 223; Alex-
ander Ross' *Adventures of the First
Settlers on the Oregon or Columbia
River*, 259; Bancroft's *Northwest Coast*,
i, 331, 339.

[2] The bill of sale was signed October 16, 1813, "at entrance of Columbia
River North West Coast of America,"
see G. C. Davidson's *The North West
Company*, 138, 139, 293, forming
vol. vii of the *University of California
Publications in History*.

[3] *Ibid.*, 164.

[4] *Treaties and Conventions* (ed. 1873)
p. 785.

[5] *Ibid.*, p. 733.

[6] *Ibid.*, 350.

[7] *Ibid.*, 365.

North West Company [1] had combined all British and Canadian fur trading interests under one extremely efficient management — and were carrying on a remarkably profitable business in the Columbia River region. As the years went by, however, they found themselves more and more hampered by the coming of American fur traders, settlers, and missionaries.

As early as 1796, when the United States took over the Northwestern posts from the British, attempts had been made to attach the Indians to American interests by establishing government trading stations, but little had been accomplished. In January, 1803, Jefferson took up the subject of western lands and Indian management with his usual mixture of altruism and advantage.[2] The tribes, he said, were becoming uneasy at the constant diminution of their hunting grounds. To counteract this restlessness they should be encouraged to apply themselves to agriculture, stock raising, and domestic manufacture. Government trading houses should be established among them to lead them to civilization and to sell them articles that they needed and that were good for them at lower rates than private traders could sell them, thus winning the good will of the Indians and disposing of the traders at the same time. This public commerce among the Indians might even be extended to the Missouri River, and a party of ten or a dozen men led by an intelligent officer might explore even as far as the "Western Ocean." A few surveying instruments, their muskets, "and light and cheap presents for the Indians would be all the apparatus they could carry."

[1] See G. C. Davidson's *North West Company*, 176 and fol. (*University of California Publications in History*, vii).

[2] See the Message in *Annals of Congress*, 7th Cong., 2nd Sess., 24–26. Jefferson also suggested that it might be well to lead the Indians into debt under the pressure of which they might be more willing to part with their lands. *Writings of Jefferson* (Congress ed.) iv, 472; ix, 460.

As to the Spaniards, they would not interfere, although Missouri still belonged to them, as they would regard the expedition as a literary pursuit.[1] Jefferson asked for an appropriation of twenty-five hundred dollars, "for the purpose of extending the external commerce of the United States." He counselled secrecy to "prevent the obstructions which interested individuals might otherwise previously prepare in its way." At the moment Jefferson had no thought of purchasing this part of Louisiana and the proposition simply was to open up the trade of a large part of Spanish America to United States merchants without the knowledge or consent of the Spaniards. Congress assented and Jefferson placed Meriwether Lewis and William Clark at the head of the expedition. He instructed them [2] to discover if possible a "practicable water-communication across the continent, for the purposes of commerce."

Starting in May, 1804, Lewis and Clark slowly ascended the Missouri River. They passed the winter in the country of the Mandan Indians not far from the present town of Bismark in North Dakota. The next spring, 1805, they pushed on and by mid-summer had gained the headwaters of that river. They supported themselves by hunting and had few excitements except an occasional encounter with grizzly bears, but the mosquitoes and "blowing" flies troubled them greatly. Arrived at the mountains they most fortunately happened on a band of Indians of the same tribe as the Indian wife of a Frenchman they had taken with them as a guide. In the mountains they made friends

---

[1] The geographical knowledge of the time is well portrayed in a map which is reproduced by photography in connection with an article by Miss A. H. Abel in the *Geographical Review*, i, 329–345. Frederick J. Teggart's "Notes Supplementary to any Edition of Lewis and Clark" (American Historical Association's *Reports*, 1908, vol. i, 185) contain an astonishing amount of information in a small compass.

[2] For the instructions, see *Writings of Jefferson* (Ford ed.), viii, 194 note.

with one Indian tribe after another, procured horses without great difficulty, but were often straitened for food. At length they came to one of the upper streams of the Columbia system that could be navigated. At this point they constructed canoes by digging or burning out the hearts of giant trees and in them floated down the streams, oftentimes encountering perils that seem incredible even in the reading. On November 7, 1805, Captain Clark wrote that they came "in *view* of the *Ocian* . . . the roreing or noise made by the waves brakeing on the rockey Shores" was heard from a great distance. The following winter, which they passed in rude huts near the sea, was most disagreeable. In July, 1806, they repassed the mountains and on September 21 regained St. Louis.[1]

In 1805, while Lewis and Clark were toiling through the Stoney Mountains, as the Rockies were usually termed in those days, Zebulon Montgomery Pike was laboriously ascending the Mississippi River to ascertain its sources and to discover the condition of trade in its upper valley. In April, 1806, he was back in St. Louis and in the following July started on an exploring expedition to the westward

---

[1] Nicholas Biddle of Philadelphia undertook to compile an account of this expedition from the journals of Lewis and Clark and their comrades and such other matter as was obtainable. He did an admirable bit of work, but the book, which was published in 1814 as *History of the Expedition under the command of Captains Lewis and Clark* has on its title-page the name of its final editor, Paul Allen. In 1893, Elliott Coues published an edition of this work with an immense amount of annotation. The most convenient reprint is that in *The Trail Makers* series. This is in three small volumes without footnotes; but each volume has a few pages of geographical identifications and the whole is preceded by Jefferson's memoir of Lewis and a succinct account of the purchase of Louisiana by Professor McMaster. In 1904–1905, there was issued a definitive edition of the Lewis and Clark journals under the editorship of Reuben Gold Thwaites giving the different accounts, word for word, with ruthless and exhausting accuracy. In 1916, his successor, M. M. Quaife, printed in the Wisconsin Historical Society's *Collections* (vol. xxii) *Journals of Captain Meriwether Lewis and Sergeant John Ordway*. C. D. Wheeler's *The Trail of Lewis and Clark* (2 vols., New York, 1904) contains a mass of useful local information mingled with extraordinary statements as to the international history of the United States.

but far to the south of the route followed by Lewis and Clark. He seems to have been despatched on this quest by General James Wilkinson, but the precise genesis of the expedition is still obscure.[1] His instructions were exceedingly vague. They directed him to go from one Indian nation to another when he would probably find himself on the headwaters of the Arkansas and Red rivers — "approximated to the settlements of New Mexico." He was ordered to be very careful to cultivate harmonious intercourse with the Spaniards. It is a curious fact that Aaron Burr began his journey at almost the same time, but whether there was any connection between the two, otherwise than indistinct relations with Wilkinson, is unknown. Before long, Pike came across the trail of a large Spanish expedition that had been operating on ground that was clearly included within the limits of the ceded province of Louisiana. On November 15, 1806, he thought he saw a mountain in the distance which appeared like a small blue cloud and was in reality the peak that bears his name, which rises eight thousand feet from the plains and fourteen thousand from the level of the sea. After wandering about in the cold of winter, climbing mountains, and going over passes, Pike built a stockaded fort on the banks of the Rio Grande at some distance above Santa Fé.[2] At this point, Dr. Robinson, a volunteer, left the expedition and alone went to Santa Fé, ostensibly to arrange some financial matters but really to apprise the Spaniards of Pike's whereabouts. Within a few days they appeared in force and invited the American to come to the Spanish

---

[1] As to the origin of this expedition see Professor I. J. Cox's informing introduction to "Papers of Zebulon M. Pike" in *American Historical Review*, xiii, 798.

[2] Professor H. E. Bolton throws a great deal of light on the doings of the Spaniards in the country north and east of the Rio Grande in the earlier time in the introduction to his *Athanase de Mézières and the Louisiana-Texas Frontier, 1768–1780* (Cleveland, 1914).

town. Arrived there, Pike exhibited surprise at finding himself on the Rio Grande instead of the Red River, but he convinced the Spanish commander of his official character and was conducted to El Paso and finally to the American posts on the Louisiana line,[1] — thus completing an extremely interesting round of international geographic exploration.

Another official exploring expedition that belongs to the same series was that of William Dunbar to the Hot Springs of Arkansas. It was begun in the autumn of 1804. Compared with the journeys of Lewis and Clark, and Pike, this expedition was mere child's play from the point of distance covered and dangers encountered. Its interest is in the scientific data gathered by the explorers and in the speculations which they aroused. They found something that looked like coal and many salt licks that might possibly develop into commercially profitable salt wells. The Hot Springs themselves were interesting and gave rise to many remarks.[2] The Spaniards told Pike of Dunbar's expedition and were evidently disposed to limit the territory acquired by the United States from France to a mere strip of land along the lower Mississippi. It was only the convulsions in Europe and in Spain that induced them to withdraw their opposition to our occupation of any portion of the western basin below the Missouri or below the Arkansas. These

---

[1] Pike prepared *An Account of Expeditions to the Sources of the Mississippi, and through the Western Parts of Louisiana*. This was first printed in 1810. An English edition with the title *Exploratory Travels through the Western Territories of North America* was brought out with some attempt at literary revision in 1811 and from this the work was translated into French and Dutch in 1811 and 1812. The English edition was reproduced, word for word, at Denver in 1889. Dr. Elliott Coues in 1895 brought out a two-volume edition of the original with an amazing amount of annotation under the title of *The Expeditions of Zebulon Montgomery Pike*.

[2] *Documents relating to The Purchase & Exploration of Louisiana*, containing I. "The Limits and Bounds of Louisiana" by Thomas Jefferson; II. "The Exploration of the *Red*, the *Black*, and the *Washita* Rivers" by William Dunbar. It was printed from the original manuscripts in the library of the American Philosophical Society (Boston and New York, 1904).

were all the official expeditions for the exploration of western
Louisiana, but before many years the fur traders were roam-
ing everywhere through that country.[1]

Of the hosts of accounts[2] of the earlier fur traders and
adventurers on the western plains, in the mountains, and on
the Pacific slope, that of Captain Bonneville stands out as
possessing interest because of the many hairbreadth adventures of the raconteur. These were due in part to his own
lack of experience, to the bad character of his employees,
and, in great measure, to the literary charm which Washington Irving threw about the narrative. Bonneville was an
officer in the United States army who thought he saw a
chance for fortune in the fur trade of the mountains. He
obtained leave of absence and proceeded northwestwardly
from St. Louis bent on adventure and gain. He left Fort
Osage, on the Missouri, on May 1, 1832, and returned three
years later having outstayed his leave and probably poorer
in purse than he was at the outset. In the interval he had
traversed mountains, voyaged down and up rivers, and encountered many Indian tribes. On one occasion he had
received hospitality at the Hudson Bay Company's post at
Walla Walla, near the present boundary line between Wash-

---

[1] John C. Luttig's *Journal of a Fur-
Trading Expedition on the Upper
Missouri, 1812–1813*, issued by the
Missouri Historical Society in 1920,
is a very lifelike picture and the "Appendix" and "Bibliography" at the
end of the volume are excellent.

[2] These are summarized, for the most
part, in Chittenden's *Fur Trade*. Of
other accounts, T. M. Marshall's "St.
Vrain's Expedition to the Gila in
1826" (*Southwestern Historical Quarterly*, xix, 251) and Elliott Coues'
Journal of Jacob Fowler and his *On
the Trail of a Spanish Pioneer* have
been found useful as giving historical
color. H. C. Dale's *The Ashley-Smith
Explorations . . . 1822–1829* goes over

some of the same ground from a very
different angle.

For the more important works of
Father De Smet, S. J., see *Letters and
Sketches: with a Narrative of a Year's
Residence among the Indian Tribes of
the Rocky Mountains* (Philadelphia,
1843) and *Oregon Missions and Travels
over the Rocky Mountains, in 1845–46*
(New-York, 1847), the latter being reprinted in French in 1848 at Ghent
in Belgium. All his works are collected into four volumes by H. M.
Chittenden and A. T. Richardson
as *Life, Letters and Travels of Father
Pierre-Jean De Smet, S. J., 1801–
1873* (New York, 1905); volume i,
144 gives an ample bibliography.

ington and Oregon; but the commandant of the post refused to give him any supplies, although he and his party were in a starving condition, for he felt that his duty to the Company forbade the sale of food and ammunition to its rivals. One portion of Bonneville's expedition, proceeding southwestwardly from the general rendezvous, passed through the Salt Lake Valley and the mountains to Monterey, in California, on the Pacific.[1] At different times Bonneville fell in with Nathaniel Wyeth. He was a Massachusetts man who had conceived the idea of establishing a trading post at the mouth of the Columbia River which would be a convenient point of supply and exchange for traders from overland and from oversea and would lead to the American occupation of the country. Wyeth had great capacity for adventure, but his means were not commensurate with his desires.[2] After sufferings and disappointments the project of the trading post was finally abandoned. Some of Wyeth's men, or of Bonneville's, or of other unmentioned expeditions may have remained in the Columbia Valley and established themselves there as farmers, as some of the Hudson Bay Company's employees did. The first organized band of American settlers came overland under the lead of Methodist missionaries to Oregon in 1834, and in 1836 another band led by Presbyterian or Congregational missionaries also came overland.[3] These proved to be the precursors of numberless migrations; in 1843 no less than

[1] *The Rocky Mountains: . . . from the Journal of Captain B. L. E. Bonneville* (2 vols., Philadelphia, 1837) by Washington Irving. This has been reprinted in many forms in his collected works and in special editions.

[2] "Correspondence and Journals of Captain Nathaniel J. Wyeth, 1831-6" (*Sources of the History of Oregon*, i); Charles Wilkes's *Narrative of the United States Exploring Expedition.*

During the Years 1838 . . . 1842 (v, ch. vi).

[3] Bancroft's *Oregon*, i, chs. iii and v, and James W. Bashford's *Oregon Missions. The Story of How the Line was Run between Canada and the United States* (New York, 1918). The earlier books on the Columbia Valley are enumerated at the beginning of Bancroft's *Oregon.* For a somewhat different view see Sir George Simp-

one thousand persons crossed the plains and mountains to the fertile valleys of Oregon. Towards the close of the first half-century, the white population west of the mountains,[1] north of the forty-second parallel and south of 54° 40' was between ten and twenty thousand souls.

Entirely unlike the history of Oregon was the early development of Texas, New Mexico, and California:[2] the first proceeded on the lines of Anglo-Saxon commercial colonization, the last three developed or failed to develop in the politico-ecclesiastical direction that seemed to be the guiding post of Spanish-American policy. From the point of view of commerce and colonization, Spain had no need of northern Mexican provinces; but from the political and ecclesiastical view-points, their acquisition and maintenance were important to Spain and to Mexico, or seemed to be. Frenchmen and later Americans were constantly intruding themselves into Texas and New Mexico, and British and, later, Americans were active on the California coast. The easiest and perhaps the only method by which Spain could secure any kind of possession of these regions was to con-

---

son's *Narrative of a Journey Round the World*, i, ch. vi; "Letters of Sir George Simpson, 1841–1843" (*American Historical Review*, xiv, 70–94); and "John McLoughlin's Last Letter" (*ibid.*, xxi, 104–134).

[1] Bancroft (*Oregon*, i, 251 *note*) estimates the population in 1841 at 500 souls, and nearly ten years later, at about 20,000 (*ibid.*, ii, 251).

[2] The books on Spanish California in the early time are really histories of the Spanish occupation of the trans-Mississippi country. Of these Charles E. Chapman's *Founding of Spanish California, the Northwestward Expansion of New Spain, 1687–1783* and Irving B. Richman's *California under Spain and Mexico, 1535–1847* contain much interesting information and are supplied with excellent bib-

liographical notes which will serve to carry the student far toward his goal. Dealing more especially with Texas, Herbert E. Bolton's *Texas in the Middle Eighteenth Century* gives one a picture of Spanish administration in any part of the world, and in a brief article in the *American Historical Review*, xxiii, 42–61, Professor Bolton has set forth vividly the character and history of the "Mission as a Frontier Institution." An excellent detailed description of the Spanish system is Herbert I. Priestley's *José de Gálvez, Visitor-General of New Spain* in the *Publications* of the University of California, v. An older book, but giving a very good brief account of the history and institutions, is George P. Garrison's *Texas; a Contest of Civilizations* (Boston, 1903).

vert the Indians to the true faith, redeem them from their wandering life, settle them around mission stations and colonize, in the vicinity, bodies of soldiers who seem to have belonged largely to the convict class, and who probably were most of them of mixed Spanish and aboriginal Mexican blood. This policy harmonized with the wish of the Church to convert the heathen and to redeem their souls from torment everlasting. Moreover, a country of missions and presidios, or military stations, would be an admirable barrier to foreign aggression from the North. Missions were established at convenient points in Texas and later in New Mexico and California. Indians were gathered around the first mission station; soldiers were established near by in a presidio, partly to protect the missionaries from Indian attack, but more especially to round up the Indians for the Fathers' ministrations and bring back such of them as wandered away from the mission. With the help of Indians already tamed, the missionaries taught the wild natives the truths of the Christian faith and habits of industry. They made good Catholics of whole Indian tribes, reclaimed them from a wandering existence, and tied them down to definite areas and to agriculture. In ten years or so lands were allotted to the natives in severalty and the mission became a parish. The missionaries with a body of tame Indians and a few soldiers then moved away to the wilderness to found a new mission, convert and civilize a new tribe of natives, and move the frontier just so far into new territory. After the missionaries and soldiers, came white men and women, and men and women of mixed blood who built a town or pueblo near by or around the mission station. The process of amalgamation and dispossession then proceeded until the natives lost their lands and their racial identity, or died out, or ran away.

In all our history there is hardly a more attractive story than that of the Texas and California missions. This is partly due to the equableness of the climate, partly to the high character of the missionaries themselves, and partly to the sad fate that overtook the converted Red Men. The system had worked well in Mexico, for there the Indians were more susceptible to the teachings of the missionaries. There also the white colonists were more under the eye of the government and were obliged to treat the natives, converted or otherwise, with some degree of humanity. In the northern provinces the Indians were wilder and more stubborn, becoming wilder and stubborner as one went farther north. In Texas, and especially in California, the whites were far removed from civil control. This irresponsibility was greatly increased by the breaking away from the Spanish empire and by the subsequent round of revolutions in Mexico and rebellions in California. The story of the devotion of Father Junipero Serra and the rest belongs to the heroic age of colonization.[1] Their ideals were high, their lives were filled with perilous services, with no hope of reward on earth, except in the satisfaction of a worthy task worthily accomplished. Their daily round of work is attractive as it appears in their accounts. There were many disappointments, but there was much joy in the doing of what they thought was good, and the little glimpses of human frailties that appear, especially among the neophytes and the soldiers, connect them with other lands, and other peoples. The time for the secularization of the California missions had arrived before Mexico split off from Spain, and the order for this had been given but had not been carried out at the time of the achievement of Mexican independence. In

---

[1] Those who wish to secure an intimate knowledge of the mission system from one of the missionaries, should go to Fr. Zephyrin Engelhardt's *The Missions and Missionaries of California* in four volumes.

due course thereafter secularization proceeded.[1] There was
nothing else to be done. The missions were not self-supporting, the Mexicans had no funds for their maintenance,
and the California colonists had eyes eagerly fixed on the
orchards and improved lands around the missions. Secularization was ordered ; the Indians, as opportunity served,
took to the hills, and the whites possessed themselves of
their lands, herds,[2] and orchards. Meantime, cultivation
and tame cattle had driven away the wild game and, within
a few years, the occupation of the foothills by the whites
deprived the natives of their supply of acorns. The herds
of the whites were the Indians' only hope — both cattle
and horses, for the natives relished one as well as the other.
As the Indians could not secure these by purchase or barter,
they stole them, and war between the Californians and the
runaway Indians began. Diseases, as the measles, small-
pox, scurvy, and pneumonia, attacked the natives and swept
them off in large numbers. Doubtless these disorders, or
some of them, had not been uncommon in the Indian villages
around the missions ; but when the natives were under the
missionaries' care they had better food and medical aid than
they could get in the mountains. In 1849 there were from
sixty to one hundred thousand Indians within the limits of
the present State of California ;[3] in 1900 there were not

[1] See "Provisional regulations for
the secularization of the missions of
Upper California promulgated by Gov-
ernor José Figueroa on the 9th of
August, 1834" in *Senate Documents*,
Rep. Com. No. 18, 31st Cong., 1st
Sess., p. 150.

[2] Walter Colton (*Three Years in
California*, 441, 443, 444, 449) gives
figures as to the numbers of cattle and
horses and sheep at different missions ;
— at Santa Clara, for instance, in 1823,
there were 22,400 calves, 74,280 cattle,
82,540 sheep, and 6125 horses.

[3] C. Hart Merriam's "Indian Population of California" (*American An-
thropologist*) vii, 594. For this citation and much valuable information
on the California Indians, I am indebted to Mr. W. H. Ellison of Santa
Barbara. Merriam (p. 598) writes
that in 1834 "the total Indian population of California . . . could hardly
have been less than 210,000." On
p. 600 he estimates it at 100,000 in
1849.

five thousand persons of tolerably pure Indian blood in that State, although there are many whites and negroes with Indian blood in their veins in California today.

The secularization of the missions and the reversion of the natives to savagery occurred during the Mexican rule, a dozen years or so before the American conquest. In 1835, when Richard H. Dana was on the coast, the missions were already dilapidated and half deserted.[1] At that time and for years thereafter, there were bands of Indians on many of the ranches or cattle farms. John A. Sutter, a German-Swiss immigrant,[2] had established a fort and trading station on the site of the modern city of Sacramento. He had collected and trained a body of Indians to take care of the cattle and to chase away any marauders who attempted to run off his cows and horses. These copper-colored retainers seemed to have lost whatever civilization they may once have had and fed like pigs from a trough.[3] After the discovery of gold in 1848, the natives were used by the miners, especially by the Californians and the Mexicans, to do the hard work. As the gold-bearing slopes and cañons were occupied by the white miners, the wild Indians were driven farther and farther into the mountains where food was scarcer than it was in the foothills. It was then that the natives began to steal and even to attack isolated parties of whites; and the miners and settlers retaliated by shooting an Indian on sight, until finally the survivors were confined on reservations.

Texas and New Mexico, as outlying parts of New Spain,

[1] See his *Two Years Before the Mast.* This remarkable book was first printed at New York in 1840, and was at once reprinted in America and in England. Other books of this time are A. Robinson's *Life in California . . . by An American* (New York, 1846; reprinted in 1891); Alexander Forbes' *California* (London, 1839); and Edwin Bryant's *What I Saw in California . . . in the Years 1846, 1847* (New York, 1848).

[2] Sutter's "Personal Reminiscences" is in the Bancroft Library.

[3] "Diary" of Col. James Clyman, p. 122 (Ms.), in the Bancroft Library.

were hardly more than geographical expressions with a few missions and trading posts thrown in. El Paso and Santa Fé were the only two towns of any importance in New Mexico and, with the exception of some cultivators and some Indian traders, about all the white inhabitants lived in those two towns. Texas had interested the Spanish authorities mainly as a buffer against possible French encroachments, and when Spain acquired Louisiana, this cause of interest disappeared. The garrisons of eastern Texas were withdrawn, the missions were starved, and there was a general backward tendency. In 1820, Moses Austin, then living in Missouri, espoused the cause of Texas colonization from the United States. At the moment, the Florida Treaty by which the United States surrendered its claims to Texas beyond the Sabine River [1] was still unratified in the hands of the Spanish government. In 1821, when Spain consented to it, Mexico or New Spain was practically independent. It was at such a moment that Austin visited Texas and applied to the representative of the dying Spanish government for a grant of land. After some demur, this was given to him in the form of permission to bring in a certain number of families. This was the last act of Moses Austin's remarkable career, as he died soon after his return to the United States. His plans were then taken up by his son, Stephen Fuller Austin.[2] When he arrived in Texas to secure a confirmation of his father's grant he found the Mexican revolutionists triumphant. He went to the City of Mexico and there secured a new grant

[1] On the boundaries of Texas, see Bolton's *Texas in the Eighteenth Century*, p. 1, and T. M. Marshall's *History of the Western Boundary of the Louisiana Purchase*. The first two paragraphs of Bolton's text state the matter admirably. It appears that when the Spaniards owned both Texas and Louisiana they talked of moving the western boundary of Louisiana westwardly to the Sabine River, but nothing was done at that time.

[2] A good, brief account of Stephen F. Austin is L. A. Wight's *Life . . . of Stephen F. Austin* in *Austin College Bulletin* for October, 1910.

from the new government. Spanish authority once over-thrown, change after change, revolutions, as they are termed, followed in Mexico. At first there was a revolutionary emperor, but in 1824 a federal republic was established, somewhat on the model of the United States. As there were not enough white inhabitants in Texas to form a separate state, it was joined with its next southern neighbor as the State of Coahuila and Texas, the capital being in the southern part. The younger Austin, thereupon, secured renewed concessions. The land system of New Spain, of the Mexican Republic, and of Coahuila and Texas was entirely unlike that of the United States.[1] Land was not granted to Austin or other leaders of colonization in fee simple; they were given the right to bring in a certain number of families and settle them within rather ill-defined boundaries, taking up specified quantities of land on account of each family. Austin and the others were termed empresarios or contractors. The financial arrangements made by Austin are impossible to unravel.[2] He undoubtedly expected to make something out of the venture, either by retaining portions of the lands or by securing contributions from his colonists. He was a man of remarkable skill in certain directions and somehow contrived to maintain himself and receive the good will of those who settled under his auspices. These colonists came from the United States, mainly from the South,[3] but there were some from New

[1] The *Laws and Decrees of the State of Coahuila and Texas* published at Houston in 1839 by order of the Texan Secretary of State contains an amazing amount of useful information. A very much briefer publication entitled *Texas Lands* contains most of the important documents.

[2] See Lester G. Bugbee's "Some Difficulties of a Texas Empresario"

in Southern History Association's *Publications* for April, 1899.

[3] Professor James E. Winston has brought forward many facts concerning the Texan colonists in *The Southwestern Historical Quarterly* for July, 1912; January, 1913; July, 1917; etc.

The following four titles have been selected from a mass of more or less contemporary material on this part of

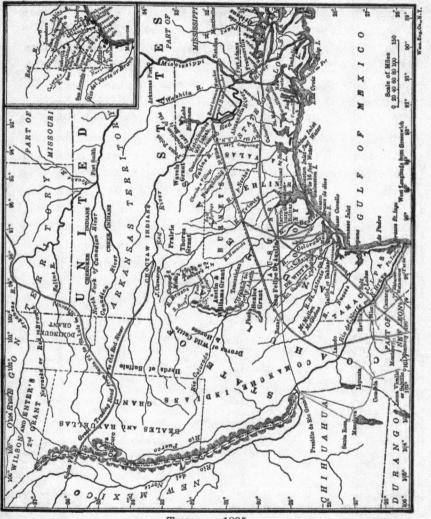

TEXAS IN 1835

(Redrawn from *A Visit to Texas*, 1834. The inset shows settled areas in 1835.)

York and New England and other parts of the North. Undoubtedly, many of them were adventurers whose absence from the United States was welcome; but the letters, diaries, and reminiscences that have come down to us give the impression that most of the colonists were hard-working, God-fearing men and women of the very best type for so arduous an enterprise. The success of Austin attracted other men of vision and also those of speculative proclivities. These obtained large grants or contracts, and colonies were formed at various places under their auspices. Looking at a map of Texas of 1830 with these "grants" marked in different colored inks, one gathers the impression of a settled area which was very far from the truth. Estimates differ widely as to the number of white inhabitants of Texas,[1] but in 1830 there were enough of them there to have a feeling of racial solidarity and of political consciousness.[2]

Meantime, one revolutionary government had succeeded another in Mexico, — this revolutionary leader and that "pronouncing" against whomsoever happened to be in power and generally attracting enough followers by the hope

Texan history, simply because they seem to shed light to the present writer's eyes: *A Visit to Texas: being the Journal of a Traveller* (New York, 1834); *Texas in 1840, or the Emigrant's Guide* (New York, 1840); *Prairiedom: Rambles and Scrambles in Texas . . . By A. Suthron* (New York, 1845); and W. B. Dewees's *Letters from an Early Settler of Texas* (Louisville, Ky., 1854.)

[1] The population of Texas in these early years has been variously estimated. The first census was taken in 1847. From that it has been deduced that Texas in 1840 had in all about 55,000 white inhabitants; in 1836 anywhere from 30,000 to 50,000; see George L. Rives's *United States and Mexico*, i, 391, 464. Yoakum states that in 1831 the "American population of Texas . . . now numbered

about twenty thousand"; *History of Texas*, i, 274 (reprinted in Wooten's *Comprehensive History of Texas*, i, 134). The largest estimate was made by F. C. Sheridan, a British official at the Barbados in 1840. He says that the population may be estimated at 150,000 souls (Texas State Historical Association's *Quarterly*, xv, 220). The editors of the *Quarterly* state that this is an excessive estimate and as late as 1847, the white population was "but a little more than a hundred thousand." See also Garrison's *Texas*, 270.

[2] W. L. McCalla's *Adventures in Texas chiefly in . . . 1840* (Philadelphia, 1841) gives a glimpse of the conditions of life in the republic in the interval between San Jacinto and annexation. ;

of public plunder to oust the existing tenant. Of these
leaders, the most remarkable was Antonio Lopez de Santa
Anna. Opinions have widely differed as to his motives
and his capacities and appraisal of them is extraordinarily
difficult, because only a person deeply versed in Spanish-
Mexican character can hope to understand them. It
seems evident that he was a man of remarkable power of
arousing enthusiasm among his own people and of making,
perhaps not the best, but something approaching it of the
people with whom he had to work. The ups and downs of
his career, his military successes and defeats, and the charm
of his personality certainly compel admiration and his
blood-thirstiness, his craftiness, and his instability belong
to his people, place, and time. It was natural that a political
and military leader of this type should feel restive under
the federal organization of the Mexican Republic which
may or may not have been a good form of government for
that country at that time.[1] It was certainly much easier
for a successful revolutionist to rule the whole republic
from Mexico City, than to have to consult the susceptibilities
of the political leaders of a score of states. At all events,
Santa Anna became the head of the Centralists and his
accession to power in 1834 meant the overthrow of the
federalist system. This movement was especially disliked by the people of California, New Mexico, and Texas.
These were so far away from the capital, not only in miles
but in modes of communication, and, so far as Texas was
concerned, so alien in political desire, that they were restive

[1] Of the innumerable books about
Mexico, the following have been use-
ful to the present writer: H. G.
Ward's *Mexico* (2nd ed., London,
1829); W. Bullock's *Six Months
Residence . . . in Mexico* (2nd ed.,
London, 1825); Mme. Calderon de
la Barca's *Life in Mexico* (Boston,
1843); Brantz Mayer's *Mexico . . .
Historical Sketch of the Late War*
(Hartford, Conn., 1852); and C. R.
Enock's *Mexico, Its Ancient and
Modern Civilisation* (London, 1912).

under domination of whatever political leader happened to make himself supreme at the capital. In Texas, also, there were other causes of dissatisfaction. The Mexican government tried to collect duties on all goods imported into Texas. This could only be done by stationing soldiers, who seem to have been generally of a very low type, in the few towns through which goods were admitted from the outside world and this greatly increased the cost of the few commodities that were brought in.[1] Under the circumstances, smuggling was inevitable and the Mexican enforcement of its laws was so spasmodic and arbitrary that added irritation was aroused. Another thing which occasioned trouble was the presence of negro slaves in Texas. In 1829, slavery was abolished throughout the Mexican Republic. So far as the Mexican portions of Mexico were concerned this did not mean very much, because the system of peonage, by which the Indians and the poorer of the mixed class were held in perpetual bondage, took the place of slavery so-called. In Texas the case was very different, for the Southern immigrants or some of them had brought their slaves with them from their old homes to their new, and not only did they desire to preserve their "property," but they dreaded above all things, the presence of free negroes. Their remonstrances were so loud that the matter was compromised and the law as to slavery was not enforced among them. Among the conditions in all these land contracts, or grants, was one requiring the colonists introduced by an empresario to be Roman Catholics. Some attention seems to have been paid to this requirement, but a rigid enforcement of it might at any time destroy many land titles in Texas so far as the new-comers were concerned. It is easy to see, bearing

[1] See Eugene C. Barker's "Difficulties of a Mexican Revenue Officer in Texas" in the *Quarterly* of the Texas Historical Association for January, 1901.

in mind the difference in race, religion, and political methods, that the Texans would become very restive whenever the authorities at Mexico City should endeavor to carry out the plain, legal requirements of their residence there.

In 1832 matters came to a crisis.[1] The Texans held a convention or consultation. They resolved to separate from Coahuila and to stand by the constitution of 1824. Stephen F. Austin proceeded to Mexico City to present an address to this effect to the successful revolutionary Centralist authorities at the capital. He was at once put in prison and measures were taken to compel the recalcitrant Texans to recognize the existing government of the Republic. After eight months' incarceration, Austin was released. He returned to Texas and advised acquiescence in the demands of the constituted authorities, at least for the time being.

As the year 1834 progressed, the strained relations between the Texans and the Mexicans increased. In October, 1835, parties of irrepressible and irresponsible Texans took the field and captured the towns of Goliad and San Antonio de Bexar. In November, the American settlers in Texas held a consultation, as they called it, because the Mexicans seemed to dislike the word convention. At this meeting, they appointed a provisional government to look after their affairs as a separate state of the Mexican Republic. In taking this action they were partly conservative as upholding the federative constitution of 1824. Otherwise, their doings were distinctly revolutionary, for they proposed to carry out their wishes as to existence apart from

[1] See Eugene C. Barker's "Organization of the Texas Revolution" and illustrative documents in the *Publications* of the Southern History Association, v, 451 and vi, 33. Professor J. E. Winston has an interesting article on the attitude of the United States newspapers toward Texan independence in the *Proceedings* of the Mississippi Valley Historical Association, viii, 160.

Coahuila and refused to recognize the existing government at Mexico City. Santa Anna was compelled to act. At this time, Mexico is supposed to have contained about seven million inhabitants and Texas from thirty to fifty thousand people. The numerical discrepancy was certainly great, but in reality the two opponents were not so unequally matched as the figures would indicate. Mexican people were sharply divided into classes and masses. The classes comprised those with European blood in their veins — more or less of it. These were the clericals, the politicians, the military officers, the civil officers, and professional and business men, together with the large land owners of the country. The masses comprised all the rest, those with a smaller amount of European blood in their veins and a good many of combined negro and Indian blood, — and there were, of course, some fairly pure-blooded Indians and pure-blooded negroes. The classes as a rule were more concerned with the perpetuation of their privileges than they were with the future of their country. Patriotism, indeed, in the present-day sense of the word was lacking and was replaced by a sentimental belief in themselves and a contempt for the outer world. Having thrown off the yoke of Spain without any preliminary training in self government, the Mexicans proved to be hopelessly inept. Revolution succeeded revolution; few presidents ever served out their terms of office, and the Army and the Church threw their weight first one way and then another, as their interests for the moment seemed to dictate. Under these circumstances, it may well be believed that the national finances were always in a hopeless condition. This meant that it was well-nigh impossible to maintain any military force in the field or any naval force on the water. We read of armies of ten thousand, of twenty thousand, of twenty-five thousand.

For the most part these were little more than collections
of half-breeds and Indians commanded by a disproportionate
number of officers who spent very little of their time in
drilling their men. There was no commissariat and no
quartermasters' department. Whenever there was any
money, some of it was given to the soldiers and they procured their own food, — at other times they seized it, or
went without. Whatever was taken on a campaign was
carried on the backs of the soldiers. These possessed astonishing marching powers; twenty or even thirty miles a day
with equipment and baggage seem to have been attained
by them. But when the fighting began, for the most
part they were helpless. They fired from the hip without
aim and bayonet practice seems to have been unknown.
The rapidity with which an army of this character disappeared while on the march and after a battle is almost
beyond belief, but the figures cannot all of them lie, — desertion was the one hope of salvation.

While Texas, New Mexico, and California had been more
or less integral parts of New Spain and were states of the
Mexican Republic, in reality they were separated geographically from the populous portion of Mexico. From
the Nueces to the Rio Grande was a desert tract that was
supposed to be valuable on account of the possibility of
obtaining salt there. South of the Rio Grande for hundreds
of miles there was little cultivation and few towns even as
far as Tampico and San Luis Potosí. Westward, the route
through Chihuahua to New Mexico and through Sonora
to California was even longer and more devoid of towns
and cultivated acres. In short, Texas, New Mexico, and
California belonged economically to the United States and
not to Mexico. The easiest approach to Texas was by
water from Vera Cruz and to California by water from

Mazatlan; but the Mexicans were no water men and, indeed, their coastal commerce was mainly carried on in American and British vessels. Constant political upheavals, continuing lack of money, and the want of any real patriotic impulse made it exceedingly difficult for any person, who happened to be momentarily in power in Mexico City, to lead an expedition of any size to any great distance from the capital, — and to send a rival in command of such a military force was merely to invite a new revolution. Nevertheless, Santa Anna, with his abounding energy and tremendous optimism, possibly spurred on by the necessity of doing something to save his position, levied an army and marched to the subjugation of Texas.

Texas accepted the challenge. In March, 1836, a convention adopted a constitution on the American model, the chief executive bearing the title of president. Military forces were called out to meet the threatened Mexican attack. The ordinary pioneer possessed courage and capacity for conflict, but he was not easily amenable to guidance, much less to discipline. Each Texan soldier was in reality a commander. The titular commander simply carried out the wishes of the majority of his men and quite likely some of the minority marched off in another direction. The result of these various factors of Mexican and Texan national and military traits might easily be foretold. Mexicans appeared in greatly superior numbers and marched from one town to another, but the Texans defended themselves with an ardor and courageous pertinacity that made one victory or two, or the capture of one town or two a matter of small moment in the final outcome. In a Mexican revolution, one set of soldiers had pointed guns at another set, and possibly had done some random shooting. Then an agreement had been reached by which a few leading men had been executed and victory had been proclaimed for one side or the other. Now, matters went very differently. The Texan defenders of San Antonio de Bexar, as their numbers dwindled, shut themselves up in an old mission building, called the Alamo, and there they fought until the last man was dead or dying, — one hundred and eighty Texans held off three thousand Mexicans for seven or eight days and then perished to a man. "Thermopylæ had her messenger of defeat — the Alamo had none," said General Edward Burleson [1] when the news of the glorious tragedy reached him at Gonzales.

By the middle of April, 1836, the Mexicans had overrun the Texo-American settlements as far as Galveston Bay. In the course of their progress, they had captured the town of Goliad with its defenders under the command of Colonel Fannin. Resistance being hopeless, the Texans had surrendered as prisoners of war. Regardless of this, the Mexicans looked upon them as fellow rebels. After a few days they marched them out onto the prairie and shot them down in cold blood, a few managing to escape by rapid flight. The Alamo, the Goliad massacre, and other bloody deeds by the Mexicans drove the Texans away from their farms and towns; they burned their buildings, destroyed their stores, and fled toward the American frontier. Santa Anna believed the rebellion was crushed and even thought of returning to Mexico to reckon with his political enemies. Then, as is so often the case in war, an accident occurred that changed the whole course of Texan history and, indeed, that of the United States and of Mexico.

The commander-in-chief of the Texan military forces, if such a phrase can be used, was Sam Houston, — once a member

---

[1] Texas State Historical Association's *Quarterly*, vii, 328. Some doubts exist as to the authorship of these words; see *ibid.*, vi, 309.

of the United States Congress and governor of Tennessee, later a chief of the Cherokee Indians, and now the leader of frontiersmen.[1] "Marital troubles" had led to his flight from Tennessee and a happy marriage in Texas at a later day gave him renewed status among his countrymen. The story of his life for this middle period is extremely uncertain. To one set of seekers he represents the highest form of statesmanship and diplomacy, playing off the United States and Great Britain, one against the other; to another, he is a mere opportunist whom chance had thrown at the head of affairs. The story of the next few weeks in the military history of Texas and of Sam Houston is equally vague. To one set of writers he is the military commander par excellence, advising and executing by his own power of mind and will. To the other set he is hardly more than the obedient executor of the commands of his own soldiers, — they and not he determining on the campaign and enforcing their own decisions. A few things seem to stand out from the general uncertainty. After the Alamo and Goliad, Houston saw that the only salvation for Texas and Texans was to stop the panic, gather the fighting men together, and strike a blow. He and his men then acted in a fortunate and skilful manner. They concentrated, with a good measure of secrecy, while the Mexicans dispersed into four bands, Santa Anna being at the head of one detachment. The movements of the hostile groups are very puzzling to trace on a map and correlate as to point of time; but it really is not necessary. Santa Anna, with perhaps eight hundred men, advanced eastwardly to the vicinity of Galveston

---

[1] There is no life of Houston at all commensurate with the possibilities of the subject. Henry Bruce's little book in the *Makers of America* series has literary merit. Houston defended his doings as commander of the Texan army in a speech delivered in the Senate on February 28, 1859; but it is not very convincing.

Bay and pitched his camp on the western bank of the San
Jacinto River, not far from its entrance into the bay. There
he was joined by another detachment bringing the number
up to eleven or twelve hundred. For some days, the consolidated Texan force having somehow slipped in between
the Mexican detachments, had been following Santa Anna
and his men. On the 20th of April they came upon them in
a sort of entrenched camp, the river and swamp being back
of the Mexican position and the front being protected by
pack saddles and other impedimenta of the expedition.
Santa Anna had selected this place because the river and
swamp protected his rear and flank; but the Texans, disdaining strategic operations, after some prolonged preliminary skirmishings, suddenly, on the afternoon of April 21,
1836, at about half-past three, yelling at the top of their
lungs, "Remember the Alamo!" "Remember Goliad!"
dashed over the obstructions and clubbing their muskets,
for they had no bayonets, beat the Mexicans from their
camp-fires and tents, killed them as they ran, and shot to
death those who tried to escape through the marsh or over
the river.[1] At the moment Santa Anna was enjoying his
siesta. Two days later, some soldiers scouting for prisoners
in the open prairie, saw a figure of a man in the grass. Receiving no reply from him, one of them kicked him and
told him to get up. He complied and, speaking to them in
Spanish, declared that he was a private soldier. As the
party entered the camp, the Mexican prisoners saluted the
captive as "El Presidente." It was, indeed, Santa Anna,
and Houston had all that he could do to preserve the life of

[1] See G. L. Rives's *United States
and Mexico*, i, ch. xiv. This account
of the battle of San Jacinto, as well as
all others, is mainly based on H.
Yoakum's *History of Texas* (ed. 1856)
ii, ch. v. Professor Eugene C. Barker
has gathered together nearly all available information in the Texas State
Historical   Association's   *Quarterly*
for April, 1901, with a convenient
"list of books" at the end.

the man responsible for the Alamo and Goliad. It would have been well, perhaps, for Mexico, Texas, and the United States had some accident removed Santa Anna from politics and war. As it was he was all compliance and ordered his subordinates to retire from Texas beyond the Rio Grande. In the battle or massacre of San Jacinto, the Texan loss was two killed and twenty-three wounded against a Mexican loss of hundreds killed and wounded, and as many more taken prisoners.[1]

The annals of Texas for the next eight years after San Jacinto are as difficult to unravel as is the story of that campaign. There were three possible courses open for Texas, or three possible positions that might be achieved. She might come to terms with Mexico and remain a part of that Republic with a good measure of home rule. She might become a part of the United States. Remaining independent, she might become the nucleus of another great North American republic, embracing all the present area of the United States to the west and south of the line of 1819 with a considerable portion of Northern Mexico in addition. Thus the new nation would include the greater part of the present State of Colorado, all of Utah, Nevada, and California on the north and extend southwardly across the Rio Grande to include the greater part of Coahuila, Chihuahua, and Sonora, — besides Texas, New Mexico, and Arizona. It was an imperial domain, equivalent in area to about one-third of the United States. As leaders of an independent republic, great careers awaited the heroes of the Texan Revolution, Houston, Anson Jones, Ashbel Smith, David G. Burnet, and the rest. Texas alone could eventually produce more cotton than all the Southern States of

[1] As to the exact figures of Mexican losses, see Yoakum's *History of Texas*, ii, 146, 501 and G. L. Rives's   *United States and Mexico*, i, 350 and note.

the American Union, at least, so it was asserted. Moreover, Texas being outside of the American Union and the Mexican Republic, could arrange her tariff system to suit her own needs and not those of Pennsylvania or New England, or of the politicians of Mexico City. It was surely an alluring prospect, and had the leaders of Texas been men of larger calibre, it might have been carried through triumphantly.

As to the first alternative, coming to some arrangement with Mexico as to more or less complete autonomy, that proved to be out of the range of possibilities. The Mexicans, while unable to compel Texas to do their bidding, were so affected by sentimental nationalism that no government could have stood a month that had come out openly for the recognition of Texan independence in any form. Isolated in their valley stronghold, the ruling classes in Mexican politics believed themselves secure from all attack. The Spaniards had tried it and been repelled, the French had tried it, and had not advanced beyond Vera Cruz. How could it be possible that the Texans, even with the aid of the United States, could ever maintain their independence? The American Army was less in size than that of Mexico and composed of German, Irish, and British renegados, of men who fought for money and not like the Mexican soldiers, for love of country! For eight years one revolutionary government after another in Mexico turned a deaf ear to all suggestions of recognition. The United States, Great Britain, France, and other countries of the world recognized Texas as an independent power; but Mexico would not. In 1843, for a moment, there appeared what looked like a change of heart. James W. Robinson, at one time high in place in Texas and now a prisoner in the fortress of Perote in Mexico, suggested to Santa Anna, who was then at the head of affairs in Mexico, that an arrangement might be made whereby Texas should acknowledge the sovereignty of Mexico and Mexico should recognize Texas as an "independent department" of the Mexican Republic. It seemed as if something might come of this project. Texas even proclaimed an armistice; but then political conditions compelled a change in Mexico's policy. Again, in 1844, this time under the guidance of the British representative in Texas, Captain Charles Elliot, Mexico listened favorably to a somewhat similar proposition, but her action was then taken too late to fend off annexation to the United States.

The third possibility was union with the United States. As far back as 1825, and again in 1827 John Quincy Adams [1] and Henry Clay had put forward propositions for the purchase of Texas from Mexico. Adams had opposed — alone in Monroe's cabinet — the giving up of Texas in 1819. He now took the first opportunity to try to retrieve what he regarded as Monroe's error, but the Mexicans would not listen. Jackson renewed the proposition in a somewhat different guise, as a rectification of the boundary,[2] for although he had approved of the Florida Treaty at the time, he had come since to regard it as a blunder. But, again, there was no response and the matter was so badly handled that added resentment was aroused on the part of the Mexicans. Then came San Jacinto and, not long thereafter, a proposition from Texas for recognition as an independent State and annexation to the American Republic. Now, Jackson, who had been eager for the acquisition of Texas by purchase and had later advocated the recognition of the new republic as an independent power, stood firmly on the obligations of the United States to Mexico. The Texans

[1] *American State Papers, Foreign Relations*, vi, 578–581; and J. Q. Adams's *Memoirs*, vii, 239, 240.

[2] See Professor E. C. Barker's "President Jackson and the Texas Revolution" in *American Historical Review* for July, 1907, and W. R. Manning's *Early Diplomatic Relations between the United States and Mexico* (Baltimore, 1916).

were disappointed but Jackson was immovable. Congress
then authorized the President to appoint a diplomatic
agent whenever he should feel satisfied as to the independence of the new republic. He at once acted by nominating a
Chargé d'Affaires to the Republic of Texas on March 3, 1837.[1]

Great Britain, on her part, pursued a fairly steady policy
of advocating Texan independence and recognition thereof
by Mexico.[2] Her statesmen preferred to see Texas an independent power, because that would have broken the
cotton monopoly of the United States. The one great
objection to it was that many of the supporters of the
Peel government that came into power in 1841 were abolitionists and an independent Texas, or a Texas annexed
to the United States, meant the perpetuation of slavery.

In 1842, Charles Elliot appeared in Texas as representative
of Great Britain. He was a naval officer of good family
who had bungled matters at the time of the opium controversy with China. Presumably, he was sent to Texas because there was no better place for him. He had been
there scarcely three months when he wrote a letter advocating the reconstruction of Texan society by the abolition of slavery and the restriction of the franchise to persons
of education and wealth ! His letters give one the impression that he was intimate with Houston. It is very possible
that the Texan revolutionist used him to draw an offer
from the British government that would be of service in
negotiations with the United States; but this theory pre-
supposes a degree of foresightedness in Houston and also
a desire for annexation to the United States which he may

[1] J. H. Smith's *Annexation of Texas*, 52–62.
[2] See Justin H. Smith's "The Mexican Recognition of Texas" in *American Historical Review*, xvi, 36; his *Annexation of Texas*; Ephraim D.
Adams's *British Interests and Activities in Texas, 1838–1846*; J. S. Reeves's *American Diplomacy under Tyler and Polk*; and G. L. Rives's *United States and Mexico*, i, chs. xv, xvi.

not have had. It is certain that the British government desired Texas to be independent, without slavery if possible, but with slavery, if necessary.[1] It was not willing to go to war with anybody on this issue. As Mexico would not recognize Texan independence unless compelled to do so, and as an open abolition propaganda seemed likely to lead to trouble with the United States, Aberdeen drew back. In this he was impelled partly by the suggestion from the British minister at Washington that his relations with the Texan representative at London and with the abolitionists were aiding the election of the pro-annexation Democratic candidate for the presidency.

In 1841, at the accession of Peel and Aberdeen to power, the relations between the United States and Great Britain were so grave that war seemed to be imminent. There were the long-standing controversies as to the Northeastern boundary and as to the division of Oregon.[2] Besides, the destruction of an American vessel by a party of Canadians

[1] Aberdeen's famous declaration is in a letter of Ashbel Smith to Anson Jones, dated Paris, July 31, 1843, in Garrison's *Diplomatic Correspondence of . . . Texas*, pp. 1116, 1117 in the American Historical Association's *Report* for 1908, vol. ii and is as follows:

" His Lordship replied, in effect, that it is the well-known policy and wish of the British Government to abolish slavery every where: that its abolition in Texas is deemed very desirable and he spoke to this point at some little length, as connected with British policy and British interests and in reference to the United States. He added, there was no disposition on the part of the British Govt to interfere improperly on this subject, and that they would not give the Texian Govt any cause to complain: 'he was not prepared to say whether the British Government would consent hereafter to make such compensation to Texas as would enable the Slaveholders to abolish slavery, the object is deemed so important perhaps they might, though he could not say certainly.' I here remarked to his Lordship, that any compensation received by Texas from a foreign power for the abolition of slavery would be derogatory to our national honor and degrade and disgrace us in the eyes of the world. He observed such things can be so done as not to be offensive, etc., but I believe his Lordship was of my opinion.

" Lord Aberdeen also stated that despatches had been recently sent to Mr. Doyle, the British Chargé d'Affaires at Mexico, instructing him to renew the tender of British Mediation based on the abolition of slavery in Texas, and declaring that abolition would be a *great moral triumph for Mexico.* Your Department will not fail to remark that this despatch to Mr. Doyle appears to introduce a new and important condition into 'mediation.' "

[2] See Note II at end of chapter.

within American territorial waters had aroused great resentment in New York.[1] At the other end of the line, the active British propaganda for the suppression of the African slave trade angered the Southerners and their feelings were not at all appeased by the release of negroes, who had captured a coasting vessel — the *Creole* — while on a voyage from Norfolk to New Orleans, by the British authorities at Nassau in the Bahamas.[2] These controversies interested the people of the North, the West, and the South. At the moment the weak government of Tyler was in office, with Daniel Webster holding on to the Secretaryship of State after all his original colleagues had resigned. Most fortunately, economic considerations, according to the financial authorities, made it practically impossible for Great Britain at this precise time to go to war with the United States. No doubt Aberdeen, the new Foreign Secretary, in succession to Palmerston was desirous of doing what was right, but in the actual condition of affairs, it would have been very difficult to have maintained the old Canning-Palmerston attitude toward the United States. It was in these circumstances that Alexander Baring, Lord Ashburton,[3] was sent on a special mission to Washington to settle as many of these questions as he could. The instructions given him were very broad and he was a man of such position and of such firmness of character that he was willing to take upon himself responsibilities that very few diplomatists had ever been willing to incur. The Oregon question proved to be insoluble at the moment and was set aside.

[1] See O. E. Tiffany's "Relations of the United States to the Canadian Rebellion of 1837-1838" in the *Publications* of the Buffalo Historical Society, viii, 1-147. There are ample footnotes to this article and there is a bibliography on p. 115. A more complete list is in *ibid.*, v, 427.

[2] J. B. Moore's *Digest of International Law*, ii, 358-361.

[3] For many years Baring had been intimately connected with American financial affairs and had married a Philadelphian who had inherited large tracts of land in the State of Maine. See the present work, vol. iv, 110.

The Northeastern boundary controversy takes one back to the Treaty of 1783.[1] The language of that instrument was certainly capable of more than one interpretation and it was found impossible to harmonize some of the geographical expressions in it with the actual topography. Commissions were appointed, but little progress was made except to ascertain the identity of the St. Croix River. This stream was small in itself, but it was of great importance in this boundary controversy, because it was from the source of this river that the boundary line between Maine and New Brunswick proceeded due north to the "angle" which was formed by its junction with the highlands that separate the rivers that flow into the St. Lawrence from those that empty themselves into "the sea" or into the Atlantic Ocean. In the War of 1812 the British had found great difficulty in reinforcing their troops in Canada and supplying them with provisions and munitions, for the St. Lawrence is navigable for only a portion of each year. It seemed to be necessary for the future of the British Empire that the Northeastern boundary should be so arranged that sufficient territory would be obtained for a military road wholly in British control from the St. Lawrence opposite Quebec to Halifax.[2] It also appeared that American settlers had

[1] See the present work, volume iii, ch. xii. The most recent treatments of this boundary dispute are H. S. Burrage's *Maine in the Northeastern Boundary Controversy* and J. F. Sprague's chapter in Hatch's *Maine, A History*, i, 247–281. Of the official documents Gallatin's *Right of the United States of America to the North-Eastern Boundary* (New York, 1840) is the most helpful. See also *The Message from the President . . . December 7, 1842* (House Document, No. 2, 27th Cong., 3rd Sess. and the *Report of the Committee on the North-Eastern Boundary* that was printed by order of the Maine Senate in 1841. A letter from Wil-

liam Pitt Preble dated at The Hague, 25th Jan., 1831, and addressed to Louis McLane, American minister at London, in the Appendix to *The Decision of the King of the Netherlands considered in reference to the rights of the United States and of the State of Maine* (Portland, 1831) gives the American side of the case most clearly. An excellent topographical treatment of the question is William F. Ganong's "Evolution of the Boundaries of the Province of New Brunswick" in the *Transactions* of the Royal Society of Canada, 2nd Series, vol. vii, Section ii.

[2] In his letter to Ashburton of March 31, 1842, Aberdeen informs him that

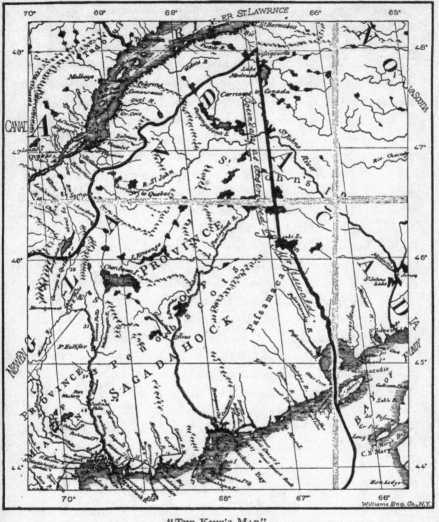

"THE KING'S MAP"

(An extract, redrawn from the colored facsimile in Col. Dudley A. Mills's article in the
United Empire, vol. ii, No. 10.)

seated themselves on territory that was clearly British at the head of the Connecticut River and at the northern end of Lake Champlain. Under these circumstances it would have been well had the British said in effect to the United States that "we want territory that clearly belongs to you, and some of your people are living within our limits. Can we not make some arrangement that will be mutually satisfactory?" Instead of doing this, successive British governments attacked the soundness of the American title. At length, in 1827, the Adams administration agreed to submit the controversy to the king of the Netherlands as arbiter, although, as Adams must have known, he was under considerable obligations to Great Britain. Instead of deciding for one party or the other, this royal arbiter undertook to divide the disputed territory between the two countries.[1] The decision was made in 1831. In 1832, President Jackson asked the Senate whether it would "advise a submission to the opinion delivered by the sovereign arbiter, and consent to its execution." On June 23 of that year, the Senators voted that they "do not advise . . . and do not consent" to the award.[2] Seven years later, in 1839, hostilities between Maine frontiersmen and British settlers in the Aroostook country had been averted only by the patriotic and skilful conduct of General Winfield Scott and Governor Harvey of New Brunswick.[3]

although a conventional line may be agreed upon "there is a limit, beyond which a regard for the safety of these Provinces must forbid us to recede"; but the whole letter should be read by any one interested in this subject. *American Historical Review*, xvii, 768.

It is worth noticing that in 1839, when there was a possibility that Webster might represent the United States at London, he had thought that "a conventional line" would better

be agreed to. Van Tyne's *Letters of Daniel Webster*, 217.

[1] J. B. Moore's *History . . . of the International Arbitrations to which the United States has been a Party*, i, pp. 1-161.

[2] See *Senate Journal*, 22nd Cong., 1st Sess., "Appendix," pp. 516-531.

[3] The seriousness of the affair comes out in the "Roster of Commissioned Officers and Enlisted Men" who were called into service in 1839 by the State

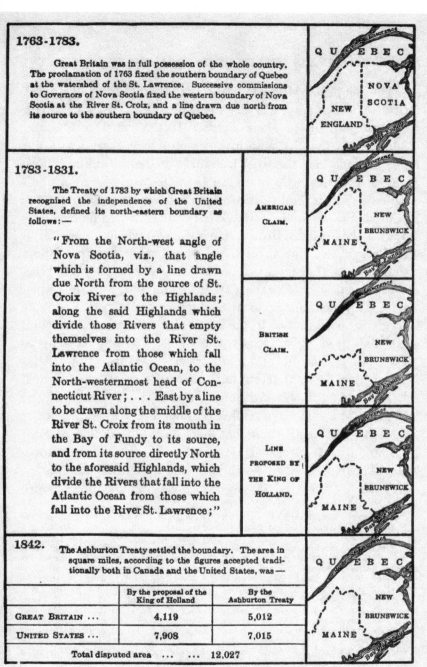

1763-1783.

Great Britain was in full possession of the whole country. The proclamation of 1763 fixed the southern boundary of Quebec at the watershed of the St. Lawrence. Successive commissions to Governors of Nova Scotia fixed the western boundary of Nova Scotia at the River St. Croix, and a line drawn due north from its source to the southern boundary of Quebec.

1783-1831.

The Treaty of 1783 by which Great Britain recognised the independence of the United States, defined its north-eastern boundary as follows:—

"From the North-west angle of Nova Scotia, viz., that angle which is formed by a line drawn due North from the source of St. Croix River to the Highlands; along the said Highlands which divide those Rivers that empty themselves into the River St. Lawrence from those which fall into the Atlantic Ocean, to the North-westernmost head of Connecticut River; . . . East by a line to be drawn along the middle of the River St. Croix from its mouth in the Bay of Fundy to its source, and from its source directly North to the aforesaid Highlands, which divide the Rivers that fall into the Atlantic Ocean from those which fall into the River St. Lawrence;"

AMERICAN CLAIM.

BRITISH CLAIM.

LINE PROPOSED BY THE KING OF HOLLAND.

1842. The Ashburton Treaty settled the boundary. The area in square miles, according to the figures accepted traditionally both in Canada and the United States, was—

	By the proposal of the King of Holland	By the Ashburton Treaty
GREAT BRITAIN ...	4,119	5,012
UNITED STATES ...	7,908	7,015
Total disputed area 12,027		

THE NORTHEASTERN BOUNDARY

(Reproduced by permission from Col. Dudley A. Mills's article in the *United Empire*, vol. ii, No. 10.)

The people of Maine thought that their State had a good title to the disputed lands and were very unwilling to do anything to lessen their rights. It happened that Jared Sparks had found a map in Paris on which there was a red line that justified the British claim.[1] For some unknown reason he had made up his mind that this was the map upon which Franklin had drawn a line showing the extent of the United States under the Treaty of Independence. Undoubtedly Franklin drew a line on a map which he presented to Vergennes; but there is no reason whatever to suppose that it was this map. It served Webster's purpose, however, because on Sparks exhibiting it to the Maine legislators, they consented to the appointment of commissioners to go to Washington to advise Webster in the negotiation. He also used it to secure the consent of the Senate to the treaty that he and Ashburton drew up; but he did not show it to Ashburton until after the treaty was signed. Earlier, in 1839, Sir Anthony Panizzi, the Director of the British Museum, had called Palmerston's attention to a map in that institution that had on it a red line marked "boundary as described by Mr. Oswald." This is known as "The King's Map." It bore out the American contention as to the line in its entirety. Palmerston at once

---

of Maine; see pamphlet entitled, *Aroostook War*, published at Augusta, Maine, in 1904.

[1] For the red-line map, see *Life and Writings of Jared Sparks*, ii, ch. xxvii; and Winsor's *Narrative and Critical History*, vii, 180. Colonel Dudley A. Mills, R.E., has printed a full-sized facsimile of the Oswald map in the *United Empire Magazine* for October, 1911. This may be compared with an extract from "Mr. Jay's Map" that is prefixed to Gallatin's *Memoir on the North-Eastern Boundary* that was printed for the New York Historical Society in 1843, and with J. D. Graham's "Map of the Boundary Lines between the United States and the Adjacent British Provinces" that was issued in March, 1843. Colonel Mills most kindly placed his Ms. notes at my disposal, and Professor Ephraim D. Adams's essay in the *American Historical Review* (xvii, 764) has been of great service. There is a list of books in the 7th volume of Winsor's *Narrative and Critical History*, and A. R. Hasse's "References" in the *Bulletin* of the New York Public Library for December, 1900, is most useful.

impounded it in the recesses of the Foreign Office and it was unknown to Aberdeen and to Ashburton until after the latter's return to England in 1843, and it was not known to students until 1896. The negotiators proceeded upon the principle that it was desirable to "draw a conventional line" that would give England the territory she wanted and would permit the Americans to stay on the lands they had occupied within British territory at the head of the Connecticut River and at the northern end of Lake Champlain. They also managed to come to an agreement as to the other disputed matters in a way, however, that was not pleasing to any one and, therefore, may have been a fair compromise. This arrangement was included in the treaty that was ratified by the Senate in 1842.

In 1843, Texan annexation became a distinct issue in American politics. John Tyler of Virginia, now President by the accidental death of William Henry Harrison, was an ardent annexationist and always had been. He believed that the United States should own not only Texas, but California as well, and with them, of course, the intervening province of New Mexico. The trouble with Tyler was that he had no party behind him and while he could block by his veto legislation proposed by the Whigs, he could not by Democratic strength get any positive measures passed through Congress. In 1843, Webster retired from the State Department, where his presence had made annexation by treaty impossible. Houston was again President of Texas and, while favoring annexation by treaty, he seemed determined to make certain beforehand of adequate protection by the United States against the wrath of the Mexican Republic before beginning active negotiations.[1] It was difficult for an executive officer at Washington to give any

[1] J. H. Smith's *Annexation of Texas*, 164, 166.

such assurance or to station soldiers and ships for the defence of Texas because the Constitution confided to Congress the power to declare war. Webster's successor in the State Department was Abel P. Upshur, a Virginian and a favorer of Tyler's plan. The treaty for the annexation of Texas as a "territory" was practically completed when the explosion of a gun on the American warship *Princeton* killed Upshur, February 28, 1844. He was succeeded by John C. Calhoun and the treaty was signed and sent to the Senate.[1] Up to this time, the prospect of the ratification of the treaty was bright.[2] It happened that Calhoun found on Upshur's desk a letter from Aberdeen to Pakenham which the latter had laid before the American Secretary of State. It was dated December 26, 1843, and was intended to allay excitement by denying that Great Britain had any "occult design" upon Mexico or upon Texas. Aberdeen avowed that he, himself, wished to see slavery abolished throughout the world, but only open and undisguised means would be adopted by Great Britain to secure "this humane and virtuous purpose." Calhoun at once undertook to answer this letter. He may have hoped to end forever the abolition propaganda; he may have expected to rally anti-abolition opinion to his side; or he may have designed to split his own country into two sections and to consolidate the national spirit of the South. In this letter, Calhoun restated the Southern view that slavery was a beneficent institution, blessed alike to the

[1] The letters and other papers that passed during the negotiations are printed in *Senate Documents*, No. 341, 28th Cong., 1st Sess.

[2] One finds articles opposing the annexation of Texas in the New England papers as early as September, 1829. In August, 1837, the Reverend William Ellery Channing addressed a letter to Henry Clay on this subject. It was widely printed and was the occasion of many replies. Among them may be mentioned *Sidney's Letters to William E. Channing . . . First Published in the "Charleston Courier."* Of the later remonstrances are *The Legion of Liberty* published in 1843; *The Texan Revolution* by "Probus," 1843 and *The Taking of Naboth's Vineyard*, printed in 1845.

slave and to the owner.[1] The avowal of Britain's desire for universal abolition necessitated the absorption of Texas into the United States to obviate so great a calamity to the world. This letter was the supreme example of Southern provincialism. For no one who had known the North or Europe and wished for Texas annexation could have written it. It aroused the anti-slavery men of the North and made abolitionists of them. It converted many a waverer on the question of Texas annexation to the theory that that movement was a conspiracy on the part of slaveholders to increase their power for evil. What had seemed to be questionable was regarded now as positively injurious. It became impossible to procure the two-thirds vote necessary in the Senate for the ratification of the treaty and it was defeated.[2] President Tyler thereupon asked Congress to provide for the annexation of Texas by joint resolution, which only required a majority vote in the two Houses. The annexation of Texas now became a distinct political issue and the presidential campaign of 1844 was fought to bring it about.

Political conditions were exceedingly peculiar at that time. Tyler, naturally enough, wished to be elected President; but his joining with the Whigs had lost him Democratic support and his refusal to approve Whig measures had made him unpopular with Clay and his followers. Enough office-holders and personal friends came together to nominate Tyler for the presidency, but his candidacy had no vitality. Clay was the inevitable candidate of the Whigs and Van Buren looked upon himself as the rightful standard bearer of the Democrats. When the Democratic convention was held, the Calhoun men, while not strong enough to nominate the South Carolinian, were

---

[1] *Senate Document*, No. 341, pp. 48, 50, 28th Cong., 1st Sess.

[2] *Journal of the Senate*, 28th Cong., 1st Sess., "Appendix," pp. 421–438.

strong enough to make Van Buren's nomination impossible
by carrying through the convention the rule that required a
two-thirds vote for the nomination. For a time it seemed
as if the nomination of any one was impossible. Suddenly,
it occurred to George Bancroft, a member of the Massachusetts delegation who combined politics with history, that
the nomination of Governor Polk of Tennessee would satisfy
all factions. Bancroft suggested this to Gideon J. Pillow,
who had formerly been Polk's law partner and in the Baltimore convention was hoping to secure for Polk the nomination to the vice-presidency. He eagerly fell in with
Bancroft's plan. The fatigued and baffled delegates received it rejoicingly and voted unanimously for Polk, who
thus became the first "dark horse" in the history of the
presidency.[1]

As soon as the nomination of Polk was made, John Tyler
withdrew from the contest. His own chances were hopeless,
and by remaining in the race he would divide the Democratic
vote. He was assured that his own friends would be taken
care of by Polk and thereby was enabled to retire grace-
fully, for Polk was also heartily in favor of the annexation
of Texas. Henry Clay seemed to have no settled opinion
on the subject. In April, 1844, he opposed it.[2] At the
moment he probably believed Southern opinion to be
doubtful. The legal status of slavery was still undeter-
mined in Texas and, in any event, that country was certain
to be a strong competitor with the existing States in the
production of cotton fibre. Clay mistook his own feelings

[1] On the nomination of Polk see
"Letters of . . . Pillow to . . . Polk,
1844" in *American Historical Review*,
xi, 832. For the Bancroft side of the
matter, see American Antiquarian Society's *Proceedings* for April, 1891,
p. 244. Polk's capacity as a politician
comes out in the letters he wrote to
Cave Johnson in the years 1833-1844
(*Tennessee Historical Magazine*, September, 1915).

[2] See the well-known "Raleigh
Letter," dated April 17, 1844, in Cal-
vin Colton's *Life of Henry Clay* (New
York, 1857), iii, 25.

for those of Southern people in general and misinterpreted political sentiment in this case as he had in many others. In reality the annexation of Texas would almost certainly add to the existing slave territory, would open new lands for colonization to the planters of the Cotton Belt, and would provide a new market for slaves to the slaveholders of the Border States.   As months went by, it became more and more evident that Clay had taken the wrong side; but his friends implored him to be silent and to write no letters, for then the Texas issue might be minimized. He could not do this and wrote other letters shifting his ground and thereby offended the abolitionists without gaining any important strength in the South.   As it was, the election was very close [1] and was determined by the action of the abolitionists in New York State. After much cogitation and with many misgivings, the anti-slavery men there determined to vote for James G. Birney for the presidency. There was no possibility of his election and the anti-slavery men by voting with the Whigs would have given the Texas annexation scheme a heavy blow; but they would not coöperate with any one who did not believe the slavery issue itself to be the most important thing at stake.[2] Birney drew enough votes away from the Whig electors in New York to give the electoral vote of that State to Polk and thereby made him President.[3]   When Congress met in December,

---

[1] An idea of the vigor with which this campaign was waged may be gained by a perusal of a series of ten papers published by a committee of the Democratic members of Congress, especially numbers 7 and 8, giving fifty reasons why Polk should be elected and Clay defeated. The means used by politicians to accomplish their purposes in those days were fully as tortuous as they were in the election of 1828. See, for example, *The Counter-*

feit Detector, or the Leaders of "The party" Exposed.

[2] Possibly the best exposition of the abolitionist view of the wickedness of slave-expansion is Loring Moody's *History of the Mexican War, or Facts for the People, showing the relation of the United States Government to Slavery* (Boston, 1848).

[3] In the New York popular vote, Polk had 237,588; Clay had 232,482; and Birney had 15,812. Adding the

Tyler urged on his scheme of annexation by resolution and in February, 1845, the two Houses passed a joint resolution for the annexation of Texas and its admission into the Union as one State.

"Who is James K. Polk?" was frequently asked and the only answer that could be given by most persons was "He is the President of the United States." That was about all that was known of him, although he had been Speaker of the Federal House of Representatives and governor of Tennessee. It was not until the publication of his "Diary" in 1910 that it was possible to make a much better appraisal, except, of course, one could rehearse the principal events of the four years of his inhabitancy of the White House. In reality Polk [1] has suffered severely at the hands of contemporaries and historians. He had no glamour of popularity about him. He shut himself up in the presidential mansion and worked sixteen hours a day, including the keeping of his "Diary." Much of his time was taken up with office hunters. Polk was a partisan and saw no virtue in Whigs; but he was thoroughly disgusted with the carrying out of this part of his duties. For the rest he gives the impression of a man who saw his duty clearly and was determined to do it. Undoubtedly, he was not of

Birney votes to the Clay votes — supposing all the anti-slavery men had voted for Clay — he would have had 248,294 votes. As the presidential electors in New York were voted for on a general ticket in that year, the 36 electoral votes of New York would have been cast for Clay instead of for Polk. Subtracting these 36 electoral votes from Polk's 170 would have left him with 134; and adding them to Clay's 105 electoral votes would have given Clay 141 and made him President. Nevertheless, it was held by the Democrats that the people in the election had approved the annexation of Texas. The above figures are taken from Greeley's *Political Text-Book*, p. 239 and *Journal of the House of Representatives*, 28th Cong., 2nd Sess., p. 372.

[1] Milo M. Quaife's "Biographical Sketch" prefixed to volume i of the *Diary* is possibly the best assessment of Polk. *The Diary of James K. Polk during his Presidency* (4 vols., Chicago, 1910) is the best memorial of him. In the *American Historical Magazine* for April, 1896, p. 154, M. W. Garrett states that President Polk was descended from "a great noble" named "Fulbert the Saxon."

great mental calibre nor of much education; but he possessed a strong will and an inflexible determination to do the right thing as he saw it. In a Cabinet council composed of Buchanan of Pennsylvania, Walker of Mississippi, Marcy of New York, Mason of Virginia, and Bancroft of Massachusetts, Polk was certainly the master spirit, and in every crisis of his administration, it was his hand that guided events. He at once proceeded to carry out "the will of the people" as expressed in his own election by pushing on the annexation of Texas.[1] The president of that country at the moment was Anson Jones. He did not favor annexation, but the voice of the Texan people was too strong for him and he was obliged to take the necessary steps to ascertain the popular wish. On July 4, 1845, a convention at San Felipe de Austin determined, with a few dissentient votes, to accept the proposal of the United States; but the later steps of actually admitting Texas to the Union were not completed until the end of that year.

[1] See the *Diary* of J. K. Polk, i, 17, etc., and some interesting letters in Massachusetts Historical Society's *Proceedings* for November, 1909, pp. 110– 121 and H. B. Learned's "Cabinet Meetings under President Polk" in American Historical Association's *Report* for 1914, vol. i, pp. 231–242.

NOTES

I. Texas Bibliography. — Our knowledge of early Texas has been derived mainly, until recent years, from the work of H. Yoakum which was published in 1856 in two volumes with the title of *History of Texas . . . to its Annexation to the United States in 1846.* This forms the basis of D. G. Wooten's *Comprehensive History of Texas.* William Kennedy's *Texas* in two volumes was published at London in 1841. He was an Englishman who had travelled extensively in America and occupied a diplomatic post in Texas under Charles Elliot, the British consul general. It is a serious painstaking work and undoubtedly represents contemporary opinion in Texas. Frank W. Johnson, who participated in the Texas Revolution, wrote out his recollections in later life and fortified them with abundant documents. Professor Eugene C. Barker edited this narrative, adding other documents. This forms volume i of *A History of Texas and Texans,* edited by Eugene C. Barker with the assistance of Ernest W. Winkler; the second volume of this work contains much instructive local information. The last three volumes are of the usual type of subscription State histories, of biographies of persons who are willing to provide material and illustrations. It differs from most of these works, however, in having an exceedingly good editor and presenting an original contemporaneous account of the origin of one of our States. Less useful books are Henry S. Foote's *Texas and the Texans; or, Advance of the Anglo-Americans to the South-west* (2 vols., Philadelphia, 1841) and J. H. Brown' *History of Texas* (2 vols., St. Louis, 1892). George P. Garrison's *Texas* in the *American Commonwealth* series has the merit of brevity, but it lacks all bibliographical apparatus.

Herbert E. Bolton of the University of California and Eugene C. Barker of the University of Texas have established new schools of research in promoting the intensive study of episodes of the early history of the Pacific Slope and the Southwest. They and their students and co-workers have explored the archives of Mexico, California, and Texas and brought to light much valuable material. They have published many studies and much original matter in the publications of the Universities of California and Texas, in *The Quarterly* of the Texas State Historical Association, and in the *Publications* of the Southern History Association. Specific references have been given to many of these articles in the preceding footnotes.

The American Historical Association has undertaken the publication of the Stephen F. Austin papers under the editorship of Professor Barker and has already printed a great mass of diplomatic papers under the editorship of the late Professor Garrison.[1]

II. The Whitman Story. — In the 1860's a story was started to the effect that Webster had been on the point of giving up Oregon in exchange for the cod fisheries, when he was compelled to desist by representations made by a missionary named Whitman, and this idea became almost an article of faith among certain good people. William I. Marshall, a Chicago school-teacher, in 1882 learned that there was no evidence to support this story and spent the rest of his life in gathering the facts and putting them together to prove the negative. See his " Marcus Whitman : a Discussion of Professor Bourne's Paper " in *Report* of the American Historical Association for 1900, pp. 221–236; in 1904 Marshall published three essays entitled *History* vs. *The Whitman Saved Oregon Story* and after his death the material that he had collected with so much labor was printed at the expense of " a number of citizens of the States of Oregon and Washington " under the title of *Acquisition of Oregon and the Long Suppressed Evidence about Marcus Whitman* (2 vols., Seattle, 1911). Not knowing of Marshall's studies, Professor Edward G. Bourne attacked the same problem and set forth the results of his research in a paper which he read at the meeting of the American Historical Association in December, 1900. This was printed in the *American Historical Review* for January, 1901, and the same matter considerably expanded is printed under the title of " The Legend of Marcus Whitman " in Bourne's *Essays in Historical Criticism,* 3–109. In this paper he acknowledges his indebtedness to Marshall and gives abundant citations.

It would seem that the fact that Whitman reached Washington City months after the ratification of the Treaty of 1842 and the departure of Ashburton for England would have caused historical students to question the accuracy of the story in other respects.

[1] American Historical Association's *Report* for 1907.

CHAPTER XVII

THE YEAR 1846

THE year 1846 is one of the most memorable in our history; it witnessed the settlement of the dispute of decades over Oregon, the occupation of California, the march of the Mormons to Utah, and the opening campaigns of the Mexican War. It was the destiny of the United States to extend to the Pacific and as far south as the arid portions of Mexico. California, New Mexico, Texas, and Oregon in its old geographical sense were all practically unutilized by man in 1835. Of course, it cannot be said that the people of the United States had any moral right to take over lands that had been practically unused by another people; but it must be said that the moral argument for the retention of these splendid lands by a people who did not and could not convert them to the benefit of humanity raises a strong presumption in favor of their acquisition by those who could make, and, as a matter of fact, have made, a good use of them.[1] The United States was ready to pay Mexico an adequate sum for their transfer. For years, there had been a continual diplomatic wrangling over the refusal of the Mexicans to treat American merchants with fairness. They encouraged them to start enterprises on Mexican soil

[1] Matias Romero's *Mexico and the United States* and his *Geographical and Statistical Notes on Mexico*, both published at New York in 1898, contain the best modern description of Mexico and her resources. Charles H. Owen gives an American view of Mexican psychology and deeds in *The Justice of the Mexican War* (New York, 1908).

and then refused them all facilities for so doing. In this way and in other ways, pecuniary claims by American citizens against Mexico arose. Allowance must be made for the disorganized political condition of the Mexican people. Their governments lacked stability and any concession to an outside power was the signal for a new revolution. Mexican politicians, therefore, were afraid to comply with the plain dictates of justice. Recognizing their weakness and helplessness, the United States yielded to the verge of ignominy. At length, in 1839, a treaty was signed providing for the arbitration [1] of the American claims. After long delays, Mexico was adjudged to pay certain sums of money and as her coffers were in the usual depleted condition, time was given for making these payments by instalments. Mexico paid one or two of them and then paid no more and further negotiations were entered into. Then, also, American citizens, who had no call to go into Mexican territory, except for the pursuit of gain, mere curiosity, or love of adventure, found themselves in Mexican prisons. Some of them were inhumanly treated. The United States protested, but received scant consideration at the hands of the Mexican authorities. The fact was that the ruling classes of Mexico had a feeling of contempt for the people of the United States, and those of them who had lived outside of Mexico and who could judge of the relative strength of the two republics either had little power in Mexico or saw that their personal advantage would not admit of their doing the right thing. This was the case, not only with the United States, but also with France and Great Britain. They, too, had claims and they also negotiated. In 1838, France lost patience and collected her claims at the cannon's mouth. British commercial interests

---

[1] *Treaties and Conventions* (ed. 1873), pp. 557, 560.

in Mexico were so large that for years that country forebore to collect what was due to her people. The annexation of Texas by the United States brought on a crisis, for the occupation of any part of it was an act of spoliation of Mexican territory, — according to Mexican belief.

In the summer of 1845, General Zachary Taylor was ordered to the Texan boundary. He was instructed to occupy a position "on or near the Rio Grande" as soon as the Texans had voted for annexation. Orders were also sent to Commodore Sloat, commanding the American naval force in the Pacific, to seize California in case of a declaration of war. In view of the probability of Mexican attack on Texas while the consideration of the annexation plan was proceeding, the strengthening of the American army in Louisiana was perfectly justifiable, if the annexation of Texas was. As the independence of the Texan Republic had been recognized by Great Britain, France, and the United States for eight years or more, and as the Texans had been governing themselves all that time without any adequate attempt on the part of Mexico to reconquer her lost province, the rightfulness of annexation would seem to be beyond the line of argument. As to California and New Mexico, which lay between that province and Texas, if Mexico made war on the United States on account of this perfectly justifiable annexation, then those provinces might be considered in the light of an indemnity for the expenditure which Mexico would force upon the United States, and in that point of view the seizure of California and New Mexico would be right and proper.

As soon as it became certain that the Texans were going to vote for annexation to the United States, Taylor made preparation for the military occupation of the new State and, by the end of July, 1845, found himself with regulars, infantry and artillery, in camp at Corpus Christi on the southwestern side of the estuary of the Nueces River, and soon afterward he was joined by a cavalry force. In October, he suggested to the government at Washington that an advance to the bank of the Rio Grande would be advisable for military reasons.[1] The Mexicans viewed with astonishment this invasion of their territory by the military forces of the United States, — for the moment Taylor crossed the Sabine, he was within Mexican territory according to Mexican belief. They determined to resist, and to attack the invader. To do this, money was appropriated by the revolutionary government then in power and soldiers were sent to Matamoros, a town on the western bank of the Rio Grande, and not far from its mouth. And so matters were in the autumn of 1845.

The winter of 1845–1846 saw two most extraordinary diplomatic or quasi-diplomatic transactions. The administration wanted Texas and California, but it did not want war, for it was quite uncertain what position the people would take on the matter, and the influence of military victories or defeats upon the fortunes of the Democratic party were exceedingly dubious. Polk determined to make one more effort to secure a peaceable settlement. At the moment there was no American representative in Mexico, but an assurance was given by the authorities there that an American minister would be received by the government. John Slidell, a New Yorker living in New Orleans, was appointed envoy to Mexico to settle all the disputes with that country or as many of them as he could. When he got there the existing government was tottering. It was unable even to appear to yield to American pressure. It tried to get out of the dilemma by asserting that it had agreed to

---

[1] *House Document* No. 60, 30th Cong., 1st Sess., p. 107.

receive a commissioner to negotiate on the Texas question and an envoy had been sent to settle everything.[1] Slidell and the Washington government exhibited a great deal of patience, but without reward, for a new Mexican regime refused to receive any diplomatic representative from the United States, no matter what he was called.

At this time Santa Anna was living in exile at Havana. In February, 1846, A. J. Atocha appeared at Washington and sought the President. Polk received him and was led to believe that Santa Anna, if he could again find himself in Mexico, would do what he could to bring about friendly relations with the United States. It is by no means clear that Atocha had any right to act in any way as the representative of the former President of the Mexican Republic, but Polk fell into the trap, — if it were a trap. He sent Alexander Slidell Mackenzie to Havana to find out the facts. Mackenzie was a naval officer of mark. He was well received by Santa Anna and given some extraordinary advice as to the best mode of attacking Mexico. Meantime, in January, 1846, at the beginning of this intrigue, a report came from Slidell that the Mexican government refused to receive him or even to listen to him. Thereupon, it was decided to reinforce diplomacy by arms. Taylor was ordered [2] (January 13, 1846) to the Rio Grande. Commodore Conner was directed to take his fleet to Vera Cruz,[3] — and later was instructed to permit Santa Anna to pass

[1] Smith's *War with Mexico*, i. 95 and fol., 436 and fol.; and George L. Rives's "Mexican Diplomacy on the Eve of War with the United States" in *American Historical Review*, xviii. 275–294. The papers are printed in *House Document*, No. 60, 30th Cong., 1st Sess., pp. 11–79.

[2] *House Document*, No. 60, 30th Cong., 1st Sess., p. 90. Pages 79–148 of this document contain the official correspondence to April 22, 1846. The papers from that date to December 29, 1846, are on pages 274–515: and the following pages to 769 relate the attempts to outfit the expedition, — a melancholy story.

[3] See P. S. P. Conner's articles on Commodore Conner in *The United Service* magazine for 1894, 1895, 1896, 1897, and see also *The Knickerbocker* for 1847.

through the blockading squadron, — but he could not have prevented the entrance of that redoubtable personage into Mexico, if he had tried. The march of Taylor and the appearance of warships off Vera Cruz produced no effect upon the Mexican rulers. The Rio Grande was a long way off and the Castle of San Juan de Ulúa in front of Vera Cruz was believed to be impregnable, for it had been greatly strengthened since the French battered it eight years before. Finally, it was inconceivable to the Mexican mind that the British would permit the Americans to work their will in Texas and in California, and the Mexicans did not believe that the Americans would fight.

In March, 1846, Taylor with his troops reached the Rio Grande opposite Matamoros and began the construction of a fort. As to Taylor [1] and his doings in Texas and Mexico great contrariety of opinion has developed. Many persons have believed that his victories were won by the display of high military qualities in spite of the lukewarm support of the administration at Washington and the removal of his best troops to carry on the Vera Cruz-Mexico City campaign. It was this belief, coupled with a certain rugged charm, that made Zachary Taylor President of the United States. At a later day, historical students have insisted that Taylor was devoid of any knowledge of warfare on any scale beyond campaigns against the Indians. They assert that he took no steps to find out what the enemy was doing and issued practically no orders.[2] Undoubtedly, Taylor surprised his contemporaries. Charles Elliot, the British

[1] A discriminating memoir by William H. Samson is prefixed to the *Letters of Zachary Taylor from the Battle-Fields of the Mexican War* (from the Bixby Collection, Rochester, 1908).

[2] General Meade, who was then a lieutenant, wrote to his wife on May 9, 1846, that during the Battle of Palo Alto he was "at the side of General Taylor, and communicating his orders." In a later letter, he stated that Taylor did not make the use of the engineers and other members of his staff that he might have done. See *Life and Letters* of G. G. Meade, i, 80, 101.

representative in Texas, declared that Taylor had too few soldiers to do anything, that too few of those he had were cavalry, and that his artillery was out of all proportion to his needs and could not be effectively used in the Texan climate. It has been said that although Taylor was a veteran of the War of 1812 he had passed the best years of his life in army posts on the frontier, superintending the petty details of his command and failing to improve himself in military science. It must be confessed that Taylor was deficient in book learning and had never exercised thousands of soldiers together. It seems true, also, that he undervalued foreknowledge of the enemies' numbers and movements. On the other side, every one admits that he was a man of unsurpassed courage and had the invaluable quality of inspiring his troops with confidence in themselves and in him. He had no brilliant staff about him, and his vigorous language attracted attention at the time and has been repeated often since. It seems safe to say that where a military commander exhibits a fairly long line of victories achieved under perilous circumstances, there must have been something in him of the soldier, that he must have issued orders, and have known what he was about. Any modern student of the campaigns of 1846 to 1848 must constantly bear in mind that, while so near to our own time, they were conducted as to transportation and intelligence with about the same facilities as General Washington had in the Revolutionary War. Moreover, the distances in Mexico and in Texas were greater than they seem to be on a map, and the Mexicans, whatever their fighting qualities may have been, possessed a mobility that could hardly have been expected by any one who had not experienced

[1] There is an interesting letter, dated September 15, 1846, from Taylor in Mrs. Chapman Coleman's *Life of John J. Crittenden*, i, 251.

it. One trouble in assessing Taylor's deeds arises from the fact that his reports were written by Major Bliss, his able adjutant, and later his son-in-law, who resembled so closely in some ways the modern publicity agent that students have not regarded them as stating the actual facts.

Taylor's base after he reached the Rio Grande was Point Isabel, which was the port of Matamoros, because the navigation of the lower reaches of the river was very uncertain.[1] Taylor blockaded the Rio Grande because the Mexican commander refused him facilities to gather supplies. There was a curious hesitation on both sides to bring matters to a decision, but finally General Arista, the Mexican commander at Matamoros, was spurred to activity by the authorities at Mexico City. An officer of the American army was murdered, reconnoitering parties were attacked, and one of these, commanded by Captain Thornton, was captured by the Mexicans after several soldiers had been killed. This was on April 25, 1846. The report of the encounter reached Washington on May 9. Two days later, President Polk informed Congress that war exists and that American blood had been shed on American soil by the Mexicans.[2] On May 13, Congress authorized the President to accept volunteers for the prosecution of the war which exists between Mexico and the United States by the act of the Republic of Mexico, and thus recognized a status of war.[3] Meantime, on the 8th and 9th of that month, Taylor had won two battles.

---

[1] On the geographical relations of these places see J. A. Stevens's *Valley of the Rio Grande*, 1–8.

[2] Richardson's *Messages and Papers*, iv, 437.

[3] *Statutes at Large*, ix, 9. On May 14, 1846, a printed "Confidential Circular" was signed by James Buchanan and sent to the diplomatic agents of the United States. In this they are informed that Mexico has "mistaken our forbearance for pusillanimity. Encouraged, probably, by this misapprehension, her army has at length passed the Del Norte, — has invaded the territory of our country, — and has shed American blood upon the American soil. . . . In conversing on

Throughout the campaign, Taylor's anxieties were mainly concerned with transportation and supplies. He was at Fort Brown with his little army and his supplies were at Point Isabel, twenty-seven miles away. Possibly in view of a threatened Mexican crossing of the Rio Grande, Taylor took by far the greater part of his force to Point Isabel for the purpose of escorting these supplies across the country to Fort Brown. It was at this point of time that Arista passed the river and, finding Taylor gone, pursued him. At the moment, Taylor was on his way back with the supply train. The two forces came together on the 8th of May at Palo Alto. The combat was a most surprising one. The Mexicans relied upon the cavalry and the lance. When they advanced to the charge, they were met by an artillery fire of an intensity that they had never dreamed of. Their ranks stood fast, men being shot down at what seemed to be a safe distance from the enemy. On the other hand, the Mexican cannon balls were propelled by such poor powder that they fell early to the earth and proceeded by leaps and bounds to the American ranks, their progress being so slow that, for the most part, it was easy to avoid them. A prairie fire, which disconcerted the Mexican plans, and a flank attack completed the affair. Night fell, and when morning dawned the Mexicans were not in their positions. Taylor, thereupon, resumed his march and some miles farther on came across the Mexicans near a ravine known as Resaca de la Palma. Here, again, the same story was repeated.[1] The American soldier as a fighter was so superior to the Mexican, that the resistance of the

the objects and purposes of the war, you will be guided by the sentiments expressed in the President's message and this dispatch." Larkin Mss. in the Bancroft Library.

[1] *Letters of Zachary Taylor* (Bixby Collection) p. 1. In the "Appendix" to this volume is a letter from Taylor to Buchanan, defending his campaigns, — but very likely it was written by his future son-in-law.

latter broke down and ended in flight to the Rio Grande and across it. In these two engagements Taylor had about 2000 men and the Mexicans numbered at least twice as many. The losses were out of all proportion, Taylor reporting 170, of whom only 38 were killed, and Arista having lost according to his own accounts 800 killed, wounded, and missing, and according to Taylor probably twice as many at least.[1]

One thing that had induced the Mexicans to attack the American soldiers had been the strong probability of war between the United States and Great Britain and a hoped-for armed intervention by the latter power between Mexico and the United States. British travellers and writers for years had lost few opportunities of saying unpleasant things about "the people of the States," [2] and the governments at Washington and London exhibited determination to maintain their respective positions as to the Oregon country. Beginning in Adams's time,[3] successive American governments had proposed to divide Oregon by extending the forty-ninth parallel from the Rocky Mountains to the Pacific Ocean. This line had been adopted in 1818 as the boundary between Canada and the United States from the Lake of the Woods to the Rocky Mountains. On the face of it, the proposition to extend this line westward to the Pacific

[1] Smith's *War with Mexico*, i, 169, 176, 466. Meade writing to his wife on May 9, reported somewhat different figures. On May 15, he stated the American force at 2000 and the Mexican at between 6000 and 7000 Meade's *Life and Letters*, i, 81, 83.

[2] Justin H. Smith sets forth the attitude of the British in these years in the *Proceedings* of the Massachusetts Historical Society for June, 1914, and at greater length in his *War with Mexico*, ch. xxxv.

Excerpts from the writings of Mrs. Trollope, Captain Basil Hall, and other British visitors may conveniently be found in a sixty-page booklet entitled

The Domestic Manners of the Americans that was published at Glasgow in 1836. and Charles Dickens's *American Notes* and *Martin Chuzzlewit* that came out in the 1840's added to the flame of indignation. A rather clumsy attempt at retaliation was *The Slaveholder Abroad; or Billy Buck's Visit, with his Master, to England* (Philadelphia, 1860) detailing in the form of letters from "Dr. Jones of Georgia" murders and other crimes that were found in a file of contemporary English newspapers.

[3] See Clay's letter to Gallatin of June 19, 1826, in *House Document*, No. 199, 20th Cong., 1st Sess.

seemed reasonable. When one looked into it closely,
however, it was found to deprive the British of all participation in the trade of the Columbia River basin, of the
navigation of Puget Sound, and to deprive them of any
control of the strait of Juan de Fuca. The British refused
again and again to accept this proposition. At one time
Tyler and Webster seemed willing to yield so far as to give
the British the northern part of the Columbia basin on
consideration of their not opposing the acquisition of San
Francisco Bay and northern California by the Americans.
Nothing came of this and the American government returned
to its old position. In his Inaugural Message, Polk declared that we had a good title to all of Oregon. As the
British had refused all offers of compromise, he withdrew
them and in December, 1845, suggested the ending of the
joint occupation. In April, 1846, the notice was given and
the United States and Great Britain stood face to face on the
Oregon question.[1] Buchanan feared that this action would
bring on war between the two countries. Polk stood firm.
He declared that the way to deal with John Bull was to
look him straight in the eye. It cannot be said that Buchanan was reassured, but the event justified Polk's position.
The English government could not involve that country
in war with the United States because the voters would not
have stood behind it. At first Aberdeen suggested arbitration, but no one in America exhibiting any interest in
that plan, he recurred to a hint that Edward Everett, the
American minister at London, had let fall some time before
and directed the British representative at Washington to

---

[1] Two related aspects of the Oregon
matter are treated in Schafer's "The
British Attitude toward the Oregon
Question" in *American Historical Review*, xvi, 273–299, and in L. B. Ship-
pee's "Federal Relations of Oregon"
in the *Quarterly* of the Oregon Historical Society, xix, 89, 189, 283. Both
articles are abundantly supplied with
citations.

suggest that the dividing line should be the forty-ninth parallel from the Rocky Mountains to the middle of the channel between the continent and Vancouver's Island and through that channel to the Pacific Ocean. He also laid down the condition that the Hudson Bay Company should enjoy the free navigation of the Columbia River. Polk at once saw the bearing of this new attitude of the British government on the Mexican War.[1] Moreover, he had become convinced that the British by making actual settlements in the country north of the forty-ninth parallel had acquired rights by settlement in that region,[2] similar to those that the United States had acquired south of that parallel. After what he had said in his Inaugural, he could hardly give way on his own part. He therefore laid the whole matter before the Senate and asked its advice as to whether he should negotiate on the terms proposed. After two days' debate the Senate advised him to do so. Three days later, on June 15, 1846, the treaty was signed and was promptly ratified.[3] Two weeks after this, but of course before the news of the actual settlement reached England, Aberdeen addressed a note to Bankhead, the British minister in Mexico, declining to interfere between Mexico and the United States. He had repeatedly warned the Mexican nation of the danger and it was in consequence of "wilful

[1] See Polk's Message of June 10, 1846, in Richardson's *Messages and Papers*, iv, 449, and Polk's *Diary*. i, 62–66, 244–253, 467. For the executive proceedings see *Journal of the Senate*, "Appendix," pp. 547, 551.

[2] Polk's *Diary*, i, p. 70.

[3] *Senate Documents*, Nos. 476, 489 (29th Cong., 1st Sess.); *Treaties and Conventions* (ed. 1873), p. 375. The Polk end of the story is in his *Diary*, (index under "Oregon").

It proved to be a difficult matter to decide precisely what was the "channel"

contemplated in the treaty. In 1871, the question was referred to the German Emperor as arbiter (*Treaties and Conventions*, 426). He decided in favor of the United States in 1872. The documents relating to this controversy were brought together in 1873 and printed by order of Parliament under the general title of *North-West American Water Boundary* (A.–G.). For an English view of the question, see Viscount Milton's *History of the San Juan Water Boundary Question* (London, 1869).

contempt of that warning" that it had plunged headlong down the precipice. If Great Britain intervened, it would mean war with the United States. He directed Bankhead to make this decision known in "explicit but courteous terms" to the Mexican government. Bankhead was also directed to assure it that Great Britain by "friendly interposition" would be willing to save Mexico as far as might yet be possible from the fatal consequences of the policy that successive Mexican governments had pursued toward Texas and the United States.

Relying on the intrigue with Santa Anna and anxious to avoid war, President Polk made one more effort for a peaceable settlement. Early in August, 1846, he asked Congress to give him money to purchase territory from Mexico.[1] When this matter was before the House of Representatives, David Wilmot of Pennsylvania moved to amend the resolution by providing "as an express and fundamental condition to the acquisition of any territory from the Republic of Mexico" that "neither slavery nor involuntary servitude shall ever exist in any part" of the territory so acquired. Wilmot was not the author of this proviso; he was a regular Democrat, and it is not clear why he took it upon himself to introduce it. A vigorous debate at once took place. Finally, the House passed the resolution with the proviso. Possibly it would have passed the Senate also had not a Massachusetts Senator prolonged the debate until the moment set for the termination of the session. Historical students have generally condemned his action. It may well be that his motive was to block any attempt to acquire territory from Mexico with or without slavery.[2] For the moment, the

---

[1] Polk's *Diary*, ii, 59–73. The President euphemistically asked for the money "to facilitate negotiations with Mexico"!

[2] The history of the Wilmot Proviso is even now practically unknown. Besides the general histories and the biographies, see C. E. Persinger on

project was dead ; but the Wilmot Proviso was moved again and again, whenever the question of the acquisition of territory from Mexico came up. On August 16 Santa Anna appeared off Vera Cruz and was allowed to pass through the blockading squadron.

Meantime, California had been occupied by American naval forces, although this was not known at Washington until September. The settlements of the whites in California were few in number and of small extent in area and population. There were a few houses at San Diego, a pueblo or village at Los Angeles, another at Santa Barbara, and a small town at Monterey, which was supposed to be the seat of government. At San Francisco, farther north, there was a dilapidated mission and at Sonoma a small collection of houses around the seat of General Vallejo, who was the richest and most respectable Hispano-Mexican-Californian in the whole country. Sutter's Fort near the confluence of the American Fork with the main stream of the Sacramento River was at the strategic point of the overland route from the United States by the way of Nevada and Utah. Two thousand would probably have included every human being possessing an appreciable amount of Caucasian blood [1] in all Alta California, or California, as we always term it. In the valleys between the ranges of mountains that roughly parallel the coast there were ranches of huge extent, pasturing thousands of cattle and horses and large flocks of

"The Origin of the Wilmot Proviso" in American Historical Association's *Report* for 1911, vol. i, 189–195. The views of a Southern Whig can be found in *Selections from the Speeches and Writings of Hon. Thomas L. Clingman*, 197. Polk's view is given in his *Diary*, ii, 75, etc.

[1] Mary Floyd Williams's "Introduction" to her *Vigilance Committee of 1851*. Larkin in his Ms. "Official Correspondence," Pt. ii, Des. 66, p. 95, gives the population of California in 1846 at 15,000 and 1000 foreigners. Dr. Marsh in a letter to Lewis Cass, written in 1846, estimates it at 7700, Elliott's *Illustrations of Contra Costa County*, p. 5, 6. Possibly the difference in figures reflects the effort to separate the pure-blooded whites from the Indian and mixed population.

sheep. The inaccessibility of California by land from Mexico and the tremendous distances in California itself made administration so difficult that it was practically independent of Mexico and, as a matter of fact, was itself subdivided into three quasi-independent areas. The revenue was derived from duties on imports which were so high that the inducement to smuggling was great. There was a governor in California who was generally some broken-down Mexican politician who came with a small band of soldiers whom the local writers generally stigmatized as convicts. The military commander in California was usually at swords' points with the governor, although the two ordinarily lived so far apart that there was not much actual collision between them. When one realizes the tremendous difficulty of getting from one part of the country to another before the days of railroads one has gone far toward realizing the facts of early California history. Furthermore, in three months of the year there is oftentimes so much rain that the streams became swollen and the roadways impassable. The people of each settlement and each ranch lived their own lives as much cut off from one another and from the world as if they were inhabitants of separate islands.

When Dana was on the coast in 1835–1836, there were few Americans in California, although there were some at each of the four towns or villages from Monterey southward. There were also some British subjects, a few Frenchmen, and fewer Germans, but put all together, the foreigners offered no occasion for jealousy to the native Californians. The dislike of outsiders appears in 1840 for almost the first time in what is known as the Graham Affair. It seems that Isaac Graham, an American, had espoused the cause of the wrong political leader. He and certain others, among them some Englishmen, were seized by the governor and sent by

sea to Mexico, but were released through the intercession
of the American and British representatives in Mexico and
some of them returned to California, with more or less
promise of compensation for their sufferings and losses.[1]
The Graham Affair was of no great consequence in itself,
but the memory of it gave point to American suspicion of
Californian good faith in the next half dozen years. In
1832, Thomas O. Larkin opened a store at Monterey. He
was a Massachusetts man who had failed in business in
South Carolina, but had somewhere acquired facility in
intercourse with men of varying nationalities and opinions.
He speedily secured the friendship of the leaders of the
different cliques in California, standing well with the
American traders, the Commandante of the Californians,
the Governor General, and the native ranchers. He supplied them all with goods on credit and talked politics with
them.[2] In 1844, he was appointed American consul at
Monterey, and this official position enabled him to extend
his trade and his influence.

After 1840, American trappers, traders, and settlers
appeared in ever increasing numbers. One party of trappers
came over the San Bernardino pass. They had been taking
fur-bearing animals in the mountains of New Mexico and
having exhausted their supplies came down to the coast.
While there they caught sea otters without a license or

---

[1] See T. H. Hittell's *History of California*, ii, 272, and Rives's *United States
and Mexico*, ii, 32, 36, 37.

[2] In 1844 it appears, from a statement in the "Larkin Manuscripts"
that he had loaned to the governor and
commandante of "this department"
no less than $3700, some of it at 12
per cent interest. It is also fairly
certain from entries in his papers and
in the California local records that
Larkin was largely interested in lands

held under grants from the Mexican
or Californian authorities. For sev-
eral entries to this effect, I am in-
debted to Mr. Owen C. Coy of the
California Historical Survey. A bio-
graphical sketch of Larkin forms
"Appendix 1" to R. W. Kelsey's
"The United States Consulate in Cali-
fornia" in the *Publications* of the
Academy of Pacific Coast History, i,
No. 5. An account of the "Larkin
Papers" is in *ibid.*, i, p. 104.

permission of any kind from any Mexican authority. They were arrested, but after some detention they were released. The story is expressive of the attitude of the American frontiersman toward the Californian. The first large American party reached the San Joaquin Valley in 1843. It came overland and was composed for the most part of persons who had originally migrated from New England and New York to the Northwest, and then had determined for no apparent reason to go to the Pacific Coast. Some of them found employment on the ranches or in the towns, and others "squatted" on lands in the vicinity of Sutter's Fort and in the country to the northward. In the next two years, 1844 and 1845, other bands arrived in California. Apparently there was no concert of action between them and they had no other motive for migration than the difficulty of making a living in the United States in the years of financial stress that followed the panic of 1837. By the beginning of 1846 there were at least five hundred Americans in California, including in that number all who had come from the United States, whether they were natives or immigrants from abroad. Their numbers were not large, but, bearing in mind the small numerical strength of the native Californians and their wide dispersal along five hundred miles from Sonoma to San Diego, the presence of even so few Americans settled within one hundred miles of Sutter's Fort was likely to arouse apprehension among the rulers of the land.

For years the Californians had been practically independent, and about the only bond they had with the Mexicans was their racial affinity. Representatives of the United States, Great Britain, and France had been throwing out suggestions of the advisability of independence from Mexico and of coöperation with the country of the speaker. James

Alexander Forbes, the British agent in California, was appealed to by a body of influential Californians who asked him whether their country could be "received under the protection of Great Britain?" He replied that he was unauthorized to enter into any such affair. He reported the matter to his superiors who, in turn, reported to Aberdeen. On December 31, 1844, the British foreign secretary replied [1] that Her Majesty's government could have nothing to do with any insurrectionary movement in California; nor did they desire their agents there to encourage such movements, for that would be contrary to good faith on the part of England. If California threw off the Mexican yoke, it would be of importance to Great Britain that that country should not assume any tie "which might prove inimical to British interests." He wrote, however, that the Californians might be informed that "Great Britain would view with much dissatisfaction the establishment of a protectoral power over California by any other foreign state." This letter reached Forbes in May, 1845, and must have been very discouraging. Sir George Seymour then commanded the British naval forces on the western American coast. He took very little interest in California before 1845. At the time the French were active among the islands of the Pacific. Seymour's principal task seems to have been to watch them and also to oppose any Russian intrigues looking to settlement below 54° 40'.[2] In December, 1845, Seymour was at Valparaiso with his vessels after a visit to

[1] E. D. Adams's *British Interests and Activities in Texas*, 247. A year and a half later, on May 14, 1846, Abel Stearns wrote to Larkin from "Angeles" that he was "certain" that overtures had been made by British agents to the government of California to declare its independence and place itself under the protection of Great Britain. "Larkin Mss."

[2] When the Russians withdrew from the Oregon country after the treaties of 1824 and 1825, they had retained a post on Bodega Bay, some sixty or seventy miles to the northward of the Golden Gate. This station had been the cause of constant expense to the Russians and they had gladly disposed of it to Captain Sutter.

Honolulu and the Friendly Islands. From that place he
addressed a letter (March, 1846) to the Admiralty asking
for an increased force. He thought that war with the
United States was possible, and he may have been led to
write this letter by the recent increase of the American
naval force in the Pacific. In June, 1846, the matter was
taken up in London. The Admiralty refused to grant any
increase unless the government would guarantee a larger
naval appropriation. The Foreign Office was appealed to
and replied that no material change in the Pacific squadron
was necessary because there was no probability of war with
the United States.[1]   In the spring of 1846 Seymour had no
greater strength and no instructions as to California or
Oregon.   In May, 1846, at about the time of Palo Alto, he
left the American fleet lying at anchor off Mazatlan and
steered southward one hundred miles or so to San Blas.[2]
He was there on June 8 when the American squadron
under Commodore Sloat left Mazatlan for Monterey in
Alta California. The story of French activities in California is even more vague. It is said that Duflot de Mofras,
an attaché of the French legation at Mexico, made some kind
of an offer of "French protection" in case the Californians
set up for themselves. He was in California in the years
1840–1842 and wrote two volumes[3] on his travels, — but
the whole matter is exceedingly uncertain.

In October, 1845, Larkin had been appointed confidential
agent by President Polk, and had been instructed to stir up
disaffection among the Californians against Mexico and to

[1] E. D. Adams's *British Interests
. . . in Texas*, 255.

[2] Justin H. Smith suggests that
Seymour went to San Blas "to wait
for orders" (*War with Mexico*, i, 531).
Josiah Royce shows conclusively that
no "race for California" or anything
approaching it occurred, in "Light
on Seizure of California" in *The Century Magazine*, for August, 1890, p.
792.

[3] Eugène Duflot de Mofras' *Exploration du Territoire de l'Orégon,
des Californies et de la Mer Vermeille,
. . . 1840, 1841 et 1842* (2 vols., Paris,
1844, with an Atlas).

induce them to seek annexation with the United States or to establish their independence under American protection. By this time Larkin had acquired great influence with the Californians, and he seems to have been possessed of power of charm and animadversion. He had been intriguing with the Californians for some time and thought that he had made such an impression upon them that by the middle of the century, at most, they would of their own accord ask, union with the Americans in one form or another.[1] He had been interfered with in his plans of conciliation and disaffection by two American officers, Commodore Ap Catesby Jones of the navy and Lieutenant John Charles Frémont of the army. Jones was on the coast in 1842 with a small naval force. He was greatly stirred by the news that came to him of exceedingly disrespectful proceedings on the part of the Mexicans toward the United States and of unusual activity on the part of the British fleet. He made up his mind that the British were on the point of seizing California and determined to forestall them, feeling certain that the United States had by this time resented the Mexican insults by war. He sailed to Monterey, landed a force, took possession of the fort and public buildings, and hoisted the American flag. After he had done all this Larkin showed him the most recent newspapers, which proved that relations between the United States and Mexico were still outwardly friendly and there was no appearance of any aggressive action on the part of the British. Indeed, as we know now, the British commodore was concerned only with Russian and French movements and had no thought whatever of seizing California. Under the circumstances the only thing that Ap Catesby Jones could do was to haul down the flag,

[1] See R. G. Cleland's "Early Sentiment for the Annexation of California" in *The Southwestern Historical Quarterly*, xviii.

reëmbark his men, apologize to the Mexican authorities,[1] and try to explain matters to his own government.

Frémont was a more enigmatical person and a more successful one. He was a South Carolinian of mixed parentage, his father being a Frenchman and his mother a Virginian, and he first saw the light of day at Savannah in Georgia.[2] He married the daughter of Senator Benton and thereby gained powerful backing for future advancement. In 1842, he was placed at the head of a western exploring expedition and in the following years led two more expeditions to the Rocky Mountains. His reports were well written and instructive.[3] They introduced the western country to the American people and thereby gained for Frémont the title of "the Pathfinder," — but the paths that he described had been familiar to trappers and to traders before he ever set eyes on them. In 1845, he was sent on his third expedition to seek the best route to the Pacific coast south of Oregon. He was then an officer in the United States army and he had with him paid employees of the United States, some thirty in number. The expedition running out of supplies, Frémont in January, 1846, visited Monterey and asked permission of Commandante-General Castro to secure the necessary supplies and equipment for his return to the

---

[1] Jesse S. Reeves in his *American Diplomacy under Tyler and Polk*, 105, says that had Jones "been right in his conjecture he might have been a precursor of Dewey; the conqueror of California and a hero in our naval history."

[2] Frémont's career either attracted or repelled literary men as it did every one else. There is no adequate memoir of him. Of the campaign lives, John Bigelow's is by far the best. The first volume of the *Memoirs of My Life* by John Charles Frémont gives his own account, somewhat dressed up by his wife, and illustrated with remarkable steel engravings. It brings his life down to 1847, and no further volumes were ever published.

[3] Frémont's reports of the expeditions of 1842 and 1843 were printed by order of the Senate in 1845 (*Senate Document*, No. 174, 28th Cong., 2nd Sess.) and also in the same year by order of the House (*Document* No. 166). They were widely reprinted in 1846 and in 1849. His *Notes of Travel in California* often cited as *Geographical Memoir upon Upper California* was dated June, 1848. The Frémont narratives were reprinted with Emory's *Overland Journey* in one convenient double columned volume at New York in 1849.

United States. Larkin acted as intermediary, but there seems to have been a misunderstanding. At all events, a few weeks later Frémont reappeared in the vicinity of Monterey with his whole expedition. The Californians were alarmed; Castro ordered Frémont away and got together what men he could to drive him off. On the other hand, Frémont, notwithstanding the advice of Larkin to retire peacefully, hoisted the American flag over his camp on Gavilan Mountain, declared himself ready to repel force by force, and then marched off to the north.

Frémont had proceeded on his northward march as far as the shores of Klamath Lake, when he was overtaken by Lieutenant Gillespie of the American navy with despatches and letters. Frémont at once retraced his steps to the vicinity of Sutter's Fort. Gillespie had made a remarkable journey from Washington. Leaving the capital early in November, 1845, he had crossed Mexico, actually outrunning the beginning of hostilities. He probably brought orders to Sloat and certainly gave a communication to Larkin from Buchanan,[1] instructing him as to his duties as confidential agent of the President in California. After he had done this, Gillespie pursued Frémont and it was after their meeting that Frémont turned back from the northward journey. It was at this time that Castro embodied an armed expedition. As no warlike movement could be performed in California without horses, he sent a party across the Sacramento River to secure them and bring them to Monterey. It is certain that what Castro had in mind was a conference, more or less preceded by warlike demonstrations with Governor Pio Pico at Los Angeles or

---

[1] The despatch of October 17, 1845, is printed from the copy sent by ship around Cape Horn in R. W. Kelsey's "The United States Consulate in California" (*Publication* of the Academy of Pacific Coast History, i, No. 5, p. 100).

somewhere between that place and Monterey. The American settlers in the Sacramento Valley suspected that his design was to drive them from their farms and prevent the coming in of any more immigrants from the United States.[1] They had some ground for their apprehension, for the Mexican government had issued stringent orders that new settlers should not be allowed to come in and that those already there should be ejected.[2] The American settlers had no legal rights to the lands they occupied, and the Graham Affair was still fresh in memory, and its details undoubtedly lost nothing in passing from man to man, especially in this time of excitement. Some of the settlers dashed down upon Castro's men as they were proceeding southward (June 10, 1846). They took the horses from them, but permitted the officer and his men to proceed to Monterey.[3] Four days later (June 14, 1846) a party of American settlers, twenty-five to forty in number, rode into Sonoma at break of day, captured General Vallejo, his brother, his son-in-law, who was an American named Jacob Leese, and some others and sent them under a guard to Sutter's Fort. There they were strictly confined. The rest of the party retained possession of the Californian village.

[1] As early as February 15, 1846, Dr. Marsh wrote to Larkin that the rumors of mighty events had induced him to leave his farm. "It appears that the present year will bring great changes over the face of California."

[2] On December 2, 1845, the Minister of Exterior Relations at Mexico City wrote to the Governor of the Department of California that, although "strangers" had established themselves on the Sacramento River, he hoped the Governor would "redouble his precautions to avoid the introduction of those strangers." The *Monterey Californian* of August 29, 1846, has a long account of the Bear Flag War which is useful as giving the local knowledge of that time. Referring to the affair of the preceding June it asserts that "An Indian" stated that two hundred or three hundred armed men on horseback were advancing up the Sacramento Valley to attack Frémont. Thereupon the Americans rushed from every direction to assist him. Furthermore, it was believed that Castro intended to build a fort near the Bear River Pass "for the purpose of preventing the ingress of the expected emigration from the United States."

[3] "New Helvetia Diary, June 10, 1846," and the *Monterey Californian*, August 29, 1846.

One of them — William B. Ide — indited a proclamation somewhat after the Mexican manner declaring the independence of the American settlements. As a sign of their new status they painted a bear and a star on a piece of white cotton cloth and hoisted this "Bear Flag" on a staff in the plaza at Sonoma.[1] Following, there were some small engagements with Californians from the southern side of San Francisco Bay, but the Americans remained in control of Sonoma and of their prisoners. Exactly what the settlers had in mind when they rode into Sonoma is unknown, possibly nothing more than to secure hostages against the vengeance of the Californians for the attack of June 10. Nor is it known exactly how far Frémont himself was implicated. It seems certain that he was consulted, and when the Americans were endangered, he undoubtedly took their part. At the moment it would appear that Frémont was intending to return to the United States and that the events of June and those of July diverted him from this purpose. It has been supposed that Frémont was acting under orders from President Polk or Senator Benton, and again that he set on foot the Bear Flag revolt to revenge himself of Castro's insult. It may well be, however, that he was really what he seemed to be, an officer of the American engineers in charge of an exploring party who had proceeded somewhat beyond his legitimate sphere of action for the purpose of getting supplies and information in a friendly country; that his turning back from his northward march was due to the

---

[1] The *Monterey Californian* for September 5, 1846. The Sonoma affair was prompted by a desire to put an end to "the oppression which they [the American settlers] had felt weighing heavily upon them — they wanted equal rights and equal laws." William Baldridge, writing years later, states that the settlers were "aroused by rumors and suspicions excited by the actions of the Spanyards." And see also William B. Ide's "Bear Flag War," p. 18, in the Bancroft Library. An excellent reminiscent pioneer account of these transactions is in the *History of San Mateo County, California* (San Francisco, 1883).

difficulties of the route, including the hostilities of the
Indians, and that his final determination to remain in
California was governed by what seemed to be the critical
condition of his fellow countrymen at the moment.[1] The
later unfortunate career of Frémont, his financial vagaries,
the mystery which has enshrouded his doings, and the extraordinary claims that were put forward in his behalf have
angered historical writers and induced them to attribute to
him qualities which he did not possess and to deny to him
qualities that he certainly had. Whatever his looseness as
to law and money may have been, he carried through
exceedingly difficult operations and bore his responsibility
with a courage that deserves commendation. Moreover,
he won the good opinion of large numbers of his fellow
countrymen who sent him to Congress as one of the first
Senators from California and put him forward as candidate
of the Republican Party for the presidency in 1856.

Commodore John D. Sloat, commander of the American
naval force on the Pacific coast, was a veteran of the War of
1812. He was in poor health, and was hampered by somewhat contradictory instructions.[2] One set directed him to
seize Californian ports when Mexico should have declared
war; but he should be careful otherwise not to do anything
that could be construed as an act of aggression. A later
set directed him to carry out these instructions "in the
event of actual hostilities." On May 17, 1846, he heard of
the disaster to the Thornton party, and on the last day of
the month of the battles of Palo Alto and Resaca de la

---

[1] From a letter from Gillespie to
Larkin, dated June 7, 1846 ("Larkin Mss." in the Bancroft Library) it
appears that at that moment Frémont
intended to return to the United
States as soon as he could.

[2] The important papers are printed
in *House Document*, No. 19, 29th

Cong., 2nd Sess., pp. 74–111, and
ibid., No. 60, 30th Cong., 1st Sess.,
pp. 230–271. Edwin A. Sherman's
*Life of the Late Rear-Admiral John
Drake Sloat* (Oakland, Cal., 1902)
has much interesting information,
largely of a pro-Sloat character.

Palma. Probably regarding these as border affairs and not as "actual hostilities" or proof of a Mexican declaration of war, he held fast to his moorings at Mazatlan. On June 7, he learned that Conner was actually blockading Vera Cruz. The next day, he weighed anchor and sailed for Monterey, which he reached on July 2. There he and Larkin had long and intimate discussions. It must be remembered that the latter had been appointed confidential agent of the President in California and that he was in possession of instructions which ordered him to conciliate the Californians and to "arouse in their bosoms that love of liberty and independence so natural to the American Continent." He was not to awaken the jealousy of the English and French agents and was to act in harmony with Lieutenant Gillespie. One can well understand the feelings of Commodore Sloat when conferring with Larkin, who had every confidence that the Californians, if left to themselves, would declare their independence from Mexico and presumably join the United States. California was a large country, Sloat had a small force at his disposal, and the example of Ap Catesby Jones was before his eyes. After five days' consideration, on July 7, in the morning he sent a party on shore, hoisted the American flag, and proclaimed possession of California for the United States. It has been supposed that Sloat acted in consequence of receiving information as to Frémont's doings. This may have been so, but he certainly had no official statement at the time he sent his men on shore.[1] On July 16, Seymour in the British ship *Collingwood* and with other vessels, greatly outnumbering the American force, anchored at Monterey. He viewed Sloat's proceedings with

---

[1] The actual facts are set forth at length in the text and foot-notes of R. W. Kelsey's article in the *Publications* of the Academy of Pacific Coast History, i, pp. 78-80. See also Edwin A. Sherman's *Life of . . . Rear-Admiral John Drake Sloat.*

great calmness.[1] Indeed, the American occupation seems to have aroused no comment on the flagship and after a week's visit there Seymour sailed away.

It was at this time that Commodore Stockton, in the frigate *Congress*, arrived from the United States after a leisurely voyage around Cape Horn. He had been directed to take over the command from Sloat, who had asked to be relieved. For a time after Stockton's arrival, Sloat seems to have hesitated about striking his flag, but by the end of the month, Stockton was in command. The appearance of a regular American force and the taking possession of Monterey had ended the Bear Flag Republic. Frémont gathered together some of the frontiersmen and with them and some of his own men rode south to Monterey and offered his services to Stockton. The other ports and Los Angeles were occupied without trouble, and there the matter should have rested. Unfortunately, however, what with Stockton's bombast and Gillespie's arbitrary action at Los Angeles, the Californians became discontented and took up arms.[2] Gillespie was forced out of the town and other places were also occupied by the "rebels." It was difficult to deal with them because Los Angeles being twenty-three miles from the sea could not be easily attacked by a naval force. In the emergency, Stockton did what he could. He landed seamen at San Diego and marched with them for the town, hauling a few guns by hand. Meantime, General Kearny of the United States army had seized Santa Fé (August 18,

[1] Clements R. Markham, President of the Royal Geographical Society, was then a midshipman on Seymour's flagship. His diary kept at the time shows no sign of excitement on the *Collingwood* when she anchored at Monterey with the American flag floating over the town. "Ms." in the Bancroft Library.

[2] Writing to his wife, while a pris-oner in the hands of the Californians, Larkin said that Captain Gillespie "punished, fined, and imprisoned who and when he pleased without any hearing." He thought that had any "proper or prudent person" been in command at Los Angeles "all this disturbance would not have happened." "Larkin Mss." under date of December 14, 1846.

1846) and ridden westward with several hundred mounted men. Unfortunately he was met (October 6, 1846) on the way by a messenger bearing the news of the complete success of the Americans in California, which was true at the time the dispatch was written. Kearny, therefore, sent back the greater part of his troopers and with only a hundred and fifty or so rode on toward San Diego. About thirty-nine miles from that place he came upon a body of armed Californians in battle array. A conflict ensued in which Kearny's men lost severely, but they maintained their position. This gave Stockton opportunity to enter Los Angeles, and liberal terms being given to the Californians they desisted from their enterprise and the conquest was completed.

The history of California in the next few years is a distressing tale of American ineptitude. Besides Kearny's small force, the Mormon Battalion, painfully reduced in numbers, reached the coast, a regiment recruited in New York came around Cape Horn, and a ship-load of artillery and munitions with some artillerymen arrived by the same route.[1] After the summer of 1847, the troubles of the Americans were not of a military kind, but were of a political and personal nature. Kearny brought with him orders constituting him commander-in-chief and military governor. Stockton had already given Frémont the title of major and some kind of political commission. Frémont refused to obey Kearny's orders and Stockton and Kearny did not get on well together. This conflict of authority was ended by the appearance of Colonel Riley with orders to assume military control and the departure of Stockton, Kearny, and Frémont overland for Washington.[2]

---

[1] It is noticeable that the orders for these preparations for war in California had been issued in June, 1846, within a few weeks of the declaration of war by Congress.

[2] Frémont's conduct was inquired into by a court, and he resigned from the service in consequence of its finding, and Senator Benton stopped visiting the White House, because

The troubles of the Americans and the Californians,
all of whom after 1846 seem to have been anxious to do the
best they could for their country — and for themselves —
were owing mainly to the inability of Americans to comprehend Californian institutions and susceptibilities and to an
equal lack of knowledge of American institutions and modes
of procedure on the part of the Californians.[1] The conquerors naturally wished to gain lands and herds, but Mexican titles were very indistinct, so that when a man had
paid good money for an estate, he found it very difficult to
discover what lands he had really bought. The leading
Spanish official in the old days had been the alcalde, for
governor and general had been hardly more than high-
sounding appellations. Stockton appointed his chaplain,
Walter Colton, alcalde of Monterey,[2] and later when affairs
had settled down somewhat an election was held and Colton
was chosen to that office by the combined votes of Californians and Americans. He has left an exceedingly interesting account of the difficulties and satisfactions of his
office. He had, as chief magistrate, to look after both civil

Polk did not intervene. All the documents and evidence are given in *Senate
Documents*, No. 33, 30th Cong., 1st
Sess. The Kearny side of the controversy is succinctly set forth by Valen-
tine M. Porter in the *Annual Publications* of the Historical Society of
Southern California, viii.

[1] Miss Mary F. Williams in the
"Introduction" to her *Vigilance Committee*, writes that "the American alcaldes inherited not only the traditional institutions of the Spanish
colonial system, but also the confusion
and abuses resulting from years of
turmoil in Mexico and the Department of California."

[2] Walter Colton's *Three Years in
California*. The duties of an alcalde
are set forth in Juan W. Barquera's
A Los Señores Alcaldes (Mexico City,
1826) and in Luis de Ezeta's *Manual

de Alcaldes y Jueces de Paz* (Mexico
City, 1845).

In the earliest days naval officers
were obliged to administer justice.
In the archives of the county clerk at
Santa Rosa, there is an illuminating
entry. The case was one of larceny,
and the court ordered "that there be
inflicted without delay fifteen lashes
by hard switches" on the culprit's
bare back. "The foregoing sentence
is approved and Lieut. Sears is directed to have it carried into execution forthwith. J. W. Revere, Lt.
U. S. Navy commanding at Sonoma."
This was communicated to me by
Mr. Coy of the California Historical
Survey. It was not until December,
1848, that local and territorial governments were organized on the American system.

and criminal affairs, arrange the marital disputes of husband and wife, and arbitrate land difficulties of neighboring ranchmen — for his jurisdiction extended for some miles inland. Unfortunately not all the alcaldes were as forceful and wise as Colton, and as Americans became more numerous, a reversion to methods more closely appealing to American ideas was necessary. Colton, himself, established jury trial, having an equal number of Americans and Californians on the jury. But any such expedients were necessarily nothing more than palliatives. Immediately after the American occupation, San Francisco, which at the time comprised only a few stores and houses, rose into importance as the best place of distribution of goods from sea-going vessels to the American settlements around the bay and on the rivers leading into it. There the difficulties of administration were most keenly felt. Affairs were in some such train as this when J. W. Marshall picked up some bits of gold in the mill-race of the saw-mill that he was constructing at Coloma about thirty miles from the fort of Colonel Sutter, his employer.

General Stephen W. Kearny's ride from Independence, Missouri, to Monterey, California, is one of the half-dozen most extraordinary episodes of the Mexican War. At the outset, the government had recognized the necessity of securing the southern overland route to California, and that meant the conquest of New Mexico and possibly of Chihuahua, the next Mexican state to the southward. Kearny was detailed for this service with some three hundred dragoons, a Missouri volunteer regiment, and other troops including the Mormon Battalion. He acted with astonishing vigor, and the people of the trans-Mississippi settlements seconded him most remarkably. He set out from Independence, a few miles from the modern Kansas City in

Missouri, and proceeded along the Santa Fé trail. After a painful beginning, the foot soldiers acquired powers of marching superior to those of the horsemen and, indeed, led the advance. Going for hundreds of miles through an uninhabited country and across large waterless spaces, it was necessary to carry provisions and sometimes water in a transport train. Everything was admirably managed and the command gained the vicinity of Santa Fé after great hardships, but without opposition. The people at that place had long been engaged in more or less illicit traffic with the Americans from St. Louis, and they also had been as thoroughly misgoverned by the representatives of Mexican politicians as any people in that Republic. The governor issued proclamations and informed his superiors at Mexico City that he was making every preparation for a glorious defence; but when Kearny actually arrived within communicating distance, he departed secretly for the South. The people welcomed the conquerors, who in turn, it must be said, in some cases behaved very badly. Later in the year, Colonel Doniphan, with a body of exceedingly irregular but hardy pioneers, left Santa Fé. On one of the last days of December, 1846, Doniphan and his men entered El Paso, practically without resistance. After a respite, they again took up the march and rode southward over mountains and across deserts to the city of Chihuahua. As they approached that place, they met sterner resistance, but their movements were so rapid and so unusual that the defenders fled into the town and for the most part surrendered at discretion, March 1, 1847. Before long it appeared that the military and territorial importance of Chihuahua had been misjudged. Doniphan, therefore, again took up the line of march and after more hardships and perils, joined Taylor's forces at Saltillo in the following May. Probably, no better

example of the evil effects of the combination of a soft climate
and continuing misgovernment can be found in our annals
than the slight resistance offered to Kearny and Doniphan.

The narrative left General Taylor with his small but effective fighting force at the mouth of the Rio Grande after the
successful encounters at Palo Alto and the Resaca in May,
1846. He occupied Matamoros on the Mexican side of the
Rio Grande without much trouble, and then month after
month through the summer remained practically stationary.
Taylor had a totally inadequate force to hold any large
extent of country and at the same time encounter hostile
armies in the field. He asked for more soldiers and was
given volunteers commanded by politicians. President
Polk seems to have thought that it was only necessary to
clothe a man more or less completely in uniform, give him a
musket, and he would do the rest. Polk even said on one
occasion that officers were not necessary. It may be that
had the soldiers gone forward, they would have found the
Mexicans in quite as moblike condition as themselves and
have settled the matter in a few months. As it was, what
with the summer heats, lack of transportation and supplies,
this was impossible; the forces of nature as well as man
had to be reckoned with. Moreover, Taylor had the prejudices of a trained soldier. Few men have shown more
courage than he, but he hesitated to advance into a very
difficult country, poorly supplied with food, and often over-
supplied with water, without having provisions and munitions with him or a line of communication with stores of
food and supplies of all kinds. At length, having received
some of the essentials of warfare, Taylor advanced up the
river and then to Monterey on the edge of the Sierra Madre
mountains in the Mexican State of Nuevo Leon. Monterey was naturally a good military position; it had been

fortified by the Mexicans and was strongly garrisoned. Taylor had with him very little siege apparatus and his troops had not acquired that military cohesion that comes only with long drilling or arduous campaigning. He attacked the town from two opposite sides at once. The courage shown by the American soldiers was admirable and the skill and tenacity of their officers remarkable, but there was lack of correlation between the two attacks, and between the units of each attacking force. It would seem that such misadventures are almost inevitable in the beginning of campaigns, and we must always remember the circumstances of the days before telegraph, telephone, wireless, and air-craft, when the horseback rider was almost the sole instrument of communication between parts of armies in the field. As it was the Americans penetrated into the town and placed it in so great jeopardy that the Mexican commander asked for a truce.[1] After some parleying, it was arranged that the Mexicans should retire without giving their paroles and that hostilities should be suspended for eight weeks or until the instructions of the respective governments could be received. It was a long way from Monterey to Washington and no orders for a resumption of hostilities could be received until Taylor got his men into fighting trim again. The President was indignant at Taylor's weakness and directed him to put an end to the armistice and renew hostilities. Now, opinion seems to be that Taylor was amply justified by the condition of his troops and of his supplies in giving the terms that he did.

Meantime, General John E. Wool, another veteran officer

---

[1] The Monterey campaign is quite fully treated in *The Life and Letters of George Gordon Meade* (New York, 1913), i, 105–150, and in John R. Kenly's *Memoirs of a Maryland Volunteer* (chs. iv–x). General O. O. Howard in his *General Taylor* (chs. xi–xiv) gives an excellent account of this part of the campaign.

of the regular army, but not a Whig, had been put in command of volunteer regiments assembling at San Antonio in the central part of the settled region of Texas. From there he was to advance to Chihuahua, apparently either to co-operate with Doniphan or to rescue him. Wool found his task rather confusing, but in time he crossed the Rio Grande and advanced to Monclova, reaching that place on October 29, 1846. While there he received orders to join Taylor, and by the end of November he was within reach of the main army. In the interval, Tampico, an important seaport about midway between the mouth of the Rio Grande and Vera Cruz, had been occupied by American naval forces. At the end of 1846, soldiers and sailors of the United States were in possession of the most important places in northern Mexico from the shores of the Pacific to the Gulf of Mexico; but the recognition of American possession of this vast region or of any part of it by the government of the Mexican Republic seemed to be as far off as it ever had been.

NOTES

I. California Bibliography. — In the Bancroft Library at Berkeley, California, there is a mass of material on the early history of that State, but the matter relating to the American occupation is disappointing. The manuscripts of Thomas O. Larkin, comprising his account-books, and letter-books, are interesting. Most of the other material consists of reminiscences of pioneers written thirty years and more after the event. The volumes on the history of California in the " Bancroft History of the Pacific States " appear to have been written by Henry L. Oak,[1] Mr. Bancroft's first assistant, and to have been printed substantially as written by him. The quotations in these volumes are very accurate, so far as they have been compared with the original manuscripts; but Mr. Oak, while painstaking and diligent, did not differentiate between matter written at the time and the recollections of old men. It is impossible to disentangle them in the notes or bibliographies of his volumes. Furthermore, as he was required to turn out ten pages of completed manuscript per diem, there was much haste and imperfect correlation. Otherwise, these volumes stand as a monument to their author.

Josiah Royce's *California* in the " American Commonwealth " series is devoted mainly to the period of the conquest. Professor Royce was born in California and grew up there. While proceeding with his work, he became intensely interested in the Frémont episode and spent much time and thought in trying to unravel it. He had access to the papers in the Bancroft Collection so far as they were then arranged, and Mr. Oak, who was then engaged in the writing of the volumes, gave him much assistance. There is no better statement of the case against Frémont than Royce's volume. T. H. Hittell's *History of California* in four volumes presents all the important facts, so far as they were known in 1885; but the book is sparsely supplied with citations. The nineteenth volume (new series) of *The Century Magazine* contains a remarkable series of articles on California. Among them may be mentioned Guadalupe Vallejo's " Ranch and Mission Days in Alta California," John Bidwell's " First Emigrant Train," and Josiah Royce's " Montgomery and Frémont." [2]

[1] See Henry L. Oak's "*Literary Industries*" *in a New Light* (San Francisco, 1893, pp. 42, 81).

[2] J. M. Cutts's *Conquest of California and New Mexico* (Philadelphia, 1847) contains a good contemporary

The bibliography of California and the Northwest Coast is extensive, as may be gathered by looking over the list of books prefixed to the volumes in the "Bancroft History." In 1914, R. E. Cowan published *A Bibliography of the History of California and the Pacific West, 1510–1906*. This includes "about 1000 titles." A list that will satisfy most students is in "Appendix 5" to Kelsey's article in the *Publications* of the Academy of Pacific Coast History, i.

Most of the important documents relating to the Mexican War in its widest aspect were printed in *House Document*, No. 60, 30th Cong., 1st Sess., and in *House Document*, No. 17, 31st Cong., 1st Sess. Other material may be found by consulting the index to the *Executive Documents* of this session that is printed therewith. Citations to other official volumes are given in the preceding foot-notes of this chapter. A great deal of information can be gathered from the pages of evidence taken in the innumerable lawsuits over lands that occupied the California courts for many years, — as those connected with the names of José Y. Limantour, the New Almaden Mine, and the opinions of Judge Hoffman in the Larkin cases.

II. The Kearny-Doniphan Expeditions. — These have attracted great attention, partly by reason of their intrinsic importance, but more especially, perhaps, because of the adventures and the hardships encountered. Probably the best account of the march from Missouri to San Diego is W. H. Emory's *Notes of a Military Reconnoissance*.[1] Most of the documents are printed in connection with the President's Message of December 22, 1846 (*House Document*, No. 19, 29th Con., 2nd Sess., pp. 1–73, and in *ibid.*, No. 60, 30th Cong., 1st Sess., pp. 149–229). R. S. Elliott participated in the Chihuahua end of the campaign and wrote most entertainingly of it in his *Notes taken in Sixty Years*, pp. 217–255. Other accounts by participants were written by John T. Hughes of the First Missouri Cavalry[2]

account, abundantly documented. *What I Saw in California . . . by Edwin Bryant, late Alcalde of St. Francisco* (New York, 1848, chs. xxiii–xxxi) contains an excellent and generally contemporaneous account of the conquest.

[1] This exists in three forms: *Senate Document*, No. 7, 30th Cong., 1st Sess.; *Executive Document*, No. 41, 30th Cong., 1st Sess.; and republished for the trade by Harpers in 1848. The first two are almost identical, but the second of them contains some supplementary reports.

[2] *Doniphan's Expedition; containing An Account of the Conquest of New Mexico*. This was first printed in 1847 at Cincinnati and was reprinted with a map at the same place in 1848, and it forms the basis of W. E. Connelley's *Doniphan's Expedition* (Topeka, Kansas, 1907).

and by F. S. Edwards, " A Volunteer." [1]   The former has some remarkable pictures that have been reproduced again and again and
the latter is provided with a really usable map. R. E. Twitchell
sets out at length the facts concerning the first part of the expedition
in his *History of the Military Occupation of the Territory of New Mexico*
(Denver, 1909).

D. Tyler's *Concise History of the Mormon Battalion* and B. H.
Robert's *Mormon Battalion, Its . . . Achievements* (Salt Lake City,
1919) bring together the leading incidents of this famous march.
The " Report of Lieut. Col. P. St. George Cooke (Commander of the
Battalion) of his March from Santa Fé, New Mexico, to San Diego,
Upper California " is sometimes printed in connection with Emory's
Notes. In April, 1907, the *Tempe Normal Student*, published at
Tempe, Arizona, printed the " Journal " kept by Captain Henry
Standage of the Battalion during the march. This gives an excellent
idea of the hardships and achievements of this part of the expedition.
For other books on the Kearny-Doniphan expeditions, see the list
prefixed to H. H. Bancroft's *Arizona and New Mexico*.

[1] *A Campaign in New Mexico with Colonel Doniphan* (Philadelphia, 1847).

CHAPTER XVIII

THE CAMPAIGN FOR MEXICO CITY

By October, 1846, the occupation of California, the seizure of Santa Fé, and the armistice following the capture of Monterey were all known at Washington. The question at once arose as to the future. All clearly available territory for American colonization was occupied, but the Mexicans would not recognize the hopelessness of the situation and confirm these territories and Texas to the United States. More coercion was clearly necessary to "conquer a peace," and the sole question was how that coercion could best be applied. Taylor suggested that the capture of Mexico City would be necessary and that this could be best accomplished by the way of Vera Cruz. The road south from Saltillo through San Luis Potosí was long and for the first part of the way devoid of supplies; for long distances it lacked even water. Moreover, so extended a line of communication would mean the utilization of large numbers of soldiers for guard post duties. This line might be shortened by using Tampico as a base; but there were several good objections to that route also. Before Taylor's letter reached Washington, Winfield Scott, the commanding general of the army, drew up a memorial as to the future operations and presented it to Marcy, the Secretary of War. Scott thought that Vera Cruz should be occupied. Probably that would bring the Mexicans to terms, as it would mean the practical isolation of the Republic. If the Mexicans did not submit, then an advance on Mexico City should at once be undertaken. Although Taylor gained the presidency, Scott was really the outstanding figure of the war.[1] In the War of 1812, while still under thirty, he had won renown at Lundy's Lane and Chippewa. He and Taylor were both Virginians by birth, but there all resemblance between them ceases, except that both were good soldiers and both were Whigs. Scott was a man of education and was a master figure wherever he happened to be. He was widely read in military lore and had travelled extensively. He had lived long in Washington and distrusted politicians of the Democratic faith. In the dearth of Democratic generals, Polk had naturally turned to the commanding officer of the army. When the two came together, the President estimated Scott as a man of scientific mind, rather than a practical soldier. In 1846, Scott wrote three letters that worked injury to him for the rest of his life. In one of them he informed a Senator that he would make no suggestions as to officers, for they were certain to be disregarded by the administration. The second letter was directed to the Secretary of War. In it he declared that unless he could have the cordial support of the administration he would prefer to have the command given to some one else, as "a fire upon my rear from Washington," of all things, was the most perilous. Marcy carried the letters to the President, who promptly withdrew his offer of active employment.[2] The news of this rebuff came to Scott as he was taking "a hasty plate of soup," to use his own words. The publication of these phrases caught the people's eye. Scott behaved very well under the provocation, keeping his mouth shut and his pen still. In the autumn, the Whigs

[1] Scott wrote his *Memoirs* in 1863. The book was published at New York in 1864 (2 vols.) and at once achieved popularity. It is interesting, but has all the defects of reminiscent compilations. The best life of Scott is that by Marcus J. Wright in the *Great Commanders* series.

[2] Polk's *Diary*, i, 413, 420, and Smith's *War with Mexico*, i, 199, 477.

began to talk of nominating Taylor for the presidency. This, with Polk's dislike of the armistice after Monterey, turned the attention of the administration back to Scott, and the thought of changing the commanding general in the field was further strengthened by some plain writing by Taylor as to the insufficiency of the means given him to do the work he was ordered to do. The President sent for Scott and there was an affecting scene in the course of which the General wept, — according to Polk. In November, 1846, Scott presented two memoranda as to the disposal of troops and a plan of operations for the coming year that gave the needed impulse to the administration.

Meantime the President had an interesting conversation with Senator Benton of Missouri, who suggested that the Vera Cruz-Mexico City campaign would be decisive of the war. Senator Benton stated that he would like to be placed in command of all the armies in the field. Polk offered to appoint him a major general;[1] but, as this would make him inferior to Scott and Taylor, a plan was hit upon to resurrect the grade of lieutenant-general. The President could then appoint Benton to this place and thus give him command over Scott and Taylor. Congress rejected this scheme; but when Scott in Mexico learned of it, his indignation knew few bounds, and he must have recurred to his statement as to the dangers of a "fire" in the rear. Scott's position and the President's and that of the Secretary of War were all natural enough. We were a peace-loving people with an ingrained dislike of regular soldiers and an utter ignorance of what war properly conducted really meant. Scott asked for more than twenty thousand men, abundant supplies of food and munitions, and also for things essential to getting an army on

---

[1] Polk's *Diary*, ii, 221 and fol., using index, and Smith's *War with Mexico*, ii, 75, 364.

shore in front of Vera Cruz. These numbers could not be supplied except by raising new regiments and stripping Taylor of his best soldiers. There seems to have been no objection on the part of the government to taking men away from Taylor. When that general found himself actually second in command in the field and relegated to a distinctly subordinate position, he felt aggrieved and stated his grievances to Scott,[1] who answered him most kindly, but insisted on having the men. There was nothing approaching a general staff in those days, and the burden placed upon the commissaries and quartermasters at Washington was too great for them. There was also a good deal of ignorance on the part of many officers, who should have known better, as to the necessities of the case, and as to the best method of going to work. When Scott finally set out from the capital, he was given instructions which practically placed all responsibility upon him.[2] Recognizing the great danger from disease at yellow fever-cursed Vera Cruz, Scott was anxious to begin his campaign in time to capture that city and gain the high lands of the interior before "yellow Jack" made his annual appearance. Delays and insubordinations on the part of political officers who felt sure of support at Washington tried Scott severely, but he proceeded with a courage and vigor that have seldom been equalled and almost never surpassed. Instead of the twenty thousand men that he desired, he never had more than ten thousand effectives at any one time during the campaign. Moreover, he was forced for months to live off the country and to fight battles in great measure with ammunition captured from the enemy.

[1] *Letters of Zachary Taylor* (Bixby Collection), p. 87–97.

[2] The soldiers' dislike of Polk and Marcy comes out in Grant's *Personal Memoirs*, i, 119–122. A trenchant criticism of this attitude is contained in *The Evolution of Myth as Exemplified in General Grant's History . . . by Senex* (Washington, 1890).

Vera Cruz is protected from the Gulf by a series of coral reefs. Upon these the Spaniards had constructed a castle — San Juan de Ulúa — which had been strengthened from time to time and very greatly improved since the French attack in 1838. The naval men thought it was out of the question to capture it from the sea; the alternative was to land on the beach, seize Vera Cruz, itself, and assail the castle on the harbor side. On March 9, 1847, the disembarkation took place on the beach to the southward of the city. Not a Mexican was in sight and the men once ashore marched over the sand hills, through the semi-tropical undergrowth of the low places, and in an almost incredibly short time had encircled the town. Storms, rain, and insects interfered with the work, but heavy guns were landed, batteries were erected, and fire opened upon the city. Eighteen days from the time that the first man leaped out of the first boat that touched the beach, Vera Cruz surrendered and with it the castle, March 27, 1847.[1]

The feeble defence of Vera Cruz by the Mexicans and the lack of any serious attempt to relieve the pressure upon the city by an attack from the interior was not what Scott had expected and is not entirely easy to understand. Santa Anna, after his return from Havana — by the grace of President Polk — had at first found himself in a difficult position. With his unexampled optimism, political audacity, and great organizing ability, he had speedily regained his position and was now again the first man in Mexico. Realizing fully the character of the coming blow, Santa Anna had

---

[1] The American loss in this operation was less than 100 killed and wounded. The Mexican loss was so indefinite that the only thing to do is to refer to Smith's *Mexico*, ii, 26–33, 341. Interesting accounts of this part of the campaign are in Robert Anderson's *An Artillery Officer in the Mexican War* (New York, 1911); and in *The Mexican War Diary of George B. McClellan*, 53–73. The account of the work of the naval battery in W. E. Griffis's *Matthew Calbraith Perry*, ch. xxiii, is graphic and authentic.

two or three modes of resistance. He might retire to the
Mexican plateau and fight the foe at the mountain passes;
he might defend Vera Cruz so stubbornly that its capture
would be very costly, if not impossible; or he might attack
and destroy isolated American forces in the north. Any
one of these courses or a combination of them was open to
him. What he did was to levy a strong army, as armies
went in those days, practically abandon Vera Cruz, and
march to the north. Santa Anna holds a low place in the
writings of American historians, but this would seem to be
somewhat undeserved. Stable political administration was
impossible in the Mexico of that day, and he treated Texan
rebels precisely as he would have treated rebels of his own
race. As to the disaster at San Jacinto, even a Mexican
president and general is obliged to leave something to his
subordinates, and neither Texan nor Mexican would have
been justified in counting upon the sudden and violent
return to the offensive on the part of Sam Houston and the
men with him. Santa Anna had a few good officers and
he had a few good soldiers, but the great mass of the human
material that he had to work with was helplessly inefficient
and hopelessly corrupt. Making what preparations he
could, he advanced at the head of a large body of troops to
San Luis Potosí. There he was about midway between
Taylor at Saltillo and Vera Cruz, where Scott might be
expected at some time in the future. It is perfectly possible
that Santa Anna, having given all the orders he could and
all the money that he could for the defence of Vera Cruz,
intended to himself march with his men to the relief of that
place whenever it should be strongly attacked. Of course,
a general should anticipate every possible movement on the
part of the enemy, and Santa Anna should have realized
that Scott would waste no time in fruitless and costly assaults

on San Juan de Ulúa; but every one before him had done exactly that thing. In reality, whatever were Santa Anna's plans, his hands were forced by an attack upon him by his political enemies which practically compelled him to put an end to preparings at San Luis and strike the enemy. The only enemy that could be struck at that moment was Taylor; and so with fifteen or sixteen thousand men Santa Anna took the northward road from San Luis Potosí for Buena Vista, Saltillo, and Monterey.

The expectation at Washington had been that Taylor would withdraw from his advanced positions and retire to Monterey. Instead, he held on at Saltillo, and kept his main forces to the southward of that place even as far as the northward edge of a waterless tract, at Agua Nueva. [1] There seems to have been great remissness in reconnoitering and guarding posts and camps. The Mexicans captured two parties of Americans and almost seized a supply depot before it could be destroyed. Taylor and his generals and his soldiers appear to have thought the Mexicans' power for the offensive had been destroyed and that whatever bodies of men might be reported from various directions were predatory bands. At length it became certain that there was a strong force of the enemy advancing from the south. Taylor at the moment was at Saltillo, and General Wool posted the soldiers to good advantage where one defender equalled three or four assailants owing to the narrowness of any possible front of attack. The scene of combat was peculiar. [2] It was in a valley about two miles wide at the

[1] The documents relating to Taylor's 1847 campaign are printed in *House Document*, No. 60, 30th Cong., 1st Sess., pp. 1092–1215, and in *Senate Document*, No. 1, 30th Cong., 1st Sess., pp. 97 and fol.

[2] Smith's *War with Mexico*, i, ch. xx. General W. B. Franklin has a succinct article on Buena Vista in *Papers of the Military Historical Society*, xiii, 543–558. Francis Baylies's *Narrative of Major General Wool's Campaign in Mexico* (Albany, 1851) is an interesting contemporaneous account of the Monclova campaign and the battle of Buena Vista. The account of Buena

ranch of Buena Vista. The road followed the bottom of the valley beside a small stream. At right angles to this little valley and the road were ten or a dozen ravines on one side and a series of gullies on the other. The only practicable way up and down the valley for horses and cannon was by the road or by the foot hills at the head of the ravines and gullies. Wool placed a battery at the narrowest point between the ravines and gullies, at a place called La Angostura. In the early afternoon of February 22, 1847, the Mexicans, having made a forced march almost without food and water, attacked along the road and were at once brought to a stop by cannon fire. The remainder of that day and all of the next, they essayed to turn one flank or the other of the American army by moving around the heads of the ravines and gullies. They succeeded in gaining positions on the slopes that made the American defence very doubtful. It was when affairs seemed most critical that Taylor, taking an advanced position on his white horse, sat there immovable, literally turning defeat into victory. Regiments that had given way returned to the battlefield and every one fought with greater vigor. At one time the Mexicans actually gained the rear of the American position, but the peculiar disposal of ravines and flat lands enabled the American artillery to be moved from one place to another. When the sun went down, the line had been restored. That night was a fearful one for the Americans. They had little food, no shelter, and disaster threatened at dawn. The sentries, as they paced their beats, watched the Mexican campfires. When the sun came up on the morning of the 24th,

Vista in Gen. S. G. French's *Two Wars: an Autobiography* (Nashville, 1901), pp. 73–84, was apparently written from notes; it certainly is clear and interesting. "An Engineer Officer's Recollections of Mexico and the Battle of Buena Vista" in *Old and New* for June and July, 1871, also appears to represent something more than reminiscence. Captain T. W. Gibson's *Letter* of March 6, 1847, dated Agua Nueva, is graphic.

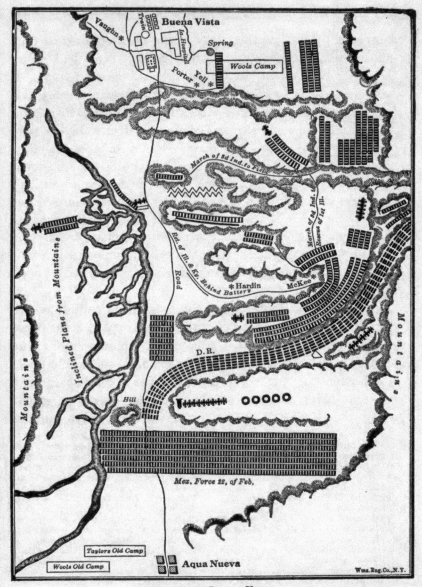

BATTLE OF BUENA VISTA

(From Gibson's *Letter*, 1847. "D.R." shows the Mexican flanking movement.)

astonished, they saw the backs of the retiring Mexican rear guard.[1] The preceding nightfall, Santa Anna had given the order for retreat, as further attacks seemed hopeless. Leaving a guard to keep up the fires, the Mexican army had moved away and, by dawn, the advance had reached Agua Nueva. There some food was found. After a day or two, the retreat was taken up again. Every mile of the way across the waterless desert to San Luis Potosí, the men fell out by the tens and hundreds. Of the fifteen to twenty thousand men that Santa Anna had with him before he set out for the North, he was able to place in the campaign for the defence of the capital only five or six thousand. Nevertheless, having captured three American guns and a standard, he announced himself the victor and was hailed as such by his countrymen.

One of the most interesting and most heartrending lessons that one draws from a study of the Mexican War is the fierce and mutual distrust of regulars and volunteers for one another.[2] This is a good place to examine the whole question because the battle of Buena Vista was won by volunteers, there not being more than six hundred soldiers of the regular army on the field. The administration at Washington

[1] The numbers are unusually vague. It would seem that Taylor had less than 5000 troops on the battle-field, first and last, and lost 673 killed and wounded, besides 1500 or 1800 who "quit the field." Smith's *Mexico*, i, 374, 396, and 561.

Of Santa Anna's 15,000 or 16,000 men who left San Luis Potosí for the north, it is unknown how many reached the actual battle-field. Smith (*ibid.*, i, 397) thinks that not less than 1800 Mexicans were killed and wounded at the battle and Santa Anna reported more than 4000 "had left him during the battle"; and probably (*ibid.*, i, 399) "not less than 3000 men" were lost on the road back to San Luis.

[2] The best way to comprehend this feeling is to read considerable portions in the diaries and memoirs of the regular and volunteer officers, as J. R. Kenly's *Memoirs of a Maryland Volunteer;* J. J. Oswandel's *Notes of the Mexican War;* and Luther Giddings's *Sketches of the Campaign in Northern Mexico* of the volunteers: the *Diary* of McClellan and *Letters* of Meade, George A. McCall's *Letters from the Frontiers*, and W. S. Henry's *Campaign Sketches* of the regulars. To these may well be added Raphael Semmes's *Service Afloat and Ashore during the Mexican War.*

seems to have had the idea that the only thing necessary to be done was to raise a large body of volunteers, officers and men, and send them to the front.[1] The diaries of many officers of the regular army who later gained distinction in the War for Southern Independence contain passage after passage referring to the lack of discipline of the volunteers, to their ignorance of military hygiene, and to their brutal treatment of the Mexicans. Scott, himself, stated that a regiment of regulars within an hour after pitching camp would be well secured and in order for any night attack, and at their comfortable supper, "merry as crickets." The volunteers, on the other hand, would eat their meat raw, lie down wet, and leave their arms and ammunition exposed to rain. He declared that "the want of the touch of the elbow . . . the want of the sure step . . . the want of military confidence in each other, and, above all, the want of reciprocal confidence between officers and men" [2] caused frightful losses in battle. There can be no doubt, whatever, that the persistent employment of volunteers in this war occasioned far greater loss in human lives and cost much more in the way of money spent than would have been the case had the new regiments received a few months' training and been commanded by officers of the regular army, assisted by such of

[1] Col. G. T. M. Davis in his *Autobiography*, pp. 96 and 110, relates that in forwarding the commission to General Shields, as Brigadier-General of Volunteers, Polk accompanied it with a statement that the appointment was a personal act and that their official relations would be of "a strictly confidential nature." It may be added that General Gideon J. Pillow had been Polk's law partner and John A. Quitman a prominent Mississippi politician. None of the three had seen any military service. The intriguing of these generals against one another and against their commander was most distressing. See, for example, J. F.

H. Claiborne's *John A. Quitman*, i, 301–307.

[2] Scott to Marcy, January 16, 1847; printed in Smith's *War with Mexico*, ii, 512.

An idea of the conditions prevailing in some volunteer regiments can be gathered from the evidence printed in *House Document*, No. 78, 30th Cong., 1st Sess. The student will also go to Davis's *Autobiography*, to Meade's *Letters* and to the "Letters of Captain E. Kirby Smith to his Wife" published under the title *To Mexico with Scott*. The first half of the last book relates to Taylor's campaign.

the volunteers as showed marked ability during the drilling period. Thousands of soldiers were sent to Taylor inadequately supplied with the impedimenta of war. They had no stretchers for the wounded and no proper equipment of medical supplies.[1] On one occasion, a volunteer officer deployed his men in such a way as to bring them directly under the enfilading fire of the enemy. And so one might go on. But the volunteers won the battle of Buena Vista and contributed most materially to the winning that of Cerro Gordo. Their losses from disease were frightful, and it must be said that the ill conduct of some of them toward the native Mexicans changed in a measure the character of the conflict, especially along the Rio Grande.

One reason why the Mexicans did not fear the military power of the United States was the fact that from one-quarter to one-third of the soldiers of the regular army were aliens — Irishmen, Englishmen, Scotsmen, and Germans. A similar condition of affairs prevailed in the navy.[2] The discipline was very severe and, as a rule, the soldiers had no love for the service. They enlisted to save themselves from starvation. Under these circumstances, desertion was by no means uncommon. Indeed, the San Patricio battalion in the Mexican service was composed of deserters from the American forces. Many of these were captured at Churubusco and elsewhere and were hanged or were flogged and branded.[3] When all has been said that can be said in their dispraise, it remains true that the gallantry, endurance, and

---

[1] On August 24, 1846, General Quitman wrote from Camargo that "the twelve-months troops are armed with refuse muskets, and their knapsacks, canteens, haversacks, and cartridge-boxes are unfit for service." Claiborne's *Quitman*, i, 242.

[2] See "Our Navy, Extracts from The Lucky Bag, on the Reorganization of the Navy." This is signed "Harry Bluff," which is supposed to have been the pen name of Lieut. M. F. Maury. It was dated "October, 1840." See also S. R. Franklin's *Memories of a Rear-Admiral*, chs. i–viii.

[3] See *Autobiography* of Col. G. T. M. Davis, 203, 205, 223–229.

general good faith of the American volunteers and regulars in these campaigns were remarkable and worthy of remembrance.

The employment of so great a proportion of volunteers had been due partly to the supposition that they were much cheaper than the regular soldiers. The armies, also, had been poorly supplied with the necessities of warfare because money was not plentiful at Washington. Polk's administration came at the end of the period of business depressions that followed the crash of 1837. The Democrats were pledged to restore the sub-treasury system and to replace the protective tariff of 1842 with a purely revenue measure.[1] The Secretary of the Treasury was Robert J. Walker, a Northern man who had gone to Mississippi and had fully identified himself with the pernicious financial system that had brought that State to repudiation. Few men in America at that time had any idea of the cost of warfare and especially of conducting campaigns at a distance from the home country. Nevertheless, the Democrats carried out their system to the letter. The sub-treasury was restored and with it the refusal of the government to accept anything except specie in payment of dues. The tariff was changed to a non-protective basis and the duties were all made ad valorem. The year 1846 saw a remarkable succession of ups and downs in business and in credit. It happened, however, that famine in Europe, especially in the British Islands, created a demand for wheat on a scale that had never been known before, and that was the real beginning of the exportation of foodstuffs in great quantities to Europe. In return, importations from Europe increased and with them the duties collected at New York and other

[1] The report of the Secretary of the Treasury and other documents setting forth the conditions under which all kinds of goods were imported and produced were printed as *Senate Document*, No. 444, 29th Cong., 1st Sess.

important centres grew and the foodstuffs that were not paid
for by the exportation of commodities from Europe were paid
for by exportation of specie. It happened, therefore, at the
precise moment when the financial task of the administration
should have been exceedingly difficult, the government was
able to borrow money at six per cent interest, — and this
at the very time when the money-lending part of the country
was lukewarm towards the war. As to the cost of the conflict, that seems to be impossible of ascertainment, but the
best estimate in round numbers gives it at one hundred
millions, including the amount paid to Mexico as the price
of the treaty. Taking everything into consideration, this
must be regarded as a small sum to pay for the acquisition of
Texas, New Mexico, Arizona, Utah, and California.

Vera Cruz in Scott's power, he pushed on in every possible
way the preparations for the advance to the interior.[1] Santa
Anna had arrived from Buena Vista and taken personal
charge of the defence of the National Road leading from
Vera Cruz to Mexico City. About fifty-five miles from
Vera Cruz the road suddenly rises into the mountains at
Cerro Gordo, the name of a height that dominated the pass.
Ten days after the triumphant entry into Vera Cruz, on
the twenty-ninth of March, 1847, the head of the American
army marched out from its camps and took its way into the
interior. At first the road was hardly more than a sandy
track, and the fatigue was great for the troops who, up to
that time, had had very little marching since landing almost
a month before. By the 11th of April, they had reached
the National Bridge and on the 13th came to the fortified
Mexican positions. The leading regiments necessarily
waited until other men and the general-in-chief came up.

[1] The correspondence between Scott
and the War Department from November 19, 1846 to February 9, 1848,
is printed in *House Document.* No.
60, 30th Cong., 1st Sess., pp. 833–
1090, 1216–1277.

Scott was most fortunate in having with him on his staff
as officers and engineers, Robert E. Lee, P. G. T. Beauregard,
George B. McClellan, George G. Meade, Zealous B. Tower,
and Isaac I. Stevens. No danger was too great to be encountered by these men, and sounder advice than they gave
to their commander has seldom been given by staff officers
to their chief. Reconnoitering, Lee discovered that a rough
way, available for artillery, could be made through the

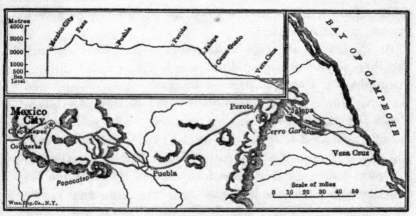

ROUTE FROM VERA CRUZ TO MEXICO CITY

woods to a point on the road in the rear of Cerro Gordo.
Scott's plan was at once formed: to send a strong force by
this road when constructed and to menace the main position in front. Unfortunately lack of obedience and lack of
professional knowledge on the part of his division commanders prevented the carrying out of the scheme in the
precise mode that had been devised. The commanding
officer on the right, seeing a good opportunity to attack
before he reached the road, made it possible for a large part
of the Mexicans to escape and entailed some loss of life.
On the left, lack of military knowledge precipitated the

assault at that point, also with unnecessary loss. Otherwise the movement succeeded beyond all reasonable anticipation. The Mexicans abandoned their positions, leaving their guns behind them, and fled in confusion, April 18, 1847, — Santa Anna himself on a mule, sliding down into a ravine.[1] After the battle, forgetting all jealousies and foregoing all recriminations, Scott and his army proceeded to Jalapa, the first large town in the interior, and then marched on by the castle or prison of Perote to the large city of Puebla, which was reached on May 15, almost exactly a month after Cerro Gordo.

At Puebla a new crisis confronted Scott. Notwithstanding the delays and disappointments, he had carried through triumphantly the first part of his task; he had captured Vera Cruz, had outrun the yellow fever, and was established in the second city of Mexico. There, however, he found himself at the head of only ten thousand troops, one-half the size of the force he had asked for. None of the new volunteers had come forward and many of the old volunteer regiments had enlisted for short terms that would be completed within a month or two. His supplies were entirely inadequate, his soldiers were badly clothed, and money was lacking. Moreover, the roads from Puebla to Vera Cruz ran through a country peculiarly favorable to guerilla warfare, and Scott's whole force might easily have been employed in guarding his communications with the coast. Finally, the exposure to a new climate and unaccustomed food and drink had brought about a great deal of sickness. A thousand of his men were in the hospitals or were unable to do duty. The government had expected that many of the volunteers would reënlist, but this they

[1] Smith (*Mexico*, ii, 44, 50, 58, 59, 347) gives the total Mexican force at from 10,000 to 15,000 men and the total loss at from 1000 to 1200. He gives Scott's force at 8500 and his loss at 64 killed and 353 wounded.

did not do to any extent. Scott, feeling that it would be
very unfair to send them to Vera Cruz in the sickly season,
decided to start them for the coast at once, while they still
had four or six weeks to serve. The government had expected him to seize food and other supplies, but Scott, thinking that it would be a great deal wiser to act with abundant
fairness to the Mexican people, had paid for whatever he
took. He now obtained money by cashing drafts on the
United States through British firms doing business in Mexico.
Calling up the garrisons he had left on the road and severing
his communications with Vera Cruz, he was able to gather
a force of 10,738 men, rank and file. Leaving the sick
and convalescents at Puebla with a guard of four hundred
sound men all under Colonel Childs, Scott set out for Mexico
City and the final conquest of seven millions of people.
Some reënforcements were on the way; 2000 of them had
already arrived at Vera Cruz and others were on shipboard
between that port and New Orleans. The time of the
arrival of these troops at the front in the heart of the Mexican
Republic, and whether they would ever arrive, being volunteers fresh from civil life led by political officers, was
questionable. It turned out to be even more questionable
than Scott could have foreseen. Nevertheless, he set out
and passed the mountainous rim of the Mexican plateau in
safety with Popocatepetl rising 18,000 feet above the sea
on the left, and the beautiful lakes of the Mexican Valley
in front. Not an attempt was made to stop him in
the rocky defiles through which the army necessarily
passed.

In the face of impending danger, Santa Anna had once
again found himself in his element. He issued appeals
to the people to come forward for the defence of their city;
he compelled the clergy — who seem to have been quite un-

willing to unite with him — to preach resistance. With
care and a good deal of skill, he fortified Peñon Mountain
on the main road leading toward the city. Scott reached
Ayotla in the Valley on August 11 and investigated the
task before him. The engineers reported that Peñon could
be successfully attacked only with great loss of life; but a
road led round the southern side of Chalco Lake and approached the city from the south instead of from the east.
Taking that route, Scott found his advance stopped by
fortifications thrown across the road at San Antonio.[1]
These extended from Lake Chalco to a large field of lava, a
pedregal as the Mexicans called it. On the other side of
this, another road led to Churubusco where the road by San
Antonio joined it. The indefatigable engineers again
exercised their abilities. They discovered a way through
the lava bed to the road in the rear of Contreras, where a
strong Mexican force had gathered to stop any advance on
that side of the pedregal. By the time that a few Americans
had struggled through the lava to the high ground, Santa
Anna with a strong body of men appeared on the other
side of a ravine, for he had come to the succor of the threatened post. Night was falling and he with his men returned to a neighboring village for shelter. More Americans joined the advance and they spent a miserable night
in the cold and wet, — without fires. At three o'clock
in the morning, without an alarm, they made their way
through a rough ravine led by an engineer and, as day broke,
advanced to the attack while the main body assailed the
position in front. The Mexicans, those of them who could
not get away, surrendered, and with their guns were found
two of the three that Taylor had lost at Buena Vista.

[1] General George H. Gordon has a
very good article on this part of the
campaign in *Proceedings* of the Military Historical Society of Massachusetts, xiii, No. xiv.

Without careful reconnoitring, Scott sent his men down the Churubusco road, and the San Antonio line also being abandoned the main body passed on there. The defences of Churubusco were far stronger than any one had anticipated. Another encircling march cleared it of the enemy. The night of August 20 found the way open to Chapultepec and the Gates of Mexico City at the cost of one thousand killed and wounded since leaving Puebla.[1] Santa Anna asked for an armistice and Scott granted the request.[2]

Meanwhile, at Washington the administration had been filled with a desire for peace. Politically, the situation was very serious in the United States, for the war was unpopular in the North and was likely to be more unpopular as taxes grew and demands for men became more insistent. There is always danger in war, and Polk had slight confidence in Scott or Taylor. Besides, if either one of them covered himself with glory, he would be a formidable Whig candidate for the presidency in 1848. The United States had been the traditional friend of Mexico, and having secured all the territory that the administration wished to have, it was time to make peace. Undoubtedly, there were leaders in Mexico, Santa Anna himself among them, who would gladly have made peace with the United States and resumed faction fighting among themselves. But after describing his defeats as

[1] Besides the authorities cited by Smith (*War with Mexico*, ii, 377) one can get a lifelike glimpse of this part of the campaign in a letter from Silas Casey to Dr. L. Goodale dated "St. Angels . . . Aug. 24, 1847" and printed in *Correspondence of the Late James Kilbourne*, 86.

[2] Taylor and Scott, both notable soldiers, entered into armistices with the enemy. These were generally condemned by politicians at that time and by historians since. It may well

be that both these remarkable men, conscious of the seriousness of the problem they had to face and of the imperfection of the weapon that was in their hands to solve it, may have taken a more serious view of the matter and a more accurate one than the administration and the historians. Probably it was the ineptitude of the Mexicans for war that made the solution less difficult than any soldier would have been justified in thinking that it would be.

victories, it was difficult for Santa Anna to place himself
openly at the head of any such movement and, indeed, he
was more fitted to stir up strife than to allay it. It was
rumored also that he had come to some kind of an agreement
with the United States. Besides those Mexicans who did
not want to make peace for what might be called patriotic
motives, there were a great many who desired the war to
continue because they were better off as they were than
when ruling themselves. Both Taylor and Scott and the
soldiers under them — with of course some exceptions —
had treated the Mexicans in the occupied towns better
than any army had ever treated them before. Not realizing all the obstacles in the way of negotiation, Polk determined to send a diplomatic agent, with the provisions of a
treaty in his portfolio, to accompany Scott on his march and
take advantage of any opening for a negotiation that might
occur. The person picked out for this extremely delicate
and difficult task was the Chief Clerk of the State Department, Nicholas P. Trist by name. He was selected because
he could be easily disavowed or recalled, as the Secretary
of State or a minister plenipotentiary could not be. Trist
was a Virginian by birth, the grandson-in-law of Thomas
Jefferson, and for a short time had been private secretary
to President Jackson — facts which he could never forget.
He had been long a minor office holder, and as consul at
Havana had been implicated in some doubtful proceedings.[1]
Trist had an idea of his own importance which oftentimes
goes with contact in a small way with great men and transactions.[2]

In April, 1847, Buchanan provided Trist with elaborate

---

[1] See *House Report*, No. 707, 26th
Cong., 1st Sess.

[2] J. S. Reeves's article on "The Treaty
of Guadalupe-Hidalgo" in the *American Historical Review*, x, 309-324

is written from the point of view of
Polk's diary. It may advantageously be read with the accounts in
Smith's *War with Mexico*, using index
under "Trist."

and well-devised instructions telling him exactly what he was to do — what terms he was to offer to the Mexicans and how much money he could offer them. It was undoubtedly supposed at Washington that he would act in harmony with Scott, who at the moment was advancing to the battle of Cerro Gordo. Arrived at Vera Cruz, Trist sent to Scott despatches, which he asked him to place in the hands of the Mexican commander; and Scott read in Marcy's explanatory letter to him that Trist was authorized to enter into arrangements for the suspension of hostilities. He at once jumped to the conclusion that his prerogative as commander in the field had been infringed. He refused to forward the papers, and he and Trist, both of them inordinate letter writers, engaged in a voluminous and acrid correspondence.[1] The Chief Clerk landed at Vera Cruz, May 6, 1847. He at once became ill and it was some time before he was able to get to Puebla. When he reached that city, Scott, who possessed the instincts of a true gentleman, personally looked after Trist's quarters and subsistence. This appealed to the latter, and in a very short time from being hostile to one another the two Virginians became fast friends, a condition of affairs that pleased Polk less than did the other. At this time the English merchants and diplomatists in Mexico City were extremely desirous of putting an end to hostilities that interfered with trade and were decidedly against the best interests of Mexico. Edward Thornton, an attaché of the British legation at Mexico City — and years later British minister at Washington — visited Trist at Puebla, on June 11, and again on the 24th of that month. Santa Anna was undoubtedly desirous of ending hostilities, and the expenditure of money among Mexican politicians was not an unusual method of bring-

[1] See *House Document*, No. 60, 30th Cong., 1st Sess., pp. 812–831.

ing about results. Somehow or other, Santa Anna, or perhaps it would be better to say Mexican circumstances, outwitted Scott and Trist, and procured the armistice and a small supply of money. But then the scene shifted. Santa Anna probably could not fulfil his engagements, or what seemed to be his engagements, and the Mexicans not adhering strictly to the conditions of the armistice, Scott put an end to it, September 6, 1847, and advanced to the attack on Mexico City itself.

The City of Mexico stood in the midst of a marsh that once had been a lake and was approached from different directions by causeways built of stone. Any advance across them was certain to be dangerous, and the choice of the point of attack was really a matter of chance. In some way, Scott's attention had been called to a group of factory buildings, the royal mill — el Molino del Rey [1] — at which the manufacture of war materials was said to be progressing. He thought it would be easy to seize the establishment and destroy it by night attack, but yielded to the suggestion that it would better be done by daylight and by a larger force of men than he had expected would be necessary. The attack was made on September 8 and succeeded, but at the cost of seven hundred and six killed and wounded. The loss was trifling as modern casualties go, but was a serious diminution of Scott's small force of some eight thousand in round numbers. Dominating the end of the two most available causeways was the hill of Chapultepec, upon which stood the buildings of a military college. The height and sharpness of the ascent made it appear easier to defend than it really was and more difficult

---

[1] General George H. Gordon has an interesting and valuable article on Molino del Rey and Chapultepec in the *Proceedings* of the Military Historical Society of Massachusetts, xiii, No. xv. Smith's account of these battles and of the entrance to the City of Mexico is much more detailed and based on much more material (*War with Mexico*, ii, ch. xxviii.)

to attack. Its occupation appeared to be necessary before an advance could be made into the city from that particular quarter and Scott ordered its capture. A number of small misadventures marred the general brilliancy of the operation, but in the end it was captured at a total loss of 450 men. In all, in these two minor operations at Molino del Rey and Chapultepec, Scott lost for the time being more than one thousand men, one-fifth of whom and probably one-quarter would never see the ranks again. This left him with less than seven thousand men to seize and hold the greatest city of Mexico, until reënforcements could arrive from the coast. Nevertheless, the troops pressed on. Advancing by two causeways, they distracted the enemy's attention, and aqueducts carried in the air by arches resting on the causeways enabled the assailants to stalk the enemy something after the mode of the Red Man of jumping from tree to tree. Reaching the fortifications at the gateways or garitas, the assailants burrowed through the walls. By nightfall (September 13) both columns were within the city walls. The next day, Scott in person took possession of the city. Then followed a period of serious disorder. The retiring Mexicans had opened the prisons, the criminals had secured arms, and attacked the invaders from the housetops and other points of vantage. Scott adopted stern measures of repression, and after a few days of cannon firing in the streets and summary shootings, the city became quiet and remained so throughout the American occupation.

When Scott had moved out from Puebla, he had left Colonel Childs there with four hundred able-bodied men to protect the sick men who were in the hospitals or were convalescent and to provide a resting-place for the volunteer regiments that would come up from the coast. Childs was an exceedingly good man, but his task was difficult, for the irregular bands of the country between Mexico City and Puebla concentrated their efforts upon the latter. Childs held them off by exceedingly good management, but the situation was perilous, especially after the fall of Mexico. Then Santa Anna, disdaining quiet, embodied a force of men, or took some of the organized units that were left, and marched to Puebla. But nothing came of this. He then continued his way toward his plantations near the coast and sought to waylay the regiments of volunteers on their march up country from Vera Cruz. Before leaving government headquarters he had resigned the presidency, and now the new government ordered him to lay down his command, return to headquarters and justify his military conduct. This Santa Anna refused to do and, instead, he proceeded to one of his plantations more or less under guard of American soldiers and soon after left the country, returning in later years again to become president in less troubled times.

Success and comparative quiet after the last strenuous weeks brought no peace to Scott, nor to his division commanders. They turned fiercely upon one another and Scott put three of them under arrest. The story is an unpleasant one of an attempt to substitute political aspirations for military obedience. General Worth, for whom Scott had done everything, turned against him, and General Pillow, formerly President Polk's law partner, ably seconded Worth in his efforts to bring into disgrace the commander-in-chief. Instead of mutual felicitations, court-martials became the order of the day. Scott, himself, was displaced by order of the President and directed to report at Washington. It was a pitiful ending of a glorious adventure and recalls to mind the measure of gratitude meted out to

Scott's illustrious predecessor, Hernan Cortez. But great in disgrace as he had been in victory, he outlived the malice of his foes and was again commander-in-chief of the American army when James Buchanan laid down the presidential office, March 4, 1861.

As was inevitable in Mexico and especially in such a crisis as that following the occupation of the capital city and the dismissal of Santa Anna, governmental affairs were in a chaotic condition. There seemed to be no settled administration that was capable of prosecuting the war or making peace. It was suggested, indeed, that the United States would be obliged to set up a government to negotiate a treaty and maintain it in power for an indefinite time to make certain that the provisions of that instrument were executed.[1] Happily this was made unnecessary by a sudden change of feeling on the part of the ruling Mexican classes. After Trist's offers had been turned down more than once and he had received his orders to return home, the Mexican Congress voted for peace and communication was once more opened with Trist. This time again the British diplomatic representatives and probably the merchants of that nation in Mexico exerted a powerful pressure on the existing government by demonstrating the necessity of peace and stating unreservedly that Great Britain would not intervene. Trist's position was extraordinary: he had been recalled and had sent a notification of his recall to the Mexican government. He felt that the putting an end to the negotiations with which he had been intrusted was done at Washing-

---

[1] The documents relating to the negotiation are printed in *Senate Document*, No. 52, 30th Cong., 1st Sess. Senator Sumner, in 1870, included a brief history of the negotiations in his report on a bill to compensate Trist for his services as negotiator (*Senate Report*, No. 261, 41st Cong., 2nd Sess.). Smith has an extended account in ch. xxxii of his *War with Mexico* and attendant notes. Julius Klein printed a long article on the subject in University of California's *Chronicle* for July, 1905 (vol. vii, No. 4).

ton under an entire misapprehension of the existing condition of affairs in Mexico. Acting on the suggestion that, as negotiations had already begun, his recall would not apply to them, and there being no means of getting away from Mexico City, he decided to go on with the parleys. As Justin H. Smith says, "it was a truly noble act," for the immediate consequences to him must be very unpleasant. This was on December 4, 1847. The terms that Trist could offer were set forth clearly in his instructions and, under the circumstances, he could not vary them. He seems to have conducted himself in an entirely dignified and considerate manner. After some weeks of conferring, the negotiations came to a deadlock, and on January 29 Trist declared them at an end. Now, again, the British intervened and arranged that one more communication should be received and also informed the government that the Americans would protect it, should the treaty be signed. Four days later, on February 2, 1848, the treaty was signed at Guadalupe Hidalgo.

President Polk's feelings may be imagined when a message was brought to him that Trist had arrived in the United States and that the treaty negotiated by him was on the way to Washington. He wrote down some severe strictures on his former Chief Clerk of the State Department. When the treaty arrived on February 19, 1848, however, it was found to be exactly what Trist had been ordered to negotiate. At first Polk did not know what to do, but finally determined to send it to the Senate and place the responsibility for peace or the continuance of the war on that body. Two-thirds of the Senators and more were distinctly of the opinion that it should be ratified with a few changes of no great importance. On March 10, 1848, they so voted, and on May 30, the amended treaty was ratified.

According to the treaty,[1] upon ratification the United States troops would be withdrawn from the occupied areas as far north as the Rio Grande del Norte. The new boundary between the two republics should follow that river from its mouth to the southern boundary of New Mexico "north of the town called Paso" and thence somewhat irregularly to the Gila River and down that stream to the Colorado and thence following the southern boundary of Upper California to the Pacific Ocean. The southern and western limits of New Mexico were defined as these were laid down in Disturnell's "Map of the United Mexican States" that was published at New York in 1847. "In consideration of the extension acquired by the boundaries of the United States" in the present treaty, the "Government of the United States" engages to pay the sum of fifteen million dollars to the Mexican Republic. Three millions were to be paid down and the other twelve in annual instalments of three million dollars each with six per cent interest. The United States also assumed the payments of the claims of American citizens against the Mexican Republic. There were many other provisions in the treaty and in the amendments made by the United States Senate; but they need not concern us here.

The boundary by the Treaty of 1848 proved to be impossible of delineation on the ground. The map was inaccurately drawn — necessarily so in the existing condition of geographical knowledge. Moreover, it soon came to the knowledge of the authorities at Washington that the best route from Texas to California followed the path or road taken by the Mormon Battalion. This proved to be south of the Gila River. This country, which was inaccurately included under the name of Mesilla Valley, was south of the

[1] *Treaties and Conventions* (ed. 1873), p. 562.

boundary line by any possible interpretation of the boundary of New Mexico as laid down on Disturnell's map.[1] In 1853, therefore, James Gadsden, acting for the United States, negotiated a treaty with the Mexicans by which for the sum of ten million dollars they ceded a roughly rectangular shaped tract that included the coveted route and mines and something more. And the line as thus drawn remains today the southwestern boundary of the United States.

In the third of the century described in the preceding pages, the American people threw off the social conditions of colonial days. They kept their old forms of government, but altered the spirit of administering them in the direction of democracy. They crossed the Appalachians in great numbers into the valley of the Mississippi and over that river into the lands that they had acquired from France. "Manifest destiny" urged them on to the acquisition of Florida, to the regaining of Texas on the South, and to the possession of the lands westward from the crest of the Rockies to the shores of the Pacific Ocean. It remained for the future to show what would be the effect of these great changes in society and these immense accessions of territory. Would the Republic remain one united country, or would it be divided according to the social and economic desires of the inhabitants of the several sections into which it was geographically divided?

[1] The reports of the different surveying parties of the boundary between the United States and Mexico are enumerated in G. K. Warren's "Memoir of Explorations and Surveys" forming Appendix F to vol. i of G. M. Wheeler's *Report Upon . . . Geographical Surveys West of the One Hundredth Meridian* (p. 584). Another enumeration is in the foot-notes to Bancroft's *Arizona and New Mexico,* 468–473, 491–494. The two most interesting reports are J. R. Bartlett's *Personal Narrative of Explorations and Incidents* (2 vols., New York, 1854) and W. H. Emory's *Report on the United States and Mexican Boundary Survey* (3 vols., Washington, 1857–1859). This forms *House Document,* No. 135, 34th Cong., 1st Sess. and is illustrated, as is Bartlett's.

NOTE

Bibliography. — For guidance in the writing of the preceding three chapters, I have relied on Justin H. Smith's remarkable history of *The War with Mexico* (2 vols., New York, 1919). It is the result of prolonged and widely extended researches. Oftentimes the most valuable information is to be found in the " Remarks " that are buried with other matter in the " Notes " at the ends of both volumes. Smith's research was so profound and his judgment generally so just that one can place peculiar reliance on his statements. At the same time, like all historical students, he has his prejudices. George L. Rives's *The United States and Mexico, 1821–1848* (2 vols., New York, 1913) is readable, but is based on insufficient evidence. Grant's account of the Mexican War in his *Personal Memoirs* (vol. i, chs. v-xiii) may almost be regarded as an historical sketch of the war and must have been based upon a considerable collection of documents.

Of the older books, one may mention Isaac I. Stevens's *Campaigns of the Rio Grande and of Mexico* (New-York, 1851) ;[1] and N. C. Brooks's *Complete History of the Mexican War* (Philadelphia, 1849). Cadmus M. Wilcox's *History of the Mexican War* (Washington, 1892) can hardly be described as readable, but it was written by a military officer who had done a great deal of preparatory research.[2] The important documents are in *House Document*, No. 60, 30th Cong., 1st Sess., and *Senate Document*, No. 1, 30th Cong., 1st Sess.

[1] This was written in reply to R. S. Ripley's *War with Mexico* (2 vols., New York, 1849). Ripley's book was prepared, apparently, to promote the fortunes of General Pillow. Were it not for its one-sidedness, it would still be a valuable work. Hazard Stevens's *Life of Isaac Ingalls Stevens* (Boston, 1900) contains an excellent account of Scott's campaign.

[2] Smith gives abundant citations in his "Notes." H. E. Haferkorn's "Select Bibliography" entitled *The War with Mexico* is very useful.

In closing this volume, the author wishes to thank numerous friends and many students, past and present, who have aided him in countless different ways. The names of some of them are included in the foot-notes. Especially he wishes again to record his obligations to his friend George Parker Winship for reading the proofs and to his secretary, Miss Eva G. Moore, to whom the accuracy of citation and statement is very largely due.

INDEX

Printed in the USA
CPSIA information can be obtained
at www.ICGtesting.com
LVHW090241251123
764662LV00004B/745